Stanford historian, **Clayborne Carson**, Ph.D., is the author and editor of several books on the civil rights struggle in the United States. In 1985, Dr Carson was invited by the King family to direct the long-term project of editing and publishing the papers of Dr Martin Luther King, Jr.

THE AUTOBIOGRAPHY OF
MARTIN LUTHER KING, JR.

EDITED BY

CLAYBORNE CARSON

IPM

INTELLECTUAL PROPERTIES MANAGEMENT, INC.

IN ASSOCIATION WITH

ABACUS

It gives me great pleasure to finally see my husband's words in autobiographical form. During the Civil Rights Movement a number of publishers and news organizations showed remarkable courage in bringing Martin's views to the public. Without these media outlets, the bits and pieces of which this autobiography is made would have been lost to posterity. Hence, my gratitude goes to Harper Collins, William Morrow, Pocket Books, Henry Holt, Pitman, University of California Press, Harper & Row, Random House, New American Library, Kennedy Presidential Library, *Albany Herald, Atlanta Journal, Christian Century, Ebony, Hindustan Times, Jet, Look, Massachusetts Review, McCall's, Montgomery Adviser, Nashville Tennessean, The Nation, New York Amsterdam News, New York Post, New York Times, Playboy, Progressive, Redbook, Saturday Review, Southern Courier, TIME,* ABC, BBC, CBC, *The Merv Griffin Show,* NBC, and WAII-TV, as well as others too numerous to mention.

Intellectual Properties Management (IPM) has made extensive efforts to identify the original source of all the material that appears in this autobiography, and to seek appropriate permission. But as with any endeavor, errors can take place. If an oversight is noted, please contact IPM so that proper credit can be made in future editions.

– Coretta Scott King, September 1998

ABACUS

First published in Great Britain by Little, Brown and Company in 1999
This paperback edition published by Abacus in 2000
Reprinted 2001, 2002, 2003, 2004, 2005, 2006, 2007, 2008

Published by arrangement with Warner Books, Inc., New York, USA

A CIP catalogue record for this book is available from the British Library

ISBN 978-0-349-11298-5

Printed and bound in Great Britain by Clays Ltd, St Ives plc

Abacus
An imprint of
Little, Brown Book Group
100 Victoria Embankment
London EC4Y 0DY

An Hachette Livre UK Company
www.hachettelivre.co.uk

www.littlebrown.co.uk

CONTENTS

EDITOR'S PREFACE

◆

I first saw Martin Luther King, Jr., from a distance. He was up on the platform in front of the Lincoln Memorial, the concluding speaker at the 1963 March on Washington for Jobs and Freedom. I was below in the vast crowd of listeners around the reflecting pool, a nineteen-year-old college student attending my first civil rights demonstration. He would become a Man of the Year, a Nobel Prize laureate, and a national icon. I would become a foot soldier in the movement he symbolized and would walk through doors of opportunity made possible by that movement.

More than two decades later, after I became a historian at Stanford University, Mrs. Coretta Scott King unexpectedly called me to offer the opportunity to edit the papers of her late husband. Since accepting her offer to become director of the King Papers Project, I have immersed myself in the documents recording his life and have gradually come to know a man I never met. The study of King has become the central focus of my scholarly life, and this project is the culmination of my career as a documentary editor. The March on Washington started me on the path to *The Autobiography of Martin Luther King, Jr.* This book is a product of King's intellectual legacy, just as I am a beneficiary of his social justice legacy.

The following narrative of King's life is based entirely on his own words. These are his thoughts about the events in his life as he expressed them at different times in various ways. Although he never wrote a comprehensive autobiography, King published three major books as well as numerous articles and essays focusing on specific periods of his life. In addition, many of his speeches, sermons, letters, and unpublished manuscripts provide revealing information. Taken together, these materials provide the basis for this approximation of the autobiography that King might have written had his life not suddenly ended.

For the most part, this book consists of autobiographical writ-

ings that were published during King's lifetime and were personally edited by him. In many instances King was assisted by others, since he made considerable use of collaborators. Nevertheless, King's papers provide ample evidence of his active involvement in the editorial processes that resulted in his most significant publications. Indeed, the preparation for this autobiography involved examining preliminary drafts (several handwritten) of King's published writings in order to determine his authorial intentions. I have included passages from such drafts when they contain revealing or clarifying information that does not appear in the published version.

Although King's published autobiographical writings provide the basic structure of this book, they constitute an incomplete narrative. In order to fill out the narrative and to include King's accounts of events that are not discussed in his published writings, I have incorporated passages from hundreds of documents and recordings, including many statements that were not intended for publication or even intended as autobiography. These passages augment the published accounts and serve as transitions between more extended narratives. In some instances, I have made editorial changes, which are explained below, in order to construct a narrative that is readable and comprehensible. This exercise of editorial craft is intended to provide readers with a readily accessible assemblage of King's writings and recorded statements that would otherwise be available only to a handful of King scholars.

I trust that readers will recognize and appreciate the fact that this narrative can never approach the coherence and comprehensiveness that would have been possible if King had been able to write a complete account of his life. Thus, this narrative understates the importance in King's life of his family. Although King often acknowledged the centrality of his wife, Coretta Scott King, in his public and private life, his extant papers rarely noted the degree to which she participated in protest activities and other public events. Similarly, King's close ties to his parents, his children, his sister Christine King Farris, and his brother A. D. King are insufficiently reflected in his papers, despite the fact that these relatives played crucial roles in his life.

The Autobiography of Martin Luther King, Jr., is, therefore,

largely a religious and political autobiography rather than an explo-
ration of a private life. It is necessarily limited to those aspects of
King's life that he chose to reveal in his papers, but King was never
garrulous about his private life and was unlikely to have chosen his
autobiography as an opportunity to reveal intimate details of his
life. In his personal papers, however, King sometimes overcame
his reticence to expose his private feelings to public view. He left
behind documents that offer information that has never previously
been published and that collectively defines his character. Although
King may have selected or utilized these materials differently than I
have, he (or researchers and co-authors working with him) would
certainly have recognized them as essential starting points for understanding his life.

   This book is an extension of my charge from the King estate to
assemble and edit King's papers. I have benefited from the long-
term, collective effort of dozens of staff members and student researchers who assisted in the search for autobiographical passages
amidst the several hundred thousand King-related documents that
the King Papers Project has identified (see Acknowledgments section). *The Autobiography of Martin Luther King, Jr.,* is one by-
product of the project's continuing effort to publish a definitive,
annotated fourteen-volume scholarly edition of *The Papers of Martin
Luther King, Jr.*

The fact that *The Autobiography of Martin Luther King, Jr.,* has been
compiled and edited after King's death warrants an explanation of
how it was constructed. Although many autobiographies are written
with some editorial assistance—from minor copyediting to extensive
rewriting of raw information (often tape-recorded recollections)
supplied by the subject—readers are rarely made aware of the significance of such assistance. The role of Alex Haley in the production
of *The Autobiography of Malcolm X* is a well-known demonstration
of the value of behind-the-scenes editorial assistance for a subject
who lacks the time or the ability to write an autobiographical narrative that is compelling and of literary value. Autobiographical editing
succeeds when the resulting narrative convinces readers that it accurately represents the thoughts of the subject.

   The authenticity of this autobiography of Martin Luther King,

Jr., derives from the fact that I have followed a consistent methodology to preserve the integrity of King's statements and writing while also merging these texts into a single narrative. Although great care has been taken to insure that this account of King's life is based on his own words, it is also the result of many challenging editorial judgments. Among these was the decision to construct a narrative that traced King's life to its end by combining source texts of many different periods in his life. The comprehensiveness of this narrative implies that King wrote it, with considerable editorial and research assistance, at the very end of his life. Although many of the source texts present King's attitudes and perspectives at earlier points in his life, King's viewpoints on major issues remained quite stable during his adult years; I feel justified in believing that King's final recounting of his beliefs would not have differed in any significant way from his earlier recollections.

The materials used to construct this narrative are the types of documentary materials that King (or those assisting him) would undoubtedly have consulted while preparing an autobiography. These source texts, which constitute the raw materials for this work, include sections and passages taken from the following types of sources:

- major autobiographical books (and draft manuscripts): *Stride Toward Freedom: The Montgomery Story* (1958), *Why We Can't Wait* (1964), and *Where Do We Go from Here: Chaos or Community?* (1967);
- articles and essays (both published and unpublished) describing specific periods and events;
- speeches, sermons, and other public statements containing autobiographical passages;
- autobiographical statements in King's published or recorded interviews;
- letters from King;
- comments by King in official documents, meeting transcripts, and various audiovisual materials.

I have tried whenever possible to track down the original publishers of these materials, but in a few instances this was virtually impossible.

To insure that this narrative accurately reflects King's autobiographical thoughts, editorial interventions have been limited to those necessary to produce a narrative that is readable, internally coherent, and lucid. I have preserved the integrity and immediacy of certain texts by inserting italicized verbatim passages into the edited narrative. Other quotations from King-authored documents have been placed in boxes at appropriate places in the autobiographical narrative.

King's recollections of episodes in his life, like all autobiographical writings, were distorted by the passage of time and the vagaries of memory. Thus I have not attempted to correct historical inaccuracies in King's account. Rather, when multiple source texts are available for a particular event, I have sought to determine which of these represent King's most vivid and reliable recollection. The resulting narrative balances several considerations in the selection of source texts, including a preference for accounts that are near to the time of the event rather than later recollections and a preference for more precise descriptions over more general, abstract ones.

After source texts were selected and placed in rough chronological order, I constructed chapter-long narratives that cover periods in King's life. In this process, I condensed some of King's source texts by removing words and details that were redundant or superfluous in the context of a comprehensive narrative. Additional editorial interventions include the following: tenses have been changed (usually from present to past or past perfect); words or brief phrases have been added to indicate or clarify time, location, or name (such as "In June"); conjunctions and other transitional words have been provided when necessary; pronouns have been replaced with proper nouns when referents are unclear ("Ralph Abernathy" rather than "he"), and vice versa when context requires; spellings have been regularized; punctuation and sentence construction have been modified in order to clarify meaning and enhance readability.

CLAYBORNE CARSON
Stanford, California
August 1, 1998

THE AUTOBIOGRAPHY OF

MARTIN LUTHER KING, JR.

1

EARLY YEARS

Of course I was religious. I grew up in the church. My father is a preacher, my grandfather was a preacher, my great-grandfather was a preacher, my only brother is a preacher, my daddy's brother is a preacher. So I didn't have much choice.

NOVEMBER 25, 1926
Michael (later Martin) Luther King, Sr., marries Alberta Williams, daughter of A. D. Williams, pastor of Ebenezer Baptist Church

JANUARY 15, 1929
Michael (later Martin) Luther King, Jr., born at Williams/King family home at 501 Auburn Avenue in Atlanta

MARCH 21, 1931
A. D. Williams dies and is succeeded as pastor of Ebenezer by King Sr.

MAY 18, 1941
King Jr.'s grandmother Jennie Celeste Williams dies and family moves to 193 Boulevard in Atlanta

APRIL 17, 1944
King Jr. travels to Dublin, Georgia, to deliver "The Negro and the Constitution" in oratory contest

I was born in the late twenties on the verge of the Great Depression, which was to spread its disastrous arms into every corner of this nation for over a decade. I was much too young to remember the beginning of this depression, but I do recall, when I was about five years of age, how I questioned my parents about the numerous

people standing in breadlines. I can see the effects of this early child-hood experience on my present anticapitalistic feelings.

My birthplace was Atlanta, Georgia, the capital of the state and the so-called "gateway to the South." Atlanta is home for me. I was born on Auburn Avenue. Our church, Ebenezer Baptist, is on Auburn Avenue. I'm now co-pastor of that church, and my office in the Southern Christian Leadership Conference is on Auburn Avenue.

I went through the public schools of Atlanta for a period, and then I went to what was then known as the Atlanta University Laboratory High School for two years. After that school closed, I went to Booker T. Washington High School.

The community in which I was born was quite ordinary in terms of social status. No one in our community had attained any great wealth. Most of the Negroes in my hometown who had attained wealth lived in a section of town known as "Hunter Hills." The community was characterized with a sort of unsophisticated simplicity. No one was in the extremely poor class. It is probably fair to class the people of this community as those of average income. It was a wholesome community, notwithstanding the fact that none of us were ever considered members of the "upper-upper class." Crime was at a minimum, and most of our neighbors were deeply religious.

From the very beginning I was an extraordinarily healthy child. It is said that at my birth the doctors pronounced me a one hundred percent perfect child, from a physical point of view. I hardly know how an ill moment feels. I guess the same thing would apply to my mental life. I have always been somewhat precocious, both physically and mentally. So it seems that from a hereditary point of view, nature was very kind to me.

My home situation was very congenial. I have a marvelous mother and father. I can hardly remember a time that they ever argued (my father happens to be the kind who just won't argue) or had any great falling out. These factors were highly significant in determining my religious attitudes. It is quite easy for me to think of a God of love mainly because I grew up in a family where love was central and where lovely relationships were ever present. It is quite easy for me to think of the universe as basically friendly mainly because of my uplifting hereditary and environmental circum-

stances. It is quite easy for me to lean more toward optimism than pessimism about human nature mainly because of my childhood experiences.

In my own life and in the life of a person who is seeking to be strong, you combine in your character antitheses strongly marked. You are both militant and moderate; you are both idealistic and realistic. And I think that my strong determination for justice comes from the very strong, dynamic personality of my father, and I would hope that the gentle aspect comes from a mother who is very gentle and sweet.

"Mother Dear"

My mother, Alberta Williams King, has been behind the scene setting forth those motherly cares, the lack of which leaves a missing link in life. She is a very devout person with a deep commitment to the Christian faith. Unlike my father, she is soft-spoken and easygoing. Although possessed of a rather recessive personality, she is warm and easily approachable.

The daughter of A. D. Williams, a successful minister, Alberta Williams grew up in comparative comfort. She was sent to the best available schools and college and was, in general, protected from the worst blights of discrimination. An only child, she was provided with all of the conveniences that any high school and college student could expect. In spite of her relatively comfortable circumstances, my mother never complacently adjusted herself to the system of segregation. She instilled a sense of self-respect in all of her children from the very beginning.

My mother confronted the age-old problem of the Negro parent in America: how to explain discrimination and segregation to a small child. She taught me that I should feel a sense of "somebodiness" but that on the other hand I had to go out and face a system that stared me in the face every day saying you are "less than," you are "not equal to." She told me about slavery and how it ended with the Civil War. She tried to explain the divided system of the South—the segregated schools, restaurants, theaters, housing; the white and colored signs on drinking fountains, waiting rooms, lavatories—as a social condition rather than a natural order. She made it clear that

she opposed this system and that I must never allow it to make me feel inferior. Then she said the words that almost every Negro hears before he can yet understand the injustice that makes them necessary: "You are as good as anyone." At this time Mother had no idea that the little boy in her arms would years later be involved in a struggle against the system she was speaking of.

"Daddy"

Martin Luther King, Sr., is as strong in his will as he is in his body. He has a dynamic personality, and his very physical presence (weighing about 220 pounds) commands attention. He has always been a very strong and self-confident person. I have rarely ever met a person more fearless and courageous than my father, notwithstanding the fact that he feared for me. He never feared the autocratic and brutal person in the white community. If they said something to him that was insulting, he made it clear in no uncertain terms that he didn't like it.

A sharecropper's son, he had met brutalities at firsthand, and had begun to strike back at an early age. His family lived in a little town named Stockbridge, Georgia, about eighteen miles from Atlanta. One day, while working on the plantation, he keenly observed that the boss was cheating his father out of some hard-earned money. He revealed this to his father right in the presence of the plantation owner. When his happened the boss angrily and furiously shouted, "Jim, if you don't keep this nigger boy of yours in his place, I am going to slap him down." Grandfather, being almost totally dependent on the boss for economic security, urged Dad to keep quiet.

My dad, looking back over that experience, says that at that moment he became determined to leave the farm. He often says humorously, "I ain't going to plough a mule anymore." After a few months he left Stockbridge and went to Atlanta determined to get an education. Although he was then eighteen—a year older than most persons finishing high school—he started out getting a high school education and did not stop until he had finished Atlanta's Morehouse College.

The thing that I admire most about my dad is his genuine Chris-

tian character. He is a man of real integrity, deeply committed to moral and ethical principles. He is conscientious in all of his undertakings. Even the person who disagrees with his frankness has to admit that his motives and actions are sincere. He never hesitates to tell the truth and speak his mind, however cutting it may be. This quality of frankness has often caused people to actually fear him. I have had young and old alike say to me, "I'm scared to death of your dad." Indeed, he is stern at many points.

My father has always had quite an interest in civil rights. He has been president of the NAACP in Atlanta, and he always stood out in social reform. From before I was born, he had refused to ride the city buses after witnessing a brutal attack on a load of Negro passengers. He led the fight in Atlanta to equalize teachers' salaries and was instrumental in the elimination of Jim Crow elevators in the courthouse.

As pastor of the Ebenezer Baptist Church, my father wielded great influence in the Negro community and perhaps won the grudging respect of the whites. At any rate, they never attacked him physically, a fact that filled my brother and sister and me with wonder as we grew up in this tension-packed atmosphere. With this heritage, it is not surprising that I also learned to abhor segregation, considering it both rationally inexplicable and morally unjustifiable.

I have never experienced the feeling of not having the basic necessities of life. These things were always provided by a father who always put his family first. My father never made more than an ordinary salary, but the secret was that he knew the art of saving and budgeting. He has always had sense enough not to live beyond his means. So for this reason he was able to provide us with the basic necessities of life with little strain. I went right on through school and never had to drop out to work or anything.

The first twenty-five years of my life were very comfortable years. If I had a problem I could always call Daddy. Things were solved. Life had been wrapped up for me in a Christmas package. This is not to say that I was born with a silver spoon in my mouth; far from it. I always had a desire to work, and I would spend my summers working.

"Doubts spring forth unrelentingly"

I joined the church at the age of five. I well remember how this event occurred. Our church was in the midst of the spring revival, and a guest evangelist had come down from Virginia. On Sunday morning the evangelist came into our Sunday school to talk to us about salvation, and after a short talk on this point he extended an invitation to any of us who wanted to join the church. My sister was the first one to join the church that morning, and after seeing her join I decided that I would not let her get ahead of me, so I was the next. I had never given this matter a thought, and even at the time of my baptism I was unaware of what was taking place. From this it seems quite clear that I joined the church not out of any dynamic conviction, but out of a childhood desire to keep up with my sister.

The church has always been a second home for me. As far back as I can remember I was in church every Sunday. My best friends were in Sunday school, and it was the Sunday school that helped me to build the capacity for getting along with people. I guess this was inevitable since my father was the pastor of my church, but I never regretted going to church until I passed through a state of skepticism in my second year of college.

The lessons which I was taught in Sunday school were quite in the fundamentalist line. None of my teachers ever doubted the infallibility of the Scriptures. Most of them were unlettered and had never heard of biblical criticism. Naturally, I accepted the teachings as they were being given to me. I never felt any need to doubt them—at least at that time I didn't. I guess I accepted biblical studies uncritically until I was about twelve years old. But this uncritical attitude could not last long, for it was contrary to the very nature of my being. I had always been the questioning and precocious type. At the age of thirteen, I shocked my Sunday school class by denying the bodily resurrection of Jesus. Doubts began to spring forth unrelentingly.

"How could I love a race of people who hated me?"

Two incidents happened in my late childhood and early adolescence that had a tremendous effect on my development. The first was the

death of my grandmother. She was very dear to each of us, but especially to me. I sometimes think I was her favorite grandchild. I was particularly hurt by her death mainly because of the extreme love I had for her. She assisted greatly in raising all of us. It was after this incident that for the first time I talked at any length on the doctrine of immortality. My parents attempted to explain it to me, and I was assured that somehow my grandmother still lived. I guess this is why today I am such a strong believer in personal immortality.

The second incident happened when I was about six years of age. From the age of three I had a white playmate who was about my age. We always felt free to play our childhood games together. He did not live in our community, but he was usually around every day; his father owned a store across the street from our home. At the age of six we both entered school—separate schools, of course. I remember how our friendship began to break as soon as we entered school; this was not my desire but his. The climax came when he told me one day that his father had demanded that he would play with me no more. I never will forget what a great shock this was to me. I immediately asked my parents about the motive behind such a statement.

We were at the dinner table when the situation was discussed, and here for the first time I was made aware of the existence of a race problem. I had never been conscious of it before. As my parents discussed some of the tragedies that had resulted from this problem and some of the insults they themselves had confronted on account of it, I was greatly shocked, and from that moment on I was determined to hate every white person. As I grew older and older this feeling continued to grow.

My parents would always tell me that I should not hate the white man, but that it was my duty as a Christian to love him. The question arose in my mind: How could I love a race of people who hated me and who had been responsible for breaking me up with one of my best childhood friends? This was a great question in my mind for a number of years.

I always had a resentment towards the system of segregation and felt that it was a grave injustice. I remember a trip to a downtown shoe store with Father when I was still small. We had sat down in

the first empty seats at the front of the store. A young white clerk came up and murmured politely:

"I'll be happy to wait on you if you'll just move to those seats in the rear."

Dad immediately retorted, "There's nothing wrong with these seats. We're quite comfortable here."

"Sorry," said the clerk, "but you'll have to move."

"We'll either buy shoes sitting here," my father retorted, "or we won't buy shoes at all."

Whereupon he took me by the hand and walked out of the store. This was the first time I had seen Dad so furious. That experience revealed to me at a very early age that my father had not adjusted to the system, and he played a great part in shaping my conscience. I still remember walking down the street beside him as he muttered, "I don't care how long I have to live with this system, I will never accept it."

And he never has. I remember riding with him another day when he accidentally drove past a stop sign. A policeman pulled up to the car and said:

"All right, boy, pull over and let me see your license."

My father instantly retorted: "Let me make it clear to you that you aren't talking to a boy. If you persist in referring to me as boy, I will be forced to act as if I don't hear a word you are saying."

The policeman was so shocked in hearing a Negro talk to him so forthrightly that he didn't quite know how to respond. He nervously wrote the ticket and left the scene as quickly as possible.

"The angriest I have ever been"

There was a pretty strict system of segregation in Atlanta. For a long, long time I could not go swimming, until there was a Negro YMCA. A Negro child in Atlanta could not go to any public park. I could not go to the so-called white schools. In many of the stores downtown, I couldn't go to a lunch counter to buy a hamburger or a cup of coffee. I could not attend any of the theaters. There were one or two Negro theaters, but they didn't get any of the main pictures. If they did get them, they got them two or three years later.

When I was about eight years old, I was in one of the downtown

stores of Atlanta and all of a sudden someone slapped me, and the only thing I heard was somebody saying, "You are that nigger that stepped on my foot." And it turned out to be a white lady. Of course I didn't retaliate at any point; I wouldn't dare retaliate when a white person was involved. I think some of it was part of my native structure—that is, that I have never been one to hit back. I finally told my mother what had happened, and she was very upset about it. But the lady who slapped me had gone, and my mother and I left the store almost immediately.

I remember another experience I used to have in Atlanta. I went to high school on the other side of town—to the Booker T. Washington High School. I had to get the bus in what was known as the Fourth Ward and ride over to the West Side. In those days, rigid patterns of segregation existed on the buses, so that Negroes had to sit in the backs of buses. Whites were seated in the front, and often if whites didn't get on the buses, those seats were still reserved for whites only, so Negroes had to stand over empty seats. I would end up having to go to the back of that bus with my body, but every time I got on that bus I left my mind up on the front seat. And I said to myself, "One of these days, I'm going to put my body up there where my mind is."

When I was fourteen, I traveled from Atlanta to Dublin, Georgia, with a dear teacher of mine, Mrs. Bradley. I participated in an oratorical contest there and I succeeded in winning the contest. My subject, ironically enough, was "The Negro and the Constitution."

We cannot have an enlightened democracy with one great group living in ignorance. We cannot have a healthy nation with one-tenth of the people ill-nourished, sick, harboring germs of disease which recognize no color lines—obey no Jim Crow laws. We cannot have a nation orderly and sound with one group so ground down and thwarted that it is almost forced into unsocial attitudes and crime. We cannot be truly Christian people so long as we flout the central teachings of Jesus: brotherly love and the Golden Rule. We cannot come to full prosperity with one great group so ill-delayed that it cannot buy goods. So as we gird ourselves to defend democracy from foreign attack, let us see to it

*that increasingly at home we give fair play and free opportunity for all
people.*

*Today thirteen million black sons and daughters of our forefathers
continue the fight for the translation of the Thirteenth, Fourteenth, and
Fifteenth Amendments from writing on the printed page to an actual-
ity. We believe with them that "if freedom is good for any it is good for
all," that we may conquer Southern armies by the sword, but it is
another thing to conquer Southern hate, that if the franchise is given to
Negroes, they will be vigilant and defend, even with their arms, the ark
of federal liberty from treason and destruction by her enemies.*

That night, Mrs. Bradley and I were on a bus returning to Atlanta. Along the way, some white passengers boarded the bus, and
the white driver ordered us to get up and give the whites our seats.
We didn't move quickly enough to suit him, so he began cursing us.
I intended to stay right in that seat, but Mrs. Bradley urged me up,
saying we had to obey the law. We stood up in the aisle for ninety
miles to Atlanta. That night will never leave my memory. It was the
angriest I have ever been in my life.

I had grown up abhorring not only segregation but also the oppressive and barbarous acts that grew out of it. I had seen police
brutality with my own eyes, and watched Negroes receive the most
tragic injustice in the courts. I can remember the organization
known as the Ku Klux Klan. It stands on white supremacy, and it
was an organization that in those days even used violent methods to
preserve segregation and to keep the Negro in his place, so to speak.
I remember seeing the Klan actually beat a Negro. I had passed spots
where Negroes had been savagely lynched. All of these things did
something to my growing personality.

I had also learned that the inseparable twin of racial injustice
was economic injustice. Although I came from a home of economic
security and relative comfort, I could never get out of my mind the
economic insecurity of many of my playmates and the tragic poverty
of those living around me. During my late teens I worked two summers (against my father's wishes—he never wanted my brother and
me to work around white people because of the oppressive conditions) in a plant that hired both Negroes and whites. Here I saw
economic injustice firsthand, and realized that the poor white was

exploited just as much as the Negro. Through these early experiences I grew up deeply conscious of the varieties of injustice in our society.

"As if the curtain had been dropped on my selfhood"

Just before going to college I went to Simsbury, Connecticut, and worked for a whole summer on a tobacco farm to earn a little school money to supplement what my parents were doing. One Sunday, we went to church in Simsbury, and we were the only Negroes there. On Sunday mornings I was the religious leader and spoke on any text I wanted to 107 boys. I had never thought that a person of my race could eat anywhere, but we ate in one of the finest restaurants in Hartford.

After that summer in Connecticut, it was a bitter feeling going back to segregation. It was hard to understand why I could ride wherever I pleased on the train from New York to Washington and then had to change to a Jim Crow car at the nation's capital in order

◆

LETTER TO MARTIN LUTHER KING, SR.

15 June 1944
Simsbury, Conn.

Dear Father:

I am very sorry I am so long about writing but I have been working most of the time. We are really having a fine time here and the work is very easy. We have to get up every day at 6:00. We have very good food. And I am working kitchen so you see I get better food.

We have service here every Sunday about 8:00 and I am the religious leader we have a Boys choir here and we are going to sing on the air soon. Sunday I went to church in Simsbury it was a white church. I could not get to Hartford to church but I am going next week. On our way here we saw some things I had never anticipated to see. After we passed Washington there was no discrimination at all the white people here are very nice. We go to any place we want to and sit any where we want to.

Tell everybody I said hello and I am still thinking of the church and reading my bible. And I am not doing any thing that I would not do in front of you.

Your Son

◆

to continue the trip to Atlanta. The first time that I was seated behind a curtain in a dining car, I felt as if the curtain had been
dropped on my selfhood. I could never adjust to the separate waiting
rooms, separate eating places, separate rest rooms, partly because
the separate was always unequal, and partly because the very idea of
separation did something to my sense of dignity and self-respect.

2

MOREHOUSE COLLEGE

My call to the ministry was not a miraculous or supernatural something. On the contrary it was an inner urge calling me to serve humanity.

SEPTEMBER 20, 1944
King begins freshman year at Morehouse College

FEBRUARY 25, 1948
Is ordained at Ebenezer

JUNE 8
Receives bachelor of arts degree in sociology from Morehouse

At the age of fifteen, I entered Morehouse College. My father and my maternal grandfather had also attended, so Morehouse has had three generations of Kings.

I shall never forget the hardships that I had upon entering college, for though I had been one of the top students in high school, I was still reading at only an eighth-grade level. I went to college from the eleventh grade. I never went to the twelfth grade, and skipped another grade earlier, so I was a pretty young fellow at Morehouse.

My days in college were very exciting ones. There was a free atmosphere at Morehouse, and it was there I had my first frank discussion on race. The professors were not caught up in the clutches of state funds and could teach what they wanted with academic freedom. They encouraged us in a positive quest for a solution to racial ills. I realized that nobody there was afraid. Important people came in to discuss the race problem rationally with us.

When I went to Morehouse as a freshman in 1944, my concern for racial and economic justice was already substantial. During my student days I read Henry David Thoreau's essay "On Civil Disobedience" for the first time. Here, in this courageous New Englander's refusal to pay his taxes and his choice of jail rather than support a war that would spread slavery's territory into Mexico, I made my first contact with the theory of nonviolent resistance. Fascinated by the idea of refusing to cooperate with an evil system, I was so deeply moved that I reread the work several times.

I became convinced that noncooperation with evil is as much a moral obligation as is cooperation with good. No other person has been more eloquent and passionate in getting this idea across than Henry David Thoreau. As a result of his writings and personal witness, we are the heirs of a legacy of creative protest. The teachings of Thoreau came alive in our civil rights movement; indeed, they are more alive than ever before. Whether expressed in a sit-in at lunch counters, a freedom ride into Mississippi, a peaceful protest in Albany, Georgia, a bus boycott in Montgomery, Alabama, these are outgrowths of Thoreau's insistence that evil must be resisted and that no moral man can patiently adjust to injustice.

As soon as I entered college, I started working with the organizations that were trying to make racial justice a reality. The wholesome relations we had in the Intercollegiate Council convinced me that we had many white persons as allies, particularly among the younger generation. I had been ready to resent the whole white race, but as I got to see more of white people, my resentment was softened, and a spirit of cooperation took its place. I was at the point where I was deeply interested in political matters and social ills. I could envision myself playing a part in breaking down the legal barriers to Negro rights.

"An inner urge calling me to serve society"

Because of the influence of my mother and father, I guess I always had a deep urge to serve humanity, but I didn't start out with an interest to enter the ministry. I thought I could probably do it better as a lawyer or doctor. One of my closest friends at Morehouse, Walter McCall, was clear about his intention of going into the ministry,

---

"KICK UP DUST"

I often find when decent treatment for the Negro is urged, a certain
class of people hurry to raise the scarecrow of social mingling and intermarriage. These questions have nothing to do with the case. And most
people who kick up this kind of dust know that it is simple dust to ob-
scure the real question of rights and opportunities. It is fair to remember
that almost the total of race mixture in America has come, not at Negro
initiative, but by the acts of those very white men who talk loudest of
race purity. We aren't eager to marry white girls, and we would like to
have our own girls left alone by both white toughs and white aristocrats.

We want and are entitled to the basic rights and opportunities of
American citizens: The right to earn a living at work for which we are
fitted by training and ability; equal opportunities in education, health,
recreation, and similar public services; the right to vote; equality before
the law; some of the same courtesy and good manners that we ourselves
bring to all human relations.

Letter to the Editor, *Atlanta Constitution*, August 6, 1946

---

but I was slow to make up my mind. I did serve as assistant to my
father for six months.

As stated above, my college training, especially the first two
years, brought many doubts into my mind. It was then that the
shackles of fundamentalism were removed from my body. More and
more I could see a gap between what I had learned in Sunday school
and what I was learning in college. My studies had made me skeptical, and I could not see how many of the facts of science could be
squared with religion.

I revolted, too, against the emotionalism of much Negro religion, the shouting and stamping. I didn't understand it, and it embarrassed me. I often say that if we, as a people, had as much religion
in our hearts and souls as we have in our legs and feet, we could
change the world.

I had seen that most Negro ministers were unlettered, not
trained in seminaries, and that gave me pause. I had been brought
up in the church and knew about religion, but I wondered whether
it could serve as a vehicle to modern thinking, whether religion
could be intellectually respectable as well as emotionally satisfying.

This conflict continued until I studied a course in Bible in which I came to see that behind the legends and myths of the Book were many profound truths which one could not escape. Two men—Dr. Mays, president of Morehouse College and one of the great influences in my life, and Dr. George Kelsey, a professor of philosophy and religion—made me stop and think. Both were ministers, both deeply religious, and yet both were learned men, aware of all the trends of modern thinking. I could see in their lives the ideal of what I wanted a minister to be.

It was in my senior year of college that I entered the ministry. I had felt the urge to enter the ministry from my high school days, but accumulated doubts had somewhat blocked the urge. Now it appeared again with an inescapable drive. I felt a sense of responsibility which I could not escape.

I guess the influence of my father had a great deal to do with my going into the ministry. This is not to say that he ever spoke to me in terms of being a minister but that my admiration for him was the great moving factor. He set forth a noble example that I didn't mind following. I still feel the effects of the noble moral and ethical ideals that I grew up under. They have been real and precious to me, and even in moments of theological doubt I could never turn away from them.

At the age of nineteen I finished college and was ready to enter seminary.

3

CROZER SEMINARY

I was well aware of the typical white stereotype of the Negro, that he is always late, that he's loud and always laughing, that he's dirty and messy, and for a while I was terribly conscious of trying to avoid identification with it. If I were a minute late to class, I was almost morbidly conscious of it and sure that everyone else noticed it. Rather than be thought of as always laughing, I'm afraid I was grimly serious for a time. I had a tendency to overdress, to keep my room spotless, my shoes perfectly shined, and my clothes immaculately pressed.

SEPTEMBER 14, 1948
King enters Crozer Theological Seminary

SPRING 1950
Hears Howard University president Mordecai Johnson lecture on Gandhi

MAY 8, 1951
Receives bachelor of divinity degree from Crozer

Not until 1948, when I entered Crozer Theological Seminary in Chester, Pennsylvania, did I begin a serious intellectual quest for a method to eliminate social evil. I turned to a serious study of the social and ethical theories of the great philosophers, from Plato and Aristotle down to Rousseau, Hobbes, Bentham, Mill, and Locke. All of these masters stimulated my thinking—such as it was—and, while finding things to question in each of them, I nevertheless learned a great deal from their study.

I spent a great deal of time reading the works of the great social

philosophers. I came early to Walter Rauschenbusch's *Christianity and the Social Crisis*, which left an indelible imprint on my thinking by giving me a theological basis for the social concern which had already grown up in me as a result of my early experiences. Of course there were points at which I differed with Rauschenbusch. I felt that he had fallen victim to the nineteenth-century "cult of inevitable progress" which led him to a superficial optimism concerning man's nature. Moreover, he came perilously close to identifying the Kingdom of God with a particular social and economic system—a tendency which should never befall the Church. But in spite of these shortcomings Rauschenbusch had done a great service for the Christian Church by insisting that the gospel deals with the whole man—not only his soul but his body; not only his spiritual well-being but his material well-being.

"The preaching ministry"

It has been my conviction ever since reading Rauschenbusch that any religion that professes concern for the souls of men and is not equally concerned about the slums that damn them, the economic conditions that strangle them, and the social conditions that cripple them is a spiritually moribund religion only waiting for the day to be buried. It well has been said: "A religion that ends with the individual, ends."

I feel that preaching is one of the most vital needs of our society, if it is used correctly. There is a great paradox in preaching: on the one hand it may be very helpful and on the other it may be very pernicious. It is my opinion that sincerity is not enough for the preaching ministry. The minister must be both sincere and intelligent. . . . I also think that the minister should possess profundity of conviction. We have too many minsters in the pulpit who are great spellbinders and too few who possess spiritual power. It is my profound conviction that I, as an aspirant for the ministry, should possess these powers.

I think that preaching should grow out of the experiences of the people. Therefore, I, as a minister, must know the problems of the people that I am pastoring. Too often do educated ministers leave the people lost in the fog of theological abstraction, rather than presenting that theology in the light of the people's experiences. It is my conviction that the minister must somehow take profound theological and philosophical

LETTER TO ALBERTA WILLIAMS KING

Dear Mother,

Your letter was received this morning. I often tell the boys around the campus I have the best mother in the world. You will never know how I appreciate the many kind things you and daddy are doing for me. So far I have gotten the money (5 dollars) every week.

As to my wanting some clippings from the newspapers, I must answer yes. I wondered why you hadn't sent many, especially the Atlanta World.

You stated that my letters aren't newsy enough. Well I don't have much news. I never go anywhere much but in these books. Some times the professor comes in class and tells us to read our assignments in Hebrew, and that is really hard.

Do you know the girl I used to date at Spelman (Gloria Royster). She is in school at Temple and I have been to see her twice. Also I met a fine chick in Phila who has gone wild over the old boy. Since Barbor told the members of his church that my family was rich, the girls are running me down. Of course, I don't ever think about them. I am too busy studying.

I hear from Christine every week. I try to answer her as regularly as possible.

Well I guess I must go back to studying. Give everybody my Regards.

Your son,

M.L.

October 1948

views and place them in a concrete framework. I must forever make the complex the simple.

Above all, I see the preaching ministry as a dual process. On the one hand I must attempt to change the soul of individuals so that their societies may be changed. On the other I must attempt to change the societies so that the individual soul will have a change. Therefore, I must be concerned about unemployment, slums, and economic insecurity. I am a profound advocate of the social gospel.

"Truth is found neither in Marxism nor in traditional capitalism"

During the Christmas holidays of 1949 I decided to spend my spare time reading Karl Marx to try to understand the appeal of commu-

nism for many people. For the first time I carefully scrutinized *Das Kapital* and *The Communist Manifesto*. I also read some interpretive works on the thinking of Marx and Lenin. In reading such Communist writings I drew certain conclusions that have remained with me as convictions to this day.

First, I rejected their materialistic interpretation of history. Communism, avowedly secularistic and materialistic, has no place for God. This I could never accept, for as a Christian I believe that there is a creative personal power in this universe who is the ground and essence of all reality—a power that cannot be explained in materialistic terms. History is ultimately guided by spirit, not matter.

Second, I strongly disagreed with communism's ethical relativism. Since for the Community there is no divine government, no absolute moral order, there are no fixed, immutable principles; consequently almost anything—force, violence, murder, lying—is a justifiable means to the "millennial" end. This type of relativism was abhorrent to me. Constructive ends can never give absolute moral justification to destructive means, because in the final analysis the end is preexistent in the means.

Third, I opposed communism's political totalitarianism. In communism the individual ends up in subjection to the state. True, the Marxist would argue that the state is an "interim" reality which is to be eliminated when the classless society emerges; but the state is the end while it lasts, and man only a means to that end. And if any man's so-called rights or liberties stand in the way of that end, they are simply swept aside. His liberties of expression, his freedom to vote, his freedom to listen to what news he likes or to choose his books are all restricted. Man becomes hardly more, in communism, than a depersonalized cog in the turning wheel of the state.

This deprecation of individual freedom was objectionable to me. I am convinced now, as I was then, that man is an end because he is a child of God. Man is not made for the state; the state is made for man. To deprive man of freedom is to relegate him to the status of a thing, rather than elevate him to the status of a person. Man must never be treated as a means to the end of the state, but always as an end within himself.

Yet, in spite of the fact that my response to communism was and is negative, and I consider it basically evil, there were points at which

I found it challenging. With all of its false assumptions and evil methods, communism grew as a protest against the hardships of the underprivileged. Communism in theory emphasized a classless society, and a concern for social justice, though the world knows from sad experience that in practice it created new classes and a new lexicon of injustice. The Christian ought always to be challenged by any protest against unfair treatment of the poor.

I also sought systematic answers to Marx's critique of modern bourgeois culture. He presented capitalism as essentially a struggle between the owners of the productive resources and the workers, whom Marx regarded as the real producers. Marx interpreted economic forces as the dialectical process by which society moved from feudalism through capitalism to socialism, with the primary mechanism of this historical movement being the struggle between economic classes whose interests were irreconcilable. Obviously this theory left out the numerous and significant complexities—political, economic, moral, religious, and psychological—which played a vital role in shaping the constellation of institutions and ideas known today as Western civilization. Moreover, it was dated in the sense that the capitalism Marx wrote about bore only a partial resemblance to the capitalism we know in this country.

But in spite of the shortcomings of his analysis, Marx had raised some basic questions. I was deeply concerned from my early teen days about the gulf between superfluous wealth and abject poverty, and my reading of Marx made me ever more conscious of this gulf. Although modern American capitalism had greatly reduced the gap through social reforms, there was still need for a better distribution of wealth. Moreover, Marx had revealed the danger of the profit motive as the sole basis of an economic system: capitalism is always in danger of inspiring men to be more concerned about making a living than making a life. We are prone to judge success by the index of our salaries or the size of our automobiles, rather than by the quality of our service and relationship to humanity. Thus capitalism can lead to a practical materialism that is as pernicious as the materialism taught by communism.

In short, I read Marx as I read all of the influential historical thinkers—from a dialectical point of view, combining a partial yes and a partial no. Insofar as Marx posited a metaphysical materialism,

an ethical relativism, and a strangulating totalitarianism, I responded with an unambiguous no; but insofar as he pointed to weaknesses of traditional capitalism, contributed to the growth of a definite self-consciousness in the masses, and challenged the social conscience of the Christian churches, I responded with a definite yes.

My reading of Marx also convinced me that truth is found neither in Marxism nor in traditional capitalism. Each represents a partial truth. Historically capitalism failed to see the truth in collective enterprise and Marxism failed to see the truth in individual enterprise. Nineteenth-century capitalism failed to see that life is social and Marxism failed and still fails to see that life is individual and personal. The Kingdom of God is neither the thesis of individual enterprise nor the antithesis of collective enterprise, but a synthesis which reconciles the truths of both.

"The only morally and practically sound method open to oppressed people"

During my stay at Crozer, I was also exposed for the first time to the pacifist position in a lecture by Dr. A. J. Muste. I was deeply moved by Dr. Muste's talk, but far from convinced of the practicability of his position. Like most of the students of Crozer, I felt that while

---

"THE SIGNIFICANT CONTRIBUTIONS OF JEREMIAH TO RELIGIOUS THOUGHT"

Again Jeremiah is a shining example of the truth that religion should never sanction the status quo. This more than anything else should be inculcated into the minds of modern religionists, for the worst disservice that we as individuals or churches can do to Christianity is to become sponsors and supporters of the status quo. How often has religion gone down, chained to a status quo it allied itself with. Therefore, we must admit that men like Jeremiah are valuable to any religion. Religion, in a sense, through men like Jeremiah, provides for its own advancement, and carries within it the promise of progress and renewed power. But what is society's reaction to such men? It has reacted, and always will react, in the only way open to it. It destroys such men. Jeremiah died a martyr.

Course paper submitted at Crozer Seminary, November 1948

war could never be a positive or absolute good, it could serve as a negative good in the sense of preventing the spread and growth of an evil force. War, horrible as it is, might be preferable to surrender to a totalitarian system—Nazi, Fascist, or Communist.

During this period I had about despaired of the power of love in solving social problems. I thought the only way we could solve our problem of segregation was an armed revolt. I felt that the Christian ethic of love was confined to individual relationships. I could not see how it could work in social conflict.

Perhaps my faith in love was temporarily shaken by the philosophy of Nietzsche. I had been reading parts of *The Genealogy of Morals* and the whole of *The Will to Power*. Nietzsche's glorification of power—in his theory, all life expressed the will to power—was an outgrowth of his contempt for ordinary mortals. He attacked the whole of the Hebraic-Christian morality—with its virtues of piety and humility, its otherworldliness, and its attitude toward suffering—as the glorification of weakness, as making virtues out of necessity and impotence. He looked to the development of a superman who would surpass man as man surpassed the ape.

Then one Sunday afternoon I traveled to Philadelphia to hear a sermon by Dr. Mordecai Johnson, president of Howard University. He was there to preach for the Fellowship House of Philadelphia. Dr. Johnson had just returned from a trip to India, and, to my great interest, he spoke of the life and teachings of Mahatma Gandhi. His message was so profound and electrifying that I left the meeting and bought a half-dozen books on Gandhi's life and works.

Like most people, I had heard of Gandhi, but I had never studied him seriously. As I read I became deeply fascinated by his campaigns of nonviolent resistance. I was particularly moved by his Salt March to the Sea and his numerous fasts. The whole concept of *Satyagraha* (*Satya* is truth which equals love, and *agraha* is force; *Satyagraha*, therefore, means truth force or love force) was profoundly significant to me. As I delved deeper into the philosophy of Gandhi, my skepticism concerning the power of love gradually diminished, and I came to see for the first time its potency in the area of social reform. Prior to reading Gandhi, I had about concluded that the ethics of Jesus were only effective in individual relationships. The "turn the other cheek" philosophy and the "love your enemies" philosophy

were only valid, I felt, when individuals were in conflict with other individuals; when racial groups and nations were in conflict a more realistic approach seemed necessary. But after reading Gandhi, I saw how utterly mistaken I was.

Gandhi was probably the first person in history to lift the love ethic of Jesus above mere interaction between individuals to a powerful and effective social force on a large scale. Love for Gandhi was a potent instrument for social and collective transformation. It was in this Gandhian emphasis on love and nonviolence that I discovered the method for social reform that I had been seeking. The intellectual and moral satisfaction that I failed to gain from the utilitarianism of Bentham and Mill, the revolutionary methods of Marx and Lenin, the social contracts theory of Hobbes, the "back to nature" optimism of Rousseau, the superman philosophy of Nietzsche, I found in the nonviolent resistance philosophy of Gandhi.

"The liberal doctrine of man"

But my intellectual odyssey to nonviolence did not end here. During my senior year in theological seminary, I engaged in the exciting reading of various theological theories. Having been raised in a rather strict fundamentalist tradition, I was occasionally shocked when my intellectual journey carried me through new and sometimes complex doctrinal lands, but the pilgrimage was always stimulating; it gave me a new appreciation for objective appraisal and critical analysis, and knocked me out of my dogmatic slumber.

When I came to Crozer, I could accept the liberal interpretation of Christianity with relative ease. Liberalism provided me with an intellectual satisfaction that I had never found in fundamentalism. I became so enamored of the insights of liberalism that I almost fell into the trap of accepting uncritically everything that came under its name. I was absolutely convinced of the natural goodness of man and the natural power of human reason.

The basic change in my thinking came when I began to question the liberal doctrine of man. My thinking went through a state of transition. At one time I found myself leaning toward a mild neo-orthodox view of man, and at other times I found myself leaning toward a liberal view of man. The former leaning may root back to

certain experiences that I had in the South, with its vicious race problem, that made it very difficult for me to believe in the essential goodness of man. The more I observed the tragedies of history and man's shameful inclination to choose the low road, the more I came to see the depths and strength of sin. Liberalism's superficial optimism concerning human nature caused it to overlook the fact that reason is darkened by sin. The more I thought about human nature, the more I saw how our tragic inclination for sin causes us to use our minds to rationalize our actions. Liberalism failed to see that reason by itself is little more than an instrument to justify man's defensive ways of thinking. Moreover, I came to recognize the complexity of man's social involvement and the glaring reality of collective evil. I came to feel that liberalism had been all too sentimental concerning human nature and that it leaned toward a false idealism. Reason, devoid of the purifying power of faith, can never free itself from distortions and rationalizations.

On the other hand, part of my liberal leaning had its source in another branch of the same root. In noticing the gradual improvements of this same race problem, I came to see some noble possibilities in human nature. Also my liberal leaning may have rooted back to the great imprint that many liberal theologians have left upon me and to my ever-present desire to be optimistic about human nature. Of course there is one phase of liberalism that I hope to cherish always: its devotion to the search for truth, its insistence on an open and analytical mind, its refusal to abandon the best light of reason. Its contribution to the philological-historical criticism of biblical literature has been of immeasurable value.

"A courageous confrontation of evil by the power of love"

During my last year in theological school, I began to read the works of Reinhold Niebuhr. The prophetic and realistic elements in Niebuhr's passionate style and profound thought were appealing to me, and made me aware of the complexity of human motives and the reality of sin on every level of man's existence. I became so enamored of his social ethics that I almost fell into the trap of accepting uncritically everything he wrote.

I read Niebuhr's critique of the pacifist position. Niebuhr had

himself once been a member of the pacifist ranks. For several years, he had been national chairman of the Fellowship of Reconciliation. His break with pacifism came in the early thirties, and the first full statement of his criticism of pacifism was in *Moral Man and Immoral Society*. Here he argued that there was no intrinsic moral difference between violent and nonviolent resistance. The social consequences of the two methods were different, he contended, but the differences were in degree rather than kind. Later Niebuhr began emphasizing the irresponsibility of relying on nonviolent resistance when there was no ground for believing that it would be successful in preventing the spread of totalitarian tyranny. It could only be successful, he argued, if the groups against whom the resistance was taking place had some degree of moral conscience, as was the case in Gandhi's struggle against the British. Niebuhr's ultimate rejection of pacifism was based primarily on the doctrine of man. He argued that pacifism failed to do justice to the reformation doctrine of justification by faith, substituting for it a sectarian perfectionism which believes "that divine grace actually lifts man out of the sinful contradictions of history and establishes him above the sins of the world."

At first, Niebuhr's critique of pacifism left me in a state of confusion. As I continued to read, however, I came to see more and more the shortcomings of his position. For instance, many of his statements revealed that he interpreted pacifism as a sort of passive nonresistance to evil expressing naive trust in the power of love. But this was a serious distortion. My study of Gandhi convinced me that true pacifism is not nonresistance to evil, but nonviolent resistance to evil. Between the two positions, there is a world of difference. Gandhi resisted evil with as much vigor and power as the violent resister, but he resisted with love instead of hate. True pacifism is not unrealistic submission to evil power, as Niebuhr contends. It is rather a courageous confrontation of evil by the power of love, in the faith that it is better to be the recipient of violence than the inflicter of it, since the latter only multiplies the existence of violence and bitterness in the universe, while the former may develop a sense of shame in the opponent, and thereby bring about a transformation and change of heart.

In spite of the fact that I found many things to be desired in Niebuhr's philosophy, there were several points at which he con-

structively influenced my thinking. Niebuhr's great contribution to
theology is that he has refuted the false optimism characteristic of a
great segment of Protestant liberalism. Moreover, Niebuhr has extraordinary insight into human nature, especially the behavior of
nations and social groups. He is keenly aware of the complexity of
human motives and of the relation between morality and power. His
theology is a persistent reminder of the reality of sin on every level
of man's existence. These elements in Niebuhr's thinking helped me
to recognize the illusions of a superficial optimism concerning
human nature and the dangers of a false idealism. While I still believed in man's potential for good, Niebuhr made me realize his
potential for evil as well. Moreover, Niebuhr helped me to recognize
the complexity of man's social involvement and the glaring reality
of collective evil.

Many pacifists, I felt, failed to see this. All too many had an
unwarranted optimism concerning man and leaned unconsciously
toward self-righteousness. After reading Niebuhr, I tried to arrive at
a realistic pacifism. In other words, I came to see the pacifist position
not as sinless but as the lesser evil in the circumstances. I do not
claim to be free from the moral dilemmas that the Christian non-
pacifist confronts, but I am convinced that the church cannot be
silent while mankind faces the threat of nuclear annihilation. I felt
that the pacifist would have a greater appeal if he did not claim
to be free from the moral dilemmas that the Christian non-pacifist
confronts.

I anticipated graduating from Crozer in May 1951. For a number of
years I had been desirous of teaching in a college or a school of
religion. Realizing the necessity for scholastic attainment in the
teaching profession, I felt that graduate work would give me a better
grasp of my field. I had a general knowledge of my field, but I had
not done adequate research to meet the scholarly issues which I
would confront in this area. I felt that a few years of intensified study
in a graduate school would give me a thorough grasp of knowledge
in my field.

My particular interest in Boston University could be summed up
in two statements. First, my thinking in philosophical areas had been
greatly influenced by some of the faculty members there, particularly

"A CONCEPTION AND IMPRESSION OF RELIGION DRAWN FROM DR. EDGAR S. BRIGHTMAN'S BOOK ENTITLED *A PHILOSOPHY OF RELIGION*"

It is religion that gives meaning to life. It is religion that gives meaning to the Universe. It is religion that is the greatest incentive for the good life. It is religion which gives us the assurance that all that is high noble and valuable will be conserved. Such fruits of religion I find to be its greatest virtues, and certainly they cannot be ignored by any sane man. I must now conclude that any atheistic view is both philosophically unsound and practically disadvantageous. How I long now for that religious experience which Dr. Brightman so cogently speaks of throughout his book. It seems to be an experience, the lack of which life becomes dull and meaningless. As I reflect on the matter, however, I do remember moments that I have been awe awakened; there have been times that I have been carried out of myself by something greater than myself and to that something I gave myself. Has this great something been God? Maybe after all I have been religious for a number of years, and am now only becoming aware of it.

From a course paper submitted at Crozer Seminary, March 28, 1951

Dr. Edgar S. Brightman. For this reason, I longed for the possibility of studying under him. Secondly, one of my professors at Crozer was a graduate of Boston University, and his great influence over me turned my eyes toward his former school. I had gotten some valuable information about Boston University from him, and I was convinced that there were definite advantages there for me.

"O THAT I KNEW WHERE I MIGHT FIND HIM"

I can remember very vividly how in my recent seminary days, I was able to strengthen my spiritual life through communing with nature. The seminary campus is a beautiful sight, particularly so in the spring. And it was at this time of year that I made it a practice to go out to the edge of the campus every afternoon for at least an hour to commune with nature. On the side of the campus ran a little tributary from the Delaware river. Every day I would sit on the edge of the campus by the side of the river and watch the beauties of nature. My friend, in this experience, I saw God. I saw him in birds of the air, the leaves of the tree, the movement of the rippling waves. . . . Sometimes I go out at night and look up at the stars as they bedeck the heavens like shining silver pins sticking in a magnificent blue pin cushion. There is God. Sometimes I watch the sun as it gets up in the morning and paints its technicolor across the eastern horizon. There is God. Sometimes I watch the moon as it walks across the sky as a queen walks across her masterly mansion. There is God. Henry Ward Beecher was right: "Nature is God's tongue."

Reminiscence about Crozer years, ca. 1953

4

BOSTON UNIVERSITY

As a young man with most of my life ahead of me, I decided early to give my life to something eternal and absolute. Not to these little gods that are here today and gone tomorrow. But to God who is the same yesterday, today, and forever.

SEPTEMBER 13, 1951
King enters Boston University's School of Theology

FEBRUARY 25, 1953
Academic advisor Edgar S. Brightman dies; Harold DeWolf becomes new advisor

JUNE 5, 1955
Receives doctorate in systematic theology from Boston University

The next stage of my intellectual pilgrimage to nonviolence came during my doctoral studies at Boston University. Here I had the opportunity to talk to many exponents of nonviolence, both students and visitors at the campus.

Boston University School of Theology, under the influence of Dean Walter Muelder and Professor Allen Knight Chalmers, had a deep sympathy for the pacifist position. Both Dean Muelder and Dr. Chalmers had a passion for social justice. One never got the impression that this passion stemmed from a superficial optimism concerning human nature, but from a deep faith in the possibilities of human beings when they allowed themselves to become co-workers with God. My association with men like that also caused me to deepen my concern, and of course many of the studies I contin-

ued to make concerning the philosophy and theory of nonviolence naturally influenced my thinking.

Theologically I found myself still holding to the liberal position. I had come to see more than ever before that there were certain enduring qualities in liberalism which all of the vociferous noises of fundamentalism and neo-orthodoxy could never destroy. However, while at Boston, I became much more sympathetic towards the neo-orthodox position than I had been in previous years. I do not mean that I accept neo-orthodoxy as a set of doctrines, but I did see in it a necessary corrective for a liberalism that had become all too shallow and that too easily capitulated to modern culture. Neo-orthodoxy certainly had the merit of calling us back to the depths of Christian faith.

I also came to see that Reinhold Niebuhr had overemphasized the corruption of human nature. His pessimism concerning human nature was not balanced by an optimism concerning divine nature. He was so involved in diagnosing man's sickness of sin that he overlooked the cure of grace.

I studied philosophy and theology at Boston University under Edgar S. Brightman and L. Harold DeWolf. I did most of my work under Dr. DeWolf, who is a very dear friend of mine, and, of course, I was greatly influenced by him and by Dr. Brightman, whom I had the privilege to study with before he passed on. It was mainly under these teachers that I studied Personalistic philosophy—the theory that the clue to the meaning of ultimate reality is found in personality. This personal idealism remains today my basic philosophical position. Personalism's insistence that only personality—finite and infinite—is ultimately real strengthened me in two convictions: it

---

MEMORIES OF HOUSING BIAS WHILE IN GRADUATE SCHOOL

I remember very well trying to find a place to live. I went into place after place where there were signs that rooms were for rent. They were for rent until they found out I was a Negro, and suddenly they had just been rented.

Quoted in *Boston Globe*, April 23, 1965

gave me metaphysical and philosophical grounding for the idea of a personal God, and it gave me a metaphysical basis for the dignity and worth of all human personality.

Just before Dr. Brightman's death, I began studying the philosophy of Hegel with him. This course proved to be both rewarding and stimulating. Although the course was mainly a study of Hegel's monumental work, *Phenomenology of Mind,* I spent my spare time reading his *Philosophy of History* and *Philosphy of Right.* There were points in Hegel's philosophy that I strongly disagreed with. For instance, his absolute idealism was rationally unsound to me because it tended to swallow up the many in the one. But there were other aspects of his thinking that I found stimulating. His contention that "truth is the whole" led me to a philosophical method of rational coherence. His analysis of the dialectical process, in spite of its shortcomings, helped me to see that growth comes through struggle.

My work at Boston University progressed very well. Both Dr. DeWolf and Dr. Brightman were quite impressed. I completed my residence work and began the process of writing my dissertation. My dissertation title was "A Comparison of the Conception of God in the Thinking of Paul Tillich and Henry Nelson Wieman." The concept of God was chosen because of the central place which it occupies in any religion and because of the ever-present need to interpret and clarify the God concept. Tillich and Wieman were chosen because they represent different types of theology and because each of them had an increasing influence upon theological and philosophical thought.

In 1954 I ended my formal training with divergent intellectual forces converging into a positive social philosophy. One of the main tenets of this philosophy was the conviction that nonviolent resistance was one of the most potent weapons available to oppressed people in their quest for social justice. Interestingly enough, at this time I had merely an intellectual understanding and appreciation of the position, with no firm determination to organize it in a socially effective situation.

"Rediscovering Lost Values"

The thing that we need in the world today, is a group of men and women who will stand up for right and be opposed to wrong, wherever

it is. A group of people who have come to see that some things are wrong, whether they're never caught up with. Some things are right, whether nobody sees you doing them or not.

All I'm trying to say is, our world hinges on moral foundations. God has made it so! God has made the universe to be based on a moral law. . . .

This universe hinges on moral foundations. There is something in this universe that justifies Carlyle in saying,

"No lie can live forever."

There is something in this universe that justifies William Cullen Bryant in saying,

"Truth, crushed to earth, will rise again."

There is something in this universe that justifies James Russell Lowell in saying,

"Truth forever on the scaffold,

Wrong forever on the throne.

With that scaffold sways the future.

Behind the dim unknown stands God,

Within the shadow keeping watch above his own."

There is something in this universe that justifies the biblical writer in saying,

"You shall reap what you sow."

As a young man with most of my life ahead of me, I decided early to give my life to something eternal and absolute. Not to these little gods that are here today and gone tomorrow. But to God who is the same yesterday, today, and forever.

I'm not going to put my ultimate faith in the little gods that can be destroyed in an atomic age, but the God who has been our help in ages past, and our hope for years to come, and our shelter in the time of storm, and our eternal home. That's the God that I'm putting my ultimate faith in. . . . The God that I'm talking about this morning is the God of the universe and the God that will last through the ages. If we are to go forward this morning, we've got to go back and find that God. That is the God that demands and commands our ultimate allegiance.

If we are to go forward, we must go back and rediscover these precious values—that all reality hinges on moral foundations and that all reality has spiritual control.

5

CORETTA

I am indebted to my wife Coretta, without whose love, sacrifices, and loyalty neither life nor work would bring fulfillment. She has given me words of consolation when I needed them and a well-ordered home where Christian love is a reality.

APRIL 27, 1927
Coretta Scott born in Heiberger, Alabama

JANUARY 1952
Coretta and Martin meet in Boston

JUNE 18, 1953
King Sr. performs marriage in Marion, Alabama

It was in Boston that I met and fell in love with the attractive singer Coretta Scott, whose gentle manner and air of repose did not disguise her lively spirit. I had met quite a few girls in Boston, but none that I was particularly fond of.

I was about to get cynical. So I asked Mary Powell, a friend from Atlanta who was also a student at the New England Conservatory of Music, "Do you know any nice, attractive young ladies?"

Mary Powell introduced us and I was fortunate enough to get Coretta's telephone number. We met over the telephone: "This is M. L. King, Jr. A mutual friend of ours told me about you and gave me your telephone number. She said some very wonderful things about you, and I'd like very much to meet you and talk to you."

We talked awhile. "You know every Napoleon has his Waterloo. I'm like Napoleon. I'm at my Waterloo, and I'm on my knees. I'd

like to meet you and talk some more. Perhaps we could have lunch tomorrow or something like that."

She agreed to see me. "I'll come over and pick you up. I have a green Chevy that usually takes ten minutes to make the trip from B.U., but tomorrow I'll do it in seven."

She talked about things other than music. I never will forget, the first discussion we had was about the question of racial and economic injustice and the question of peace. She had been actively engaged in movements dealing with these problems.

After an hour, my mind was made up. I said, "So you can do something else besides sing? You've got a good mind also. You have everything I ever wanted in a woman. We ought to get married someday."

I didn't want a wife I couldn't communicate with. I had to have a wife who would be as dedicated as I was. I wish I could say that I led her down this path, but I must say we went down it together because she was as actively involved and concerned when we met as she is now.

I told my mother, "Coretta is going to be my wife." On June 18, 1953, we were married. Although we had returned to Marion to be married by my father on the Scotts' spacious lawn, it was in Boston that we began our married life together.

"Corrie"

Coretta Scott is a native of the South. She is from Marion, Alabama, and she went to college in Ohio, Antioch College. Having inherited a talent for music from her mother, Bernice Scott, as well as the strength of quiet determination, she had then gone on with the aid of a scholarship to work her way through the New England Conservatory in Boston. She wanted to be a concert singer. She was a mezzo-soprano and I'm sure she would have gone on into this area if a Baptist preacher hadn't interrupted her life.

Coretta's father, Obie Scott, a short, stocky man of dark complexion, is a strong and courageous man. People are strongly attracted to him because of his warm personality. He loves people and is always ready to help someone in need. Although reared on a farm, Obie Scott was always concerned about going into business for him-

LETTER TO CORETTA

Darling, I miss you so much. In fact, much too much for my own good. I never realized that you were such an intimate part of my life. My life without you is like a year without a spring time which comes to give illumination and heat to the atmosphere saturated by the dark cold breeze of winter. . . . O excuse me, my darling. I didn't mean to go off on such a poetical and romantic flight. But how else can we express the deep emotions of life other than in poetry? Isn't love too ineffable to be grasped by the cold calculating hands of intellect?

By the way (to turn to something more intellectual) I have just completed Bellamy's *Looking Backward*. It was both stimulating and fascinating. There can be no doubt about it. Bellamy had the insight of a social prophet as well as the fact finding mind of the social scientist. I welcomed the book because much of its content is in line with my basic ideas. I imagine you already know that I am much more socialistic in my economic theory than capitalistic. And yet I am not so opposed to capitalism that I have failed to see its relative merits. It started out with a noble and high motive, viz., to block the trade monopolies of nobles, but like most human systems it fell victim to the very thing it was revolting against. So today capitalism has out-lived its usefulness. It has brought about a system that takes necessities from the masses to give luxuries to the classes. So I think Bellamy is right in seeing the gradual decline of capitalism.

I think you noticed that Bellamy emphasized that the change would be evolutionary rather than revolutionary. This, it seems to me, is the most sane and ethical way for social change to take place.

Eternally Yours,
Martin

Atlanta, July 18, 1952

self. He finally succeeded and operated a trucking business, a combination filling station and grocery store, and a chicken farm. Despite the reprisals and physical threats of his white competitors, he attempted to get ahead in these various businesses and dared to make a decent living for his family. He has never been an Uncle Tom, but he had to suffer certain insults and even humiliation in order to survive in his community. The amazing thing is that he came through all of this with his courage undaunted, without becoming

bitter. Coretta often made comparison between me and her father. Even in the early days of our courtship, she used to say, "You remind me so much of my father." I don't suppose any compliment could be more inflating to the male ago.

Coretta's mother, Bernice Scott, is quite different from her father in many respects. In contrast to his overflowing personality she is rather shy. She is an attractive woman, fair in complexion, possessing narrow features and long black straight hair. In knowing her, one soon detects that she is a person of courage, determination, and amazing internal strength. She is deeply devoted to her family, always willing to sacrifice her needs to those of her children. More than anyone else, she taught Coretta her moral and ethical values, not by what she said alone, but also by her example.

"Staying with the struggle to the end"

My devoted wife has been a constant source of consolation to me through all the difficulties. In the midst of the most tragic experiences, she never became panicky or overemotional. I have come to see the real meaning of that rather trite statement: a wife can either make or break a husband. My wife was always stronger than I was through the struggle. While she had certain natural fears and anxieties concerning my welfare, she never allowed them to hamper my active participation in the movement. Corrie proved to be that type of wife with qualities to make a husband when he could have been so easily broken. In the darkest moments, she always brought the light of hope. I am convinced that if I had not had a wife with the fortitude, strength, and calmness of Corrie, I could not have withstood the ordeals and tensions surrounding the movement.

She saw the greatness of the movement and had a unique willingness to sacrifice herself for its continuation. If I have done anything in this struggle, it is because I have had behind me and at my side a devoted, understanding, dedicated, patient companion in the person of my wife. I can remember times when I sent her away for safety. I would look up a few days later, and she was back home, because she wanted to be there.

LETTER TO CORETTA

July 23, 1954
Boston

Darling,

How goes everything? I received your special and naturally I was over-joyed to hear from you. I was happy to know that the Women's Day went over in a big way. Your analysis of Gardner's sermon was very good. I see you are a very keen observer.

I am doing quite well, and studying hard as usual. I have plenty of privacy here and nobody to bother me.

All of your friends that I have seen are doing fine. Everybody asks about you.

We had our Philosophy Club Monday night and it was well attended. Brother Satterwhite did the paper.

How are all of the folks?

I will be arriving in Atlanta by plane at 1:25 A.M. Friday night or rather Saturday morning. You all be sure to meet me at the airport. We will leave for Montgomery sometime Saturday morning, that is, if you can go.

Give everybody my regards and let me hear from you soon. Let me know how you are doing.

Be sweet and I will see you soon.

Your Darling,
Martin

Coretta was never satisfied in being away from me, but she could not always be with me because she had to stay home with our four rather young children. She did join me on some occasions, and she was always a deep consolation to me, supporting my every move. I didn't have the problem of having a wife who was afraid and trying to run from the situation. And that was a great help in all of the difficulties that I confronted.

Coretta had to settle down to a few concerts here and there. Basically she has been a pastor's wife and mother of our four children, Martin Luther III, Dexter Scott, Yolanda Denise, and Bernice Albertine.

When I thought of my future, I also thought of my family. I had to think of what's best for them also. One of the frustrating aspects

of my life has been the great demands that come as a result of my involvement in the civil rights movement and the struggle for justice and peace. I have to be away from home a great deal and that takes me away from the family so much. It's just impossible to carry out the responsibilities of a father and husband when you have these kinds of demands. But fortunately I have a most understanding wife who has tried to explain to the children why I have to be absent so much. I think in some way they understand, even though it's pretty hard on them.

6

DEXTER AVENUE
BAPTIST CHURCH

*You the people of Dexter Avenue Baptist Church have called me to
serve as pastor of your historic church; and I have gladly accepted the
call. It is with more than perfunctory gratitude that I offer my appreciation to you for bestowing upon me this great honor. I accept the pastorate dreadfully aware of the tremendous responsibilities accompanying
it. Contrary to some shallow thinking, the responsibilities of the pastorate both stagger and astound the imagination. They tax the whole man.*

JANUARY 24, 1954
King delivers trial sermon at Dexter Avenue Baptist Church in
Montgomery, Alabama

FEBRUARY 28
Delivers guest sermon at Second Baptist Church in Detroit,
Michigan

APRIL 14
Accepts call to Dexter's pastorate

MAY 2
Delivers first sermon as Dexter's minister

OCTOBER 31
Offically becomes pastor of Dexter; King Sr. delivers installation
sermon

AUGUST 26, 1955
Rosa Parks, secretary of Montgomery NAACP chapter, informs
King of his election to executive committee

NOVEMBER 17
First child, Yolanda Denise, is born

A fter being in school twenty-one years without a break, I reached the satisfying moment of completing the residential require-ments for the Ph.D. degree. The major job that remained was to write my doctoral thesis. In the meantime I felt that it would be wise to start considering a job. I was not sure what area of the ministry I wanted to settle down in. I had had a great deal of satisfaction in the pastorate and had almost come to the point of feeling that I could best render my service in this area. I never could quite get the idea out of my mind that I should do some teaching, yet I felt a great deal of satisfaction with the pastorate.

Two churches in the East—one in Massachusetts and one in New York—had expressed an interest in calling me. Three colleges had offered attractive and challenging posts—one a teaching post, one a deanship, and the other an administrative position. In the midst of thinking about each of these positions, I received a letter from the officers of the Dexter Avenue Baptist Church of Montgomery, saying that they were without a pastor and that they would be glad to have me preach when I was again in that section of the country. They had heard of me through my father in Atlanta. I wrote immediately say-ing that I would be home in Atlanta for the Christmas holidays, and that I would be happy to come to Montgomery to preach one Sun-day in January.

The Dexter Avenue Baptist Church had a rich history. Many out-standing ministers served there, including Dr. Vernon Johns. It was a very fine church with even greater possibilities.

"Asking for God's guidance"

On a cool Saturday afternoon in January 1954, I set out to drive from Atlanta, Georgia, to Montgomery, Alabama. It was one of those clear wintry days when the sun bedecked the skies with all of its radiant beauty. After starting out on the highway, I happened to have turned on the radio. Fortunately, the Metropolitan Opera was on the air with a performance of one of my favorite operas—Donizetti's *Lucia di Lammermoor*. So with the captivating beauty of the countryside, the inspiration of Donizetti's inimitable music, and the matchless splendor of the skies, the usual monotony that accom-

panies a relatively long drive—especially when one is alone—was absorbed into meaningful diversions.

After about a four-hour drive, I arrived in Montgomery. Although I had passed through the city before, I had never been there on a real visit. Now I would have the opportunity to spend a few days in this beautiful little town, which has the distinction of being one of the oldest cities in the United States. It occupies an undulating site around a sharp bend in the Alabama River in the midst of rich and fertile farmland.

Not long after I arrived a friend was gracious enough to take me by the Dexter Avenue Baptist Church where I was to preach the following morning. A solid brick structure erected in Reconstruction days, it stood at one corner of a handsome square not far from the center of town. As we drove up, I noticed diagonally across the square a stately white building of impressive proportions and arresting beauty, the State Capitol—one of the finest examples of classical Georgian architecture in America. Here on January 7, 1861, Alabama voted to secede from the Union, and on February 18, on the steps of the portico, Jefferson Davis took his oath of office as President of the Confederate States. For this reason, Montgomery has been known across the years as the Cradle of the Confederacy. Here the first Confederate flag was made and unfurled. I was to see this imposing reminder of the Confederacy from the steps of the Dexter Avenue Baptist Church many times in the following years.

Saturday evening, as I began going over my sermon, I was aware of a certain anxiety. Although I had preached many times before— having served as associate pastor of my father's church in Atlanta for four years, and actually doing all of the preaching there for three straight summers—I had never preached in a situation in which I was being considered for the pastorate of a church. In such a situation one cannot but be conscious of the fact that he is on trial. Many questions came to my mind. How could I best impress the congregation? Should I attempt to interest it with a display of scholarship? Or should I preach just as I had always done, depending finally on the inspiration of the spirit of God? I decided to follow the latter course. I said to myself over and over again, "Keep Martin Luther King in the background and God in the foreground and everything will be all right. Remember you are a channel of the gospel and not

the source." With these words on my lips I knelt and prayed my regular evening prayer. I closed the prayer by asking for God's guidance and His abiding presence as I confronted the congregation of His people on the next morning. With the assurance that always comes to me after sincere prayer, I rose from my knees to the comfortable bed, and in almost an instant I fell asleep.

I arose early on Sunday morning—a custom I follow every Sunday in order to have an hour of quiet meditation. It was a beautiful morning. From my window I watched the sun rise in the eastern horizon and move out as if to point its Technicolor across the lofty blue. I went over my sermon one more time.

Eleven o'clock soon came around and I found myself in the pulpit of Dexter Avenue Baptist Church. A large congregation turned out that morning. My sermon topic was "The Three Dimensions of a Complete Life." The congregation was receptive, and I left with the feeling that God had used me well. I was also greatly impressed with Dexter and its vast possibilities. Later in the day the pulpit committee asked me if I would accept the pastorate in the event they saw fit to call me. I answered that I would give such a call my most prayerful and serious consideration. After this meeting, I left Montgomery for Atlanta, and then took a flight back to Boston.

About a month later I received an air-mail, special-delivery letter from Montgomery, telling me that I had been unanimously called to

---

"THE THREE DIMENSIONS OF A COMPLETE LIFE"

The Length of Life, as we shall use it, is not its duration, not its longevity. It is rather the push of a life forward to its personal ends and ambitions. It is the inward concern for one's personal welfare. The Breadth of Life is the outward concern for the welfare of others. The Height of Life is the upward reach toward God. These are the three dimensions of life, and, without the due development of all, no life becomes complete. Life at its best is a great triangle. At one angle stands the individual person, at the other angle stands other persons, and at the tip top stands God. Unless these three are concatenated, working harmoniously together in a single life, that life is incomplete.

From sermon delivered at Dexter, January 24, 1954

the pastorate of the Dexter Avenue Baptist Church. I was very happy to have this offer, but I did not answer immediately. Now I had to face up to the problem of what to do about the several offers that had come my way. It so happened that I was to take a flight to Detroit, Michigan, the next day, where I was to preach the following Sunday. I thought about this important matter all the way to Detroit. It was one of those turbulent days in which the clouds were hovering very low, but as the plane lifted itself above the clouds, the choppiness of the flight soon passed away. As I sailed along noticing the shining silvery sheets of the clouds below and the dark deep shadow of the blue above, several things came to my mind.

At this time I was torn in two directions. On the one hand I was inclined toward the pastorate; on the other hand, toward educational work. Which way should I go? And if I accepted a church, should it be one in the South, with all the tragic implications of segregation, or one of the two available pulpits in the North? Now, I thought, as the plane carried me toward Detroit, I had a chance to escape from the long night of segregation. Could I return to a society that condoned a system I had abhorred since childhood?

These questions were still unanswered when I returned to Boston. I discussed them with my wife, Coretta (we had been married less than a year), to find that she too was hesitant about returning south. We discussed the all-important question of raising children in the bonds of segregation. We reviewed our own growth in the South, and the many advantages that we had been deprived of as a result of segregation. The question of my wife's musical career came up. She was certain that a Northern city would afford a greater opportunity for continued study than any city in the deep South. For several days we talked and thought and prayed over each of these matters.

Finally we agreed that, in spite of the disadvantages and inevitable sacrifices, our greatest service could be rendered in our native South. We came to the conclusion that we had something of a moral obligation to return—at least for a few years.

The South, after all, was our home. Despite its shortcomings, we had a real desire to do something about the problems that we had felt so keenly as youngsters. We never wanted to be considered detached spectators. Since racial discrimination was most intense in

the South, we felt that some of the Negroes who had received a portion of their training in other sections of the country should return to share their broader contacts and educational experience. Moreover, despite having to sacrifice much of the cultural life we loved, despite the existence of Jim Crow, which kept reminding us at all times of the color of our skin, we had the feeling that something remarkable was unfolding in the South, and we wanted to be on hand to witness it.

With this decision my inclination toward the pastorate temporarily won out over my desire to teach, and I decided to accept the call to Dexter for a few years and satisfy my fondness for scholarship later by turning to the teaching field.

So I went back to Montgomery. Because of my desire to spend at least four more months of intensive work on my doctoral thesis, I asked for and was granted the condition that I would not be required to take up the full-time pastorate until September 1, 1954. I agreed, however, to come at least once a month to keep things running smoothly during this interim period. For the next four months I commuted by plane between Boston and Montgomery.

On a Sunday in May 1954 I preached my first sermon as minister of the Dexter Avenue Baptist Church:

It is a significant fact that I come to the pastorate of Dexter at a most crucial hour of our world's history; at a time when the flame of war might arise at any time to redden the skies of our dark and dreary world; at a time when men know all too well that without the proper guidance the whole of civilization can be plunged across the abyss of destruction; at a time when men are experiencing in all realms of life disruption and conflict, self-destruction, and meaningless despair and anxiety. Today men who were but yesterday ridiculing the Church of Christ are now asking the Church the way to the paradise of peace and happiness. We must somehow give our generation an answer. Dexter, like all other churches, must somehow lead men and women of a decadent generation to the high mountain of peace and salvation. We must give men and women, who are all but on the brink of despair, a new bent on life. I pray God that I will be able to lead Dexter in this urgent mission.

I come to you with nothing so special to offer. I have no pretense to

being a great preacher or even a profound scholar. I certainly have no pretense to infallibility—that is reserved for the height of the Divine, rather than the depth of the human. At every moment, I am conscious of my finiteness, knowing so clearly that I have never been bathed in the sunshine of omniscience or baptized in the waters of omnipotence. I come to you with only the claim of being a servant of Christ, and a feeling of dependence on his grace for my leadership. I come with a feeling that I have been called to preach and to lead God's people. I have felt like Jeremiah, "The word of God is in my heart like burning fire shut up in my bones." I have felt with Amos that when God speaks who can but prophesy? I have felt with Jesus that the spirit of the Lord is upon me, because he hath anointed me to preach the gospel to the poor, to heal the brokenhearted, to preach deliverance to the captives and to set at liberty those that are bruised.

"I began my full-time pastorate"

Montgomery was not unfamiliar to Coretta, for her home was just eighty miles away. (I teased her that she had better be thankful. If she hadn't married me, she'd still be back in Marion, Alabama, picking cotton.) Since her teens she had breathed the free air of unsegregated colleges, and stayed as a welcome guest in white homes. Now in preparation for our long-term return to the South, she visited the Negro section of town where we would be living without choice. She saw the Negroes crowded into the backs of segregated buses and knew that she would be riding there too. But on the same visit she was introduced to the church and cordially received by its fine congregation. And with her sense of optimism and balance, which were to be my constant support in the days to come, she placed her faith on the side of the opportunities and the challenge for Christian service that were offered by Dexter and the Montgomery community.

The church work was stimulating from the beginning. The first few weeks of the autumn of 1954 were spent formulating a program that would be meaningful to this particular congregation. I was anxious to change the impression in the community that Dexter was a sort of silk-stocking church catering only to a certain class. Often it was referred to as the "big folk church." Revolting against this idea, I was convinced that worship at its best is a social experience with

people of all levels of life coming together to realize their oneness and unity under God. Whenever the church, consciously or unconsciously, caters to one class it loses the spiritual force of the "whosoever will, let him come" doctrine, and is in danger of becoming little more than a social club with a thin veneer of religiosity.

For several months I had to divide my efforts between completing my thesis and carrying out my duties with the church. I continued to study hard as usual. I rose every morning at five-thirty and spent three hours writing the thesis, returning to it late at night for another three hours. The remainder of the day was given to church work, including, besides the weekly service, marriages, funerals, and personal conferences. One day each week was given over to visiting and praying with members who were either sick or otherwise confined to their homes.

On September 1, 1954, we moved into the parsonage and I began my full-time pastorate. The first months were busy with the usual chores of getting to know a new house, a new job, a new city. There were old friendships to pick up and new ones to be made, and little time to look beyond our private lives to the general community around us.

My installation at Dexter was held on October 31. Daddy came down to preach the sermon and brought about a hundred people. It was a great success. Members of Ebenezer Baptist were present and contributed. Their presence in large numbers meant much to me at the beginning of my pastorate. Their generosity and bigheartedness were in the forefront and continued to prove to me that there was but one Ebenezer. I felt greatly indebted. I would remember that occasion so long as the cords of memory would lengthen.

I took an active part in current social problems. I insisted that every church member become a registered voter and a member of the NAACP and organized within the church a social and political action committee—designed to keep the congregation intelligently informed on the social, political, and economic situations. The duties of the Social and Political Action Committee were, among others, to keep before the congregation the importance of the NAACP and the necessity of being registered voters, and—during state and national elections—to sponsor forums and mass meetings to discuss the major issues. Two members of the Social and Political Action

"LOOKING BEYOND YOUR CIRCUMSTANCES"

The Negro who experiences bitter and agonizing circumstances as a result of some ungodly white person is tempted to look upon all white persons as evil, if he fails to look beyond his circumstances. But the minute he looks beyond his circumstances and sees the whole of the situation, he discovers that some of the most implacable and vehement advocates of racial equality are consecrated white persons. We must never forget that such a noble organization as the National Association for the Advancement of Colored People was organized by whites, and even to this day gains a great deal of support from Northern and Southern white persons.

Sermon delivered at Dexter, 1955

Committee—Jo Ann Robinson and Rufus Lewis—were among the first people to become prominent in the bus boycott that was soon to mobilize the latent strength of Montgomery's Negro community.

I joined the local branch of the NAACP and began to take an active interest in implementing its program in the community itself. By attending most of the monthly meetings I was brought face-to-face with some of the racial problems that plagued the community, especially those involving the courts.

Around the time that I started working with the NAACP, the Alabama Council on Human Relations also caught my attention. This interracial group was concerned with human relations in Alabama and employed educational methods to achieve its purpose. It sought to attain, through research and action, equal opportunity for all the people of Alabama. After working with the Council for a few months, I was elected to the office of vice-president. Although the Council never had a large membership, it played an important role. As the only truly interracial group in Montgomery, it served to keep the desperately needed channels of communication open between the races.

I was surprised to learn that many people found my dual interest in the NAACP and the Council inconsistent. Many Negroes felt that integration could come only through legislation and court action—

the chief emphases of the NAACP. Many white people felt that integration could come only through education—the chief emphasis of the Council on Human Relations. How could one give his allegiance to two organizations whose approaches and methods seemed so diametrically opposed?

This question betrayed an assumption that there was only one approach to the solution of the race problem. On the contrary, I felt that both approaches were necessary. Through education we seek to change attitudes and internal feelings (prejudice, hate, etc.); through legislation and court orders we seek to regulate behavior. Anyone who starts out with the conviction that the road to racial justice is only one lane wide will inevitably create a traffic jam and make the journey infinitely longer.

After I lived in Montgomery about a year, I became the proud father of a little daughter—Yolanda Denise. "Yoki" was a big little girl—she weighed nine pounds and eleven ounces. She kept her father quite busy walking the floor.

And then, the bus boycott began.

7

MONTGOMERY
MOVEMENT BEGINS

While the nature of this account causes me to make frequent use of the pronoun "I," in every important part of the story it should be "we." This is not a drama with only one actor. More precisely it is the chronicle of fifty thousand Negroes who took to heart the principles of nonviolence, who learned to fight for their rights with the weapon of love, and who, in the process, acquired a new estimate of their own human worth.

DECEMBER 1, 1955
Rosa Parks arrested for violating segregation laws

DECEMBER 5
King elected head of newly formed protest group, the Montgomery Improvement Association (MIA)

On December 1, 1955, Mrs. Rosa Parks refused to move when she was asked to get up and move back by the bus operator. Mrs. Parks was sitting in the first seat in the unreserved section. All of the seats were taken, and if Mrs. Parks had followed the command of the bus operator she would have stood up and given up her seat for a *male* white passenger, who had just boarded the bus. In a quiet, calm, dignified manner, so characteristic of the radiant personality of Mrs. Parks, she refused to move. The result was her arrest.

One can never understand the action of Mrs. Parks until one realizes that eventually the cup of endurance runs over, and the human personality cries out, "I can't take it no longer." Mrs. Parks's

refusal to move back was her intrepid and courageous affirmation
to the world that she had had enough. (No, she was not planted
there by the NAACP or any other organization; she was planted
there by her sense of dignity and self-respect.) She was a victim of
both the forces of history and the forces of destiny. Mrs. Parks was
ideal for the role assigned to her by history. Her character was im-
peccable and her dedication deep-rooted. All of these traits made
her one of the most respected people in the Negro community.

Her trial was set for Monday, December 5.

Only E. D. Nixon—the signer of Mrs. Parks's bond—and one or
two other persons were aware of the arrest when it occurred early
Thursday evening. Nixon had always been a foe of injustice. You
could look at the face of this tall, dark-skinned, graying man and tell
that he was a fighter. In his work as a Pullman porter, he was in
close contact with organized labor. He had served as state president
of the NAACP and also as president of the Montgomery branch.
Through each of these mediums E. D. Nixon worked fearlessly to
achieve the rights of his people, and to rouse the Negroes from their
apathy.

Early Friday morning, December 2, Nixon called me. He was so
caught up in what he was about to say that he forgot to greet me
with the usual hello but plunged immediately into the story of what
had happened to Mrs. Parks the night before. I listened, deeply
shocked, as he described the humiliating incident. "We have taken
this type of thing too long already," Nixon concluded, his voice
trembling. "I feel that the time has come to boycott the buses. Only
through a boycott can we make it clear to the white folks that we
will not accept this type of treatment any longer."

I agreed that some protest was necessary and that the boycott
method would be an effective one.

Just before calling me Nixon had discussed the idea with Rev.
Ralph Abernathy, the young minister of Montgomery's First Baptist
Church who was to become one of the central figures in the protest.
Abernathy also felt a bus boycott was our best course of action. So
for thirty or forty minutes the three of us telephoned back and forth
concerning plans and strategy. Nixon suggested that we call a meeting of all the ministers and civic leaders that same evening in order

to get their thinking on the proposal, and I offered my church as the meeting place.

As the hour for the meeting arrived, I approached the church with some apprehension, wondering how many of the leaders would respond to our call. More than forty people, from every segment of Negro life, were crowded into the large church meeting room. The largest number there was from the Christian ministry. I was filled with joy when I found so many of them there; for then I knew that something unusual was about to happen.

Rev. L. Roy Bennett, president of Montgomery's Interdenominational Alliance and minister of the Mt. Zion A.M.E. Church, presented the proposal that the Negro citizens of Montgomery should boycott the buses on Monday in protest. "Now is the time to move," he concluded. "This is no time to talk; it is time to act." He appointed a committee, including myself, to prepare the statement. Our final message read as follows:

> Don't ride the bus to work, to town, to school, or any place Monday, December 5. Another Negro woman has been arrested and put in jail because she refused to give up her bus seat. Don't ride the buses to work, to town, to school, or anywhere on Monday. If you work, take a cab, or share a ride, or walk. Come to a mass meeting, Monday at 7:00 P.M., at the Holt Street Baptist Church for further instruction.

I was so excited that I slept very little that night, and early the next morning I was on my way to the church to get the leaflets out. By eleven o'clock an army of women and young people had taken the seven thousand leaflets off to distribute by hand.

"Put justice in business"

The bus situation was one of the sore spots of Montgomery. If a visitor had come to Montgomery before the bus boycott, he would have heard bus operators referring to Negro passengers as "niggers," "black apes," and "black cows." He would have frequently noticed Negro passengers getting on at the front door and paying their fares, and then being forced to get off and go to the back doors to board the bus, and often he would have noticed that before the Negro

passenger could get to the back door, the bus rode off with his fare in the box. But even more, that visitor would have noticed Negro passengers standing over empty seats. No matter if a white person never got on the bus and the bus was filled up with Negro passengers, these Negro passengers were prohibited from sitting in the first four seats because they were only for white passengers. It even went beyond this. If the reserved section for whites was filled up with white persons, and additional white persons boarded the bus, then Negro passengers sitting in the unreserved section were often asked to stand up and give their seats to white persons. If they refused to do this, they were arrested.

After a heavy day of work, I went home late Sunday afternoon and sat down to read the morning paper. There was a long article on the proposed boycott. Implicit throughout the article, I noticed, was the idea that the Negroes were preparing to use the same approach to their problem as the White Citizens Councils used.

As a result of reading that article, I was forced for the first time to think seriously on the nature of the boycott method. Up to this time I had uncritically accepted this method as our best course of action. Now certain doubts began to bother me. Were we following an ethical course of action? Is the boycott method basically unchristian? Isn't it a negative approach to the solution of a problem? Was it true that we would be following the course of some of the White Citizens Councils? Even if lasting practical results came from such a boycott, would immoral means justify moral ends? Each of these questions demanded honest answers.

I had to recognize that the boycott method could be used to unethical and unchristian ends. I had to concede, further, that this was the method used so often by White Citizens Councils to deprive many Negroes, as well as white persons of goodwill, of the basic necessities of life. But certainly, I said to myself, our pending actions could not be interpreted in this light. Our purposes were altogether different. We would use this method to give birth to justice and freedom, and also to urge men to comply with the law of the land. Our concern would not be to put the bus company out of business, but to put justice in business.

As I thought further, I came to see that what we were really doing was withdrawing our cooperation from an evil system, rather

than merely withdrawing our support from the bus company. The bus company, being an external expression of the system, would naturally suffer, but the basic aim was to refuse to cooperate with evil. At this point I began to think about Thoreau's "Essay on Civil Disobedience." I became convinced that what we were preparing to do in Montgomery was related to what Thoreau had expressed. We were simply saying to the white community, "We can no longer lend our cooperation to an evil system." From this moment on I conceived of our movement as an act of massive noncooperation. From then on I rarely used the word "boycott."

"A miracle had taken place"

Wearied, but no longer doubtful about the morality of our proposed protest, I prepared to retire early. But, soon after I was in bed, two-week-old Yolanda Denise began crying and the telephone started ringing. Clearly condemned to stay awake for some time longer, I used the time to think about other things. My wife and I discussed the possible success of the protest. Coretta and I agreed that if we could get 60 percent cooperation the protest would be a success.

Around midnight a call from one of the committee members informed me that every Negro taxi company in Montgomery had agreed to support the protest on Monday morning. After midnight the phone stopped ringing and Yoki stopped crying. Wearily, I said good night to Coretta, and with a strange mixture of hope and anxiety, I fell asleep.

My wife and I awoke earlier than usual on Monday morning. We were up and fully dressed by five-thirty. The day for the protest had arrived, and we were determined to see the first act of this unfolding drama.

Fortunately, a bus stop was just five feet from our house. We could observe the opening stages from our front window. And so we waited through an interminable half hour. I was in the kitchen drinking my coffee when I heard Coretta cry, "Martin, Martin, come quickly!" I put down my cup and ran toward the living room. As I approached the front window Coretta pointed joyfully to a slowly moving bus: "Darling, it's empty!" I could hardly believe what I saw. I knew that the South Jackson line, which ran past our house, carried

more Negro passengers than any other line in Montgomery, and that this first bus was usually filled with domestic workers going to their jobs. Would all of the other buses follow the pattern that had been set by the first? Eagerly we waited for the next bus. In fifteen minutes it rolled down the street, and, like the first, it was empty. A third bus appeared, and it too was empty of all but two white passengers.

I jumped in my car and for almost an hour I cruised down every major street and examined every passing bus. At the peak of the morning traffic, I saw no more than eight Negro passengers riding the buses. Instead of the 60 percent cooperation we had hoped for, it was becoming apparent that we had reached almost 100 percent. A miracle had taken place. The once dormant and quiescent Negro community was now fully awake.

All day long it continued. At the afternoon peak the buses were still as empty of Negro passengers as they had been in the morning. Students of Alabama State College were cheerfully walking or thumbing rides. Job holders had either found other means of transportation or made their way on foot. Men were seen riding mules to work, and more than one horse-drawn buggy drove the streets of Montgomery that day.

During the rush hours the sidewalks were crowded with laborers and domestic workers trudging patiently to their jobs and home again, sometimes as much as twelve miles. They knew why they walked, and the knowledge was evident in the way they carried themselves. And as I watched them I knew that there is nothing more majestic than the determined courage of individuals willing to suffer and sacrifice for their freedom and dignity.

Around nine-thirty in the morning I tore myself from the action of the city streets and headed for the crowded police court. Here Mrs. Parks was being tried for disobeying the city segregation ordinance. After the judge heard the arguments, he found Mrs. Parks guilty and fined her $10.00 and court costs (a total of $14.00). She appealed the case. This was one of the first clear-cut instances in which a Negro had been convicted for disobeying the segregation law. In the past, either cases like this had been dismissed or the people involved had been charged with disorderly conduct. So in a real sense the arrest and conviction of Mrs. Parks had a twofold impact: it was a precipitating factor to arouse the Negroes to positive

action; and it was a test of the validity of the segregation law itself. I am sure that supporters of such prosecutions would have acted otherwise if they had had the prescience to look beyond the moment.

Leaving Mrs. Parks's trial, Ralph Abernathy, E. D. Nixon, and Rev. E. N. French—then minister of the Hilliard Chapel A.M.E. Zion Church—discussed the need for some organization to guide and direct the protest. Up to this time things had moved forward more or less spontaneously. These men were wise enough to see that the moment had now come for a clearer order and direction.

Meanwhile Roy Bennett had called several people together at three o'clock to make plans for the evening mass meeting. Everyone present was elated by the tremendous success that had already attended the protest. But beneath this feeling was the question, where do we go from here? When E. D. Nixon reported on his discussion with Abernathy and French earlier in the day, and their suggestions for an ad hoc organization, the group responded enthusiastically. The new organization needed a name, and several were suggested. Someone proposed the Negro Citizens Committee; but this was rejected because it resembled too closely the White Citizens Councils. Other suggestions were made and dismissed until finally Ralph Abernathy offered a name that was agreeable to all—the Montgomery Improvement Association (MIA). The next job was to elect the officers.

As soon as Bennett had opened the nominations for president, Rufus Lewis spoke from the far corner of the room: "Mr. Chairman, I would like to nominate Reverend M. L. King for president." The motion was seconded and carried, and in a matter of minutes I was unanimously elected.

The action had caught me unawares. It had happened so quickly that I did not even have time to think it through. It is probable that if I had, I would have declined the nomination. They probably picked me because I had not been in town long enough to be identified with any particular group or clique. Just three weeks before, several members of the local chapter of the NAACP had urged me to run for the presidency of that organization, assuring me that I was certain of election. After my wife and I discussed the matter, we agreed that I should not then take on any heavy community responsibilities, since I had so recently finished my thesis, and

needed to give more attention to my church work. Coretta's opposition probably resulted in one of the luckiest decisions of my life. For when the bus protest movement broke out, I would hardly have been able to accept the presidency of the Montgomery Improvement Association without lending weight to the oft-made white contention that the whole thing was an NAACP conspiracy.

With these organizational matters behind us, we turned to a discussion of the evening meeting. Several people, not wanting the reporters to know our future moves, suggested that we just sing and pray; if there were specific recommendations to be made to the people, these could be mimeographed and passed out secretly during the meeting. This, they felt, would leave the reporters in the dark. Others urged that something should be done to conceal the true identity of the leaders, feeling that if no particular name was revealed it would be safer for all involved. After a rather lengthy discussion, E. D. Nixon rose impatiently:

"We are acting like little boys," he said. "Somebody's name will have to be known, and if we are afraid we might just as well fold up right now. We must also be men enough to discuss our recommendations in the open; this idea of secretly passing something around on paper is a lot of bunk. The white folks are eventually going to find it out anyway. We'd better decide now if we are going to be fearless men or scared boys."

With this forthright statement the air was cleared. Nobody would again suggest that we try to conceal our identity or avoid facing the issue head-on. Nixon's courageous affirmation had given new heart to those who were about to be crippled by fear.

It was unanimously agreed that the protest should continue until certain demands were met, and that a committee under the chairmanship of Ralph Abernathy would draw up these demands in the form of a resolution and present them to the evening mass meeting for approval. Someone suggested that perhaps we should reconsider our decision to continue the protest. "Would it not be better," said the speaker, "to call off the protest while it is still a success rather than let it go on a few more days and fizzle out? We have already proved our united strength to the white community. If we stop now we can get anything we want from the bus company, simply because they will have the feeling that we can do it again. But if we continue,

and most of the people return to the buses tomorrow or the next day, the white people will laugh at us, and we will end up getting nothing." This argument was so convincing that we almost resolved to end the protest. But we finally agreed to let the mass meeting—which was only about an hour off—be our guide. If the meeting was well attended and the people were enthusiastic, we would continue; otherwise we would call off the protest that night.

"The most decisive speech of my life"

I went home for the first time since seven that morning, and found Coretta relaxing from a long day of telephone calls and general excitement. After we had brought each other up to date on the day's developments, I told her, somewhat hesitantly—not knowing what her reaction would be—that I had been elected president of the new association. I need not have worried. Naturally surprised, she still saw that since the responsibility had fallen on me, I had no alternative but to accept it. She did not need to be told that we would now have even less time together, and she seemed undisturbed at the possible danger to all of us in my new position. "You know," she said quietly, "that whatever you do, you have my backing."

Reassured, I went to my study and closed the door. The minutes were passing fast. I had only twenty minutes to prepare the most decisive speech of my life. I became possessed by fear. Now I was faced with the inescapable task of preparing, in almost no time at all, a speech that was expected to give a sense of direction to a people imbued with a new and still unplumbed passion for justice. I was also conscious that reporters and television men would be there with their pencils and sound cameras poised to record my words and send them across the nation.

I was now almost overcome, obsessed by a feeling of inadequacy. In this state of anxiety, I wasted five minutes of the original twenty. With nothing left but faith in a power whose matchless strength stands over against the frailties and inadequacies of human nature, I turned to God in prayer. My words were brief and simple, asking God to restore my balance and to be with me in a time when I needed His guidance more than ever.

With less than fifteen minutes left, I began preparing an outline.

In the midst of this, however, I faced a new and sobering dilemma: how could I make a speech that would be militant enough to keep my people aroused to positive action and yet moderate enough to keep this fervor within controllable and Christian bounds? I knew that many of the Negro people were victims of bitterness that could easily rise to flood proportions. What could I say to keep them courageous and prepared for positive action and yet devoid of hate and resentment? Could the militant and the moderate be combined in a single speech?

I decided that I had to face the challenge head-on, and attempt to combine two apparent irreconcilables. I would seek to arouse the group to action by insisting that their self-respect was at stake and that if they accepted such injustices without protesting, they would betray their own sense of dignity and the eternal edicts of God Himself. But I would balance this with a strong affirmation of the Christian doctrine of love. By the time I had sketched an outline of the speech in my mind, my time was up. Without stopping to eat supper (I had not eaten since morning) I said good-bye to Coretta and drove to the Holt Street Church. Within five blocks of the church I noticed a traffic jam. Cars were lined up as far as I could see on both sides of the street.

It took fully fifteen minutes to push my way through to the pastor's study. By now my doubts concerning the continued success of our venture were dispelled. The question of calling off the protest was now academic. The enthusiasm of these thousands of people swept everything along like an onrushing tidal wave.

It was some time before the remaining speakers could push their way to the rostrum through the tightly packed church. When the meeting began it was almost half an hour late. The opening hymn was the old familiar "Onward Christian Soldiers," and when that mammoth audience stood to sing, the voices outside swelling the chorus in the church, there was a mighty ring like the glad echo of heaven itself.

The chairman introduced me. I rose and stood before the pulpit. Television cameras began to shoot from all sides. The crowd grew quiet.

Without manuscript or notes, I told the story of what had hap-

pened to Mrs. Parks. Then I reviewed the long history of abuses and insults that Negro citizens had experienced on the city buses:

We are here this evening for serious business. We are here in a general sense because first and foremost we are American citizens and we are determined to apply our citizenship to the fullness of its meaning. We are here also because of our love for democracy, because of our deep-seated belief that democracy transformed from thin paper to thick action is the greatest form of government on earth. . . .

You know, my friends, there comes a time when people get tired of being trampled over by the iron feet of oppression. There comes a time, my friends, when people get tired of being plunged across the abyss of humiliation, where they experience the bleakness of nagging despair. There comes a time when people get tired of being pushed out of the glittering sunlight of life's July, and left standing amid the piercing chill of an alpine November.

And we are not wrong. We are not wrong in what we are doing. If we are wrong, the Supreme Court of this nation is wrong. If we are wrong, the Constitution of the United States is wrong. If we are wrong, God Almighty is wrong. If we are wrong, Jesus of Nazareth was merely a utopian dreamer that never came down to earth. And we are determined here in Montgomery to work and fight until justice runs down like water and righteousness like a mighty stream.

I want to say that in all of our actions we must stick together. Unity is the great need of the hour, and if we are united we can get many of the things that we not only desire but which we justly deserve. And don't let anybody frighten you. We are not afraid of what we are doing, because we are doing it within the law. There is never a time in our American democracy that we must ever think we're wrong when we protest. We reserve that right.

We, the disinherited of this land, we who have been oppressed so long, are tired of going through the long night of captivity. And now we are reaching out for the daybreak of freedom and justice and equality. May I say to you, my friends, as I come to a close . . . that we must keep . . . God in the forefront. Let us be Christian in all of our actions. But I want to tell you this evening that it is not enough for us to talk about love. Love is one of the pivotal points of the Christian faith. There is another side called justice.

Standing beside love is always justice and we are only using the

tools of justice. Not only are we using the tools of persuasion but we've come to see that we've got to use the tools of coercion. Not only is this thing a process of education but it is also a process of legislation.

As we stand and sit here this evening and as we prepare ourselves for what lies ahead, let us go out with a grim and bold determination that we are going to stick together. We are going to work together. Right here in Montgomery, when the history books are written in the future, somebody will have to say, "There lived a race of people, a black people, 'fleecy locks and black complexion,' a people who had the moral courage to stand up for their rights. And thereby they injected a new meaning into the veins of history and of civilization."

As I took my seat the people rose to their feet and applauded. I was thankful to God that the message had gotten over and that the task of combining the militant and the moderate had been at least partially accomplished. The people had been as enthusiastic when I urged them to love as they were when I urged them to protest.

As I sat listening to the continued applause I realized that this speech had evoked more response than any speech or sermon I had ever delivered, and yet it was virtually unprepared. I came to see for the first time what the older preachers meant when they said, "Open your mouth and God will speak for you." While I would not let this experience tempt me to overlook the need for continued preparation, it would always remind me that God can transform man's weakness into his glorious opportunity.

Now the time had come for the all-important resolution. Ralph Abernathy read the words slowly and forcefully. The resolution called upon the Negroes not to resume riding the buses until (1) courteous treatment by the bus operators was guaranteed; (2) passengers were seated on a first-come, first-served basis—Negroes seating from the back of the bus toward the front, whites from the front toward the back; (3) Negro bus operators were employed on predominantly Negro routes. At the words, "All in favor of the motion stand," every person to a man stood up, and those who were already standing raised their hands. Cheers began to ring out from both inside and outside.

As I drove away my heart was full. I had never seen such enthusiasm for freedom. And yet this enthusiasm was tempered by amazing

REFLECTIONS ON FIRST BOYCOTT MEETING

The deliberations of that brisk and cold night in December will long be stenciled on the mental sheets of succeeding generations. Little did we know on that night that we were starting a movement that would rise to international proportions; a movement whose lofty echos would ring in the ears of people of every nation; a movement that would stagger and astound the imagination of the oppressor, while leaving a glittering star of hope etched in the midnight skies of the oppressed. Little did we know that night that we were starting a movement that would gain the admiration of men of goodwill all over the world. But God still has a mysterious way to perform His wonders. It seems that God decided to use Montgomery as the proving ground for the struggle and triumph of freedom and justice in America. It is one of the ironies of our day that Montgomery, the Cradle of the Confederacy, is being transformed into Montgomery, the cradle of freedom and justice.

Address at First Institute for Nonviolence and Social Change, December 3, 1956

self-discipline. The unity of purpose and esprit de corps of these people had been indescribably moving. No historian would ever be able fully to describe this meeting and no sociologist would ever be able to interpret it adequately. One had to be a part of the experience really to understand it.

The day of days, December 5, 1955, was drawing to a close. We all prepared to go to our homes, not yet fully aware of what had happened. I said to myself, the victory is already won, no matter how long we struggle to attain the three points of the resolution. It is a victory infinitely larger than the bus situation. The real victory was in the mass meeting, where thousands of black people stood revealed with a new sense of dignity and destiny. That night we were starting a movement that would gain national recognition; whose echoes would ring in the ears of people of every nation; a movement that would astound the oppressor, and bring new hope to the oppressed. That night was Montgomery's moment in history.

8

THE VIOLENCE OF DESPERATE MEN

Along the way of life, someone must have sense enough and morality enough to cut off the chain of hate and evil. The greatest way to do that is through love. I believe firmly that love is a transforming power than can lift a whole community to new horizons of fair play, good-will, and justice.

DECEMBER 17, 1955
King and other MIA leaders meet with white representatives in unsuccessful attempt to resolve bus dispute

JANUARY 26, 1956
During "Get Tough" campaign, King is arrested and jailed for speeding

JANUARY 28
Receives $14 fine for speeding

JANUARY 30
After his home is bombed, King pleads for nonviolence

After ascending the mountain on Monday night, I woke up Tuesday morning urgently aware that I had to leave the heights and come back to earth. I was faced with a number of organizational decisions. The movement could no longer continue without careful planning.

I began to think of the various committees necessary to give the movement guidance and direction. First we needed a more permanent transportation committee, since the problem of getting the ex–

bus riders about the city was paramount. We would also need to raise money to carry on the protest. Therefore, a finance committee was necessary. Since we would be having regular mass meetings, there must be a program committee for these occasions. And then, I reasoned, from time to time strategic decisions would have to be made; we needed the best minds of the association to think them through and then make recommendations to the executive board. So I felt that a strategy committee was essential.

"The response was tremendous"

From the beginning of the protest Ralph Abernathy was my closest associate and most trusted friend. We prayed together and made important decisions together. His ready good humor lightened many tense moments. Whenever I went out of town I always left him in charge of the important business of the association, knowing that it was in safe hands. After Roy Bennett left Montgomery, Ralph became first vice president of the MIA, and has held that position ever since with dignity and efficiency.

In the early stages of the protest the problem of transportation demanded most of our attention. The labor and ingenuity that went into that task is one of the most interesting sides of the Montgomery story. For the first few days we had depended on the Negro taxi companies who had agreed to transport the people for the same ten-cent fare that they paid on the buses. But during the first "negotiation meeting" that we held with the city commission on Thursday, December 8, Police Commissioner Sellers mentioned in passing that there was a law that limited the taxis to a minimum fare. I caught this hint and realized that Commissioner Sellers would probably use this point to stop the taxis from assisting in the protest.

At that moment I remembered that some time previously my good friend the Reverend Theodore Jemison had led a bus boycott in Baton Rouge, Louisiana. Knowing that Jemison and his associates had set up an effective private car pool, I put in a long-distance call to ask him for suggestions for a similar pool in Montgomery. As I expected, his painstaking description of the Baton Rouge experience was invaluable. I passed on word of Sellers's remark and Jemison's advice to the transportation committee and suggested that we imme-

diately begin setting up a pool in order to offset the confusion which
could come if the taxis were eliminated from service.

Fortunately, a mass meeting was being held that night. There I
asked all those who were willing to offer their cars to give us their
names, addresses, telephone numbers, and the hours that they could
drive, before leaving the meeting. The response was tremendous.
More than a hundred and fifty signed slips volunteering their automobiles. Some who were not working offered to drive in the car
pool all day; others volunteered a few hours before and after work.
Practically all of the ministers offered to drive whenever they were
needed.

On Friday afternoon, as I had predicted, the police commissioner issued an order to all of the cab companies reminding them
that by law they had to charge a minimum fare of forty-five cents,
and that failure to comply would be a legal offense. This brought an
end to the cheap taxi service.

Our answer was to call hastily on our volunteers, who responded
immediately. They started out simply by cruising the streets of
Montgomery with no particular system. On Saturday the ministers
agreed to go to their pulpits the following day and seek additional
recruits. Again the response was tremendous. With the new addi-
tions, the number of cars swelled to about three hundred.

Thousands of mimeographed leaflets were distributed throughout the Negro community with a list of the forty-eight dispatch and
the forty-two pick-up stations. In a few days this system was working
astonishingly well. The white opposition was so impressed at this
miracle of quick organization that they had to admit in a White
Citizens Council meeting that the pool moved with "military preci-
sion." The MIA had worked out in a few nights a transportation
problem that the bus company had grappled with for many years.

Despite this success, so profoundly had the spirit of the protest
become a part of the people's lives that sometimes they even preferred to walk when a ride was available. The act of walking, for
many, had become of symbolic importance. Once a pool driver
stopped beside an elderly woman who was trudging along with obvious difficulty.

"Jump in, Grandmother," he said. "You don't need to walk."

She waved him on. "I'm not walking for myself," she explained.

"I'm walking for my children and my grandchildren." And she continued toward home on foot.

While the largest number of drivers were ministers, their ranks were augmented by housewives, teachers, businessmen, and unskilled laborers. At least three white men from the air bases drove in the pool during their off-duty hours. One of the most faithful drivers was Mrs. A. W. West, who had early shown her enthusiasm for the protest idea by helping to call the civic leaders to the first organizing meeting. Every morning she drove her large green Cadillac to her assigned dispatch station, and for several hours in the morning and again in the afternoon one could see this distinguished and handsome gray-haired chauffeur driving people to work and home again.

Another loyal driver was Jo Ann Robinson. Attractive, fair-skinned, and still youthful, Jo Ann came by her goodness naturally. She did not need to learn her nonviolence from any book. Apparently indefatigable, she, perhaps more than any other person, was active on every level of the protest. She took part in both the executive board and the strategy committee meetings. When the MIA newsletter was inaugurated a few months after the protest began, she became its editor. She was sure to be present whenever negotiations were in progress. And although she carried a full teaching load at Alabama State, she still found time to drive both morning and afternoon.

The ranks of our drivers were further swelled from an unforeseen source. Many white housewives, whatever their commitment to segregation, had no intention of being without their maids. And so every day they drove to the Negro sections to pick up their servants and return them at night. Certainly, if selfishness was a part of the motive, in many cases affection for a faithful servant also played its part. There was some humor in the tacit understandings—and sometimes mutually accepted misunderstandings—between these white employers and their Negro servants. One old domestic, an influential matriarch to many young relatives in Montgomery, was asked by her wealthy employer, "Isn't this bus boycott terrible?"

The old lady responded: "Yes, ma'am, it sure is. And I just told all my young'uns that this kind of thing is white folks' business and we just stay off the buses till they get this whole thing settled."

"The inspiration of Mahatma Gandhi"

From the beginning a basic philosophy guided the movement. This guiding principle has since been referred to variously as nonviolent resistance, noncooperation, and passive resistance. But in the first days of the protest none of these expressions was mentioned; the phrase most often heard was "Christian love." It was the Sermon on the Mount, rather than a doctrine of passive resistance, that initially inspired the Negroes of Montgomery to dignified social action. It was Jesus of Nazareth that stirred the Negroes to protest with the creative weapon of love.

As the days unfolded, however, the inspiration of Mahatma Gandhi began to exert its influence. I had come to see early that the Christian doctrine of love operating through the Gandhian method of nonviolence was one of the most potent weapons available to the Negro in his struggle for freedom. About a week after the protest started, a white woman who understood and sympathized with the Negroes' efforts wrote a letter to the editor of the *Montgomery Advertiser* comparing the bus protest with the Gandhian movement in India. Miss Juliette Morgan, sensitive and frail, did not long survive the rejection and condemnation of the white community, but long before she died in the summer of 1957 the name of Mahatma Gandhi was well known in Montgomery. People who had never heard of the little brown saint of India were now saying his name with an air of familiarity. Nonviolent resistance had emerged as the technique of the movement, while love stood as the regulating ideal. In other words, Christ furnished the spirit and motivation while Gandhi furnished the method.

People responded to this philosophy with amazing ardor. To be sure, there were some who were slow to concur. Occasionally members of the executive board would say to me in private that we needed a more militant approach. They looked upon nonviolence as weak and compromising. Others felt that at least a modicum of violence would convince the white people that the Negroes meant business and were not afraid. A member of my church came to me one day and solemnly suggested that it would be to our advantage to "kill off" eight or ten white people. "This is the only language these white folks will understand," he said. "If we fail to do this they will

think we're afraid. We must show them we're not afraid any longer." Besides, he thought, if a few white persons were killed the federal government would inevitably intervene and this, he was certain, would benefit us.

Still others felt that they could be nonviolent only if they were not attacked personally. They would say: "If nobody bothers me, I will bother nobody. If nobody hits me, I will hit nobody. But if I am hit I will hit back." They thus drew a moral line between aggressive and retaliatory violence. But in spite of these honest disagreements, the vast majority were willing to try the experiment.

In a real sense, Montgomery's Negroes showed themselves willing to grapple with a new approach to the crisis in race relations. It is probably true that most of them did not believe in nonviolence as a philosophy of life, but because of their confidence in their leaders and because nonviolence was presented to them as a simple expression of Christianity in action, they were willing to use it as a technique. Admittedly, nonviolence in the truest sense is not a strategy that one uses simply because it is expedient at the moment; nonviolence is ultimately a way of life that men live by because of the sheer morality of its claim. But even granting this, the willingness to use nonviolence as a technique is a step forward. For he who goes this far is more likely to adopt nonviolence later as a way of life.

"I almost broke down under the continual battering"

In spite of the fact that the bus protest had been an immediate success, the city fathers and the bus officials felt that it would fizzle out in a few days. They were certain that the first rainy day would find the Negroes back on the buses. But the first rainy day came and passed and the buses remained empty.

In the meantime, the city fathers and the bus officials had expressed their first willingness to negotiate. At a special session of the MIA executive board a negotiating committee of twelve was appointed and I was chosen to serve as their spokesman. It was agreed that we would present three proposals: (1) a guarantee of courteous treatment; (2) passengers to be seated on a first-come first-served basis, the Negroes seating from the back; and (3) employment of Negro bus operators on predominantly Negro routes. The aim of

these proposals was frankly no more than a temporary alleviation of the problem that we confronted. We never felt that the first-come first-served seating arrangement would provide a final solution, since this would eventually have to depend on a change in the law. We were sure, however, that the Rosa Parks case, which was by then in the courts, would be the test that would ultimately bring about the defeat of bus segregation itself.

We arrived at the city hall and were directed to the Commissioners' Chamber. We sat down near the front. The mayor then turned to the Negro delegation and demanded: "Who is the spokesman?" When all eyes turned toward me, the mayor said: "All right, come forward and make your statement." In the glare of the television lights, I walked slowly toward the front of the room and took a seat at the opposite end.

I opened by stating briefly why we found it necessary to "boycott" the buses. I made it clear that the arrest of Mrs. Parks was not the cause of the protest, but merely the precipitating factor. "Our action," I said, "is the culmination of a series of injustices and indignities that have existed over the years."

As soon as I finished the mayor opened the meeting to general discussion. The commissioners and the attorney for the bus company began raising questions. They challenged the legality of the seating arrangement that we were proposing. They contended that the Negroes were demanding something that would violate the law. We answered by reiterating our previous argument that a first-come first-served seating arrangement could exist entirely within the segregation law, as it did in many Southern cities.

It soon became clear that Jack Crenshaw, the attorney for the bus company, was our most stubborn opponent. Doggedly he sought to convince the group that there was no way to grant the suggested seating proposal without violating the city ordinance. The more Crenshaw talked, the more he won the city fathers to his position. Eventually I saw that the meeting was getting nowhere, and suggested that we bring it to a close.

I soon saw that I was the victim of an unwarranted pessimism because I had started out with an unwarranted optimism. I had gone to the meeting with a great illusion. I had believed that the privileged would give up their privileges on request. This experience, however,

taught me a lesson. I came to see that no one gives up his privileges without strong resistance. I saw further that the underlying purpose of segregation was to oppress and exploit the segregated, not simply to keep them apart. Even when we asked for justice *within* the segregation laws, the "powers that be" were not willing to grant it. Justice and equality, I saw, would never come while segregation remained, because the basic purpose of segregation was to perpetuate injustice and inequality.

Shortly after this first negotiating conference, I called a meeting of the executive board of the MIA to report the results. The members were disappointed, but agreed that we should stand firm on our three proposals. In the meantime, the mayor sent word that he was calling a citizens committee to meet with the bus officials and Negro leaders on the morning of December 17. Over a week had passed since the first conference and the protest had still shown no signs of faltering.

White members of the committee began to lash out against me. They contended that I was the chief stumbling block to a real solution of the problem. For a moment it appeared that I was alone. Nobody came to my rescue, until suddenly Ralph Abernathy was on the floor in my defense. He pointed out that, since I was the spokesman for the group, I naturally had to do most of the talking, but this did not mean that I did not have the support of the rest of the committee. By trying to convince the Negroes that I was the main obstacle to a solution, the white committee members had hoped to divide us among ourselves. But Ralph's statement left no doubt. From this moment on, the white group saw the futility of attempting to negotiate us into a compromise.

That Monday I went home with a heavy heart. I was weighted down by a terrible sense of guilt, remembering that on two or three occasions I had allowed myself to become angry and indignant. I had spoken hastily and resentfully. Yet I knew that this was no way to solve a problem. "You must not harbor anger," I admonished myself. "You must be willing to suffer the anger of the opponent, and yet not return anger. You must not become bitter. No matter how emotional your opponents are, you must be calm."

After the opposition had failed to negotiate us into a compro-

mise, it turned to subtler means for blocking the protest; namely, to conquer by dividing. False rumors were spread concerning the leaders of the movement. During this period the rumor was spread that I had purchased a brand-new Cadillac for myself and a Buick station wagon for my wife. Of course none of this was true.

Not only was there a conscious attempt to raise questions about the integrity of the Negro leaders, and thereby cause their followers to lose faith in them, there was also an attempt to divide the leaders among themselves. Prominent white citizens went to many of the older Negro ministers and said: "If there has to be a protest, you should be the leaders. It is a shame for you, who have been in the community for so many years, to have your own people overlook you and choose these young upstarts to lead them." Certain members of the white community tried to convince several of the other protest leaders that the problem could be solved if I were out of the picture. "If one of you," they would say, "took over the leadership, things would change overnight."

I almost broke down under the continual battering of this argument. I began to think that there might be some truth in it, and I also feared that some were being influenced by this argument. After two or three troubled days and nights of little sleep, I called a meeting of the executive board and offered my resignation. I told them that I would be the last person to want to stand in the way of a solution to the problem which plagued our community, and that maybe a more mature person could bring about a speedier conclusion. I further assured the board that I would be as active in the background as I had been in the position of spokesman. But I had barely finished talking before board members began to urge me from every side to forget the idea of resignation. With a unanimous vote of confidence, they made it clear that they were well pleased with the way I was handling things, and that they would follow my leadership to the end.

Afterward, as I drove up to the parsonage, more at peace than I had been in some time, I could hear Coretta's high, true soprano through the living room window. In the back bedroom Yoki, now more than a month old, was wide awake and busy discovering her fingers. I picked her up and walked to the front room, bouncing her in time to Coretta's song.

Such moments together had become rare. We could never plan them, for I seldom knew from one hour to the next when I would be home. Many times Coretta saw her good meals grow dry in the oven when a sudden emergency kept me away. Yet she never complained, and she was always there when I needed her. Yoki and Beethoven, she said, kept her company when she was alone. Calm and unruffled, Coretta moved quietly about the business of keeping the household going. When I needed to talk things out, she was ready to listen, or to offer suggestions when I asked for them.

"Conquer by dividing"

The height of the attempt to conquer by dividing came on Sunday, January 22, when the city commissioners shocked the Negro community by announcing in the local newspaper that they had met with a group of prominent Negro ministers and worked out a settlement. Many people were convinced the boycott was over. It was soon clear that this announcement was a calculated design to get the Negroes back on the buses Sunday morning. The city commission felt certain that once a sizable number of Negroes began riding the buses, the boycott would end.

I began to wonder whether any of my associates had betrayed me and made an agreement in my absence. I needed to find out if a group of Negro ministers had actually met with the city commission. After about an hour of calling here and there we were able to identify the "three prominent Negro ministers." They were neither prominent nor were they members of the MIA.

It was now about eleven o'clock on Saturday night. Something had to be done to let the people know that the article they would read the next morning was false. I asked one group to call all the Negro ministers of the city and urge them to announce in church Sunday morning that the protest was still on. Another group joined me on a tour of the Negro nightclubs and taverns to inform those present of the false statement. For the first time I had a chance to see the inside of most of Montgomery's night spots. As a result of our fast maneuvering, the word got around so well that the next day the buses were empty as usual.

With the failure of the attempted hoax, the city fathers lost face.

They were now desperate. Their answer was to embark on a "get-tough" policy. The mayor went on television and denounced the boycott. The vast majority of white Montgomerians, he declared, did not care if a Negro ever rode the buses again, and he called upon the white employers to stop driving Negro employees to and from work. During this period all three city commissioners let it be known that they had joined the White Citizens Council.

The "get-tough" policy turned out to be a series of arrests for minor and often imaginary traffic violations. Faced with these difficulties, the volunteer car pool began to weaken. Some drivers became afraid that their licenses would be revoked or their insurance canceled. Many of the drivers quietly dropped out of the pool. It became more and more difficult to catch a ride. Complaints began to rise. From early morning to late at night my telephone rang and my doorbell was seldom silent. I began to have doubts about the ability of the Negro community to continue the struggle.

"Going to jail"

I did not suspect that I myself was soon to face arrest as a result of the "get-tough" operation. One afternoon in the middle of January, after several hours of work at my church office, I started driving home with a friend, Robert Williams, and the church secretary, Mrs. Lilie Thomas. Before leaving the downtown district, I decided to make a quick trip to the parking lot to pick up a few people going in my direction. As we entered the lot, I noticed four or five policemen questioning the drivers. I picked up three passengers and drove to the edge of the lot, where I was stopped by one of these officers. While he asked to see my license and questioned me concerning the ownership of the car, I heard a policeman across the street say, "That's that damn King fellow."

Leaving the lot, I noticed two motorcycle policemen behind me. One was still following three blocks later. When I told Bob Williams that we were being trailed, he said, "Be sure that you follow every traffic regulation." Slowly and meticulously I drove toward home, with the motorcycle behind me. Finally, as I stopped to let my passengers out, the policeman pulled up and said, "Get out, King; you are under arrest for speeding thirty miles an hour in a twenty-five

mile zone." Without a question I got out of the car, telling Bob
Williams and Mrs. Thomas to drive on and notify my wife. Soon a
patrol car came. Two policemen got out and searched me from top
to bottom, put me in the car, and drove off.

As we drove off, presumably to the city jail, a feeling of panic
began to come over me. The jail was in the downtown section of
Montgomery. Yet we were going in a different direction. The more
we rode, the farther we were from the center of town. In a few minutes we turned into a dark and dingy street that I had never seen
and headed under a desolate old bridge. By this time I was convinced
that these men were carrying me to some faraway spot to dump me
off. "But this couldn't be," I said to myself. "These men are officers
of the law." Then I began to wonder whether they were driving me
out to some waiting mob, planning to use the excuse later on that
they had been overpowered. I found myself trembling within and
without. Silently, I asked God to give me the strength to endure
whatever came.

By this time we were passing under the bridge. I was sure now
that I was going to meet my fateful hour on the other side. But as I
looked up I noticed a glaring light in the distance, and soon I saw
the words "Montgomery City Jail." I was so relieved that it was some
time before I realized the irony of my position: going to jail at that
moment seemed like going to some safe haven!

A policeman ushered me in. After depositing my things and giving the jailer the desired information, I was led to a dingy and odor-
ous cell. As the big iron door swung open the jailer said to me: "All
right, get on in there with all the others." For the moment strange
gusts of emotion swept through me like cold winds on an open prairie. For the first time in my life I was thrown behind bars.

As I entered the crowded cell, I recognized two acquaintances,
one a teacher, who had also been arrested on pretexts connected
with the protest. In the democracy of the jail they were packed together with vagrants and drunks and serious lawbreakers. But democracy did not go so far as to break the rules of segregation. Here
whites and Negroes languished in separate enclosures.

When I began to look around I was so appalled at the conditions
I saw that I soon forgot my own predicament. I saw men lying on
hard wood slats, and others resting on cots with torn-up mattresses.

The toilet was in one corner of the cell without a semblance of an enclosure. I said to myself that no matter what these men had done, they shouldn't be treated like this.

They all gathered around to find out why I was there, and showed some surprise that the city had gone so far as to arrest me. Soon one man after another began talking to me about his reason for being in jail and asking if I could help him out. I turned to the group and said: "Fellows, before I can assist in getting any of you out, I've got to get my ownself out." At this they laughed.

Shortly after, the jailer came to get me. As I left the cell, wondering where he was going to take me, one of the men called after me: "Don't forget us when you get out." I assured them that I would not forget. The jailer led me down a long corridor into a little room in the front of the jail. He ordered me to be seated, and began rubbing my fingers on an ink pad. I was about to be fingerprinted like a criminal.

By this time the news of my arrest had spread over Montgomery, and a number of people had headed for the city jail. The first to arrive was my good friend Ralph Abernathy. He immediately sought to sign my bond, but the officials told him that he had to bring a certified statement from the court asserting that he owned a sufficient amount of property to sign a bond. Ralph pointed out that since it was almost six-thirty at night, the courthouse was already closed.

Indifferently, the official retorted: "Well, you will just have to wait till tomorrow morning."

Ralph then asked if he could see me.

The jailer replied: "No, you can't see him until ten o'clock tomorrow."

"Well, is it possible," said Abernathy, "to pay a cash bond?"

The jailer reluctantly answered yes. Ralph rushed to call someone who could produce the cash.

Meanwhile a number of people had assembled in front of the jail. Soon the crowd had become so large that the jailer began to panic. Rushing into the fingerprinting room he said, "King, you can go now," and before I could half get my coat on, he was ushering me out, released on my own bond.

As I walked out and noticed the host of friends and well-wishers,

I regained the courage that I had temporarily lost. I knew that I did not stand alone. After a brief statement to the crowd, I was driven home. My wife greeted me with a kiss. Many members of my church were waiting anxiously to hear the outcome. Their words of encouragement gave me further assurance that I was not alone.

From that night on my commitment to the struggle for freedom was stronger than ever before. Before retiring I talked with Coretta, and, as usual, she gave me the reassurance that can only come from one who is as close to you as your own heartbeat. Yes, the night of injustice was dark: the "get-tough" policy was taking its toll. But in the darkness I could see a radiant star of unity.

"I heard the voice of Jesus saying still to fight on"

Almost immediately after the protest started we had begun to receive threatening telephone calls and letters. They increased as time went on. By the middle of January, they had risen to thirty and forty a day.

From the beginning of the protest both my parents and Coretta's parents always had the unconscious, and often conscious, fear that something fatal might befall us. They never had any doubt about the rightness of our actions but they were concerned about what might happen to us. My father made a beaten path between Atlanta and Montgomery throughout the days of the protest. Every time I saw him I went through a deep feeling of anxiety, because I knew that my every move was driving him deeper and deeper into a state of worry. During those days he could hardly mention the many harassments that Coretta, the baby, and I were subjected to without shedding tears.

As the weeks passed, I began to see that many of the threats were in earnest. Soon I felt myself faltering and growing in fear. One day, a white friend told me that he had heard from reliable sources that plans were being made to take my life. For the first time I realized that something could happen to me.

One night at a mass meeting, I found myself saying: "If one day you find me sprawled out dead, I do not want you to retaliate with a single act of violence. I urge you to continue protesting with the

same dignity and discipline you have shown so far." A strange silence came over the audience.

One night toward the end of January I settled into bed late, after a strenuous day. Coretta had already fallen asleep and just as I was about to doze off the telephone rang. An angry voice said, "Listen, nigger, we've taken all we want from you; before next week you'll be sorry you ever came to Montgomery." I hung up, but I couldn't sleep. It seemed that all of my fears had come down on me at once. I had reached the saturation point.

I got out of bed and began to walk the floor. I had heard these things before, but for some reason that night it got to me. I turned over and I tried to go to sleep, but I couldn't sleep. I was frustrated, bewildered, and then I got up. Finally I went to the kitchen and heated a pot of coffee. I was ready to give up. With my cup of coffee sitting untouched before me I tried to think of a way to move out of the picture without appearing a coward. I sat there and thought about a beautiful little daughter who had just been born. I'd come in night after night and see that little gentle smile. I started thinking about a dedicated and loyal wife, who was over there asleep. And she could be taken from me, or I could be taken from her. And I got to the point that I couldn't take it any longer. I was weak. Something said to me, "You can't call on Daddy now, you can't even call on Mama. You've got to call on that something in that person that your Daddy used to tell you about, that power that can make a way out of no way." With my head in my hands, I bowed over the kitchen table and prayed aloud. The words I spoke to God that midnight are still vivid in my memory: "Lord, I'm down here trying to do what's right. I think I'm right. I am here taking a stand for what I believe is right. But Lord, I must confess that I'm weak now, I'm faltering. I'm losing my courage. Now, I am afraid. And I can't let the people see me like this because if they see me weak and losing my courage, they will begin to get weak. The people are looking to me for leadership, and if I stand before them without strength and courage, they too will falter. I am at the end of my powers. I have nothing left. I've come to the point where I can't face it alone."

It seemed as though I could hear the quiet assurance of an inner voice saying: "Martin Luther, stand up for righteousness. Stand up

for justice. Stand up for truth. And lo, I will be with you. Even until the end of the world."

I tell you I've seen the lightning flash. I've heard the thunder roar. I've felt sin breakers dashing trying to conquer my soul. But I heard the voice of Jesus saying still to fight on. He promised never to leave me alone. At that moment I experienced the presence of the Divine as I had never experienced Him before. Almost at once my fears began to go. My uncertainty disappeared. I was ready to face anything.

"The bombing"

Three nights later, on January 30, I left home a little before seven to attend our Monday evening mass meeting at the First Baptist Church. A member of my congregation had come to the parsonage to keep my wife company in my absence. About nine-thirty they heard a noise in front that sounded as though someone had thrown a brick. In a matter of seconds an explosion rocked the house. A bomb had gone off on the porch.

After word of the bombing reached the mass meeting, everybody attempted to keep it from me. People looked at me and then away; one or two seemed about to approach me and then changed their minds. Soon I noticed several of my fellow ministers going in and out of the church in a rather unusual manner, and from this I surmised that something had happened. Unable to restrain my curiosity any longer, I called three of my closest associates and urged them to tell me what had happened. I assured them that I was prepared for whatever it was. Ralph Abernathy said hesitantly, "Your house has been bombed."

STATEMENT AT MIA MASS MEETING

I want you to know that if M. L. King had never been born this movement would have taken place. I just happened to be here. You know there comes a time when time itself is ready for change. That time has come in Montgomery, and I had nothing to do with it.

Statement at MIA Mass Meeting, January 30, 1956

I asked if my wife and baby were all right.

They said, "We are checking on that now."

Strangely enough, I accepted the word of the bombing calmly. My religious experience a few nights before had given me the strength to face it. I urged each person to go straight home after the meeting and adhere strictly to our philosophy of nonviolence. I admonished them not to become panicky and lose their heads. "Let us keep moving," I urged them, "with the faith that what we are doing is right, and with the even greater faith that God is with us in the struggle."

I was immediately driven home. As we neared the scene I noticed hundreds of people with angry faces in front of the house. The policemen were trying, in their usual rough manner, to clear the streets, but they were ignored by the crowd. One Negro was saying to a policeman, who was attempting to push him aside: "I ain't gonna move nowhere. That's the trouble now; you white folks is always pushin' us around. Now you got your .38 and I got mine; so let's battle it out." As I walked toward the front porch, I realized that many people were armed. Nonviolent resistance was on the verge of being transformed into violence.

I rushed into the house to see if Coretta and Yoki were safe. When I walked into the bedroom and saw my wife and daughter uninjured, I drew my first full breath in many minutes. Coretta was neither bitter nor panicky. She had accepted the whole thing with unbelievable composure. As I noticed her calmness I became more calm myself.

The mayor, the police commissioner, and several white reporters had reached the house before I did and were standing in the dining room. After reassuring myself about my family's safety, I went to speak to them. They expressed their regret that "this unfortunate incident has taken place in our city." One of the trustees of my church turned to the mayor and said: "You may express your regrets, but you must face the fact that your public statements created the atmosphere for this bombing. This is the end result of your 'get-tough' policy."

By this time the crowd outside was getting out of hand. The policemen had failed to disperse them, and throngs of additional people were arriving every minute. The white reporters were afraid

to face the angry crowd. The mayor and police commissioner, though they might not have admitted it, were very pale.

In this atmosphere I walked out to the porch and asked the crowd to come to order. In less than a moment there was complete silence. Quietly I told them that I was all right and that my wife and baby were all right.

We believe in law and order. Don't get panicky. Don't do anything panicky at all. Don't get your weapons. He who lives by the sword will perish by the sword. Remember that is what God said. We are not advocating violence. We want to love our enemies. I want you to love our enemies. Be good to them. Love them and let them know you love them.

I did not start this boycott. I was asked by you to serve as your spokesman. I want it known the length and breadth of this land that if I am stopped this movement will not stop. If I am stopped our work will not stop. For what we are doing is right. What we are doing is just. And God is with us.

As I finished speaking there were shouts of "Amen" and "God bless you." I could hear voices saying: "We are with you all the way, Reverend." I looked out over that vast throng of people and noticed tears on many faces.

After our many friends left the house late that evening, Coretta, Yoki, and I were driven to the home of one of our church members to spend the night. I could not get to sleep. While I lay in that quiet front bedroom, with a distant street lamp throwing a reassuring glow through the curtained window, I began to think of the viciousness of people who would bomb my home. I could feel the anger rising when I realized that my wife and baby could have been killed. I thought about the city commissioners and all the statements that they had made about me and the Negro generally. I was once more on the verge of corroding hatred. And once more I caught myself and said: "You must not allow yourself to become bitter."

Midnight had long since passed. Coretta and the baby were sound asleep. I turned over in bed and fell into a dazed slumber. But the night was not yet over. Some time later Coretta and I were awakened by a slow, steady knocking at the front door. Through the window we could see the dark outline of a figure on the front porch. I

MEANING OF THE BOYCOTT

There are those who would try to make of this a hate campaign. This is not war between the white and the Negro but a conflict between justice and injustice. This is bigger than the Negro race revolting against the white. We are seeking to improve not the Negro of Montgomery but the whole of Montgomery.

If we are arrested every day, if we are exploited every day, if we are trampled over every day, don't ever let anyone pull you so low as to hate them. We must use the weapon of love. We must have compassion and understanding for those who hate us. We must realize so many people are taught to hate us that they are not totally responsible for their hate. But we stand in life at midnight, we are always on the threshold of a new dawn.

Quoted in the *New York Times*, February 24, 1956

---

pulled myself out of bed, peered through the curtains, and recognized the stocky, reassuring back of Coretta's father.

Obie Scott had heard the news of the bombing over the radio and had driven to Montgomery. He came in the house with an obvious sign of distress on his face. After talking with us a while he turned and said: "Coretta, I came to take you and the baby back home with me until this tension cools off." In a calm but positive manner Coretta answered: "I'm sorry, Dad, but I can't leave Martin now. I must stay here with him through this whole struggle." And so Obie Scott drove back to Marion alone.

Just two nights later, a stick of dynamite was thrown on the lawn of E. D. Nixon. Fortunately, again no one was hurt. Once more a large crowd of Negroes assembled, but they did not lose control. And so nonviolence had won its first and its second tests.

After the bombings, many of the officers of my church and other trusted friends urged me to hire a bodyguard and armed watchmen for my house. When my father came to town, he concurred with both of these suggestions. I tried to tell them that I had no fears now and consequently needed no weapons for protection. This they would not hear. They insisted that I protect the house and family, even if I didn't want to protect myself. In order to satisfy the wishes of these close friends and associates, I decided to consider the ques-

tion of an armed guard. I went down to the sheriff's office and applied for a license to carry a gun in the car; but this was refused.

Meanwhile I reconsidered. How could I serve as one of the leaders of a nonviolent movement and at the same time use weapons of violence for my personal protection? Coretta and I talked the matter over for several days and finally agreed that arms were no solution. We decided then to get rid of the one weapon we owned. We tried to satisfy our friends by having floodlights mounted around the house, and hiring unarmed watchmen around the clock. I also promised that I would not travel around the city alone.

I was much more afraid in Montgomery when I had a gun in my house. When I decided that I couldn't keep a gun, I came face-to-face with the question of death and I dealt with it. From that point on, I no longer needed a gun nor have I been afraid. Had we become distracted by the question of my safety we would have lost the moral offensive and sunk to the level of our oppressors.

9

DESEGREGATION
AT LAST

We came to see that, in the long run, it is more honorable to walk in dignity than ride in humiliation. So in a quiet dignified manner, we decided to substitute tired feet for tired souls, and walk the streets of Montgomery until the sagging walls of injustice had been crushed by the battering rams of surging justice.

FEBRUARY 21, 1956
Montgomery grand jury indicts King and other MIA leaders for violating antiboycott law

MARCH 22
King is found guilty of leading illegal boycott and sentenced to $500 fine or 386 days in jail; the case is appealed

NOVEMBER 13
U.S. Supreme Court declares bus segregation laws unconstitutional

DECEMBER 21
After MIA votes to end boycott, King is one of first passengers to ride desegregated buses

When the opposition discovered that violence could not block the protest, they resorted to mass arrests. As early as January 9, a Montgomery attorney had called the attention of the press to an old state law against boycotts. On February 13 the Montgomery County Grand Jury was called to determine whether Negroes who were boycotting the buses were violating this law. After about a week

of deliberations, the jury, composed of seventeen whites and one Negro, found the boycott illegal and indicted more than one hundred persons. My name, of course, was on the list.

At the time of the indictments I was at Fisk University in Nashville, giving a series of lectures. During this period I was talking to Montgomery on the phone at least three times a day in order to keep abreast of developments. Thus I heard of the indictments first in a telephone call from Ralph Abernathy, late Tuesday night, February 21. He said that the arrests were scheduled to begin the following morning. Knowing that he would be one of the first to be arrested, I assured him that I would be with him and the others in my prayers. As usual he was unperturbed.

All night long I thought of the people in Montgomery. Would these mass arrests so frighten them that they would urge us to call off the protest? I knew how hard-pressed they had been. For more than thirteen weeks they had walked, and sacrificed, and worn down their cars. They had been harassed and intimidated on every hand. And now they faced arrest on top of all this. Would they become battle-weary, I wondered. Would they give up in despair? Would this be the end of our movement?

"The point of no return"

I arose early Wednesday morning and flew to Atlanta to pick up my wife and daughter, whom I had left at my parents' home while I was in Nashville. My wife, my mother and father met me at the airport. I had told them about the indictments over the phone, and they had gotten additional information from a radio broadcast. Coretta showed her usual composure, but my parents' faces wore signs of deep perturbation.

My father, so unafraid for himself, had fallen into a constant state of worry for me and my family. Many times he sat in on our councils and had never shown any doubt about the justice of our actions. Yet this stern and courageous man had reached the point where he could scarcely mention the protest without tears. My mother too had suffered. Like all parents, she was afraid for her son and his family. After the bombing she had had to take to bed under doctor's orders, and she was often ill later. During this period I piled

up high long distance telephone bills calling between Atlanta and Montgomery—knowing that if Mother could hear my voice on the telephone she would be temporarily consoled. My parents' expressions—even the way they walked as they came toward me at the airport—had begun to show the strain.

As we drove toward my parents' home, my father said that he thought it would be unwise for me to return to Montgomery now. "Although many others have been indicted," he said, "their main concern is to get you. They might even put you in jail without a bond." He went on to tell me that the law enforcement agencies in Montgomery had been trying to find something on my record in Atlanta that would make it possible to have me deported from Alabama. They had gone to the Atlanta police department, and were disappointed when they learned that I did not have even a minor police record. "All of this shows," my father concluded, "that they are out to get you."

I listened to him attentively, and yet I knew that I could not follow his suggestion and stay in Atlanta. I was profoundly concerned about my parents. I was worried about their worry. These were difficult days for me. On the one hand I had to be concerned about keeping my emotional and psychological balance; on the other hand I was deeply concerned about my mother's worrying. But if I eased out now I would be plagued by my own conscience, reminding me that I lacked the moral courage to stand by a cause to the end. No one can understand my conflict who has not looked into the eyes of those he loves, knowing that he has no alternative but to take a dangerous stand that leaves them tormented.

We continued our drive from the airport and soon arrived at my parents' house. I went directly upstairs to see my daughter, Yoki, now three months old. The innocence of her smile and the warmth of her affection brought temporary relief to my tension.

My father asked several trusted friends to come to the house in the early afternoon to discuss the whole issue. Feeling that this exchange of ideas might help to relieve his worries, I readily agreed to stay over and talk to them. Among those who came were A. T. Walden, distinguished attorney; C. R. Yates and T. M. Alexander, both prominent businessmen; C. A. Scott, editor of the *Atlanta Daily World*; Bishop Sherman L. Green of A.M.E. Church; Benjamin E.

Mays, president of Morehouse College; and Rufus E. Clement, president of Atlanta University. Coretta and my mother joined us.

My father explained to the group that because of his respect for their judgment he was calling on them for advice on whether I should return to Montgomery. He gave them a brief history of the attempts that had been made to get me out of Montgomery. He admitted that the fear of what might happen to me caused him and my mother many restless nights. He concluded by saying that he had talked to a liberal white attorney a few hours earlier, who had confirmed his feeling that I should not go back at this time.

There were murmurs of agreement in the room, and I listened as sympathetically and objectively as I could while two of the men gave their reasons for concurring. These were my elders, leaders among my people. Their words commanded respect. But soon I could not restrain myself any longer. "I must go back to Montgomery," I protested. "My friends and associates are being arrested. It would be the height of cowardice for me to stay away. I would rather be in jail ten years than desert my people now. I have begun the struggle, and I can't turn back. I have reached the point of no return." In the moment of silence that followed I heard my father break into tears. I looked at Dr. Mays, one of the great influences in my life. Perhaps he heard my unspoken plea. At any rate, he was soon defending my position strongly. Then others joined him in supporting me. They assured my father that things were not so bad as they seemed. Mr. Walden put through two calls on the spot to Thurgood Marshall, general counsel of the NAACP, and Arthur Shores, NAACP counsel in Alabama, both of whom assured him that I would have the best legal protection. In the face of all of these persuasions, my father began to be reconciled to my return to Montgomery.

Characteristically, my father, having withdrawn his objections to our return to Montgomery, decided to go along with us, unconcerned with any possible danger or unpleasantness to himself. Ralph Abernathy, released on bail after his arrest the previous day, came to the house. With Ralph and my father, I set out for the county jail, several of my church members following after.

"I was proud of my crime"

At the jail, an almost holiday atmosphere prevailed. People had rushed down to get arrested. No one had been frightened. No one had tried to evade arrest. Many Negroes had gone voluntarily to the sheriff's office to see if their names were on the list, and were even disappointed when they were not. A once fear-ridden people had been transformed. Those who had previously trembled before the law were now proud to be arrested for the cause of freedom. With this feeling of solidarity around me, I walked with firm steps toward the rear of the jail. After I had been photographed and fingerprinted, one of my church members paid my bond and I left for home.

The trial was set for March 19. Friends from all over the country came to Montgomery to be with us during the proceedings. Judge Eugene Carter brought the court to order, and after the necessary preliminaries the state called me up as the first defendant. For four days I sat in court listening to arguments and waiting for a verdict. On Thursday afternoon, March 22, both sides rested. All eyes were turned toward Judge Carter, as with barely a pause he rendered his verdict: "I declare the defendant guilty of violating the state's anti-boycott law." The penalty was a fine of $500 and court costs, or 386 days at hard labor in the county of Montgomery. Then Judge Carter announced that he was giving a minimum penalty because of what I had done to prevent violence. In the cases of the other Negroes charged with the same violation, Judge Carter entered a continuance until a final appeal was complete in my case.

In a few minutes several friends had come up to sign my bond, and the lawyers had notified the judge that the case would be appealed. I left the courtroom with my wife at my side and a host of friends following. In front of the courthouse hundreds of Negroes and whites, including television cameramen and photographers, were waiting. As I waved my hand, they began to sing, "We ain't gonna ride the buses no more."

Ordinarily, a person leaving a courtroom with a conviction behind him would wear a somber face. But I left with a smile. I knew that I was a convicted criminal, but I was proud of my crime. It was the crime of joining my people in a nonviolent protest against injus-

tice. It was the crime of seeking to instill within my people a sense of dignity and self-respect. It was the crime of desiring for my people the unalienable rights of life, liberty, and the pursuit of happiness. It was above all the crime of seeking to convince my people that noncooperation with evil is just as much a moral duty as is cooperation with good.

So ended another effort to halt the protest. I had faith that as the case was appealed and went up through the higher courts, the decision would be reversed. Instead of stopping the movement, the opposition's tactics had only served to give it greater momentum, and to draw us closer together. On that cloudy afternoon in March, Judge Carter had convicted more than Martin Luther King, Jr., Case No. 7399; he had convicted every Negro in Montgomery. It is no wonder that the movement couldn't be stopped. It was too large to be stopped. Its links were too well bound together in a powerfully effective chain. There is amazing power in unity. Where there is true unity, every effort to disunite only serves to strengthen the unity. What the opposition failed to see was that our mutual sufferings had wrapped us all in a single garment of destiny. What happened to one happened to all.

The members of the opposition had also revealed that they did not know the Negroes with whom they were dealing. They thought they were dealing with a group who could be cajoled or forced to do whatever the white man wanted them to do. They were not aware that they were dealing with Negroes who had been freed from fear. And so every move they made proved to be a mistake. It could not be otherwise, because their methods were geared to the "old Negro," and they were dealing with a "new Negro."

I have always felt that ultimately along the way of life an individual must stand up and be counted and be willing to face the consequences whatever they are. And if he is filled with fear he cannot do it. My great prayer is always for God to save me from the paralysis of crippling fear, because I think when a person lives with the fears of the consequences for his personal life he can never do anything in terms of lifting the whole of humanity and solving many of the social problems which we confront in every age and every generation.

In this crisis the members of my church were always nearby to lend their encouragement and active support. As I gradually lost my

role as husband and father, having to be away from home for hours and sometimes days at a time, women came into the house to keep Coretta company. Many of the men took turns as watchmen. My day-to-day contact with my parishioners had almost ceased. I had become no more than a Sunday preacher. But my church willingly shared me with the community, and threw their own considerable resources of time and money into the struggle.

White friends, too, came forward with their support. Often they called to say an encouraging word, and when the house was bombed several of them, known and unknown to us, came by to express their regret.

Through all of these trying and difficult days, Coretta remained amazingly calm and even-tempered. In the midst of the most tragic experiences, she never became panicky or overemotional. She was always strong and courageous. While she had certain natural fears and anxieties concerning my welfare, she never allowed them to hamper my active participation in the movement. And she seemed to have no fear for herself. She was always a deep consolation to me and supported my every move. Occasionally, I would send Coretta and Yoki to Atlanta to stay with my parents or to Marion to stay with hers in order to give them some relief from the heat of the struggle. However, she was never satisfied being away from me. She always insisted on coming back and staying with the struggle to the end. I am convinced that if I had not had a wife with the fortitude, strength, and calmness of Coretta, I could not have stood up amid the ordeals and tensions surrounding the Montgomery movement. In the darkest moments, she always brought the light of hope.

"Segregation must die"

Let's not fool ourselves, we haven't reached the promised land, North or South. We still confront segregation in the South in its glaring and conspicuous forms. We still confront it in the North in its subtle and hidden forms. Segregation is still a fact. Now it might be true that old man segregation is on its deathbed. But history has proven that social systems have a great last-minute breathing power. And the guardians of the status-quo are always on hand with their oxygen tents to keep the old order alive. But if democracy is to live, segregation must die.

The underlying philosophy of democracy is diametrically opposed to the underlying philosophy of segregation, and all of the dialectics of the logicians cannot make them lie down together. Segregation is an evil, segregation is a cancer in the body politic which must be removed before our democratic health can be realized.

There was a time that we attempted to live with segregation. There were those who felt that we could live by a doctrine of separate but equal and so back in 1896, the Supreme Court of this nation through the Plessy v. Ferguson decision established the doctrine of separate but equal as the law of the land. But we all know what happened as a result of that doctrine; there was always a strict enforcement of the separate without the slightest intention to abide by the equal. And so as a result of the old Plessy doctrine, we ended up being plunged across the abyss of exploitation, where we experienced the bleakness of nagging injustice.

But even if it had been possible to provide the Negro with equal facilities in terms of external construction and quantitative distribution we would have still confronted inequality. If it had been possible to give Negro children the same number of schools proportionately and the same type of buildings as white children, the Negro children would have still confronted inequality in the sense that they would not have had the opportunity of communicating with all children. You see, equality is not only a matter of mathematics and geometry, but it's a matter of psychology. It's not only a quantitative something but it is a qualitative something; and it is possible to have quantitative equality and qualitative inequality. The doctrine of separate but equal can never be.

I experienced this the other day. I left Montgomery, Alabama, Thursday morning, September 27, via Eastern Air Lines en route to Virginia. In Atlanta I changed from Eastern to Capitol Air Lines. Just as we were about to take off we discovered that we had generator trouble which necessitated our deplaning and going back in the waiting room. We were to have lunch on the flight and so while we were waiting they gave all of us tickets to go in the Dobbs House in the Atlanta airport and have lunch. I was the only Negro passenger on the plane, and I followed everybody else going into the Dobbs House to get lunch. When I got there one of the waiters ushered me back and I thought they were giving me a very nice comfortable seat with everybody else and I discovered they were leading me to a compartment in the back. And

this compartment was around you, you were completely closed in, cut off from everybody else, so I immediately said that I couldn't afford to eat there. I went on back and took a seat out in the main dining room with everybody else and I waited there, and nobody served me. I waited a long time, everybody else was being served. So finally I asked for the manager and he came out and started talking, and I told him the situation and he talked in very sympathetic terms. And I never will forget what he said to me.

He said, "Now Reverend, this is the law; this is the state law and the city ordinance and we have to do it. We can't serve you out here but now everything is the same. Everything is equal back there; you will get the same food; you will be served out of the same dishes and everything else; you will get the same service as everybody out here."

And I looked at him and started wondering if he really believed that. And I started talking with him. I said, "I don't see how I can get the same service. Number one, I confront aesthetic inequality. I can't see all these beautiful pictures that you have around the walls here. We don't have them back there. But not only that, I just don't like sitting back there and it does something to me. It makes me almost angry. I know that I shouldn't get angry. I know that I shouldn't become bitter, but when you put me back there something happens to my soul, so that I confront inequality in the sense that I have a greater potential for the accumulation of bitterness because you put me back there. And then not only that, I met a young man from Mobile who was my seat mate, a white fellow from Mobile, Alabama, and we were discussing some very interesting things. And when we got in the dining room, if we followed what you're saying, we would have to be separated. And this means that I can't communicate with this young man. I am completely cut off from communication. So I confront inequality on three levels: I confront aesthetic inequality; I confront inequality in the sense of a greater potential for the accumulation of bitterness; and I confront inequality in the sense that I can't communicate with the person who was my seat mate."

And I came to see what the Supreme Court meant when they came out saying that separate facilities are inherently unequal. There is no such thing as separate but equal.

"A glorious daybreak"

The battle was not yet won. We would have to walk and sacrifice for several more months, while the city appealed the case. But at least we could walk with new hope. Now it was only a matter of time. The summer days gave way to the shorter cooler days of an Alabama autumn. The Supreme Court decision on our appeal was still pending. Meanwhile we were facing continued attempts to block the car pool. Insurance agents decided, almost overnight, to refuse to insure our station wagons, contending that the risk was too high. Finally the company that held our liability insurance notified us that all the policies would be canceled as of September 15. A Northern friend who had read of our trouble wrote suggesting that we contact Lloyds of London. A few days later I talked to T. M. Alexander, an insurance broker in Atlanta, who approved of the idea and agreed to make the contact for us. In a few days he was able to tell us that Lloyds of London would take the insurance.

But we were in for even greater difficulties. The city decided to take legal action against the car pool itself. We tried to block this maneuver by filing a request in the federal court for an order restraining the city from interfering with the pool. But U.S. District Judge Frank M. Johnson refused to grant the request. Soon several of us received subpoenas; the city had filed the petition. The hearing was set for Tuesday, November 13.

The night before the hearing I had to go before the mass meeting to warn the people that the car pool would probably be enjoined. I knew that they had willingly suffered for nearly twelve months, but how could they function at all with the car pool destroyed? Could we ask them to walk back and forth every day to their jobs? And if not, would we then be forced to admit that the protest had failed in the end? For the first time in our long struggle together, I almost shrank from appearing before them.

The evening came, and I mustered up enough courage to tell them the truth. I tried, however, to end on a note of hope. "This may well be," I said, "the darkest hour just before dawn. We have moved all of these months with the daring faith that God was with us in our struggle. The many experiences of days gone by have vindicated that faith in a most unexpected manner. We must go out with

the same faith, the same conviction. We must believe that a way will be made out of no way." But in spite of these words, I could feel the cold breeze of pessimism passing through the audience. It was a dark night—darker than a thousand midnights. It was a night in which the light of hope was about to fade away and the lamp of faith about to flicker. We went home with nothing before us but a cloud of uncertainty.

Tuesday morning found us in court, once again before Judge Carter. The city's petition was directed against the MIA and several churches and individuals. It asked the court to grant the city compensation for damages growing out of the car pool operation. As chief defendant I sat at the front table with the prosecuting and defense attorneys.

Around twelve o'clock—during a brief recess—I noticed unusual commotion in the courtroom. Both Commissioner Sellers and Mayor Gayle were called to a back room, followed by two of the city attorneys. Several reporters moved excitedly in and out of the room.

I turned to my attorneys, Fred Gray and Peter Hall, and said: "Something is wrong."

Before I could fully get these words out, Rex Thomas—a reporter for Associated Press—came up to me with a paper in his hand.

"Here is the decision that you have been waiting for. Read this release."

Quickly, with a mixture of anxiety and hope, I read these words: "The United States Supreme Court today affirmed a decision of a special three-judge U.S. District Court in declaring Alabama's state and local laws requiring segregation on buses unconstitutional. The Supreme Court acted without listening to any argument; it simply said 'the motion to affirm is granted and the judgment is affirmed.'"

At this moment my heart began to throb with an inexpressible joy. At once I told the news to the attorneys at the table. Then I rushed to the back of the room to tell my wife, Ralph Abernathy, and E. D. Nixon. Soon the word had spread to the whole courtroom. The faces of the Negroes showed that they had heard. "God Almighty has spoken from Washington, D.C.," said one joyful bystander.

After a few minutes Judge Carter called the court to order again, and we settled down to the case at hand for the remainder of the

day. About five o'clock both sides rested, and the judge's decision came in a matter of minutes: As we had all expected, the city was granted a temporary injunction to halt the motor pool. But the decision was an anticlimax. Tuesday, November 13, 1956, will always remain an important and ironic date in the history of the Montgomery bus protest. On that day two historic decisions were rendered—one to do away with the pool; the other to remove the underlying conditions that made it necessary. The darkest hour of our struggle had become the hour of victory. Disappointment, sorrow, and despair are born at midnight, but morning follows.

I rushed home and notified the press that I was calling the Negro citizens together on Wednesday night, November 14, to decide whether to call off the protest. In order to accommodate as many people as possible, two simultaneous meetings were scheduled, one on each side of town, with the speakers traveling from one meeting to the other. In the meantime, the executive board decided, on the advice of counsel, to recommend that the official protest be ended immediately, but that the return to the buses be delayed until the mandatory order arrived from the Supreme Court in Washington. It was expected in a few days.

The eight thousand men and women who crowded in and around the two churches were in high spirits. At the first meeting it was clear that the news of the decision had spread fast. Each of the meetings accepted the recommendations of the executive board to call off the protest but refrain from riding the buses until the mandate reached Alabama. It was a glorious daybreak to end a long night of enforced segregation.

That night the Ku Klux Klan rode. The radio had announced their plan to demonstrate throughout the Negro community, and threats of violence and new bombings were in the air. For a short period during the late summer and early fall, there had been a decline in harassments, but they started again when the Supreme Court rendered its verdict. The evening after the decision my telephone rang almost every five minutes. One caller said to me, "If you allow the niggers to go back to the buses and sit on the front seat, we are going to burn down more than fifty nigger houses in one night, including yours." I said to him very calmly that that wasn't the way to solve the problem. Before I could complete my sentence, he said,

"Shut up your mouth, nigger, or we will come out there and blow you up right now." Another caller spent his time cursing the Supreme Court. He told me that he had evidence that all the Supreme Court justices were Communists. He closed his bitter statement by saying: "We are just waiting for that damn Hugo Black to come back to Alabama, and we are going to hang you and him on the same tree."

Ordinarily, threats of Klan action were a signal to the Negroes to go into their houses, close the doors, pull the shades, or turn off the lights. Fearing death, they played dead. But this time they had prepared a surprise. When the Klan arrived—according to the newspapers "about forty carloads of robed and hooded members"—porch lights were on and doors open. As the Klan drove by, the Negroes behaved as though they were watching a circus parade. Concealing the effort it cost them, many walked about as usual; some simply watched from their steps; a few waved at the passing cars. After a few blocks, the Klan, nonplussed, turned off into a side street and disappeared into the night.

Meanwhile we went to work to prepare the people for integrated buses. In mass meeting after mass meeting we stressed nonviolence. The prevailing theme was that "we must not take this as a victory over the white man, but as a victory for justice and democracy." We hammered away at the point that "we must not go back on the buses and push people around unnecessarily, boasting of our rights. We must simply sit where there is a vacant seat."

In spite of all of our efforts to prepare the Negroes for integrated buses, not a single white group would take the responsibility of preparing the white community. We tried to get the white ministerial alliance to make a simple statement calling for courtesy and Christian brotherhood, but in spite of the favorable response of a few ministers, the majority "dared not get involved in such a controversial issue." This was a deep disappointment.

"Our faith seems to be vindicated"

On December 20, 1956, the bus integration order finally reached Montgomery. A mass meeting was immediately scheduled for that evening, to give the people final instructions before returning to the

buses the following day. I called and asked the manager of the bus company to be sure to have service restored on all of the major lines. With evident relief, he agreed.

To the overflow crowd at the St. John A.M.E. Church I read the following message that I had carefully prepared in the afternoon:

These twelve months have not at all been easy. Our feet have often been tired. We have struggled against tremendous odds to maintain alternative transportation. There have been moments when roaring waters of disappointment poured upon us in staggering torrents. We can remember days when unfavorable court decisions came upon us like tidal waves, leaving us treading in the deep and confused waters of despair. But amid all of this we have kept going with the faith that as we struggle, God struggles with us, and that the arc of the moral universe, although long, is bending toward justice. We have lived under the agony and darkness of Good Friday with the conviction that one day the heightening glow of Easter would emerge on the horizon. We have seen truth crucified and goodness buried, but we have kept going with the conviction that truth crushed to earth will rise again.

Now our faith seems to be vindicated. This morning the long awaited mandate from the United States Supreme Court concerning bus segregation came to Montgomery. Our experience and growth during this past year of united nonviolent protest has been of such that we cannot be satisfied with a court "victory" over our white brothers. We must respond to the decision with an understanding of those who have oppressed us and with an appreciation of the new adjustments that the court order poses for them. We must be able to face up honestly to our own shortcomings. We must act in such a way as to make possible a coming together of white people and colored people on the basis of a real harmony of interests and understanding. We seek an integration based on mutual respect.

This is the time that we must evince calm dignity and wise restraint. Emotions must not run wild. Violence must not come from any of us, for if we become victimized with violent intents, we will have walked in vain, and our twelve months of glorious dignity will be transformed into an eve of gloomy catastrophe. As we go back to the buses let us be loving enough to turn an enemy into a friend. We must now move from protest to reconciliation. It is my firm conviction that God is working in Montgomery. Let all men of goodwill, both Negro and white, con-

tinue to work with Him. With this dedication we will be able to emerge from the bleak and desolate midnight of man's inhumanity to man to the bright and glittering daybreak of freedom and justice.

The audience stood and cheered loudly. This was the moment toward which they had pressed for more than a year. The return to the buses, on an integrated basis, was a new beginning. But it was a conclusion too, the end of an effort that had drawn Montgomery's Negroes together as never before. It had been gratifying to know how the idea of nonviolence had gradually seeped into the hearts and souls of the people. There had been an amazing amount of discipline on the part of our people. I felt that the whole struggle had given the Negro a new sense of dignity and destiny. To many of those present the joy was not unmixed. Some perhaps feared what might happen when they began to ride the buses again the next day. Others had found a spiritual strength in sacrifice to a cause; now the sacrifice was no longer necessary. Like many consummations, this one left a slight aftertaste of sadness.

I had decided that after many months of struggling with my people for the goal of justice I should not sit back and watch, but should lead them back to the buses myself. I asked Ralph Abernathy, E. D. Nixon, and Glenn Smiley to join me in riding on the first integrated bus. They reached my house around 5:45 on Friday morning. Television cameras, photographers, and news reporters were hovering outside the door. At 5:55 we walked toward the bus stop, the cameras shooting, the reporters bombarding us with questions. Soon the bus appeared; the door opened, and I stepped on. The bus driver greeted me with a cordial smile. As I put my fare in the box he said:

"I believe you are Reverend King, aren't you?"

I answered: "Yes I am."

"We are glad to have you this morning," he said.

I thanked him and took my seat, smiling now too. Abernathy, Nixon, and Smiley followed, with several reporters and television men behind them. Glenn Smiley sat next to me. So I rode the first integrated bus in Montgomery with a white minister, and a native Southerner, as my seat mate.

Downtown we transferred to one of the buses that serviced the white residential section. As the white people boarded, many took seats as if nothing were going on. Others looked amazed to see Ne-

groes sitting in front, and some appeared peeved to know that they either had to sit behind Negroes or stand. One elderly man stood up by the conductor, despite the fact that there were several vacant seats in the rear. When someone suggested to him that he sit in back, he responded: "I would rather die and go to hell than sit behind a nigger." A white woman unknowingly took a seat by a Negro. When she noticed her neighbor, she jumped up and said in a tone of obvious anger: "What are these niggers gonna do next?"

But despite such signs of hostility there were no major incidents on the first day. Many of the whites responded to the new system calmly. Several deliberately and with friendly smiles took seats beside Negroes. True, one Negro woman was slapped by a white man as she alighted, but she refused to retaliate. Later she said: "I could have broken that little fellow's neck all by myself, but I left the mass meeting last night determined to do what Reverend King asked." The *Montgomery Advertiser* reported at the end of the first day: "The calm but cautious acceptance of this significant change in Montgomery's way of life came without any major disturbance."

"A courageous new Negro"

Montgomery marked the first flash of organized, sustained, mass action and nonviolent revolt against the Southern way of life. In Montgomery, there emerged courageous and collective challenge to and protest against the American order, which promised so much for all, while perpetuating indignities and brutalities on the oppressed minority.

Montgomery marked the psychological turning point for the American Negro in his struggle against segregation. The revolution birthed in Montgomery was unlike the isolated, futile, and violent slave revolts. It was also unlike the many sporadic incidents of revolt against segregation by individuals, resisting in their own way the forces of oppression pinning them down. In Montgomery, all across the board, at one and the same time, the rank and file rose up and revolted, by refusing to ride the buses. By walking instead, and by brilliant use of car pools and improvising, the boycotters sustained their revolt all the way to victory.

Also, Montgomery contributed a new weapon to the Negro revo-

lution. This was the social tool of nonviolent resistance. It was a weapon first applied on the American scene and in a collective way in Montgomery. In that city too, it was honed well for future use. It was effective in that it had a way of disarming the opponent. It exposed his moral defenses. It weakened his morale, and at the same time it worked on his conscience. It also provided a method for Negroes to struggle to secure moral ends through moral means. Thus, it provided a creative force through which men could channel their discontent.

Ultimately, victory in Montgomery came with the United States Supreme Court's decision; however, in a real sense, the victory had already come to the boycotters, who had proven to themselves, the community, and the world that Negroes could join in concert and sustain collective action against segregation, carrying it through until the desired objective was reached. In conclusion, then, Montgomery gave forth, for all the world to see, a courageous new Negro. He emerged, etched in sharpest relief, a person whom whites had to confront and even grudgingly respect, and one whom Negroes admired and, then, emulated. He had thrust off his stagnant passivity and deadening complacency, and emerged with a new sense of dignity and destiny. The Montgomery Negro had acquired a new sense of somebodiness and self-respect, and had a new determination to achieve freedom and human dignity no matter what the cost.

10

THE EXPANDING STRUGGLE

History has thrust upon our generation an indescribably important destiny—to complete a process of democratization which our nation has too long developed too slowly, but which is our most powerful weapon for world respect and emulation. How we deal with this crucial situation will determine our moral health as individuals, our cultural health as a region, our political health as a nation, and our prestige as a leader of the free world.

FEBRUARY 14, 1957
King becomes head of Southern Leaders Conference (later SCLC)

MAY 17
Delivers address at Prayer Pilgrimage for Freedom in Washington, D.C.

SEPTEMBER 25
Applauds President Eisenhower's decision to use force to integrate Little Rock's Central High School

OCTOBER 23
Martin Luther King III is born

JUNE 23, 1958
King and other civil rights leaders meet with Eisenhower

On January 9, 1957, Ralph Abernathy and I went to Atlanta to prepare for a meeting of Negro leaders that I had called for the following day. In the middle of the night we were awakened by a

telephone call from Ralph's wife, Juanita. I knew that only some new disaster would make her rouse us at two in the morning. When Ralph came back, his sober face told part of the story. "My home has been bombed," he said, "and three or four other explosions have been heard in the city, but Juanita doesn't know where yet." I asked about Juanita and their daughter. "Thank God, they are safe." Before we could talk any more, the telephone rang a second time. It was Juanita again, saying that the First Baptist Church had been hit. Ralph's home and his church had been bombed in one night. I knew no words to comfort him. There in the early morning hours we prayed to God together, asking for the power of endurance, the strength to carry on.

Ralph and I arranged to fly back, leaving the meeting of Southern leaders to begin without us. From the Montgomery airport we drove directly to Ralph's house. The street was roped off, and hundreds of people stood staring at the ruins. The front porch had been almost completely destroyed, and things inside the house were scattered from top to bottom. Juanita, though shocked and pale, was fairly composed.

The rest of the morning was spent in a grim tour of the other bombings. The Bell Street and Mt. Olive Baptist churches had been almost completely destroyed. The other two churches were less severely damaged, but nevertheless faced great losses.

That afternoon, I returned to Atlanta to make at least an appearance at the meeting of Negro leaders. There I found an enthusiastic group of almost a hundred men from all over the South, committed to the idea of a Southern movement to implement the Supreme Court's decision against bus segregation through nonviolent means. We wired President Dwight D. Eisenhower, asking him to come south immediately, to make a major speech in a major Southern city urging all Southerners to accept and to abide by the Supreme Court's decisions as the law of the land. We further urged him to use the weight of his great office to point out to the South the moral nature of the problems posed at home and abroad by the unsolved civil rights issue. Before adjourning they voted to form the Southern Leaders Conference (later the Southern Christian Leadership Conference or SCLC), a permanent organization to facilitate coordinated

action of local protest groups. I became the group's president, a position I still hold.

"Wave of terror"

When I returned to Montgomery over the weekend I found the Negro community in low spirits. After the bombings the city commission had ordered all buses off the streets; and it now appeared that the city fathers would use this reign of violence as an excuse to cancel the bus company's franchise. As a result, many were coming to feel that all our gains had been lost; I myself started to fear that we were in for another long struggle to get bus service renewed. I was also beginning to wonder whether the virulent leaflets that were bombarding the Negro community might be having their effect. Discouraged, and still revolted by the bombings, for some strange reason I began to feel a personal sense of guilt for everything that was happening.

In this mood I went to the mass meeting on Monday night. There for the first time, I broke down in public. I had invited the audience to join me in prayer, and had begun by asking God's guidance and direction in all our activities. Then, in the grip of an emotion I could not control, I said, "Lord, I hope no one will have to die as a result of our struggle for freedom in Montgomery. Certainly I don't want to die. But if anyone has to die, let it be me." The audience was in an uproar. Shouts and cries of "no, no" came from all sides. So intense was the reaction, that I could not go on with my prayer. Two of my fellow ministers came to the pulpit and suggested that I take a seat. For a few minutes I stood with their arms around me, unable to move. Finally, with the help of my friends, I sat down. It was this scene that caused the press to report mistakenly that I had collapsed.

Unexpectedly, this episode brought me great relief. Many people came up to me after the meeting and many called the following day to assure me that we were all together until the end. For the next few days, the city was fairly quiet. Bus service was soon resumed, though still on a daytime schedule only.

Then another wave of terror hit. Early in the morning of January 28, the People's Service Station and Cab Stand was bombed, and

LETTER TO MRS. FANNIE E. SCOTT [CORETTA'S GRANDMOTHER]

Dear Mrs. Scott:

Thanks for your very kind letter of recent date. I am very happy to
know of your interest here in Montgomery. May I assure you that things
are going very well with me and the family. Coretta and the baby are
doing fine. We are determined as ever before to continue to struggle for
freedom and justice here in Montgomery. The impression that the paper
gave a few days ago was totally false. I neither collapsed nor broke
down in tears. I am still as strong and healthy as ever before. Be sure to
keep us in your prayers.

January 28, 1957

another bomb fell at the home of a sixty-year-old Negro hospital
worker. The same morning an unexploded bomb, crudely assembled
from twelve sticks of dynamite, was found still smoldering on my
porch.

I was staying with friends on the other side of town, and Coretta
and Yoki were in Atlanta. So once more I heard the news first on the
telephone. On my way home, I visited the other scenes of disaster
nearby, and found to my relief that no one had been hurt.

At home I addressed the crowd from my porch, where the mark
of the bomb was clear. "We must not return violence under any
condition. I know this is difficult advice to follow, especially since
we have been the victims of no less than ten bombings. But this is
the way of Christ; it is the way of the cross. We must somehow
believe that unearned suffering is redemptive." Then, since it was
Sunday morning, I urged the people to go home and get ready for
church. Gradually they dispersed.

With these bombings the community came to see that Montgomery
was fast being plunged into anarchy. Finally, the city began to inves-
tigate in earnest. Rewards of $4,000 were offered for information
leading to the arrest and conviction of the bombers. On January 31,
the Negro community was surprised to hear that seven white men
had been arrested in connection with the bombings.

The defense attorneys spent two days attempting to prove the

innocence of their clients, arguing that the bombings had been carried out by the MIA in order to inspire new outside donations for their dwindling treasury. At the end of the second day I was called to the witness stand by the defense. For more than an hour I was questioned on things which had no relevance to the bombing case. The lawyers lifted statements of mine out of context to give the impression that I was a perpetrator of hate and violence. At many points they invented derogatory statements concerning white people, and attributed them to me. The men had signed confessions. But in spite of all the evidence, the jury returned a verdict of not guilty.

Justice had once more miscarried. But the diehards had made their last stand. The disturbances ceased abruptly. Desegregation on the buses proceeded smoothly. In a few weeks transportation was back to normal, and people of both races rode together wherever they pleased. The skies did not fall when integrated buses finally traveled the streets of Montgomery.

"A symbol of a movement"

After *Time* magazine published a cover story on our movement in February 1957, I thought I observed a lessening of tensions and feelings against me and the movement itself.

TO CORETTA SCOTT KING

14 February 1957
New Orleans, La.

MRS CORETTA KING =
309 SOUTH JACKSON ST MONTGOMERY ALA =

MY DARLING IT IS A PLEASURE FOR ME TO PAUSE WHILE ATTENDING TO IMPORTANT BUSINESS WHICH AFFECTS THE WELFARE OF THIS NATION AND ATTEND TO THE MOST IMPORTANT BUSINESS IN THE WORLD NAMELY CHOOSING AS MY VALENTINE THE SWEETEST AND MOST LOVELY WIFE AND MOTHER IN ALL THE WORLD AS THE DAYS GO BY MY LOVE GROWS EVEN GREATER FOR YOU WILL ALWAYS BE MY VALENTINE =

MARTIN =

During this period, I could hardly go into any city or any town in this nation where I was not lavished with hospitality by peoples of all races and of all creeds. I could hardly go anywhere to speak in this nation where hundreds and thousands of people were not turned away because of lack of space. And then after speaking, I often had to be rushed out to get away from the crowd rushing for autographs. I could hardly walk the street in any city of this nation where I was not confronted with people running up the street: "Isn't this Reverend King of Alabama?" And living under this it was easy to feel that I was something special.

When you are aware that you are a symbol, it causes you to search your soul constantly—to go through this job of self-analysis, to see if you live up to the high and noble principles that people surround you with, and to try at all times to keep the gulf between the public self and the private self at a minimum.

One of the prayers that I prayed to God every day was: "Oh God, help me to see myself in my true perspective. Help me, oh God, to see that I'm just a symbol of a movement. Help me to see that I'm the victim of what the Germans call a *Zeitgeist* and that something was getting ready to happen in history. And that a boycott would have taken place in Montgomery, Alabama, if I had never come to Alabama. Help me to realize that I'm where I am because of the forces of history and because of the fifty thousand Negroes of Alabama who will never get their names in the papers and in the headlines. Oh, God, help me to see that where I stand today, I stand because others helped me to stand there and because the forces of history projected me there."

"New Negro in the South"

It was clear that things were much better than they were before December 5, 1955, but Montgomery's racial problems were still far from solved. The problem in Montgomery was merely symptomatic of the larger national problem. Forces maturing for years had given rise to a crisis in race relations. The social upheavals of the two world wars, the Great Depression, and the spread of the automobile had made it both possible and necessary for the Negro to move away from his former isolation on the rural plantation. The decline of

◆

THE CONSEQUENCES OF FAME

One of the frustrations of any young man is to approach the heights at such an early age. The average man reaches this point maybe in his late forties or early fifties. But when you reach it so young, your life becomes a kind of decrescendo. You feel yourself fading from the screen at a time you should just be starting to work toward your goal.

Frankly, I'm worried to death. A man who hits the peak at twenty-seven has a tough job ahead. People will be expecting me to pull rabbits out of the hat for the rest of my life. If I don't or there are no rabbits to be pulled, then they'll say I'm no good.

Quoted in the *New York Post*, April 14, 1957

◆

agriculture and the parallel growth of industry had drawn large numbers of Negroes to urban centers and brought about a gradual improvement in their economic status. New contacts had led to a broadened outlook and new possibilities for educational advance.

All of these factors conjoined to cause the Negro to take a fresh look at himself. His expanding life experiences had created within him a consciousness that he was an equal element in a larger social compound and accordingly should be given rights and privileges commensurate with his new responsibilities. Once plagued with a tragic sense of inferiority resulting from the crippling effects of slavery and segregation, the Negro was driven to reevaluate himself. He had come to feel that he was somebody.

This growing self-respect has inspired the Negro with a new determination to struggle and sacrifice until first-class citizenship becomes a reality. This is the true meaning of the Montgomery Story. One can never understand the bus protest in Montgomery without understanding that there is a new Negro in the South, with a new sense of dignity and destiny.

Along with the Negro's changing image of himself has come an awakening moral consciousness on the part of millions of white Americans concerning segregation. Ever since the signing of the Declaration of Independence, America has manifested a schizophrenic personality on the question of race. She has been torn between selves—a self in which she has proudly professed democracy

and a self in which she has sadly practiced the antithesis of democracy. The reality of segregation, like slavery, has always had to confront the ideals of democracy and Christianity. Indeed, segregation and discrimination are strange paradoxes in a nation founded on the principle that all men are created equal.

Climaxing this process was the Supreme Court's decision outlawing segregation in the public schools. For all men of goodwill May 17, 1954, marked a joyous end to the long night of enforced segregation. In unequivocal language the Court affirmed that "separate but equal" facilities are inherently unequal, and that to segregate a child on the basis of his race is to deny that child equal protection of the law. This decision brought hope to millions of disinherited Negroes who had formerly dared only to dream of freedom. It further enhanced the Negro's sense of dignity and gave him even greater determination to achieve justice.

This determination of Negro Americans to win freedom from all forms of oppression springs from the same deep longing that motivates oppressed peoples all over the world. The rumblings of discontent in Asia and Africa are expressions of a quest for freedom and human dignity by people who have long been the victims of colonialism and imperialism. So, in a real sense, the racial crisis in America is a part of the larger world crisis.

"Give us the ballot!"

On the seventeenth of May, 1957, civil rights advocates commemorated the third anniversary of the Supreme Court's momentous decision outlawing segregation by leading a Prayer Pilgrimage to Washington, D.C. On that day thousands of Negroes and white persons of goodwill from all over the country assembled at the Lincoln Memorial and had a service about two hours in length. We received strong and powerful support from organized labor. Walter Reuther, for instance, sent letters to all of his locals requesting them to send delegations and also money. The overall purpose of this pilgrimage was to arouse the conscience of the nation in favor of racial justice. The more specific purposes were to demonstrate the unity of the Negro in the struggle for freedom, the violence and terror which we suffer in the southland at this time, and to appeal to Congress to

pass the Civil Rights Bill, which was being bottled up in committees by Southern congressmen.

In the midst of these prevailing conditions, we came to Washington to say to the men in the forefront of our government, that the civil rights issue was not an ephemeral, evanescent domestic issue that could be kicked about by reactionary guardians of the status quo; it was rather an eternal moral issue which may well determine the destiny of our nation in the ideological struggle with Communism.

Our most urgent request to the President of the United States and every member of Congress is to give us the right to vote. Give us the ballot and we will no longer have to worry the federal government about our basic rights. Give us the ballot and we will no longer plead to the federal government for passage of an anti-lynching law; we will by the power of our vote write the law on the statute books of the South and bring an end to the dastardly acts of the hooded perpetrators of violence. Give us the ballot and we will transform the salient misdeeds of bloodthirsty mobs into the calculated good deeds of orderly citizens. Give us the ballot and we will fill our legislative halls with men of goodwill and send to the sacred halls of Congress men who will not sign a Southern manifesto because of their devotion to the manifesto of justice. Give us the ballot and we will place judges on the benches of the South who will do justly and love mercy, and we will place at the head of the Southern states governors who will, who have felt not only the tang of the human, but the glow of the Divine. Give us the ballot and we will quietly and nonviolently, without rancor or bitterness, implement the Supreme Court's Decision of May 17, 1954. . . .

If the executive and legislative branches of the government were as concerned about the protection of our citizenship rights as the federal courts have been, then the transition from a segregated to an integrated society would be infinitely smoother. But we so often look to Washington in vain for this concern. In the midst of the tragic breakdown of law and order, the executive branch of the government is all too silent and apathetic. In the midst of the desperate need for civil rights legislation, the legislative branch of the government is all too stagnant and hypocritical.

This dearth of positive leadership from the federal government is not confined to one particular political party. Both political parties have

betrayed the cause of justice. The Democrats have betrayed it by capitu-
lating to the prejudices and undemocratic practices of the southern Dix-
iecrats. The Republicans have betrayed it by capitulating to the blatant
hypocrisy of right wing, reactionary Northerners. These men so often
have a high blood pressure of words and an anemia of deeds.

"Crusade for Citizenship"

During the summer of 1957 the SCLC made plans for a Crusade for
Citizenship, a new Southwide educational and action campaign for
the enforcement of Negro voting rights. The recently enacted Civil
Rights law would be meaningless unless it was translated into action
by Negroes exercising their right to vote. The main purpose of the
Crusade for Citizenship was to get Negroes throughout the South to
exercise that right.

It was my firm conviction that if the Negro achieved the ballot
throughout the South, many of the problems which we faced would
be solved. Once we gained the ballot, we would see a new day in the
South. I had come to see that one of the most decisive steps that the
Negro could take was a short walk to the voting booth. Until we
gained the ballot and placed proper public officials in office, this
condition would continue to exist.

In September 1957 I thought it was quite regrettable and unfortunate that young high school students in Little Rock, Arkansas, had
to go to school under the protection of federal troops. But I thought
it was even more unfortunate that Arkansas Governor Orval Faubus,
through irresponsible actions, left the president of the United States
with no other alternative. I believe firmly in nonviolence, but, at the
same time, I am not an anarchist. I believe in the intelligent use of
police force. And I thought that was all we had in Little Rock. It
wasn't an army fighting against a nation or a race of people. It was
just police force, seeking to enforce the law of the land. It was high
time that a man as popular in the world as Eisenhower—a man with
his moral influence—speak out and take a stand against what was
happening all over the South. So I backed the President, and I sent
him a telegram commending him for the positive and forthright
stand that he took in the Little Rock school situation. He showed

the nation and the world that the United States was a nation dedicated to law and order rather than mob rule.

Nevertheless, it was strange to me that the federal government was more concerned about what happened in Budapest than what happened in Birmingham. I thought Eisenhower believed that integration would be a fine thing. But I thought he felt that the more you push it, the more tension it would create, so, just wait a few more years and it will work itself out. I didn't think that Eisenhower felt like being a crusader for integration. President Eisenhower was a man of integrity and goodwill, but I am afraid that on the question of integration he didn't understand the dimensions of social change involved nor how the problem was to be worked out.

11

BIRTH OF A NEW NATION

Ghana has something to say to us. It says to us first that the oppressor never voluntarily gives freedom to the oppressed. You have to work for it. Freedom is never given to anybody. Privileged classes never give up their privileges without strong resistance.

MARCH 4, 1957
King party arrives in Gold Coast for independence celebration

MARCH 6
Attends midnight ceremony marking Ghana's independence

MARCH 12
Departs from Accra to Rome, by way of Nigeria

MARCH 26
Returns to New York after stays in Paris and London

The minute I knew I was coming to Ghana I had a very deep emotional feeling. A new nation was being born. It symbolized the fact that a new order was coming into being and an old order was passing away. So I was deeply concerned about it. I wanted to be involved in it, be a part of it, and notice the birth of this new nation with my own eyes. The trip, which included visits to other countries of Africa and several stops in Europe, was of tremendous cultural value and made possible many contacts of lasting significance.

Struggling had been going on in Ghana for years. The British

Empire saw that it could no longer rule the Gold Coast and agreed that on the sixth of March, 1957, it would release the nation. All of this was because of the persistent protest, the continual agitation, of Prime Minister Kwame Nkrumah and the other leaders who worked along with him and the masses of people who were willing to follow.

"A new age coming into being"

So that day finally came. About midnight on a dark night in 1957, a new nation came into being. That was a great hour. As we walked out, we noticed all over the polo grounds almost a half million people. They had waited for this hour and this moment for years.

People came from all over the world—seventy nations—to say to this new nation: "We greet you and give you our moral support. We hope for you God's guidance as you move now into the realm of independence." It was a beautiful experience to see some of the leading persons on the scene of civil rights in America on hand: to my left was Charles Diggs, to my right were Adam Powell and Ralph Bunche. All of these people from America: Mordecai Johnson, Horace Mann Bond, A. Philip Randolph; then you looked out and saw the vice-president of the United States.

A handsome black man walked out on the platform, and he was followed by eight or ten other men. He stood there and said, "We are no longer a British colony. We are a free and sovereign people." When he uttered those words, we looked back and saw an old flag coming down and a new flag going up. And I said to myself, "That old flag coming down doesn't represent the meaning of this drama taking place on the stage of history, for it is the symbol of an old order passing away. That new flag going up is the symbol of a new age coming into being." I could hear people shouting all over that vast audience, "Freedom! Freedom! Freedom!"

Before I knew it, I started weeping. I was crying for joy. And I knew about all of the struggles, all of the pain, and all of the agony that these people had gone through for this moment.

After Nkrumah made that final speech, we walked away, and we could hear little children six years old and old people eighty and ninety years old walking the streets of Accra crying: "Freedom! Freedom!" They were crying it in a sense that they had never heard it

SERMON ON GHANA

It seems this morning that I can hear God speaking. I can hear him speaking throughout the universe, saying, "Be still and know that I am God. And if you don't stop, if you don't straighten up, if you don't stop exploiting people, I'm going to rise up and break the backbone of your power. And your power will be no more!" And the power of Great Britain is no more. I looked at France. I looked at Britain. And I thought about the Britain that could boast, "The sun never sets on our great Empire." And I say now she had gone to the level that the sun hardly rises on the British Empire.

April 7, 1957

before. And I could hear that old Negro spiritual once more crying out: "Free at last, free at last, Great God Almighty, I'm free at last." They were experiencing that in their very souls. And everywhere we turned, we could hear it ringing out from the housetops. We could hear it from every corner, every nook and crook of the community. "Freedom! Freedom!" This was the breaking loose from Egypt.

The thing that impressed me more than anything else that night was when Nkrumah and his other ministers who had been in prison with him walked in. They didn't come in with the crowns and all of the garments of kings. They walked in with prison caps. Nkrumah stood up and made his closing speech to Parliament with the little cap that he wore in prison for several months and the coat that he wore in prison for several months. Often the path to freedom will carry you through prison.

Nkrumah had started out in a humble way. His mother and father were illiterate, not chiefs at all, but humble people. He went to school for a while in Africa and then he decided to work his way to America. He went to the Lincoln University in Pennsylvania, and took his theology degree there. He preached a while in Philadelphia. He went to the University of Pennsylvania and took a master's degree there in philosophy and sociology.

He always realized that colonialism was made for domination and exploitation. It was made to keep a certain group down and exploit that group economically for the advantage of another. He

studied and thought about all of this, and one day he decided to go back to Africa.

He was immediately elected the executive secretary of the United Party of the Gold Coast, and he worked hard getting a following. And the people in this party—the old, the people who had had their hands on the plow for a long time—thought he was pushing a little too fast, and they got a little jealous of his influence. So finally he had to break from the United Party of the Gold Coast, and in 1949 he organized the Convention People's Party. It was this party that started out working for the independence of the Gold Coast.

He urged his people to unite for freedom and urged the officials of the British Empire to give them freedom. The officials were slow to respond, but the masses of people were with him, and they had united to become the most powerful and influential party that had ever been organized in that section of Africa.

Nkrumah himself was finally placed in jail for several years. He was an agitator. He was imprisoned on the basis of sedition, but he had inspired some people outside of prison. They got together just a few months after he had been in prison and elected him the prime minister. The British Empire saw that they had better let him out. He was placed there for fifteen years, but he only served eight or nine months. He came out the prime minister of the Gold Coast.

"A symbol of hope"

I thought that this event, the birth of this new nation, would give impetus to oppressed peoples all over the world. I thought it would have worldwide implications and repercussions—not only for Asia and Africa, but also for America. Just as in 1776, when America received its independence, the harbor of New York became sort of a beacon of hope for thousands of oppressed people of Europe, I thought Ghana would become a symbol of hope for hundreds and thousands of oppressed peoples all over the world as they struggled for freedom.

The birth of this new nation renewed my conviction in the ultimate triumph of justice. And it seemed to me, this was fit testimony to the fact that eventually the forces of justice triumph in the uni-

verse, and somehow the universe itself is on the side of freedom and justice. This gave new hope to me in the struggle for freedom.

Wednesday morning the official opening of Parliament was held, and we were able to get on the inside. There Nkrumah, now the Prime Minister of the Gold Coast, with no superior, made his first speech. The Duchess of Kent, who represented the Queen of England, walked in. She was just a passing visitor now—like M. L. King and Ralph Bunche and Coretta King and everybody else—because this was a new nation. After Parliament was open, and Nkrumah drove out, the people standing around the streets of the city cried out: "All hail, Nkrumah!" Everybody was crying his name because they knew he had suffered for them, he had sacrificed for them, he'd gone to jail for them.

This nation was now out of Egypt and had crossed the Red Sea. Now it would confront its wilderness. Nkrumah realized that. For instance, Ghana was a one-crop country, cocoa mainly. In order to make the economic system more stable, it would be necessary to industrialize. Nkrumah said to me that one of the first things that he would do would be to work toward industrialization.

Ninety percent of the people were illiterate, and it was necessary to lift the whole cultural standard of the community in order to make it possible to stand up in the free world. It was my hope that even people from America would go to Africa as immigrants. American Negroes could lend their technical assistance to a growing new nation. I was very happy to see people who had moved in. A doctor from Brooklyn, New York, had just come in that week. His wife was a dentist, and they were living there, and the people loved them. Nkrumah made it very clear to me that he would welcome any persons coming there as immigrants.

I realized that there would be difficulties. Whenever you have a transition, whenever you are moving from one system to another there will be definite difficulties, but I thought that there was enough brainpower, enough determination, enough courage and faith to meet the difficulties as they developed.

When I hear, "People aren't ready," that's like telling a person who is trying to swim, "Don't jump in that water until you learn how to swim." When actually you will never learn how to swim until

you get in the water. People have to have an opportunity to develop themselves and govern themselves.

I am often reminded of the statement made by Nkrumah: "I prefer self-government with danger to servitude with tranquility." I think that's a great statement. They were willing to face the dangers and difficulties, but I thought that Ghana would be able to profit by the mistakes of other nations that had existed over so many years and develop into a great nation.

After meeting Kwame Nkrumah, we stopped in Nigeria for a day or so. Then we went to Europe and then back to America to deal with the problems there.

12

BRUSH WITH DEATH

This was a rather difficult year for me. I have had to confront the brutality of police officers, an unwarranted arrest, and a near fatal stab wound by a mentally deranged woman. These things were poured upon me like staggering torrents on a cold, wintry day.

SEPTEMBER 3, 1958
King is arrested in Montgomery

SEPTEMBER 4
After his conviction for failing to obey an officer, King's fine is paid by Montgomery police commissioner

SEPTEMBER 20
Is stabbed in Harlem

OCTOBER 3
After release from Harlem Hospital, begins convalescing at the home of the Reverend Sandy F. Ray

OCTOBER 24
Returns to Montgomery to continue recuperation

On a Saturday afternoon in 1958, I sat in a Harlem department store, surrounded by hundreds of people. I was autographing copies of *Stride Toward Freedom*, my book about the Montgomery bus boycott. And while sitting there, a demented black woman came up. The only question I heard from her was, "Are you Martin Luther King?"

I was looking down writing, and I said "Yes." And the next minute, I felt something sharp plunge forcefully into my chest. Before I

knew it, I had been stabbed with a letter opener by a woman who would later be judged insane, Mrs. Izola Ware Curry.

Rushed by ambulance to Harlem Hospital, I lay in a bed for hours while preparations were made to remove the keen-edged knife from my body. Days later, when I was well enough to talk with Dr. Aubrey Maynard, the chief of the surgeons who performed the delicate, dangerous operation, I learned the reason for the long delay that preceded surgery. He told me that the razor tip of the instrument had been touching my aorta and that my whole chest had to be opened to extract it.

"If you had sneezed during all those hours of waiting," Dr. Maynard said, "your aorta would have been punctured and you would have drowned in your own blood."

It came out in the *New York Times* the next morning that, if I had sneezed, I would have died.

About four days later, after the operation, after my chest had been opened, and the blade had been taken out, they allowed me to move around in the wheelchair in the hospital and read some of the kind letters that came from all over the States, and the world. I read a few, but one of them I will never forget. There was a letter from a young girl who was a student at the White Plains High School. It said simply, "Dear Dr. King: I am a ninth-grade student at the White Plains High School." She said, "While it should not matter, I would like to mention that I am a white girl. I read in the paper of your misfortune, and of your suffering. And I read that if you had sneezed, you would have died. And I'm simply writing you to say that I'm so happy that you didn't sneeze."

"Uncertain but promising future"

If I demonstrated unusual calm during the recent attempt on my life, it was certainly not due to any extraordinary powers that I possess. Rather, it was due to the power of God working through me. Throughout this struggle for racial justice I have constantly asked God to remove all bitterness from my heart and to give me the strength and courage to face any disaster that came my way. This constant prayer life and feeling of dependence on God have given me the feeling that I have divine

---

TO THE MASS MEETING OF THE MONTGOMERY IMPROVEMENT ASSOCIATION

My Dear Friends and Co-Workers of the MIA:

While convalescing here in New York from an act of violence which was inflicted upon me two weeks ago, my mind inevitably turns toward you. Over and over again during these difficult days I have thought of you and our long association together.

First, let me relieve your minds by saying that I am doing quite well. The five physicians who have been at my side from the moment of the operation have all agreed that I have made an amazing recovery. I am gradually regaining my strength and the natural pain that follows an operation is gradually passing away. . . .

May I urge you to continue in the noble struggle for freedom and justice that has been so courageously started in the Cradle of the Confederacy. Fortunately, God has given Montgomery several marvelous leaders and my absence does not in any way have to impede the program of our movement. . . . Our final destination is the City of Freedom and we must not stop until we have entered the sublime and lofty Metropolis. . . .

Your servant in the cause of Christ and Freedom,

Martin Luther King, Jr.

October 6, 1958

---

companionship in the struggle. I know no other way to explain it. It is the fact that in the midst of external tension, God can give an inner peace.

As far as the repeated attacks on me and my family, I must say that here again God gives one the strength to adjust to such acts of violence. None of these attacks came as a total surprise to me, because I counted the cost early in the struggle. To believe in nonviolence does not mean that violence will not be inflicted upon you. The believer in nonviolence is the person who will willingly allow himself to be the victim of violence but will never inflict violence upon another. He lives by the conviction that through his suffering and cross bearing, the social situation may be redeemed.

The experience I had in New York gave me time to think. I became convinced that if the movement held to the spirit of nonviolence, our struggle and example would challenge and help redeem not only America but the world. It was my hope that we would

remove from our souls the shackles of fear and the manacles of despair, and move on into the uncertain but promising future with the faith that the dawn of a new day was just around the horizon.

The pathetic aspect of the experience was not the injury to one individual. It demonstrated to me that a climate of hatred and bitterness so permeated areas of our nation that inevitably deeds of extreme violence must erupt. I saw its wider social significance. The lack of restraint upon violence in our society along with the defiance of law by men in high places cannot but result in an atmosphere which engenders desperate deeds.

I was intensely impatient to get back to continue the work we all knew had to be done regardless of the cost. So I rejoined the ranks of those who were working ceaselessly for the realization of the ideals of freedom and justice for all men. I did not have the slightest intention of turning back at that point.

13

PILGRIMAGE TO NONVIOLENCE

It was a marvelous experience to meet and talk with the great leaders of India, to meet and talk with and speak to thousands and thousands of people all over that vast country. These experiences will remain dear to me as long as the cords of memory shall lengthen.

FEBRUARY 3, 1959
The Kings, accompanied by Dr. L. D. Reddick, embark for India

FEBRUARY 10
After stay in Paris, King party arrives in India and has dinner with Prime Minister Nehru

MARCH 10
Departure from India to Jerusalem and Cairo

MARCH 18
Return to United States

For a long time I had wanted to take a trip to India. Even as a child, the entire Orient held a strange fascination for me—the elephants, the tigers, the temples, the snake charmers, and all the other storybook characters.

While the Montgomery boycott was going on, India's Gandhi was the guiding light of our technique of nonviolent social change. So as soon as our victory over bus segregation was won, some of my friends said: "Why don't you go to India and see for yourself what the Mahatma, whom you so admire, has wrought?"

In 1956 when Pandit Jawaharlal Nehru, India's prime minister, made a short visit to the United States, he was gracious enough to say that he wished that he and I had met. His diplomatic representatives made inquiries as to the possibility of my visiting his country some time. Our former American ambassador to India, Chester Bowles, wrote me along the same lines.

But every time that I was about to make the trip, something would interfere. At one time it was my visit by prior commitment to Ghana. At another time my publishers were pressing me to finish writing *Stride Toward Freedom*. Then along came Mrs. Izola Ware Curry. She not only knocked out the travel plans that I had but almost everything else as well.

After I recovered from this near-fatal encounter and was finally released by my doctors, it occurred to me that it might be better to get in the trip to India before plunging too deeply once again into the sea of the Southern segregation struggle.

I preferred not to take this long trip alone and asked my wife and my friend, Lawrence Reddick, to accompany me. Coretta was particularly interested in the women of India, and Dr. Reddick in the history and government of that great country. He had written my biography, *Crusader Without Violence*, and said that my true test would come when the people who knew Gandhi looked me over and passed judgment upon me and the Montgomery movement. The three of us made up a sort of three-headed team with six eyes and six ears for looking and listening.

And so on February 3, 1959, just before midnight, we left New York by plane. En route we stopped in Paris with Richard Wright, an old friend of Reddick's, who brought us up to date on European attitudes on the Negro question and gave us a taste of the best French cooking.

We missed our plane connection in Switzerland because of fog, and arrived in India after a roundabout route, two days late. But from the time we came down out of the clouds at Bombay on February 10, until March 10, when we waved good-bye at the New Delhi airport, we had one of the most concentrated and eye-opening experiences of our lives.

"We were looked upon as brothers"

We had a grand reception in India. The people showered upon us the most generous hospitality imaginable. Almost every door was open so that our party was able to see some of India's most important social experiments and talk with leaders in and out of government, ranging from Prime Minister Nehru, to village councilmen and Vinoba Bhave, the sainted leader of the land reform movement. Since our pictures were in the newspapers very often it was not unusual for us to be recognized by crowds in public places and on public conveyances. Occasionally I would take a morning walk in the large cities, and out of the most unexpected places someone would emerge and ask: "Are you Martin Luther King?"

We had hundreds of invitations that the limited time did not allow us to accept. We were looked upon as brothers, with the color of our skins as something of an asset. But the strongest bond of fraternity was the common cause of minority and colonial peoples in America, Africa, and Asia struggling to throw off racism and imperialism.

We had the opportunity to share our views with thousands of Indian people through endless conversations and numerous discussion sessions. I spoke before university groups and public meetings all over India. Because of the keen interest that the Indian people have in the race problem these meetings were usually packed. Occasionally interpreters were used, but on the whole I spoke to audiences that understood English.

The Indian people love to listen to the Negro spirituals. Therefore, Coretta ended up singing as much as I lectured. We discovered that autograph seekers are not confined to America. After appearances in public meetings and while visiting villages, we were often besieged for autographs. Even while riding planes, more than once pilots came into the cabin from the cockpit requesting our signatures. We got good press throughout our stay. Thanks to the Indian papers, the Montgomery bus boycott was already well known in that country. Indian publications perhaps gave a better continuity of our 381-day bus strike than did most of our papers in the United States.

We held press conferences in all of the larger cities—Delhi, Cal-

REFLECTIONS ON INDIA TRIP

How can one avoid being depressed when he discovers that of India's 400 million people, more than 365 million make an annual income of less than sixty dollars a year? Most of these people have never seen a doctor or a dentist.

As I looked at these conditions, I found myself saying that we in America cannot stand idly by and not be concerned. Then something within me cried out, "Oh, no, because the destiny of the United States is tied up with the destiny of India—with the destiny of every other nation." And I remembered that we spend more than a million dollars a day to store surplus food in this country. I said to myself, "I know where we can store that food free of charge—in the wrinkled stomachs of the millions of people who go to bed hungry at night." Maybe we spend too much of our national budget building military bases around the world rather than bases of genuine concern and understanding.

Address at Lincoln University, June 6, 1961

cutta, Madras, and Bombay—and talked with newspapermen almost everywhere we went. They asked sharp questions and at times appeared to be hostile, but that was just their way of bringing out the story that they were after. As reporters, they were scrupulously fair with us and in their editorials showed an amazing grasp of what was going on in America and other parts of the world.

"Crowded humanity"

India is a vast country with vast problems. We flew over the long stretches, from north to south, east to west; we took trains for shorter jumps and used automobiles and jeeps to get us into the less accessible places.

Everywhere we went we saw crowded humanity—on the roads, in the city streets and squares, even in the villages. Most of the people were poor and poorly dressed. In the city of Bombay, for example, over a half million people—mostly unattached, unemployed, or partially employed males—slept out of doors every night.

Great ills flowed from the poverty of India but strangely there was relatively little crime. This was another concrete manifestation

of the wonderful spiritual quality of the Indian people. They were poor, jammed together, and half-starved, but they did not take it out on each other.

In contrast to the poverty-stricken, there were Indians who were rich, had luxurious homes, landed estates, fine clothes, and showed evidence of overeating. The bourgeoise—white, black, or brown—behaves about the same the world over.

India's leaders, in and out of government, were conscious of their country's other great problems and were heroically grappling with them. The country seemed to be divided. Some said that India should become Westernized and modernized as quickly as possible so that she might raise her standards of living. On the other hand, there were others—perhaps the majority—who said that Westernization would bring with it the evils of materialism, cutthroat competition, and rugged individualism. They said that India would lose her soul if she took to chasing Yankee dollars, and that the big machine would only raise the living standard of the comparatively few workers who got jobs, but the greater number of people would be displaced.

Prime Minister Nehru, at once an intellectual and a man charged with the practical responsibility of heading the government, seemed to steer a middle course between these extreme attitudes. In our talk with him he indicated that he felt that some industrialization was absolutely necessary; that there were some things that only big or heavy industry could do for the country but that if the state kept a watchful eye on the developments, most of the pitfalls might be avoided. At the same time, Mr. Nehru gave support to the movement that would encourage and expand the handicraft arts such as spinning and weaving in homes and villages and thus leave as much economic self-help and autonomy as possible to the local community.

That night we had dinner with Prime Minister Nehru; with us as a guest was Lady Mountbatten, the wife of Lord Mountbatten, who was viceroy of India when it received its independence. They were lasting friends only because Gandhi followed the way of love and nonviolence. The aftermath of nonviolence is the creation of the beloved community, so that when the battle is over, a new relationship comes into being between the oppressed and the oppressor.

"The Bhoodanists"

There was a great movement in India that is almost unknown in America. At its center was the campaign for land reform known as Bhoodan. It would solve India's great economic and social change by consent, not by force. The Bhoodanists were led by the sainted Vinoba Bhave and Jayaprakash Narayan, a highly sensitive intellectual who was trained in American colleges. Their ideal was the self-sufficient village. Their program envisioned persuading large landowners to give up some of their holdings to landless peasants; persuading small landowners to give up their individual ownership for common cooperative ownership by the villages; and encouraging farmers and villagers to spin and weave the cloth for their own clothes during their spare time from their agricultural pursuits. Since these measures would answer the questions of employment, food, and clothing, the village could then, through cooperative action, make just about everything that it would need or get it through barter or exchange from other villages. Accordingly, each village would be virtually self-sufficient and would thus free itself from the domination of the urban centers that were like evil loadstones drawing the people away from the rural areas, concentrating them in city slums, and debauching them with urban vices. At least this was the argument of the Bhoodanists and other Gandhians.

Such ideas sound strange and archaic to Western ears. However, the Indians have already achieved greater results than we Americans would ever expect. For example, millions of acres of land have been given up by rich landlords and additional millions of acres have been given up to cooperative management by small farmers. On the other hand, the Bhoodanists shrink from giving their movement the organization and drive that we in America would venture to guess that it must have in order to keep pace with the magnitude of the problems that everybody is trying to solve.

It would be a boon to democracy if one of the great nations of the world, with almost four hundred million people, proves that it is possible to provide a good living for everyone without surrendering to a dictatorship of either the "right" or "left." India is a tremendous force for peace and nonviolence, at home and abroad. It is a land where the idealist and the intellectual are yet respected. We

should want to help India preserve her soul and thus help to save our own.

"The light that can shine through all the darkness"

On February 22, Mrs. King and I journeyed down to a city in India called Trivandrum. Then we went from Trivandrum down to a point known as Cape Comorin. This is where the mass of India ends and the vast rolling waters of the ocean have their beginning. It is one of the most beautiful parts of all the world. Three great bodies of water meet together in all of their majestic splendor: the Bay of Bengal, the Arabian Sea, and the Indian Ocean.

I remember how we went out there and looked at the big old rocks, a sight that was truly incredible, out into the waters, out into the ocean. Seated on a huge rock that slightly protruded into the ocean, we were enthralled by the vastness of the ocean and its terrifying immensities. We looked at the waves of those great bodies of water as they unfolded in almost rhythmic suspension. As the waves crashed against the base of the rock on which we were seated, an oceanic music brought sweetness to the ear. To the west we saw the magnificent sun, a red cosmic ball of fire, appear to sink into the very ocean itself. Just as it was almost lost from sight, Coretta touched me and said, "Look, Martin, isn't that beautiful!" I looked around and saw the moon, another ball of scintillating beauty. As the sun appeared to be sinking into the ocean, the moon appeared to be rising from the ocean. When the sun finally passed completely beyond sight, darkness engulfed the earth, but in the east the radiant light of the rising moon shone supreme. This was, as I said, one of the most beautiful parts in all the world, and that happened to be one of those days when the moon was full. This is one of the few points in all the world where you can see the setting of the sun and the rising of the moon simultaneously.

I looked at that and something came to my mind and I had to share it with Coretta, Dr. Reddick, and other people who were accompanying us around at that point. God has the light that can shine through all the darkness. We have experiences when the light of day vanishes, leaving us in some dark and desolate midnight—moments when our highest hopes are turned into shambles of de-

---

SERMON ON MAHATMA GANDHI

If you ask people in India why is it that Mahatma Gandhi was able to do what he did in India, they will say they followed him because of his absolute sincerity and his absolute dedication. Here was a man who achieved in his lifetime this bridging of the gulf between the ego and the id. Gandhi had the amazing capacity for self-criticism. This was true in individual life, in his family life, and was true in his people's life. Gandhi criticized himself when he needed it. And whenever he made a mistake, he confessed it publicly. Here was a man who would say to his people: I'm not perfect, I'm not infallible, I don't want you to start a religion around me, I'm not a god. And I'm convinced today that there would be a religion around Gandhi, if Gandhi had not insisted, all through his life: I don't want a religion around me because I'm too human, I'm too fallible, never think I'm infallible. And any time he made a mistake, even in his personal life, or even a decision that he made in the independence struggle, he came out in the public and said, "I made a mistake."

March 22, 1959, Montgomery

---

spair or when we are victims of some tragic injustice and some terrible exploitation. During such moments our spirits are almost overcome by gloom and despair, and we feel that there is no light anywhere. But ever and again, we look toward the east and discover that there is another light which shines even in the darkness, and "the spear of frustration" is transformed "into a shaft of light."

"Gandhians accepted us with open arms"

On March 1 we had the privilege of spending a day at the Amniabad ashram and stood there at the point where Gandhi started his walk of 218 miles to a place called Bambi. He started there walking with eight people. Gradually the number grew to millions and millions. Gandhi went on and reached down in the river and brought up a little salt in his hands to demonstrate and dramatize the fact that they were breaking this law in protest against the injustices they had faced over all the years with these salt laws. And Gandhi said to his people: "If you are hit, don't hit back; even if they shoot at you,

don't shoot back. If they curse you, don't curse back. Just keep moving. Some of us might have to die before we get there. Some of us might be thrown in jail before we get there, but let's just keep moving." And they kept moving and walked and walked, and millions of them came together.

STATEMENT ON LEAVING INDIA

I wish to make a plea to the people and government of India. The issue of world peace is so critical that I feel compelled to offer a suggestion that came to me during the course of our conversations with Vinoba Bhave. The peace-loving peoples of the world have not yet succeeded in persuading my own country, America, and Soviet Russia to eliminate fear and disarm themselves. Unfortunately, as yet America and the Soviet Union have not shown the faith and moral courage to do this. Vinoba Bhave has said that India or any other nation that has the faith and moral courage could disarm itself tomorrow, even unilaterally. It may be that just as India had to take the lead and show the world that national independence could be achieved nonviolently, so India may have to take the lead and call for universal disarmament, and if no other nation will join her immediately, India should declare itself for disarmament unilaterally. Such an act of courage would be a great demonstration of the spirit of the Mahatma and would be the greatest stimulus to the rest of the world to do likewise.

March 9, 1959

Gandhi was able to mobilize and galvanize more people in his lifetime than any other person in the history of this world. And just with a little love and understanding goodwill and a refusal to cooperate with an evil law, he was able to break the backbone of the British Empire. This, I think, was one of the most significant things that ever happened in the history of the world. More than 390 million people achieved their freedom, and they achieved it nonviolently.

I was delighted that the Gandhians accepted us with open arms. They praised our experiment with the nonviolent resistance technique at Montgomery. They seemed to look upon it as an outstanding example of the possibilities of its use in Western civilization. To them, as to me, it also suggested that nonviolent resistance *when*

planned and positive in action could work effectively even under totalitarian regimes.

We argued this point at some length with the groups of African students who were studying in India. They felt that nonviolent resistance could only work in a situation where the resisters had a potential ally in the conscience of the opponent. We soon discovered that they, like many others, tended to confuse passive resistance with nonresistance. This is completely wrong. True nonviolent resistance is not unrealistic submission to evil power. It is rather a courageous confrontation of evil by the power of love, in the faith that it is better to be the recipient of violence than the inflicter of it, since the latter only multiplies the existence of violence and bitterness in the universe, while the former may develop a sense of shame in the opponent, and thereby bring about a transformation and change of heart.

"The problem of the untouchables"

We went in some little villages, and in these villages, we saw hundreds of people sleeping on the ground; they didn't have any beds to sleep in. There was no running water there, nothing to wash with. We looked in these villages and we saw people there in their little huts and their little rooms, and their cows slept in the same room with them. If they had a few chickens—the chickens slept in the same room with them. We looked at these people. They had nothing that we would consider convenient, none of the comforts of life. Here they were, sleeping in the same room with the beasts of the field; this was all they had.

Pretty soon we discovered that these people were the untouchables. This caste system had existed for years. These were the people who worked hardest, and they were trampled over even by the Indian people themselves.

Gandhi looked at this system and couldn't stand it. He looked at his people and said, "Now you have selected me, and you've asked me to free you from the political domination and the economic exploitation inflicted upon you by Britain, and here you are, trampling over and exploiting seventy million of your brothers." And he decided that he would not ever adjust to that system, and that he would speak against it and stand up against it the rest of his life.

At age two, with sister Christine. (Courtesy of CSK Collection)

have a marvelous mother
d father. I can hardly
member a time that they ever
gued or had any great falling
it." Martin Luther Sr. and
lberta Williams King at
lebration of their twenty-fifth
edding anniversary in 1951.
ourtesy of CSK Collection)

"It was in my senior year of college that I entered the ministry. I felt a sense of responsibility which I could not escape." With parents, brother A. D. King, sister Christine, and uncle Joel King, on Morehouse campus in 1948. (Courtesy of CSK Collection)

"My devoted wife has been a constant source of consolation to me through all the difficulties." At wedding party on June 18, 1953 *(left to right)* father-in-law Obadiah Scott, Alberta Williams King, Bernice Scott, Alveda King, sister-in-law Edythe Scott, King Sr., Coretta Scott King, sister-in-law Naomi Barbert King, Betty Ann Hill, A. D. King, and Christine King. (Courtesy of CSK Collection)

'I began to think of the viciousness of people who would bomb my home. I could feel the anger rising when I realized that my wife and baby could have been killed." With Coretta and Yolanda at the Dexter Avenue Baptist Church in 1956. (Photo by Dan Weiner – courtesy Sandra Weiner)

"Ordinarily, a person leaving a courtroom with a conviction behind him would wear a somber face. But I left with a smile." Greeted by Coretta after conviction in antiboycott trial in March 1956. (AP/Wide World Photos)

Arrested for loitering while attempting to gain admittance to the trial of Ralph Abernathy in Montgomery, Alabama, on September 3, 1958, with Coretta nearby. (Charles Moore/Black Star)

(opposite) "In 1960 an electrifying movement of Negro students shattered the placid surface of campuses and communities across the South." Attending a meeting with Atlanta student activists in 1960. (Howard Sochurek, *Life* Magazine © Time Inc.

"After they transferred me to Reidsville, Harris Wofford and others strongly urged Mr. Kennedy to try to use his influence to do something about it, and he finally agreed." Greeted by family and friends after being released from Georgia State Prison at Reidsville, after serving time for a traffic violation in 1960. (AP/Wide World)

"Darling, it is extremely difficult for me to think of being away from you and my Yoki and Marty." Spending time with Martin III (age three), Yolanda (age five), and Coretta in 1960. (Don Uhrbrock, *Life* Magazine © Time Inc.)

With the inspiring Jackie Robinson in the 1960s. (AP/Wide World)

"I had used the phrase 'I have a dream' many times before, and I just felt that I wanted to use it here." At March on Washington for Jobs and Freedom in August 1963. (Archive Photos)

"I met Malcolm X once in Washington, but circumstances didn't enable me to talk with him for more than a minute." Encounter with Malcolm X in March 1964. (AP/Wide World)

"I AM AN UNTOUCHABLE"

I remember when Mrs. King and I were in India, we journeyed down one afternoon to the southernmost part of India, the state of Kerala, the city of Trivandrum. That afternoon I was to speak in one of the schools, what we would call high schools in our country, and it was a school attended by and large by students who were the children of former untouchables. . . .

The principal introduced me and then as he came to the conclusion of his introduction, he says, "Young people, I would like to present to you a fellow untouchable from the United States of America." And for a moment I was a bit shocked and peeved that I would be referred to as an untouchable. . . .

I started thinking about the fact: twenty million of my brothers and sisters were still smothering in an airtight cage of poverty in an affluent society. I started thinking about the fact: these twenty million brothers and sisters were still by and large housed in rat-infested, unendurable slums in the big cities of our nation, still attending inadequate schools faced with improper recreational facilities. And I said to myself, "Yes, I am an untouchable, and every Negro in the United States of America is an untouchable."

From sermon at Ebenezer Baptist Church, July 4, 1965

The first thing he did was to adopt an untouchable girl as his daughter. His wife—a member of one of the high castes—thought he was going crazy. She said, "What in the world are you doing adopting an untouchable? We are not supposed to touch these people." And he said, "I am going to have this young lady as my daughter." He brought her into his ashram, and she lived there. He demonstrated in his own life that untouchability had to go.

One day Mahatma Gandhi stood before his people and said: "You are exploiting these untouchables. Even though we are fighting with all that we have of our bodies and our souls to break loose from the bondage of the British Empire, we are exploiting these people and we are taking from them their selfhood and their self-respect." He said, "I will refuse to eat until the leaders of the caste system will come to me with the leaders of the untouchables and say that there will be an end to untouchability and the Hindu temples of India will open their doors to the untouchables." And he refused to eat, and

days passed. Finally when Gandhi was about to breathe his last breath, and his body was all but gone, a group from the untouchables and a group from the Brahmin caste came to him and signed a statement saying that they would no longer adhere to the caste system. The priest of the temple came to him and said, "Now the temples will be opened to the untouchables." That afternoon, untouchables from all over India went into the temples and all of these thousands and millions of people put their arms around the Brahmins and people of other castes. Hundreds of millions of people who had never touched each other for two thousand years were now singing and praising all together. This was a great contribution that Mahatma Gandhi brought about.

"Atoning for the injustices"

India appeared to be integrating its untouchables faster than the United States was integrating its Negro minority. Both countries had

SERMON ON GANDHI

The world doesn't like people like Gandhi. That's strange, isn't it? They don't like people like Christ; they don't like people like Lincoln. They killed him—this man who had done all of that for India, who gave his life and who mobilized and galvanized 400 million people for independence. . . . One of his own fellow Hindus felt that he was a little too favorable toward the Moslems, felt that he was giving in too much for the Moslems. . . . Here was the man of nonviolence, falling at the hands of a man of violence. Here was a man of love falling at the hands of a man with hate. This seems the way of history. And isn't it significant that he died on the same day that Christ died? It was on Friday. And this is the story of history, but thank God it never stopped here. Thank God Good Friday is never the end. The man who shot Gandhi only shot him into the hearts of humanity. Just as when Abraham Lincoln was shot, mark you, for the same reason that Mahatma Gandhi was shot—that is, the attempt to heal the wounds of the divided nation—when Abraham Lincoln was shot, Secretary Stanton stood by and said, "Now he belongs to the ages." The same thing could be said about Mahatma Gandhi now: He belongs to the ages.

March 22, 1959, in Montgomery

federal laws against discrimination, but in India the leaders of government, of religious, educational, and other institutions, had publicly endorsed the integration laws. The prime minister admitted to me that many Indians still harbored a prejudice against these long-oppressed people, but that it had become unpopular to exhibit this prejudice in any form. In part, this change in climate was created through the moral leadership of the late Mahatma Gandhi. In part, it was the result of the Indian Constitution, which specified that discrimination against the untouchables is a crime, punishable by imprisonment.

The Indian government spent millions of rupees annually developing housing and job opportunities in villages heavily inhabited by untouchables. Moreover, the prime minister said, if two applicants compete for entrance into a college or university, one of the applicants being an untouchable and the other of high caste, the school is required to accept the untouchable.

Professor Lawrence Reddick, who was with me during the interview, asked: "But isn't that discrimination?"

"Well, it may be," the prime minister answered. "But this is our way of atoning for the centuries of injustices we have inflicted upon these people."

From the prime minister down to the village councilmen, everybody declared publicly that untouchability is wrong. But in the United States some of our highest officials declined to render a moral judgment on segregation, and some from the South publicly boasted of their determination to maintain segregation. That would be unthinkable in India.

Although discrimination has not yet been eliminated in India, it is a crime to practice discrimination against an untouchable. But even without this coercion, so successfully has the government made the issue a matter of moral and ethical responsibility that no government figure or political leader on any level would dare defend discriminatory practices. One could wish that we here in the United States had reached this level of morality. America must seek its own ways of atoning for the injustices she has inflicted upon her Negro citizens.

The spirit of Gandhi was very much alive in India. Some of his disciples remembered the drama of the fight for national indepen-

dence and, when they look around, find no one who comes near the stature of the Mahatma. But any objective observer must report that Gandhi is not only the greatest figure in India's history, but his influence is felt in almost every aspect of life and public policy.

The trip had a great impact upon me personally. It was wonderful to be in Gandhi's land, to talk with his son, his grandsons, his cousin, and other relatives; to share the reminiscences of his close comrades; to visit his ashram; to see the countless memorials for him; and, finally, to lay a wreath on his entombed ashes at Rajghat. We had learned a lot, but we were not rash enough to presume that we knew India—a vast subcontinent with all of its people, problems, contrasts, and achievements.

I left India more convinced than ever before that nonviolent resistance was the most potent weapon available to oppressed people in their struggle for freedom. It was a marvelous thing to see the amazing results of a nonviolent campaign. India won her independence, but without violence on the part of Indians. The aftermath of hatred and bitterness that usually follows a violent campaign was found nowhere in India. The way of acquiescence leads to moral and spiritual suicide. The way of violence leads to bitterness in the survivors and brutality in the destroyers. But the way of nonviolence leads to redemption and the creation of the beloved community.

I returned to America with a greater determination to achieve freedom for my people through nonviolent means. As a result of my visit to India, my understanding of nonviolence became greater and my commitment deeper.

14

THE SIT-IN MOVEMENT

A generation of young people has come out of decades of shadows to face naked state power; it has lost its fears, and experienced the majestic dignity of a direct struggle for its own liberation. These young people have connected up with their own history—the slave revolts, the incomplete revolution of the Civil War, the brotherhood of colonial colored men in Africa and Asia. They are an integral part of the history which is reshaping the world, replacing a dying order with modern democracy.

FEBRUARY 1, 1960
King moves with family to Atlanta; in Greensboro, North Carolina, lunch counter sit-in movement begins

FEBRUARY 17
Is arrested and charged with falsifying his 1956 and 1958 Alabama state income tax returns

APRIL 15
Speaks at founding conference of the Student Nonviolent Coordinating Committee (SNCC)

MAY 28
Is acquitted of tax evasion by an all-white jury in Montgomery

After four years as president of the Montgomery Improvement Association and five years as a resident of Montgomery, I decided to move from Montgomery to Atlanta. I would become co-pastor of the Ebenezer Baptist Church in Atlanta and thereby have more time and a better location to direct the Southwide campaigns of the SCLC.

For a year the Southern Christian Leadership Conference had been pleading with me to give it the maximum of my time, since the time was ripe for expanded militant action across the South. After giving the request serious and prayerful consideration, I came to the conclusion that I had a moral obligation to give more of my time and energy to the whole South. This was only possible by moving closer to the headquarters where transportation was more flexible and time hitherto consumed in longer travel could be saved and utilized for planning, directing, and supervising.

So I had the painful experience of having to leave Montgomery for Atlanta. It was not easy for me to decide to leave a community where bravery, resourcefulness, and determination had shattered the girders of the old order and weakened confidence of the rulers, despite their centuries of unchallenged rule. It was not easy to decide to leave a city whose Negroes resisted injustice magnificently and followed a method of nonviolent struggle that became one of the glowing epics of the twentieth century. I hated to leave Montgomery, but the people there realized that the call from the whole South was one that could not be denied.

This was the creative moment for a full-scale assault on the system of segregation. The time had come for a bold, broad advance of the Southern campaign for equality.

FAREWELL MESSAGE TO DEXTER CONGREGATION

Unknowingly and unexpectedly, I was catapulted into the leadership of the Montgomery Movement. At points I was unprepared for the symbolic role that history had thrust upon me. But there was no way out. I, like everybody in Montgomery, was pulled into the mainstream by the rolling tides of historical necessity. As a result of my leadership in the Montgomery movement, my duties and activities tripled. A multiplicity of new responsibilities poured in upon me in almost staggering torrents. So I ended up futilely attempting to be four or five men in one. One would have expected that many of these responsibilities would have tapered off after the boycott. But now, three years after the termination of the bus struggle, the same situation stands. At points the demands have increased.

November 29, 1959

I felt terribly frustrated over my inability to retreat, concentrate, and reflect. Even when I was writing *Stride Toward Freedom* I would only take off one or two weeks at a time. After returning from India I decided that I would take one day a week as a day of silence and meditation. This I attempted on several occasions, but things began to pile up so much that I found myself using that particular day as a time to catch up on so many things that had accumulated. I knew that I could not continue to live with such a tension-filled schedule. My whole life seemed to be centered around giving something out and only rarely taking something in. My failure to reflect would do harm not only to me as a person, but to the total movement. For that reason I felt a moral obligation to do it.

One of my reasons for moving to Atlanta was to meet this problem head-on. I felt that I would have more time to meditate and think through the total struggle ahead. Unfortunately, however, things happened which made my schedule more crowded in Atlanta than it was in Montgomery.

"The student demonstrations"

In 1960 an electrifying movement of Negro students shattered the placid surface of campuses and communities across the South. The young students of the South, through sit-ins and other demonstrations, gave America a glowing example of disciplined, dignified nonviolent action against the system of segregation. Though confronted in many places by hoodlums, police guns, tear gas, arrests, and jail sentences, the students tenaciously continued to sit down and demand equal service at variety store lunch counters, and they extended their protest from city to city. Spontaneously born, but guided by the theory of nonviolent resistance, the lunch counter sit-ins accomplished integration in hundreds of communities at the swiftest rate of change in the civil rights movement up to that time. In communities like Montgomery, Alabama, the whole student body rallied behind expelled students and staged a walkout while state government intimidation was unleashed with a display of military force appropriate to a wartime invasion. Nevertheless, the spirit of self-sacrifice and commitment remained firm, and the state govern-

ments found themselves dealing with students who had lost the fear of jail and physical injury.

The campuses of Negro colleges were infused with a dynamism of both action and philosophical discussion. Even in the thirties, when the college campus was alive with social thought, only a minority were involved in action. During the sit-in phase, when a few students were suspended or expelled, more than one college saw the total student body involved in a walkout protest. This was a change in student activity of profound significance. Seldom, if ever, in American history had a student movement engulfed the whole student body of a college.

Many of the students, when pressed to express their inner feelings, identified themselves with students in Africa, Asia, and South America. The liberation struggle in Africa was the great single international influence on American Negro students. Frequently, I heard them say that if their African brothers could break the bonds of colonialism, surely the American Negro could break Jim Crow.

I felt we had to continue to challenge the system of segregation, whether it was in the schools, public parks, churches, lunch counters, or public libraries. Segregation had to be removed from our

---

STATEMENT AT YOUTH MARCH FOR INTEGRATED SCHOOLS

As June approaches, with its graduation ceremonies and speeches, a thought suggests itself. You will hear much about careers, security, and prosperity. I will leave the discussion of such matters to your deans, your principals, and your valedictorians. But I do have a graduation thought to pass along to you. Whatever career you may choose for yourself—doctor, lawyer, teacher—let me propose an avocation to be pursued along with it. Become a dedicated fighter for civil rights. Make it a central part of your life.

It will make you a better doctor, a better lawyer, a better teacher. It will enrich your spirit as nothing else possibly can. It will give you that rare sense of nobility that can only spring from love and selflessly helping your fellow man. Make a career of humanity. Commit yourself to the noble struggle for equal rights. You will make a greater person of yourself, a greater nation of your country, and a finer world to live in.

April 18, 1959, Washington, D.C.

society. And Negroes had to be prepared to suffer, sacrifice, and even die to gain their goals. We could not rest until we had achieved the ideals of our democracy. I prayed much over our Southern situation, and I came to the conclusion that we were in for a season of suffering.

I urged students to continue the struggle on the highest level of dignity. They had rightly chosen to follow the path of nonviolence. Our ultimate aim was not to defeat or humiliate the white man but to win his friendship and understanding. We had a moral obligation to remind him that segregation is wrong. We protested with the ultimate aim of being reconciled with our white brothers.

A period began in which the emphasis shifted from the slow court process to direct action in the form of bus protests, economic boycotts, and mass marches to and demonstrations in the nation's capital and state capitals. The most significant aspect of this student movement was that the young people knocked some of the oldsters out of their state of apathy and complacency. What we saw was that segregation could not be maintained in the South without resultant chaos and social disintegration. One may wonder why the movement started with the lunch counters. The answer lay in the fact that there the Negro had suffered indignities and injustices that could not be justified or explained. Almost every Negro had experienced the tragic inconveniences of lunch counter segregation. He could not understand why he was welcomed with open arms at most counters in the store, but was denied service at a certain counter because it happened to be selling food and drink. In a real sense the "sit-in" represented more than a demand for service; it represented a demand for respect.

I was convinced that the student movement that was taking place all over the South in 1960 was one of the most significant developments in the whole civil rights struggle. It was no overstatement to characterize these events as historic. Never before in the United States had so large a body of students spread a struggle over so great an area in pursuit of a goal of human dignity and freedom. The student movement finally refuted the idea that the Negro was content with segregation. The students had taken the struggle for justice into their own hands. Negro freedom fighters revealed to the nation

and the world their determination and courage. They were moving away from tactics which were suitable merely for gradual and long-term change. This was an era of offensive on the part of oppressed people. All peoples deprived of dignity and freedom marched on every continent throughout the world.

"A turning point in my life"

I can recall what may very well have been a turning point in my life as a participant in the Negro struggle in the South. It was the year 1960, in Montgomery, Alabama, when the glorious sit-ins at lunch

---

STATEMENT AT FOUNDING CONFERENCE OF STUDENT NONVIOLENT COORDINATING COMMITTEE

Today the leaders of the sit-in movement are assembled here from ten states and some forty communities to evaluate these recent sit-ins and to chart future goals. They realize that they must now evolve a strategy for victory. Some elements which suggest themselves for discussion are: (1) The need for some type of continuing organization. . . . (2) The students must consider calling for a nationwide campaign of "selective buying." . . . It is immoral to spend one's money where one cannot be treated with respect. (3) The students must seriously consider training a group of volunteers who will willingly go to jail rather than pay bail or fines. This courageous willingness to go to jail may well be the thing to awaken the dozing conscience of many of our white brothers. We are in an era in which a prison term for a freedom struggle is a badge of honor. (4) The youth must take the freedom struggle into every community in the South without exception. The struggle must be spread into every nook and cranny. Inevitably, this broadening of the struggle and the determination which it represents will arouse vocal and vigorous support and place pressure on the federal government that will compel its intervention. (5) The students will certainly want to delve deeper into the philosophy of nonviolence. It must be made palpably clear that resistance and nonviolence are not in themselves good. There is another element that must be present in our struggle that then makes our resistance and nonviolence truly meaningful. That element is reconciliation. Our ultimate end must be the creation of the beloved community.

April 15, 1960, in Raleigh, North Carolina

counters had seized the attention of all Americans. The white Southern power structure, in an attempt to blunt and divert that effort, indicted me for perjury and openly proclaimed that I would be imprisoned for at least ten years.

This case was tried before an all-white Southern jury. All of the State's witnesses were white. The judge and the prosecutor were white. The courtroom was segregated. Passions were inflamed. Feelings ran high. The press and other communications media were hostile. Defeat seemed certain, and we in the freedom struggle braced ourselves for the inevitable. There were two men among us who persevered with the conviction that it was possible, in this context, to marshal facts and law and thus win vindication. These men were our lawyers—Negro lawyers from the North: William Ming of Chicago and Hubert Delaney from New York.

They brought to the courtroom wisdom, courage, and a highly developed art of advocacy; but most important, they brought the lawyers' indomitable determination to win. After a trial of three days, by the sheer strength of their legal arsenal, they overcame the most vicious Southern taboos festering in a virulent and inflamed atmosphere and they persuaded an all-white jury to accept the word of a Negro over that of white men. The jury, after a few hours of deliberation, returned a verdict of acquittal.

I am frank to confess that on this occasion I learned that truth and conviction in the hands of a skillful advocate could make what started out as a bigoted, prejudiced jury, choose the path of justice. I cannot help but wish in my heart that the same kind of skill and devotion which Bill Ming and Hubert Delaney accorded to me could be available to thousands of civil rights workers, to thousands of ordinary Negroes, who are every day facing prejudiced courtrooms.

15

ATLANTA ARREST AND PRESIDENTIAL POLITICS

I fear that there is a dearth of vision in our government, a lack of a sense of history and genuine morality.

JUNE 23, 1960
King discusses civil rights with presidential candidate Senator John F. Kennedy

OCTOBER 19
Is arrested at Atlanta sit-in

OCTOBER 25
Charges are dropped for sit-in arrest but King is held for violating probation for earlier traffic offense and transferred to Reidsville State Prison

OCTOBER 26
Presidential candidate John F. Kennedy calls Coretta Scott King to express sympathy and offer assistance; Robert Kennedy calls Georgia governor S. Ernest Vandiver and Judge Oscar Mitchell seeking King's release on bail

OCTOBER 27
King's attorney Donald L. Hollowell arranges release from prison

NOVEMBER 1
King applauds Senator Kennedy for support

NOVEMBER 8
Kennedy wins close election, receiving strong support from black voters

My first contact with John Kennedy was when he was a senator seeking the nomination for President. For several months, we had tried to work out a meeting and every time I could go he was away. Finally we worked out an engagement at his apartment in New York. That was June of 1960, about a month before the convention.

We talked for about an hour over the breakfast table. I was very frank about what I thought: that there was a need for a strong executive leadership and that we hadn't gotten this during the Eisenhower administration. If we didn't get it in the new administration, we would be set back even more. I was very impressed by the forthright and honest manner in which he discussed the civil rights question, and with his concern and his willingness to learn more about civil rights.

I specifically mentioned a need for an executive order outlawing discrimination in federally assisted housing. I also mentioned to him the need for strong civil rights legislation, and I stressed voting issues because we were deeply involved at that time in voter registration drives and had encountered a number of difficulties in states like Alabama and Mississippi.

As I recall, he agreed with all of these things. He agreed that there was a need for strong executive leadership and that this had not existed, and he felt if he received the nomination and was elected he could give this kind of leadership. He assured me also that he felt the whole question of the right to vote was a key and basic, and that this would be one of the immediate things that he would look into. He said that he had voted consistently for civil rights. I raised the question with him about 1957, when he voted against what we considered as a very important section of the civil rights bill. He said that since that time, if he had to face the issue again, he would reverse his position because many of the developments during the sit-in movement had pointed up the injustices and indignities that Negroes were facing all over the South, and for this reason he had reevaluated many of these things.

John Kennedy did not have the grasp and the comprehension of the depths of the problem at that time, as he later did. He knew that segregation was morally wrong and he certainly intellectually

committed himself to integration, but I could see that he didn't have the emotional involvement then. He had not really been involved enough in and with the problem. He didn't know too many Negroes personally. He had never really had the personal experience of knowing the deep groans and passionate yearnings of the Negro for freedom, because he just didn't know Negroes generally and he hadn't had any experience in the civil rights struggle. So I felt that it was an intellectual commitment.

A few months later, after he had been nominated, I talked with him over at his house in Georgetown, and in that short period he had really learned a great deal about civil rights and had been advised rather well. I'd had little enthusiasm when he first announced his candidacy, but I had no doubt that he would do the right thing on the civil rights issue, if he were elected President.

He was very much concerned then about the election and possibly losing. Some of his friends were concerned about this and felt he had to do something dramatic to convince the nation of his commitment to civil rights. Some of the advisors thought that he should come South and make a civil rights speech right here in the South which would really convince people. They wanted him to come under my auspices to speak for a board meeting or a dinner sponsored by SCLC. I told him I just couldn't do that unless Mr. Nixon came, because we were a nonpartisan organization. I said, "Now Nixon may not come but I would have to invite him." But they felt, naturally, that it wouldn't work that way. So I kind of backed out on that idea because I thought it would be a mistake.

For many months during the election campaign, my close friends urged me to declare my support for John Kennedy. I spent many troubled hours searching for the responsible and fair decision. I was impressed by his qualities, by many elements in his record, and by his program. I had learned to enjoy and respect his charm and his incisive mind. But I made very clear to him that I did not endorse candidates publicly and that I could not come to the point that I would change my views on this.

"I didn't know where they were taking me"

Nevertheless, I was grateful to Senator Kennedy for the genuine concern he expressed about my arrest in October 1960 because of my

participation in nonviolent efforts to integrate lunch counters in Atlanta, Georgia. I took part in the lunch counter sit-ins at Rich's department store as a follower, not a leader. I did not initiate the thing. It came into being with the students discussing the issues involved. They called me and asked me to join in. They wanted me to be in it, and I felt a moral obligation to be in it with them.

I was arrested along with some two hundred eighty students in a sit-in demonstration seeking to integrate lunch counters. I said when I went in Fulton County Jail that I could not in all good conscience post bail and that I would stay and serve the time if it was one year, five, or ten years. Of course the students agreed to stay also.

If, by chance, Your Honor, we are guilty of violating the law, please be assured that we did it to bring the whole issue of racial injustice under the scrutiny of the conscience of Atlanta. I must honestly say that we firmly believe that segregation is evil, and that our Southland will never reach its full potential and moral maturity until this cancerous disease is removed. We do not seek to remove this unjust system for ourselves alone but for our white brothers as well. The festering sore of segregation debilitates the white man as well as the Negro. So, if our actions in any way served to bring this issue to the forefront of the conscience of the community, they were not undertaken in vain.

And, sir, I know you have a legal obligation facing you at this hour. This judicial obligation may cause you to hand us over to another court rather than dismiss the charges. But, sir, I must say that I have a moral obligation facing me at this hour. This imperative drives me to say that if you find it necessary to set a bond, I cannot in all good conscience have anyone go buy my bail. I will choose jail rather than bail, even if it means remaining in jail a year or even ten years. Maybe it will take this type of self-suffering on the part of numerous Negroes to finally expose the moral defense of our white brothers who happen to be misguided and thusly awaken the dozing conscience of our community.

When they came to see after five or six days that we were not coming out and that the community was getting very much concerned, the merchants dropped the charges, which meant that everybody was released without bail immediately. But when I was released, they served me with papers stating that I had violated my probation and

that I would be transferred to DeKalb jail and go on trial in the court there.

On the night of May 4, 1960, police stopped me in DeKalb County and discovered I still had an Alabama driver's license. Because of this, they gave me a ticket. I had gone to court, and I didn't even know it at the time but the lawyer pleaded guilty for me and they had fined me something like $25 or $50 and placed me on probation for I guess six months. I didn't even pay attention to the case, it was such a minor case; I didn't pay attention to it and never knew that the lawyer had really pleaded guilty. He had just told me, "I've got everything worked out." He made me think it was clear and all I needed to do was pay. Actually they later admitted in court

---

LETTER TO CORETTA

Reidsville, Georgia

Hello Darling,

Today I find myself a long way from you and the children. I am at the State Prison in Reidsville which is about 230 miles from Atlanta. They picked me up from the DeKalb jail about 4 o'clock this morning. I know this whole experience is very difficult for you to adjust to, especially in your condition of pregnancy, but as I said to you yesterday this is the cross that we must bear for the freedom of our people. So I urge you to be strong in faith, and this will in turn strengthen me. I can assure you that it is extremely difficult for me to think of being away from you and my Yoki and Marty for four months, but I am asking God hourly to give me the power of endurance. I have the faith to believe that this excessive suffering that is now coming to our family will in some little way serve to make Atlanta a better city, Georgia a better state, and America a better country. Just how I do not yet know, but I have faith to believe it will. If I am correct then our suffering is not in vain.

I understand that I can have visitors twice a month—the second and fourth Sunday. However, I understand that everybody—white and colored—can have visitors this coming Sunday. I hope you can find some way to come down. I know it will be a terrible inconvenience in your condition, but I want to see you and the children very badly.

Eternally Yours,
Martin

October 26, 1960

that they had never fined or arrested anybody on a charge like that, and they really had nothing on the statute to reveal how long you had to be in Atlanta before changing your license. So it was obviously a case of persecution.

I sat in the back of the courtroom while Mr. Charles M. Clayton, a Negro attorney who represented me, talked with the judge. We had this big trial and I had my lawyers arguing the case brilliantly and after all of that the judge said six months of hard labor, and this was not appealable.

So they took me back upstairs and put me in jail in the DeKalb County Jail. Then early in the morning, about three o'clock in the morning, they came and got me and took me to Reidsville. That was the state prison some two hundred and twenty miles from Atlanta. On the way, they dealt with me just like I was some hardened criminal. They had me chained all the way down to my legs, and they tied my legs to something in the floor so there would be no way for me to escape.

They talked with themselves. It was a long ride. I didn't know where they were taking me; but finally I assumed it must be to one of the state prisons after we had been gone so long. That kind of mental anguish is worse than dying, riding for mile after mile, hungry and thirsty, bound and helpless, waiting and not knowing what you're waiting for. And all over a traffic violation.

"Kennedy exhibited moral courage"

When people found out that they had taken me out in the wee hours of the morning and transferred me, there was real resentment all over. I think people had already started talking to both Nixon and Kennedy about doing something even when we were still in the Fulton County Jail—saying to them that they should make a statement about it. After they transferred me to Reidsville—in a segregated cell-block, a place where inmates who had attacked guards, psychotics, and other special cases were housed—Harris Wofford and others strongly urged Mr. Kennedy to try to use his influence to do something about it, and he finally agreed.

The first thing he did was call my wife. She was pregnant, and this was kind of a rough experience for her, so he called her and

expressed his concern. He said that he would do whatever he could and that he would think this over with his brother and try to use his influence to get me released.

In the meantime, Robert Kennedy called the judge to find out about the bond. I understand Robert Kennedy was really angry about it, when they got it over to him and let him know all of the facts in the situation. In that spirit of anger, he called the judge. I don't know what he said in that conversation with the judge, but it was later revealed his main point was "Why can't he be bonded out?" I was released the next day. It was about two weeks before the election.

Senator Kennedy had served as a great force in making my release from Reidsville Prison possible. I was personally obligated to him and his brother for their intervention during my imprisonment. He did it because of his great concern and his humanitarian bent. I would like to feel that he made the call because he was concerned. He had come to know me as a person then. He had been in the debates and had done a good job when he talked about civil rights and what the Negro faces. Harris and others had really been talking with him about it. At the same time, I think he naturally had political considerations in mind. He was running for an office, and he needed to be elected, and I'm sure he felt the need for the Negro votes. So I think that he did something that expressed deep moral concern, but at the same time it was politically sound. It did take a little courage to do this; he didn't know it was politically sound.

I always felt that Nixon lost a real opportunity to express support of something much larger than an individual, because this expressed support for the movement for civil rights. It indicated the direction that this man would take, if he became president.

And I had known Nixon longer. He had been supposedly close to me, and he would call me frequently about things, seeking my advice. And yet, when this moment came, it was like he had never heard of me. So this is why I really considered him a moral coward and one who was really unwilling to take a courageous step and take a risk. And I am convinced that he lost the election because of that. Many Negroes were still on the fence, still undecided, and they were leaning toward Nixon.

ON RICHARD NIXON

First, I must admit that I was strongly opposed to Vice President Nixon before meeting him personally. I went to him with an initial bias. I remembered his statements against Helen Gahegen Douglas and also the fact that he voted with the right wing of the Republican Party. These were almost unforgivable sins for me at that time. After meeting the vice president, however, I must admit that my impression somewhat changed. I have frankly come to feel that the position and the world contacts of the vice president have matured his person and judgment. Whether he can have experienced a complete conversion, I cannot say. But I do believe that he has grown a great deal and has changed many of his former opinions.

Since I am quite interested in civil rights, I might say just a word concerning his views at this point. I am coming to believe that Nixon is absolutely sincere about his views on this issue. His travels have revealed to him how the race problem is hurting America in international relations and it is altogether possible that he has no basic racial prejudice. Nixon happens to be a Quaker and there are very few Quakers who are prejudiced from a racial point of view. I also feel that Nixon would have done much more to meet the present crisis in race relations than President Eisenhower has done. . . .

Finally, I would say that Nixon has a genius for convincing one that he is sincere. When you are close to Nixon he almost disarms you with his apparent sincerity. You never get the impression that he is the same man who campaigned in California a few years ago, and who made a tear-jerking speech on television in the 1952 campaign to save himself from an obvious misdeed. And so I would conclude by saying that if Richard Nixon is not sincere, he is the most dangerous man in America.

Letter to Earl Mazo, September 2, 1958

My father had endorsed Nixon until that call. He knew about my relations with Nixon, and I think he felt that Nixon would do a good job on the civil rights question. I guess deep down within there may have been a little of the religious feeling that a Catholic should not be president. I'm sure my father had been somewhat influenced by this, so that he had gone on record endorsing Nixon. After that call, he changed, and he made a very strong statement.

I was grateful to Senator Kennedy for the genuine concern he expressed in my arrest. After the call I made a statement to the press

thanking him but not endorsing him. Very frankly, I did not feel at that time that there was much difference between Kennedy and Nixon. I could find some things in the background of both men that I didn't particularly agree with. Remembering what Nixon had done out in California to Helen Gahegen Douglas, I felt that he was an opportunist at many times who had no real grounding in basic convictions, and his voting record was not good. He improved when he became vice president, but, when he was a congressman and a senator, he didn't have a good voting record.

With Mr. Kennedy, after I looked over his voting record, I felt at points that he was so concerned about being president of the United States that he would compromise basic principles to become president. But I had to look at something else beyond the man—the people who surrounded him—and I felt that Kennedy was surrounded by better people. It was on that basis that I felt that Kennedy would make the best president.

I never came out with an endorsement. My father did, but I never made one. I took this position in order to maintain a nonpartisan posture, which I have followed all along in order to be able to look objectively at both parties at all times. As I said to him all along, I couldn't, and I never changed that even after he made the call during my arrest. I made a statement of thanks, and I expressed my gratitude for the call, but in the statement I made it clear that I did not endorse any candidate and that this was not to be interpreted as an endorsement.

I had to conclude that the then known facts about Kennedy were not adequate to make an unqualified judgment in his favor. I do feel that, as any man, he grew a great deal. After he became president I thought we really saw two Kennedys—a Kennedy the first two years and another Kennedy emerging in 1963. He was getting ready to throw off political considerations and see the real moral issues. Had President Kennedy lived, I would probably have endorsed him in 1964. But, back at that time, I concluded that there was something to be desired in both candidates.

16

THE ALBANY MOVEMENT

Why Albany? Because Albany symbolizes the bastions of segregation set upon by the compounded forces of morality and justice.

JANUARY 30, 1961
Kings' third child, Dexter Scott, is born

MAY 21
After the initial group of Freedom Riders seeking to integrate bus terminals are assaulted in Alabama, King addresses mass rally at mob-besieged Montgomery church

DECEMBER 15
King arrives in Albany in response to telegram from Dr. W. G. Anderson, head of the Albany Movement

DECEMBER 16
Is arrested with more than 700 Albany protesters

JULY 10, 1962
With Ralph Abernathy, is convicted of leading December protest; begins serving a 45-day sentence

JULY 12
Leaves jail after his fine is paid by unidentified person

JULY 25
After outbreak of racial violence in Albany, calls for Day of Penance to atone for violence

JULY 27
Albany city hall prayer vigil ends in arrest

AUGUST 10
Leaves jail and agrees to halt demonstrations

I n 1961 the Kennedy administration waged an essentially cautious and defensive struggle for civil rights against an unyielding adversary. As the year unfolded, executive initiative became increasingly feeble, and the chilling prospect emerged of a general administration retreat.

Negroes had manifested their faith by racking up a substantial majority of their votes for President Kennedy. They had expected more of him than of the previous administration. His administration appeared to believe it was doing as much as was politically possible and had, by its positive deeds, earned enough credit to coast on civil rights. Politically, perhaps, this was not a surprising conclusion. How many people understood, during the first two years of the Kennedy administration, that the Negroes' "Now" was becoming as militant as the segregationists' "Never"?

Despite tormenting handicaps, Negroes moved from sporadic, limited actions to broadscale activities different in kind and degree from anything done in the past. A new spirit was manifest in the Negro's willingness to demonstrate in the streets of communities in which, by tradition, he was supposed to step aside when a white man strode toward him.

Areas such as Mississippi and rural Georgia, hitherto quiescent, were churned into turbulence by registration campaigns and freedom rides. The change in spirit was even more dramatically exemplified by the Negroes' willingness, in communities such as Albany, Georgia, to endure mass jailing.

Albany, Georgia, was a distillation of the tensions and conflicts straining the social fabric of the contemporary South. On one side were the segregationists who thought granite stubbornness was a policy. On the other side were Negroes marching forward utilizing nonviolence. Discrimination of all kinds had been simultaneously brought under our sights: school segregation, denial of voting rights, segregation in parks, libraries, restaurants, and buses.

The Negroes of Albany suffered in quiet silence. The throbbing pain of segregation could be felt but not seen. It scarred Negroes in every experience of their lives. They lived in segregation; they ate in

segregation; they learned in segregation; they prayed, and rode and worked and died in segregation. And in silence. A corroding loss of self-respect rusted their moral fiber. Their discontent was turned inward on themselves. But an end came with the beginning of protest.

"I knew I had to stay"

As Rosa Parks triggered the Montgomery bus protest, so the arrival in December 1961 of eleven Freedom Riders had triggered the now historic nonviolent thrust in Albany. This Freedom Ride movement came into being to reveal the indignities and the injustices which Negro people faced as they attempted to do the simple thing of traveling through the South as interstate passengers. The Freedom Rides, which were begun by the young, grew to such proportion that they eventually encompassed people of all ages. As a result of this movement, many achievements had come into being. The Interstate Commerce Commission had said in substance that all bus terminals must be integrated. The dramatic Albany Movement was the climax to this psychological forward thrust.

The Albany Movement, headed by Dr. W. G. Anderson, was already functional and had developed a year-long history on the part of the Negro community to seek relief of their grievance. The presence of staff and personnel of variegated human relations fields gave rise to the notion that Albany had been made a target city, with the ominous decision having been made months before—probably in a "smoke-filled New York hotel room." The truth is, Albany had become a symbol of segregation's last stand almost by chance. The ferment of a hundred years' frustration had come to the fore. Sociologically, Albany had all the ingredients of a target city, but it could just as easily have been one of a hundred cities throughout the deep and mid South. Twenty-seven thousand Negroes lived in Albany, Georgia, but a hundred years of political, economic, and educational suppression had kept them hopelessly enslaved to a demonic, though sophisticated, system of segregation which sought desperately and ruthlessly to perpetuate these deprivations.

Negroes, wielding nonviolent protest in its most creative utilization to date, challenged discrimination in public places, denial of

voting rights, school segregation, and the deprivation of free speech
and assembly. On that broad front, the Albany Movement used all
the methods of nonviolence: direct action expressed through mass
demonstrations; jail-ins; sit-ins; wade-ins, and kneel-ins; political action; boycotts and legal actions. In no other city of the deep South
had all those methods of nonviolence been simultaneously exercised.

The city authorities were wrestling with slippery contradictions,
seeking to extend municipal growth and expansion while preserving
customs suitable only in a backward and semi-feudal society. Confronted by the potency of the nonviolent protest movement, the city
fathers sought to project an image of unyielding mastery. But in
truth they staggered from blunder to blunder, losing their cocksure-
ness and common sense as they built retaining walls of slippery sand
to shore up a crumbling edifice of injustice.

The Southern Christian Leadership Conference gave full moral
and financial support to the Albany Movement and the noble efforts
of that community to realize justice, equal rights, and an end to
second-class citizenship.

For us the first stage of victory required that Negroes break the
barrier of silence and paralysis which for decades suppressed them
and denied them the simplest of improvements. This victory was
achieved when nonviolent protest aroused every element of the
community: the youth, the elderly, men and women in the tens of
thousands. Class distinctions were erased in the streets and in jail as
domestics, professionals, workers, businessmen, teachers, and laun-
dresses were united as cellmates, charged together with the crime of
seeking human justice.

On December 16, 1961, the Negro community of that city made
its stride toward freedom. Citizens from every quarter of the community made their moral witness against the system of segregation.
They willingly went to jail to create an effective protest.

I too was jailed on charges of parading without a permit, disturbing the peace, and obstructing the sidewalk. I refused to pay the fine
and had expected to spend Christmas in jail. I hoped thousands
would join me. I didn't come to be arrested. I had planned to stay a
day or so and return home after giving counsel. But after seeing
negotiations break down, I knew I had to stay. My personal reason
for being in Albany was to express a personal witness of a situation

I felt was very important to me. As I, accompanied by over one hundred spirited Negroes, voluntarily chose jail to bail, the city officials appeared so hardened to all appeals to conscience that the confidence of some of our supporters was shaken. They nervously counted heads and concluded too hastily that the movement was losing momentum.

I shall never forget the experience of seeing women over seventy, teenagers, and middle-aged adults—some with professional degrees in medicine, law, and education, some simple housekeepers and laborers—crowding the cells. This development was an indication that the Negro would not rest until all the barriers of segregation were broken down. The South had to decide whether it would comply with the law of the land or drift into chaos and social stagnation.

One must search for words in an attempt to describe the spirit of enthusiasm and majesty engendered in the next mass meeting, on that night when seven hundred Negro citizens were finally released from prison. Out from the jails came those men and women—doctors, ministers, housewives—all of whom had joined ranks with a gallant student leadership in an exemplary demonstration of nonviolent resistance to segregation.

Before long the merchants were urging a settlement upon the city officials and an agreement was finally wrung from their unwilling hands. That agreement was dishonored and violated by the city. It was inevitable that the sweep of events would see a resumption of the nonviolent movement, and when cases against the seven hundred odd prisoners were not dropped and when the city council refused to negotiate to end discrimination in public places, actions began again.

When the Albany Movement, true to its promise, resumed protest activity in July 1962, it invited the Southern Christian Leadership Conference to share leadership with it. As president of the SCLC, I marshaled our staff of personnel experienced in nonviolent action, voter registration, and law.

Ralph and I had been called to trial along with two other Albany citizens in February. Recorder's Court Judge A. N. Durden deferred judgment until Tuesday, July 10.

Jail Diary for July 10–July 11

Tuesday, July 10: *We left Atlanta in a party of seven via Southern Airlines to attend court trial in Albany, Georgia. The party included Juanita and Ralph Abernathy, Wyatt Walker, Ted Brown, Vincent Harding, Coretta, and myself. We left Atlanta around 7:45 A.M. and arrived in Albany promptly at 8:50. We were met at the airport by Andy Young, who had preceded us the night before, Dr. William Anderson, and the two detectives who had been assigned to us by the city. We proceeded directly to Dr. Anderson's residence. There we had breakfast and discussed our possible action in the event we were convicted. Dr. Anderson brought us up to date on the temper of the Negro community. He assured us that the people were generally enthusiastic and determined to stick with us to the end. He mentioned that several people had made it palpably clear that they would go to jail again and stay indefinitely. From all of these words we gradually concluded that we had no alternative but to serve the time if we were sentenced. Considering church and organizational responsibilities we concluded that we could not stay in more than three months. But if the sentence were three months or less we would serve the time. With this decision we left for court.*

At 10:00 A.M. Judge Durden called the court to order. He immediately began by reading a prepared statement. It said in short that he had found all four defendants guilty. The four defendants were Ralph Abernathy, Eddie Jackson, Solomon Walker, and myself. Ralph and I were given a fine of $178 or forty-five days on the streets. Jackson and Walker were given lesser fines and days, since, according to the judge, they were not the leaders.

Ralph and I immediately notified the court that we could not in all good conscience pay the fine, and thereby chose to serve the time. Eddie Jackson joined us in this decision. Mr. Walker decided to appeal.

After a brief press conference in the vestibule of the court we were brought immediately to the Albany City Jail which is in the basement of the same building which houses the court and the city hall. This jail is by far the worst I've ever been in. It is a dingy, dirty hole with nothing suggestive of civilized society. The cells are saturated with filth, and what mattresses there are for the bunks are as hard as solid rocks and as nasty as anything that one has ever seen. The companionship of

MESSAGE FROM JAIL

Our course of action was decided after very careful soul searching. There was the consideration of our wives and families, our respective pulpits, our official responsibility as chief officers of SCLC, and many long-standing commitments. However, in the face of all these, we were overwhelmed by some other primary concerns that could be resolved in no other way.

We chose to serve our time because we feel so deeply about the plight of more than seven hundred others who have yet to be tried. The fine and appeal for this number of people would make the cost astronomical. We have experienced the racist tactics of attempting to bankrupt the movement in the South through excessive bail and extended court fights. The time has now come when we must practice civil disobedience in a true sense or delay our freedom thrust for long years.

July 14, 1962

roaches and ants is not at all unusual. In several of the cells there are no mattresses at all. The occupants are compelled to sleep on the bare hard steel.

When we entered our cell—Ralph and I were placed together in a single cell—we found it as filthy as all the rest. However, conscious of the fact that he had some political prisoners on hand who could make these conditions known around the nation, the Chief immediately ordered the entire cell block to be cleaned. So with water, soap, and Lysol the boys got to work and gave the cleaning it so desperately needed.

The rest of the day was spent getting adjusted to our home for the next forty-five days. There is something inherently depressing about jail, especially when one is confined to his cell. We soon discovered that we would not be ordered to work on the streets because, according to the Chief, "it would not be safe." This, to me, was bad news. I wanted to work on the streets at least to give some attention to the daily round. Jail is depressing because it shuts off the world. It leaves one caught in the dull monotony of sameness. It is almost like being dead while one still lives. To adjust to such a meaningless existence is not easy. The only way that I adjust to it is to constantly remind myself that this self-imposed suffering is for a great cause and purpose. This realization takes a little of the agony and a little of the depression away. But, in

spite of this, the painfulness of the experience remains. It is something like the mother giving birth to a child. While she is temporarily consoled by the fact that her pain is not just bare meaningless pain, she nevertheless experiences the pain. In spite of the fact that she realizes that beneath her pain is the emergence of life in a radiant infant, she experiences the agony right on. So is the jail experience. It is life without the singing of a bird, without the sight of the sun, moon, and stars, without the felt presence of the fresh air. In short, it is life without the beauties of life; it is bare existence—cold, cruel, and degenerating.

One of the things that takes the monotony out of jail is the visit of a relative or friend. About 1:30—three hours after we were arrested— our wives came by to see us. As usual Coretta was calm and sweet, encouraging me at every point. God blessed me with a great and wonderful wife. Without her love, understanding, and courage, I would have faltered long ago. I asked about the children. She told me that Yolanda cried when she discovered that her daddy was in jail. Somehow, I have never quite adjusted to bringing my children up under such inexplicable conditions. How do you explain to a little child why you have to go to jail? Coretta developed an answer. She told them that daddy has gone to jail to help the people.

The rest of the day was spent sleeping, adjusting to the unbearable heat, and talking with other friends—Wyatt, Dr. Anderson, Andy Young, Ted Brown, Vincent Harding, and Atty. King—who floated in. Around 11:00 P.M. I fell asleep. Never before have I slept under more miserable conditions. My bed was so hard, my back was so sore, and the jail was so ugly.

Wednesday, July 11: I awoke bright and early. It was around 6:00 to be exact. My back was still sore. Around 8:00 breakfast came. We had fasted all day Tuesday in order to prepare ourselves, spiritually, for the ordeals ahead. We broke the fast by eating breakfast. The food is generally good in this jail. This may be due to the fact that the food is cooked, not in the jail itself, but in a cafe, adjacent to the jail. For breakfast we had link sausage, eggs, and grits. I was pleasantly surprised when I discovered that the coffee had cream and sugar. In all the jails that I have inhabited we were not permitted to have sugar or cream in the coffee.

At 10:00 we had a visit from C. K. Steele, Andy Young, and Henry Elkins, my summer assistant pastor. He had brought me some articles that my wife sent from Atlanta. They told us about the mass meeting. It was lively and extremely well attended. They whispered to us that a group was planning to march to the city hall around noon.

Around noon the group did march. They were led by C. K. Steele. All were arrested—about fifty. They were first brought to the city jails. We heard them as they approached singing freedom songs. Naturally this was a big lift for us.

As the group neared the jail, two of the jailers came over and ordered Ralph and I to move over to what is known as the bull pen. This is a dark and desolate cell that holds nine persons. It is unbelievable that such a cell could exist in a supposedly civilized society.

About seven-thirty on the morning of July 13, we were called and notified that Chief Pritchett wanted to see us. They asked us to dress in our civilian clothes. We did that and went to see Chief Pritchett at about nine o'clock. At which time, the Chief said to us that we had been released, in other words that our fine had been paid. I said, "Well, Chief, we want to serve this time, we feel that we owe it to ourselves and the seven hundred and some-odd people of this community who still have these cases hanging over them." His only response then was, "God knows, Reverend, I don't want you in my jail." This was one time that I was out of jail and I was not happy to be out. Not that I particularly enjoyed the inconveniences and the discomforts of jail, but I did not appreciate the subtle and conniving tactics used to get us out of jail. We had witnessed persons being kicked off lunch counter stools during the sit-ins, ejected from churches during the kneel-ins, and thrown into jail during the Freedom Rides. But for the first time, we witnessed being kicked out of jail.

On July 24, officials unleashed force against our peaceful demonstration, brutally beating a pregnant woman and caning one of our lawyers. Some of the Negro onlookers, not our demonstrators, seething with resentment, hurled bottles and stones at the police. At that point, I temporarily halted mass demonstrations, and for several days, I visited homes, clubs, and pool rooms, urging that no retaliation be tolerated, and even the angriest of men acceded.

"Day of Penance"

While we are certain that neither the peaceful demonstrators nor persons active in the Albany Movement were involved in the violence that erupted last night, we abhor violence so much that when it occurs in the ranks of the Negro community, we assume part of the responsibility for it.

In order to demonstrate our commitment to nonviolence and our determination to keep our protest peaceful, we declare a "Day of Penance" beginning at 12 noon today. We are calling upon all members and supporters of the Albany Movement to pray for their brothers in the Negro community who have not yet found their way to the nonviolent discipline during this Day of Penance. We feel that as we observe this Day of Penance, the City Commission and white people of goodwill should seriously examine the problems and conditions existing in Albany. We must honestly say that the City Commission's arrogant refusal to talk with the leaders of the Albany Movement, the continued suppression of the Negro's aspiration for freedom, and the tragic attempt on the part of the Albany police officials to maintain segregation at any cost, all serve to create the atmosphere for violence and bitterness.

While we will preach and teach nonviolence to our people with every ounce of energy in our bodies, we fear that these admonitions will fall on some deaf ears if Albany does not engage in good-faith negotiations.

Albany city officials were quick to recognize that the watching and concerned millions across the nation would sense the moral righteousness of our conduct. Quickly, they became converted to nonviolence, and without embarrassment, Sheriff Pritchett declared to the press that he too was an advocate of nonviolence. An equilibrium, in which the external use of force was excluded, settled over the troubled city.

Jail Diary for July 27–August 10

Friday, July 27: *Ralph Abernathy and I were arrested again in Albany at 3:15 P.M. (for the second time in July and the third time since last December). We were accompanied by Dr. W. G. Anderson, Slater King,*

the Rev. Ben Gay, and seven ladies. This group held a prayer vigil in
front of City Hall, seeking to appeal to the City Commission to negotiate with leaders of the Albany Movement. When we arrived at the city
hall, the press was on hand in large numbers and Police Chief Laurie
Pritchett came directly over to us and invited us into his office. When
we declined, he immediately ordered us arrested.

Around 9 P.M., one of the officers came to the cell and said Chief
Pritchett wanted to see me in his office. I responded suspiciously, remembering that two weeks ago, we were summoned to Pritchett's office,
only to discover that we were being tricked out of jail. (A mysterious
donor paid the fine, $178 for each of us.) Today, we were determined
that this would not happen again. So, I told the officer that Pritchett
would have to step back to our cell. The officer reacted very bitterly,
but he apparently got the message to Pritchett because the Chief came
immediately and said: "Come on, Doctor. I am not trying to get you to
leave. There is a long-distance call for you from a man named Spivak."

The call turned out to be Lawrence Spivak from the Meet the Press
TV program. I was scheduled to be on the program, Sunday, July 29.
He was very upset and literally begged me to come out on bond. I
immediately called Atty. (C. B.) King and the Rev. Wyatt Walker, my
assistant, to the jail and sought their advice. We all agreed that I should
not leave and suggested that Dr. Anderson, president of the Albany
Movement, get out on bond and substitute for me. Dr. Anderson agreed
and I decided to remain in jail.

Saturday, July 28: I was able to arrange with Chief Pritchett for
members of my staff to consult with me at any time. We held our staff
meetings right there in jail. My wife, Coretta, also came to see me twice
today before returning to Atlanta.

When Wyatt came to the jail, I emphasized that more demonstrations must be held with smaller numbers in front of the city hall instead
of large marches because there is so much tension in the town.

A little while after I talked with Wyatt, fifteen more demonstrators
were arrested as they appeared before City Hall and they all came in
the jail singing loudly. This was a big lift for us. This group was immediately shipped out to another jail in the state.

Later that day. Pritchett came and asked me to leave jail for good.
He said that someone had actually sent the cash money for my bond

and technically he could make me leave. I told him I certainly did not want to be put in the position of being dragged out of jail, but that I had no intention of leaving because I wanted to serve my sentence.

Prichett told us: "You don't know how tense things are, do you? Do you know what happened?" When we said no, he replied: "Somebody almost busted C. B. King's head wide open." It sounded horrible and we became excited. I asked him who and he said calmly: "The sheriff over in the County Jail." I immediately sent for Wyatt and asked him to send a telegram to the President and to call Atty. Gen. Robert Kennedy and Burke Marshall of the Justice Dept. I told them I was very much concerned about this kind of brutality by law enforcement agencies and that something had to be done.

Sunday, July 29: *Everything was rather quiet this morning. We had our regular devotional services among all the prisoners. I read from the Book of Job. We hold services every morning and evening and sing whenever we feel like it. Since only Ralph and I are in a cell together, we can't see the other prisoners, but we can always hear them. Slater is two cells away. Marvin Rich, Ed Dickenson, and Earl Gorden (some white demonstrators) are across the hall in another cell block but they join us in services. After devotion, I started reading some of the books I had with me.*

They brought us the usual breakfast at 8 o'clock. It was one link sausage, one egg and some grits, two pieces of bread on a tin plate with a tin cup of coffee. We were astonished when the jailer returned at ten minutes after 10 this morning with a plate of hash, peas and rice and corn bread. He said it was supper and the last meal we were going to get that day because the cook was getting off early. Soon, the Rev. Mr. Walker came over with Dr. Roy C. Bell from Atlanta and Larry Still, a writer from Jet. Roy inspected Ralph's teeth and said he would arrange with Chief Pritchett to get us some "food packages." I told him this was needed because we would starve on the jail house food. The Albany Jail is dirty, filthy, and ill-equipped. I have been in many jails and it is really the worst I have ever seen.

Monday, July 30: *I spent most of the day reading and writing my book on Negro sermons before our hearing in federal court started. The heat was so unbearable, I could hardly get anything done. I think we had the hottest cell in the jail because it is back in a corner. There are*

four bunks in our cell, but for some reason, they never put anybody in with us. Ralph says every time we go to the wash bowl we bump into each other. He is a wonderful friend and really keeps our spirits going. The food seemed to be worse than usual today. I could only drink the coffee.

I talked with Wyatt and he told me the demonstrations were still going as planned. We soon heard about them because they brought in about fifteen more they had arrested. We were then told to get ready to go to court to begin the hearing on the city's request for a federal injunction against the demonstrations. I was informed that Atty. Connie Motley was here from the New York office of the NAACP and I was very happy. Lawyers King and Donald L. Hollowell of Atlanta came to see me before the hearing started. We discussed how the Albany battle must be waged on all four fronts. A legal battle in the courts; with demonstrations and kneel-ins and sit-ins; with an economic boycott; and, finally, with an intense voter registration campaign. This is going to be a long summer.

Tuesday, July 31: I was very glad to get to court today because I had a chance to see my wife and my friends and associates who are keeping the Albany Movement going. I also had a chance to consult with Wyatt during the recesses. He told us demonstrations were going on while we were in court and that some of the youth groups led by the Student Nonviolent Coordinating Committee were testing places like drugstores and drive-ins and motels.

Later, my father came to me with the Rev. Allen Middleton, head of Atlanta's SCLC chapter. I was happy to hear that my mother has adjusted to my role in the Albany Movement. She understood that I still had to remain in jail as long as necessary. I told Dad to invite some preachers in to help him carry on the church, but he told me, "As long as you carry on in jail, I'll carry on outside."

Wednesday, August 1: My father and Dr. Middleton came to see me again this morning and told me they spoke at the mass meeting last night at Mt. Zion Baptist Church. The crowd was so large they overflowed into Shiloh Baptist across the street, where nightly mass meetings are usually held. Dad said he would remain through today's hearing and listen to Chief Pritchett's testimony about how he had to arrest Negroes to protect the white people from beating them. Dad said he

told the people I didn't come to Albany on my own but I was invited there by the city officials to visit their jail.

Thursday, August 2: *I learned about President Kennedy saying that the commissioners of Albany ought to talk to the Negro leaders. I felt this was a very forthright statement and immediately dictated a statement to the President commending him on his action.*

Friday, August 3: *They recessed the court hearing until Tuesday. I still have the feeling it is too long and drawn out and that the people should keep demonstrating no matter what happens.*

Saturday, August 4: *More demonstrators were arrested all day today and later on Pritchett came back and asked them to sing for him. "Sing that song about 'Ain't Going to Let Chief Pritchett Turn Me Around,'" he asked. I think he really enjoyed hearing it. The other jailers would just stare and listen.*

Sunday, August 5: *Today was a big day for me, because my children—Yolanda, Martin Luther III, and Dexter—came to see me. I had not seen them for five weeks. We had about twenty-five minutes together. They certainly gave me a lift.*

Monday, August 6: *I saw Coretta again before she left to take the children back to Atlanta. I devoted most of the day to reading newspapers and letters from all over the world. Some of them were just addressed to "Nation's No. 1 Troublemaker, Albany," without any state. I got a few bad ones like this, but most of them were good letters of encouragement from Negroes and whites. After dinner and devotional period I continued writing on my book. I had planned to finish it this summer, but I have only written eleven of the eighteen sermons to be*

TELEGRAM TO PRESIDENT KENNEDY

DEAR MR PRESIDENT, GRATIFIED BY DIRECTNESS OF YOUR STATE-
MENT TO ALBANY CRISIS. REV ABERNATHY AND I EARNESTLY HOPE
YOU WILL CONTINUE TO USE THE GREAT MORAL INFLUENCE OF
YOUR OFFICE TO HELP THIS CRITICAL SITUATION.

August 2, 1962

included. I have written three sermons in jail. They all deal with how to make the Christian gospel relevant to the social and economic life of man. This means how the Christian should deal with race relations, war and peace, and economic injustices. They are all based on sermons I have preached. The sermons I wrote in jail are called "A Tender Heart and A Tough Mind," "Love in Action," and "Loving Your Enemies." I think I will name the book Loving Your Enemies.

Tuesday, August 7: *We went back to court today. As I listened to the testimony of the State's witnesses about how they were trying to prevent violence and protect the people, I told Ralph it was very depressing to see city officials make a farce of the court.*

Wednesday, August 8: *Today was the last day of the hearing and Ralph and I testified. Although the federal court hearing offered some relief from the hot jail, I was glad the hearings were over. It was always miserable going back to the hot cell from the air-conditioned courtroom. I was so exhausted and sick that Dr. Anderson had to come and treat me for the second time.*

Thursday, August 9: *Even though we decided to remain in jail, "We Woke Up This Morning with Our Mind on Freedom." Everyone appeared to be in good spirits and we had an exceptionally good devotional program and sang all of our freedom songs.*
Later, Wyatt and Dr. Anderson came and told me that two marches were being planned if Ralph and I were sentenced to jail tomorrow. All of the mothers of many prisoners agreed to join their families in jail including my wife, Mrs. Anderson, Wyatt's wife, Young's wife, Ralph's wife, and the wife of Atty. William Kunstler.

Friday, August 10: *The suspended sentence today did not come as a complete surprise to me. I still think the sentence was unjust and I want to appeal but our lawyers have not decided. Ralph and I agreed to call off the marches and return to our churches in Atlanta to give the Commission a chance to "save face" and demonstrate good faith with the Albany Movement.*

I thought the federal government could do more, because basic constitutional rights were being denied. The persons who were protesting in Albany, Georgia, were merely seeking to exercise constitu-

TERRIBLE COST OF THE BALLOT

Tears welled up in my heart and my eyes last week as I surveyed the shambles of what had been the Shady Grove Baptist Church of Leesburg, Georgia. I had been awakened shortly after daybreak by my executive assistant, the Rev. Wyatt Tee Walker, who informed me that a SNCC staffer had just called and reported that the church where their organization had been holding voting clinics and registration classes had been destroyed by fire and/or dynamite. . . .

The naked truth is that whether the object of the Negro community's efforts are directed at lunch counters or interstate buses, First Amendment privileges or pilgrimages of prayer, school desegregation or the right to vote—he meets an implacable foe in the Southern white racist. No matter what it is we seek, if it has to do with full citizenship, self-respect, human dignity, and borders on changing the "Southern way of life," the Negro stands little chance, if any, of securing the approval, consent, or tolerance of the segregationist white South—Exhibit "A": the charred remains of Shady Grove Baptist Church, Lee County, Georgia. This is the terrible cost of the ballot in the deep South.

From newspaper column, September 1, 1962

TELEGRAM TO PRESIDENT KENNEDY

I HAVE LEARNED FROM AUTHENTIC SOURCES THAT NEGROES ARE ARMING THEMSELVES IN MANY QUARTERS WHERE THIS REIGN OF TERROR IS ALIVE. I WILL CONTINUE TO URGE MY PEOPLE TO BE NONVIOLENT IN THE FACE OF BITTEREST OPPOSITION, BUT I FEAR THAT MY COUNSEL WILL FALL ON DEAF EARS IF THE FEDERAL GOVERNMENT DOES NOT TAKE DECISIVE ACTION. IF NEGROES ARE TEMPTED TO TURN TO RETALIATORY VIOLENCE, WE SHALL SEE A DARK NIGHT OF RIOTING ALL OVER THE SOUTH.

September 11, 1962

tional rights through peaceful protest, nonviolent protest. I thought that the people in Albany were being denied their rights on the basis of the first amendment of the Constitution. I thought it would be a very good thing for the federal government to take a definite stand on that issue, even if it meant joining with Negro attorneys who were working on the situation.

"The people of Albany had straightened their backs"

Our movement aroused the Negro to a spirited pitch in which more than 5 percent of the Negro population voluntarily went to jail. At the same time, about 95 percent of the Negro population boycotted buses, and shops where humiliation, not service, was offered. Those boycotts were remarkably effective. The buses were off the streets and rusting in garages, and the line went out of business. Other merchants watched the sales of their goods decline week by week. National concerns even changed plans to open branches in Albany because the city was too unstable to encourage business to invest there. To thwart us, the opposition had closed parks and libraries, but in the process, they closed them for white people as well, thus they had made their modern city little better than a rural village without recreational and cultural facilities.

When months of demonstrations and jailings failed to accomplish the goals of the movement, reports in the press and elsewhere pronounced nonviolent resistance a dead issue.

There were weaknesses in Albany, and a share of the responsibility belongs to each of us who participated. There is no tactical theory so neat that a revolutionary struggle for a share of power can be won merely by pressing a row of buttons. Human beings with all their faults and strengths constitute the mechanism of a social movement. They must make mistakes and learn from them, make more mistakes and learn anew. They must taste defeat as well as success, and discover how to live with each. Looking back over it, I'm sorry I was bailed out. I didn't understand at the time what was happening. We lost an initiative that we never regained. We attacked the political power structure instead of the economic power structure. You don't win against a political power structure where you don't have the votes.

If I had that to do again, I would guide that community's Negro leadership differently than I did. The mistake I made there was to protest against segregation generally rather than against a single and distinct facet of it. Our protest was so vague that we got nothing, and the people were left very depressed and in despair. It would have been much better to have concentrated upon integrating the buses or the lunch counters. One victory of this kind would have been symbolic, would have galvanized support and boosted morale. But I don't mean that our work in Albany ended in failure. And what we learned from our mistakes in Albany helped our later campaigns in other cities to be more effective. We never since scattered our efforts in a general attack on segregation, but focused upon specific, symbolic objectives.

Yet, the repeal of Albany's segregation laws indicated clearly that the city fathers were realistically facing the legal death of segregation. After the "jail-ins," the City Commission repealed the entire section of the city code that carried segregation ordinances. The public library was opened on a thirty-day "trial" basis—integrated! To be sure, neither of these events could be measured as a full victory, but neither did they smack of defeat.

When we planned our strategy for Birmingham months later, we spent many hours assessing Albany and trying to learn from its errors. Our appraisals not only helped to make our subsequent tactics more effective, but revealed that Albany was far from an unqualified failure. Though lunch counters remained segregated, thousands of Negroes were added to the voting registration rolls. In the gubernatorial elections that followed our summer there, a moderate candidate confronted a rabid segregationist. By reason of the expanded Negro vote, the moderate defeated the segregationist in the city of Albany, which in turn contributed to his victory in the state. As a result, Georgia elected its first governor pledged to respect and enforce the law equally.

In short, our movement had taken the moral offensive, enriching our people with a spirit of strength to fight for equality and freedom even if the struggle is to be long and arduous. The people of Albany had straightened their backs, and, as Gandhi had said, no one can ride on the back of a man unless it is bent.

The atmosphere of despair and defeat was replaced by the surg-

ing sense of strength of people who had dared to defy tyrants, and had discovered that tyrants could be defeated. To the Negro in the South, staggering under a burden of centuries of inferiority, to have faced his oppressor squarely, absorbed his violence, filled the jails, driven his segregated buses off the streets, worshiped in a few white churches, rendered inoperative parks, libraries, and pools, shrunken his trade, revealed his inhumanity to the nation and the world, and sung, lectured, and prayed publicly for freedom and equality—these were the deeds of a giant. No one would silence him up again. That was the victory which could not be undone. Albany would never be the same again. We had won a partial victory in Albany, and a partial victory to us was not an end but a beginning.

17

THE BIRMINGHAM
CAMPAIGN

In the entire country, there was no place to compare with Birmingham. The largest industrial city in the South, Birmingham had become, in the thirties, a symbol for bloodshed when trade unions sought to organize. It was a community in which human rights had been trampled on for so long that fear and oppression were as thick in its atmosphere as the smog from its factories. Its financial interests were interlocked with a power structure which spread throughout the South and radiated into the North. The challenge to nonviolent, direct action could not have been staged in a more appropriate arena.

MARCH 28, 1963
The Kings' fourth child, Bernice Albertine, is born

APRIL 2
Albert Boutwell wins runoff election over Police Commissioner Eugene "Bull" Connor for mayor of Birmingham, but Connor and other city commissioners refuse to leave office

APRIL 3
After delays in order to avoid interfering with election, SCLC and Alabama Christian Movement for Human Rights launch protest campaign in Birmingham

APRIL 12
After violating a state circuit court injunction against protests, King is arrested

APRIL 15
President Kennedy calls Coretta Scott King expressing concern for her jailed husband

I f you had visited Birmingham before the third of April in the
one-hundredth-anniversary year of the Negro's emancipation,
you might have come to a startling conclusion. You might have concluded that here was a city which had been trapped for decades in a
Rip Van Winkle slumber; a city whose fathers had apparently never
heard of Abraham Lincoln, Thomas Jefferson, the Bill of Rights, the
Preamble to the Constitution, The Thirteenth, Fourteenth, and Fifteenth Amendments, or the 1954 decision of the United States Supreme Court outlawing segregation in the public schools.

If your powers of imagination are great enough to enable you to
place yourself in the position of a Negro baby born and brought up
to physical maturity in Birmingham, you would picture your life in
the following manner:

You would be born in a Jim Crow hospital to parents who probably lived in a ghetto. You would attend a Jim Crow school. You
would spend your childhood playing mainly in the streets because
the "colored" parks were abysmally inadequate. When a federal
court order banned park segregation, you would find that Birmingham closed down its parks and gave up its baseball team rather
than integrate them.

If you went shopping with your mother or father, you would
trudge along as they purchased at every counter except one, in the
large or small stores. If you were hungry or thirsty, you would have
to forget about it until you got back to the Negro section of town,
for in your city it was a violation of the law to serve food to Negroes
at the same counter with whites.

If your family attended church, you would go to a Negro church.
If you attended your own Negro church and wanted to play safe,
you might select a church that didn't have a pastor with a reputation
for speaking out on civil rights. If you wanted to visit a church attended by white people, you would not be welcome. For although
your white fellow citizens would insist that they were Christians,
they practiced segregation as rigidly in the house of God as they did
in the theater.

If you wanted to contribute to and be a part of the work of the
National Association for the Advancement of Colored People, you
would not have been able to join a local branch. In the state of

Alabama, segregationist authorities had been successful in enjoining the NAACP from performing its civil rights work by declaring it a "foreign corporation" and rendering its activities illegal.

If you wanted a job in this city—one of the greatest iron- and steel-producing centers in the nation—you had better settle on doing menial work as a porter or laborer. If you were fortunate enough to get a job, you could expect that promotions to a better status or more pay would come, not to you, but to a white employee regardless of your comparative talents.

If you believed your history books and thought of America as a country whose governing officials—whether city, state, or nation—are selected by the governed, you would be swiftly disillusioned when you tried to exercise your right to register and vote. Your race, constituting two-fifths of the city's population, would have made up one-eighth of its voting strength.

You would be living in a city where brutality directed against Negroes was an unquestioned and unchallenged reality. One of the city commissioners, a member of the body that ruled municipal affairs, would be Eugene "Bull" Connor, a racist who prided himself on knowing how to handle the Negro and keep him in his "place." As commissioner of public safety, Bull Connor, entrenched for many years in a key position in the Birmingham power structure, displayed as much contempt for the rights of the Negro as he did defiance for the authority of the federal government.

You would have found a general atmosphere of violence and brutality in Birmingham. Local racists intimidated, mobbed, and even killed Negroes with impunity. One of the more vivid examples of the terror of Birmingham was the castration of a Negro man, whose mutilated body had then been abandoned on a lonely road. No Negro home was protected from bombings and burnings. From the year 1957 through January 1963, while Birmingham was still claiming that its Negroes were "satisfied," seventeen unsolved bombings of Negro churches and homes of civil rights leaders occurred.

In Connor's Birmingham, the silent password was fear. It was a fear not only on the part of the black oppressed, but also in the hearts of the white oppressors. Certainly Birmingham had its white moderates who disapproved of Bull Connor's tactics. Certainly Bir-

mingham had its decent white citizens who privately deplored the maltreatment of Negroes. But they remained publicly silent. It was a silence born of fear—fear of social, political, and economic reprisals. The ultimate tragedy of Birmingham was not the brutality of the bad people, but the silence of the good people.

In Birmingham, you would be living in a community where the white man's long-lived tyranny had cowed your people, led them to abandon hope, and developed in them a false sense of inferiority. You would be living in a city where the representatives of economic and political power refused to even discuss social justice with the leaders of your people.

You would be living in the largest city of a police state, presided over by a governor—George Wallace—whose inauguration vow had been a pledge of "segregation now, segregation tomorrow, segregation forever!" You would be living, in fact, in the most segregated city in America.

"Project C"

There was one threat to the reign of white supremacy in Birmingham. As an outgrowth of the Montgomery bus boycott, protest movements had sprung up in numerous cities across the South. In Birmingham, one of the nation's most courageous freedom fighters, the Reverend Fred Shuttlesworth, had organized the Alabama Christian Movement for Human Rights—ACHR—in the spring of 1956. Shuttlesworth, a wiry, energetic, and indomitable man, had set out to change Birmingham and to end for all time the terrorist, racist rule of Bull Connor.

When Shuttlesworth first formed his organization—which soon became one of the eighty-five affiliates of our Southern Christian Leadership Conference—Bull Connor doubtless regarded the group as just another bunch of troublesome "niggers." It soon became obvious even to Connor, however, that Shuttlesworth was in dead earnest. Back at Christmas 1956, Shuttlesworth's home was bombed and completely demolished. In the winter of 1956, his church, Bethel Baptist, was dynamited by racists, and later in 1957, Shuttlesworth and his wife were mobbed, beaten, and stabbed. They were also jailed eight times, four times during the Freedom Rides.

At the May 1962 board meeting of SCLC at Chattanooga, we decided to give serious consideration to joining Shuttlesworth and the ACHR in a massive direct action campaign to attack segregation in Birmingham. Along with Shuttlesworth, we believed that while a campaign in Birmingham would surely be the toughest fight of our civil rights careers, it could, if successful, break the back of segregation all over the nation. A victory there might well set forces in motion to change the entire course of the drive for freedom and justice. Because we were convinced of the significance of the job to be done in Birmingham, we decided that the most thorough planning and prayerful preparation must go into the effort. We began to prepare a top secret file which we called "Project C"—the "C" for Birmingham's *Confrontation* with the fight for justice and morality in race relations.

In preparation for our campaign, I called a three-day retreat and planning session with SCLC staff and board members at our training center near Savannah, Georgia. Here we sought to perfect a timetable and discuss every possible eventuality. In analyzing our campaign in Albany, Georgia, we decided that one of the principal mistakes we had made there was to scatter our efforts too widely. We had been so involved in attacking segregation in general that we had failed to direct our protest effectively to any one main facet. We concluded that in hard-core communities, a more effective battle could be waged if it was concentrated against one aspect of the evil and intricate system of segregation. We decided, therefore, to center the Birmingham struggle on the business community, for we knew that the Negro population had sufficient buying power so that its withdrawal could make the difference between profit and loss for many businesses.

Two weeks after the retreat, I went to Birmingham with my able executive assistant, the Reverend Wyatt Tee Walker, and my abiding friend and fellow campaigner from the days of Montgomery, the Reverend Ralph Abernathy, SCLC's treasurer. There we began to meet with the board of ACHR to assist in preparing the Negro community for what would surely be a difficult, prolonged, and dangerous campaign.

We met in the now famous Room 30 of the Gaston Motel. This room, which housed Ralph and myself, and served as the headquar-

ters for all the strategy sessions in subsequent months, would later be the target of one of the bombs on the fateful and violent Saturday night of May 11, the eve of Mother's Day.

The first major decision we faced was setting the date for launching of "Project C." Since it was our aim to bring pressure to bear on the merchants, we felt that our campaign should be mounted around the Easter season—the second biggest shopping period of the year. If we started the first week of March, we would have six weeks to mobilize the community before Easter, which fell on April 14. But at this point we were reminded that a mayoralty election was to be held in Birmingham on March 5.

The leading candidates were Albert Boutwell, Eugene "Bull" Connor, and Tom King. All were segregationists, running on a platform to preserve the status quo. Yet both King and Boutwell were considered moderates in comparison to Connor. We were hopeful that Connor would be so thoroughly defeated that at least we would not have to deal with him. Since we did not want our campaign to be used as a political football, we decided to postpone it, planning to begin demonstrations two weeks after the election.

By March 1, 1963, the project was in high gear and the loose ends of organizational structure were being pulled together. Some 250 people had volunteered to participate in the initial demonstrations and had pledged to remain in jail at least five days.

At this point the results of the March 5 election intervened to pose a serious new problem. No candidate had won a clear victory. There would have to be a runoff vote, to be held the first week in April. The competing candidates were to be Boutwell and Connor.

Again we had to remap strategy. Had we moved in while Connor and Boutwell were electioneering, Connor would undoubtedly have capitalized on our presence by using it as an emotion-charged issue for his own political advantage, waging a vigorous campaign to persuade the white community that he, and he alone, could defend the city's official policies of segregation. We might actually have had the effect of helping Connor win. Reluctantly, we decided to postpone the demonstrations until the day after the runoff.

We left Birmingham sadly, realizing that after this second delay the intensive groundwork we had done in the Negro community might not bring the effective results we sought. We were leaving

some 250 volunteers who had been willing to join our ranks and to go to jail. Now we might lose contact with these recruits for several weeks. Yet we dared not remain. It was agreed that no member of the SCLC staff would return to Birmingham until after the runoff.

In New York City, Harry Belafonte, an old friend and supporter of SCLC, agreed to call a meeting at his apartment. Approximately seventy-five leading New Yorkers were present. Fred Shuttlesworth and I spoke of the problems then existing in Birmingham and those we anticipated. We explained why we had delayed taking action until after the runoff, and why we felt it necessary to proceed with our plans whether Connor or Boutwell was the eventual victor. When we had finished, the most frequent question was: "What can we do to help?"

We answered that we were certain to need tremendous sums of money for bail bonds. We might need public meetings to organize more support. On the spot, Harry Belafonte organized a committee, and money was pledged that same night. For the next three weeks, Belafonte, who never did anything without getting totally involved, gave up his career to organize people and money. With these contacts established, the time had come to return to Birmingham. The runoff election was April 2. We flew in the same night. By word of mouth, we set about trying to make contact with our 250 volunteers for an unadvertised meeting. About sixty-five came out. The following day, with the modest task force, we launched the direct-action campaign in Birmingham.

"People came forward to join our army"

On Wednesday, April 3, 1963, the Birmingham *News* appeared on the stands, its front page bright with a color drawing showing a golden sun rising over the city. It was captioned: "New Day Dawns for Birmingham," and celebrated Albert Boutwell's victory in the runoff vote for mayor. The golden glow of racial harmony, the headline implied, could now be expected to descend on the city. As events were to show, it was indeed a new day for Birmingham; but not because Boutwell had won the election.

For all the optimism expressed in the press and elsewhere, we were convinced that Albert Boutwell was, in Fred Shuttlesworth's

apt phrase, "just a dignified Bull Connor." We knew that the former state senator and lieutenant governor had been the principal author of Alabama's Pupil Placement Law, and was a consistent supporter of segregationist views. His statement a few days after election that "we citizens of Birmingham respect and understand one another" showed that he understood nothing about two-fifths of Birmingham's citizens, to whom even polite segregation was no respect.

Meanwhile, despite the results of the runoff, the city commissioners, including Bull Connor, had taken the position that they could not legally be removed from office until 1965. They would go into the courts to defend their position, and refused in the interim to move out of their City Hall offices. If they won in court they would remain in office for another two years. If they lost, their terms would still not expire until April 15, the day after Easter. In either case, we were committed to enter a situation in which a city was operating literally under two governments.

We had decided to limit the first few days' efforts to sit-ins. Being prepared for a long struggle, we felt it best to begin modestly, with a limited number of arrests each day. By rationing our energies in this manner, we would help toward the buildup and drama of a growing campaign. The first demonstrations were, accordingly, not spectacular, but they were well organized. After the first day we held a mass meeting, the first of sixty-five nightly meetings conducted at various churches in the Negro community. Through these meetings we were able to generate the power and depth which finally galvanized the entire Negro community. I spoke at the mass meetings nightly on the philosophy of nonviolence and its methods.

"The soul of the movement"

An important part of the mass meetings was the freedom songs. In a sense the freedom songs are the soul of the movement. They are more than just incantations of clever phrases designed to invigorate a campaign; they are as old as the history of the Negro in America. They are adaptations of songs the slaves sang—the sorrow songs, the shouts for joy, the battle hymns, and the anthems of our movement. I have heard people talk of their beat and rhythm, but we in the movement are as inspired by their words. "Woke Up This Morning

with My Mind Stayed on Freedom" is a sentence that needs no music to make its point. We sing the freedom songs for the same reason the slaves sang them, because we too are in bondage and the songs add hope to our determination that "We shall overcome, Black and white together, We shall overcome someday." These songs bound us together, gave us courage together, helped us march together. We could walk toward any Gestapo force. We had cosmic companionship, for we were singing, "Come By Me, Lord, Come By Me."

With this music, a rich heritage from our ancestors who had the stamina and the moral fiber to be able to find beauty in broken fragments of music, whose illiterate minds were able to compose eloquently simple expressions of faith and hope and idealism, we can articulate our deepest groans and passionate yearnings—and end always on a note of hope that God is going to help us work it out, right here in the South where evil stalks the life of a Negro from the time he is placed in his cradle. Through this music, the Negro is able to dip down into wells of a deeply pessimistic situation and danger-fraught circumstances and to bring forth a marvelous, sparkling, fluid optimism. He knows it is still dark in his world, but somehow, he finds a ray of light.

Toward the end of the mass meetings, Abernathy or Shuttlesworth or I would extend an appeal for volunteers to serve in our nonviolent army. We made it clear that we would not send anyone out to demonstrate who had not convinced himself and us that he could accept and endure violence without retaliating. At the same time, we urged the volunteers to give up any possible weapons that they might have on their persons. Hundreds of people responded to this appeal. Some of those who carried penknives, Boy Scout knives—all kinds of knives—had them not because they wanted to use them against the police or other attackers, but because they wanted to defend themselves against Mr. Connor's dogs. We proved to them that we needed no weapons—not so much as a toothpick. We proved that we possessed the most formidable weapon of all—the conviction that we were right. We had the protection of our knowledge that we were more concerned about realizing our righteous aims than about saving our skins.

The invitational periods at the mass meetings, when we asked

for volunteers, were much like those invitational periods that occur every Sunday morning in Negro churches, when the pastor projects the call to those present to join the church. By twenties and thirties and forties, people came forward to join our army. We did not hesitate to call our movement an army. It was a special army, with no supplies but its sincerity, no uniform but its determination, no arsenal except its faith, no currency but its conscience. It was an army that would move but not maul. It was an army that would sing but not slay.

We were seeking to bring about a great social change which could only be achieved through unified effort. Yet our community was divided. Our goals could never be attained in such an atmosphere. It was decided that we would conduct a whirlwind campaign of meetings with organizations and leaders in the Negro community, to seek to mobilize every key person and group behind our movement.

Along with members of my staff, I began addressing numerous groups representing a cross section of our people in Birmingham. I spoke to business and professional people, and I talked to a gathering of two hundred ministers. I met with many smaller groups, during a hectic one-week schedule. In most cases, the atmosphere when I entered was tense and chilly, and I was aware that there was a great deal of work to be done.

I went immediately to the point, explaining why we had been forced to proceed without letting them know the date in advance. I dealt with the argument of timing. To the ministers I stressed the need for a social gospel to supplement the gospel of individual salvation. I suggested that only a "dry as dust" religion prompts a minister to extol the glories of heaven while ignoring the social conditions that cause men an earthly hell. I pleaded for the projections of strong, firm leadership by the Negro minister, pointing out that he is freer, more independent, than any other person in the community.

I challenged those who had been persuaded that I was an "outsider." I pointed out that as president of SCLC, I had come in the interests of aiding an SCLC affiliate. I expounded on the weary and worn "outsider" charge, which we have faced in every community where we have gone to try to help. No Negro, in fact, no American, is an outsider when he goes to any community to aid the cause of

freedom and justice. No Negro anywhere, regardless of his social standing, his financial status, his prestige and position, is an outsider so long as dignity and decency are denied to the humblest black child in Mississippi, Alabama, or Georgia.

Somehow God gave me the power to transform the resentments, the suspicions, the fears, and the misunderstanding I found that week into faith and enthusiasm. I spoke from my heart, and out of each meeting came firm endorsements and pledges of participation and support. With the new unity that developed, and now poured fresh blood into our protest, the foundations of the old order were doomed. A new order was destined to be born, and not all the powers of bigotry or Bull Connor could abort it.

"At the center of all that my life had brought me to be"

By the end of the first three days of lunch counter sit-ins, there had been thirty-five arrests. On Saturday, April 6, 1963, we began the next stage of our crusade with a march on City Hall. From then on, the daily demonstrations grew stronger. Our boycott of the downtown merchants was proving amazingly effective. A few days before Easter, a careful check showed less than twenty Negroes entering all the stores in the downtown area. Meanwhile, with the number of volunteers increasing daily, we were able to launch campaigns against a variety of additional objectives: kneel-ins at churches; sit-ins at the library; a march on the county building to mark the opening of a voter registration drive. And all the time the jails were slowly but steadily filling up.

Birmingham residents of both races were surprised at the restraint of Connor's men at the beginning of the campaign. True, police dogs and clubs made their debut on Palm Sunday, but their appearance that day was brief, and they quickly disappeared. What observers probably did not realize was that the commissioner was trying to take a leaf from the book of Police Chief Laurie Pritchett of Albany. Chief Pritchett felt that by directing his police to be nonviolent, he had discovered a new way to defeat the demonstrations. Mr. Connor, as it developed, was not to adhere to nonviolence long; the dogs were baying in kennels not far away; the hoses were primed.

A second reason Bull Connor had held off at first was that he

thought he had found another way out. This became evident on April 10, when the city government obtained a court injunction directing us to cease our activities until our right to demonstrate had been argued in court. The time had now come for us to counter their legal maneuver with a strategy of our own. Two days later, we did an audacious thing, something we had never done in any other crusade. We disobeyed a court order.

I had intended to be one of the first to set the example of civil disobedience. Ten days after the demonstrations began, between four hundred and five hundred people had gone to jail; some had been released on bail, but about three hundred remained. Now that the job of unifying the Negro community had been accomplished, my time had come. We decided that, because of its symbolic significance, April 12, Good Friday, would be the day that Ralph Abernathy and I would present our bodies as personal witness in this crusade.

STATEMENT ON INJUNCTION

We cannot in all good conscience obey such an injunction which is an unjust, undemocratic, and unconstitutional misuse of the legal process.

We do this not out of any disrespect for the law but out of the highest respect for the law. This is not an attempt to evade or defy the law or engage in chaotic anarchy. Just as in all good conscience we cannot obey unjust laws, neither can we respect the unjust use of the courts.

We believe in a system of law based on justice and morality. Out of our great love for the Constitution of the U.S. and our desire to purify the judicial system of the state of Alabama, we risk this critical move with an awareness of the possible consequences involved.

April 11, 1963

Soon after we announced our intention to lead a demonstration on April 12 and submit to arrest, we received a message so distressing that it threatened to ruin the movement. Late Thursday night, the bondsman who had been furnishing bail for the demonstrators notified us that he would be unable to continue. The city notified him that his financial assets were insufficient. Obviously, this was another move on the part of the city to hurt our cause.

It was a serious blow. We had used up all the money we had on hand for cash bonds. We had a moral responsibility for our people in jail. Fifty more were to go in with Ralph and me. This would be the largest single group to be arrested to date. Without bail facilities, how could we guarantee their eventual release?

Good Friday morning, early, I sat in Room 30 of the Gaston Motel discussing this crisis with twenty-four key people. As we talked, a sense of doom began to pervade the room. I looked about me and saw that for the first time our most dedicated and devoted leaders were overwhelmed by a feeling of hopelessness. No one knew what to say, for no one knew what to do. Finally someone spoke up and, as he spoke, I could see that he was giving voice to what was on everyone's mind.

"Martin," he said, "this means you can't go to jail. We need money. We need a lot of money. We need it now. You are the only one who has the contacts to get it. If you go to jail, we are lost. The battle of Birmingham is lost."

I sat there, conscious of twenty-four pairs of eyes. I thought about the people in the jail. I thought about the Birmingham Negroes already lining the streets of the city, waiting to see me put into practice what I had so passionately preached. How could my failure now to submit to arrest be explained to the local community? What would be the verdict of the country about a man who had encouraged hundreds of people to make a stunning sacrifice and then excused himself?

Then my mind began to race in the opposite direction. Suppose I went to jail? What would happen to the three hundred? Where would the money come from to assure their release? What would happen to our campaign? Who would be willing to follow us into jail, not knowing when or whether he would ever walk out once more into the Birmingham sunshine?

I sat in the midst of the deepest quiet I have ever felt, with two dozen others in the room. There comes a time in the atmosphere of leadership when a man surrounded by loyal friends and allies realizes he has come face-to-face with himself and with ruthless reality. I was alone in that crowded room.

I walked to another room in the back of the suite, and I stood in the center of the floor. I thought I was standing at the center of all

that my life had brought me to be. I thought of the twenty-four people, waiting in the next room. I thought of the three hundred, waiting in prison. I thought of the Birmingham Negro community, waiting. Then my tortured mind leaped beyond the Gaston Motel, past the city jail, past the city and state lines, and I thought of the twenty million black people who dreamed that someday they might be able to cross the Red Sea of injustice and find their way into the promised land of integration and freedom. There was no more room for doubt.

I whispered to myself, "I must go."

The doubt, the fear, the hesitation was gone. I pulled off my shirt and pants, got into work clothes, and went back to the other room.

"Friends," I said, "I've made my decision. I have to make a faith act. I don't know what will happen or what the outcome will be. I don't know where the money will come from."

I turned to Ralph Abernathy. "I know you have a need to be in your pulpit on Easter Sunday, Ralph. But I am asking you to take this faith act with me."

As Ralph stood up, unquestioningly, without hesitation, we all linked hands involuntarily, almost as if there had been some divine signal, and twenty-five voices in Room 30 at the Gaston Motel in Birmingham, Alabama, chanted the battle hymn of our movement, "We Shall Overcome."

"Held incommunicado, solitary confinement"

We rode from the motel to the Zion Hill church, where the march would begin. Many hundreds of Negroes had turned out to see us, and great hope grew within me as I saw those faces smiling approval as we passed. It seemed that every Birmingham police officer had been sent into the area. Leaving the church, where we were joined by the rest of our group of fifty, we started down the forbidden streets that lead to the downtown sector. It was a beautiful march. We were allowed to walk farther than the police had ever permitted before. We were singing, and occasionally the singing was interspersed with bursts of applause from the sidewalks.

As we neared the downtown area, Bull Connor ordered his men to arrest us, and somebody from the police force leaned over and

reminded Mr. Connor, "Mr. Connor, we ain't got nowhere to put 'em." Ralph and I were hauled off by two muscular policemen, clutching the backs of our shirts in handfuls. All the others were promptly arrested. In jail Ralph and I were separated from everyone else and later from each other.

For more than twenty-four hours, I was held incommunicado, in solitary confinement. No one was permitted to visit me, not even my lawyers. Those were the longest, most frustrating and bewildering hours I have lived. Having no contact of any kind, I was besieged with worry. How was the movement faring? Where would Fred and the other leaders get the money to have our demonstrators released? What was happening to the morale in the Negro community?

I suffered no physical brutality at the hands of my jailers. Some of the prison personnel were surly and abusive, but that was to be expected in Southern prisons. Solitary confinement, however, was brutal enough. In the mornings the sun would rise, sending shafts of light through the window high in the narrow cell which was my home. You will never know the meaning of utter darkness until you have lain in such a dungeon, knowing that sunlight is streaming overhead and still seeing only darkness below. You might have thought I was in the grip of a fantasy brought on by worry. I did worry. But there was more to the blackness than a phenomenon conjured up by a worried mind. Whatever the cause, the fact remained that I could not see the light.

When I had left my Atlanta home some days before, my wife, Coretta, had just given birth to our fourth child. As happy as we were about the new little girl, Coretta was disappointed that her condition would not allow her to accompany me. She had been my strength and inspiration during the terror of Montgomery. She had been active in Albany, Georgia, and was preparing to go to jail with the wives of other civil rights leaders there, just before the campaign ended.

Now, not only was she confined to our home, but she was denied even the consolation of a telephone call from her husband. On the Sunday following our jailing, she decided she must do something. Remembering the call that John Kennedy had made to her when I was jailed in Georgia during the 1960 election campaign, she placed a call to the President. Within a few minutes, his brother, Attorney

General Robert Kennedy, phoned back. She told him that she had learned that I was in solitary confinement and was afraid for my safety. The attorney general promised to do everything he could to have my situation eased. A few hours later President Kennedy himself called Coretta from Palm Beach, and assured her that he would look into the matter immediately. Apparently the President and his brother placed calls to officials in Birmingham; for immediately after Coretta heard from them, my jailers asked if I wanted to call her. After the President's intervention, conditions changed considerably.

TELEGRAM TO PRESIDENT KENNEDY

I AM DEEPLY GRATEFUL TO YOU FOR TAKING TIME OUT OF YOUR EASTER WEEKEND TO TELEPHONE MY WIFE CONCERNING THE BIRMINGHAM SITUATION. YOUR ENCOURAGING WORDS AND THOUGHTFUL CONCERN GAVE HER RENEWED STRENGTH TO FACE THE DIFFICULT MOMENTS THROUGH WHICH WE ARE NOW PASSING. SUCH MORAL SUPPORT GREATLY ENHANCES OUR HUMBLE EFFORTS TO MAKE THE AMERICAN DREAM A REALITY.

April 16, 1963

Meanwhile, on Easter Sunday afternoon, two of our attorneys, Orzell Billingsley and Arthur Shores, had been allowed to visit me. They told me that Clarence B. Jones, my friend and lawyer, would be coming in from New York the following day. When they left, none of the questions tormenting me had been answered. When Clarence Jones arrived the next day, before I could even tell him how happy I was to see him, he said a few words that lifted a thousand pounds from my heart:

"Harry Belafonte has been able to raise fifty thousand dollars for bail bonds. It is available immediately. And he says that whatever else you need, he will raise it."

I found it hard to say what I felt. Jones's message had brought me more than relief from the immediate concern about money, more than gratitude for the loyalty of friends far away, more than confirmation that the life of the movement could not be snuffed out. What silenced me was a profound sense of awe. I was aware of a feeling that had been present all along below the surface of con-

sciousness, pressed down under the weight of concern for the movement: I had never been truly in solitary confinement. God's companionship does not stop at the door of a jail cell. God had been my cellmate. When the decision came—in Room 30 on Good Friday—that we must commit a faith act, God was there. And he was also present in a Fifth Avenue, New York City, apartment where a dedicated young star had worked night and day, telephoning everyone he could think of to demand that they send him some money for bail bonds in Alabama. In the midst of deepest midnight, daybreak had come. I did not know whether the sun was shining at that moment. But I knew that once again I could see the light.

18

LETTER FROM
BIRMINGHAM JAIL

I remember saying in that letter that so often I have been disappointed because we have not received the cooperation of the Church. I remember saying that so often the Church in our struggle had been a taillight, rather than a headlight. The Church had so often been an echo, rather than a voice.

APRIL 12, 1963
White Birmingham ministers write to King calling for end of demonstrations

APRIL 16
King writes letter of response

I will never forget that one morning, I think the next morning after I was placed in the cell in solitary confinement, a newspaper was slipped in to me. I turned it over and found a kind of advertisement that had been placed there, taken out by eight clergyman of all of the major religious faiths in our nation. They were criticizing our demonstrations. They were calling us extremists. They were calling us law breakers and believers in anarchy and all of these things. And when I read it, I became so concerned and even upset and at points so righteously indignant that I decided to answer the letter.

My response to the published statement by eight fellow clergymen from Alabama (Bishop C.C.J. Carpenter, Bishop Joseph A. Durick, Rabbi Hilton L. Grafman, Bishop Paul Hardin, Bishop Holan B. Harmon, the Reverend George M. Murray, the Reverend

Edward V. Ramage, and the Reverend Earl Stallings) was composed under somewhat constricting circumstances. I didn't have anything at my disposal like a pad or writing paper. Begun on the margins of the newspaper in which the statement appeared, the letter was continued on scraps of writing paper supplied by a friendly Negro trusty, and concluded on a pad my attorneys were eventually permitted to leave me. I was able to slip it out of the jail to one of my assistants through the lawyer.

Although the text remains in substance unaltered, I have indulged in the author's prerogative of polishing it.

April 16, 1963

MY DEAR FELLOW CLERGYMEN:

While confined here in the Birmingham city jail, I came across your recent statement calling my present activities "unwise and untimely." Seldom do I pause to answer criticism of my work and ideas. If I sought to answer all the criticisms that cross my desk, my secretaries would have little time for anything other than such correspondence in the course of the day, and I would have no time for constructive work. But since I feel that you are men of genuine goodwill and that your criticisms are sincerely set forth, I want to try to answer your statements in what I hope will be patient and reasonable terms.

I think I should indicate why I am here in Birmingham, since you have been influenced by the view which argues against "outsiders coming in." I have the honor of serving as president of the Southern Christian Leadership Conference, an organization operating in every Southern state, with headquarters in Atlanta, Georgia. We have some eight-five affiliated organizations across the South, and one of them is the Alabama Christian Movement for Human Rights. Frequently we share staff, educational and financial resources with our affiliates. Several months ago the affiliate here in Birmingham asked us to be on call to engage in a nonviolent direct-action program if such were deemed necessary. We readily consented, and when the hour came we lived up to our promise. So I, along with several members of my staff, am here because I was invited here. I am here because I have organizational ties here.

But more basically, I am in Birmingham because injustice is here.

Just as the prophets of the eighth century B.C. left their villages and carried their "thus saith the Lord" far beyond the boundaries of their hometowns, and just as the Apostle Paul left his village of Tarsus and carried the gospel of Jesus Christ to the far corners of the Greco-Roman world, so am I compelled to carry the gospel of freedom beyond my own hometown. Like Paul, I must constantly respond to the Macedonian call for aid.

Moreover, I am cognizant of the interrelatedness of all communities and states. I cannot sit idly by in Atlanta and not be concerned about what happens in Birmingham. Injustice anywhere is a threat to justice everywhere. We are caught in an inescapable network of mutuality, tied in a single garment of destiny. Whatever affects one directly, affects all indirectly. Never again can we afford to live with the narrow, provincial "outside agitator" idea. Anyone who lives inside the United States can never be considered an outsider anywhere within its bounds.

You deplore the demonstrations taking place in Birmingham. But your statement, I am sorry to say, fails to express a similar concern for the conditions that brought about the demonstrations. I am sure that none of you would want to rest content with the superficial kind of social analysis that deals merely with effects and does not grapple with underlying causes. It is unfortunate that demonstrations are taking place in Birmingham, but it is even more unfortunate that the city's white power structure left the Negro community with no alternative.

In any nonviolent campaign there are four basic steps: collection of the facts to determine whether injustices exist; negotiation; self-purification; and direct action. We have gone through all these steps in Birmingham. There can be no gainsaying the fact that racial injustice engulfs this community. Birmingham is probably the most thoroughly segregated city in the United States. Its ugly record of brutality is widely known. Negroes have experienced grossly unjust treatment in the courts. There have been more unsolved bombings of Negro homes and churches in Birmingham than in any other city in the nation. These are the hard, brutal facts of the case. On the basis of these conditions, Negro leaders sought to negotiate with the city fathers. But the latter consistently refused to engage in good-faith negotiation.

Then, last September, came the opportunity to talk with leaders of Birmingham's economic community. In the course of the negotiations, certain promises were made by the merchants—for example, to remove

the stores' humiliating racial signs. On the basis of these promises, the Reverend Fred Shuttlesworth and the leaders of the Alabama Christian Movement for Human Rights agreed to a moratorium on all demonstrations. As the weeks and months went by, we realized that we were the victims of a broken promise. A few signs, briefly removed, returned; the others remained.

As in so many past experiences, our hopes had been blasted, and the shadow of deep disappointment settled upon us. We had no alternative except to prepare for direct action, whereby we would present our very bodies as a means of laying our case before the conscience of the local and the national community. Mindful of the difficulties involved, we decided to undertake a process of self-purification. We began a series of workshops on nonviolence, and we repeatedly asked ourselves: "Are you able to accept blows without retaliating?" "Are you able to endure the ordeal of jail?" We decided to schedule our direct-action program for the Easter season, realizing that except for Christmas, this is the main shopping period of the year. Knowing that a strong economic-withdrawal program would be the by-product of direct action, we felt that this would be the best time to bring pressure to bear on the merchants for the needed change.

Then it occurred to us that Birmingham's mayoralty election was coming up in March, and we speedily decided to postpone action until after election day. When we discovered that the commissioner of public safety, Eugene "Bull" Connor, had piled up enough votes to be in the run-off, we decided again to postpone action until the day after the run-off so that the demonstrations could not be used to cloud the issues. Like many others, we waited to see Mr. Connor defeated, and to this end we endured postponement after postponement. Having aided in this community need, we felt that our direct-action program could be delayed no longer.

You may well ask: "Why direct action? Why sit-ins, marches, and so forth? Isn't negotiation a better path?" You are quite right in calling for negotiation. Indeed, this is the very purpose of direct action. Nonviolent direct action seeks to create such a crisis and foster such a tension that a community which has constantly refused to negotiate is forced to confront the issue. It seeks to dramatize the issue so that it can no longer be ignored. My citing the creation of tension as part of the work of the nonviolent resister may sound rather shocking. But I must confess that

I am not afraid of the word "tension." I have earnestly opposed violent tension, but there is a type of constructive, nonviolent tension which is necessary for growth. Just as Socrates felt that it was necessary to create a tension in the mind so that individuals could rise from the bondage of myths and half-truths to the unfettered realm of creative analysis and objective appraisal, so must we see the need for nonviolent gadflies to create the kind of tension in society that will help men rise from the dark depths of prejudice and racism to the majestic heights of understanding and brotherhood.

The purpose of our direct-action program is to create a situation so crisis-packed that it will inevitably open the door to negotiation. I therefore concur with you in your call for negotiation. Too long has our beloved Southland been bogged down in a tragic effort to live in monologue rather than dialogue.

One of the basic points in your statement is that the action that I and my associates have taken in Birmingham is untimely. Some have asked: "Why didn't you give the new city administration time to act?" The only answer that I can give to this query is that the new Birmingham administration must be prodded about as much as the outgoing one, before it will act. We are sadly mistaken if we feel that the election of Albert Boutwell as mayor will bring the millennium to Birmingham. While Mr. Boutwell is a much more gentle person than Mr. Connor, they are both segregationists, dedicated to maintenance of the status quo. I have hope that Mr. Boutwell will be reasonable enough to see the futility of massive resistance to desegregation. But he will not see this without pressure from devotees of civil rights. My friends, I must say to you that we have not made a single gain in civil rights without determined legal and nonviolent pressure. Lamentably, it is an historical fact that privileged groups seldom give up their privileges voluntarily. Individuals may see the moral light and voluntarily give up their unjust posture; but, as Reinhold Neibuhr has reminded us, groups tend to be more immoral than individuals.

We know through painful experience that freedom is never voluntarily given by the oppressor; it must be demanded by the oppressed. Frankly, I have yet to engage in a direct-action campaign that was "well timed" in the view of those who have not suffered unduly from the disease of segregation. For years now I have heard the word "Wait!" It rings in the ear of every Negro with piercing familiarity. This "Wait"

has almost always meant "Never." We must come to see, with one of
our distinguished jurists, that "justice too long delayed is justice denied."

We have waited for more than 340 years for our constitutional and
God-given rights. The nations of Asia and Africa are moving with jet-
like speed toward gaining political independence, but we still creep at
horse-and-buggy pace toward gaining a cup of coffee at a lunch
counter. Perhaps it is easy for those who have never felt the stinging
darts of segregation to say, "Wait." But when you have seen vicious
mobs lynch your mothers and fathers at will and drown your sisters
and brothers at whim; when you have seen hate-filled policemen curse,
kick, and even kill your black brothers and sisters; when you see the
vast majority of your twenty million Negro brothers smothering in an
airtight cage of poverty in the midst of an affluent society; when you
suddenly find your tongue twisted and your speech stammering as you
seek to explain to your six-year-old daughter why she can't go to the
public amusement park that has just been advertised on television, and
see tears welling up in her eyes when she is told that Funtown is closed
to colored children, and see ominous clouds of inferiority beginning to
form in her little mental sky, and see her beginning to distort her personality by developing an unconscious bitterness toward white people;
when you have to concoct an answer for a five-year-old son who is
asking: "Daddy, why do white people treat colored people so mean?";
when you take a cross-county drive and find it necessary to sleep night
after night in the uncomfortable corners of your automobile because no
motel will accept you; when you are humiliated day in and day out by
nagging signs reading "white" and "colored"; when your first name
becomes "nigger," your middle names becomes "boy" (however old you
are), and your last name becomes "John," and your wife and mother
are never given the respected title "Mrs."; when you are harried by day
and haunted by night by the fact that you are a Negro, living constantly
at tiptoe stance, never quite knowing what to expect next, and are
plagued with inner fears and outer resentments; when you are forever
fighting a degenerating sense of "nobodiness"—then you will understand why we find it difficult to wait. There comes a time when the cup
of endurance runs over, and men are no longer willing to be plunged
into the abyss of despair. I hope, sirs, you can understand our legitimate
and unavoidable impatience.

You express a great deal of anxiety over our willingness to break laws. This is certainly a legitimate concern. Since we so diligently urge people to obey the Supreme Court's decision of 1954 outlawing segregation in the public schools, at first glance it may seem rather paradoxical for us consciously to break laws. One may well ask: "How can you advocate breaking some laws and obeying others?" The answer lies in the fact that there are two types of laws: just and unjust. I would be the first to advocate obeying just laws. One has not only a legal but a moral responsibility to obey just laws. Conversely, one has a moral responsibility to disobey unjust laws. I would agree with St. Augustine that "an unjust law is no law at all."

Now, what is the difference between the two? How does one determine whether a law is just or unjust? A just law is a man-made code that squares with the moral law or the law of God. An unjust law is a code that is out of harmony with the moral law. To put it in the terms of Saint Thomas Aquinas: an unjust law is a human law that is not rooted in eternal and natural law. Any law that uplifts human personality is just. Any law that degrades human personality is unjust. All segregation statutes are unjust because segregation distorts the soul and damages the personality. It gives the segregator a false sense of superiority and the segregated a false sense of inferiority. Segregation, to use the terminology of the Jewish philosopher Martin Buber, substitutes an "I-it" relationship for an "I-thou" relationship and ends up relegating persons to the status of things. Hence segregation is not only politically, economically, and sociologically unsound, it is morally wrong and sinful. Paul Tillich has said that sin is separation. Is not segregation an existential expression of man's tragic separation, his awful estrangement, his terrible sinfulness? Thus it is that I can urge men to obey the 1954 decision of the Supreme Court, for it is morally right; and I can urge them to disobey segregation ordinances, for they are morally wrong.

Let us consider a more concrete example of just and unjust laws. An unjust law is a code that a numerical or power majority group compels a minority group to obey but does not make binding on itself. This is difference made legal. By the same token, a just law is a code that a majority compels a minority to follow that it is willing to follow itself. This is sameness made legal.

Let me give another explanation. A law is unjust if it is inflicted on

a minority that, as a result of being denied the right to vote, had no part in enacting or devising the law. Who can say that the legislature of Alabama which set up that state's segregation laws was democratically elected? Throughout Alabama all sorts of devious methods are used to prevent Negroes from becoming registered voters, and there are some counties in which, even though Negroes constitute a majority of the population, not a single Negro is registered. Can any law enacted under such circumstances be considered democratically structured?

Sometimes a law is just on its face and unjust in its application. For instance, I have been arrested on a charge of parading without a permit. Now, there is nothing wrong in having an ordinance which requires a permit for a parade. But such an ordinance becomes unjust when it is used to maintain segregation and to deny citizens the First Amendment privilege of peaceful assembly and protest.

I hope you are able to see the distinction I am trying to point out. In no sense do I advocate evading or defying the law, as would the rabid segregationist. That would lead to anarchy. One who breaks an unjust law must do so openly, lovingly, and with a willingness to accept the penalty. I submit that an individual who breaks a law that conscience tells him is unjust, and who willingly accepts the penalty of imprisonment in order to arouse the conscience of the community over its injustice, is in reality expressing the highest respect for law.

Of course, there is nothing new about this kind of civil disobedience. It was evidenced sublimely in the refusal of Shadrach, Meshach, and Abednego to obey the laws of Nebuchadnezzar, on the ground that a higher moral law was at stake. It was practiced superbly by the early Christians, who were willing to face hungry lions and the excruciating pain of chopping blocks rather than submit to certain unjust laws of the Roman Empire. To a degree, academic freedom is a reality today because Socrates practiced civil disobedience. In our own nation, the Boston Tea Party represented a massive act of civil disobedience.

We should never forget that everything Adolf Hitler did in Germany was "legal" and everything the Hungarian freedom fighters did in Hungary was "illegal." It was "illegal" to aid and comfort a Jew in Hitler's Germany. Even so, I am sure that, had I lived in Germany at the time, I would have aided and comforted my Jewish brothers. If today I lived in a Communist country where certain principles dear to

the Christian faith are suppressed, I would openly advocate disobeying that country's antireligious laws.

I must make two honest confessions to you, my Christian and Jewish brothers. First, I must confess that over the past few years I have been gravely disappointed with the white moderate. I have almost reached the regrettable conclusion that the Negro's great stumbling block in his stride toward freedom is not the White Citizen's Counciler or the Ku Klux Klanner, but the white moderate, who is more devoted to "order" than to justice; who prefers a negative peace which is the absence of tension to a positive peace which is the presence of justice; who constantly says: "I agree with you in the goal you seek, but I cannot agree with your methods of direct action"; who paternalistically believes he can set the timetable for another man's freedom; who lives by a mythical concept of time and who constantly advises the Negro to wait for a "more convenient season." Shallow understanding from people of good will is more frustrating than absolute misunderstanding from people of ill will. Lukewarm acceptance is much more bewildering than outright rejection.

I had hoped that the white moderate would understand that law and order exist for the purpose of establishing justice and that when they fail in this purpose they become the dangerously structured dams that block the flow of social progress. I had hoped that the white moderate would understand that the present tension in the South is a necessary phase of the transition from an obnoxious negative peace, in which the Negro passively accepted his unjust plight, to a substantive and positive peace, in which all men will respect the dignity and worth of human personality. Actually, we who engage in nonviolent direct action are not the creators of tension. We merely bring to the surface the hidden tension that is already alive. We bring it out in the open, where it can be seen and dealt with. Like a boil that can never be cured so long as it is covered up but must be opened with all its ugliness to the natural medicines of air and light, injustice must be exposed, with all the tension its exposure creates, to the light of human conscience and the air of national opinion before it can be cured.

In your statement you assert that our actions, even though peaceful, must be condemned because they precipitate violence. But is this a logical assertion? Isn't this like condemning a robbed man because his possession of money precipitated the evil act of robbery? Isn't this like

condemning Socrates because his unswerving commitment to truth and his philosophical inquiries precipitated the act by the misguided populace in which they made him drink hemlock? Isn't this like condemning Jesus because his unique God-consciousness and never-ceasing devotion to God's will precipitated the evil act of crucifixion? We must come to see that, as the federal courts have consistently affirmed, it is wrong to urge an individual to cease his efforts to gain his basic constitutional rights because the quest may precipitate violence. Society must protect the robbed and punish the robber.

I had also hoped that the white moderate would reject the myth concerning time in relation to the struggle for freedom. I have just received a letter from a white brother in Texas. He writes: "All Christians know that the colored people will receive equal rights eventually, but it is possible that you are in too great a religious hurry. It has taken Christianity almost two thousand years to accomplish what it has. The teachings of Christ take time to come to earth." Such an attitude stems from a tragic misconception of time, from the strangely irrational notion that there is something in the very flow of time that will inevitably cure all ills. Actually, time itself is neutral; it can be used either destructively or constructively. More and more I feel that the people of ill will have used time much more effectively than have the people of good will. We will have to repent in this generation not merely for the hateful words and actions of the bad people but for the appalling silence of the good people. Human progress never rolls in on wheels of inevitability; it comes through the tireless efforts of men willing to be co-workers with God, and without this hard work, time itself becomes an ally of the forces of social stagnation. We must use time creatively, in the knowledge that the time is always ripe to do right. Now is the time to make real the promise of democracy and transform our pending national elegy into a creative psalm of brotherhood. Now is the time to lift our national policy from the quicksand of racial injustice to the solid rock of human dignity.

You speak of our activity in Birmingham as extreme. At first I was rather disappointed that fellow clergymen would see my nonviolent efforts as those of an extremist. I began thinking about the fact that I stand in the middle of two opposing forces in the Negro community. One is a force of complacency, made up in part of Negroes who, as a result of long years of oppression, are so drained of self-respect and a

sense of "somebodiness" that they have adjusted to segregation; and in part of a few middle-class Negroes who, because of a degree of academic and economic security and because in some ways they profit by segregation, have become insensitive to the problems of the masses. The other force is one of bitterness and hatred, and it comes perilously close to advocating violence. It is expressed in the various black nationalist groups that are springing up across the nation, the largest and best-known being Elijah Muhammad's Muslim movement. Nourished by the Negro's frustration over the continued existence of racial discrimination, this movement is made up of people who have lost faith in America, who have absolutely repudiated Christianity, and who have concluded that the white man is an incorrigible "devil."

I have tried to stand between these two forces, saying that we need emulate neither the "do-nothingism" of the complacent nor the hatred and despair of the black nationalist. For there is the more excellent way of love and nonviolent protest. I am grateful to God that, through the influence of the Negro church, the way of nonviolence became an integral part of our struggle.

If this philosophy had not emerged, by now many streets of the South would, I am convinced, be flowing with blood. And I am further convinced that if our white brothers dismiss as "rabble-rousers" and "outside agitators" those of us who employ nonviolent direct action, and if they refuse to support our nonviolent efforts, millions of Negroes will, out of frustration and despair, seek solace and security in black nationalist ideologies—a development that would inevitably lead to a frightening racial nightmare.

Oppressed people cannot remain oppressed forever. The yearning for freedom eventually manifests itself, and that is what has happened to the American Negro. Something within has reminded him of his birthright of freedom, and something without has reminded him that it can be gained. Consciously or unconsciously, he has been caught up by the Zeitgeist, and with his black brothers of Africa and his brown and yellow brothers of Asia, South America, and the Caribbean, the United States Negro is moving with a sense of great urgency toward the promised land of racial justice. If one recognizes this vital urge that has engulfed the Negro community, one should readily understand why public demonstrations are taking place. The Negro has many pent-up resentments and latent frustrations, and he must release them. So let

him march; let him make prayer pilgrimages to the city hall; let him go on freedom rides—and try to understand why he must do so. If his repressed emotions are not released in nonviolent ways, they will seek expression through violence; this is not a threat but a fact of history. So I have not said to my people: "Get rid of your discontent." Rather, I have tried to say that this normal and healthy discontent can be channeled into the creative outlet of nonviolent direct action. And now this approach is being termed extremist.

But though I was initially disappointed at being categorized as an extremist, as I continued to think about the matter I gradually gained a measure of satisfaction from the label. Was not Jesus an extremist for love: "Love your enemies, bless them that curse you, do good to them that hate you, and pray for them which despitefully use you, and persecute you." Was not Amos an extremist for justice: "Let justice roll down like waters and righteousness like an ever-flowing stream." Was not Paul an extremist for the Christian gospel: "I bear in my body the marks of the Lord Jesus." Was not Martin Luther an extremist: "Here I stand; I cannot do otherwise, so help me God." And John Bunyan: "I will stay in jail to the end of my days before I make a butchery of my conscience." And Abraham Lincoln: "This nation cannot survive half slave and half free." And Thomas Jefferson: "We hold these truths to be self-evident, that all men are created equal . . ." So the question is not whether we will be extremists, but what kind of extremists we will be. Will we be extremists for hate or for love? Will we be extremists for the preservation of injustice or for the extension of justice? In that dramatic scene on Calvary's hill three men were crucified. We must never forget that all three were crucified for the same crime—the crime of extremism. Two were extremists for immorality, and thus fell below their environment. The other, Jesus Christ, was an extremist for love, truth, and goodness, and thereby rose above his environment. Perhaps the South, the nation, and the world are in dire need of creative extremists.

I had hoped that the white moderate would see this need. Perhaps I was too optimistic; perhaps I expected too much. I suppose I should have realized that few members of the oppressor race can understand the deep groans and passionate yearnings of the oppressed race, and still fewer have the vision to see that injustice must be rooted out by strong, persistent, and determined action. I am thankful, however, that

some of our white brothers in the South have grasped the meaning of this social revolution and committed themselves to it. They are still too few in quantity, but they are big in quality. Some—such as Ralph McGill, Lillian Smith, Harry Golden, James McBride Dabbs, Ann Braden, and Sarah Patton Boyle—have written about our struggle in eloquent and prophetic terms. Others have marched with us down nameless streets of the South. They have languished in filthy, roach-infested jails, suffering the abuse and brutality of policemen who view them as "dirty nigger lovers." Unlike so many of their moderate brothers and sisters, they have recognized the urgency of the moment and sensed the need for powerful "action" antidotes to combat the disease of segregation.

Let me take note of my other major disappointment. I have been so greatly disappointed with the white church and its leadership. Of course, there are some notable exceptions. I am not unmindful of the fact that each of you has taken some significant stands on this issue. I commend you, Reverend Stallings, for your Christian stand on this past Sunday, in welcoming Negroes to your worship service on a nonsegregated basis. I commend the Catholic leaders of this state for integrating Spring Hill College several years ago.

But despite these notable exceptions, I must honestly reiterate that I have been disappointed with the Church. I do not say this as one of those negative critics who can always find something wrong with the Church. I say this as a minister of the gospel, who loves the Church; who was nurtured in its bosom; who has been sustained by its spiritual blessings and who will remain true to it as long as the cord of life shall lengthen.

When I was suddenly catapulted into the leadership of the bus protest in Montgomery, Alabama, a few years ago, I felt we would be supported by the white church. I felt that the white ministers, priests, and rabbis of the South would be among our strongest allies. Instead, some have been outright opponents, refusing to understand the freedom movement and misrepresenting its leaders; all too many others have been more cautious than courageous and have remained silent behind the anesthetizing security of stained-glass windows.

In spite of my shattered dreams, I came to Birmingham with the hope that the white religious leadership of this community would see the justice of our cause and, with deep moral concern, would serve as the channel through which our just grievances could reach the power

structure. I had hoped that each of you would understand. But again I have been disappointed.

I have heard numerous Southern religious leaders admonish their worshipers to comply with a desegregation decision because it is the law, but I have longed to hear white ministers declare: "Follow this decree because integration is morally right and because the Negro is your brother." In the midst of blatant injustices inflicted upon the Negro, I have watched white churchmen stand on the sideline and mouth pious irrelevancies and sanctimonious trivialities. In the midst of a mighty struggle to rid our nation of racial and economic injustice, I have heard many ministers say: "Those are social issues, with which the gospel has no real concern." And I have watched many churches commit themselves to a completely otherworldly religion which makes a strange, un-Biblical distinction between body and soul, between the sacred and the secular.

I have traveled the length and breadth of Alabama, Mississippi, and all the other Southern states. On sweltering summer days and crisp autumn mornings I have looked at the South's beautiful churches with their lofty spires pointing heavenward. I have beheld the impressive outlines of her massive religious-education buildings. Over and over I have found myself asking: "What kind of people worship here? Who is their God? Where were their voices when the lips of Governor Barnett dripped with words of interposition and nullification? Where were they when Governor Wallace gave a clarion call for defiance and hatred? Where were their voices of support when bruised and weary Negro men and women decided to rise from the dark dungeons of complacency to the bright hills of creative protest?"

Yes, these questions are still in my mind. In deep disappointment I have wept over the laxity of the Church. But be assured that my tears have been tears of love. There can be no deep disappointment where there is not deep love. Yes, I love the Church. How could I do otherwise? I am in the rather unique position of being the son, the grandson, and the great-grandson of preachers. Yes, I see the Church as the body of Christ. But, oh! How we have blemished and scarred that body through social neglect and through fear of being nonconformists.

There was a time when the Church was very powerful—in the time when the early Christians rejoiced at being deemed worthy to suffer for what they believed. In those days the church was not merely a ther-

mometer that recorded the ideas and principles of popular opinion; it was a thermostat that transformed the mores of society. Whenever the early Christians entered a town, the people in power became disturbed and immediately sought to convict the Christians for being "disturbers of the peace" and "outside agitators." But the Christians pressed on, in the conviction that they were "a colony of heaven," called to obey God rather than man. Small in number, they were big in commitment. They were too God-intoxicated to be "astronomically intimidated." By their effort and example they brought an end to such ancient evils as infanticide and gladiatorial contests.

Things are different now. So often the contemporary Church is a weak, ineffectual voice with an uncertain sound. So often it is an arch-defender of the status quo. Far from being disturbed by the presence of the Church, the power structure of the average community is consoled by the Church's silent—and often even vocal—sanction of things as they are.

But the judgment of God is upon the Church as never before. If today's Church does not recapture the sacrificial spirit of the early Church, it will lose its authenticity, forfeit the loyalty of millions, and be dismissed as an irrelevant social club with no meaning for the twentieth century. Every day I meet young people whose disappointment with the Church has turned into outright disgust.

Perhaps I have once again been too optimistic. Is organized religion too inextricably bound to the status quo to save our nation and the world? Perhaps I must turn my faith to the inner spiritual church, the church within the church, as the true ecclesia and the hope of the world. But again I am thankful to God that some noble souls from the ranks of organized religion have broken loose from the paralyzing chains of conformity and joined us as active partners in the struggle for freedom. They have left their secure congregations and walked the streets of Albany, Georgia, with us. They have gone down the highways of the South on tortuous rides for freedom. Yes, they have gone to jail with us. Some have been dismissed from their churches, have lost the support of their bishops and fellow ministers. But they have acted in the faith that right defeated is stronger than evil triumphant. Their witness has been the spiritual salt that has preserved the true meaning of the gospel in these troubled times. They have carved a tunnel of hope through the dark mountain of disappointment.

I hope the Church as a whole will meet the challenge of this decisive hour. But even if the Church does not come to the aid of justice, I have no despair about the future. I have no fear about the outcome of our struggle in Birmingham, even if our motives are at present misunderstood. We will reach the goal of freedom in Birmingham and all over the nation, because the goal of America is freedom. Abused and scorned though we may be, our destiny is tied up with America's destiny. Before the pilgrims landed at Plymouth, we were here. Before the pen of Jefferson etched the majestic words of the Declaration of Independence across the pages of history, we were here. For more than two centuries our forebears labored in this country without wages; they made cotton king; they built the homes of their masters while suffering gross injustice and shameful humiliation—and yet out of a bottomless vitality they continued to thrive and develop. If the inexpressible cruelties of slavery could not stop us, the opposition we now face will surely fail. We will win our freedom because the sacred heritage of our nation and the eternal will of God are embodied in our echoing demands.

Before closing I feel impelled to mention one other point in your statement that has troubled me profoundly. You warmly commended the Birmingham police force for keeping "order" and "preventing violence." I doubt that you would have so warmly commended the police force if you had seen its dogs sinking their teeth into unarmed, nonviolent Negroes. I doubt that you would so quickly commend the policemen if you were to observe their ugly and inhumane treatment of Negroes here in the city jail; if you were to watch them push and curse old Negro women and young Negro girls; if you were to see them slap and kick old Negro men and young boys; if you were to observe them, as they did on two occasions, refuse to give us food because we wanted to sing our grace together. I cannot join you in your praise of the Birmingham police department.

It is true that the police have exercised a degree of discipline in handling the demonstrators. In this sense they have conducted themselves rather "nonviolently" in public. But for what purpose? To preserve the evil system of segregation. Over the past few years I have consistently preached that nonviolence demands that the means we use must be as pure as the ends we seek. I have tried to make clear that it is wrong to use immoral means to attain moral ends. But now I must affirm that it is just as wrong, or perhaps even more so, to use moral

means to preserve immoral ends. Perhaps Mr. Connor and his police-men have been rather nonviolent in public, as was Chief Pritchett in Albany, Georgia, but they have used the moral means of nonviolence to maintain the immoral end of racial injustice. As T. S. Eliot has said: "The last temptation is the greatest treason: To do the right deed for the wrong reason."

I wish you had commended the Negro sit-inners and demonstrators of Birmingham for their sublime courage, their willingness to suffer, and their amazing discipline in the midst of great provocation. One day the South will recognize its real heros. They will be the James Merediths, with the noble sense of purpose that enables them to face jeering and hostile mobs, and with the agonizing loneliness that characterizes the life of the pioneer. They will be old, oppressed, battered Negro women, symbolized in a seventy-two-year-old woman in Montgomery, Ala-bama, who rose up with a sense of dignity and with her people decided not to ride segregated buses, and who responded with ungrammatical profundity to one who inquired about her weariness: "My feets is tired, but my soul is at rest." They will be the young high school and college students, the young ministers of the gospel and a host of their elders, courageously and nonviolently sitting in at lunch counters and willingly going to jail for conscience's sake. One day the South will know that when these disinherited children of God sat down at lunch counters, they were in reality standing up for what is best in the American dream and for the most sacred values in our Judeo-Christian heritage, thereby bringing our nation back to those great wells of democracy which were dug deep by the founding fathers in their formulation of the Constitu-tion and the Declaration of Independence.

Never before have I written so long a letter. I'm afraid it is much too long to take your precious time. I can assure you that it would have been much shorter if I had been writing from a comfortable desk, but what else can one do when he is alone in a narrow jail cell, other than write long letters, think long thoughts, and pray long prayers?

If I have said anything in this letter that overstates the truth and indicates an unreasonable impatience, I beg you to forgive me. If I have said anything that understates the truth and indicates my having a patience that allows me to settle for anything less than brotherhood, I beg God to forgive me.

I hope this letter finds you strong in the faith. I also hope that

circumstances will soon make it possible for me to meet each of you, not as an integrationist or a civil rights leader but as a fellow clergyman and a Christian brother. Let us all hope that the dark clouds of racial prejudice will soon pass away and the deep fog of misunderstanding will be lifted from our fear-drenched communities, and in some not too distant tomorrow the radiant stars of love and brotherhood will shine over our great nation with all their scintillating beauty.

Yours for the cause of Peace and Brotherhood,

Martin Luther King, Jr.

19

FREEDOM NOW!

I have had many experiences in my relatively young life, but I have never in my life had an experience like I am having in Birmingham, Alabama. This is the most inspiring movement that has ever taken place in the United States of America.

APRIL 19, 1963
King and Ralph Abernathy are released on bond

MAY 2–7
Birmingham police use fire hoses and dogs against "Children's Crusade"; over 1,000 youngsters arrested

MAY 8
Protest leaders suspend mass demonstrations

MAY 11
After tentative settlement is reached, segregationists bomb the Gaston Motel where King was staying and the home of King's brother, the Reverend A. D. King

MAY 13
Federal troops arrive in Birmingham

After eight days of imprisonment, Ralph Abernathy and I accepted bond to come out of jail for two purposes. It was necessary for me to regain communication with the SCLC officers and our lawyers in order to map the strategy for the contempt cases that would be coming up shortly in the circuit court. Also, I had decided to put into operation a new phase of our campaign, which I felt would speed victory.

I called my staff together and repeated a conviction I had been

voicing ever since the campaign began. If our drive was to be successful, we must involve the students of the community. Even though we realized that involving teenagers and high school students would bring down upon us a heavy fire of criticism, we felt that we needed this dramatic new dimension. Our people were demonstrating daily and going to jail in numbers, but we were still beating our heads against the brick wall of the city officials' stubborn resolve to maintain the status quo. Our fight, if won, would benefit people of all ages. But most of all we were inspired with the desire to give to our young a true sense of their own stake in freedom and justice. We believed they would have the courage to respond to our call.

"Children understood the stakes"

SCLC staff members James Bevel, Andy Young, Bernard Lee, and Dorothy Cotton began visiting colleges and high schools in the area. They invited students to attend after-school meetings at churches. The word spread fast, and the response from Birmingham's youngsters exceeded our fondest dreams. By the fifties and by the hundreds, these youngsters attended mass meetings and training sessions. They listened eagerly as we talked of bringing freedom to Birmingham, not in some distant time, but right now. We taught them the philosophy of nonviolence. We challenged them to bring their exuberance, their youthful creativity, into the disciplined dedication of the movement. We found them eager to belong, hungry for participation in a significant social effort. Looking back, it is clear that the introduction of Birmingham's children into the campaign was one of the wisest moves we made. It brought a new impact to the crusade, and the impetus that we needed to win the struggle.

Immediately, of course, a cry of protest went up. Although by the end of April the attitude of the national press had changed considerably, so that the major media were according us sympathetic coverage, yet many deplored our "using" our children in this fashion. Where had these writers been, we wondered, during the centuries when our segregated social system had been misusing and abusing Negro children? Where had they been with their protective words when, down through the years, Negro infants were born into ghettos, taking their first breath of life in a social atmosphere where

the fresh air of freedom was crowded out by the stench of discrimination?

The children themselves had the answer to the misguided sympathies of the press. One of the most ringing replies came from a child of no more than eight who walked with her mother one day in a demonstration. An amused policeman leaned down to her and said with mock gruffness: "What do you want?"

The child looked into his eyes, unafraid, and gave her answer.

"F'eedom," she said.

She could not even pronounce the word, but no Gabriel trumpet could have sounded a truer note.

Even children too young to march requested and earned a place in our ranks. Once when we sent out a call for volunteers, six tiny youngsters responded. Andy Young told them that they were not old enough to go to jail but that they could go to the library. "You won't get arrested there," he said, "but you might learn something." So these six small children marched off to the building in the white district, where, up to two weeks before, they would have been turned away at the door. Shyly but doggedly, they went to the children's room and sat down, and soon they were lost in their books. In their own way, they had struck a blow for freedom.

The children understood the stakes they were fighting for. I think of one teenage boy whose father's devotion to the movement turned sour when he learned that his son had pledged himself to become a demonstrator. The father forbade his son to participate.

"Daddy," the boy said, "I don't want to disobey you, but I have made my pledge. If you try to keep me home, I will sneak off. If you think I deserve to be punished for that, I'll just have to take the punishment. For, you see, I'm not doing this only because I want to be free. I'm doing it also because I want freedom for you and Mama, and I want it to come before you die."

That father thought again, and gave his son his blessing.

The movement was blessed by the fire and excitement brought to it by young people such as these. And when Birmingham youngsters joined the march in numbers, a historic thing happened. For the first time in the civil rights movement, we were able to put into effect the Gandhian principle: "Fill up the jails."

Jim Bevel had the inspiration of setting a "D" Day, when the

students would go to jail in historic numbers. When that day arrived, young people converged on the Sixteenth Street Baptist Church in wave after wave. Altogether on "D" Day, May 2, more than a thousand young people demonstrated and went to jail. At one school, the principal gave orders to lock the gates to keep the students in. The youngsters climbed over the gates and ran toward freedom. The assistant superintendent of schools threatened them with expulsion, and still they came, day after day. At the height of the campaign, by conservative estimates, there were 2,500 demonstrators in jail at one time, a large proportion of them young people.

Serious as they were about what they were doing, these teenagers had that marvelous humor that arms the unarmed in the face of danger. Under their leaders, they took delight in confusing the police. A small decoy group would gather at one exit of the church, bringing policemen streaming in cars and on motorcycles. Before the officers knew what was happening, other groups, by the scores, would pour out of other exits and move, two by two, toward our goal in the downtown section.

Many arrived at their destination before the police could confront and arrest them. They sang as they marched and as they were loaded into the paddy wagons. The police ran out of paddy wagons and had to press sheriff's cars and school buses into service.

Watching those youngsters in Birmingham, I could not help remembering an episode in Montgomery during the bus boycott. Someone had asked an elderly women why she was involved in our struggle.

"I'm doing it for my children and for my grandchildren," she had replied.

Seven years later, the children and grandchildren were doing it for themselves.

"The pride and the power of nonviolence"

With the jails filling up and the scorching glare of national disapproval focused on Birmingham, Bull Connor abandoned his posture of nonviolence. The result was an ugliness too well known to Americans and to people all over the world. The newspapers of May 4 carried pictures of prostrate women, and policemen bending over

STATEMENT AT SIXTEENTH STREET BAPTIST CHURCH

The reason I can't follow the old eye-for-an-eye philosophy is that it ends up leaving everybody blind. Somebody must have sense and somebody must have religion. I remember some years ago, my brother and I were driving from Atlanta to Chattanooga, Tennessee. And for some reason the drivers that night were very discourteous or they were forgetting to dim their lights. . . . And finally A.D. looked over at me and he said, "I'm tired of this now, and the next car that comes by here and refuses to dim the lights, I'm going to refuse to dim mine." I said, "Wait a minute, don't do that. Somebody has to have some sense on this highway and if somebody doesn't have sense enough to dim the lights, we'll all end up destroyed on this highway." And I'm saying the same thing for us here in Birmingham. We are moving up a mighty highway toward the city of Freedom. There will be meandering points. There will be curves and difficult moments, and we will be tempted to retaliate with the same kind of force that the opposition will use. But I'm going to say to you, "Wait a minute, Birmingham. Somebody's got to have some sense in Birmingham."

May 3, 1963

them with raised clubs; of children marching up to the bared fangs of police dogs; of the terrible force of pressure hoses sweeping bodies into the streets.

This was the time of our greatest stress, and the courage and conviction of those students and adults made it our finest hour. We did not fight back, but we did not turn back. We did not give way to bitterness. Some few spectators, who had not been trained in the discipline of nonviolence, reacted to the brutality of the policemen by throwing rocks and bottles. But the demonstrators remained nonviolent. In the face of this resolution and bravery, the moral conscience of the nation was deeply stirred and, all over the country, our fight became the fight of decent Americans of all races and creeds.

The moral indignation which was spreading throughout the land, the sympathy created by the children, the growing involvement of the Negro community—all these factors were mingling to create a certain atmosphere inside our movement. It was a pride in progress and a conviction that we were going to win. It was a mounting

◆

STATEMENT AT MASS MEETING

There are those who write history. There are those who make history. There are those who experience history. I don't know how many historians we have in Birmingham tonight. I don't know how many of you would be able to write a history book, but you are certainly making history and you are experiencing history. And you will make it possible for the historians of the future to write a marvelous chapter. Never in the history of this nation have so many people been arrested for the cause of freedom and human dignity.

May 5, 1963

◆

optimism which gave us the feeling that the implacable barriers that confronted us were doomed and already beginning to crumble. We were advised, in the utmost confidence, that the white business structure was weakening under the adverse publicity, the pressure of our boycott, and a parallel falling-off of white buying.

Strangely enough, the masses of white citizens in Birmingham were not fighting us. This was one of the most amazing aspects of the Birmingham crusade. Only a year or so ago, had we begun such a campaign, Bull Connor would have had his job done for him by murderously angry white citizens. Now, however, the majority were maintaining a strictly hands-off policy. I do not mean to insinuate that they were in sympathy with our cause or that they boycotted stores because we did. I simply suggest that it was powerfully symbolic of shifting attitudes in the South that the majority of the white citizens of Birmingham remained neutral through our campaign. This neutrality added force to our feeling that we were on the road to victory.

On one dramatic occasion even Bull Connor's men were shaken. It was a Sunday afternoon, when several hundred Birmingham Negroes had determined to hold a prayer meeting near the city jail. They gathered at the New Pilgrim Baptist Church and began an orderly march. Bull Connor ordered out the police dogs and fire hoses. When the marchers approached the border between the white and Negro areas, Connor ordered them to turn back. The Reverend Charles Billups, who was leading the march, politely refused. En-

raged, Bull Connor whirled on his men and shouted: "Dammit. Turn on the hoses."

What happened in the next thirty seconds was one of the most fantastic events of the Birmingham story. Bull Connor's men stood facing the marchers. The marchers, many of them on their knees, ready to pit nothing but the power of their bodies and souls against Connor's police dogs, clubs, and fire hoses, stared back, unafraid and unmoving. Slowly the Negroes stood up and began to advance. Connor's men, as though hypnotized, fell back, their hoses sagging uselessly in their hands while several hundred Negroes marched past them, without further interference, and held their prayer meeting as planned. I felt there, for the first time, the pride and the power of nonviolence.

"The beginning of the end"

Even though pressure on Birmingham's business community was intense, there were stubborn men in its midst who seemed to feel they would rather see their own enterprises fail than sit across the table and negotiate with our leadership. However, when national pressure began to pile up on the White House, climaxing with the infamous day of May 3, the adminstration was forced to act. On

---

STATEMENT AT BIRMINGHAM MASS MEETING

Don't worry about your children, they're gonna be all right. Don't hold them back if they want to go to jail. For they are doing a job not only for themselves but for all of America and for all mankind. Somewhere we read, "A little child shall lead them." Remember there was another little child just twelve years old and he got involved in a discussion back in Jerusalem. . . . He said, "I must be about my father's business." These young people are about their fathers' business. And they are carving a tunnel of hope through the great mountain of despair. . . . We are going to see that they are treated right, don't worry about that . . . and go on and not only fill up the jails around here, but just fill up the jails all over the state of Alabama if necessary.

May 5, 1963

May 4, the attorney general dispatched Burke Marshall, his chief civil rights assistant, and Joseph F. Dolan, assistant deputy attorney general, to seek a truce in the tense racial situation. Though Marshall had no ultimate power to impose a solution, he had full authority to represent the President in the negotiations. It was one of the first times the federal government had taken so active a role in such circumstances.

I must confess that although I appreciated the fact that the administration had finally made a decisive move, I had some initial misgivings concerning Marshall's intentions. I was afraid that he had come to urge a "cooling off" period—to ask us to declare a one-sided truce as a condition to negotiations. To his credit, Marshall did not adopt such a position. Rather, he did an invaluable job of opening channels of communication between our leadership and the top people in the economic power structure. Said one staunch defender of segregation, after conferring with Marshall: "There is a man who listens. I had to listen back, and I guess I grew up a little."

With Burke Marshall as catalyst, we began to hold secret meetings with the Senior Citizens Committee. At these sessions, unpromising as they were at the outset, we laid the groundwork for the agreement that would eventually accord us all of our major demands.

Meanwhile, however, for several days violence swept through the streets of Birmingham. An armored car was added to Bull Connor's strange armament. And some Negroes, not trained in our nonviolent methods, again responded with bricks and bottles. On one of these days, when the pressure in Connor's hoses was so high that it peeled the bark off the trees, Fred Shuttlesworth was hurled by a blast of water against the side of a building. Suffering injuries in his chest, he was carried away in an ambulance. Connor, when told, responded in characteristic fashion. "I wish he'd been carried away in a hearse," he said. Fortunately, Shuttlesworth was resilient and though still in pain he was back at the conference table the next day.

Terrified by the very destructiveness brought on by their own acts, the city police appealed for state troopers to be brought into the area. Many of the white leaders now realized that something had to be done. Yet there were those among them who were still adamant. But one other incident was to occur that would transform

recalcitrance into good faith. On Tuesday, May 7, the Senior Citizens Committee had assembled in a downtown building to discuss our demands. In the first hours of this meeting, they were so intransigent that Burke Marshall despaired of a pact. The atmosphere was charged with tension, and tempers were running high.

In this mood, these 125-odd business leaders adjourned for lunch. As they walked out on the street, an extraordinary sight met their eyes. On that day several thousand Negroes had marched on the town. The jails were so full that the police could only arrest a handful. There were Negroes on the sidewalks, in the streets, standing, sitting in the aisles of downtown stores. There were square blocks of Negroes, a veritable sea of black faces. They were committing no violence; they were just present and singing. Downtown Birmingham echoed to the strains of the freedom songs.

Astounded, these businessmen, key figures in a great city, suddenly realized that the movement could not be stopped. When they returned—from the lunch they were unable to get—one of the men who had been in the most determined opposition cleared his throat and said: "You know, I've been thinking this thing through. We ought to be able to work something out."

That admission marked the beginning of the end. Late that afternoon, Burke Marshall informed us that representatives from the business and industrial community wanted to meet with the movement leaders immediately to work out a settlement. After talking with these men for about three hours, we became convinced that they were negotiating in good faith. On the basis of this assurance we called a twenty-four-hour truce on Wednesday morning.

That day President Kennedy devoted the entire opening statement of his press conference to the Birmingham situation, emphasizing how vital it was that the problems be squarely faced and resolved and expressing encouragement that a dialogue now existed between the opposing sides. Even while the president spoke, the truce was briefly threatened when Ralph and I were suddenly clapped into jail on an old charge. Some of my associates, feeling that they had again been betrayed, put on their walking shoes and prepared to march. They were restrained, however; we were swiftly bailed out, and negotiations were resumed.

After talking all night Wednesday, and practically all day and

night Thursday, we reached an accord. On Friday, May 10, this agreement was announced. It contained the following pledges:

1. The desegregation of lunch counters, rest rooms, fitting rooms, and drinking fountains, in planned stages within ninety days after signing.
2. The upgrading and hiring of Negroes on a nondiscriminatory basis throughout the industrial community of Birmingham, to include hiring of Negroes as clerks and salesmen within sixty days after signing of the agreement—and the immediate appointment of a committee of business, industrial, and professional leaders to implement an area-wide program for the acceleration of upgrading and employment of Negroes in job categories previously denied to them.
3. Official cooperation with the movement's legal representatives in working out the release of all jailed persons on bond or on their personal recognizance.
4. Through the Senior Citizens Committee or Chamber of Commerce, communications between Negro and white to be publicly established within two weeks after signing, in order to prevent the necessity of further demonstrations and protests.

I am happy to report to you this afternoon that we have commitments that the walls of segregation will crumble in Birmingham, and they will crumble soon. Now let nobody fool you. These walls are not crumbling just to be crumbling. They are breaking down and falling down, because in this community more people have been willing to stand up for freedom and to go to jail for that freedom than in any city at any time in the United States of America.

"Brutal answer to the pact"

Our troubles were not over. The announcement that a peace pact had been signed in Birmingham was flashed across the world by the hundred-odd foreign correspondents then covering the campaign on the crowded scene. It was headlined in the nation's press and heralded on network television. Segregationist forces within the city were consumed with fury. They vowed reprisals against the white

businessmen who had "betrayed" them by capitulating to the cause of Negro equality.

On Saturday night, they gave their brutal answer to the pact. I had not gotten more than two hours' sleep a single night for the past four or five nights. I was about to close my eyes for an evening of good sleep, only to get a telephone call. Following a Ku Klux Klan meeting on the outskirts of town, the home of my brother, the Reverend A. D. King, was bombed. That same night a bomb was planted near the Gaston Motel, a bomb placed so as to kill or seriously wound anyone who might have been in Room 30—my room. Evidently the would-be assassins did not know I was in Atlanta that night.

The bombing had been well timed. The bars in the Negro district close at midnight, and the bombs exploded just as some of Birmingham's Saturday-night drinkers came out of the bars. Thousands of Negroes poured into the streets. Wyatt Walker, my brother, and others urged them to go home, but they were not under the discipline of the movement and were in no mood to listen to counsels of peace. Fighting began. Stones were hurled at the police. Cars were wrecked and fires started. Whoever planted the bombs had *wanted* the Negroes to riot. They wanted the pact upset.

Governor George Wallace's state police and "conservation men" sealed off the Negro area and moved in with their bullies and pistols. They beat numerous innocent Negroes; among their acts of chivalry was the clubbing of the diminutive Anne Walker, Wyatt's wife, as she was about to enter her husband's quarters at the partially bombed-out Gaston Motel. They further distinguished themselves by beating Wyatt when he was attempting to drive back home after seeing his wife to the hospital.

I shall never forget the phone call my brother placed to me in Atlanta that violent Saturday night. His home had just been destroyed. Several people had been injured at the motel. I listened as he described the erupting tumult and catastrophe in the streets of the city. Then, in the background as he talked, I heard a swelling burst of beautiful song. Feet planted in the rubble of debris, threatened by criminal violence and hatred, followers of the movement were singing "We Shall Overcome." I marveled that in a moment of

such tragedy the Negro could still express himself with hope and with faith.

The following evening, a thoroughly aroused President told the nation that the federal government would not allow extremists to sabotage a fair and just pact. He ordered three thousand federal troops into position near Birmingham and made preparations to federalize the Alabama National Guard. This firm action stopped the troublemakers in their tracks.

Yet the segregationist diehards were to attempt still once more to destroy the peace. On May 20, the headlines announced that more than a thousand students who had participated in the demonstrations had been either suspended or expelled by the city's Board of Education. I was convinced that this was another attempt to drive the Negro community to an unwise and impulsive move. The plot might have worked; there were some people in our ranks who sincerely felt that, in retaliation, all the students of Birmingham should stay out of school and that demonstrations should be resumed.

I was out of the city at the time, but I rushed back to Birmingham to persuade the leaders that we must not fall into the trap. We decided to take the issue into the courts and did so, through the auspices of the NAACP Legal Defense and Educational Fund. On May 22, the local federal district court judge upheld the Birmingham Board of Education. But that same day, Judge Elbert P. Tuttle, of the Fifth Circuit Court of Appeals, not only reversed the decision of the district judge but strongly condemned the Board of Education for its action. In a time when the nation was trying to solve the problem of school dropouts, Judge Tuttle's ruling indicated, it was an act of irresponsibility to drive those youngsters from school in retaliation for having engaged in a legally permissible action to achieve their constitutional rights. The night this ruling was handed down, we had a great mass meeting. It was a jubilant moment, another victory in the titanic struggle.

The following day, in an appropriate postscript, the Alabama Supreme Court ruled Eugene "Bull" Connor and his fellow commissioners out of office, once and for all.

I could not close an account of events in Birmingham without noting the tremendous moral and financial support which poured in

upon us from all over the world during the six weeks of demonstrations and in the weeks and months to follow. Although we were so preoccupied with the day-to-day crises of the campaign that we did not have time to send out a formal plea for funds, letters of encouragement and donations ranging from pennies taken from piggy banks to checks of impressive size flowed into our besieged command post at the Gaston Motel and our Atlanta headquarters.

One of the most gratifying developments was the unprecedented show of unity that was displayed by the national Negro community in support of our crusade. From all over the country came Negro ministers, civil rights leaders, entertainers, star athletes, and ordinary citizens, ready to speak at our meetings or join us in jail. The NAACP Legal Defense and Educational Fund came to our aid several times both with money and with resourceful legal talent. Many other organizations and individuals contributed invaluable gifts of time, money, and moral support.

The signing of the agreement was the climax of a long struggle for justice, freedom, and human dignity. The millennium still had not come, but Birmingham had made a fresh, bold step toward equality.

Birmingham is by no means miraculously desegregated. There is still resistance and violence. The last-ditch struggle of a segregationist governor still soils the pages of current events and it is still necessary for a harried President to invoke his highest powers so that a Negro child may go to school with a white child in Birmingham. But these factors only serve to emphasize the truth that even the segregationists know: The system to which they have been committed lies on its deathbed. The only imponderable is the question of how costly they will make the funeral.

I like to believe that Birmingham will one day become a model in Southern race relations. I like to believe that the negative extremes of Birmingham's past will resolve into the positive and utopian extreme of her future; that the sins of a dark yesterday will be redeemed in the achievements of a bright tomorrow. I have this hope because, once on a summer day, a dream came true. The city of Birmingham discovered a conscience.

20

MARCH ON WASHINGTON

There can be no doubt, even in the true depths of the most prejudiced minds, that the August 28 March on Washington was the most significant and moving demonstration for freedom and justice in all the history of this country.

JUNE 11, 1963
President Kennedy announces new civil rights proposal

JUNE 12
Assassin kills NAACP leader Medgar Evers

JUNE 22
King meets with Kennedy

AUGUST 28
Addresses the March on Washington for Jobs and Freedom

In the summer of 1963 a great shout for freedom reverberated across the land. It was a shout from the hearts of a people who had been too patient, too long. It was a shout which arose from the North and from the South. It was a shout which reached the ears of a President and stirred him to unprecedented statesmanship. It was a shout which reached the halls of Congress and brought back to the legislative chambers a resumption of the Great Debate. It was a shout which awoke the consciences of millions of white Americans and caused them to examine themselves and to consider the plight of twenty million black disinherited brothers. It was a shout which

brought men of God down out of their pulpits, where they had been preaching only a Sunday kind of love, out into the streets to practice a Monday kind of militancy. Twenty million strong, militant, marching blacks, flanked by legions of white allies, were volunteers in an army which had a will and a purpose—the realization of a new and glorious freedom.

The shout burst into the open in Birmingham. The contagion of the will to be free, the spreading virus of the victory which was proven possible when black people stood and marched together with love in their hearts instead of hate, faith instead of fear—that virus spread from Birmingham across the land and a summer of blazing discontent gave promise of a glorious autumn of racial justice. The Negro revolution was at hand.

Birmingham had made it clear that the fight of the Negro could be won if he moved that fight out to the sidewalks and the streets, down to the city halls and the city jails and—if necessary—into the martyred heroism of a Medgar Evers. The Negro revolution in the South had come of age. It was mature. It was courageous. It was epic—and it was in the American tradition, a much delayed salute to the Bill of Rights, the Declaration of Independence, the Constitution, and the Emancipation Proclamation.

The Negro in the North came to the shocking realization that the subtle and hidden discrimination of the North was as humiliating and vicious as the obvious and overt sins of the South. In the South, the shout was being heard for public rights—nondiscrimination in hotels, motels, schools, parks. In the North, the shout was raised for private advancement—the elimination of de facto school segregation, the wiping out of housing and job discrimination. In Chicago, Illinois, intensified situations involving residential bias came to the fore.

Seen in perspective, the summer of 1963 was historic because it witnessed the first offensive in history launched by Negroes along a broad front. The heroic but spasmodic and isolated slave revolts of the antebellum South had fused, more than a century later, into a simultaneous, massive assault against segregation. And the virtues so long regarded as the exclusive property of the white South—gallantry, loyalty, and pride—had passed to the Negro demonstrators in the heat of the summer's battles.

In assessing the summer's events, some observers have tended to diminish the achievement by treating the demonstrations as an end in themselves. The heroism of the march, the drama of the confrontation, became in their minds the total accomplishment. It is true that these elements have meaning, but to ignore the concrete and specific gains in dismantling the structure of segregation is like noticing the beauty of the rain, but failing to see that it has enriched the soil. A social movement that only moves people is merely a revolt. A movement that changes both people and institutions is a revolution.

The summer of 1963 was a revolution because it changed the face of America. Freedom was contagious. Its fever boiled in nearly one thousand cities, and by the time it had passed its peak, many thousands of lunch counters, hotels, parks, and other places of public accommodation had become integrated.

The sound of the explosion in Birmingham reached all the way to Washington, where the Kennedy administration, which had firmly declared that civil rights legislation would have to be shelved for 1963, hastily reorganized its priorities and placed a strong civil rights bill at the top of the top of the Congressional calendar.

"Free in '63"

The thundering events of the summer required an appropriate climax. The dean of Negro leaders, A. Philip Randolph, whose gifts of imagination and tireless militancy had for decades dramatized the civil rights struggle, once again provided the uniquely suitable answer. He proposed a March on Washington to unite in one luminous action all of the forces along the far-flung front.

It took daring and boldness to embrace the idea. The Negro community was firmly united in demanding a redress of grievances, but it was divided on tactics. It had demonstrated its ability to organize skillfully in single communities, but there was no precedent for a convocation of national scope and gargantuan size. Complicating the situation were innumerable prophets of doom who feared that the slightest incidence of violence would alienate Congress and destroy all hope of legislation. Even without disturbances, they were afraid that inadequate support by Negroes would reveal weaknesses that were better concealed.

The debate on the proposal neatly polarized positions. Those with faith in the Negro's abilities, endurance, and discipline welcomed the challenge. On the other side were the timid, confused, and uncertain friends, along with those who had never believed in the Negro's capacity to organize anything of significance. The conclusion was never really in doubt, because the powerful momentum of the revolutionary summer had swept aside all opposition.

The shout had roared across America. It reached Washington, the nation's capital, on August 28 when more than two hundred thousand people, black and white, people of all faiths, people of every condition of life, stood together before the stone memorial to Abraham Lincoln. The enemies of racial justice had not wanted us to come. The enemies of civil rights legislation had warned us not to come. There were dire predictions of mass rioting and dark Southern hints of retaliation.

Even some friends of our cause had honest fears about our coming. The President of the United States publicly worried about the wisdom of such a project, and congressmen from states in which liberality supposedly prevailed broadly hinted that such a march would have no effect on their deliberative process. The sense of purpose which pervaded preparations for the march had an infectious quality that made liberal whites and leaders of great religious organizations realize that the oncoming march could not be stopped. Like some swelling chorus promising to burst into glorious song, the endorsement and pledges of participation began.

Just as Birmingham had caused President Kennedy to completely reverse his priorities with regard to seeking legislation, so the spirit behind the ensuing march caused him to become a strong ally on its execution. The President's reversal was characterized by a generous and handsome new interest not only in seeing the march take place but in the hope that it would have a solid impact on the Congress.

Washington is a city of spectacles. Every four years imposing Presidential inaugurations attract the great and the mighty. Kings, prime ministers, heroes, and celebrities of every description have been feted there for more than 150 years. But in its entire glittering history, Washington had never seen a spectacle of the size and grandeur that assembled there on August 28, 1963. Among the nearly 250,000 peo-

ple who journeyed that day to the capital, there were many dignitaries and many celebrities, but the stirring emotion came from the mass of ordinary people who stood in majestic dignity as witnesses to their single-minded determination to achieve democracy in their time.

They came from almost every state in the union; they came in every form of transportation; they gave up from one to three days' pay plus the cost of transportation, which for many was a heavy financial sacrifice. They were good-humored and relaxed, yet disciplined and thoughtful. They applauded their leaders generously, but the leaders, in their own hearts, applauded their audience. Many a Negro speaker that day had his respect for his own people deepened as he felt the strength of their dedication. The enormous multitude was the living, beating heart of an indefinitely noble movement. It was an army without guns, but not without strength. It was an army into which no one had to be drafted. It was white, and Negro, and of all ages. It had adherents of every faith, members of every class, every profession, every political party, united by a single ideal. It was a fighting army, but no one could mistake that its most powerful weapon was love.

One significant element of the march was the participation of white churches. Never before had they been so fully, so enthusiastically, so directly involved. One writer observed that the march "brought the country's three major religious faiths closer than any other issue in the nation's peacetime history." I venture to say that no single factor which emerged in the summer of 1963 gave so much momentum to the on-rushing revolution and to its aim of touching the conscience of the nation as the decision of the religious leaders of this country to defy tradition and become an integral part of the quest of the Negro for his rights.

In unhappy contrast, the National Council of the AFL-CIO declined to support the march and adopted a position of neutrality. A number of international unions, however, independently declared their support, and were present in substantial numbers. In addition, hundreds of local unions threw their full weight into the effort.

We had strength because there were so many of us, representing so many more. We had dignity because we knew our cause was just. We had no anger, but we had a passion—a passion for freedom. So

we stood there, facing Mr. Lincoln and facing ourselves and our own destiny and facing the future and facing God.

I prepared my speech partially in New York City and partially in Washington, D.C. The night of the twenty-seventh I got in to Washington about ten o'clock and went to the hotel. I thought through what I would say, and that took an hour or so. Then I put the outline together, and I guess I finished it about midnight. I did not finish the complete text of my speech until 4:00 A.M. on the morning of August 28.

Along with other participant speakers, I was requested by the national March on Washington Committee to furnish the press liaison with a summary or excerpts of my intended speech by the late afternoon or evening of August 27. But, inasmuch as I had not completed my speech by the evening before the march, I did not forward any portion of my remarks which I had prepared until the morning of August 28.

"I have a dream"

I started out reading the speech, and read it down to a point. The audience's response was wonderful that day, and all of a sudden this thing came to me. The previous June, following a peaceful assemblage of thousands of people through the streets of downtown Detroit, Michigan, I had delivered a speech in Cobo Hall, in which I used the phrase "I have a dream." I had used it many times before, and I just felt that I wanted to use it here. I don't know why. I hadn't thought about it before the speech. I used the phrase, and at that point I just turned aside from the manuscript altogether and didn't come back to it.

I am happy to join with you today in what will go down in history as the greatest demonstration for freedom in the history of our nation.

Five score years ago, a great American, in whose symbolic shadow we stand today, signed the Emancipation Proclamation. This momentous decree came as a great beacon light of hope to millions of Negro slaves, who had been seared in the flames of withering injustice. It came as a joyous daybreak to end the long night of their captivity.

But one hundred years later, the Negro still is not free. One hun-

dred years later, the life of the Negro is still sadly crippled by the manacles of segregation and the chains of discrimination. One hundred years later, the Negro lives on a lonely island of poverty in the midst of a vast ocean of material prosperity. One hundred years later, the Negro is still languished in the corners of American society and finds himself an exile in his own land.

And so we've come here today to dramatize a shameful condition. In a sense, we've come to our nation's capital to cash a check. When the architects of our republic wrote the magnificent words of the Constitution and the Declaration of Independence, they were signing a promissory note to which every American was to fall heir. This note was a promise that all men, yes, black men as well as white men, would be guaranteed the unalienable rights of "Life, Liberty and the pursuit of Happiness."

It is obvious today that America has defaulted on this promissory note insofar as her citizens of color are concerned. Instead of honoring this sacred obligation, America has given the Negro people a bad check, a check which has come back marked "insufficient funds." But we refuse to believe that the bank of justice is bankrupt. We refuse to believe that there are insufficient funds in the great vaults of opportunity of this nation. So we've come to cash this check, a check that will give us upon demand the riches of freedom and the security of justice.

We have also come to this hallowed spot to remind America of the fierce urgency of now. This is no time to engage in the luxury of cooling off or to take the tranquilizing drug of gradualism. Now is the time to make real the promises of democracy. Now is the time to rise from the dark and desolate valley of segregation to the sunlit path of racial justice. Now is the time to lift our nation from the quicksands of racial injustice to the solid rock of brotherhood. Now is the time to make justice a reality for all of God's children.

It would be fatal for the nation to overlook the urgency of the moment. This sweltering summer of the Negro's legitimate discontent will not pass until there is an invigorating autumn of freedom and equality. Nineteen sixty-three is not an end but a beginning. Those who hope that the Negro needed to blow off steam and will now be content will have a rude awakening if the nation returns to business as usual.

There will be neither rest nor tranquility in America until the Negro is granted his citizenship rights. The whirlwinds of revolt will continue

to shake the foundations of our nation until the bright day of justice emerges.

But there is something that I must say to my people, who stand on the warm threshold which leads into the palace of justice: in the process of gaining our rightful place, we must not be guilty of wrongful deeds. Let us not seek to satisfy our thirst for freedom by drinking from the cup of bitterness and hatred. We must forever conduct our struggle on the high plane of dignity and discipline. We must not allow our creative protest to degenerate into physical violence. Again and again, we must rise to the majestic heights of meeting physical force with soul force.

The marvelous new militancy which has engulfed the Negro community must not lead us to a distrust of all white people, for many of our white brothers, as evidenced by their presence here today, have come to realize that their destiny is tied up with our destiny. They have come to realize that their freedom is inextricably bound to our freedom. We cannot walk alone. And as we walk, we must make the pledge that we shall always march ahead. We cannot turn back.

There are those who are asking the devotees of civil rights, "When will you be satisfied?" We can never be satisfied as long as the Negro is the victim of the unspeakable horrors of police brutality. We can never be satisfied as long as our bodies, heavy with the fatigue of travel, cannot gain lodging in the motels of the highways and the hotels of the cities. We cannot be satisfied as long as the Negro's basic mobility is from a smaller ghetto to a larger one. We can never be satisfied as long as our children are stripped of their selfhood and robbed of their dignity by signs stating "For Whites Only." We cannot be satisfied as long as a Negro in Mississippi cannot vote and a Negro in New York believes he has nothing for which to vote. No, no, we are not satisfied and we will not be satisfied until justice rolls down like waters and righteousness like a mighty stream.

I am not unmindful that some of you have come here out of great trials and tribulations. Some of you have come fresh from narrow jail cells. Some of you have come from areas where your quest for freedom left you battered by the storms of persecution and staggered by the winds of police brutality. You have been the veterans of creative suffering. Continue to work with the faith that unearned suffering is redemptive.

Go back to Mississippi, go back to Alabama, go back to South Caro-

lina, go back to Georgia, go back to Louisiana, go back to the slums and ghettos of our northern cities, knowing that somehow this situation can and will be changed.

Let us not wallow in the valley of despair. I say to you today, my friends: so even though we face the difficulties of today and tomorrow, I still have a dream. It is a dream deeply rooted in the American dream.

I have a dream that one day this nation will rise up and live out the true meaning of its creed—we hold these truths to be self-evident that all men are created equal.

I have a dream that one day on the red hills of Georgia the sons of former slaves and the sons of former slave owners will be able to sit down together at the table of brotherhood.

I have a dream that one day even the state of Mississippi, a state sweltering with the heat of injustice, sweltering with the heat of oppression, will be transformed into an oasis of freedom and justice.

I have a dream that my four little children will one day live in a nation where they will not be judged by the color of their skin but by the content of their character.

I have a dream today!

I have a dream that one day, down in Alabama, with its vicious racists, with its governor having his lips dripping with the words of interposition and nullification; one day right there in Alabama little black boys and black girls will be able to join hands with little white boys and white girls as sisters and brothers.

I have a dream today!

I have a dream that one day every valley shall be exalted, every hill and mountain shall be made low, the rough places will be made plain and the crooked places will be made straight and the glory of the Lord shall be revealed and all flesh shall see it together.

This is our hope. This is the faith that I will go back to the South with. With this faith we will be able to hew out of the mountain of despair a stone of hope.

With this faith we will be able to transform the jangling discords of our nation into a beautiful symphony of brotherhood. With this faith we will be able to work together, to pray together, to struggle together, to go to jail together, to stand up for freedom together, knowing that we will be free one day.

This will be the day, this will be the day when all of God's children

*will be able to sing with new meaning: "My country 'tis of thee, sweet
land of liberty, of thee I sing. Land where my fathers died, land of the
Pilgrim's pride, from every mountainside, let freedom ring!" And if
America is to be a great nation, this must become true.*

*And so let freedom ring from the prodigious hilltops of New Hamp-
shire.*

Let freedom ring from the mighty mountains of New York.

Let freedom ring from the heightening Alleghenies of Pennsylvania.

Let freedom ring from the snow-capped Rockies of Colorado.

Let freedom ring from the curvaceous slopes of California.

But not only that.

Let freedom ring from Stone Mountain of Georgia.

Let freedom ring from Lookout Mountain of Tennessee.

*Let freedom ring from every hill and molehill of Mississippi, from
every mountainside, let freedom ring!*

*And when this happens, when we allow freedom to ring, when we
let it ring from every village and every hamlet, from every state and
every city, we will be able to speed up that day when all of God's children, black men and white men, Jews and Gentiles, Protestants and
Catholics, will be able to join hands and sing in the words of the old
Negro spiritual, "Free at last, free at last. Thank God Almighty, we are
free at last."*

If anyone had questioned how deeply the summer's activities had
penetrated the consciousness of white America, the answer was evident in the treatment accorded the March on Washington by all the
media of communication. Normally Negro activities are the object
of attention in the press only when they are likely to lead to some
dramatic outbreak, or possess some bizarre quality. The march was
the first organized Negro operation that was accorded respect and
coverage commensurate with its importance. The millions who
viewed it on television were seeing an event historic not only because
of the subject but because it was being brought into their homes.

Millions or white Americans, for the first time, had a clear, long
look at Negroes engaged in a serious occupation. For the first time
millions listened to the informed and thoughtful words of Negro
spokesmen, from all walks of life. The stereotype of the Negro suffered a heavy blow. This was evident in some of the comments,

which reflected surprise at the dignity, the organization, and even the wearing apparel and friendly spirit of the participants. If the press had expected something akin to a minstrel show, or a brawl, or a comic display of odd clothes and bad manners, they were disappointed. A great deal has been said about a dialogue between Negro and white. Genuinely to achieve it requires that all the media of communications open their channels wide as they did on that radiant August day.

As television beamed the image of this extraordinary gathering across the border oceans, everyone who believed in man's capacity to better himself had a moment of inspiration and confidence in the future of the human race. And every dedicated American could be proud that a dynamic experience of democracy in the nation's capital had been made visible to the world.

21

DEATH OF ILLUSIONS

Man's inhumanity to man is not only perpetrated by the vitriolic actions of those who are bad. It is also perpetrated by the vitiating inaction of those who are good.

SEPTEMBER 15, 1963
Dynamite blast kills four young black girls in Sunday school at Birmingham's Sixteenth Street Baptist Church

SEPTEMBER 19
King and other civil rights leaders meet with President John F. Kennedy

SEPTEMBER 22
Delivers eulogy for the four children

NOVEMBER 22
Assassination of President Kennedy; Lyndon B. Johnson becomes president

It would have been pleasant to relate that Birmingham settled down after the storm, and moved constructively to justify the hopes of the many who wished it well. It would have been pleasant, but it would not be true. After partial and grudging compliance with some of the settlement terms, the twentieth-century night riders had yet another bloodthirsty turn on the stage. On one horror-filled September morning they blasted the lives from four innocent girls, at Birmingham's Sixteenth Street Baptist Church: Addie Mae Collins, Denise McNair, Carole Robertson, and Cynthia Wesley. Police killed another child in the streets, and hate-filled white youths climaxed

the day with the wanton murder of a Negro boy harmlessly riding his bicycle.

I shall never forget the grief and bitterness I felt on that terrible September morning. I think of how a woman cried out crunching through broken glass, "My God, we're not even safe in church!" I think of how that explosion blew the face of Jesus Christ from a stained glass window. I can remember thinking, was it all worth it? Was there any hope?

In Birmingham, which we had believed to be a city redeemed, a crucifixion had taken place. The children were the victims of a brutality which echoed around the world. Where was God in the midst of falling bombs?

In every battle for freedom there are martyrs whose lives are forfeited and whose sacrifice endorses the promise of liberty. The girls died as a result of the Holy Crusade of black men to be free. They were not civil rights leaders, as was Medgar Evers. They were not crusaders of justice, as was William Moore—a Baltimore postman who was gunned down as he sought to deliver the message of democracy to the citadel of injustice. They were youngsters—a tiny bit removed from baby food—and babies, we are told, are the latest news from heaven.

So, children are a glorious promise, and no one could tell what those children could have become—another Mary Bethune or Mahalia Jackson. But, they became the most glorious that they could have become. They became symbols of our crusade. They gave their lives to insure our liberty. They did not do this deliberately. They did it because something strange, something incomprehensible to man is reenacted in God's will, and they are home today with God.

"So they did not die in vain"

Perhaps the poverty of conscience of the white majority in Birmingham was most clearly illustrated at the funeral of the child martyrs. No white official attended. No white faces could be seen save for a pathetically few courageous ministers. More than children were buried that day; honor and decency were also interred.

Our tradition, our faith, our loyalty were taxed that day as we

gazed upon the caskets which held the bodies of those children. Some of us could not understand why God permitted death and destruction to come to those who had done no man harm.

This afternoon we gather in the quiet of this sanctuary to pay our last tribute of respect to these beautiful children of God. They entered the stage of history just a few years ago, and in the brief years that they were privileged to act on this mortal stage, they played their parts exceedingly well. Now the curtain falls; they move through the exit; the drama of their earthly life comes to a close. They are now committed back to that eternity from which they came.

These children—unoffending, innocent, and beautiful—were the victims of one of the most vicious, heinous crimes ever perpetrated against humanity.

Yet they died nobly. They are the martyred heroines of a holy crusade for freedom and human dignity. So they have something to say to us in their death. They have something to say to every minister of the gospel who has remained silent behind the safe security of stained-glass windows. They have something to say to every politician who has fed his constituents the stale bread of hatred and the spoiled meat of racism. They have something to say to a federal government that has compromised with the undemocratic practices of Southern Dixiecrats and the blatant hypocrisy of right-wing Northern Republicans. They have something to say to every Negro who passively accepts the evil system of segregation and stands on the sidelines in the midst of a mighty struggle for justice. They say to each of us, black and white alike, that we must substitute courage for caution. They say to us that we must be concerned not merely about who murdered them, but about the system, the way of life, and the philosophy which produced the murderers. Their death says to us that we must work passionately and unrelentingly to make the American dream a reality.

So they did not die in vain. God still has a way of wringing good out of evil. History has proven over and over again that unmerited suffering is redemptive. The innocent blood of these little girls may well serve as the redemptive force that will bring new light to this dark city. The holy Scripture says, "A little child shall lead them." The death of these little children may lead our whole Southland from the low road

of man's inhumanity to man to the high road of peace and brotherhood. These tragic deaths may lead our nation to substitute an aristocracy of character for an aristocracy of color. The spilt blood of these
innocent girls may cause the whole citizenry of Birmingham to transform the negative extremes of a dark past into the positive extremes of
a bright future. Indeed, this tragic event may cause the white South to
come to terms with its conscience.

So in spite of the darkness of this hour we must not despair. We
must not become bitter; nor must we harbor the desire to retaliate with
violence. We must not lose faith in our white brothers. Somehow we
must believe that the most misguided among them can learn to respect
the dignity and worth of all human personality.

May I now say a word to you, the members of the bereaved families.
It is almost impossible to say anything that can console you at this
difficult hour and remove the deep clouds of disappointment which are
floating in your mental skies. But I hope you can find a little consolation from the universality of this experience. Death comes to every
individual. There is an amazing democracy about death. It is not an
aristocracy for some of the people, but a democracy for all of the people.
Kings die and beggars die; rich men die and poor men die; old people
die and young people die; death comes to the innocent and it comes to
the guilty. Death is the irreducible common denominator of all men.

I hope you can find some consolation from Christianity's affirmation that death is not the end. Death is not a period that ends the great
sentence of life, but a comma that punctuates it to more lofty significance. Death is not a blind alley that leads the human race into a state
of nothingness, but an open door which leads man into life eternal. Let
this daring faith, this great invincible surmise, be your sustaining power
during these trying days.

"Accomplices to murder"

As did most citizens of the United States, I looked to the White
House for solace in this moment of crisis. The White House could
never restore the lives of these four unoffending children. But, in my
mind and in my heart and in my soul, there was a dream and a hope
that out of this unbelievable horror would come lasting good. When
the President summoned me and leaders of the Birmingham move-

ment to confer with him, this dream became more poignant and this hope more real.

We come to you today because we feel that the Birmingham situation is so serious that it threatens not only the life and stability of Birmingham and Alabama but our whole nation. The destiny of our nation is involved. We feel that Birmingham has reached a state of civil disorder. There are many things that would justify our coming to this conclusion.

The real problem that we face is this: the Negro community is about to reach a breaking point and a great deal of frustration is there and confusion. And there is a feeling of being alone and not being protected. If you walk the streets, you are not safe; if you stay at home, you are not safe; if you are in church, you are not safe. So that the Negro feels that everywhere he goes that if he remains stationary, he is in danger of some physical problem.

Now this presents a real problem for those of us who find ourselves in leadership positions, because we are preaching the philosophy and method of nonviolence. We have been consistent in standing up for nonviolence. But more and more we are faced with the problem of our people saying, "What's the use?" And we find it a little more difficult to get over nonviolence. And I am convinced that if something isn't done to give the Negro a new sense of hope and a sense of protection, there is a danger we will face the worse race riot we have ever seen in this country.

When I left the White House, I left with an almost audacious faith that, finally, something positive, something definitive, something real would be done by the leadership of this nation to redeem the community in which horror had come to make its home. I exercised what I believed to be a tremendous restraint. In doing so, I acted contrary to the wishes of those who had marched with me in the dangerous campaigns for freedom. I was certain that my silence and restraint were misunderstood by many who were loyal enough not to express their doubts. I did this because I was naive enough to believe that the proof of good faith would emerge.

It became obvious that this was a mistake. It began to become obvious when I realized that the mayor who had wept on television had not even had the common decency to come or to send an emissary to the funerals of these murdered innocents. I looked back and

noted that the administration itself endorsed the pattern of segregation by having separate—and I wonder if they were equal—meetings with the white and colored leadership. The presidential envoys seemed to believe that, by meeting with white people at one hour and Negroes at another, they could bring about a redemptive understanding. This, we knew, they could not do. This, surely, the President must have understood, was impossible.

CHRISTMAS LETTER TO THE FAMILY OF DENISE MCNAIR

Dear Mr. and Mrs. McNair:

Here in the midst of the Christmas season my thoughts have turned to you. This has been a difficult year for you. The coming Christmas, when the family bonds are normally more closely knit, makes the loss you have sustained even more painful. Yet, with the sad memories there are the memories of the good days when Denise was with you and your family.

As you know, many of us are giving up our Christmas as a memorial for the great sacrifices made this year in the Freedom Struggle. I know there is nothing that can compensate for the vacant place in your family circle, but we did want to share a part of our sacrifice this year with you. Perhaps there is some small thing dear to your heart in which this gift can play a part.

We knew, when we went into Birmingham, that this was the test, the acid test of whether the Negro Revolution would succeed. If the forces of reaction which were seeking to nullify and cancel out all of the gains made in Birmingham were allowed to triumph, the day was lost in this battle for freedom. We were faced with an extreme situation, and our remedies had to be extreme.

I fear that, from the White House down to the crocodile-weeping city administration of Birmingham, the intent and the intensity of the Negro has been misunderstood. So, I must serve notice on this nation, I must serve notice on the White House. I must serve notice on the city administration of Birmingham. I must serve notice on the conscience of the American people. On August 28, we had marched on our capital. It was a peaceful march; it was a quiet march; it was a tranquil march. And I am afraid that some people, from the White House down, misunderstood the peace and the quiet and the tranquility of that march.

They must have believed that it meant that the Revolution was all over, that its fires were quenched, that its marvelous militancy had died. They could have made no greater error. Our passion to be free; our determination to walk with dignity and justice have never abated. We are more determined than ever before that nonviolence is the way. Let them bring on their bombs. Let them sabotage us with the evil of cooperation with segregation. We intend to be free.

"Assassinated by a morally inclement climate"

Negroes tragically know political assassination well. In the life of Negro civil rights leaders, the whine of the bullet from ambush, the roar of the bomb have all too often broken the night's silence. They have replaced lynching as a political weapon. More than a decade ago, sudden death came to Mr. and Mrs. Harry T. Moore, NAACP leaders in Florida. The Reverend George Lee of Belzoni, Mississippi, was shot to death on the steps of a rural courthouse. The bombings multiplied. Nineteen sixty-three was a year of assassinations. Medgar Evers in Jackson, Mississippi; William Moore in Alabama; six Negro children in Birmingham—and who could doubt that these too were political assassinations?

The unforgivable default of our society has been its failure to apprehend the assassins. It is a harsh judgment, but undeniably true, that the cause of the indifference was the identity of the victims. Nearly all were Negroes. And so the plague spread until it claimed the most eminent American, a warmly loved and respected President. The words of Jesus, "Inasmuch as ye have done it unto one of the least of these my brethren, ye have done it unto me" were more than a figurative expression; they were a literal prophecy.

Men everywhere were stunned into sober confusion at the news of the assassination of President Jack Kennedy. We watched the thirty-fifth President of our nation go down like a great cedar. The personal loss was deep and crushing; the loss to the world was overpowering. It is still difficult to believe that one so saturated with vim, vitality, and vigor is no longer in our midst.

President Kennedy was a strongly contrasted personality. There were in fact two John Kennedys. One presided in the first two years under pressure of the uncertainty caused by his razor-thin margin

of victory. He vacillated, trying to sense the direction his leadership could travel while retaining and building support for his administration. However, in 1963, a new Kennedy had emerged. He had found that public opinion was not in a rigid mold. American political thought was not committed to conservatism, nor radicalism, nor moderation. It was above all fluid. As such it contained trends rather than hard lines, and affirmative leadership could guide it into constructive channels.

President Kennedy was not given to sentimental expressions of feeling. He had, however, a deep grasp of the dynamics of and the necessity for social change. His work for international amity was a bold effort on a world scale. His last speech on race relations was the most earnest, human, and profound appeal for understanding and justice that any President has uttered since the first days of the republic. Uniting his flair for leadership with a program of social progress, he was at his death undergoing a transformation from a hesitant leader with unsure goals to a strong figure with deeply appealing objectives.

The epitaph of John Kennedy reveals that he was a leader unafraid of change. He came to the presidency in one of the most turbulent and cataclysmic periods of human history, a time when the problems of the world were gigantic in intent and chaotic in detail. On the international scene there was the ominous threat of mankind being plunged into the abyss of nuclear annihilation. On the domestic scene the nation was reaping the harvest of its terrible injustice toward the Negro. John Kennedy met these problems with a depth of concern, a breath of intelligence, and a keen sense of history. He had the courage to be a friend of civil rights and a stalwart advocate of peace. The unmistakable cause of the sincere grief expressed by so many millions was more than simple emotion. It revealed that President Kennedy had become a symbol of people's yearnings for justice, economic well-being, and peace.

Our nation should do a great deal of soul-searching as a result of President Kennedy's assassination. The shot that came from the fifth-story building cannot be easily dismissed as the isolated act of a madman. Honesty impels us to look beyond the demented mind that executed this dastardly act. While the question "Who killed President

Kennedy?" is important, the question "What killed him?" is more important.

Our late President was assassinated by a morally inclement climate. It is a climate filled with heavy torrents of false accusation, jostling winds of hatred, and raging storms of violence.

It is a climate where men cannot disagree without being disagreeable, and where they express dissent through violence and murder. It is the same climate that murdered Medgar Evers in Mississippi and six innocent Negro children in Birmingham, Alabama.

So in a sense we are all participants in that horrible act that tarnished the image of our nation. By our silence, by our willingness to compromise principle, by our constant attempt to cure the cancer of racial injustice with the Vaseline of gradualism, by our readiness to allow arms to be purchased at will and fired at whim, by allowing our movie and television screens to teach our children that the hero is one who masters the art of shooting and the technique of killing, by allowing all these developments, we have created an atmosphere in which violence and hatred have become popular pastimes.

So President Kennedy has something important to say to each of us in his death. He has something to say to every politician who has fed his constituents the stale bread of racism and the spoiled meat of hatred. He has something to say to every clergyman who observed racial evils and remained silent behind the safe security of stained glass windows. He has something to say to the devotees of the extreme right who poured out venomous words against the Supreme Court and the United Nations, and branded everyone a communist with whom they disagree. He has something to say to a misguided philosophy of communism that would teach man that the end justifies the means, and that violence and the denial of basic freedom are justifiable methods to achieve the goal of a classless society.

He says to all of us that this virus of hate that has seeped into the veins of our nation, if unchecked, will lead inevitably to our moral and spiritual doom.

Thus the epitaph of John Kennedy's life illuminates profound truths that challenge us to set aside our grief of a season and move forward with more determination to rid our nation of the vestiges of racial segregation and discrimination.

The assassination of President Kennedy killed not only a man but a complex of illusions. It demolished the myth that hate and violence can be confined in an airtight chamber to be employed against but a few. Suddenly the truth was revealed that hate is a contagion; that it grows and spreads as a disease; that no society is so healthy that it can automatically maintain its immunity. If a smallpox epidemic had been raging in the South, President Kennedy would have been urged to avoid the area. There was a plague afflicting the South, but its perils were not perceived.

We were all involved in the death of John Kennedy. We tolerated hate; we tolerated the sick simulation of violence in all walks of life; and we tolerated the differential application of law, which said that a man's life was sacred only if we agreed with his views. This may explain the cascading grief that flooded the country in late November. We mourned a man who had become the pride of the nation, but we grieved as well for ourselves because we knew we were sick.

22

ST. AUGUSTINE

The bill now pending in Congress is the child of a storm, the product of the most turbulent motion the nation has ever known in peacetime.

FEBRUARY 9, 1964
Segregationist violence prompts St. Augustine, Florida, civil rights leader Robert Hayling to invite SCLC to join struggle

MAY 28
After the jailing of hundreds of demonstrators in St. Augustine, King appeals for outside assistance

JUNE 11
After King's arrest in St. Augustine, bi-racial committee is formed

JUNE
Why We Can't Wait is published

JULY 2
Attends the signing of Civil Rights Act of 1964

When 1963 came to a close, more than a few skeptical voices asked what substantial progress had been achieved through the demonstrations that had drawn more than a million Negroes into the streets. By the close of 1964, the pessimistic clamor was stilled by the music of major victories. Taken together, the two years marked a historical turning point for the civil rights movement; in the previous century no comparable change for the Negro had occurred. Now, even the most cynical acknowledged that at Birmingham, as at Concord, a shot had been fired that was heard around the world.

In the bursting mood that had overtaken the Negro, the words "compromise" and "retreat" were profane and pernicious. Our revolution was genuine because it was born from the same womb that always gives birth to massive social upheavals—the womb of intolerable conditions and unendurable situations. The Negro was determined to liberate himself. His cry for justice had hardened into a palpable, irresistible force. He was unwilling to retrogress or even mark time.

The mainstay of the SCLC program was still in the area of nonviolent direct action. Our feeling was that this method, more than any other, was the best way to raise the problems of the Negro people and the injustices of our social order before the court of world opinion, and to require action.

"Four Hundred Years of Bigotry and Hate"

St. Augustine, Florida, a beautiful town and our nation's oldest city, was the scene of raging tempers, flaring violence, and the most corrupt coalition of segregationist opposition outside of Mississippi. It was a stronghold of the Ku Klux Klan and the John Birch Society. There the Klan made a last-ditch stand against the nonviolent movement. They flocked to St. Augustine's Slave Market Plaza from all across north Florida, Georgia, and Alabama. Klansmen abducted four Negroes and beat them unconscious with clubs, ax handles, and pistol butts.

Florida responded out of a concern for its tourist trade. But when Governor Bryant realized that justice was the price to be paid for a good image, he resorted to the Old South line of attempting to crush those seeking their constitutional rights. Only Judge Bryan Simpson of the federal district court, a Republican appointee, proved to be free enough of the "system" to preserve constitutional rights for St. Augustine's Negroes.

SCLC came to St. Augustine at the request of the local unit which was seeking: (1) a bi-racial committee; (2) desegregation of public accommodations; (3) hiring of policemen, firemen, and office workers in municipal jobs; and (4) dropping of charges against persons peacefully protesting for their constitutional rights.

St. Augustine was a testing ground. Can the Deep South change?

Could southern states maintain law and order in the face of change? Could local citizens, black and white, work together to make democracy a reality throughout America? These were the questions the nonviolent movement sought to answer with a resounding: "Yes—God willing!"

Once in St. Augustine, SCLC uncovered a sore of hatred, violence, and ignorance which spread its venom throughout the business and political life of Florida and reached subtly into the White House. St. Augustine's 3,700 Negro citizens waged a heroic campaign in the midst of savage violence and brutality condoned and committed by police. We faced some lawlessness and violence that we hadn't faced before, even in Birmingham. Night after night, Negroes marched by the hundreds amidst showers of bricks, bottles, and insults. Day by day, Negroes confronted restaurants, beaches, and the Slave Market where they spoke and sang of their determination to be free.

After several months of raging violence in America's oldest city, in which more than three hundred SCLC-led demonstrators were arrested and scores of others injured by Klansmen wielding tire chains and other weapons, we were able to proclaim a relative victory in that rock-bound bastion of segregation and discrimination.

In combination with the local defense fund, we began to pave the way for compliance with the civil rights bill and rush through its passage. The legal and action strategies together had given us a body of precedent for dealing with hard-core communities who allowed vigilante mobs to preserve the Old South traditions.

We communicated with state and federal officials concerning conditions in St. Augustine. After tireless efforts, we succeeded in getting the governor of the state to persuade four distinguished citizens of St. Augustine to serve on a biracial committee to discuss ways to solve the racial problems of St. Augustine. In order to demonstrate our good faith, and show that we were not seeking to wreck St. Augustine, as some mistakenly believed, we agreed to call off demonstrations while the committee sought to work out a settlement. As the saying goes, "Every thousand-mile journey begins with the first step." This development was merely the first step in a long journey toward freedom and justice in St. Augustine, but it was an

important first step, for it at least opened the channels of communication—something that St. Augustine needed for so long.

When we left St. Augustine, we were about to get a civil rights bill that would become the law of the land. The Civil Rights Act was signed by President Lyndon Johnson two days before the Fourth of July. The businessmen in St. Augustine said before we left that they would comply with the civil rights bill, and we were very happy about this. It represented a degree of progress, and I said to myself maybe St. Augustine is now coming to terms with its conscience.

"A legislative achievement of rare quality"

Both houses of Congress approved a monumental, indeed, historic affirmation of Jefferson's ringing truth that "all men are created equal." First recommended and promoted by President Kennedy, this bill was passed because of the overwhelming support and perseverance of millions of Americans, Negro and white. It came as a bright interlude in the long and sometimes turbulent struggle for civil rights: the beginning of a second emancipation proclamation providing a comprehensive legal basis for equality of opportunity. With the bill's passage, we stood at an auspicious position, a momentous time for thanksgiving and rededication, rather than intoxication and relaxation. The bill was born of the "blood, sweat, toil, and tears" of countless congressmen of both major parties, legions of amateur lobbyists, and great volumes of grassroots sentiment. Supporters, black and white, did themselves honor as they sowed the seeds of protest and political persuasion, reaping this glorious harvest in law. Furthermore, the bill's germination could be traced to the Negro revolt of 1963, epitomized in Birmingham's fire hoses, police dogs, and thousands of "not-to-be-denied" demonstrations; to the massive militancy of the majestic March on Washington; to a martyred President; to his successor, a Southern-sired President who carried on and enhanced the Kennedy legacy; and to the memories of bygone martyrs whose blood was shed so that America might find remission for her sins of segregation.

I had been fortunate enough to meet Lyndon Johnson during his tenure as vice president. He was not then a presidential aspirant, and he was searching for his role under a man who not only had a four-

year term to complete but was confidently expected to serve out yet another term as chief executive. Therefore, the essential issues were easier to reach, and were unclouded by political considerations.

His approach to the problem of civil rights was not identical with mine—nor had I expected it to be. Yet his careful practicality was nonetheless clearly no mask to conceal indifference. His emotional and intellectual involvement were genuine and devoid of adornment. It was conspicuous that he was searching for a solution to a problem he knew to be a major shortcoming in American life. I came away strengthened in my conviction that an undifferentiated approach to white Southerners could be a grave error, all too easy for Negro leaders in the heat of bitterness. Later, it was Vice President Johnson I had in mind when I wrote in *The Nation* that the white South was splitting, and that progress could be furthered by driving a wedge between the rigid segregationists and the new white elements whose love of their land was stronger than the grip of old habits and customs.

The dimensions of Johnson's leadership spread from a region to a nation. His expressions, public and private, indicated that he had a comprehensive grasp of contemporary problems. He saw that poverty and unemployment were grave and growing catastrophes, and he was aware that those caught most fiercely in the grip of this economic holocaust were Negroes. Therefore, he had set the twin goal of a battle against discrimination within the war on poverty.

I had no doubt that we might continue to differ concerning the tempo and the tactical design required to combat the impending crisis. But I did not doubt that the President was approaching the solution with sincerity, with realism, and thus far with wisdom. I hoped his course would be straight and true. I would do everything in my power to make it so by outspoken agreement whenever proper, and determined opposition whenever necessary.

I had the good fortune of standing there with President Johnson when he signed that bill. Certainly one of the things that I will hold among my most cherished possessions is the pen that President Johnson used to sign this bill. It was a great moment. The legislature had joined the judiciary's long line of decisions invalidating state-compelled segregation, and the office of the President with its great tradition of executive actions, including Lincoln's Emancipation

Proclamation, Roosevelt's war decree banning employment discrimination, Truman's mandate ending segregated Armed Forces units, and Kennedy's order banning discrimination in federally aided housing.

"Legislation was first written in the streets"

Would the slower processes of legislation and law enforcement ultimately have accomplished greater results more painlessly? Demonstrations, experience has shown, are part of the process of stimulating legislation and law enforcement. The federal government reacts to events more quickly when a situation of conflict cries out for its intervention. Beyond this, demonstrations have a creative effect on the social and psychological climate that is not matched by the legislative process. Those who have lived under the corrosive humiliation of daily intimidation are imbued by demonstrations with a sense of courage and dignity that strengthen their personalities. Through demonstrations, Negroes learn that unity and militance have more force than bullets. They find that the bruises of clubs, electric cattle prods, and fists hurt less than the scars of submission. And segregationists learn from demonstrations that Negroes who have been taught to fear can also be taught to be fearless. Finally, the millions of Americans on the sidelines learn that inhumanity wears an official badge and wields the power of law in large areas of the democratic nation of their pride.

What specifically did we accomplish in 1963–64? The Civil Rights Act of 1964 is important even beyond its far-reaching provisions. It is historic because its enhancement was generated by a massive coalition of white and Negro forces. Congress was aroused from a century of slumber to a legislative achievement of rare quality. These multitudinous sponsors to its enactment explain why sections of the Civil Rights Act were complied with so hastily even in some hard-core centers of the South.

The Civil Rights Act was expected by many to suffer the fate of the Supreme Court decisions on school desegregation. In particular, it was thought that the issue of public accommodations would encounter massive defiance. But this pessimism overlooked a factor of supreme importance. The legislation was not a product of the char-

ity of white America for a supine black America, nor was it the result of enlightened leadership by the judiciary. This legislation was first written in the streets. The epic thrust of the millions of Negroes who demonstrated in 1963 in hundreds of cities won strong white allies to the cause. Together they created a "coalition of conscience" which awoke a hitherto somnolent Congress. The legislation was polished and refined in the marble halls of Congress, but the vivid marks of its origin in the turmoil of mass meetings and marches were on it, and the vigor and momentum of its turbulent birth carried past the voting and insured substantial compliance.

Apart from its own provisions, the new law stimulated and focused attention on economic needs. An assault on poverty was planned. The fusing of economic measures with civil rights needs; the boldness to penetrate every region of the Old South; and the undergirding of the whole by the massive Negro vote, both North and South, all placed the freedom struggle on a new elevated level.

23

THE MISSISSIPPI CHALLENGE

The future of the United States of America may well be determined here, in Mississippi, for it is here that Democracy faces its most serious challenge. Can we have government in Mississippi which represents all of the people? This is the question that must be answered in the affirmative if these United States are to continue to give moral leadership to the Free World.

JUNE 21, 1964
On the eve of the "Freedom Summer" campaign in Mississippi, three civil rights workers are reported missing after their arrest in Philadelphia, Mississippi

JULY 16
King asserts that nomination of Senator Barry Goldwater by Republicans will aid racists

JULY 20
Arrives in Mississippi to assist civil rights effort

AUGUST 4
The bodies of missing civil rights workers are discovered

AUGUST 22
Testifies at Democratic convention on behalf of Mississippi Freedom Democratic Party

In 1964 the meaning of so-called Negro revolution became clear for all to see and was given legislative recognition in the civil rights law. Yet, immediately following the passage of this law, a series

of events shook the nation, compelling the grim realization that the revolution would continue inexorably until total slavery had been replaced by total freedom.

The new events to which I refer were: the Republican Convention held in San Francisco; the hideous triple lynchings in Mississippi; and the outbreak of riots in several Northern cities.

The Republican Party geared its appeal and program to racism, reaction, and extremism. All people of goodwill viewed with alarm and concern the frenzied wedding at the Cow Palace of the KKK with the radical right. The "best man" at this ceremony was a senator whose voting record, philosophy, and program were anathema to all the hard-won achievements of the past decade.

It was both unfortunate and disastrous that the Republican Party nominated Barry Goldwater as its candidate for President of the United States. In foreign policy Mr. Goldwater advocated a narrow nationalism, a crippling isolationism, and a trigger-happy attitude that could plunge the whole world into the dark abyss of annihilation. On social and economic issues, Mr. Goldwater represented an unrealistic conservatism that was totally out of touch with the realities of the twentieth century. The issue of poverty compelled the attention of all citizens of our country. Senator Goldwater had neither the concern nor the comprehension necessary to grapple with this problem of poverty in the fashion that the historical moment dictated. On the urgent issue of civil rights, Senator Goldwater represented a philosophy that was morally indefensible and socially suicidal. While not himself a racist, Mr. Goldwater articulated a philosophy which gave aid and comfort to the racist. His candidacy and philosophy would serve as an umbrella under which extremists of all stripes would stand. In the light of these facts and because of my love for America, I had no alternative but to urge every Negro and white person of goodwill to vote against Mr. Goldwater and to withdraw support from any Republican candidate that did not publicly disassociate himself from Senator Goldwater and his philosophy.

While I had followed a policy of not endorsing political candidates, I felt that the prospect of Senator Goldwater being President of the United States so threatened the health, morality, and survival

of our nation, that I could not in good conscience fail to take a stand against what he represented.

The celebration of final enactment of the civil rights bill curdled and soured. Rejoicing was replaced by a deep and frightening concern that the counter-forces to Negro liberation could flagrantly nominate for the highest office in the land one who openly clasped the racist hand of Strom Thurmond. A cold fear touched the hearts of twenty million Negroes. They had only begun to come out of the dark land of Egypt where so many of their brothers were still in bondage—still denied elementary dignity. The forces to bar the freedom road, to drive us back to Egypt, seemed so formidable, so high in authority, and so determined.

"Mississippi's New Negroes"

A handsome young Negro, dressed in slacks and short-sleeve shirt, wiped his brow and addressed the police chief, "Now look here, chief, there's no need in trying to blow at us. Everybody scared of white folks has moved north, and you just as well realize that you've got to do right by the rest of us."

This comment by Aaron Henry of Clarksdale, Mississippi, was typical of Mississippi's New Negroes. And in spite of the threat of death, economic reprisals, and continuous intimidation, they were pressing hard toward the high call of freedom.

The remarkable thing was that the Negro in Mississippi had found for himself an effective way to deal with his problems and had organized efforts across the entire state. As part of SCLC's "people-to-people" program, several members of our staff and I had traveled the fertile and sometimes depressing Mississippi Delta country in 1962. That trip provided me with an opportunity to talk with thousands of people on a personal basis. I talked with them on the farms and in the village stores, on the city streets and in the city churches. I listened to their problems, learned of their fears, felt the yearnings of their hope.

There were some flesh-and-blood scenes that I can never dispel from my memory. One of our earliest stops was a Catholic school that included the elementary and high school grades. The sister in charge in each classroom asked the question, "Where are you going

tonight?" The answer was chorused, "To the Baptist Church!" They were referring to the Baptist Church where I was to speak for the mass meeting. The sister had urged them to attend. How marvelous that the struggle for freedom and human dignity rose above the communions of Catholic and Protestant. This was a bit of the hope that I glimpsed in the Mississippi Delta. Then, of course, there was the pathos. How sobering it was to meet people who work only six months in the year and whose annual income averaged $500 to $600.

Along with the economic exploitation that the whole state of Mississippi inflicts upon the Negro, there was the ever-present problem of physical violence. As we rode along the dusty roads of the Delta country, our companions cited unbelievable cases of police brutality and incidents of Negroes being brutally murdered by white mobs.

In spite of this, there was a ray of hope. This ray of hope was seen in the new determination of the Negroes themselves to be free.

Under the leadership of Bob Moses, a team of more than a thousand Northern white students and local Negro citizens had instituted a program of voter registration and political action that was one of the most creative attempts I had seen to radically change the oppressive life of the Negro in that entire state and possibly the entire nation. The Negroes in Mississippi had begun to learn that change would come in that lawless, brutal police state only as Negroes reformed the political structure of the area. They had begun this reform in 1964 through the Freedom Democratic Party.

The enormity of the task was inescapable. We would have had to put the field staffs of SCLC, NAACP, CORE, SNCC, and a few other agencies to work in the Delta alone. However, no matter how big and difficult a task it was, we began. We encouraged our people in Mississippi to rise up by the hundreds and thousands and demand their freedom—now!

Nothing had inspired me so much for some time as my tour of Mississippi in July 1964 on behalf of the Mississippi Freedom Democratic Party. These were a great people who had survived a concentration camp existence by the sheer power of their souls. They had no money, no guns, very few votes and yet they were then the number-one power in the nation; for they were organized and

moving by the thousands to rid the nation of its most violent racist element.

When I was about to visit Mississippi, I was told that a sort of guerrilla group was plotting to take my life during the visit. I was urged to cancel the trip, but I decided that I had no alternative but to go on into Mississippi, because I had a job to do. If I were constantly worried about death, I could not function. After a while, if your life is more or less constantly in peril, you come to a point where you accept the possibility of death philosophically.

We landed in Greenwood, the home of Byron de la Beckwith, indicted murderer of Medgar Evers. The sullen white crowd stood on one side of the gate and a cheering integrated crowd on the other. Two years ago this would not have been possible, for the first white persons to work in civil rights were thrown in jail for eating in a Negro restaurant.

We spent five days touring Jackson, Vicksburg, and Meridian. We walked the streets, preached on front porches, at mass meetings, or in the pool halls, and always God's children flocked by the thousands to learn of freedom. We stopped off in Philadelphia and visited the burned church which Andrew Goodman, James Chaney, and Michael Schwerner were investigating when they were so savagely murdered in June.

I was proud to be with the workers of the Council of Federated Organizations and students of the Summer Project, to work with them through the Freedom Democratic Party to make democracy a reality. Those young people made up a domestic Peace Corps. Our nation had sent our Peace Corps volunteers throughout the underdeveloped nations of the world and none of them had experienced the kind of brutality and savagery that the voter registration workers suffered in Mississippi.

The church burnings, harassment, and murders in this state were direct results of the fact that Negro citizens could not vote and participate in electing responsible public officials who would protect the rights of all the people. Many thousands had tried to register—in spite of violence, economic reprisals, and other forms of intimidation—yet in 1963 only 1,636 Negro persons were registered in the entire state.

The federal government had a choice of working toward the gradual political reform of Mississippi through the civil process and through representative institutions such as the Freedom Democratic Party, or to send federal troops anytime a constitutional issue arose. The Freedom Democratic Party hoped to unite all persons of good-will in the state of Mississippi under the platform and program of the National Democratic Party. We intended to send a delegation to Atlantic City and urge that they be seated. Our nation needed at least one party which was free of racism, and the National Democratic Party could make a significant step in this direction by recognizing the Mississippi Freedom Democratic Party as the official Mississippi delegation.

"Beacon light of hope"

Everyone expected the Democratic Convention to be very dull and routine. Lyndon Johnson would name his running mate personally, and there were no issues which loomed as controversial enough to stir the convention. But everyone underestimated the Mississippi Freedom Democratic Party. The group of sixty-eight Negroes from Mississippi descended on the convention with a display of power, which even Lyndon Johnson had difficulty coping with. Their power was the moral power on which this nation was built. They deliberately ignored the man-made rules of the convention and appealed directly to the heart and soul of America and her people. What we experienced in Atlantic City was a classical illustration of the power of nonviolence, in the political arena. Many Americans became aware of the facts for the first time as the Mississippi Freedom Democratic Party took its case before the nation and the credentials committee of the National Democratic Party.

The people of Mississippi knew they were in a police state. They realized that politics provided the avenue for educating their children, providing homes and jobs for their families, and literally making over the whole climate of the state of Mississippi. This is a lesson that all Americans needed to learn, especially those of us who had been deprived because of color.

Ladies and Gentlemen of the Credentials Committee, if you value the future of democratic government, you have no alternative but to recognize, with full voice and vote, the Mississippi Freedom Democratic Party.

This is in no way a threat. It is the most urgent moral appeal that I can make to you. The question cannot be decided by the splitting of legal hairs or by seemingly expedient political compromises. For what seems to be expedient today will certainly prove disastrous tomorrow, unless it is based on a sound moral foundation.

This is no empty moral admonition. The history of men and of nations has proven that failure to give men the right to vote, to govern themselves and to select their own representatives brings certain chaos to the social, economic, and political institution which allows such an injustice to prevail.

And finally this is no mean issue. The recognition of the Mississippi Freedom Democratic Party has assumed symbolic value for oppressed people the world over. Seating this delegation would become symbolic of the intention of this country to bring freedom and democracy to all people. It would be a declaration of political independence to under-privileged citizens long denied a voice in their own destinies. It would be a beacon light of hope for all the disenfranchised millions of this earth whether they be in Mississippi and Alabama, behind the Iron Curtain, floundering in the mire of South African apartheid, or freedom-seeking persons in Cuba. Recognition of the Freedom Democratic Party would say to them that somewhere in this world there is a nation that cares about justice, that lives in a democracy, and that insures the rights of the downtrodden.

The Freedom Democratic Party found itself immersed in the world of practical politics almost immediately. The strong moral appeal before the credentials committee had to be backed up with political support. The following days involved gaining enough persons on the committee to submit a minority report before the convention body, and then enough states to support us to demand a roll call vote which would make each state take sides openly. In general the sentiment of the convention was for the Freedom Party, but the fact that Lyndon Johnson had to run against Goldwater made everybody cautious, lest the entire South bolt the party with Mississippi.

Finally, a compromise emerged which required the regular party to take a loyalty oath, and granted delegate-at-large status to two of the Freedom Party. This was a significant step. It was not a great victory, but it was symbolic, and it involved the pledge of high party officials to work with the Freedom Party for the next four years to gain registered voters and political strength in Mississippi. But there was no compromise for these persons who had risked their lives to get this far. Had I been a member of the delegation, I would probably have advised them to accept this as an offer in good faith and attempted to work to strengthen their position. But life in Mississippi had involved too many compromises already, and too many promises had come from Washington for them to take these seriously; so their skepticism must be viewed sympathetically.

We will never forget Aaron Henry and Fannie Lou Hamer. Their testimony educated a nation and brought the political powers to their knees in repentance, for the convention voted never again to seat a delegation that was racially segregated. But the true test of their message would be whether or not Negroes in Northern cities heard them and would register and vote.

"Promising aspects of the elections"

In San Francisco, the Republican Party had taken a giant stride away from its Lincoln tradition, and the results of election day graphically illustrate how tragic this was for the two-party system in America. Those who sought to turn back the tide of history suffered a bitter defeat, and in the process degraded themselves and their party in a manner seldom witnessed on our national political scene. The forces of goodwill and progress dealt a telling blow to the fanaticism of the right, and Americans swallowed their prejudices in the interests of progress, prosperity, and world peace.

One of the more promising aspects of the election was that the grand alliance of labor, civil rights forces, intellectual and religious leaders was provided with its second major victory within a year. This was the coalition which had to continue to grow in depth and breadth, if we were to overcome the problems which confronted us.

President Johnson had the opportunity to complete the job which was started by Roosevelt and interrupted by the war. Our very

survival as a nation depended on the success of several rather radical reforms. The key to progress was still to be found in the states which President Johnson lost to Goldwater. Until the Southern power block was broken and the committees of our Congress freed from the domination of racists and reactionaries within the Democratic Party, we could not expect the kind of imagination and creativity which this period in history demanded from our federal government.

The problems of poverty, urban life, unemployment, education, housing, medical care, and flexible foreign policy were dependent on positive and forthright action from the federal government. But so long as men like Senators Eastland, Russell, Byrd, and Ellender held the positions of power in our Congress, the entire progress of our nation was in as grave a danger as the election of Senator Goldwater might have produced. The battle was far from won. It had only begun. The main burden of reform would still be upon the Negro.

24

THE NOBEL
PEACE PRIZE

*Occasionally in life there are those moments of unutterable fulfill-
ment which cannot be completely explained by those symbols called
words. Their meaning can only be articulated by the inaudible language of the heart.*

DECEMBER 10, 1964
King receives Nobel Peace Prize in Oslo

DECEMBER 11
Delivers Nobel Lecture at University of Oslo

JANUARY 27, 1965
Integrated dinner in Atlanta honors King

After many months of exhausting activity in the civil rights movement, I had reluctantly checked into the hospital for a rest and
complete physical check-up. The following morning I was awakened
by a telephone call from my wife. She had received a call from a New
York television network. It had been announced in Oslo, Norway,
by the Norwegian Parliament that I was the recipient of the Nobel
Prize for Peace for 1964.

My eyes were hardly open, and I could not be sure whether this
was merely a dream or if I was hearing correctly. I was stunned at
first. I had known of my nomination for this honor, but in the rush
of responsibilities of a movement such as ours, one does not have
time to contemplate honors, so I was quite unprepared psychologically.

But then I realized that this was no mere recognition of the contribution of one man on the stage of history. It was a testimony to the magnificent drama of the civil rights movement and the thousands of actors who had played their roles extremely well. In truth, it is these "noble" people who had won this Nobel Prize.

"A reward for the ground crew"

Many friends, members of my congregation, staff members of the Southern Christian Leadership Conference—and just people in various cities—asked me the same question: "How does it feel to win the Nobel Peace Prize, the world's most coveted award? What does it mean to you?"

I felt so humbly grateful to have been selected for this distinguished honor that it was hard to form in my mind a lucid manner of expressing "what it meant to me." Sitting in my church study, plunged into one of those rare periods of solitude and contemplation, I found the answer.

I recalled that, some years ago, I was seated in a huge jet at O'Hare Field in Chicago. In a matter of moments, the mighty plane was to take off for Los Angeles. From the speaker we heard the announcement that there would be a delay in departure. There was some mechanical difficulty which would be repaired within a brief time. Looking out of the window, I saw half a dozen men approaching the plane. They were dressed in dirty, greasy overalls. They assembled around the plane and began to work. Someone told me this was the ground crew.

All during that flight, I am sure that there were some on the plane who were grateful for our competent pilot. Others were aware that there was an able co-pilot. The stewardesses were charming and gracious. I am sure that many of the passengers were conscious of the pilot, the co-pilot, and the stewardesses. But, in my mind, first and foremost, was the memory of the ground crew.

There are many wonderful pilots today, charting the sometimes rocky, sometimes smooth course of human progress; pilots like Roy Wilkins and Whitney Young and A. Philip Randolph. And yet, if it were not for the ground crew, the struggle for human dignity and social justice would not be in orbit.

That is why I thought of the Nobel Peace Prize as a prize, a reward, for the ground crew: fifty thousand Negro people in Montgomery, Alabama, who came to discover that it is better to walk in dignity than to ride in buses; the students all over this nation who, in sitting down in restaurants and department stores were actually standing up for the true American Dream; the Freedom Riders who knew that this nation cannot hope to conquer outer space until the hearts of its citizens have won inner peace; Medgar Evers, slain; the three Mississippi martyrs, slain; Americans, colored and white, who marched on Washington.

In the final analysis, it must be said that this Nobel Prize was won by a movement of great people, whose discipline, wise restraint, and majestic courage has led them down a nonviolent course in seeking to establish a reign of justice and a rule of love across this nation of ours: Herbert Lee, Fannie Lou Hamer, Medgar Evers, Chaney, Goodman and Schwerner, and the thousands of children in Birmingham, Albany, St. Augustine, and Savannah who had accepted physical blows and jail and had discovered that the power of the soul is greater than the might of violence. These unknown thousands had given this movement the international acclaim, which we received from the Norwegian Parliament.

Members of the ground crew would not win the Nobel Peace Prize. Their names would not go down in history. They were unknown soldiers in the second great American Revolution. Yet, when years have rolled past and when the blazing light of truth is focused on this marvelous age in which we are now living—men and women will know and children will be taught that we have a finer land, a better people, a more noble civilization—because of the ground crew which made possible the jet flight to the clear skies of brotherhood. On December 10 in Oslo, I would receive—for the ground crew—a significant symbol, which was not for me, really.

I was greatly humbled, yet tremendously gratified by the visit to Oslo for the Nobel Prize. The response to our cause in London, Stockholm, and Paris, as well as in Oslo, was far beyond even my imagination. These great world capitals looked upon racism in this nation with horror and revulsion, but also with a certain amount of hope that America could solve this problem and point the way to

the rest of the world. I assured them that this was our intention in the civil rights movement and among those forces within the churches and the labor and intellectual communities who have pledged themselves to this challenge.

The Nobel Prize for Peace placed a new dimension in the civil rights struggle. It reminded us graphically that the tide of world opinion was in our favor. Though people of color are a minority here in America, there are billions of colored people who look to the United States and to her Negro population to demonstrate that color is no obstacle or burden in the modern world.

The nations of Northern Europe had proudly aligned themselves with our struggle and challenged the myths of race the world over. This was the promise of a strong international alliance for peace and brotherhood in the world. Northern Europe, Africa, and Latin America all indicated a willingness to confront the problem of racism in the world. This was the starting point of a peaceful world. The Negro had to look abroad also. Poverty and hunger were not peculiar to Harlem and the Mississippi Delta. India, Mexico, the Congo, and many other nations faced essentially the same problems that we faced.

From the moment it was announced that the Norwegian Parliament had chosen me as winner of the 1964 Prize, demands for my involvement in national and international affairs began to mushroom. En route to Oslo I had the opportunity to discuss racial matters with the lord chancellor of Britain and with members of the British Parliament. I also participated in the organization of a movement to bring together colored people in the London area. It included West Indians, Pakistanis, Indians, and Africans who, together, were fighting racial injustice in Britain.

In our struggle for freedom and justice in the U.S., which has also been so long and arduous, we feel a powerful sense of identification with those in the far more deadly struggle for freedom in South Africa. We know how Africans there, and their friends of other races, strove for half a century to win their freedom by nonviolent methods. We have honored Chief Lutuli for his leadership, and we know how this nonviolence was only met by increasing violence from the State, increasing repression, culminating in the shootings of Sharpeville and all that has happened since.

Playing baseball with son Martin III in 1964. (© 1986 – Flip Schulke. All reproduction and/or storage rights reserved)

Playing with youngest
daughter Bernice.

Eating Sunday supper with
family, with photograph of
Mahatma Gandhi overhead.

With youngest son Dexter. (© 1986 – Flip Schulke. All reproduction and/or storage rights
reserved)

"I fought hard to hold back the tears. My emotions were about to overflow." Displaying the Nobel Prize medallion after ceremony in December 1964. (AP/Wide World)

"I would rather die on the highways of Alabama than make a butchery of my conscience." Marching from Selma to Montgomery in 1965. (AP/Wide World)

"Segregation is on its deathbed in Alabama and the only thing uncertain about it is how costly the segregationists and Wallace will make the funeral." Attacked while attempting to register at the Hotel Albert in Selma. (AP/Wide World)

"The same president who told me in his office that it was impossible to get a voting rights bill was on television calling for the passage of a voting rights bill in Congress. And it did pass two months later." President Lyndon Johnson offering the pen with which he signed into law the Voting Rights Act of 1965. (Archive Photos)

"One young man said to me, 'We won!' I said, 'What do you mean, "We won"?'"
Speaking to residents of Watts after the riots in 1965. (Corbis)

With *(left to right)* Simone Signoret, Harry Belafonte, Yves Montand, Professor Jacques Monod, and Coretta at 1966 civil rights rally. (Agence France Presse/Archive Photos)

(overleaf)
"I am in Birmingham because injustice is here." Serving a five-day prison sentence in 1967 for contempt of court, resulting from Birmingham demonstrations of 1963. (Corbis)

Today great leaders—Nelson Mandela and Robert Sobukwé—are among the hundreds wasting away in Robben Island prison. Against the massively armed and ruthless State, which uses torture and sadistic forms of interrogation to crush human beings—even driving some to suicide—the militant opposition inside South Africa seems for the moment to be silenced.

It is in this situation, with the great mass of South Africans denied their humanity, denied their dignity, denied opportunity, denied all human rights; it is in this situation, with many of the bravest and best South Africans serving long years in prison, with some already executed; in this situation we in America and Britain have a unique responsibility. For it is we, through our investments, through our governments' failure to act decisively, who are guilty of bolstering up the South African tyranny.

Our responsibility presents us with a unique opportunity. We can join in the one form of nonviolent action that could bring freedom and justice to South Africa, the action which African leaders have appealed for: a massive movement for economic sanctions.

"I accept this award with an abiding faith"

This was, for most of us, our first trip to Scandinavia, and we looked forward to making many new friends. We felt we had much to learn from Scandinavia's democratic socialist tradition and from the manner in which they had overcome many of the social and economic problems that still plagued far more powerful and affluent nations. In both Norway and Sweden, whose economies are literally dwarfed by the size of our affluence and the extent of our technology, they have no unemployment and no slums. Their men, women, and children have long enjoyed free medical care and quality education. This contrast to the limited, halting steps taken by our rich nation deeply troubled me.

I brought greetings from many Americans of goodwill, Negro and white, who were committed to the struggle for brotherhood and to the crusade for world peace. On their behalf I had come to Oslo to accept the Nobel Peace Prize. It was indeed a privilege to receive the Nobel Prize on behalf of the nonviolent movement, and I

pledged that the entire prize of approximately $54,000 would be used to further the movement.

I accept this award today with an abiding faith in America and an audacious faith in the future of mankind. I refuse to accept the idea that the "is-ness" of man's present nature makes him morally incapable of reaching up for the eternal "ought-ness" that forever confronts him. I refuse to accept the idea that man is mere flotsam and jetsam in the river of life which surrounds him. I refuse to accept the view that mankind is so tragically bound to the starless midnight of racism and war that the bright daybreak of peace and brotherhood can never become a reality. I believe that even amid today's mortar bursts and whining bullets, there is still hope for a brighter tomorrow. I believe that wounded justice, lying prostrate on the blood-flowing streets of our nations, can be lifted from this dust of shame to reign supreme among the children of men. I have the audacity to believe that peoples everywhere can have three meals a day for their bodies, education and culture for their minds, and dignity, equality, and freedom for their spirits. I believe that what self-centered men have torn down, other-centered men can build up. I still believe that one day mankind will bow down before the altars of God and be crowned triumphant over war and bloodshed, and nonviolent redemptive goodwill will proclaim the rule of the land. I still believe that we shall overcome. This faith can give us courage to face the uncertainties of the future. It will give our tired feet new strength as we continue our forward stride toward the City of Freedom.

Today I come to Oslo as a trustee, inspired and with renewed dedication to humanity. I accept this prize on behalf of all men who love peace and brotherhood.

I fought hard to hold back the tears. My emotions were about to overflow. Whatever I was, I owed to my family and to all those who struggled with me. But my biggest debt I owed to my wife. She was the one who gave my life meaning. All I could pledge to her, and to all those millions, was that I would do all I could to justify the faith that she, and they, had in me. I would try more than ever to make my life one of which she, and they, could be proud. I would do in private that which I knew my public responsibility demanded.

"What now?"

The Nobel Peace Prize was a proud honor, but not one with which we began a "season of satisfaction" in the civil rights movement. We

returned from Oslo not with our heads in the clouds, congratulating ourselves for marvelous yesterdays and tempted to declare a holiday in our struggle, but with feet even more firmly on the ground, convictions strengthened and determinations driven by dreams of greater and brighter tomorrows.

In accepting the 1964 Nobel Peace Prize, I asked why such an honor had been awarded to a movement which remained beleaguered and committed to unrelenting struggle; to a movement which was surging forward with majestic scorn for risk and danger; to a movement which had not won the very peace and brotherhood which were the essence of Count Alfred Nobel's great legacy.

I suggested then that the prize was not given merely as recognition of past achievement, but also as recognition, a more profound recognition, that the nonviolent way, the American Negro's way, was the answer to the crucial political and moral question of our time: the need for man to overcome oppression and violence without resorting to violence and oppression.

In almost every press conference after my return from Oslo I was asked, "What now? In what direction is the civil rights movement headed?" I could not, of course, speak to for the entire civil rights movement. There were several pilots; I was but one, and the organization of which I was president, the Southern Christian Leadership

---

LECTURE AT UNIVERSITY OF OSLO

The time has come for an all-out world war against poverty. The rich nations must use their vast resources of wealth to develop the underdeveloped, school the unschooled, and feed the unfed. Ultimately a great nation is a compassionate nation. No individual or nation can be great if it does not have a concern for "the least of these." Deeply etched in the fiber of our religious tradition is the conviction that men are made in the image of God and that they are souls of infinite metaphysical value, the heirs of a legacy of dignity and worth. If we feel this as a profound moral fact, we cannot be content to see men hungry, to see men victimized with starvation and ill health when we have the means to help them. The wealthy nations must go all out to bridge the gulf between the rich minority and the poor majority.

December 11, 1964

Conference, was, mainly, a Southern organization seeking solutions to the peculiar problems of the South.

Pressure continued to build for SCLC to open offices in various cities of the North. We reached a decision on this after the "Jobs and Freedom Tour" of ten Northern cities that spring. Even though SCLC's main base of operations remained in the South, where we could most effectively assault the roots of racial evils, we became involved to a much greater extent with the problems of the urban North.

On another level, I now had to give a great deal of attention to the three problems which I considered as the largest of those that confront mankind: racial injustice around the world, poverty, and war. Though each appeared to be separate and isolated, all were interwoven into a single garment of man's destiny.

Whatever measure of influence I had as a result of the importance which the world attaches to the Nobel Peace Prize would have to be used to bring the philosophy of nonviolence to all the world's people who grapple with the age-old problem of racial injustice. I would have to somehow convince them of the effectiveness of this weapon that cuts without wounding, this weapon that ennobles the man who wields it.

I found myself thinking more and more about what I consider mankind's second great evil: the evil of poverty. This is an evil which exists in Indiana as well as in India; in New Orleans as well as in New Delhi.

Cannot we agree that the time has indeed come for an all-out war on poverty—not merely in President Johnson's "Great Society," but in every town and village of the world where this nagging evil exists? Poverty—especially that found among thirty-five million persons in the United States—is a tragic deficit of human will. We have, it seems, shut the poor out of our minds and driven them from the mainstream of our society. We have allowed the poor to become invisible, and we have become angry when they make their presence felt. But just as nonviolence has exposed the ugliness of racial injustice, we must now find ways to expose and heal the sickness of poverty—not just its symptoms, but its basic causes.

The third great evil confronting mankind was one about which I was deeply concerned. It was the evil of war. At Oslo I suggested that

the philosophy and strategy of nonviolence become immediately a subject for study and serious experimentation in every field of human conflict, including relations between nations. This was not, I believed, an unrealistic suggestion.

World peace through nonviolent means is neither absurd nor unattainable. All other methods have failed. Thus we must begin anew. Nonviolence is a good starting point. Those of us who believe in this method can be voices of reason, sanity, and understanding amid the voices of violence, hatred, and emotion. We can very well set a mood of peace out of which a system of peace can be built.

Racial injustice around the world. Poverty. War. When man solves these three great problems he will have squared his moral progress with his scientific progress. And, more importantly, he will have learned the practical art of living in harmony.

The Nobel Peace Prize had given me even deeper personal faith that man would indeed rise to the occasion and give new direction to an age drifting rapidly to its doom.

Wherever I traveled abroad, I had been made aware that America's integrity in all of its world endeavors was being weighed on the scales of racial justice. This was dramatically and tragically evidenced when that travesty of lawlessness and callousness in Meridian, Mississippi, was headlined in Oslo on the very day of the Nobel Peace Prize ceremonies. On the same day the civil rights movement was receiving the Nobel Peace Prize, a U.S. commissioner in Mississippi dismissed charges against nineteen of the men arrested by the FBI in connection with the brutal slaying of three civil rights voter registration workers in Mississippi the previous summer. I was convinced that the whole national conscience must be mobilized to deal with the tragic situation of violence, terror, and blatant failure of justice in Mississippi. We considered calling for a nationwide boycott of Mississippi products.

Aside from the proposed boycott, however, there was a more immediate opportunity for Congress to speak out in a way that would remedy the root cause of Mississippi's injustices—the total denial of the right to vote to her Negro citizens. On Monday, January 4, 1965, the House of Representatives had the opportunity to challenge the seating of the entire Mississippi delegation in the

ADDRESS AT RECOGNITION DINNER IN ATLANTA

I must confess that I have enjoyed being on this mountaintop and I am tempted to want to stay here and retreat to a more quiet and serene life. But something within reminds me that the valley calls me in spite of all its agonies, dangers, and frustrating moments. I must return to the valley. Something tells me that the ultimate test of a man is not where he stands in moments of comfort and moments of convenience, but where he stands in moments of challenge and moments of controversy. So I must return to the valley—a valley filled with misguided bloodthirsty mobs, but a valley filled at the same time with little Negro boys and girls who grow up with ominous clouds of inferiority forming in their little mental skies; a valley filled with millions of people who, because of economic deprivation and social isolation, have lost hope, and see life as a long and desolate corridor with no exit sign. I must return to the valley—a valley filled with literally thousands of Negroes in Alabama and Mississippi who are brutalized, intimidated, and sometimes killed when they seek to register and vote. I must return to the valley all over the South and in the big cities of the North—a valley filled with millions of our white and Negro brothers who are smothering in an airtight cage of poverty in the midst of an affluent society.

January 27, 1965

House. Under the provisions of the Act of February 23, 1870, readmitting Mississippi to representation in the Congress, it was stipulated that the principal condition for readmission was that all citizens twenty-one years or older, who had resided in the state for six months or more and who were neither convicts nor insane, be allowed to vote freely. Mississippi had deliberately and repeatedly ignored this solemn pact with the nation for more than fifty years and maintained seats to which she was not entitled in an indifferent Congress. The conscience of America, troubled by the twin Mississippi tragedies of the presence of violence and the absence of law, could have expressed itself in supporting this moral challenge to immoral representation.

25

MALCOLM X

He was an eloquent spokesman for his point of view and no one can honestly doubt that Malcolm had a great concern for the problems that we face as a race. While we did not always see eye to eye on methods to solve the race problems, I always had a deep affection for Malcolm and felt that he had the great ability to put his finger on the existence and root of the problem.

MARCH 26, 1964
After press conference at U.S. Senate, King has brief encounter with Malcolm X

FEBRUARY 5, 1965
Coretta Scott King meets with Malcolm X in Selma, Alabama

FEBRUARY 21
Malcolm X is assassinated in Harlem

I met Malcolm X once in Washington, but circumstances didn't enable me to talk with him for more than a minute.

He is very articulate, but I totally disagree with many of his political and philosophical views—at least insofar as I understand where he now stands. I don't want to sound self-righteous, or absolutist, or that I think I have the only truth, the only way. Maybe he does *have some of the answers. I know that I have often wished that he would talk less of violence, because violence is not going to solve our problem. And, in his litany of articulating the despair of the Negro without offering any positive, creative alternative, I feel that Malcolm has done himself and our*

people a great disservice. Fiery, demagogic oratory in the black ghettos, urging Negroes to arm themselves and prepare to engage in violence, as he has done, can reap nothing but grief.

In the event of a violent revolution, we would be sorely outnumbered. And when it was all over, the Negro would face the same unchanged conditions, the same squalor and deprivation—the only difference being that his bitterness would be even more intense, his disenchantment even more abject. Thus, in purely practical as well as moral terms, the American Negro has no rational alternative to nonviolence.

When they threw eggs at me in New York, I think that was really a result of the Black Nationalist groups. They had heard all of these things about my being soft, my talking about love, and they transferred that bitterness toward the white man to me. They began to feel that I was saying to love this person that they had such a bitter attitude toward. In fact, Malcolm X had a meeting the day before, and he talked about me a great deal and told them that I would be there the next night and said, "You ought to go over there and let old King know what you think about him." And he had said a great deal about nonviolence, criticizing nonviolence, and saying that I approved of Negro men and women being bitten by dogs and the firehoses. So I think this kind of response grew out of all of the talk about my being a sort of polished Uncle Tom.

My feeling has always been that they have never understood what I was saying. They did not see that there's a great deal of difference between nonresistance to evil and nonviolent resistance. Certainly I'm not saying that you sit down and patiently accept injustice. I'm talking about a very strong force, where you stand up with all your might against an evil system, and you're not a coward. You are resisting, but you come to see that tactically as well as morally it is better to be nonviolent. Even if one didn't want to deal with the moral question, it would just be impractical for the Negro to talk about making his struggle violent.

But I think one must understand that Malcolm X was a victim of the despair that came into being as a result of a society that gives so many Negroes the nagging sense of "nobody-ness." Just as one condemns the philosophy, which I did constantly, one must be as

vigorous in condemning the continued existence in our society of the conditions of racist injustice, depression, and man's inhumanity to man.

"A product of the hate and violence"

The ghastly nightmare of violence and counter-violence is one of the most tragic blots to occur on the pages of the Negro's history in this country. In many ways, however, it is typical of the misplacement of aggressions which has occurred throughout the frustrated circumstances of our existence.

How often have the frustrations of second-class citizenship and humiliating status led us into blind outrage against each other and the real cause and course of our dilemma been ignored? It is sadly ironic that those who so clearly pointed to the white world as the seed of evil should now spend their energies in their own destruction.

Malcolm X came to the fore as a public figure partially as a result of a TV documentary entitled "The Hate That Hate Produced." That title points clearly to the nature of Malcolm's life and death. He was clearly a product of the hate and violence invested in the Negro's blighted existence in this nation. He, like so many of our number, was a victim of the despair that inevitably derives from the conditions of oppression, poverty, and injustice which engulf the masses of our race. But in his youth, there was no hope, no preaching, teaching, or movements of nonviolence. He was too young for the Garvey Movement, too poor to be a Communist—for the Communists geared their work to Negro intellectuals and labor without realizing that the masses of Negroes were unrelated to either—and yet he possessed a native intelligence and drive which demanded an outlet and means of expression. He turned first to the underworld, but this did not fulfill the quest for meaning which grips young minds. It was a testimony to Malcolm's personal depth and integrity that he could not become an underworld czar, but turned again and again to religion for meaning and destiny. Malcolm was still turning and growing at the time of his brutal and meaningless assassination.

* * *

I was in jail when he was in Selma, Alabama. I couldn't block his coming, but my philosophy was so antithetical to the philosophy of Malcolm X that I would never have invited Malcolm X to come to Selma when we were in the midst of a nonviolent demonstration. This says nothing about the personal respect I had for him.

During his visit to Selma, he spoke at length to my wife Coretta about his personal struggles and expressed an interest in working more closely with the nonviolent movement, but he was not yet able to renounce violence and overcome the bitterness which life had invested in him. There were also indications of an interest in politics as a way of dealing with the problems of the Negro. All of these were signs of a man of passion and zeal seeking for a program through which he could channel his talents.

But history would not have it so. A man who lived under the torment of knowledge of the rape of his grandmother and murder of his father under the conditions of the present social order, does not readily accept that social order or seek to integrate into it. And so Malcolm was forced to live and die as an outsider, a victim of the violence that spawned him, and which he courted through his brief but promising life.

The assassination of Malcolm X was an unfortunate tragedy. Let us learn from this tragic nightmare that violence and hate only breed violence and hate, and that Jesus' word still goes out to every potential Peter, "Put up thy sword." Certainly we will continue to disagree, but we must disagree without becoming violently disagreeable. We will still suffer the temptation to bitterness, but we must learn that hate is too great a burden to bear for a people moving on toward their date with destiny.

The American Negro cannot afford to destroy its leadership. Men of talent are too scarce to be destroyed by envy, greed, and tribal rivalry before they reach their full maturity. Like the murder of Patrice Lamumba in the Congo, the murder of Malcolm X deprived the world of a potentially great leader. I could not agree with either of these men, but I could see in them a capacity for leadership which I could respect and which was only beginning to mature in judgment and statesmanship.

I think it is even more unfortunate that this great tragedy occurred at a time when Malcolm X was reevaluating his own philo-

sophical presuppositions and moving toward a greater understanding of the nonviolent movement and toward more tolerance of white people generally.

I think there is a lesson that we can all learn from this: that violence is impractical and that now, more than ever before, we must pursue the course of nonviolence to achieve a reign of justice and a rule of love in our society, and that hatred and violence must be cast into the unending limbo if we are to survive.

In a real sense, the growth of black nationalism was symptomatic of the deeper unrest, discontent, and frustration of many Negroes because of the continued existence of racial discrimination. Black nationalism was a way out of that dilemma. It was based on an unrealistic and sectional perspective that I condemned both publicly and privately. It substituted the tyranny of black supremacy for the tyranny of white supremacy. I always contended that we as a race must not seek to rise from a position of disadvantage to one of advantage, but to create a moral balance in society where democracy and brotherhood would be a reality for all men.

26

SELMA

In 1965 the issue is the right to vote and the place is Selma, Alabama. In Selma, we see a classic pattern of disenfranchisement typical of the Southern Black Belt areas where Negroes are in the majority.

FEBRUARY 1, 1965
King is jailed with more than two hundred others after voting rights march in Selma, Alabama

FEBRUARY 26
Jimmie Lee Jackson dies after being shot by police during demonstration in Marion, Alabama

MARCH 7
Voting rights marchers are beaten at Edmund Pettus Bridge

MARCH 11
Rev. James Reeb dies after beating by white racists

MARCH 25
Selma-to-Montgomery march concludes with address by King; hours afterward, Klan night riders kill Viola Gregg Liuzzo while she transports marchers back to Selma

When I was coming from Scandinavia in December 1964, I stopped by to see President Johnson and we talked about a lot of things, but finally we started talking about voting.

And he said, "Martin, you're right about that. I'm going to do it eventually, but I can't get a voting rights bill through in this session of Congress." He said, "Now, there's some other bills that I have here that I want to get through in my Great Society program, and I

think in the long run they'll help Negroes more, as much as a voting rights bill. And let's get those through and then the other."

I said, "Well, you know, political reform is as necessary as anything if we're going to solve all these other problems."

"I can't get it through," he said, "because I need the votes of the Southern bloc to get these other things through. And if I present a voting rights bill, they will block the whole program. So it's just not the wise and the politically expedient thing to do."

I left simply saying, "Well, we'll just have to do the best we can."

I left the mountaintop of Oslo and the mountaintop of the White House, and two weeks later went on down to the valley of Selma, Alabama, with Ralph Abernathy and the others. Something happened down there. Three months later, the same President who told me in his office that it was impossible to get a voting rights bill was on television singing in speaking terms, "We Shall Overcome," and calling for the passage of a voting rights bill in Congress. And it did pass two months later.

The President said nothing could be done. But we started a movement.

"The ugly pattern of denial"

Selma, Alabama, was to 1965 what Birmingham was to 1963. The right to vote was the issue, replacing public accommodation as the mass concern of a people hungry for a place in the sun and a voice in their destiny.

In Selma, thousands of Negroes were courageously providing dramatic witness to the evil forces that bar our way to the all-important ballot box. They were laying bare for all the nation to see, for all the world to know, the nature of segregationist resistance. The ugly pattern of denial flourished with insignificant differences in thousands of Alabama, Louisiana, Mississippi, and other Southern communities.

The pattern of denial depended upon four main roadblocks.

First, there was the Gestapo-like control of county and local government by the likes of Sheriff Jim Clark of Selma, and Sheriff Rainey of Philadelphia, Mississippi. There was a carefully cultivated

mystique behind the power and brutality of these men. The gun, the club, and the cattle prod produced the fear that was the main barrier to voting—a barrier erected by 345 years' exposure to the psychology and brutality of slavery and legal segregation. It was a fear rooted in feelings of inferiority.

Secondly, city ordinances were contrived to make it difficult for Negroes to move in concert. So-called parade ordinances and local laws making public meetings subject to surveillance and harassment by public officials were used to keep Negroes from working out a group plan of action against injustice. These laws deliberately ignored and defied the First Amendment of our Constitution.

After so many years of intimidation, the Negro community had learned that its only salvation was in united action. When one Negro stood up, he was run out of town; if a thousand stood up together, the situation was bound to be drastically overhauled.

The third link in the chain of slavery was the slow pace of the registrar and the limited number of days and hours during which the office was open. Out of 15,000 Negroes eligible to vote in Selma and the surrounding Dallas County, less than 350 were registered. This was the reason why the protest against the limited number of opportunities for registration had to continue.

The fourth link in the chain of disenfranchisement was the literacy test. This test was designed to be difficult, and the Justice Department had been able to establish that in a great many counties these tests were not administered fairly.

Clearly, the heart of the voting problem lay in the fact that the machinery for enforcing this basic right was in the hands of state-appointed officials answerable to the very people who believed they could continue to wield power in the South only so long as the Negro was disenfranchised. No matter how many loopholes were plugged, no matter how many irregularities were exposed, it was plain that the federal government must withdraw that control from the states or else set up machinery for policing it effectively.

The patchwork reforms brought about by the laws of 1957, 1960, and 1964 had helped, but the denial of suffrage had gone on too long, and had caused too deep a hurt for Negroes to wait out the time required by slow, piecemeal enforcement procedures. What was

needed was the new voting rights legislation promised for the 1965 session of Congress.

Our Direct Action Department, under the direction of Rev. James Bevel, then decided to attack the very heart of the political structure of the state of Alabama and the Southland through a campaign for the right to vote. Planning for the voter registration project in Selma started around the seventeenth of December, 1964, but the actual project started on the second of January, 1965. Our affiliate organization, the Dallas County Voters League, invited us to aid and assist in getting more Negroes registered to vote. We planned to have Freedom Days, days of testing and challenge, to arouse people all over the community. We decided that on the days that the county and the state had designated as registration days, we would assemble at the Brown Chapel A.M.E. Church and walk together to the courthouse. More than three thousand were arrested in Selma and Marion together. I was arrested in one of those periods when we were seeking to go to the courthouse.

"Selma Jail"

When the king of Norway participated in awarding the Nobel Peace Prize to me he surely did not think that in less than sixty days I would be in jail. They were little aware of the unfinished business in the South. By jailing hundreds of Negroes, the city of Selma, Alabama, had revealed the persisting ugliness of segregation to the nation and the world.

When the Civil Rights Act of 1964 was passed, many decent Americans were lulled into complacency because they thought the day of difficult struggle was over. But apart from voting rights, merely to be a person in Selma was not easy. When reporters asked Sheriff Clark if a woman defendant was married, he replied, "She's a nigger woman and she hasn't got a Miss or a Mrs. in front of her name."

This was the U.S.A. in 1965. We were in jail simply because we could not tolerate these conditions for ourselves or our nation. There was a clear and urgent need for new and improved federal

◆

INSTRUCTIONS FROM SELMA JAIL TO MOVEMENT ASSOCIATES

Do following to keep national attention focused on Selma:

1. *Joe Lowery:* Make a call to Florida Governor Leroy Collins and urge him to make a personal visit to Selma, to talk with city and county authorities concerning speedier registration and more days for registering.

2. *Walter Fauntroy:* Follow through on suggestion of having a congressional delegation to come in for personal investigation. They should also make an appearance at a mass meeting if they come.

3. *Lowery, via Lee White:* Make a personal call to President Johnson and urge him to intervene in some way (send a personal emissary to Selma, get the Justice Department involved, make a plea to Dallas and Selma officials in a press conference).

4. *Chuck Jones:* Urge lawyers to go to the 5th Circuit if Judge Thomas does not issue an immediate injunction against the continued arrests and speed up registration.

5. *Bernard Lafayette:* Keep some activity alive every day this week.

6. Consider a night march to the city jail protesting my arrest. Have another march to the courthouse to let Clark show true colors.

7. Stretch every point to get teachers to march.

8. *Clarence Jones:* Immediately post bond for staff members essential for mobilization who are arrested.

9. *Atlanta Office:* Call C. T. Vivian and have him return from California in case other staff is put out of circulation.

12. Local Selma editor sent a telegram to the President calling for a Congressional committee to come out and study the situation of Selma. We should join in calling for this. By all means, we cannot let them get the offensive. I feel they were trying to give the impression that they were orderly and that Selma was a good community because they integrated public accommodations. We have to insist that voting is the issue and here Selma has dirty hands. We should not be too soft. We have the offensive. We cannot let Baker control our movement. In a crisis, we needed a sense of drama.

13. Ralph to call Sammy Davis and ask him to do a Sunday benefit in Atlanta to raise money for the Alabama project. I find that all of these fellows respond better when I am in a jail or in a crisis.

February 1965

◆

legislation and for expanded law enforcement measures to finally eliminate all barriers to the right to vote.

A brief statement I read to the press tried to interpret what we sought to do:

For the past month the Negro citizens of Selma and Dallas County have been attempting to register by the hundreds. To date only 57 persons have entered the registrar's office, while 280 have been jailed. Of the 57 who have attempted to register, none have received notice of successful registration, and we have no reason to hope that they will be registered. The registration test is so difficult and so ridiculous that even Chief Justice Warren might fail to answer some questions.

In the past year Negroes have been beaten by Sheriff Clark and his posse, they have been fired from their jobs, they have been victimized by the slow registration procedure and the difficult literacy test, all because they have attempted to vote.

Now we must call a halt to these injustices. Good men of the nation cannot sit idly by while the democratic process is defied and prostituted in the interests of racists. Our nation has declared war against totalitarianism around the world, and we call upon President Johnson, Governor Wallace, the Supreme Court, and the Congress of this great nation to declare war against oppression and totalitarianism within the shores of our country.

If Negroes could vote, there would be no Jim Clarks, there would be no oppressive poverty directed against Negroes. Our children would not be crippled by segregated schools, and the whole community might live together in harmony.

This is our intention: to declare war on the evils of demagoguery. The entire community will join in this protest, and we will not relent until there is a change in the voting process and the establishment of democracy.

When I left jail in Selma on Friday, February 5, I stated that I would fly to Washington. On Tuesday afternoon I met with Vice President Hubert H. Humphrey in his capacity as chairman of the newly created Council for Equal Opportunity and with Attorney General Nicholas Katzenbach. My colleagues and I made clear to the vice president and the attorney general our conviction that all citizens must be free to exercise their right and responsibility to vote

without delays, harassment, economic intimidation, and police brutality.

I indicated that while there had been some progress in several Southern states in voter registration in previous years, in other states, new crippling legislation had been instituted since 1957 precisely to frustrate Negro registration. At a recent press conference President Johnson stated that another evil was the "slow pace of registration for Negroes." This snail's pace was clearly illustrated by the ugly events in Selma. Were this pace to continue, it would take another hundred years before all eligible Negro voters were registered.

There were many more Negroes in jail in Selma than there were Negroes registered to vote. This slow pace was not accidental. It was the result of a calculated and well-defined pattern which used many devices and tactics to maintain white political power in many areas of the South. I emphatically stated that the problem of securing voting rights could not be cured by patchwork or piecemeal legislation programs. We needed a basic legislative program to insure procedures for achieving the registration of Negroes in the South without delay or harassment. I expressed my conviction that the voting sections of the 1957, 1960, and 1964 Civil Rights Acts were inadequate to secure voting rights for Negroes in many key areas of the South.

I told Mr. Humphrey and General Katzenbach how pleased I was that the Department of Justice had under consideration legislation pertaining to voting which would implement President Johnson's State of the Union declaration, namely: "I propose we eliminate every remaining obstacle in the right and opportunity to vote."

I asked the attorney general to seek an injunction against the prosecution of the more than three thousand Negro citizens of Selma, who otherwise would face years of expensive and frustrating litigation before the exercise of their guaranteed right to vote was vindicated. Moreover, to the extent that existing laws were inadequate or doubtful to accomplish this all-important purpose, I asked the vice president and the attorney general to include in the administration's legislative program new procedures which would invest the attorney general and private citizens with the power to avoid the oppression and delays of spurious state court prosecution.

In a meeting with President Johnson, Vice President Humphrey,

Attorney General Katzenbach, and Florida Governor Leroy Collins, chairman of the newly created Community Relations Service, I urged the administration to offer a voting rights bill which would secure the right to vote without delay and harassment.

"Events leading to the confrontation"

During the course of our struggle to achieve voting rights for Negroes in Selma, Alabama, it was reported that a "delicate understanding" existed between myself, Alabama state officials, and the federal government to avoid the scheduled march to Montgomery on Tuesday, March 9.

On the basis of news reports of my testimony in support of our petition for an injunction against state officials, it was interpreted in some quarters that I worked with the federal government to throttle the indignation of white clergymen and Negroes. I was concerned about this perversion of the facts, and for the record would like to sketch in the background of the events leading to the confrontation of marchers and Alabama state troopers at Pettus Bridge in Selma, and our subsequent peaceful turning back.

The goal of the demonstrations in Selma, as elsewhere, was to dramatize the existence of injustice and to bring about the presence of justice by methods of nonviolence. Long years of experience indicated to us that Negroes could achieve this goal when four things occured:

1. nonviolent demonstrators go into the streets to exercise their constitutional rights;
2. racists resist by unleashing violence against them;
3. Americans of good conscience in the name of decency demand federal intervention and legislation;
4. the administration, under mass pressure, initiates measures of immediate intervention and supports remedial legislation.

The working out of this process has never been simple or tranquil. When nonviolent protests were countered by local authorities with harassment, intimidation, and brutality, the federal government always first asked the Negro to desist and leave the streets rather than bring pressure to bear on those who commit the crimi-

nal acts. We were always compelled to reject vigorously such federal requests and relied on our allies, the millions of Americans across the nation, to bring pressure on the federal government for protective action in our behalf. Our position always was that there is a wrong and right side to the questions of full freedom and equality for millions of Negro Americans and that the federal government did not belong in the middle on this issue.

During our nonviolent direct-action campaigns we were advised, and again we were so advised in Selma, that violence might ensue. Herein lay a dilemma: of course, there always was the likelihood that, because of the hostility to our demonstrations, acts of lawlessness may be precipitated. We realized that we had to exercise extreme caution so that the direct-action program would not be conducted in a manner that might be considered provocative or an invitation to violence. Accordingly, each situation had to be studied in detail: the strength and the temper of our adversaries had to be estimated and any change in any of these factors would affect the details of our strategy. Nevertheless, we had to begin a march without knowing when or where it would actually terminate.

How were these considerations applied to our plans for the march from Selma to Montgomery?

My associates and friends were constantly concerned about my personal safety, and in the light of recent threats of death, many of them urged me not to march that Sunday for the fear that my presence in the line would lead to assassination attempts. However, as a matter of conscience, I could not always respond to the wishes of my staff and associates; in this case, I made the decision to lead the march on Sunday and was prepared to do so in spite of any possible danger to my person.

In working out a time schedule, I had to consider my church responsibilities. Because I was so frequently out of my pulpit and because my life was so full of emergencies, I was always on the horns of a dilemma. I had been away for two straight Sundays and therefore felt that I owed it to my parishioners to be there. It was arranged that I take a chartered plane to Montgomery after the morning service and lead the march out of Selma, speak with a group for three

or four hours, and take a chartered flight back in order to be on hand for the Sunday Communion Service at 7:30 P.M.

When Governor Wallace issued his ban on the march, it was my view and that of most of my associates that the state troopers would deal with the problem by arresting all of the people in the line. We never imagined that they would use the brutal methods to which they actually resorted to repress the march. I concluded that if I were arrested it would be impossible for me to get back to the evening service at Ebenezer to administer the Lord's Supper and baptism. Because of this situation, my staff urged me to stay in Atlanta and lead a march on Monday morning. This I agreed to do. I was prepared to go to jail on Monday but at the same time I would have met my church responsibilities. If I had had any idea that the state troopers would use the kind of brutality they did, I would have felt compelled to give up my church duties altogether to lead the line. It was one of those developments that none of us anticipated. We felt that the state troopers, who had been severely criticized over their terrible acts two weeks earlier even by conservative Alabama papers, would never again engage in that kind of violence.

I shall never forget my agony of conscience for not being there when I heard of the dastardly acts perpetrated against nonviolent demonstrators that Sunday, March 7. As a result, I felt that I had to lead a march on the following Tuesday and decided to spend Monday mobilizing for it.

The march on Tuesday, March 9, illustrated the dilemma we often face. Not to try to march again would have been unthinkable. However, whether we were marching to Montgomery or to a limited point within the city of Selma could not be determined in advance; the only certain thing was that we had to begin, so that a confrontation with injustice would take place in full view of the millions looking on throughout this nation.

The next question was whether the confrontation had to be a violent one; here the responsibility of weighing all factors and estimating the consequences rests heavily on the civil rights leaders. It is easy to decide on either extreme. To go forward recklessly can have terrible consequences in terms of human life and also can cause friends and supporters to lose confidence if they feel a lack of re-

sponsibility exists. On the other hand, it is ineffective to guarantee that no violence will occur by the device of not marching or undertaking token marches avoiding direct confrontation.

On Tuesday, March 9, Judge Frank M. Johnson of the federal district court in Montgomery issued an order enjoining me and the local Selma leadership of the nonviolent voting rights movement from peacefully marching to Montgomery. The issuance of Judge Johnson's order caused disappointment and bitterness to all of us. I felt that as a result of the order we had been put in a very difficult position. I felt that it was like condemning the robbed man for getting robbed. It was one of the most painful decisions I ever made—to try on the one hand to do what I felt was a practical matter of controlling a potentially explosive situation, and at the same time, not defy a federal court order. We had looked to the federal judiciary in Alabama to prevent the unlawful interference with our program to expand elective franchise for Negroes throughout the Black Belt.

I consulted with my lawyers and trusted advisors both in Selma and other parts of the country and discussed what course of action we should take. Information came in that troopers of the Alabama State Police and Sheriff James Clark's possemen would be arrayed in massive force across Highway 80 at the foot of Pettus Bridge in Selma. I reflected upon the role of the federal judiciary as a protector of the rights of Negroes. I also gave thoughtful consideration to the hundreds of clergymen and other persons of goodwill who had come to Selma to make a witness with me in the cause of justice by participating in our planned march to Montgomery. Taking all of this into consideration, I decided that our plans had to be carried out and that I would lead our march to a confrontation with injustice to make a witness to our countrymen and the world of our determination to vote and be free.

As my associates and I were spiritually preparing ourselves for the task ahead, Governor Collins of the Community Relations Service and John Doar, acting assistant attorney general, Civil Rights Division, came to see me to dissuade me from the course of action which we had painfully decided upon.

Governor Collins affirmed and restated the commitment of President Johnson to the achievement of full equality for all persons

without regard to race, color, or creed, and his commitment to securing the right to vote for all persons eligible to do so. He mentioned the fact that the situation was explosive, and it would tarnish
the image of our nation if the events of Sunday were repeated. He
very strongly urged us not to march. I listened attentively to both
Mr. Doar and Governor Collins. I said at that point, "I think instead
of urging us not to march, you should urge the state troopers not to
be brutal toward us if we do march, because we have got to march."
I explained to them why, as a matter of conscience, I felt it was
necessary to seek a confrontation with injustice on Highway 80. I
felt that I had a moral obligation to the movement, to justice, to our
nation, to the health of our democracy, and above all to the philosophy of nonviolence to keep the march peaceful. I felt that, if I had
not done it, the pent-up emotions would have exploded into retaliatory violence. Governor Collins realized at this point that we were
determined to march and left the room, saying that he would do
what he could to prevent the state troopers from being violent.

*I say to you this afternoon that I would rather die on the highways
of Alabama than make a butchery of my conscience. I say to you, when
we march, don't panic and remember that we must remain true to
nonviolence. I'm asking everybody in the line, if you can't be nonviolent, don't get in here. If you can't accept blows without retaliating,
don't get in the line. If you can accept it out of your commitment to
nonviolence, you will somehow do something for this nation that may
well save it. If you can accept it, you will leave those state troopers
bloodied with their own barbarities. If you can accept it, you will do
something that will transform conditions here in Alabama.*

Just as we started to march, Governor Collins rushed to me and
said that he felt everything would be all right. He gave me a small
piece of paper indicating a route that I assumed Mr. Baker, public
safety director of Selma, wanted us to follow. It was the same route
that had been taken the previous Sunday. The press, reporting this
detail, gave the impression that Governor Collins and I had sat down
and worked out some compromise. There were no talks or agreement between Governor Collins and me beyond the discussions I
have just described. I held on to my decision to march despite the
fact that many people in the line were concerned about breaking the

court injunction issued by one of the strongest and best judges in the South. I felt that we had to march at least to the point where the troopers had brutalized the people, even if it meant a recurrence of violence, arrest, or even death. As a nonviolent leader, I could not advocate breaking through a human wall set up by the policemen. While we desperately desired to proceed to Montgomery, we knew before we started our march that this human wall set up on Pettus Bridge would make it impossible for us to go beyond it. It was not that we didn't intend to go on to Montgomery, but that, in consideration of our commitment to nonviolent action, we knew we could not go under those conditions.

We sought to find a middle course. We marched until we faced the troopers in their solid line shoulder to shoulder across Highway 80. We did not disengage until they made it clear they were going to use force. We disengaged then because we felt we had made our point, we had revealed the continued presence of violence.

On March 11, I received the shocking information that the Reverend James Reeb had just passed away as a result of the dastardly act of brutality visited upon him in Selma. Those elements that had constantly harassed us and who did their cowardly work by night, went to the Walkers' Café and followed three clergymen and beat them brutally. Two of them were from Boston—the Reverend Miller and the Reverend Reeb—and Reverend Clark Olson was from Berkeley, California.

This murder, like so many others, is the direct consequence of the reign of terror in some parts of our nation. This unprovoked attack on the streets of an Alabama city cannot be considered an isolated incident in a smooth sea of tolerance and understanding. Rather, it is a result of a malignant sickness in our society that comes from the tolerance of organized hatred and violence. We must all confess that Reverend Reeb was murdered by a morally inclement climate—a climate filled with torrents of hatred and jostling winds of violence. He was murdered by an atmosphere of inhumanity in Alabama that tolerated the vicious murder of Jimmy Lee Jackson in Marion and the brutal beatings of Sunday in Selma. Had police not brutally beaten unarmed nonviolent persons desiring the right to vote on Sunday, it is doubtful whether this act of murder would have taken place on Tuesday. This is additional

proof that segregation knows no color line. It attempts to control the movement and mind of white persons as well as Negroes. When it cannot dominate, it murders those that dissent.

"From Selma to Montgomery"

As soon as we had won legal affirmation on March 11 of our right to march to Montgomery, the next phase hinged on the successful completion of our mission to petition the governor to take meaningful measures to abolish voting restrictions, the poll tax, and police brutality. The President and federal judiciary had spoken affirmatively of the cause for which we struggled. All citizens had to make their personal witness. We could no longer accept the injustices that we had faced from Governor Wallace. We could no longer adjust to the evils that we had faced all of these years.

We made it very clear that this was a march of goodwill and to stimulate the Negro citizenry of Montgomery to make use of the new opportunity that had been provided through the federal court. We had a legal and constitutional right to march from Selma to Montgomery. We were very serious in saying that we planned to walk to Montgomery, and we went through a great deal of work and spent a lot of time planning the route, the stopping points, the tents and where they would be. We felt this would be a privilege that citizens could engage in as long as they didn't tie up traffic and walk out on the main highway but on the side of the road. Hosea Williams reported to me that there were three bridges, but that one could walk across these bridges single file rather than two or three abreast.

Things were shaping up beautifully. We had people coming in from all over the country. I suspected that we would have representatives from almost every state in the union, and naturally a large number from the state of Alabama. We hoped to see, and we planned to see, the greatest witness for freedom that had ever taken place on the steps of the capitol of any state in the South. And this whole march added drama to this total thrust. I think it will go down in American history on the same level as the March to the Sea did in Indian history.

Some of us started out on March 21 marching from Selma, Ala-

bama. We walked through desolate valleys and across tiring hills. We walked on meandering highways and rested our bodies on rocky byways. Some of our faces were burnt from the outpourings of the sweltering sun. Some literally slept in the mud. We were drenched by the rain. Our bodies were tired. Our feet were sore. The thousands of pilgrims had marched across a route traveled by Sherman a hundred years before. But in contrast to a trail of destruction and bloodshed, they watered the red Alabama clay with tears of joy and love overflowing, even for those who taunted and jeered along the sidelines. Not a shot was fired. Not a stone displaced. Not a window broken. Not a person abused or insulted. This was certainly a triumphant entry into the "Cradle of the Confederacy." And an entry destined to put an end to that racist oligarchy once and for all.

It was with great optimism that we marched into Montgomery on March 25. The smell of victory was in the air. Voting rights legislation loomed as a certainty in the weeks ahead. Fifty thousand nonviolent crusaders from every county in Alabama and practically every state in the union gathered in Montgomery on a balmy spring afternoon to petition Governor Wallace.

"How long? Not long"

So I stand before you this afternoon with the conviction that segregation is on its deathbed in Alabama and the only thing uncertain about it is how costly the segregationists and Wallace will make the funeral.

Our whole campaign in Alabama has been centered around the right to vote. In focusing the attention of the nation and the world today on the flagrant denial of the right to vote, we are exposing the very origin, the root cause, of racial segregation in the Southland.

The threat of the free exercise of the ballot by the Negro and the white masses alike resulted in the establishing of a segregated society. They segregated Southern money from the poor whites; they segregated Southern churches from Christianity; they segregated Southern minds from honest thinking; and they segregated the Negro from everything.

We have come a long way since that travesty of justice was perpetrated upon the American mind. Today I want to tell the city of Selma, today I want to tell the state of Alabama, today I want to say to the people of America and the nations of the world: We are not about to

turn around. We are on the move now. Yes, we are on the move and no wave of racism can stop us.

We are on the move now. The burning of our churches will not deter us. We are on the move now. The bombing of our homes will not dissuade us. We are on the move now. The beating and killing of our clergymen and young people will not divert us. We are on the move now. The arrest and release of known murderers will not discourage us. We are on the move now.

Like an idea whose time has come, not even the marching of mighty armies can halt us. We are moving to the land of freedom.

Let us therefore continue our triumph and march to the realization of the American dream. Let us march on segregated housing until every ghetto of social and economic depression dissolves and Negroes and whites live side by side in decent, safe, and sanitary housing.

Let us march on segregated schools until every vestige of segregated and inferior education becomes a thing of the past and Negroes and whites study side by side in the socially healing context of the classroom.

Let us march on poverty until no American parent has to skip a meal so that their children may eat. March on poverty until no starved man walks the streets of our cities and towns in search of jobs that do not exist.

Let us march on ballot boxes, march on ballot boxes until race baiters disappear from the political arena. Let us march on ballot boxes until the Wallaces of our nation tremble away in silence.

Let us march on ballot boxes until we send to our city councils, state legislatures, and the United States Congress men who will not fear to do justice, love mercy, and walk humbly with their God. Let us march on ballot boxes until all over Alabama God's children will be able to walk the earth in decency and honor.

For all of us today the battle is in our hands. The road ahead is not altogether a smooth one. There are no broad highways to lead us easily and inevitably to quick solutions. We must keep going.

My people, my people, listen! The battle is in our hands. The battle is in our hands in Mississippi and Alabama, and all over the United States.

So as we go away this afternoon, let us go away more than ever before committed to the struggle and committed to nonviolence. I must admit to you there are still some difficulties ahead. We are still in for a

season of suffering in many of the black belt counties of Alabama, many areas of Mississippi, many areas of Louisiana.

I must admit to you there are still jail cells waiting for us, dark and difficult moments. We will go on with the faith that nonviolence and its power transformed dark yesterdays into bright tomorrows. We will be able to change all of these conditions.

Our aim must never be to defeat or humiliate the white man but to win his friendship and understanding. We must come to see that the end we seek is a society at peace with itself, a society that can live with its conscience. That will be a day not of the white man, not of the black man. That will be the day of man as man.

I know you are asking today, "How long will it take?" I come to say to you this afternoon however difficult the moment, however frustrating the hour, it will not be long, because truth pressed to earth will rise again.

How long? Not long, because no lie can live forever.

How long? Not long, because you still reap what you sow.

How long? Not long. Because the arm of the moral universe is long, but it bends toward justice.

How long? Not long, because mine eyes have seen the glory of the coming of the Lord, trampling out the vintage where the grapes of wrath are stored. He has loosed the fateful lightning of his terrible swift sword. His truth is marching on.

He has sounded forth the trumpets that shall never call retreat. He is lifting up the hearts of men before His judgment seat. Oh, be swift, my soul, to answer Him. Be jubilant, my feet. Our God is marching on.

As the trains loaded and the busses embarked for their destinations, as the inspired throng returned to their homes to organize the final phase of political activity which would complete the revolution so eloquently proclaimed by the word and presence of the multitude in Montgomery, the scent of victory in the air gave way to the stench of death. We were reminded that this was not a march to the capital of a civilized nation, as was the March on Washington. We had marched through a swamp of poverty, ignorance, race hatred, and sadism.

We were reminded that the only reason that this march was possible was due to the presence of thousands of federalized troops,

marshals, and a federal court. We were reminded that the troops would soon be going home, and that in the days to come we had to renew our attempts to organize the very county in which Mrs. Viola Liuzzo was murdered. If they murdered a white woman for standing up for the Negro's right to vote, what would they do to Negroes who attempted to register and vote?

Certainly it should not have been necessary for more of us to die, to suffer jailings and beatings at the hands of sadistic savages in uniforms. The Alabama voting project had been total in its commitment to nonviolence, and yet people were beginning to talk more and more of arming themselves. The people who followed along the fringe of the movement, who seldom came into the nonviolent training sessions, were growing increasingly bitter and restless. But we could not allow even the thought or spirit of violence to creep into our movement.

When we marched from Selma to Montgomery, Alabama, I remember that we had one of the most magnificent expressions of the ecumenical movement that I've ever seen. Protestants, Catholics, and Jews joined together in a beautiful way to articulate the injustices and the indignities that Negroes were facing in the state of Alabama and all over the South on the question of the right to vote. I had seen many clergymen come to the forefront who were not there some years ago. The march gave new relevance to the gospel. Selma brought into being the second great awakening of the church in America. Long standing aside and giving tacit approval to the civil rights struggle, the church finally marched forth like a mighty army and stood beside God's children in distress.

Stalwart nonviolent activists within our ranks had brought about a coalition of the nation's conscience on the infamous stretch of highway between Selma and Montgomery. The awakening of the church also brought a new vitality to the labor movement, and to intellectuals across the country. A little known fact was that forty of the nation's top historians took part in the march to Montgomery.

One can still hear the tramping feet and remember the glowing eyes filled with determination and hope which said eloquently, "*We must be free,*" a sound which echoed throughout this nation, and yes, even throughout the world. My mind still remembers vividly

the ecumenicity of the clergy, the combined forces of labor, civil
rights organizations, and the academic community which joined our
ranks and said in essence, "Your cause is morally right, and we are
with you all the way."

After the march to Montgomery, there was a delay at the airport
and several thousand demonstrators waited more than five hours,
crowding together on the seats, the floors, and the stairways of the
terminal building. As I stood with them and saw white and Negro,
nuns and priests, housemaids and shop workers brimming with vitality and enjoying a rare comradeship, I knew I was seeing a micro-
cosm of the mankind of the future in that moment of luminous and
genuine brotherhood.

"Selma brought us a voting bill"

In his address to the joint session of Congress on March 15, 1965,
President Johnson made one of the most eloquent, unequivocal, and
passionate pleas for human rights ever made by a President of the
United States. He revealed an amazing understanding of the depth
and dimension of the problem of racial justice. His tone and his
delivery were sincere. He rightly praised the courage of the Negro
for awakening the conscience of the nation. He declared that the
national government must by law insure every Negro his full rights
as a citizen. When he signed the measure, the President announced
that, "Today is a triumph for freedom as huge as any victory that's
ever been won on any battlefield. Today we strike away the last
major shackle of fierce and ancient bonds."

We were happy to know that our struggle in Selma had brought
the whole issue of the right to vote to the attention of the nation. It
was encouraging to know that we had the support of the President
in calling for immediate relief of the problems of the disinherited
people of our nation.

When SCLC went into Selma in January 1965, it had limited
objectives. It sought primarily to correct wrongs existing in that
small city. But our adversaries met us with such unrestrained brutality that they enlarged the issues to a national scale. The ironic and
splendid result of the small Selma project was nothing less than the
Voting Rights Act of 1965. For the aid Governor Wallace and Sheriff

Clark gave us in our legislative objectives, SCLC tendered them its warm appreciation.

In conclusion, Selma brought us a voting bill, and it also brought us the grand alliance of the children of light in this nation and made possible changes in our political and economic life heretofore undreamed of. With President Johnson, SCLC viewed the Voting Rights Act of 1965 as "one of the most monumental laws in the history of American freedom." We had a federal law which could be used, and use it we would. Where it fell short, we had our tradition of struggle and the method of nonviolent direct action, and these too we would use.

Let us not mark this great movement only by bloodshed and brutality. We certainly can never forget those who gave their lives in this struggle and who suffered in jail, but let us especially mark the sacrifices of Jimmie Lee Jackson, Rev. James Reeb, and Mrs. Viola Liuzzo as the martyrs of the faith. Cities that had been citadels of the status quo became the unwilling birthplace of a significant national legislation. Montgomery led to the Civil Rights Acts of 1957 and 1960; Birmingham inspired the Civil Rights Act of 1964; and Selma produced the Voting Rights Act of 1965.

When President Johnson declared that Selma, Alabama, is joined in American history with Lexington, Concord, and Appomattox, he honored not only our embattled Negroes, but the overwhelming majority of the nation, Negro and white. The victory in Selma is now being written in the Congress. Before long, more than a million Negroes will be new voters—and psychologically, new people. Selma is a shining moment in the conscience of man. If the worst in American life lurked in the dark streets of Selma, the best of American democratic instincts arose from across the nation to overcome it.

27

WATTS

As soon as we began to see our way clear in the South, the shock and horror of Northern riots exploded before our eyes and we saw that the problems of the Negro go far beyond mere racial segregation. The catastrophe in Los Angeles was a result of seething and rumbling tensions throughout our nation and, indeed, the world.

AUGUST 11–15, 1965
Widespread racial violence in Los Angeles results in more than 30 deaths

AUGUST 17
King arrives in Los Angeles at the invitation of local groups

As we entered the Watts area of Los Angeles, all seemed quiet, but there could still be sensed raging hostility which had erupted in volcanic force in the days previous. What had been an inferno of flame and smoke a few nights before was now an occupied territory. National Guardsmen in groups of three and four stood posted on each street corner. People, black and white, meandered through the charred remains of the Watts business district.

I had been warned not to visit. We were told that the people were in no mood to hear talk of nonviolence. There had been wild threats hurled at all Negro leaders and many were afraid to venture into the area. But I had visited Watts on many occasions and received the most generous of acclamations. One of the most responsive and enthusiastic gatherings I ever saw was our meeting in Watts during the "Get-Out-the-Vote" tour in 1964. So, despite the warn-

ings, I was determined to hear firsthand from the people involved, just what the riot was all about.

Let me say first of all that I profoundly deplore the events that have occurred in Los Angeles in these last few tragic days. I believe and have said on many occasions that violence is not the answer to social conflict whether it is engaged in by white people in Alabama or by Negroes in Los Angeles. Violence is all the more regrettable in this period in light of the tremendous nonviolent sacrifices that both Negro and white people together have endured to bring justice to all men.

But it is equally clear, as President Johnson pointed out yesterday, that it is the job of all Americans "to right the wrong from which such violence and disorder spring." The criminal responses which led to the tragic outbreaks of violence in Los Angeles are environmental and not racial. The economic deprivation, racial isolation, inadequate housing, and general despair of thousands of Negroes teaming in Northern and Western ghettoes are the ready seeds which gave birth to tragic expressions of violence. By acts of commission and omission none of us in this great country has done enough to remove injustice. I therefore humbly suggest that all of us accept our share of responsibility for these past days of anguish.

"Stirring of a deprived people"

After visiting Watts and talking with hundreds of persons of all walks of life, it was my opinion that the riots grew out of the depths of despair which afflict a people who see no way out of their economic dilemma.

There were serious doubts that the white community was in any way concerned. There also was a growing disillusionment and resentment toward the Negro middle class and the leadership which it had produced. This ever-widening breach was a serious factor which led to a feeling on the part of ghetto-imprisoned Negroes that they were alone in their struggle and had to resort to any method to gain attention to their plight.

The nonviolent movement of the South meant little to them since we had been fighting for rights which theoretically were already theirs; therefore, I believed what happened in Los Angeles was of grave national significance. What we witnessed in the Watts area was

the beginning of a stirring of a deprived people in a society who had been by-passed by the progress of the previous decade. I would minimize the racial significance and point to the fact that these were the rumblings of discontent from the "have nots" within the midst of an affluent society.

The issue of police brutality loomed as one of major significance. The slightest discourtesy on the part of an officer of the law was a deprivation of the dignity that most of the residents of Watts came west seeking. Whether it was true or not, the Negro of the ghetto was convinced that his dealings with the police denied him the dignity and respect to which he was entitled as a citizen and a human being. This produced a sullen, hostile attitude, which resulted in a spiral of hatred on the part of both the officer and the Negro. This whole reaction complex was often coupled with fear on the part of both parties. Every encounter between a Negro and the police in the hovering hostility of the ghetto was a potential outburst.

A misguided fire truck, a conflict in arrest, a sharp word between a store owner and customer—the slightest incident can trigger a riot in a community, but events converge in such a cataclysmic manner that often the situation seems to be the result of a planned organized attempt at insurrection. This was the term used by Mayor Sam Yorty—an insurrection staged by a group of organized criminals.

I am afraid that this was too superficial an explanation. Two separate and distinct forces were operating in Los Angeles. One was a hardened criminal element incapable of restraint by appeals to reason or discipline. This was a small number in contrast to the large number involved. The larger group of participants were not criminal elements. I was certain that the majority of the more than four thousand persons arrested in Los Angeles were being arrested for the first time. They were the disorganized, the frustrated, and the oppressed. Their looting was a form of social protest. Forgotten by society, taunted by the affluence around them, but effectively barred from its reach, they were acting out hostilities as a method of relief and to focus attention.

The objective of the people with whom I talked was consistently work and dignity. It was as though the speeches had been rehearsed, but on every corner the theme was the same. Unless some work could be found for the unemployed and underemployed, we would

continually face the possibility of this kind of outbreak at every encounter with police authority. At a time when the Negro's aspirations were at a peak, his actual conditions of employment, education, and housing were worsening. The paramount problem is one of economic stability for this sector of our society. All other advances in education, family life, and the moral climate of the community were dependent upon the ability of the masses of Negroes to earn a living in this wealthy society of ours.

In the South there is something of shared poverty, Negro and white. In the North, white existence, only steps away, glares with conspicuous consumption. Even television becomes incendiary, when it beams pictures of affluent homes and multitudinous consumer products at the aching poor, living in wretched homes. In these terms, Los Angeles could have expected riots because it is the luminous symbol of luxurious living for whites. Watts is closer to it, and yet farther from it, than any other Negro community in the country. The looting in Watts was a form of social protest very common through the ages as a dramatic and destructive gesture of the poor toward symbols of their needs.

ENCOUNTER IN WATTS

I was out in Watts during the riots. One young man said to me—and Andy Young, Bayard Rustin, and Bernard Lee, who were with me—"We won!" I said, "What do you mean, 'we won'? Thirty-some people dead—all but two are Negroes. You've destroyed your own. What do you mean, 'we won'?" And he said, "We made them pay attention to us."

When people are voiceless, they will have temper tantrums like a little child who has not been paid attention to. And riots are massive temper tantrums from a neglected and voiceless people.

July 1967

There was joy among the rioters of Watts, not shame. They were completely oblivious to the destruction of property in their wake. They were destroying a physical and emotional jail; they had asserted themselves against a system which was quietly crushing them into oblivion and now they were "somebody." As one young man put it,

"We know that a riot is not the answer, but we've been down here suffering for a long time and nobody cared. Now at least they know we're here. A riot may not be *the* way, but it is *a* way." This was the new nationalist mood gripping a good many ghetto inhabitants. It rejected the alliance with white liberals as a means of social change. It affirms the fact that black men act alone in their own interest only, because nobody really cares.

Amazingly enough, and in spite of the inflammatory assertions to the contrary, these were not murderous mobs. They were destructive of property, but with all of the reports of thousands of violent people on the loose, very few people were killed, and almost all of them by the police. Certainly, had the intention of the mob been to murder, many more lives would have been lost.

What I emphasized is that, in spite of all of the hostility that some Negroes felt, and as violent and destructive as the mood temporarily became, it was not yet a blind and irredeemable condition. The people of Watts were hostile to nonviolence, but when we actually went to them and emphasized the dangers of hatred and violence, the same people cheered. Only minutes before the air had been thick with tension, but when they were reminded of the Rev. James Reeb and Viola Liuzzo, the martyrs of the Selma campaign, they cheered the thought that white people can and do cooperate with us in our search for jobs and dignity.

But let no one think that this is a defense of riots. The wake of destruction of property where many Negroes were employed and where many more were served consumer goods was one of the most tragic sights I ever witnessed. It was second only to the thought of thirty-seven persons dying needlessly in an uncontrolled tantrum of devastation and death. This was more human loss than had been suffered in ten years of nonviolent direct action, which produced the revolutionary social changes in the South.

Violence only serves to harden the resistance of the white reactionary and relieve the white liberal of guilt, which might motivate him to action and thereby leaves the condition unchanged and embittered. The backlash of violence is felt far beyond the borders of the community where it takes place. Whites are arming themselves in Selma and across Alabama in the expectation that rioting would spread South. In this kind of atmosphere a single drunken disorderly

Negro could set off the panic button that might result in the killing of many innocent Negroes.

However, a mere condemnation of violence is empty without understanding the daily violence that our society inflicts upon many of its members. The violence of poverty and humiliation hurts as intensely as the violence of the club. This is a situation that calls for statesmanship and creative leadership, of which I did not see evidence in Los Angeles. What we did find was a blind intransigence and ignorance of the tremendous social forces that were at work there. And so long as this stubborn attitude was maintained by responsible authorities, I could only see the situation worsening.

"A crisis for the nonviolent movement"

Los Angeles could have expected the holocaust when its officials tied up federal aid in political manipulation, when the rate of Negro unemployment soared above depression levels of the twenties, and when the population density of Watts became the worst in the nation. Yet even these tormenting physical conditions are less than the full sign. California in 1964 repealed its law forbidding racial discrimination in housing. It was the first major state in the country to take away gains Negroes had won at a time when progress was visible and substantial elsewhere, and especially in the South. California by that callous act voted for ghettos. The atrociousness of some deeds may be concealed by legal ritual, but the destructiveness is felt with bitter force by its victims. When all is finally entered into the annals of sociology; when philosophers, politicians, and preachers have all had their say, we must return to the fact that a person participates in this society primarily as an economic entity. At rock bottom we are neither poets, athletes, nor artists; our existence is centered in the fact that we are consumers, because we first must eat and have shelter to live. This is a difficult confession for a preacher to make, and it is a phenomenon against which I will continue to rebel, but it remains a fact that "consumption" of goods and services is the raison d'être of the vast majority of Americans. When persons are for some reason or other excluded from the consumer circle, there is discontent and unrest.

Watts was not only a crisis for Los Angeles and the Northern

cities of our nation: It was a crisis for the nonviolent movement. I tried desperately to maintain a nonviolent atmosphere in which our nation could undergo the tremendous period of social change which confronts us, but this was mainly dependent on the obtaining of tangible progress and victories, if those of us who counsel reason and love were to maintain our leadership. However, the cause was not lost. In spite of pockets of hostility in ghetto areas such as Watts, there was still overwhelming acceptance of the ideal of nonviolence.

I was in touch with the White House on the matter and asked that the President do everything in his power to break the deadlock which had prevented the poverty program from entering Los Angeles. I also asked that the government's efforts be vastly increased toward obtaining full employment for both the Negro and white poor in our country. The President was sensitive to this problem and was prepared to give us the kind of leadership and vision which we needed in those turbulent times.

All in all, my visit to Watts was a tremendous help to me personally. I prayed that somehow leadership and statesmanship would emerge in the places of public office, the press, the business community, and among the Negro leadership and people of Watts, to avoid further conflict. Such a conflict would bring only bloodshed and shame to our entire nation's image abroad.

28

CHICAGO CAMPAIGN

It is reasonable to believe that if the problems of Chicago, the nation's second largest city, can be solved, they can be solved everywhere.

JULY 26, 1965
King leads march to Chicago City Hall and addresses a rally sponsored by Chicago's Coordinating Council of Community Organizations (CCCO)

JANUARY 7, 1966
Announces the start of the Chicago Campaign

JULY 10
At "Freedom Sunday" rally at Soldier's Field, launches drive to make Chicago an "open city" for housing

JULY 12-14
Racial rioting on Chicago's West Side results in two deaths and widespread destruction

AUGUST 5
Angry whites attack civil rights march through Chicago's southwest side

AUGUST 26
Arranges "Summit Agreement" with Mayor R. Daley and other Chicago leaders

In the early summer of 1965 we received invitations from Negro leaders in the city of Chicago to join with them in their fight for quality integrated education. We had watched this movement with interest, and members of the staff of the Southern Christian Leader-

ship Conference had maintained constant communication with the leadership. As a result of meetings between members of my staff and leaders of Chicago civil rights organizations, I agreed to accept the invitation to spend some time in Chicago, beginning July 24.

Later in the year, after careful deliberation with my staff, the SCLC decided to begin a concentrated effort to create a broadly based, vibrant, nonviolent movement in the North. Our efforts would be directed at the social ills which plagued Chicago—the potentially explosive ghetto pathology of the Northern Negro.

My concern for the welfare of Negroes in the North was no less than that for Negroes in the South, and my conscience dictated that I should commit as much of my personal and organizational resources to their cause as was humanly possible. Our primary objective was to bring about the unconditional surrender of forces dedicated to the creation and maintenance of slums and ultimately to make slums a moral and financial liability upon the whole community. Chicago was not alone among cities with a slum problem, but certainly we knew that slum conditions there were the prototype of those chiefly responsible for the Northern urban race problem.

"Breaking down the infamous wall of segregation"

We worked under the Coordinating Council of Community Organizations, a coalition of local civil rights groups, convened by Al Raby, a former Chicago public school teacher. Our main concentration would be on the school issue—a fight for quality integrated education which had been waged in that city for more than five years. This did not mean that we would stop there, because it was painfully clear that the school issue was merely symptomatic of a system which relegated thousands of Negroes into economic and spiritual deprivation.

The only solution to breaking down the infamous wall of segregation in Chicago rested in our being able to mobilize both the white and black communities into a massive nonviolent movement, which would stop at nothing short of changing the ugly face of the black ghetto into a community of love and justice. Essentially it meant removing future generations from dilapidated tenements, opening the doors of job opportunities to all regardless of their color, and

making the resources of all social institutions available for their uplifting into the mainstream of American life.

No longer could we afford to isolate a major segment of our
society in a ghetto prison and expect its spiritually crippled wards to
accept the advanced social responsibilities of the world's leading nation. Birmingham, Alabama, once the most segregated city in the
South, had been our target city for public accommodations, and our
nonviolent movement there gave birth to the Civil Rights Bill of
1964. Selma, Alabama, had been our pilot city for the Voting Rights
Bill of 1965, and I had faith that Chicago, considered one of the
most segregated cities in the nation, could well become the metropolis where a meaningful nonviolent movement could arouse the conscience of this nation to deal realistically with the Northern ghetto.

We had no illusions that we could undertake alone such a mammoth task; therefore, our advance SCLC team headed by the Rev.
James Bevel laid the groundwork for our movement. We were confident that a convergence of many forces—religious, civic, political,
and academic—would come about to demand a solution to Chicago's problems.

It did not require an in-depth evaluation to determine what evils
had to be eliminated from our society. Any efforts made to extend
and prolong the suffering of Negroes imprisoned in the ghetto
would be a flagrant attempt to perpetuate a social crisis capable of
exploding in our faces and searing the very soul of this nation. In
this regard, it was neither I, nor SCLC, that decided to go north, but
rather, existing deplorable conditions and the conscience of good to
the cause that summoned us.

"Lawndale was truly an island of poverty"

During 1966 I lived and worked in Chicago. The civil rights movement had too often been middle-class oriented and had not moved
to the grassroots levels of our communities. So I thought the great
challenge facing the civil rights movement was to move into these
areas to organize and gain identity with ghetto dwellers and young
people in the ghetto. This was one of the reasons why I felt that in
moving to Chicago I would live in the very heart of the ghetto. I

would not only experience what my brothers and sisters experience in living conditions, but I would be able to live with them.

In a big city like Chicago it is hard to do it overnight, but I thought that all of the civil rights organizations had to work more to organize the grassroots levels of our communities. There, the problems of poverty and despair were more than an academic exercise. The phone rang daily with stories of the most drastic forms of man's inhumanity to man and I found myself fighting a daily battle against the depression and hopelessness which the heart of our cities pumps into the spiritual bloodstream of our lives. The problems of poverty and despair were graphically illustrated. I remember a baby attacked by rats in a Chicago slum. I remember a young Negro murdered by a gang in Cicero, where he was looking for a job.

The slum of Lawndale was truly an island of poverty in the midst of an ocean of plenty. Chicago boasted the highest per capita income of any city in the world, but you would never believe it looking out of the windows of my apartment in the slum of Lawndale. From this vantage point you saw only hundreds of children playing in the streets. You saw the light of intelligence glowing in their beautiful dark eyes. Then you realized their overwhelming joy because someone had simply stopped to say hello; for they lived in a world where even their parents were often forced to ignore them. In the tight squeeze of economic pressure, their mothers and fathers both had to work; indeed, more often than not, the father will hold two jobs, one in the day and another at night. With the long distances ghetto parents had to travel to work and the emotional exhaustion that comes from the daily struggle to survive in a hostile world, they were left with too little time or energy to attend to the emotional needs of their growing children.

Too soon you began to see the effects of this emotional and environmental deprivation. The children's clothes were too skimpy to protect them from the Chicago wind, and a closer look revealed the mucus in the corners of their bright eyes, and you were reminded that vitamin pills and flu shots were luxuries which they could ill afford. The "runny noses" of ghetto children became a graphic symbol of medical neglect in a society which had mastered most of the diseases from which they will too soon die. There was something wrong in a society which allowed this to happen.

My neighbors paid more rent in the substandard slums of Lawndale than the whites paid for modern apartments in the suburbs. The situation was much the same for consumer goods, purchase prices of homes, and a variety of other services. This exploitation was possible because so many of the residents of the ghetto had no personal means of transportation. It was a vicious circle. You could not get a job because you were poorly educated, and you had to depend on welfare to feed your children; but if you received public aid in Chicago, you could not own property, not even an automobile, so you were condemned to the jobs and shops closest to your home. Once confined to this isolated community, one no longer participated in a free economy, but was subject to price fixing and wholesale robbery by many of the merchants of the area.

Finally, when a man was able to make his way through the maze of handicaps and get just one foot out of the jungle of poverty and exploitation, he was subject to the whims of the political and economic giants of the city, which moved in impersonally to crush the little flower of success that had just begun to bloom.

It is a psychological axiom that frustration generates aggression. Certainly, the Northern ghetto daily victimized its inhabitants. The Chicago West Side with its concentration of slums, the poor, and the young, represented in grotesque exaggeration the suppression that Negroes of all classes feel within the ghetto.

The Northern ghetto had become a type of colonial area. The colony was powerless because all important decisions affecting the community were made from the outside. Many of its inhabitants even had their daily lives dominated by the welfare worker and the policeman. The profits of landlord and merchant were removed and seldom if ever reinvested. The only positive thing the larger society saw in the slum was that it was a source of cheap surplus labor in times of economic boom. Otherwise, its inhabitants were blamed for their own victimization.

"An emotional pressure cooker"

This type of daily frustration was violence visited upon the slum inhabitants. Our society was only concerned that the aggressions thus generated did not burst outward. Therefore, our larger society

had encouraged the hostility it created within slum dwellers to turn inward—to manifest itself in aggression toward one another or in self-destruction and apathy. The larger society was willing to let the frustrations born of racism's violence become internalized and consume its victims. America's horror was only expressed when the aggression turned outward, when the ghetto and its controls could no longer contain its destructiveness. In many a week as many Negro youngsters were killed in gang fights as were killed in the riots. Yet there was no citywide expression of horror.

Our own children lived with us in Lawndale, and it was only a few days before we became aware of the change in their behavior. Their tempers flared, and they sometimes reverted to almost infantile behavior. During the summer, I realized that the crowded flat in which we lived was about to produce an emotional explosion in my own family. It was just too hot, too crowded, too devoid of creative forms of recreation. There was just not space enough in the neighborhood to run off the energy of childhood without running into busy, traffic-laden streets. And I understood anew the conditions which make of the ghetto an emotional pressure cooker.

In all the speaking that I have done in the United States before varied audiences, including some hostile whites, the only time that I have ever been booed was one night in our regular weekly mass meeting by some angry young men of our movement. I went home that night with an ugly feeling. Selfishly, I thought of my sufferings and sacrifices over the last twelve years. Why would they boo one so close to them? But as I lay awake thinking, I finally came to myself, and I could not for the life of me have less than patience and understanding for those young people.

For twelve years I, and others like me, had held out radiant promises of progress. I had preached to them about my dream. I had lectured to them about the not too distant day when they would have freedom, "all, here and now." I had urged them to have faith in America and in white society. Their hopes had soared. They booed because they felt that we were unable to deliver on our promises, and because we had urged them to have faith in people who had too often proved to be unfaithful. They were hostile because they were watching the dream that they had so readily accepted turn into a frustrating nightmare.

When we first went to Chicago, there were those who were saying that the nonviolent movement couldn't work in the North, that problems were too complicated and that they were much different from the South and all that. I contended that nonviolence could work in the North.

This is no time to engage in the luxury of cooling off or to take the tranquilizing drug of gradualism. Now is the time to make real the promises of democracy, now is the time to open the doors of opportunity to all of God's children. Now is the time to end the long and desolate night of slumism. Now is the time to have a confrontation between the forces resisting change and the forces demanding change. Now is the time to let justice roll down like water and righteousness like a mighty stream.

We also come here today to affirm that we will no longer sit idly by in agonizing deprivation and wait on others to provide our freedom. We will be sadly mistaken if we think freedom is some lavish dish that the federal government and the white man will pass out on a silver platter while the Negro merely furnishes the appetite. Freedom is never voluntarily granted by the oppressor. It must be demanded by the oppressed.

"Resorting to violence against oppression"

The responsibility for the social eruption in July 1966 lay squarely upon the shoulders of those elected officials whose myopic social vision had been further blurred by political expedience rather than commitment to the betterment of living conditions and dedication to the eradication of slums and the forces which create and maintain slum communities. It must be remembered that genuine peace is not the absence of tension, but the presence of justice. Justice was not present on Chicago's West Side, or for that matter, in other slum communities.

Riots grow out of intolerable conditions. Violent revolts are generated by revolting conditions and there is nothing more dangerous than to build a society with a large segment of people who feel they have no stake in it, who feel they have nothing to lose. To the young victim of the slums, this society has so limited the alternatives of his

life that the expression of his manhood is reduced to the ability to defend himself physically. No wonder it appears logical to him to strike out, resorting to violence against oppression. That is the only way he thinks he gets recognition.

After the riot in Chicago that summer, I was greatly discouraged. But we had trained a group of about two thousand disciplined devotees of nonviolence who were willing to take blows without retaliating. We started out engaging in constitutional privileges, marching before real estate offices in all-white communities. And that nonviolent, disciplined, determined force created such a crisis in the city of Chicago that the city had to do something to change conditions. We didn't have any Molotov cocktails, we didn't have any bricks, we didn't have any guns, we just had the power of our bodies and our souls. There was power there, and it was demonstrated once more.

I remember when the riot broke out that summer, some of the gang leaders and fellows were out there encouraging the riot. I'd been trying to talk to them, and I couldn't get to them. Then they sent the National Guard in, and that night I said, "Well, why aren't you all out there tonight? Now what you've got to do is join with us and let us get a movement that the National Guard can't stop. This is what we've got to do. I'm going on with nonviolence because I've tried it so long. I've come to see how far it has brought us. And I'm not going to turn my back on it now."

In the aftermath of the riot there were concerted attempts to discredit the nonviolent movement. Scare headlines announced paramilitary conspiracies—only to have the attorney general of the United States announce that these claims were totally unfounded. More seriously, there was a concerted attempt to place the responsibility for the riot upon the nonviolent Chicago Freedom Movement and upon myself. Both of these maneuvers were attempts to dodge the fundamental issue of racial subjugation. They represented an unwillingness to do anything more than put the lid back on the pot and a refusal to make fundamental structural changes required to right our racial wrongs.

The Chicago Freedom Movement would not be dampened by these phony accusations. We would not divert our energies into meaningless introspection. The best remedy we had to offer for riots

was to press our nonviolent program even more vigorously. We stepped up our plans for nonviolent direct actions to make Chicago an open and just city.

"Demonstrations for open housing"

Mid-summer of 1966 saw the boil of Northern racism burst and spread its poisons throughout the streets of Chicago as thousands of Negro and white marchers began their demonstrations for open housing. When we were demonstrating around the whole issue of open housing, we were confronted with massive violence as we marched into certain areas. We suffered in the process of trying to dramatize the issue through our marches into all-white areas that denied us access to houses and where real estate agents would not allow us to see the listings.

Bottles and bricks were thrown at us; we were often beaten. Some of the people who had been brutalized in Selma and who were present at the Capitol ceremonies in Montgomery led marchers in the suburbs of Chicago amid a rain of rocks and bottles, among burning automobiles, to the thunder of jeering thousands, many of them waving Nazi flags. Swastikas bloomed in Chicago parks like misbegotten weeds. Our marchers were met by a hailstorm of bricks, bottles, and firecrackers. "White power" became the racist catcall, punctuated by the vilest of obscenities—most frequently directly at Catholic priests and nuns among the marchers. I've been in many demonstrations all across the South, but I can say that I had never seen, even in Mississippi, mobs as hostile and as hate-filled as in Chicago.

When we had our open housing marches many of our white liberal friends cried out in horror and dismay: "You are creating hatred and hostility in the white communities in which you are marching. You are only developing a white backlash." They failed to realize that the hatred and the hostilities were already latently or subconsciously present. Our marches merely brought them to the surface.

What insane logic it is to condemn the robbed man because his possession of money precipitates the evil act of robbery. Society must condemn the robber and never the robbed. What insane logic it is to

condemn Socrates because his philosophical delving precipitated the evil act of making him drink the hemlock. What an insane logic it is to condemn Jesus Christ because his love for God and Truth precipitated the evil act of his crucifixion. We must condemn those who are perpetuating the violence, and not those individuals who engage in the pursuit of their constitutional rights.

We were the social physicians of Chicago revealing that there was a terrible cancer. We didn't cause it. This cancer was not in its terminal state, it was in its early stages and might be cured if we got at it. Not only were we the social physicians, in the physical sense, but we were the social psychiatrists, bringing out things that were in the subconscious all along. Those people probably had latent hostilities toward Negroes for many, many years. As long as the struggle was down in Alabama and Mississippi, they could look afar and think about it and say how terrible people are. When they discovered brotherhood had to be a reality in Chicago and that brotherhood extended to next door, then those latent hostilities came out.

Day after day during those Chicago marches, I never saw anyone retaliate with violence. There were lots of provocations, not only screaming white hoodlums lining the sidewalks, but also groups of Negro militants talking about guerrilla warfare. We had some gang leaders and members marching with us. I remember walking with the Blackstone Rangers while bottles were flying from the sidelines, and I saw their noses being broken and blood flowing from their wounds; and I saw them continue and not retaliate, not one of them, with violence. I am convinced that even violent temperaments can be channeled through nonviolent discipline, if they can act constructively and express through an effective channel their very legitimate anger.

In August, after being out a few days in Mississippi for the annual convention of the Southern Christian Leadership Conference, I was back in Chicago. The Board of Realtors of the Real Estate Board of the City of Chicago made certain statements concerning a willingness to do things that had not been done before. We wanted to see if they were serious about it. A meeting on August 17 lasted almost ten hours. It was a fruitful meeting, but we didn't get enough out of that meeting to merit calling off our demonstrations, so our demonstrations continued.

I just want to warn the city that it would be an act of folly, in the midst of seeking to negotiate a solution to this problem, to go seek an injunction, because if they don't know it, we are veteran jail-goers. And for us, jail cells are not dungeons of shame, they are havens of freedom and human dignity. I've been to jail in Alabama, I've been to jail in Florida, I've been to jail in Georgia, I've been to jail in Mississippi, I've been to jail in Virginia, and I'm ready to go to jail in Chicago. All I'm saying, my friends, is very simple: we sing a song in this movement, "Ain't Gonna Let Nobody Turn Me 'Round."

We had almost round-the-clock negotiations and hammered out what would probably stand out as the most significant and far-reaching victory that has ever come about in a Northern community on the whole question of open housing. For the first time in the city of Chicago, and probably any other city, the whole power structure was forced by the power of the nonviolent movement to sit down and negotiate and capitulate, and made concessions that had never been made before. Our nonviolent marches in Chicago of the summer brought about a housing agreement which, if implemented, would have been the strongest step toward open housing taken in any city in the nation.

"A drive to end slums"

When we first joined forces with the Coordinating Council of Community Organizations, we outlined a drive to end slums. We viewed slums and slumism as more than a problem of dilapidated, inadequate housing. We understood them as the end product of domestic colonialism: slum housing and slum schools, unemployment and underemployment, segregated and inadequate education, welfare dependency and political servitude. Because no single attack could hope to deal with this overwhelming problem, we established a series of concurrent projects aimed at each facet. Two significant programs were developed to this end.

We had a vigorous, turbulent campaign to make Chicago an open city. We knew that in spite of a marvelous open housing agreement on paper that we reached in Chicago, open housing was not going to be a reality in Chicago in the next year or two. We knew that it was going to take time to really open that city, and we could

not neglect those who lived in the ghetto communities in the process.

At the same time Negro neighborhoods had to be made more hospitable for those who remained. Tenant unions, modeled after labor organizations, became the collective bargaining agents between landlord and resident. This program had remarkable success. In less than a year, unions were formed in three of the city's worst slum and ghetto areas. The collective bargaining contracts also included such measures as rent freezes and stabilization, daily janitorial and sanitation services, and immediate repairs of facilities that jeopardized health and safety. Twelve other smaller tenants unions also sprung up in various communities throughout the city. All met regularly in an informal federation.

Another phase of the housing thrust concerned neighborhood rehabilitation. The unique aspect of this program lay in the fact that the rehabilitated buildings would be turned over to housing cooperatives organized in each of the neighborhoods. The residents therefore gained their much-needed voice in management and administration of the properties. It was through such moves that we hoped to break the cycle of defeatism and psychological servitude that marked the mentality of slumism, achieving human as well as housing renewal.

The most spectacularly successful program in Chicago was Operation Breadbasket. Operation Breadbasket had a very simple program but a powerful one: "If you respect my dollar, you must respect my person." The philosophical undergirding of Operation Breadbasket rested in the belief that many retail business and consumer goods industries depleted the ghetto by selling to Negroes without returning to the community any of the profits through fair hiring practices. To reverse this pattern Operation Breadbasket committees selected a target industry, then obtained the employment statistics of individual companies within it. If the proportion of Negro employees was unsatisfactory, or if they were confined to the menial jobs, the company was approached to negotiate a more equitable employment practice. Leverage was applied where necessary through selective buying campaigns organized by the clergymen through their congregations and through the movement. They sim-

ply said, "We will no longer spend our money where we cannot get substantial jobs."

By 1967 SCLC had Operation Breadbasket functioning in some twelve cities, and the results were remarkable. In Chicago, Operation Breadbasket successfully completed negotiations with three major industries: milk, soft drinks, and chain grocery stores. Four of the companies involved concluded reasonable agreements only after short "don't buy" campaigns. Seven other companies were able to make the requested changes across the conference table, without necessitating a boycott. Two other companies, after providing their employment information to the ministers, were sent letters of commendation for their healthy equal-employment practices. The net results added up to approximately eight hundred new and upgraded jobs for Negro employees, worth a little over $7 million in new annual income for Negro families. We added a new dimension to Operation Breadbasket. Along with requesting new job opportunities, we requested that businesses with stores in the ghetto deposit the income for those establishments in Negro-owned banks, and that Negro-owned products be placed on the counters of all their stores.

"A special and unique relationship to Jews"

When we were working in Chicago, we had numerous rent strikes on the West Side, and it was unfortunately true that, in most instances, the persons we had to conduct these strikes against were Jewish landlords. There was a time when the West Side of Chicago was a Jewish ghetto, and when the Jewish community started moving out into other areas, they still owned the property there, and all of the problems of the landlord came into being.

We were living in a slum apartment owned by a Jew and a number of others, and we had to have a rent strike. We were paying $94 for four run-down, shabby rooms, and we would go out on our open housing marches on Gage Park and other places and we discovered that whites with five sanitary, nice, new rooms, apartments with five rooms, were paying only $78 a month. We were paying 20 percent tax.

The Negro ends up paying a color tax, and this has happened in instances where Negroes actually confronted Jews as the landlord or

the storekeeper. The irrational statements that have been made are the result of these confrontations.

The limited degree of Negro anti-Semitism is substantially a Northern ghetto phenomenon; it virtually does not exist in the South. The urban Negro has a special and unique relationship to Jews. He meets them in two dissimilar roles. On the one hand, he is associated with Jews as some of his most committed and generous partners in the civil rights struggle. On the other hand, he meets them daily as some of his most direct exploiters in the ghetto as slum landlords and gouging shopkeepers. Jews have identified with Negroes voluntarily in the freedom movement, motivated by their religious and cultural commitment to justice. The other Jews who are engaged in commerce in the ghettos are remnants of older communities. A great number of Negro ghettos were formerly Jewish neighborhoods; some storekeepers and landlords remained as population changes occurred. They operate with the ethics of marginal business entrepreneurs, not Jewish ethics, but the distinction is lost on some Negroes who are maltreated by them. Such Negroes, caught in frustration and irrational anger, parrot racial epithets. They foolishly add to the social poison that injures themselves and their own people.

It would be a tragic and immoral mistake to identify the mass of Negroes with the very small number that succumb to cheap and dishonest slogans, just as it would be a serious error to identify all Jews with the few who exploit Negroes under their economic sway.

Negroes cannot irrationally expect honorable Jews to curb the few who are rapacious; they have no means of disciplining or suppressing them. We can only expect them to share our disgust and disdain. Negroes cannot be expected to curb and eliminate the few who are anti-Semitic, because they are subject to no controls we can exercise. We can, however, oppose them, and we have in concrete ways. There has never been a instance of articulated Negro anti-Semitism that was not swiftly condemned by virtually all Negro leaders with the support of the overwhelming majority. I have myself directly attacked it within the Negro community, because it is wrong. I will continue to oppose it, because it is immoral and self-destructive.

"A year of beginnings and of transition"

In March 1967 we announced my resumption of regular activities in Chicago on a schedule similar to that I maintained from January through November of the previous year. I took a brief leave of absence from our civil rights action program in order to write a book on the problems and progress of the movement during the past few years. I spent the months of January and February completing my book, entitled *Where Do We Go from Here, Chaos or Community?* In March I met with Al Raby and Chicago's other outstanding and committed civil rights leaders to evaluate the progress of our several ongoing programs and to lay plans for the next phase of our drive to end slums.

It was clear to me that city agencies had been inert in upholding their commitment to the open housing pact. I had to express our swelling disillusionment with the foot-dragging negative actions of agencies such as the Chicago Housing Authority, Department of Urban Renewal, and the Commission on Human Relations. It appeared that, for all intents and purposes, the public agencies had reneged on the agreement and had in fact given credence to the apostles of social disorder who proclaimed the housing agreement a sham and a batch of false promises. The city's inaction was not just a rebuff to the Chicago Freedom Movement or a courtship of the white backlash, but also another hot coal on the smoldering fires of discontent and despair that are rampant in our black communities. For more than a month during the marches we were told to come to the bargaining table, that compromise and negotiation were the only ways to solve the complex, multi-layered problems of open occupancy. We came, we sat, we negotiated. We reached the summit and then nearly seven months later we found that much of the ground had been cut out from beneath us.

I could not say that all was lost. There were many decent respected and sincere persons on the Leadership Council who had not broken faith. I pleaded with those responsible and responsive persons to take a good long hard look at the facts and act now in an effort to regain the spirit of good faith that existed when we began. It was not too late, even with the failures of yesterday to renew the effort and take some first steps toward the goals pledged last August.

Open housing had to become more than a meaningless scrap of paper. It had to become a reality if this city was to be saved. Our minds and our hearts were open for some real good faith reevaluation and determination to move on, but we also were ready to expose this evil. I had about reached the conclusion that it was going to be almost necessary to engage in massive demonstrations to deal with the problem.

We look back at 1966 as a year of beginnings and of transition. For those of us who came to Chicago from Georgia, Mississippi, and Alabama, it was a year of vital education. Our organization, carried out in conjunction with the very capable local leadership, experienced fits and starts, setbacks and positive progress. We found ourselves confronted by the hard realities of a social system in many ways more resistant to change than the rural South.

While we were under no illusions about Chicago, in all frankness we found the job greater than even we imagined. And yet on balance we believed that the combination of our organization and the wide-ranging forces of goodwill in Chicago produced the basis for changes.

I am thinking now of some teenage boys in Chicago. They have nicknames like "Tex," and "Pueblo," and "Goat" and "Teddy." They hail from the Negro slums. Forsaken by society, they once proudly fought and lived for street gangs like the Vice Lords, the Roman Saints, the Rangers. I met these boys and heard their stories in discussions we had on some long, cold nights at the slum apartment I rented in the West Side ghetto of Chicago.

I was shocked at the venom they poured out against the world. At times I shared their despair and felt a hopelessness that these young Americans could ever embrace the concept of nonviolence as the effective and powerful instrument of social reform. All their lives, boys like this have known life as a madhouse of violence and degradation. Some have never experienced a meaningful family life. Some have police records. Some dropped out of the incredibly bad slum schools, then were deprived of honorable work, then took to the streets.

But this year, they gave us all the gift of nonviolence, which is indeed the gift of love. The Freedom Movement has tried to bring a message to boys like Tex. First we explained that violence can be put down by armed might and police work, that physical force can never solve the

underlying social problems. Second, we promised them we could prove, by example, that nonviolence works.

The young slum dweller has good reason to be suspicious of promises. But these young people in Chicago agreed last winter to give nonviolence a test. Then came the very long, very tense, hot summer of 1966, and the first test for many Chicago youngsters: the Freedom March through Mississippi. Gang members went there in carloads.

Those of us who had been in the movement for years were apprehensive about the behavior of the boys. Before the march ended, they were to be attacked by tear gas. They were to be called upon to protect women and children on the march, with no other weapon than their own bodies. To them, it would be a strange and possibly nonsensical way to respond to violence.

But they reacted splendidly! They learned in Mississippi, and returned to teach in Chicago, the beautiful lesson of acting against evil by renouncing force.

29

BLACK POWER

Negroes can still march down the path of nonviolence and interracial amity if white America will meet them with honest determination to rid society of its inequality and inhumanity.

JUNE 6, 1966
James Meredith, who integrated the University of Mississippi in 1962, is wounded by a sniper during his "March Against Fear" designed to encourage black voting in Mississippi; King and other civil rights leaders agree to continue the march

JUNE 16
Stokely Carmichael ignites controversy by using the "Black Power" slogan

---

J ames Meredith has been shot!"

It was about three o'clock in the afternoon on a Monday in June 1966, and I was presiding over the regular staff meeting of the Southern Christian Leadership Conference in our Atlanta headquarters. When we heard that Meredith had been shot in the back only a day after he had begun his Freedom March through Mississippi, there was a momentary hush of anger and dismay throughout the room. Our horror was compounded by the fact that the early reports announced that Meredith was dead. Soon the silence was broken, and from every corner of the room came expressions of outrage. The business of the meeting was forgotten in the shock of this latest evidence that a Negro's life is still worthless in many parts of his own country.

When order was finally restored, our executive staff immediately

agreed that the march must continue. After all, we reasoned, Meredith began his lonely journey as a pilgrimage against fear. Wouldn't failure to continue only intensify the fears of the oppressed and deprived Negroes of Mississippi? Would this not be a setback for the whole civil rights movement and a blow to nonviolent discipline?

After several calls between Atlanta and Memphis, we learned that the earlier reports of Meredith's death were false and that he would recover. This news brought relief, but it did not alter our feeling that the civil rights movement had a moral obligation to continue along the path that Meredith had begun.

The next morning I was off to Memphis along with several members of my staff. Floyd McKissick, national director of CORE, flew in from New York and joined us on the flight from Atlanta to Memphis. After landing we went directly to the Municipal Hospital to visit Meredith. We were happy to find him resting well. After expressing our sympathy and gratitude for his courageous witness, Floyd and I shared our conviction with him that the march should continue in order to demonstrate to the nation and the world that Negroes would never again be intimidated by the terror of extremist white violence. Realizing that Meredith was often a loner and that he probably wanted to continue the march without a large group, we felt that it would take a great deal of persuasion to convince him that the issue involved the whole civil rights movement. Fortunately, he soon saw this and agreed that we should continue without him. We spent some time discussing the character and logistics of the march, and agreed that we would consult with him daily on every decision.

As we prepared to leave, the nurse came to the door and said, "Mr. Meredith, there is Mr. Carmichael in the lobby who would like to see you and Dr. King. Should I give him permission to come in?" Meredith consented. Stokely Carmichael entered with his associate, Cleveland Sellers, and immediately reached out for Meredith's hand. He expressed his concern and admiration and brought messages of sympathy from his colleagues in the Student Nonviolent Coordinating Committee. After a brief conversation we all agreed that James should get some rest and that we should not burden him with any additional talk. We left the room assuring him that we would conduct the march in his spirit and would seek as never before to expose

the ugly racism that pervaded Mississippi and to arouse a new sense of dignity and manhood in every Negro who inhabited the bastion of man's inhumanity to man.

In a brief conference Floyd, Stokely and I agreed that the march would be jointly sponsored by CORE, SNCC, and SCLC, with the understanding that all other civil rights organizations would be invited to join. It was also agreed that we would issue a national call for support and participation.

One hour later, after making staff assignments and setting up headquarters at the Rev. James Lawson's church in Memphis, a group of us packed into four automobiles and made our way to that desolate spot on Highway 51 where James Meredith had been shot the day before. So began the second stage of the Meredith Mississippi Freedom March.

"Disappointment produces despair and despair produces bitterness"

As we walked down the meandering highway in the sweltering heat, there was much talk and many questions were raised.

"I'm not for that nonviolence stuff anymore," shouted one of the younger activists.

"If one of those damn white Mississippi crackers touches me, I'm gonna knock the hell out of him," shouted another.

Later on a discussion of the composition of the march came up.

"This should be an all-black march," said one marcher. "We don't need any more white phonies and liberals invading our movement. This is our march."

Once during the afternoon we stopped to sing, "We Shall Overcome." The voices rang out with all of the traditional fervor, the glad thunders and the gentle strength that had always characterized the singing of this noble song. But when we came to the stanza which speaks of "black and white together," the voices of a few of the marchers were muted. I asked them later why they refused to sing that verse. The retort was, "This is a new day, we don't sing those words anymore. In fact, the whole song should be discarded. Not 'We Shall Overcome,' but 'We Shall Overrun.'"

As I listened to all these comments, the words fell on my ears

like strange music from a foreign land. My hearing was not attuned to the sound of such bitterness. I guess I should not have been surprised. I should have known that in an atmosphere where false promises are daily realities, where deferred dreams are nightly facts, where acts of unpunished violence toward Negroes are a way of life, nonviolence would eventually be seriously questioned. I should have been reminded that disappointment produces despair and despair produces bitterness, and that the one thing certain about bitterness is its blindness. Bitterness has not the capacity to make the distinction between some and *all*. When some members of the dominant group, particularly those in power, are racist in attitude and practice, bitterness accuses the whole group.

At the end of the march that first day we all went back to Memphis and spent the night in a Negro motel, since we had not yet secured the tents that would serve as shelter each of the following nights on our journey. The discussion continued at the motel. I decided that I would plead patiently with my brothers to remain true to the time-honored principle of our movement. I began with a plea for nonviolence. This immediately aroused some of our friends from the Deacons for Defense, who contended that self-defense was essential and that therefore nonviolence should not be a prerequisite for participation in the march. They were joined in this view by some of the activists from CORE and SNCC.

I tried to make it clear that besides opposing violence on principle, I could imagine nothing more impractical and disastrous than for any of us, through misguided judgment, to precipitate a violent confrontation in Mississippi. We had neither the resources nor the techniques to win. Furthermore, I asserted, many Mississippi whites, from the government on down, would enjoy nothing more than for us to turn to violence in order to use this as an excuse to wipe out scores of Negroes in and out of the march. Finally, I contended that the debate over the question of self-defense was unnecessary since few people suggested that Negroes should not defend themselves as individuals when attacked. The question was not whether one should use his gun when his home was attacked, but whether it was tactically wise to use a gun while participating in an organized demonstration. If they lowered the banner of nonviolence, I said, Missis-

sippi injustice would not be exposed and the moral issues would be obscured.

Next the question of the participation of whites was raised. Stokely Carmichael contended that the inclusion of whites in the march should be de-emphasized and that the dominant appeal should be made for black participation. Others in the room agreed. As I listened to Stokely, I thought about the years that we had worked together in communities all across the South, and how joyously we had then welcomed and accepted our white allies in the movement. What accounted for this reversal in Stokely's philosophy?

I surmised that much of the change had its psychological roots in the experience of SNCC in Mississippi during the summer of 1964, when a large number of Northern white students had come down to help in that racially torn state. What the SNCC workers saw was the most articulate, powerful, and self-assured young white people coming to work with the poorest of the Negro people—and simply overwhelming them. That summer Stokely and others in SNCC had probably unconsciously concluded that this was no good for Negroes, for it simply increased their sense of their own inadequacies. Of course, the answer to this dilemma was not to give up, not to conclude that blacks must work with blacks in order for Negroes to gain a sense of their own meaning. The answer was only to be found in persistent trying, perpetual experimentation, persevering togetherness.

Like life, racial understanding is not something that we find but something that we must create. What we find when we enter these mortal plains is existence; but existence is the raw material out of which all life must be created. A productive and happy life is not something you find; it is something you make. And so the ability of Negroes and whites to work together, to understand each other, will not be found ready-made; it must be created by the fact of contact.

Along these lines, I implored everyone in the room to see the morality of making the march completely interracial. Consciences must be enlisted in our movement, I said, not merely racial groups. I reminded them of the dedicated whites who had suffered, bled, and died in the cause of racial justice, and suggested that to reject white

participation now would be a shameful repudiation of all for which they had sacrificed.

Finally, I said that the formidable foe we now faced demanded more unity than ever before and that I would stretch every point to maintain this unity, but that I could not in good conscience agree to continue my personal involvement and that of SCLC in the march if it were not publicly affirmed that it was based on nonviolence and the participation of both black and white. After a few more minutes of discussion, Floyd and Stokely agreed that we could unite around these principles as far as the march was concerned. The next morning, we had a joint press conference affirming that the march was nonviolent and that whites were welcomed.

Now I've said all along and I still say it, that no individual in our movement can change Mississippi. No one organization in our movement can do the job in Mississippi alone. I have always contended that if all of us get together, we can change the face of Mississippi. This isn't any time for organizational conflicts, this isn't any time for ego battles over who's going to be the leader. We are all the leaders here in this struggle in Mississippi. You see, to change Mississippi we've got to be together. We aren't dealing with a force that has little power. We are dealing with powerful political dynasties, and somehow we must set out to be that David of Truth sent out against the Goliath of Injustice. And we can change this state. And I believe firmly that if we will stick together like this, we are going to do it.

"Black Power!"

As the day progressed, debates and discussions continued, but they were usually pushed to the background by the on-rush of enthusiasm engendered by the large crowds that turned out to greet us in every town. We had been marching for about ten days when we passed through Grenada on the way to Greenwood. Stokely did not conceal his growing eagerness to reach Greenwood. This was SNCC territory, in the sense that the organization had worked courageously there during that turbulent summer of 1964.

As we approached the city, large crowds of old friends and new turned out to welcome us. At a huge mass meeting that night, which was held in a city park, Stokely mounted the platform and after

arousing the audience with a powerful attack on Mississippi justice, he proclaimed: "What we need is black power." Willie Ricks, the fiery orator of SNCC, leaped to the platform and shouted, "What do you want?" The crowd roared "Black Power." Again and again Ricks cried, "What do you want?" and the response "Black Power" grew louder and louder, until it had reached fever pitch.

So Greenwood turned out to be the arena for the birth of the Black Power slogan in the civil rights movement. The phrase had been used long before by Richard Wright and others, but never until that night had it been used as a slogan in the civil rights movement. For people who had been crushed so long by white power and who had been taught that black was degrading, this slogan had a ready appeal.

Immediately, however, I had reservations about its use. I had the deep feeling that it was an unfortunate choice of words for a slogan. Moreover, I saw it bringing about division within the ranks of the marchers. For a day or two there was fierce competition between those who were wedded to the Black Power slogan and those wedded to Freedom Now. Speakers on each side sought desperately to get the crowds to chant their slogan the loudest.

Now, there is a kind of concrete, real black power that I believe in. I don't believe in black separatism, I don't believe in black power that would have racist overtones, but certainly if black power means the amassing of political and economic power in order to gain our just and legitimate goals, then we all believe in that. And I think that all white people of goodwill believe in that.

We are 10 percent of the population of this nation and it would be foolish for me to stand up and tell you we are going to get our freedom by ourselves. There's going to have to be a coalition of conscience and we aren't going to be free here in Mississippi and anywhere in the United States until there is a committed empathy on the part of the white man of this country, and he comes to see along with us that segregation denigrates him as much as it does the Negro. I would be misleading you if I made you feel that we could win a violent campaign. It's impractical even to think about it. The minute we start, we will end up getting many people killed unnecessarily. Now, I'm ready to die myself. Many other committed people are ready to die. If you believe in something firmly, if you believe in it truly, if you believe it in your

heart, you are willing to die for it, but I'm not going to advocate a method that brings about unnecessary death.

Sensing this widening split in our ranks, I asked Stokely and Floyd McKissick to join me in a frank discussion of the problem. We met the next morning, along with members of each of our staffs, in a small Catholic parish house in Yazoo City. For five long hours I pleaded with the group to abandon the Black Power slogan. It was my contention that a leader has to be concerned about the problem of semantics. Each word, I said, has a denotative meaning—its explicit and recognized sense—and a connotative meaning—its suggestive sense. While the concept of legitimate black power might be denotatively sound, the slogan "Black Power" carried the wrong connotations. I mentioned the implications of violence that the press had already attached to the phrase. And I went on to say that some of the rash statements on the part of a few marchers only reinforced this impression.

Stokely replied by saying that the question of violence versus nonviolence was irrelevant. The real question was the need for black people to consolidate their political and economic resources to achieve power. "Power," he said, "is the only thing respected in this world, and we must get it at any cost." Then he looked me squarely in the eye and said, "Martin, you know as well as I do that practically every other ethnic group in America has done just this. The Jews, the Irish, and the Italians did it, why can't we?"

"That is just the point," I answered. "No one has ever heard the Jews publicly chant a slogan of Jewish power, but they have power. Through group unity, determination, and creative endeavor, they have gained it. The same thing is true of the Irish and Italians. Neither group has used a slogan of Irish or Italian power, but they have worked hard to achieve it. This is exactly what we must do," I said. "We must use every constructive means to amass economic and political power. This is the kind of legitimate power we need. We must work to build racial pride and refute the notion that black is evil and ugly. But this must come through a program, not merely through a slogan."

Stokely and Floyd insisted that the slogan itself was important. "How can you arouse people to unite around a program without a

slogan as a rallying cry? Didn't the labor movement have slogans? Haven't we had slogans all along in the freedom movement? What we need is a new slogan with 'black' in it."

I conceded the fact that we must have slogans. But why have one that would confuse our allies, isolate the Negro community, and give many prejudiced whites, who might otherwise be ashamed of their anti-Negro feeling, a ready excuse for self-justification?

Throughout the lengthy discussion, Stokely and Floyd remained adamant, and Stokely concluded by saying, with candor, "Martin, I deliberately decided to raise this issue on the march in order to give it a national forum, and force you to take a stand for Black Power."

I laughed. "I have been used before," I said to Stokely. "One more time won't hurt."

The meeting ended with the SCLC staff members still agreeing with me that the slogan was unfortunate and would only divert attention from the evils of Mississippi while most CORE and SNCC staff members joined Stokely and Floyd in insisting that it should be projected nationally. In a final attempt to maintain unity I suggested that we compromise by not chanting either "Black Power" or "Freedom Now" for the rest of the march. In this way, neither the people nor the press would be confused by the apparent conflict, and staff members would not appear to be at loggerheads. They all agreed with this compromise.

"A cry of disappointment"

But while the chant died out, the press kept the debate going. News stories now centered, not on the injustices of Mississippi, but on the apparent ideological division in the civil rights movement. Every revolutionary movement has its peaks of united activity and its valleys of debate and internal confusion. This debate might well have been little more than a healthy internal difference of opinion, but the press loves the sensational and it could not allow the issue to remain within the private domain of the movement. In every drama there has to be an antagonist and a protagonist, and if the antagonist is not there the press will find and build one.

So Black Power is now a part of the nomenclature of the national community. To some it is abhorrent, to others dynamic; to some it

is repugnant, to others exhilarating; to some it is destructive, to others it is useful. Since Black Power means different things to different people and indeed, being essentially an emotional concept, can mean different things to the same person on differing occasions, it is impossible to attribute its ultimate meaning to any single individual or organization. One must look beyond personal styles, verbal flourishes, and the hysteria of the mass media to assess its values, its assets and liabilities honestly.

First, it is necessary to understand that Black Power is a cry of disappointment. The Black Power slogan did not spring full grown from the head of some philosophical Zeus. It was born from the wounds of despair and disappointment. It was a cry of daily hurt and persistent pain. For centuries the Negro has been caught in the tentacles of white power. Many Negroes have given up faith in the white majority because white power with total control has left them empty-handed. So in reality the call for Black Power is a reaction to the failure of white power.

Many of the young people proclaiming Black Power today were but yesterday the devotees of black-white cooperation and nonviolent direct action. With great sacrifice and dedication and a radiant faith in the future they labored courageously in the rural areas of the South; with idealism they accepted blows without retaliating; with dignity they allowed themselves to be plunged into filthy, stinking jail cells; with a majestic scorn for risk and danger they nonviolently confronted the Jim Clarks and the Bull Connors of the South, and exposed the disease of racism in the body politic. If they are America's angry children today, this anger is not congenital. It is a response to the feeling that a real solution is hopelessly distant because of the inconsistencies, resistance, and faintheartedness of those in power. If Stokely Carmichael now says that nonviolence is irrelevant, it is because he, as a dedicated veteran of many battles, has seen with his own eyes the most brutal white violence against Negroes and white civil rights workers, and he has seen it go unpunished.

Their frustration is further fed by the fact that even when blacks and whites die together in the cause of justice, the death of the white person gets more attention and concern than the death of the black person. Stokely and his colleagues from SNCC were with us in Alabama when Jimmy Lee Jackson, a brave young Negro man, was killed and

*when James Reeb, a committed Unitarian white minister, was fatally
clubbed to the ground. They remembered how President Johnson sent
flowers to the gallant Mrs. Reeb, and in his eloquent "We Shall Overcome" speech paused to mention that one person, James Reeb, had
already died in the struggle. Somehow the President forgot to mention
Jimmy, who died first. The parents and sister of Jimmy received no
flowers from the President. The students felt this keenly. Not that they
felt that the death of James Reeb was less than tragic, but because they
felt that the failure to mention Jimmy Jackson only reinforced the impression that to white America the life of a Negro is insignificant and
meaningless.*

"Powerlessness into creative and positive power"

Second, Black Power, in its broad and positive meaning, was a call
to black people to amass the political and economic strength to
achieve their legitimate goals. No one could deny that the Negro was
in dire need of this kind of legitimate power. Indeed, one of the
great problems that the Negro confronted was his lack of power.
From the old plantations of the South to the newer ghettos of the
North, the Negro was confined to a life of voicelessness and powerlessness. Stripped of the right to make decisions concerning his life
and destiny, he was subject to the authoritarian and sometimes
whimsical decisions of the white power structure. The plantation
and the ghetto were created by those who had power both to confine
those who had no power and to perpetuate their powerlessness. The
problem of transforming the ghetto was, therefore, a problem of
power—a confrontation between the forces of power demanding
change and the forces of power dedicated to preserving the status
quo.

Power, properly understood, is the ability to achieve purpose. It
is the strength required to bring about social, political, or economic
changes. In this sense power is not only desirable but necessary in
order to implement the demands of love and justice. One of the
greatest problems of history is that the concepts of love and power
are usually contrasted as polar opposites. Love is identified with a
resignation of power and power with a denial of love. What is
needed is a realization that power without love is reckless and abu-

sive and that love without power is sentimental and anemic. Power
at its best is love implementing the demands of justice. Justice at its
best is love correcting everything that stands against love.

There is nothing essentially wrong with power. The problem is
that in America power is unequally distributed. This has led Negro
Americans in the past to seek their goals through love and moral
suasion devoid of power and white Americans to seek their goals
through power devoid of love and conscience. It has led a few extremists to advocate for Negroes the same destructive and con-
scienceless power that they justly abhorred in whites. It is precisely
this collision of immoral power with powerless morality which con-
stitutes the major crisis of our times.

"THE NECESSITY FOR TEMPORARY SEGREGATION"

There are points at which I see the necessity for temporary segregation in order to get to the integrated society. I can point to some cases.
I've seen this in the South, in schools being integrated, and I've seen it
with Teachers' Associations being integrated. Often when they merge,
the Negro is integrated without power. . . . We don't want to be integrated *out* of power; we want to be integrated *into* power.

And this is why I think it is absolutely necessary to see integration in
political terms, to see that there are some situations where separation
may serve as a temporary way-station to the ultimate goal which we
seek, which I think is the only answer in the final analysis to the problem of a truly integrated society.

March 25, 1968

In his struggle for racial justice, the Negro must seek to transform his condition of powerlessness into creative and positive
power. To the extent that Black Power advocated the development
of political awareness and strength in the Negro community, the
election of blacks to key positions, and the use of the bloc vote to
liberalize the political climate and achieve our just aspirations for
freedom and human dignity, it was a positive and legitimate call to
action.

Black Power was also a call for the pooling of black financial
resources to achieve economic security. While the ultimate answer
to the Negroes' economic dilemma was in a massive federal program

for all the poor along the lines of A. Philip Randolph's Freedom Budget, a kind of Marshall Plan for the disadvantaged, there was something that the Negro himself could do to throw off the shackles of poverty.

Finally, Black Power was a psychological call to manhood. For years the Negro had been taught that he was nobody, that his color was a sign of his biological depravity, that his being was stamped with an indelible imprint of inferiority, that his whole history was soiled with the filth of worthlessness. All too few people realize how slavery and racial segregation scarred the soul and wounded the spirit of the black man. The whole dirty business of slavery was based on the premise that the Negro was a thing to be used, not a person to be respected. Black Power assumed that Negroes would be slaves unless there was a new power to counter the force of the men who are still determined to be masters rather than brothers.

Black Power was a psychological reaction to the psychological indoctrination that led to the creation of the perfect slave. While this reaction often led to negative and unrealistic responses and frequently brought about intemperate words and actions, one must not overlook the positive value in calling the Negro to a new sense of manhood, to a deep feeling of racial pride, and to an audacious appreciation of his heritage. The Negro had to be grasped by a new realization of his dignity and worth. He had to stand up amid a system that still oppresses him and develop an unassailable and majestic sense of his own value. He could no longer be ashamed of being black.

The job of arousing manhood within a people that had been taught for so many centuries that they were nobody is not easy. Even semantics conspire to make that which is black seem ugly and degrading. In Roget's *Thesaurus* there are some 120 synonyms for "blackness" and at least 60 of them are offensive—such words as "blot," "soot," "grime," "devil," and "foul." There are some 134 synonyms for "whiteness," and all are favorable, expressed in such words as "purity," "cleanliness," "chastity," and "innocence." A white lie is better than a black lie. The most degenerate member of a family is the "black sheep," not the "white sheep."

The history books, which had almost completely ignored the contribution of the Negro in American history, only served to inten-

sify the Negroes' sense of worthlessness and to augment the anachro-
nistic doctrine of white supremacy. All too many Negroes and whites
are unaware of the fact that the first American to shed blood in the
revolution which freed this country from British oppression was a
black seaman named Crispus Attucks. Negroes and whites are almost totally oblivious of the fact that it was a Negro physician, Dr.
Daniel Hale Williams, who performed the first successful operation
on the heart in America. Another Negro physician, Dr. Charles
Drew, was largely responsible for developing the method of separating blood plasma and storing it on a large scale, a process that saved
thousands of lives in World War II and has made possible many of
the important advances in postwar medicine. History books have
virtually overlooked the many Negro scientists and inventors who
have enriched American life. Although a few refer to George Washington Carver, whose research in agricultural products helped to re-
vive the economy of the South when the throne of King Cotton
began to totter, they ignore the contribution of Norbert Rillieux,
whose invention of an evaporating pan revolutionized the process of
sugar refining. How many people know that the multimillion-dollar
United Shoe Machinery Company developed from the shoe-lasting
machine invented in the last century by a Negro from Dutch Guiana,
Jan Matzeliger; or that Granville T. Woods, an expert in electric mo-
tors, whose many patents speeded the growth and improvement of
the railroads at the beginning of this century, was a Negro?

Even the Negroes' contribution to the music of America is sometimes overlooked in astonishing ways. In 1965 my oldest son and
daughter entered an integrated school in Atlanta. A few months later
my wife and I were invited to attend a program entitled "Music that
has made America great." As the evening unfolded, we listened to
the folk songs and melodies of the various immigrant groups. We
were certain that the program would end with the most original of
all American music, the Negro spiritual. But we were mistaken. Instead, all the students, including our children, ended the program by
singing "Dixie."

As we rose to leave the hall, my wife and I looked at each other
with a combination of indignation and amazement. All the students,
black and white, all the parents present that night, and all the faculty
members had been victimized by just another expression of Ameri-

ca's penchant for ignoring the Negro, making him invisible and
making his contributions insignificant. I wept within that night. I
wept for my children and all black children who have been denied a
knowledge of their heritage; I wept for all white children, who,
through daily miseducation, are taught that the Negro is an irrelevant entity in American society; I wept for all the white parents and
teachers who are forced to overlook the fact that the wealth of cultural and technological progress in America is a result of the com-
monwealth of inpouring contributions.

"A slogan that cannot be implemented into a program"

Nevertheless, in spite of the positive aspects of Black Power, which
were compatible with what we have sought to do in the civil rights
movement without the slogan, its negative values, I believed, prevented it from having the substance and program to become the
basic strategy for the civil rights movement.

Beneath all the satisfaction of a gratifying slogan, Black Power
was a nihilistic philosophy born out of the conviction that the Negro
can't win. It was, at bottom, the view that American society is so
hopelessly corrupt and enmeshed in evil that there is no possibility
of salvation from within. Although this thinking is understandable
as a response to a white power structure that never completely committed itself to true equality for the Negro, and a die-hard mentality
that sought to shut all windows and doors against the winds of
change, it nonetheless carried the seeds of its own doom.

Before this century, virtually all revolutions had been based on
hope and hate. The hope was expressed in the rising expectation
of freedom and justice. What was new about Mahatma Gandhi's
movement in India was that he mounted a revolution on hope and
love, hope and nonviolence. This same new emphasis characterized
the civil rights movement in our country dating from the Montgomery bus boycott of 1956 to the Selma movement of 1965. We
maintained the hope while transforming the hate of traditional revolutions into positive nonviolent power. As long as the hope was fulfilled there was little questioning of nonviolence. But when the hopes
were blasted, when people came to see that in spite of progress their
conditions were still insufferable, when they looked out and saw

more poverty, more school segregation, and more slums, despair began to set in.

But revolution, though born of despair, cannot long be sustained by despair. This was the ultimate contradiction of the Black Power movement. It claimed to be the most revolutionary wing of the social revolution taking place in the United States. Yet it rejected the one thing that keeps the fire of revolutions burning: the ever-present flame of hope. When hope dies, a revolution degenerates into an undiscriminating catchall for evanescent and futile gestures. The Negro cannot entrust his destiny to a philosophy nourished solely on despair, to a slogan that cannot be implemented into a program.

Over cups of coffee in my home in Atlanta and my apartment in Chicago, I often talked late at night and over into the small hours of the morning with proponents of Black Power who argued passionately about the validity of violence and riots. They didn't quote Gandhi or Tolstoy. Their Bible was Frantz Fanon's *The Wretched of the Earth.* This black psychiatrist from Martinique, who went to Algeria to work with the National Liberation Front in its fight against the French, argued in his book—a well-written book, incidentally, with many penetrating insights—that violence is a psychologically healthy and tactically sound method for the oppressed. And so, realizing that they are a part of that vast company of the "wretched of the earth," young American Negroes, who were involved in the Black Power movement, often quoted Fanon's belief that violence is the only thing that will bring about liberation.

The plain, inexorable fact was that any attempt of the American Negro to overthrow his oppressor with violence would not work. We did not need President Johnson to tell us this by reminding Negro rioters that they were outnumbered ten to one. The courageous efforts of our own insurrectionist brothers, such as Denmark Vesey and Nat Turner, should be eternal reminders to us that violent rebellion is doomed from the start. Anyone leading a violent rebellion must be willing to make an honest assessment regarding the possible casualties to a minority population confronting a well-armed, wealthy majority with a fanatical right wing that would delight in exterminating thousands of black men, women, and children.

Occasionally Negroes contended that the 1965 Watts riot and

other riots in various cities represented effective civil rights action. But those who expressed this view always ended up with stumbling words when asked what concrete gains were won as a result. At best the riots produced a little additional anti-poverty money, allotted by frightened government officials, and a few water sprinklers to cool the children of the ghettos. Nowhere did the riots win any concrete improvement such as did the organized protest demonstrations.

When one tries to pin down advocates of violence as to what acts would be effective, the answers are blatantly illogical. Sometimes they talk of overthrowing racist state and local governments. They fail to see that no internal revolution has ever succeeded in overthrowing a government by violence unless the government had already lost the allegiance and effective control of its armed forces. Anyone in his right mind knows that this will not happen in the United States.

Nonviolence is power, but it is the right and good use of power. Constructively it can save the white man as well as the Negro. Racial segregation is buttressed by such irrational fears as loss of preferred economic privilege, altered social status, intermarriage, and adjustment to new situations. Through sleepless nights and haggard days, numerous white people struggled pitifully to combat these fears. By following the path of escape, some seek to ignore questions of race relations, and to close their minds to the issues involved. Others, placing their faith in legal maneuvers, counsel massive resistance. Still others hope to drown their fears by engaging in acts of meanness and violence toward their Negro brethren. But, how futile are all these remedies! Instead of eliminating fear, they instill deeper and more pathological fears. The white man, through his own efforts, through education and goodwill, through searching his conscience and through confronting the fact of integration, must do a great deal to free himself of these paralyzing fears. But to master fear he must also depend on the spirit the Negro generates toward him. Only through our adherence to nonviolence—which also means love in its strong and commanding sense—will the fear in the white community be mitigated.

"A genuine leader is not a searcher for consensus"

People have said to me, "Since violence is the new cry, isn't there a danger that you will lose touch with the people in the ghetto and

be out of step with the times if you don't change your views on nonviolence?"

My answer is always the same. While I am convinced that the vast majority of Negroes reject violence, even if they did not I would not be interested in being a consensus leader. I refuse to determine what is right by taking a Gallup poll of the trends of the time. I imagine that there were leaders in Germany who sincerely opposed what Hitler was doing to the Jews. But they took their poll and discovered that anti-Semitism was the prevailing trend. In order to "be in step with the times," in order to "keep in touch," they yielded to one of the most ignominious evils that history has ever known.

Ultimately, a genuine leader is not a searcher for consensus but a molder of consensus. If every Negro in the United States turns to violence, I will choose to be that one lone voice preaching that this is the wrong way. Maybe this sounds like arrogance. But it is not intended that way. It is simply my way of saying that I would rather be a man of conviction than a man of conformity. Occasionally in life one develops a conviction so precious and meaningful that he will stand on it till the end. This is what I have found in nonviolence.

I cannot make myself believe that God wanted me to hate. I'm tired of violence, I've seen too much of it. I've seen such hate on the faces of too many sheriffs in the South. And I'm not going to let my oppressor dictate to me what method I must use. Our oppressors have used violence. Our oppressors have used hatred. Our oppressors have used rifles and guns. I'm not going to stoop down to their level. I want to rise to a higher level. We have a power that can't be found in Molotov cocktails.

One of the greatest paradoxes of the Black Power movement was that it talked unceasingly about not imitating the values of white society, but in advocating violence it was imitating the worst, the most brutal, and the most uncivilized value of American life. American Negroes had not been mass murderers. They had not murdered children in Sunday school, nor had they hung white men on trees bearing strange fruit. They had not been hooded perpetrators of violence, lynching human beings at will and drowning them at whim.

I am concerned that Negroes achieve full status as citizens and as human beings here in the United States. But I am also concerned about our moral uprightness and the health of our souls. Therefore I must oppose any attempt to gain our freedom by the methods of malice, hate, and violence that have characterized our oppressors.

Hate is just as injurious to the hater as it is to the hated. Like an unchecked cancer, hate corrodes the personality and eats away its vital unity. Many of our inner conflicts are rooted in hate. This is why the psychiatrists say, "Love or perish." Hate is too great a burden to bear.

Humanity is waiting for something other than blind imitation of the past. If we want truly to advance a step further, if we want to turn over a new leaf and really set a new man afoot, we must begin to turn mankind away from the long and desolate night of violence. May it not be that the new man the world needs is the nonviolent man? Longfellow said, "In this world a man must either be an anvil or a hammer." We must be hammers shaping a new society rather than anvils molded by the old. This not only will make us new men, but will give us a new kind of power. It will not be Lord Acton's image of power that tends to corrupt or absolute power that corrupts absolutely. It will be power infused with love and justice, that will change dark yesterdays into bright tomorrows, and lift us from the fatigue of despair to the buoyancy of hope. A dark, desperate, confused, and sin-sick world waits for this new kind of man and this new kind of power.

30

BEYOND VIETNAM

Today, young men of America are fighting, dying, and killing in Asian jungles in a war whose purposes are so ambiguous the whole nation seethes with dissent. They are told they are sacrificing for democracy, but the Saigon regime, their ally, is a mockery of democracy and the black American soldier has himself never experienced democracy.

AUGUST 12, 1965
King calls for halt to U.S. bombing of North Vietnam to encourage negotiated settlement of conflict

JANUARY 10, 1966
Backs Georgia State Senator-elect Julian Bond's right to oppose war

MAY 29
Urges halt to bombing on *Face the Nation* televised interview

APRIL 4, 1967
Delivers his first public antiwar speech at New York's Riverside Church

All my adult life I have deplored violence and war as instruments for achieving solutions to mankind's problems. I am firmly committed to the creative power of nonviolence as the force which is capable of winning lasting and meaningful brotherhood and peace. As a minister, a Nobel Prize holder, a civil rights leader, a Negro, a father, and above all as an American, I have wrestled with my conscience.

Despite this—whether right or wrong—in the summer and fall

of 1965, after President Johnson declared himself willing to negotiate, I believed that it was essential for all Americans to publicly avoid the debate on why we were waging war in the far-off lands of Vietnam. I believed that the crucial problem which faced Americans was how to move with great speed and without more bloodshed from the battlefield to the peace table. The issues of culpability and morality, while important, had to be subordinated lest they divert or divide. The President's strong declaration to negotiate, to talk peace, and thus end the death and destruction, had to be accepted, honored, and implemented.

Accepting this premise, my public statements, while condemning all militarism, were directed mainly to the mechanics for achieving an immediate cessation of hostilities. I did not march, I did not demonstrate, I did not rally. I petitioned in direct meetings with the President, and at his invitation with U.N. Ambassador Arthur Goldberg. In my meeting with Ambassador Goldberg, in September 1965, I urged that our efforts to seek peace by negotiations could be speeded by agreeing to negotiate directly with the National Liberation Front, by admitting Red China to the U.N., and by halting the bombing of North Vietnam.

For a while, knowing that my wife shares my passion for peace, I decided that I would leave it to her to take the stands and make the meetings on the peace issue and leave me to concentrate on civil rights. But as the hopeful days became disappointing months, I began the agonizing measurement of government promising words of peace against the baneful, escalating deeds of war. Doubts gnawed at my conscience. Uncertain, but still trusting, we watched setbacks in the search for peace and advances in the search for military advantage.

Some of my friends of both races and others who do not consider themselves my friends expressed disapproval because I had been voicing concern over the war in Vietnam. In newspaper columns and editorials, both in the Negro and general press, it was indicated that Martin King, Jr., is "getting out of his depth." I was chided, even by fellow civil rights leaders, members of Congress, and brothers of the cloth for "not sticking to the business of civil rights."

I agonized a great deal over this whole problem. I went away for two months to do a lot of thinking, but basically to write a book. I

had a chance to reflect, to meditate, and to think. I thought about civil rights and I thought about the world situation and I thought about America.

Something said to me, "Martin, you have got to stand up on this. No matter what it means." I didn't rush into it. I didn't just decide to do it on a moment's notice. I had my own vacillations and I asked questions of whether on the one hand I should do it or whether I shouldn't.

As I went through this period one night I picked up an article entitled "The Children of Vietnam," and I read it. And after reading that article, I said to myself, "Never again will I be silent on an issue that is destroying the soul of our nation and destroying thousands and thousands of little children in Vietnam." I came to the conclusion that there is an existential moment in your life when you must decide to speak for yourself; nobody else can speak for you.

"I was a loud speaker but a quiet actor"

In February 1967, the slender cord which held me threatened to break as our government spurned the simple peace offer—conveyed by one no less than the authorized head of the Soviet Union—to halt our bombing of North Vietnam, not the bombing of all of Vietnam, in return for fully occupied seats at a peace table. We rejected it by demanding a military quid pro quo.

As I look back, I acknowledge that this end of faith was not sudden; it came like the ebbing of a tide. As I reviewed the events, I saw an orderly buildup of evil, an accumulation of inhumanities, each of which alone was sufficient to make men hide in shame. What was woeful, but true, was that my country was only talking peace but was bent on military victory. Inside the glove of peace was the clenched fist of war. I now stood naked with shame and guilt, as indeed every German should have when his government was using its military power to overwhelm other nations. Whether right or wrong, I had for too long allowed myself to be a silent onlooker. At best, I was a loud speaker but a quiet actor, while a charade was being performed.

So often I had castigated those who by silence or inaction condoned and thereby cooperated with the evils of racial injustice. Had

I not, again and again, said that the silent onlooker must bear the responsibility for the brutalities committed by the Bull Connors, or by the murderers of the innocent children in a Birmingham church? Had I not committed myself to the principle that looking away from evil is, in effect, a condoning of it? Those who lynch, pull the trigger, point the cattle prod, or open the fire hoses act in the name of the silent. I had to therefore speak out if I was to erase my name from the bombs which fall over North or South Vietnam, from the canisters of napalm. The time had come—indeed it was past due—when I had to disavow and dissociate myself from those who in the name of peace burn, maim, and kill.

More than that, I had to go from the pulpits and platforms. I had to return to the streets to mobilize men to assemble and petition, in the spirit of our own revolutionary history, for the immediate end of this bloody, immoral, obscene slaughter—for a cause which cries out for a solution before mankind itself is doomed. I could do no less for the salvation of my soul.

I had lived and worked in ghettos throughout the nation, and I traveled tens of thousands of miles each month into dozens of Northern and Southern Negro communities. My direct personal experience with Negroes in all walks of life convinced me that there was deep and widespread disenchantment with the war in Vietnam—first, because they were against war itself, and second, because they felt it has caused a significant and alarming diminishing of concern and attention to civil rights progress. I had held these views for a long time, but Negroes in so many circles urged me to articulate their concern and frustration. They felt civil rights was well on its way to becoming a neglected and forgotten issue long before it was even partially solved.

The great tragedy was that our government declared a war against poverty, and yet it only financed a skirmish against poverty. And this led to great despair. It led to great cynicism and discontent throughout the Negro community. I had lived in the ghettos of Chicago and Cleveland, and I knew the hurt and the cynicism and the discontent. And the fact was that every city in our country was sitting on a potential powderkeg.

*   *   *

As I moved to break the betrayal of my own silences and to speak from the burnings of my own heart—as I called for radical departures from the destruction of Vietnam—many persons questioned me about the wisdom of my path. At the heart of their concern, this query has often loomed large and loud: "Why are you speaking about the war, Dr. King? Why are you joining the voices of dissent?" "Peace and civil rights don't mix," they say. And when I hear them, though I often understand the source of their concern, I nevertheless am greatly saddened that such questions mean that the inquirers have not really known me, my commitment, or my calling. They seem to forget that before I was a civil rights leader, I answered a call, and when God speaks, who can but prophesy. I answered a call which left the spirit of the Lord upon me and anointed me to preach the gospel. And during the early days of my ministry, I read the Apostle Paul saying, "Be ye not conformed to this world, but be ye transformed by the renewing of minds." I decided then that I was going to tell the truth as God revealed it to me. No matter how many people disagreed with me, I decided that I was going to tell the truth.

I believe that the path from Dexter Avenue Baptist Church—the church in Montgomery, Alabama, where I began my pastorate—leads clearly to this sanctuary tonight.

There is . . . a very obvious and almost facile connection between the war in Vietnam and the struggle I and others have been waging in America. A few years ago there was a shining moment in that struggle. It seemed as if there was a real promise of hope for the poor—both black and white—through the poverty program. There were experiments, hopes, new beginnings. Then came the buildup in Vietnam, and I watched this program broken and eviscerated as if it were some idle political plaything of a society gone mad on war. And I knew that America would never invest the necessary funds or energies in rehabilitation of its poor so long as adventures like Vietnam continued to draw men and skills and money like some demonic, destructive suction tube. So I was increasingly compelled to see the war as an enemy of the poor and to attack it as such.

Perhaps a more tragic recognition of reality took place when it became clear to me that the war was doing far more than devastating the hopes of the poor at home. It was sending their sons and their brothers

and their husbands to fight and to die in extraordinarily high proportions relative to the rest of the population. We were taking the black
young men who had been crippled by our society and sending them
eight thousand miles away to guarantee liberties in Southeast Asia
which they had not found in southwest Georgia and East Harlem. So
we have been repeatedly faced with the cruel irony of watching Negro
and white boys on TV screens as they kill and die together for a nation
that has been unable to seat them together in the same schools. So we
watch them in brutal solidarity burning the huts of a poor village, but
we realize that they would hardly live on the same block in Chicago. I
could not be silent in the face of such cruel manipulation of the
poor. . . .

As I have walked among the desperate, rejected, and angry young
men, I have told them that Molotov cocktails and rifles would not solve
their problems. I have tried to offer them my deepest compassion while
maintaining my conviction that social change comes most meaningfully
through nonviolent action. But they asked, and rightly so, "What about
Vietnam?" They asked if our own nation wasn't using massive doses of
violence to solve its problems, to bring about the changes it wanted.
Their questions hit home, and I knew that I could never again raise my
voice against the violence of the oppressed in the ghettos without having
first spoken clearly to the greatest purveyor of violence in the world
today: my own government. For the sake of those boys, for the sake of
this government, for the sake of the hundreds of thousands trembling
under our violence, I cannot be silent.

Now, it should be incandescently clear that no one who has any
concern for the integrity and life of America today can ignore the present war. If America's soul becomes totally poisoned, part of the autopsy
must read "Vietnam." It can never be saved so long as it destroys the
deepest hopes of men the world over. So it is that those of us who are
yet determined that "America will be" are led down the path of protest
and dissent, working for the health of our land.

As if the weight of such a commitment to the life and health of
America were not enough, another burden of responsibility was placed
upon me in 1964; and I cannot forget that the Nobel Peace Prize was
also a commission, a commission to work harder than I had ever
worked before for the brotherhood of man. This is a calling that takes
me beyond national allegiances.

But even if it were not present, I would yet have to live with the meaning of my commitment to the ministry of Jesus Christ. To me the relationship of this ministry to the making of peace is so obvious that I sometimes marvel at those who ask me why I am speaking against the war. Could it be that they do not know that the Good News was meant for all men—for communist and capitalist, for their children and ours, for black and for white, for revolutionary and conservative? Have they forgotten that my ministry is in obedience to the one who loved his enemies so fully that He died for them? What then can I say to the Vietcong or to Castro or to Mao as a faithful minister of this one? Can I threaten them with death or must I not share with them my life?

Finally, as I try to explain for you and for myself the road that leads from Montgomery to this place, I would have offered all that was most valid if I simply said that I must be true to my conviction that I share with all men the calling to be a son of the living God. Beyond the calling of race or nation or creed is this vocation of sonship and brotherhood. Because I believe that the Father is deeply concerned especially for His suffering and helpless and outcast children, I come tonight to speak for them. This I believe to be the privilege and the burden of all of us who deem ourselves bound by allegiances and loyalties which are broader and deeper than nationalism and which go beyond our nation's self-defined goals and positions. We are called to speak for the weak, for the voiceless, for the victims of our nation, for those it calls "enemy," for no document from human hands can make these humans any less our brothers. . . .

The war in Vietnam is but a symptom of a far deeper malady within the American spirit, and if we ignore this sobering reality, we will find ourselves organizing Clergy and Laymen Concerned committees for the next generation. They will be concerned about Guatemala and Peru. They will be concerned about Thailand and Cambodia. They will be concerned about Mozambique and South Africa. We will be marching for these and a dozen other names and attending rallies without end unless there is a significant and profound change in American life and policy. So such thoughts take us beyond Vietnam, but not beyond our calling as sons of the living God.

In 1957, a sensitive American official overseas said that it seemed to him that our nation was on the wrong side of a world revolution. During the past ten years we have seen emerge a pattern of suppression

which has now justified the presence of U.S. military advisors in Vene-
zuela. This need to maintain social stability for our investment accounts
for the counter-revolutionary action of American forces in Guatemala.
It tells why American helicopters are being used against guerrillas in
Cambodia and why American napalm and Green Beret forces have
already been active against rebels in Peru.

It is with such activity in mind that the words of the late John F.
Kennedy come back to haunt us. Five years ago he said, "Those who
make peaceful revolution impossible will make violent revolution inevitable." Increasingly, by choice or by accident, this is the role our nation
has taken: the role of those who make peaceful revolution impossible by
refusing to give up the privileges and the pleasures that come from the
immense profits of overseas investments. I am convinced that if we are
to get on the right side of the world revolution, we as a nation must
undergo a radical revolution of values. We must rapidly begin the shift
from a thing-oriented society to a person-oriented society. When ma-
chines and computers, profit motives and property rights, are considered
more important than people, the giant triplets of racism, extreme materialism, and militarism are incapable of being conquered.

A true revolution of values will soon cause us to question the fair-
ness and justice of many of our past and present policies. On the one
hand we are called to play the Good Samaritan on life's roadside, but
that will be only an initial act. One day we must come to see that the
whole Jericho Road must be transformed so that men and women will
not be constantly beaten and robbed as they make their journey on life's
highway. True compassion is more than flinging a coin to a beggar. It
comes to see that an edifice which produces beggars needs restructuring.

A true revolution of values will soon look uneasily on the glaring
contrast of poverty and wealth. With righteous indignation, it will look
across the seas and see individual capitalists of the West investing huge
sums of money in Asia, Africa, and South America, only to take the
profits out with no concern for the social betterment of the countries,
and say: "This is not just." It will look at our alliance with the landed
gentry of South America and say: "This is not just." The Western arrogance of feeling that it has everything to teach others and nothing to
learn from them is not just.

A true revolution of values will lay hands on the world order and
say of war: "This way of settling differences is not just." This business

of burning human beings with napalm, of filling our nation's homes with orphans and widows, of injecting poisonous drugs of hate into the veins of peoples normally humane, of sending men home from dark and bloody battlefields physically handicapped and psychologically deranged, cannot be reconciled with wisdom, justice, and love. A nation that continues year after year to spend more money on military defense than on programs of social uplift is approaching spiritual death.

America, the richest and most powerful nation in the world, can well lead the way in this revolution of values. There is nothing except a tragic death wish to prevent us from reordering our priorities, so that the pursuit of peace will take precedence over the pursuit of war. There is nothing to keep us from molding a recalcitrant status quo with bruised hands until we have fashioned it into a brotherhood. . . .

These are revolutionary times. All over the globe men are revolting against old systems of exploitation and oppression, and, out of the wounds of a frail world, new systems of justice and equality are being born. The shirtless and barefoot people of the land are rising up as never before. The people who sat in darkness have seen a great light. We in the West must support these revolutions.

It is a sad fact that because of comfort, complacency, a morbid fear of communism, and our proneness to adjust to injustice, the Western nations that initiated so much of the revolutionary spirit of the modern world have now become the arch anti-revolutionaries. This has driven many to feel that only Marxism has a revolutionary spirit. Therefore, communism is a judgment against our failure to make democracy real and follow through on the revolutions that we initiated. Our only hope today lies in our ability to recapture the revolutionary spirit and go out into a sometimes hostile world declaring eternal hostility to poverty, racism, and militarism. With this powerful commitment we shall boldly challenge the status quo and unjust mores, and thereby speed the day when "every valley shall be exalted, and every mountain and hill shall be made low, the crooked shall be made straight, and the rough places plain."

A genuine revolution of values means in the final analysis that our loyalties must become ecumenical rather than sectional. Every nation must now develop an overriding loyalty to mankind as a whole in order to preserve the best in their individual societies. . . .

We must move past indecision to action. We must find new ways to speak for peace in Vietnam and justice throughout the developing world, a world that borders on our doors. If we do not act, we shall surely be dragged down the long, dark, and shameful corridors of time reserved for those who possess power without compassion, might without morality, and strength without sight.

Now let us begin. Now let us rededicate ourselves to the long and bitter, but beautiful, struggle for a new world. This is the calling of the sons of God, and our brothers wait eagerly for our response. Shall we say the odds are too great? Shall we tell them the struggle is too hard? Will our message be that the forces of American life militate against their arrival as full men, and we send our deepest regrets? Or will there be another message—of longing, of hope, of solidarity with their yearnings, of commitment to their cause, whatever the cost? The choice is ours, and though we might prefer it otherwise, we must choose in this crucial moment of human history.

When I first took my position against the war in Vietnam, almost every newspaper in the country criticized me. It was a low period in my life. I could hardly open a newspaper. It wasn't only white people either; it was Negroes. But then I remember a newsman coming to me one day and saying, "Dr. King, don't you think you're going to have to change your position now because so many people are criticizing you? And people who once had respect for you are going to lose respect for you. And you're going to hurt the budget, I understand, of the Southern Christian Leadership Conference; people have cut off support. And don't you think that you have to move now more in line with the administration's policy?" That was a good question, because he was asking me the question of whether I was going to think about what happens to me or what happens to truth and justice in this situation.

On some positions, Cowardice asks the question, "Is it safe?" Expediency asks the question, "Is it politic?" And Vanity comes along and asks the question, "Is it popular?" But Conscience asks the question, "Is it right?" And there comes a time when one must take a position that is neither safe, nor politic, nor popular, but he must do it because Conscience tells him it is right.

The ultimate measure of a man is not where he stands in moments of convenience, but where he stands in moments of challenge, moments

*of great crisis and controversy. And this is where I choose to cast my lot
today. And this is why I wanted to go through with this, because I think
this is where SCLC should be. There may be others who want to go
another way, but when I took up the cross I recognized its meaning. It
is not something that you merely put your hands on. It is not something
that you wear. The cross is something that you bear and ultimately that
you die on. The cross may mean the death of your popularity. It may
mean the death of your bridge to the White House. It may mean the
death of a foundation grant. It may cut your budget down a little, but
take up your cross and just bear it. And that is the way I have decided
to go. Come what may, it doesn't matter now.*

A myth about my views on Vietnam credited me with advocating
the fusion of the civil rights and peace movements, and I was criticized for such a "serious tactical mistake." I held no such view. In a
formal public resolution, my organization, SCLC, and I explicitly
declared that we had no intention of diverting or diminishing our
activities in civil rights, and we outlined extensive programs for the
immediate future in the South as well as in Chicago.

I was saddened that the board of directors of the NAACP, a fellow civil rights organization, would join in the perpetuation of the
myth about my views. They challenged and repudiated a nonexistent
proposition. SCLC and I expressed our view on the war and drew
attention to its damaging effects on civil rights programs, a fact we
believed to be incontrovertible and, therefore, mandatory to express
in the interest of the struggle for equality. I challenged the NAACP
and other critics of my position to take a forthright stand on the
rightness or wrongness of this war, rather than going off creating a
nonexistent issue.

*I am a clergyman as well as a civil rights leader and the moral roots
of our war policy are not unimportant to me. I do not believe our
nation can be a moral leader of justice, equality, and democracy if it is
trapped in the role of a self-appointed world policeman. Throughout
my career in the civil rights movement I have been concerned about
justice for all people. For instance, I strongly feel that we must end not
merely poverty among Negroes but poverty among white people. Likewise, I have always insisted on justice for all the world over, because
justice is indivisible. And injustice anywhere is a threat to justice everywhere. I will not stand idly by when I see an unjust war taking place*

"SO PRECIOUS THAT YOU WILL DIE FOR IT"

I say to you, this morning, that if you have never found something so dear and so precious to you that you will die for it, then you aren't fit to live. You may be thirty-eight years old, as I happen to be, and one day, some great opportunity stands before you and calls upon you to stand up for some great principle, some great issue, some great cause. And you refuse to do it because you are afraid. You refuse to do it because you want to live longer. You're afraid that you will lose your job, or you are afraid that you will be criticized or that you will lose your popularity, or you're afraid that somebody will stab you or shoot at you or bomb your house. So you refuse to take the stand. Well, you may go on and live until you are ninety, but you are just as dead at thirty-eight as you would be at ninety. And the cessation of breathing in your life is but the belated announcement of an earlier death of the spirit. You died when you refused to stand up for right. You died when you refused to stand up for truth. You died when you refused to stand up for justice. . . .

Don't ever think that you're by yourself. Go on to jail if necessary, but you never go alone. Take a stand for that which is right, and the world may misunderstand you, and criticize you. But you never go alone, for somewhere I read that one with God is a majority. And God has a way of transforming a minority into a majority. Walk with him this morning and believe in him and do what is right, and He'll be with you even until the consummation of the ages. Yes, I've seen the lightning flash. I've heard the thunder roll. I've felt sin breakers dashing, trying to conquer my soul, but I heard the voice of Jesus saying, still to fight on. He promised never to leave me alone, never to leave me alone. No, never alone. No, never alone.

Sermon at Ebenezer, November 5, 1967

without in any way diminishing my activity in civil rights, just as millions of Negro and white people are doing day in and day out.

This war played havoc with the destiny of the entire world. It tore up the Geneva Agreement, seriously impaired the United Nations, exacerbated the hatreds between continents and, worse still, between races. It frustrated our development at home, telling our own underprivileged citizens that we place insatiable military demands above their most critical needs; it greatly contributed to the forces of reaction in America and strengthened the military-

industrial complex against which even President Eisenhower solemnly warned us; it practically destroyed Vietnam and left thousands of American and Vietnamese youth maimed and mutilated; and it exposed the whole world to the risk of nuclear warfare.

The Johnson Administration seemed amazingly devoid of statesmanship, and when creative statesmanship wanes, irrational militarism increases. President Kennedy was a man who was big enough to admit when he was wrong—as he did after the Bay of Pigs incident. But Johnson seemed to be unable to make this kind of statesmanlike gesture in connection with Vietnam. Even when he could readily summon popular support to end the bombing in Vietnam, he persisted. Yet bombs in Vietnam also exploded at home; they destroyed the hopes and possibilities for a decent America.

I followed a policy of being very honest with President Johnson when he consulted me about civil rights. I went to the White House when he invited me. I made it very clear to him why I had taken a stand against the war in Vietnam. I had a long talk with him on the telephone about this and made it clear to him I would be standing up against it even more. I was not centering this on President Johnson. I thought there was collective guilt. Four Presidents participated in some way leading us to the war in Vietnam. So, I am not going to put it all on President Johnson. What I was concerned about was that we end the nightmarish war and free our souls.

There isn't a single official of our country that can go anywhere in the world without being stoned and eggs being thrown at him. It's because we have taken on to ourselves a kind of arrogance of power. We've ignored the mandates of justice and morality. And I don't know about you, but I wish I could make a witness more positive about this thing. I wish I was of draft age. I wish I did not have my ministerial exemption. I tell you this morning, I would not fight in the war in Vietnam. I'd go to jail before I'd do it. And I say to the federal government or anybody else: they can do to me what they did to Dr. Spock and William Sloan Coffin, my good friend, the chaplain of Yale. They can just as well get ready to convict me, because I'm going to continue to say to young men, that if you feel it in your heart that this war is wrong, unjust, and objectionable, don't go and fight in it. Follow the path of Jesus Christ.

31

THE POOR PEOPLE'S CAMPAIGN

We have moved into an era where we are called upon to raise certain basic questions about the whole society. We are still called upon to give aid to the beggar who finds himself in misery and agony on life's highway. But one day, we must ask the question of whether an edifice which produces beggars must not be restructured and refurbished. That is where we are now.

MAY 31, 1967
At an SCLC staff retreat King calls for a radical redistribution of economic and political power

DECEMBER 4
Launches the Poor People's Campaign

MARCH 18, 1968
Speaks to striking sanitation workers in Memphis

MARCH 28
Leads Memphis march that is disrupted by violence

In November 1967 the staff of the Southern Christian Leadership Conference held one of the most important meetings we ever convened. We had intensive discussions and analyses of our work and of the challenges which confront us and our nation. At the end, we made a decision: the SCLC would lead waves of the nation's poor and disinherited to Washington, D.C., in the spring of 1968 to demand redress of their grievances by the United States government and to secure at least jobs or income for all.

We had learned from hard and bitter experience in our movement that our government did not move to correct a problem involving race until it was confronted directly and dramatically. It
required a Selma before the fundamental right to vote was written
into the federal statutes. It took a Birmingham before the government moved to open doors of public accommodations to all human
beings. What we now needed was a new kind of Selma or Birmingham to dramatize the economic plight of the Negro, and compel the government to act.

We would go to Washington and demand to be heard, and we
would stay until America responded. If this meant forcible repression of our movement, we would confront it, for we have done this
before. If this meant scorn or ridicule, we embrace it for that is what
America's poor now receive. If it meant jail, we accepted it willingly,
for the millions of poor were already imprisoned by exploitation and
discrimination. But we hoped, with growing confidence, that our
campaign in Washington would receive a sympathetic understanding across our nation, followed by dramatic expansion of nonviolent
demonstrations in Washington and simultaneous protests elsewhere.
In short we would be petitioning our government for specific reforms, and we intended to build militant nonviolent actions until
that government moves against poverty.

We intended to channel the smouldering rage and frustration of
Negro people into an effective, militant, and nonviolent movement
of massive proportions in Washington and other areas. Similarly, we
would be calling on the swelling masses of young people in this
country who were disenchanted with this materialistic society and
asking them to join us in our new Washington movement. We also
looked for participation by representatives of the millions of non-
Negro poor—Indians, Mexican-Americans, Puerto Ricans, Appala-
chians, and others. And we welcomed assistance from all Americans
of goodwill.

And so, we decided to go to Washington and to use any means
of legitimate nonviolent protest necessary to move our nation and
our government on a new course of social, economic, and political
reform. In the final analysis, SCLC decided to go to Washington
because, if we did not act, we would be abdicating our responsibilities as an organization committed to nonviolence and freedom. We

were keeping that commitment, and we called on America to join us in our Washington campaign. In this way, we could work creatively against the despair and indifference that so often caused our nation to be immobilized during the cold winter and shaken profoundly in the hot summer.

"New tactics which do not count on government goodwill"

The policy of the federal government is to play Russian roulette with riots; it is prepared to gamble with another summer of disaster. Despite two consecutive summers of violence, not a single basic cause of riots has been corrected. All of the misery that stoked the flames of rage and rebellion remains undiminished. With unemployment, intolerable housing, and discriminatory education, a scourge in Negro ghettos, Congress and the administration still tinker with trivial, halfhearted measures.

Yet only a few years ago, there was discernible, if limited, progress through nonviolence. Each year, a wholesome, vibrant Negro self-confidence was taking shape. The fact is inescapable that the tactic of nonviolence, which had then dominated the thinking of the civil rights movement, has in the last two years not been playing its transforming role. Nonviolence was a creative doctrine in the South because it checkmated the rabid segregationists who were thirsting for an opportunity to physically crush Negroes. Nonviolent direct action enabled the Negro to take to the streets in active protest, but it muzzled the guns of the oppressor because even he could not shoot down in daylight unarmed men, women, and children. This is the reason there was less loss of life in ten years of Southern protest than in ten days of Northern riots. . . .

I agree with the President's National Advisory Commission on Civil Disorders that our nation is splitting into two hostile societies and that the chief destructive cutting edge is white racism. We need, above all, effective means to force Congress to act resolutely—but means that do not involve the use of violence.

The time has come for a return to mass nonviolent protest. Accordingly, we are planning a series of such demonstrations this spring and summer, to begin in Washington, D.C. They will have Negro and white participation, and they will seek to benefit the poor of both races.

"A TESTAMENT OF HOPE"

The nation waited until the black man was explosive with fury before stirring itself even to partial concern. Confronted now with the interrelated problems of war, inflation, urban decay, white backlash, and a climate of violence, it is now *forced* to address itself to race relations and poverty, and it is tragically unprepared. What might once have been a series of separate problems now merge into a social crisis of almost stupefying complexity.

I am not sad that black Americans are rebelling; this was not only inevitable but eminently desirable. Without this magnificent ferment among Negroes, the old evasions and procrastinations would have continued indefinitely. Black men have slammed the door shut on a past of deadening passivity. Except for the Reconstruction years, they have never in their long history on American soil struggled with such creativity and courage for their freedom. These are our bright years of emergence; though they are painful ones, they cannot be avoided.

1968

"Find a way to put pressure on them"

We know from past experience that Congress and the President wouldn't do anything until we developed a movement around which people of goodwill could find a way to put pressure on them, because it really meant breaking that coalition in Congress. It was still a coalition-dominated, rural-dominated, basically Southern Congress. There were Southerners there with committee chairmanships, and they were going to stand in the way of progress as long as they could. They got enough right-wing Midwestern or Northern Republicans to go along with them.

This really meant making the movement powerful enough, dramatic enough, morally appealing enough so that people of goodwill—the churches, labor, liberals, intellectuals, students, poor people themselves—began to put pressure on congressmen to the point that they could no longer elude our demands.

Our idea was to dramatize the whole economic problem of the poor. We felt there was a great deal that we needed to do to appeal to Congress itself. The early demonstrations would be more geared

toward educational purposes—to educate the nation on the nature of the problem and the crucial aspects of it, the tragic conditions that we confront in the ghettos. After that, if we had not gotten a response from Congress, we would branch out. And we were honest enough to feel that we weren't going to get any instantaneous results from Congress, knowing its recalcitrant nature on this issue, and knowing that so many resources and energies were being used in Vietnam rather than on the domestic situation. So we didn't have any illusions about moving Congress in two or three weeks. But we did feel that, by starting in Washington, centering on Congress and departments of the government, we would be able to do a real educational job.

We called our demonstration a campaign for jobs and income because we felt that the economic question was the most crucial that black people, and poor people generally, were confronting. There was a literal depression in the Negro community. When you have mass unemployment in the Negro community, it's called a social problem; when you have mass unemployment in the white community, it's called a depression.

We would begin activity around Washington, but as that activity was beginning, some people would be talking to Washington. Some would be coming on mules to Washington. Some would be in their buggies being pulled by the mules. And we would have a mule train, all moving toward Washington, so that we would have forces moving out of the South—Mississippi joining forces with Alabama, Alabama joining with Georgia, Georgia joining with South Carolina, South Carolina with North Carolina with Virginia, and right on into Washington. Other forces would be coming up out of Chicago and Detroit and Cleveland and Milwaukee, others coming down from Boston, New York, Philadelphia, Baltimore—all moving toward Washington.

We would place the problems of the poor at the seat of government of the wealthiest nation in the history of mankind. If that power refused to acknowledge its debt to the poor, it would have failed to live up to its promise to insure "life, liberty, and the pursuit of happiness" to its citizens. If this society fails, I fear that we will hear very shortly that racism is a sickness unto death.

The American people are infected with racism—that is the peril.

Paradoxically, they are also infected with democratic ideals—that is the hope. While doing wrong, they have the potential to do right. But they do not have a millennium to make changes. Nor have they a choice of continuing in the old way. The future they are asked to inaugurate is not so unpalatable that it justifies the evils that beset the nation. To end poverty, to extirpate prejudice, to free a tormented conscience, to make a tomorrow of justice, fair play, and creativity—all these are worthy of the American ideal.

We have, through massive nonviolent action, an opportunity to avoid a national disaster and create a new spirit of class and racial harmony. We can write another luminous moral chapter in American history. All of us are on trial in this troubled hour, but time still permits us to meet the future with a clear conscience.

We have the power to change America and give a kind of new vitality to the religion of Jesus Christ. And we can get those young men and women who've lost faith in the church to see that Jesus was a serious man precisely because he dealt with the tang of the human amid the glow of the Divine and that he was concerned about their problems. He was concerned about bread; he opened and started Operation Breadbasket a long time ago. He initiated the first sit-in movement. The greatest revolutionary that history has ever known. And when people tell us when we stand up that we got our inspiration from this or that, go back and let them know where we got our inspiration.

I read Das Kapital and The Communist Manifesto years ago when I was a student in college. And many of the revolutionary movements in the world came into being as a result of what Marx talked about.

The great tragedy is that Christianity failed to see that it had the revolutionary edge. You don't have to go to Karl Marx to learn how to be a revolutionary. I didn't get my inspiration from Karl Marx; I got it from a man named Jesus, a Galilean saint who said he was anointed to heal the broken-hearted. He was anointed to deal with the problems of the poor. And that is where we get our inspiration. And we go out in a day when we have a message for the world, and we can change this world and we can change this nation.

"A great movement in Memphis"

During one week in March 1968 I made about thirty-five speeches. I started out on Thursday in Grosse Point, Michigan. I had to speak

---

RESOLUTIONS

And I'm simply saying this morning, that you should resolve that you will never become so secure in your thinking or your living that you forget the least of these. . . . In some sense, all of us are the least of these, but there are some who are least than the least of these. I try to get it over to my children early, morning after morning, when I get a chance. As we sit at the table, as we did this morning in morning devotions, I couldn't pray my prayer without saying, "God, help us, as we sit at this table to realize that there are those who are less fortunate than we are. And grant that we will never forget them, no matter where we are." And I said to my little children, "I'm going to work and do everything that I can do to see that you get a good education. I don't ever want you to forget that there are millions of God's children who will not and cannot get a good education, and I don't want you feeling that you are better than they are. For you will never be what you ought to be until they are what they ought to be."

From sermon on January 7, 1968

---

four times in Detroit on Friday. Saturday I went to Los Angeles. I had to speak five times. Then on Sunday I preached in three churches in Los Angeles. And I flew from there to Memphis.

As I came in to Memphis, I turned around and said to Ralph Abernathy, "They really have a great movement here in Memphis." The issue was the refusal of Memphis to be fair and honest in its dealings with its public servants, who happened to be sanitation workers. One thousand three hundred sanitation workers were on strike, and Memphis was not being fair to them. They were demonstrating something there that needed to be demonstrated all over our country. They were demonstrating that we can stick together and they were demonstrating that we are all tied in a single garment of destiny, and that if one black person suffers, if one black person is down, we are all down. The Negro "haves" must join hands with the Negro "have-nots." And armed with the compassionate traveler's check, they must journey into that other country of their brother's denial and hurt and exploitation. One day our society will come to respect the sanitation worker if it is to survive, for the person

who picks up our garbage is in the final analysis as significant as the physician, for if he doesn't do his job, diseases are rampant. All labor has dignity.

Now let me say a word to those of you who are on strike. You have been out now for a number of days, but don't despair. Nothing worthwhile is gained without sacrifice. The thing for you to do is stay together and say to everybody in this community that you are going to stick it out to the end until every demand is met, and that you are going to say, "We ain't gonna let nobody turn us around." Let it be known everywhere that along with wages and all of the other securities that you are struggling for, you are also struggling for the right to organize and to be recognized.

We can all get more together than we can apart. And this is the way we gain power. Power is the ability to achieve purpose, power is the ability to affect change, and we need power. And I want you to stick it out so that you will be able to make Mayor Loeb and others say "Yes," even when they want to say "No."

Now the other thing is that nothing is gained without pressure. Don't let anybody tell you to go back on the job and paternalistically say, "Now you are my men and I'm going to do the right thing for you. Just come on back on the job." Don't go back on the job until the demands are met. Never forget that freedom is not something that is voluntarily given by the oppressor. It is something that must be demanded by the oppressed. Freedom is not some lavish dish that the power structure and the white forces in policy-making positions will voluntarily hand out on a silver platter while the Negro merely furnishes the appetite. If we are going to get equality, if we are going to get adequate wages, we are going to have to struggle for it. . . .

You know Jesus reminded us in a magnificent parable one day that a man went to hell because he didn't see the poor. His name was Dives. And there was a man by the name of Lazarus who came daily to his gate in need of the basic necessities of life and Dives didn't do anything about it. And he ended up going to hell. There is nothing in that parable which says that Dives went to hell because he was rich. Jesus never made a universal indictment against all wealth. It is true that one day a rich young ruler came to Him talking about eternal life and he ad-

vised him to sell all, but in that instance Jesus was prescribing individual surgery, not setting forth a universal diagnosis. If you will go on and read that parable in all of its dimensions and its symbolism you will remember that a conversation took place between heaven and hell. And on the other end of that long distance call between heaven and hell was Abraham in heaven talking to Dives in hell. It wasn't a millionaire in hell talking with a poor man in heaven, it was a little millionaire in hell talking with a multimillionaire in heaven. Dives didn't go to hell because he was rich. His wealth was his opportunity to bridge the gulf that separated him from his brother Lazarus. Dives went to hell because he allowed Lazarus to become invisible. Dives went to hell because he allowed the means by which he lived to outdistance the ends for which he lived. Dives went to hell because he sought to be a conscientious objector in the war against poverty.

And I come by here to say that America too is going to hell if she doesn't use her wealth. If America does not use her vast resources of wealth to end poverty and make it possible for all of God's children to have the basic necessities of life, she too will go to hell. I will hear America through her historians, years and generations to come, saying, "We built gigantic buildings to kiss the skies. We built gargantuan bridges to span the seas. Through our space ships we were able to carve highways through the stratosphere. Through our submarines we were able to penetrate oceanic depths." It seems that I can hear the God of the universe saying, "Even though you have done all of that, I was hungry and you fed me not. I was naked and you clothed me not. The children of my sons and daughters were in need of economic security and you didn't provide it for them. And so you cannot enter the kingdom of greatness." This may well be the indictment on America. And that same voice says in Memphis to the mayor, to the power structure, "If you do it unto the least of these of my children you do it unto me."

. . . Having to live under the threat of death every day, sometimes I feel discouraged. Having to take so much abuse and criticism, sometimes from my own people, sometimes I feel discouraged. Having to go to bed so often frustrated with the chilly winds of adversity about to stagger me, sometimes I feel discouraged and feel my work's in vain.

But then the holy spirit revives my soul again. In Gilead, there is

balm to make the wounded whole. If we will believe that, we will build a new Memphis. And bring about the day when every valley shall be exalted. Every mountain and hill will be made low. The rough places will be made plain, and the crooked places straight. And the glory of the Lord shall be revealed, and all flesh shall see it together.

32

UNFULFILLED DREAMS

APRIL 3, 1968
Delivers final address at Bishop Charles J. Mason Temple in
Memphis

APRIL 4
Is assassinated at Loraine Hotel

I guess one of the great agonies of life is that we are constantly trying to finish that which is unfinishable. We are commanded to do that. And so we, like David, find ourselves in so many instances having to face the fact that our dreams are not fulfilled.

Life is a continual story of shattered dreams. Mahatma Gandhi labored for years and years for the independence of his people. But Gandhi had to face the fact that he was assassinated and died with a broken heart, because that nation that he wanted to unite ended up being divided between India and Pakistan as a result of the conflict between the Hindus and the Moslems.

Woodrow Wilson dreamed a dream of a League of Nations, but he died before the promise was delivered.

The Apostle Paul talked one day about wanting to go to Spain. It was Paul's greatest dream to go to Spain, to carry the gospel there. Paul never got to Spain. He ended up in a prison cell in Rome. This is the story of life.

So many of our forebears used to sing about freedom. And they dreamed of the day that they would be able to get out of the bosom of slavery, the long night of injustice. And they used to sing little songs:

"Nobody knows de trouble I seen, nobody knows but Jesus." They thought about a better day as they dreamed their dream. And they would say, "I'm so glad the trouble don't last always. By and by, by and by I'm going to lay down my heavy load." And they used to sing it because of a powerful dream. But so many died without having the dream fulfilled.

And each of you in some way is building some kind of temple. The struggle is always there. It gets discouraging sometimes. It gets very disenchanting sometimes. Some of us are trying to build a temple of peace. We speak out against war, we protest, but it seems that your head is going against a concrete wall. It seems to mean nothing. And so often as you set out to build the temple of peace you are left lonesome; you are left discouraged; you are left bewildered.

Well, that is the story of life. And the thing that makes me happy is that I can hear a voice crying through the vista of time, saying: "It may not come today or it may not come tomorrow, but it is well that it is within thine heart. It's well that you are trying." You may not see it. The dream may not be fulfilled, but it's just good that you have a desire to bring it into reality. It's well that it's in thine heart.

Now let me bring out another point. Whenever you set out to build a creative temple, whatever it may be, you must face the fact that there is a tension at the heart of the universe between good and evil. Hinduism refers to this as a struggle between illusion and reality. Platonic philosophy used to refer to it as a tension between body and soul. Zoroastrianism, a religion of old, used to refer to it as a tension between the god of light and the god of darkness. Traditional Judaism and Christianity refer to it as a tension between God and Satan. Whatever you call it, there is a struggle in the universe between good and evil.

Now not only is that struggle structured out somewhere in the external forces of the universe, it's structured in our own lives. Psychologists have tried to grapple with it in their way, and so they say various things. Sigmund Freud used to say that this tension is a tension between what he called the id and the superego. Some of us feel that it's a tension between God and man. And in every one of us, there's a war going on. It's a civil war. I don't care who you are, I don't care where you live, there is a civil war going on in your life. And every time you set out to be good, there's something pulling on you, telling you to be evil. It's

going on in your life. Every time you set out to love, something keeps pulling on you, trying to get you to hate. Every time you set out to be kind and say nice things about people, something is pulling on you to be jealous and envious and to spread evil gossip about them. There's a civil war going on. There is a schizophrenia, as the psychologists or the psychiatrists would call it, going on within all of us. And there are times that all of us know somehow that there is a Mr. Hyde and a Dr. Jekyll in us. And we end up having to cry out with Ovid, the Latin poet, "I see and approve the better things of life, but the evil things I do." We end up having to agree with Plato that the human personality is like a charioteer with two headstrong horses, wanting to go in different directions. Or sometimes we even have to end up crying out with Saint Augustine as he said in his Confessions, "Lord, make me pure, but not yet." We end up crying out with the Apostle Paul, "The good that I would I do not: And the evil that I would not, that I do." Or we end up having to say with Goethe that "there's enough stuff in me to make both a gentleman and a rogue." There's a tension at the heart of human nature. And whenever we set out to dream our dreams and to build our temples, we must be honest enough to recognize it.

In the final analysis, God does not judge us by the separate incidents or the separate mistakes that we make, but by the total bent of our lives. In the final analysis, God knows that his children are weak and they are frail. In the final analysis, what God requires is that your heart is right.

And the question I want to raise with you: is your heart right? If your heart isn't right, fix it up today; get God to fix it up. Get somebody to be able to say about you: "He may not have reached the highest height, he may not have realized all of his dreams, but he tried." Isn't that a wonderful thing for somebody to say about you? "He tried to be a good man. He tried to be a just man. He tried to be an honest man. His heart was in the right place." And I can hear a voice saying, crying out through the eternities, "I accept you. You are a recipient of my grace because it was in your heart. And it is so well that it was within thine heart."

I don't know about you, but I can make a testimony. You don't need to go out saying that Martin Luther King is a saint. Oh, no. I want you to know this morning that I'm a sinner like all of God's

children. But I want to be a good man. And I want to hear a voice saying to me one day, "I take you in and I bless you, because you tried. It is well that it was within thine heart."

"I've been to the mountaintop"

And you know, if I were standing at the beginning of time with the possibility of taking a kind of general and panoramic view of the whole human history up to now, and the Almighty said to me, "Martin Luther King, which age would you like to live in?" I would take my mental flight by Egypt, and I would watch God's children in their magnificent trek from the dark dungeons of Egypt across the Red Sea, through the wilderness, on toward the promised land. And in spite of its magnificence, I wouldn't stop there.

I would move on by Greece, and take my mind to Mount Olympus. And I would see Plato, Aristotle, Socrates, Euripides, and Aristophanes assembled around the Parthenon, and I would watch them around the Parthenon as they discussed the great and eternal issues of reality. But I wouldn't stop there.

I would go on even to the great heyday of the Roman Empire and I would see developments around there, through various emperors and leaders. But I wouldn't stop there.

I would even come up to the day of the Renaissance, and get a quick picture of all that the Renaissance did for the cultural and aesthetic life of man. But I wouldn't stop there.

I would even go by the way that the man for whom I'm named had his habitat, and I would watch Martin Luther as he tacks his ninety-five theses on the door at the church in Wittenberg. But I wouldn't stop there.

I would come on up even to 1863 and watch a vacillating President by the name of Abraham Lincoln finally come to the conclusion that he had to sign the Emancipation Proclamation. But I wouldn't stop there.

I would even come up to the early thirties and see a man grappling with the problems of the bankruptcy of his nation, and come with an eloquent cry that "we have nothing to fear but fear itself." But I wouldn't stop there.

Strangely enough, I would turn to the Almighty and say, "If you

allow me to live just a few years in the second half of the twentieth century, I will be happy."

Now that's a strange statement to make, because the world is all messed up. The nation is sick; trouble is in the land, confusion all around. That's a strange statement. But I know, somehow, that only when it is dark enough can you see the stars. And I see God working in this period of the twentieth century. Something is happening in our world. The masses of people are rising up. And wherever they are assembled today, whether they are in Johannesburg, South Africa; Nairobi, Kenya; Accra, Ghana; New York City; Atlanta, Georgia; Jackson, Mississippi; or Memphis, Tennessee, the cry is always the same: "We want to be free."

And another reason that I'm happy to live in this period is that we have been forced to a point where we are going to have to grapple with the problems that men have been trying to grapple with through history. Survival demands that we grapple with them. Men for years now have been talking about war and peace. But now, no longer can they just talk about it. It is no longer a choice between violence and nonviolence in this world; it's nonviolence or nonexistence. That is where we are today.

And also in the human rights revolution, if something isn't done, and done in a hurry, to bring the colored peoples of the world out of their long years of poverty, their long years of hurt and neglect, the whole world is doomed. Now, I'm just happy that God has allowed me to live in this period, to see what is unfolding. And I'm happy that he's allowed me to be in Memphis.

I can remember, I can remember when Negroes were just going around, as Ralph has said so often, scratching where they didn't itch and laughing when they were not tickled. But that day is all over. We mean business now and we are determined to gain our rightful place in God's world. And that's all this whole thing is about. We aren't engaged in any negative protest and in any negative arguments with anybody. We are saying that we are determined to be men. We are determined to be people. We are saying, we are saying that we are God's children. And if we are God's children, we don't have to live like we are forced to live.

Now, what does all of this mean in this great period of history? It means that we've got to stay together. We've got to stay together and

maintain unity. You know, whenever Pharaoh wanted to prolong the period of slavery in Egypt, he had a favorite formula for doing it. What was that? He kept the slaves fighting among themselves. But whenever the slaves get together, something happens in Pharaoh's court, and he cannot hold the slaves in slavery. When the slaves get together, that's the beginning of getting out of slavery. Now let us maintain unity.

We aren't going to let any mace stop us. We are masters in our nonviolent movement in disarming police forces; they don't know what to do. I've seen them so often. I remember in Birmingham, Alabama, when we were in that majestic struggle there, we would move out of the Sixteenth Street Baptist Church day after day. By the hundreds we would move out, and Bull Connor would tell them to send the dogs forth, and they did come. But we just went before the dogs singing, "Ain't gonna let nobody turn me around." Bull Connor next would say, "Turn the firehoses on." And as I said to you the other night, Bull Connor didn't know history. He knew a kind of physics that somehow didn't relate to the transphysics that we knew about. And that was the fact that there was a certain kind of fire that no water could put out. And we went before the firehoses. We had known water. If we were Baptist or some other denomination, we had been immersed. If we were Methodist, and some others, we had been sprinkled—but we knew water. That couldn't stop us.

And we just went on before the dogs, and we would look at them; and we'd go on before the water hoses, and we would look at them. And we'd just go on singing, "Over my head, I see freedom in the air." And then we would be thrown in the paddy wagons, and sometimes we were stacked in there like sardines in a can. And they would throw us in, and old Bull would say, "Take 'em off." And they did, and we would just go on in the paddy wagon singing, "We shall overcome." And every now and then we'd get in jail, and we'd see the jailers looking through the windows being moved by our prayers and being moved by our words and our songs. And there was a power there which Bull Connor couldn't adjust to, and so we ended up transforming Bull into a steer, and we won our struggle in Birmingham.

We've got to give ourselves to this struggle until the end. Nothing would be more tragic than to stop at this point in Memphis. We've got to see it through. When we have our march, you need to be there. If it

means leaving work, if it means leaving school, be there. Be concerned about your brother. You may not be on strike, but either we go up together or we go down together. Let us develop a kind of dangerous unselfishness.

One day a man came to Jesus and he wanted to raise some questions about some vital matters of life. At points he wanted to trick Jesus, and show him that he knew a little more than Jesus knew and throw him off base. Now that question could have easily ended up in a philosophical and theological debate. But Jesus immediately pulled that question from midair and placed it on a dangerous curve between Jerusalem and Jericho. And he talked about a certain man who fell among thieves. You remember that a Levite and a priest passed by on the other side—they didn't stop to help him. Finally, a man of another race came by. He got down from his beast, decided not to be compassionate by proxy. But he got down with him, administered first aid, and helped the man in need. Jesus ended up saying this was the good man, this was the great man, because he had the capacity to project the "I" into the "thou," and to be concerned about his brother.

Now you know, we use our imagination a great deal to try to determine why the priest and the Levite didn't stop. At times we say they were busy going to a church meeting, an ecclesiastical gathering, and they had to get on down to Jerusalem so they wouldn't be late for their meeting. At other times we would speculate that there was a religious law that one who was engaged in religious ceremonies was not to touch a human body twenty-four hours before the ceremony. And every now and then we begin to wonder whether maybe they were not going down to Jerusalem, or down to Jericho, rather, to organize a Jericho Road Improvement Association. That's a possibility. Maybe they felt it was better to deal with the problem from the causal root, rather than to get bogged down with an individual effect.

But I'm going to tell you what my imagination tells me. It's possible that those men were afraid. You see, the Jericho Road is a dangerous road. I remember when Mrs. King and I were first in Jerusalem. We rented a car and drove from Jerusalem down to Jericho. And as soon as we got on that road I said to my wife, "I can see why Jesus used this as a setting for his parable." It's a winding, meandering road. It's really conducive for ambushing. You start out in Jerusalem, which is about twelve hundred miles, or rather, twelve hundred feet above sea level.

And by the time you get down to Jericho, fifteen or twenty minutes later, you're about twenty-two hundred feet below sea level. That's a dangerous road. In the days of Jesus it came to be known as the "Bloody Pass." And you know, it's possible that the priest and the Levite looked over that man on the ground and wondered if the robbers were still around. Or it's possible that they felt that the man on the ground was merely faking. And he was acting like he had been robbed and hurt, in order to seize them over there, lure them there for quick and easy seizure. (Oh yeah.) And so the first question that the priest asked, the first question that the Levite asked was, "If I stop to help this man, what will happen to me?"

But then the Good Samaritan came by, and he reversed the question: "If I do not stop to help this man, what will happen to him?"

That's the question before you tonight. Not, "If I stop to help the sanitation workers, what will happen to my job?" Not, "If I stop to help the sanitation workers, what will happen to all of the hours that I usually spend in my office every day and every week as a pastor?" The question is not, "If I stop to help this man in need, what will happen to me?" The question is, "If I do not stop to help the sanitation workers, what will happen to them?" That's the question.

Let us rise up tonight with a greater readiness. Let us stand with a greater determination. And let us move on in these powerful days, these days of challenge, to make America what it ought to be. We have an opportunity to make America a better nation. And I want to thank God, once more, for allowing me to be here with you.

You know, several years ago I was in New York City autographing the first book that I had written. And while sitting there autographing books, a demented black woman came up. The only question I heard from her was, "Are you Martin Luther King?" And I was looking down writing and I said, "Yes."

And the next minute I felt something beating on my chest. Before I knew it I had been stabbed by this demented woman. I was rushed to Harlem Hospital. It was a dark Saturday afternoon. And that blade had gone through, and the X rays revealed that the tip of the blade was on the edge of my aorta, the main artery. And once that's punctured, you drown in your own blood; that's the end of you. It came out in the

New York Times *the next morning that if I had merely sneezed, I would have died.*

Well, about four days later, they allowed me, after the operation, after my chest had been opened and the blade had been taken out, to move around in the wheelchair in the hospital. They allowed me to read some of the mail that came in, and from all over the states and the world kind letters came in. I read a few, but one of them I will never forget. I had received one from the President and the Vice President; I've forgotten what those telegrams said. I'd received a visit and a letter from the governor of New York, but I've forgotten what the letter said.

But there was another letter that came from a little girl, a young girl who was a student at the White Plains High School. And I looked at the letter and I'll never forget it. It said simply, "Dear Dr. King: I am a ninth-grade student at the White Plains High School." She said, "While it should not matter, I would like to mention that I'm a white girl. I read in the paper of your misfortune and of your suffering. And I read that if you had sneezed, you would have died. And I'm simply writing to you to say that I'm so happy that you didn't sneeze."

I want to say that I too am happy that I didn't sneeze. Because if I had sneezed, I wouldn't have been around here in 1960, when students all over the South started sitting in at lunch counters. And I knew that as they were sitting in, they were really standing up for the best in the American Dream and taking the whole nation back to those great wells of democracy which were dug deep by the founding fathers in the Declaration of Independence and the Constitution.

If I had sneezed, I wouldn't have been around here in 1961, when we decided to take a ride for freedom and ended segregation in interstate travel.

If I had sneezed, I wouldn't have been around here in 1962, when Negroes in Albany, Georgia, decided to straighten their backs up. And whenever men and women straighten their backs up, they are going somewhere, because a man can't ride your back unless it is bent.

If I had sneezed, I wouldn't have been here in 1963, when the black people of Birmingham, Alabama, aroused the conscience of this nation and brought into being the Civil Rights Bill.

If I had sneezed, I wouldn't have had a chance later that year, in August, to try to tell America about a dream that I had had.

If I had sneezed, I wouldn't have been down in Selma, Alabama, to see the great movement there.

If I had sneezed, I wouldn't have been in Memphis to see a community rally around those brothers and sisters who are suffering. I'm so happy that I didn't sneeze.

I left Atlanta this morning, and as we got started on the plane—there were six of us—the pilot said over the public address system, "We are sorry for the delay, but we have Dr. Martin Luther King on the plane. And to be sure that all of the bags were checked and to be sure that nothing would be wrong on the plane, we had to check out everything carefully. And we've had the plane protected and guarded all night."

And then I got into Memphis. And some began to say the threats, or talk about the threats that were out, or what would happen to me from some of our sick white brothers.

Well, I don't know what will happen now; we've got some difficult days ahead. But it really doesn't matter with me now, because I've been to the mountaintop. And I don't mind. Like anybody, I would like to live a long life—longevity has its place. But I'm not concerned about that now. I just want to do God's will. And He's allowed me to go up to the mountain. And I've looked over, and I've seen the promised land. I may not get there with you. But I want you to know tonight, that we, as a people, will get to the promised land. And I'm happy tonight. I'm not worried about anything. I'm not fearing any man. Mine eyes have seen the glory of the coming of the Lord.

"A drum major for righteousness"

Every now and then I guess we all think realistically about that day when we will be victimized with what is life's final common denominator—that something we call death. We all think about it. And every now and then I think about my own death, and I think about my own funeral. And I don't think of it in a morbid sense. Every now and then I ask myself, "What is it that I would want said?" And I leave the word to you this morning.

I'd like somebody to mention that day, that Martin Luther King, Jr., tried to give his life serving others.

I'd like for somebody to say that day, that Martin Luther King, Jr., tried to love somebody.

I want you to say that day, that I tried to be right on the war question.

I want you to be able to say that day, that I did try to feed the hungry.

And I want you to be able to say that day, that I did try, in my life, to clothe those who were naked.

I want you to say, on that day, that I did try, in my life, to visit those who were in prison.

I want you to say that I tried to love and to serve humanity.

Yes, if you want to say that I was a drum major, say that I was a drum major for justice. Say that I was a drum major for peace. I was a drum major for righteousness. And all of the other shallow things will not matter. I won't have any money to leave behind. I won't have the fine and luxurious things of life to leave behind. But I just want to leave a committed life behind. And that's all I wanted to say.

If I can help somebody as I pass along, if I can cheer somebody with a word or song, if I can show somebody he's traveling wrong, then my living will not be in vain. If I can do my duty as a Christian ought, if I can bring salvation to a world once wrought, if I can spread the message as the master taught, then my living will not be in vain.

EDITOR'S
ACKNOWLEDGMENTS

◆

The Autobiography of Martin Luther King, Jr. is an outgrowth of discussions involving myself and members of the King family. In 1992
I proposed to the family several ideas for increasing public understanding of King's life and thought. As director of the Martin Luther
King, Jr., Papers Project, I was aware of the enormous quantity of
documents that existed regarding King; yet I also knew that these
documents were available mainly to scholars who were able to travel
to archives. Although the King Project's fourteen-volume edition of
The Papers of Martin Luther King, Jr. was intended as a way to make
these documents more widely available, this long-term effort will
not be completed for many years. Designed as an essential foundation for future studies of King and his times, the project's annotated
edition of King's writings and public statements has more often attracted the attention of researchers rather than casual readers, and
many of the important revelations that have resulted from the King
Project's research are not widely known outside the community of
King scholars. Thus I urged the King family to join with me in developing innovative, popularly accessible ways to present the findings
of the project.

The first result of these discussions was the development of a
docudrama, *Passages of Martin Luther King.* With the assistance of
Stanford drama professor Dr. Victor Leo Walker and Stanford undergraduate researcher Heather Williams, I explored ways of telling
the story of King's life through his own words and the words of
those who knew him best. After several dramatic readings at Stanford, *Passages* was produced by the Stanford drama department in
April 1993. Revised versions were presented as dramatic readings at
Dartmouth College and the University of Washington in January
1996 and 1998, respectively. I am grateful for the contributions of

all of the individuals who participated in these presentations, which increased my familiarity with the documentary resources concerning King and prepared a foundation for this comprehensive autobiographical account of King's life.

Soon after Dexter King became the president and chief executive officer of the King Center in 1995, I found that we shared a common interest in facilitating the dissemination of King's ideas through various media. In association with Philip Jones, president and CEO of Intellectual Properties Management (IPM) and the manager of the King literary estate, Mr. King established a partnership with Warner Books that will result in increasing public awareness of King's ideas and achievements. I have greatly enjoyed the opportunity to work closely with Dexter and Philip to achieve our common goals, including the publication of this work. At every stage in the development of this work, their support and advice have been essential and available. Their energy and enthusiasm have been contagious.

My agent, Sandra Dijkstra, provided continuous encouragement for this project since its inception. Her expertise and that of her able staff made it possible for me to concentrate on research while they handled the financial and contractual matters. I especially appreciated the opportunity to work with a former student of mine, Rebecca Lowen, who is now with the Dijkstra Literary Agency.

Even before the book contract was signed, I became deeply involved in the task of searching for the source texts for the autobiography from the hundreds of thousands of King-related documents. My initial research assistant was Jennifer Marcus, a dedicated and talented researcher who helped produce the original prospectus for the autobiography and who remained involved in the project for most of her Stanford University undergraduate career.

Once I formally agreed to produce the autobiography in little more than a year, Randy Gellerman Mont-Reynaud became the principal researcher for the book. Randy examined thousands of documents and listened to hundreds of audio recordings to identify texts for possible inclusion and then assembled these texts in a preliminary chronological narrative. She brought to this difficult and daunting task considerable energy and enthusiasm—essential qualities for any effort of this scope.

The autobiography owes its completion to the extensive involve-

ment of various members of the King Project staff. In particular, managing editor and archivist Susan Carson provided her unparalleled knowledge of the more than twenty thousand cataloged documents in the project's database. During the final stages of manuscript preparation, she and researcher Erin Wood contributed valuable suggestions for revision, supervised the effort to locate appropriate additional documents, and checked the manuscript for accuracy.

Other King Project staff also made this book possible. I wish to thank especially Adrienne Clay, Kerry Taylor, and Elizabeth Baez who, despite the other demands of the project's documentary edition, volunteered to read chapters and suggest necessary improvements. My assistant Vicki Brooks also contributed by proofreading chapters and by bringing a measure of organization to my office. Barbara Ifejika volunteered to help during the final stages of manuscript preparation.

Undergraduate and graduate student researchers have contributed to this work in a variety of ways. The following individuals have made significant contributions through the Martin Luther King, Jr., Research Fellowship summer internship program: Tenisha Armstrong (University of California, Santa Cruz), Brandi Brimmer (University of California, Los Angeles), Joy Clinkscales (American University), Andrew Davidson (Cornell University), Julian Davis (Brown University), Rashann Duvall (Yale University), Patrick Guarasci (Macalaster College), Lisa Marley (Brown University), and Maria-Theresa Robinson (Spelman College). Stanford students who worked on this volume include Stephanie Baca-Delancey, Joe Crespino, Elsa Cruz-Pearson, Nancy Farghalli, Hanan Hardy, Shaw-San Liu, Naila Moseley, Megan Thompkins, and Ali Zaidi.

I also appreciate the assistance of the following: Jeff Shram, Gail Westergard, and Christopher Carson.

Several others offered helpful comments on earlier versions of this manuscript. My editor at Warner Books, Rick Horgan, gave useful and tactful suggestions at various stages of manuscript preparation. I appreciate and benefited from the constructive criticisms of Candace Falk of the University of California, Berkeley, and of Michael Honey of the University of Washington, Tacoma. I am especially grateful for Coretta Scott King's willingness to read this

manuscript with the painstaking care and sensitive understanding
that only she could provide.

Finally, I appreciate the remarkable fact that Martin Luther King,
Jr., had the foresight to create and leave behind the autobiographical
documents on which this book is based.

SOURCE NOTES

◆

Abbreviations of Collections and Repositories:

ABSP, DHU   Arthur B. Spingarn Papers, Howard University, Washington, D.C.

AC, InU-N   Audiotape Collection, Indiana University, Northwest Regional Campus, Gary, Indiana

ACA-ARC, LNT   American Committee on Africa Papers, Amistad Research Center, Tulane University, New Orleans, Louisiana

AFSCR, AFSCA   American Friends Service Committee Records, AFSC Archives, Philadelphia, Pennsylvania

CB, CtY   Chester Bowles Collection, Yale University, New Haven, Connecticut

CSKC, INP   Coretta Scott King Collection (in private hands)

DABCC, INP   Dexter Avenue King Memorial Baptist Church Collection (in private hands)

DCST, AB   Dallas County Sheriff's Department Surveillance Tape, Birmingham Public Library, Birminghan, Alabama

DHSTR, WHi   Donald H. Smith Tape Recordings, State Historical Society, Madison, Wisconsin

DJG, INP   David J. Garrow Collection (in private hands)

EMBC, INP   Etta Moten Barnett Collection (in private hands)

HG, GAMK   Hazel Gregory Papers, Martin Luther King, Jr., Center for Nonviolent Change, Inc., Atlanta, Georgia

JFKP, MWalk   John F. Kennedy Miscellaneous Papers, John F. Kennedy Library, Waltham, Massachusetts

JWWP, DHU   Julius Waties Waring Papers, Howard University, Washington, D.C.

MLKP, MBU   Martin Luther King, Jr., Papers, 1954–1968, Boston University, Boston, Massachusetts

MLKEC, INP   Martin Luther King Estate Collection (in private hands)

MLKJP, GAMK   Martin Luther King, Jr., Papers, 1954–1968, King Center, Atlanta, Georgia

MMFR, INP   Montgomery to Memphis Film Research Files (in private hands)

MVC, TMM   Mississippi Valley Collection, Memphis State University, Memphis, Tennessee

NAACPP, DLC   National Association for the Advancement of Colored People Papers, Library of Congress, Washington, D.C.

NBCC, NNNBC   National Broadcasting Company, Inc., Collection, NBC Library, New York, New York

NF, GEU   *Newsweek* File, Emory University Special Collections, Atlanta, Georgia

OGCP, MBU   Office of General Council Papers, Boston University, Boston, Massachusetts

PHBC, INP   Paul H. Brown Collection (in private hands)

SAVFC, WHi   Social Action Vertical File, State Historical Society, Madison, Wisconsin

SCLCT, INP   Southern Christian Leadership Conference Tapes (in private hands)

TWUC, NNU-T   Transport Workers Union Collection, Tamiment Library, New York University, New York, New York

UPWP, WHi   United Packinghouse Workers Union Papers, State Historical Society, Madison, Wisconsin

WAR, INP   William A. Robinson Miscellaneous Papers (in private hands)

1. EARLY YEARS

PRINCIPAL SOURCES:

"An Autobiography of Religious Development," November 1950, in Clayborne Carson, Ralph E. Luker, and Penny A. Russell, eds., *The Papers of Martin*

Luther King, Jr., Volume I: Called to Serve, January 1929–June 1951 (Berkeley: University of California Press, 1992), pp. 359–363.

Stride Toward Freedom: The Montgomery Story (New York: Harper and Row, 1958), chapter 1; "Family in Siege," drafts for *Stride Toward Freedom* (MLKP, MBU).

OTHER SOURCES:

"Facing the Challenge of the New Age," address at NAACP Emancipation Day Rally, Atlanta, January 1, 1957 (PHBC, INP).

"Why Jesus Called a Man a Fool," sermon at Mount Pisgah Missionary Baptist Church, Chicago, Autust 27, 1967, in Clayborne Carson and Peter Holloran, eds., *A Knock at Midnight: Inspiration from the Great Sermons of Reverend Martin Luther King, Jr.* (New York: IPM/Warner Books, 1998), pp. 145–164.

Interview with Edward T. Ladd on *Profile*, WAII-TV, at Emory University, Atlanta, April 12, 1964 (MLKEC, INP).

Interview with John Freeman on BBC's *Face to Face*, London, England, October 24, 1961 (MLKJP, GAMK).

Interview with Alex Haley, *Playboy* 12 (January 1965): 65–68, 70–74, 76–78.

Statement on Meredith March, Grenada, Mississippi, June 16, 1966 (MLKJP, GAMK).

Quoted in Ted Poston, "Fighting Pastor," *New York Post,* April 10, 1957.

"The Negro and the Constitution," May 1944, *Papers I,* pp. 110–111.

Letters to Alberta Williams King, June 11 and 18, 1944; Martin Luther King, Sr., June 15, 1944, *Papers I,* pp. 112–116.

2. MOREHOUSE COLLEGE

PRINCIPAL SOURCE:

"An Autobiography of Religious Development."

OTHER SOURCES:

Stride Toward Freedom, pp. 91, 145.

"A Legacy of Creative Protest," in *Massachusetts Review* 4 (September 1962): 43.

"Martin Luther King Explains Nonviolent Resistance," in William Katz, *The Negro in American History* (New York: Pitman, 1967), pp. 511–513.

"May 17—11 Years Later," *New York Amsterdam News,* May 22, 1965.

Interview with Edward T. Ladd.

Interview with John Freeman.

Quoted in Ted Poston, "Fighting Pastor" and "The Boycott and the 'New Dawn,'" *New York Post,* May 13, 1956.

Quoted in William Peters, "'Our Weapon Is Love,'" *Redbook* 107 (August 1956): 42–43, 71–73.

Quoted in L. D. Reddick, *Crusader Without Violence* (New York: Harper and Brothers, 1959), p. 74.

"Kick Up Dust," Letter to Editor, *Atlanta Constitution,* August 6, 1946, *Papers I,* p. 121.

3. CROZER SEMINARY

PRINCIPAL SOURCES:

Stride Toward Freedom, chapter 6.

"Pilgrimage to Nonviolence," *Christian Century* 77 (April 13, 1960): 439–441; "How my mind has changed," draft of *Christian Century* article (MLKP, MBU).

Strength to Love (New York: Harper and Row, 1963), chapter 17.

OTHER SOURCES:

"Autobiography of Religious Development."

"Preaching Ministry," 1949(?), course paper submitted at Crozer Theological Seminary, Chester, Pennsylvania (CSKC, INP).

"How Modern Christians Should Think of Man," 1949–50, *Papers I,* pp. 273–279.

"His Influence Speaks to World Conscience," *Hindustan Times,* January 30, 1958.

"The Theology of Reinhold Niebuhr," 1954(?), in Clayborne Carson, Ralph E. Luker, Penny A. Russell, and Peter Holloran, eds., *The Papers of Martin Luther King, Jr., Volume II: Rediscovering Precious Values, July 1951–November 1955* (Berkeley: University of California Press, 1994), pp. 269–279.

Fragment of Application to Boston University, December 1950(?), *Papers I,* p. 390.

Letter to Sankey L. Blanton, January 1951, *Papers I,* p. 391.

Letter to Alberta Williams King, October 1948, *Papers I,* p. 161.

Quoted in Peters, "'Our Weapon Is Love.'"

"The Significant Contributions of Jeremiah to Religious Thought," November 1948, *Papers I,* pp. 181–194.

"A Conception and Impression of Religion Drawn from Dr. Edgar S. Brightman's Book Entitled 'A Philosophy of Religion,'" March 28, 1951, *Papers I,* pp. 407–416.

4. BOSTON UNIVERSITY

PRINCIPAL SOURCE:

Stride Toward Freedom, chapter 6.

OTHER SOURCES:

"Rediscovering Lost Values," sermon at Second Baptist Church, Detroit, Michigan, February 28, 1954, *Papers II,* pp. 248–256.

Press conference on donation of papers to Boston University, Boston, Massachusetts, September 11, 1964 (OGCP, MBU).

Letter to George W. Davis, December 1, 1953, *Papers II,* pp. 223–224.

Abstract of "A Comparison of the Conceptions of God in the Thinking of Paul Tillich and Henry Nelson Wieman," April 15, 1955, *Papers II,* pp. 545–548.

"Memories of Housing Bias in Boston," *Boston Globe,* April 23, 1965.

5. CORETTA

PRINCIPAL SOURCES:

Stride Toward Freedom, chapter 1, and "Family in siege," unpublished draft.

Coretta Scott King, *My Life with Martin* (New York: Henry Holt, 1969, rev. 1993), chapter 3.

Interview with Edward T. Ladd.

Interview with Arnold Michaelis, *Martin Luther King, Jr.: A Personal Portrait* (videotape), December 1966 (MLKEC, INP).

OTHER SOURCES: .

"Remarks in Acceptance of the NAACP Spingarn Medal," Detroit, Michigan, June 28, 1957 (ABSP, DHU).

Interview with Martin Agronsky, NBC's *Look Here,* Montgomery, October 27, 1957 (NBCC, NNNBC).

Interview with John Freeman.

Quoted in Poston, "Fighting Pastor."

Letter to Coretta Scott King, Atlanta, July 18, 1952; and letter to Coretta Scott King, Boston, July 23, 1954 (CSKC, INP).

6. DEXTER AVENUE BAPTIST CHURCH

PRINCIPAL SOURCE:

Stride Toward Freedom, chapters 1, and 2; and "Montgomery Before the Protest," unpublished draft of *Stride Toward Freedom* (MLKP, MBU).

OTHER SOURCES:

"Recommendations to the Dexter Avenue Baptist Church for the Fiscal Year 1954–
    55," September 5, 1954, *Papers II*, pp. 287–294.

Address to Dexter Avenue Baptist Church Congregation, Montgomery, May 2,
    1954 (CSKC, INP).

"The Three Dimensions of a Complete Life," sermon at Dexter Avenue Baptist
    Church, Montgomery, January 24, 1954 (CSKC, INP).

"Looking Beyond Your Circumstances," sermon at Dexter Avenue Baptist Church,
    September 18, 1955 (CSKC, INP).

Letter to Francis E. Stewart, July 26, 1954, *Papers II*, pp. 280–281.

Letter to Walter R. McCall, October 19, 1954, *Papers II*, pp. 301–302.

Letter to Ebenezer Baptist Church Members, November 6, 1954, *Papers II*,
    pp. 313–314.

Letter to Howard Thurman, October 31, 1955, *Papers II*, pp. 583–584.

Letter to John Thomas Porter, November 18, 1955, *Papers II*, p. 590.

Letter to L. Harold DeWolf, January 4, 1957 (MLKP, MBU).

Letter to Edward H. Whitaker, November 30, 1955, *Papers II*, p. 593.

Quoted in Poston, "The Boycott and the New Dawn."

Quoted in "My Life with Martin Luther King, Jr.," interview with Coretta Scott
    King, SCLC radio program, December 1969 (SCLCT, INP).

7. MONTGOMERY MOVEMENT BEGINS

PRINCIPAL SOURCES:

Stride Toward Freedom, chapters 1 and 2; and "The Decisive Arrest," unpublished
    draft of *Stride Toward Freedom*, May 1958 (MLKP, MBU).

"The Montgomery Story," address at Forty-seventh Annual NAACP Convention,
    San Francisco, California, June 27, 1956, in Clayborne Carson, Stewart Burns,
    Susan Carson, Peter Holloran, and Dana L. H. Powell, eds., *The Papers of
    Martin Luther King, Jr., Volume III: Birth of a New Age, December 1955–
    December 1956* (Berkeley: University of California Press, 1997), pp. 299–310.

OTHER SOURCES:

Address at Montgomery Improvement Association Mass Meeting at Holt Street
    Baptist Church, December 5, 1955, *Papers III*, pp. 71–79.

"Facing the Challenge of a New Age," address at First Institute for Nonviolence
    and Social Change, Atlanta, December 3, 1956, *Papers III*, pp. 451–463.

Quoted in Poston, "Fighting Pastor."

8. THE VIOLENCE OF DESPERATE MEN

PRINCIPAL SOURCE:

Stride Toward Freedom, chapters 5, 7, and 8; and "Family in Siege," draft.

OTHER SOURCES:

"Walk for Freedom," May 1956, *Papers III*, pp. 277–280.
"Why Jesus Called a Man a Fool."
"A Testament of Hope," *Playboy* 16 (January 1969): 175.
"Nonviolence: The Only Road to Freedom," *Ebony* 21 (October 1966): pp. 27–30.
Notes on MIA Executive Board Meeting, by Donald T. Ferron, January 30, 1956; and notes on MIA Mass Meeting at First Baptist Church, by Willie Mae Lee, January 30, 1956, *Papers III*, pp. 109–112, 113–114.
Interview with Martin Agronsky.
Quoted in Joe Azbell, "Blast Rocks Residence of Bus Boycott Leader," *Montgomery Advertiser*, Montgomery, January 31, 1956, *Papers III*, pp. 114–115.
Quoted in Wayne Phillips, "Negroes Pledge to Keep Boycott," *New York Times*, February 24, 1956. *Papers III*, pp. 135–136.

9. DESEGREGATION AT LAST

PRINCIPAL SOURCE:

Stride Toward Freedom, chapters 8 and 9; "Family in Siege," unpublished draft; and "The Violence of Desperate Men," unpublished draft (MLKP-MBU).

OTHER SOURCES:

Statement on ending the bus boycott, Montgomery, December 20, 1956, *Papers III*, pp. 485–487.
"Montgomery Sparked a Revolution," *Southern Courier*, December 11–12, 1965.
Reactions to Conviction, *Papers III*, pp. 198–199.
"A Knock at Midnight," in *Strength to Love*, chapter 6.
"The Montgomery Story."
Letter to Lillian Eugenia Smith, May 24, 1956, *Papers III*, pp. 273–274.
Letter to Sylvester S. Robinson, October 3, 1956, *Papers III*, pp. 391–393.
Interview with Joe Azbell, Montgomery, March 23, 1956, *Papers III*, pp. 202–203.
"Desegregation and the Future," address at annual luncheon of National Committee for Rural Schools, New York, December 15, 1956, *Papers III*, pp. 472–473.
Quoted in L. D. Reddick, *Crusader Without Violence*.

10. THE EXPANDING STRUGGLE

PRINCIPAL SOURCE:

Stride Toward Freedom, chapters 9–11.

OTHER SOURCES:

"Conquering Self-Centeredness," sermon at Dexter Avenue Baptist Church, Montgomery, August 11, 1957 (MLKJP, GAMK).

"The Future of Integration," address to the United Packinghouse Workers of America, AFL-CIO, Chicago, October 2, 1957 (UPWP, WHi).

"Facing the Challenge of a New Age," December 3, 1956.

"Facing the Challenge of a New Age," January 1, 1957.

"Give Us the Ballot," address at the Prayer Pilgrimage for Freedom, Washington, D.C., May 17, 1957 (MLKJP, GAMK).

"South-Wide Conference to Draft Final Plans for a Voting Rights Campaign," press release, Montgomery, October 30, 1957 (UPWP, WHi).

Letter to O. Clay Maxwell, November 20, 1958 (MLKP, MBU).

Letter to Frank J. Gregory, May 7, 1957 (MLKJP, GAMK).

Letter to Dwight D. Eisenhower, November 5, 1957 (NAACPP, DLC).

Letter to Fannie E. Scott, January 28, 1957 (MLKP, MBU).

Telegram to Coretta Scott King, New Orleans, February 14, 1957 (CSKC, INP).

Interview with Mike Wallace, "Does Desegregation Equal Integration?" *New York Post,* July 11, 1958.

Interview with Mike Wallace, "Self-Portrait of a Symbol: Martin Luther King," *New York Post,* February 15, 1961.

Interview with Martin Agronsky.

"The Consequences of Fame," *New York Post,* April 14, 1957.

Quoted in Poston, "Where Does He Go from Here?" *New York Post,* April 14, 1957.

11. BIRTH OF A NEW NATION

PRINCIPAL SOURCES:

"The Birth of a New Nation," sermon at Dexter Avenue Baptist Church, Montgomery, April 7, 1957 (MLKEC, INP).

Interview with Etta Moten Barnett, Accra, Ghana, March 6, 1957 (EMBC, INP).

OTHER SOURCES:

"Concerning Southern Civil Rights," address at Mississippi Freedom Party rally, Jackson, Mississippi, July 25, 1964 (MMFR, INP).

Why We Can't Wait (New York: New American Library, 1964), p. 21.

Annual Report, Dexter Avenue Baptist Church, Montgomery, November 1, 1956–
    October 31, 1957 (DABCC, INP).

12. BRUSH WITH DEATH

PRINCIPAL SOURCES:

Why We Can't Wait, p. 17

"I've Been to the Mountaintop," address at the Bishop Charles J. Mason Temple,
    Memphis, Tennessee, April 3, 1968 (MLKJP, GAMK).

"Advice for Living," *Ebony* 14 (December, 1958): 159.

OTHER SOURCES:

Annual Report, Dexter Avenue Baptist Church, Montgomery, November 1, 1957–
    November 30, 1958 (DABCC, INP).

Letter to the mass meeting of the Montgomery Improvement Association, October
    6, 1958 (HG, GAMK).

Interview on assassination attempt by Izola Curry, New York, September 30, 1958
    (MMFR, INP).

Statement issued from Harlem Hospital, New York, September 30, 1958 (MLKP,
    MBU).

Statement upon return to Montgomery, Montgomery, October 24, 1958 (MLKJP,
    GAMK).

13. PILGRIMAGE TO NONVIOLENCE

PRINCIPAL SOURCES:

"My Trip to the Land of Gandhi," *Ebony* 20 (July 1959): 84–86.

"Sermon on Mahatma Gandhi," at Dexter Avenue Baptist Church, Montgomery,
    March 22, 1959 (MLKJP, GAMK).

"A Walk Through the Holy Land," at Dexter Avenue Baptist Church, Montgom-
    ery, March 29, 1959 (MLKJP, GAMK).

"The Death of Evil upon the Seashore," in *Strength to Love*, chapter 8.

OTHER SOURCES:

"Remaining Awake Through a Great Revolution," sermon at National Cathedral,
    Washington, D.C., March 31, 1968 (MLKJP, GAMK).

"The American Dream," address at Lincoln University, Pennsylvania, June 6, 1961
    (MLKP, MBU).
"The American Dream," sermon at Ebenezer Baptist Church, Atlanta, July 4, 1965
    (MLKEC, INP).
"Equality Now: The President Has the Power," *Nation* 192 (February 4, 1961):
    91–95.
Statement on leaving India, New Delhi, March 9, 1959 (MLKP, MBU).
Quoted in the Tour Diary of James Bristol, March 10, 1959 (AFSCR, AFSCA).
"Pilgrimage to Nonviolence."
Letter to G. Ramachandran, May 19, 1959 (MLKP, MBU).
Why We Can't Wait, p. 135.

14. THE SIT-IN MOVEMENT

PRINCIPAL SOURCES:

"The Burning Truth in the South," *Progressive* 24 (May 1960): 8–10.
Annual Address on the Fourth Anniversary of the Montgomery Improvement
    Association, December 3, 1959 (MLKJP, GAMK).
"Foreword," in William Kunstler, ed., *Deep in My Heart* (New York: William
    Morrow, 1966), pp. 21–26.

OTHER SOURCES:

"The Time for Freedom Has Come," *New York Times Magazine,* September 10,
    1961. Copyright © 1961 by the New York Times Co. Reprinted by permission.
"A Creative Protest," address in Durham, North Carolina, February 16, 1960
    (DJG, INP).
Why We Can't Wait, chapter 2.
Statement at Youth March for Integrated Schools, Washington, D.C., April 18,
    1959 (MLKJP, GAMK).
Statement to press at beginning of the Youth Leadership Conference, Raleigh,
    North Carolina, April 15, 1960 (MLKP, MBU).
Farewell Message to Dexter Avenue Baptist Church Congregation, November 29,
    1959 (MLKJP, GAMK).
Letter to Allan Knight Chalmers, April 18, 1960 (MLKP, MBU).
Letter to James W. Shaeffer, December 4, 1959 (MLKP, MBU).
Form letter to supporters, June 1960 (MLKP, MBU).
Letter to William Herbert Gray, April 6, 1960 (MLKP, MBU).
Quoted in "King Accepts Atlanta Job; Leaving City," *Montgomery Advertiser,* No-
    vember 30, 1959.

15. ATLANTA ARREST AND PRESIDENTIAL POLITICS

PRINCIPAL SOURCE:

Interview with Berl I. Bernhard for John F. Kennedy Presidential Library, Atlanta, March 9, 1964 (MLKJP, GAMK).

OTHER SOURCES:

Why We Can't Wait, p. 147.

Why We Chose Jail, Not Bail: Statement to judge after the arrests at Rich's, Atlanta, October 19, 1960 (CSKC, INP).

"Out on Bond," *Atlanta Journal,* October 28, 1960.

Letter to Irl G. Whitchurch, August 6, 1959 (MLKP, MBU).

Letter to Chester Bowles, June 24, 1960 (CB, CtY).

Letter to Mrs. Frank Skeller, January 30, 1961 (MLKP, MBU).

Quoted in Andrew Young, *An Easy Burden* (New York: HarperCollins, 1996), p. 175.

16. THE ALBANY MOVEMENT

PRINCIPAL SOURCES:

Diary in Albany Jail, July 10–11, July 27–August 10, 1962 (CSKC, INP).

"Why It's Albany," *New York Amsterdam News,* August 18, 1962.

"Fumbling on the New Frontier," *Nation,* 194 (March 3, 1962): 190–193.

"Albany, Georgia—Tensions of the South," draft of article for *New York Times Magazine,* August 20, 1962 (MLKJP, GAMK).

Why We Can't Wait, chapters 1 and 2.

Address to District 65-AFL-CIO at Laurels Country Club, Monticello, New York, September 8, 1962 (MLKJP, GAMK).

OTHER SOURCES:

Letter to Earl Mazo, September 2, 1958 (MLKP, MBU).

Form letter to supporters, December 19, 1961 (JWWP, DHU).

"America's Great Crisis," address to Transport Workers Union Convention, New York, October 5, 1961 (TWUC, NNU-T).

"Solid Wall of Segregation Cracks at Albany," *SCLC Newsletter,* March, 1963 (MLKJP, GAMK).

Quoted in Vic Smith, "Peace Prevails," *Albany Herald,* December 18, 1961.

"Turning Point of Civil Rights," *New York Amsterdam News,* February 3, 1962.

"A Message from Jail," *New York Amsterdam News,* July 14, 1962.

"The Case against Tokenism," *New York Times Magazine,* August 5, 1962. Copyright © 1962 by the New York Times Co. Reprinted by permission.

"Terrible Cost of the Ballot," *New York Amsterdam News,* September 1, 1962 (MLKJP, GAMK).

Statement on release from jail, Albany, Georgia, July 13, 1962 (MLKJP, GAMK).

Address and responses to questions at National Press Club, Washington, D.C., July 19, 1962 (MLKP, MBU).

Statement on Violence in Albany, with W. G. Anderson, July 25, 1962 (CSKC, INP).

Telegram to John F. Kennedy, August 2, 1962 (JFKP, MWalK).

Telegram to John F. Kennedy, September 11, 1962 (JFKP, MWalK).

Interview with Alex Haley.

Quoted in *Time,* January 3, 1964, p. 15.

"Interview, Man of the Year," *Time* 83 (January 3, 1964): 13–16, 25–27.

17. THE BIRMINGHAM CAMPAIGN

PRINCIPAL SOURCE:

Why We Can't Wait, chapters 3 and 4; and draft of *Why We Can't Wait* (MLKP, MBU).

OTHER SOURCES:

Statement on Injunction, April 11, 1963, in Alan F. Westin and Barry Mahoney, *The Trial of Martin Luther King* (New York: Crowell, 1974), p. 79.

"Most Abused Man in Nation," *New York Amsterdam News,* March 31, 1962.

Address at Mass Meeting at St. Luke's Baptist Church, Birmingham, May 5, 1963 (MLKJP, GAMK).

Address at Mass Meeting, Yazoo City, Mississippi, June 21, 1966 (MLKJP, GAMK).

Telegram to John F. Kennedy, April 16, 1963 (JFKP, MWalK).

18. LETTER FROM BIRMINGHAM JAIL

PRINCIPAL SOURCE:

Why We Can't Wait, chapter 5.

OTHER SOURCES:

Address and press conference at St. John Baptist Church, Gary, Indiana, July 1, 1966 (AC, InU-N).

19. FREEDOM NOW!

PRINCIPAL SOURCE:

Why We Can't Wait, chapter 6.

OTHER SOURCES:

Statement at Sixteenth Street Baptist Church, Birmingham, May 3, 1963 (DCST, AB).

Statement at Mass Meeting at St. Luke's Baptist Church.

Statement at Mass Meeting, Birmingham, May 10, 1963 (MLKEC, INP).

"What a Mother Should Tell Her Child," sermon at Ebenezer Baptist Church, Atlanta, May 12, 1963 (MLKJP, GAMK).

Interview with Kenneth B. Clark, in *King, Malcolm, Baldwin: Three Interviews by Kenneth B. Clark* (Middletown, Connecticut, 1963), p. 27.

Interview with Alex Haley.

Press Conference USA, videotaped interview, Washington, D. C., July 5, 1963 (DJG, INP).

20. MARCH ON WASHINGTON

PRINCIPAL SOURCES:

Why We Can't Wait, chapter 7; and "A Summer of Discontent," draft for *Why We Can't Wait*, September 1963 (MLKP, MBU).

Address at March on Washington for Jobs and Freedom, Washington, D.C., August 28, 1963 (SCLCT, INP).

OTHER SOURCES:

Interview with Donald H. Smith, Altanta, November 29, 1963 (DHSTR, WHi).

Affidavit, Martin Luther King, Jr., vs. Mister Maestro, Inc. and Twentieth Century Fox Record Corporation, U.S. District Court, S.D. of New York, December 16, 1963 (MLKEC, INP).

21. DEATH OF ILLUSIONS

PRINCIPAL SOURCES:

Why We Can't Wait, chapter 8.

"Epitaph and Challenge," *SCLC Newsletter*, November–December 1963.

"Eulogy for the Martyred Children," Birmingham, September 18, 1963 (MLKJP, GAMK).

Meeting with John F. Kennedy and civil rights leaders, audio recording, Washington, D.C., September 19, 1963 (JFKP, MWalK).

OTHER SOURCES:

Annual Address to Seventh Annual Convention of SCLC, Virginia Union, Richmond, September 27, 1963 (MLKJP, GAMK).

Interview with Alex Haley.

Address on Three of the Children Killed at Sixteenth Street Baptist Church, Birmingham, September 18, 1963 (MLKP, MBU).

Handwritten Notes on John F. Kennedy assassination, November 1963 (MLKJP, GAMK).

"What Killed JFK?" *New York Amsterdam News,* December 21, 1963.

Christmas letter to the Family of Denise McNair, December 1963 (MLKJP, GAMK).

22. ST. AUGUSTINE

PRINCIPAL SOURCES:

Why We Can't Wait, chapter 8.

"Let Justice Roll Down," *Nation* 200 (March 15, 1965): 269–274. Copyright © 1965. Reprinted by permission.

"St. Augustine Florida, 400 Years of Bigotry and Hate," *SCLC Newsletter,* June 1964.

Statement on St. Augustine, Atlanta, June 17, 1964 (MLKJP, GAMK).

Annual Address to Eighth Annual Convention of SCLC, Savannah, Georgia, October 1, 1964 (SAVFC, WHi).

Passage of 1964 Civil Rights Act, Atlanta, July 2, 1964 (MLKJP, GAMK).

OTHER SOURCES:

"Hammer of Civil Rights," *Nation* 198 (March 9, 1964): 230–234.

Statement on Goldwater and St. Augustine, ABC interview, St. Augustine, Florida, July 16, 1964 (MLKJP, GAMK).

"Quest for Peace and Justice," Nobel Prize Lecture at University of Oslo, Oslo, Norway, December 11, 1964 (MLKJP, GAMK).

23. THE MISSISSIPPI CHALLENGE

PRINCIPAL SOURCES:

Statement in support of Freedom Democratic Party, Jackson, Mississippi, July 22, 1964 (MLKJP, GAMK).

Annual Address to Eighth Annual Convention of SCLC.

Address to Southern Association of Political Scientists, November 13, 1964 (MLKJP, GAMK).

"Ready in Mississippi," *New York Amsterdam News,* August 29, 1964.

"Pathos and Hope," *New York Amsterdam News,* March 3, 1962.

"People to People," *New York Amsterdam News,* September 1964.

OTHER SOURCES:

"Passage of 1964 Civil Rights Act," July 2, 1964.

Statement before the Credentials Committee, Democratic National Committee, Atlantic City, New Jersey, August 22, 1964 (MLKJP, GAMK).

24. THE NOBEL PEACE PRIZE

PRINCIPAL SOURCES:

"Mighty Army of Love," *New York Amsterdam News,* November 7, 1964.

"What the Nobel Prize Means to Me," *New York Amsterdam News,* November 28, 1964.

Acceptance Address at Nobel Peace Prize Ceremony, Oslo, Norway, December 10, 1964 (MLKJP, GAMK).

Statement Concerning Nobel Prize Money, Oslo, Norway, December 17, 1964 (MLKJP, GAMK).

"Dreams of Brighter Tomorrows," *Ebony* 20 (March 1965): 43.

OTHER SOURCES:

"Quest for Peace and Justice."

Address on South African Independence, London, England, December 7, 1964 (ACA-ARC, LNT).

Statement on the Nobel Peace Prize, Forneby, Norway, December 9, 1964 (MLKJP, GAMK).

Address upon Acceptance of the New York City Medallion, New York, December 17, 1964 (MLKJP, GAMK).

"The Nobel Prize," *Liberation* (January 1965): 28–29.

"Struggle for Racial Justice," address at Recognition Dinner, Atlanta, January 27, 1965 (NF, GEU).

"After the Nobel Ceremony, A Tender Moment Is Shared," *Ebony* 20 (March 1965): 38.

25. MALCOLM X

PRINCIPAL SOURCES:

Interview with Alex Haley.

"The Nightmare of Violence," *New York Amsterdam News,* February 25, 1965.

Press conference on the Death of Malcolm X, the Nation of Islam and Violence, Los Angeles, February 24, 1965 (MLKJP, GAMK).

OTHER SOURCES:

Telegram to Betty Shabazz, February 26, 1965 (MLKJP, GAMK).

Letter to Edward D. Ball, December 14, 1961 (MLKP, MBU).

Transcript, Testimony in *Williams v. Wallace,* March 11, 1965 (MLKJP, GAMK).

Interview with Robert Penn Warren, in *Who Speaks for the Negro?,* Robert Penn Warren, ed. (New York: Random House, 1965), pp. 203–221.

26. SELMA

PRINCIPAL SOURCES:

"Movement to Washington," Address at SCLC's Ministers Leadership Training Program, Miami, February 23, 1968 (MLKEC, INP).

"Selma—The Shame and the Promise," *Industrial Unions Department Agenda* 1 (March 1965): 18–21.

"Civil Rights No. 1—The Right to Vote," *New York Times Magazine,* March 14, 1965, p. 26. Copyright © 1965 by the New York Times Co. Reprinted by permission.

Transcript, Testimony in *Williams v. Wallace.*

Meeting scheduled with Hubert Humphrey, press release, Washington, D.C., February 7, 1965 (MLKJP, GAMK).

"Behind the Selma March," *Saturday Review* 48 (April 3, 1965): 16–17.

"After the March—An Open Letter to the American People," Atlanta, April 1, 1965 (MLKJP, GAMK).

Annual Address to Ninth Annual Convention of SCLC, Birmingham, Alabama, August 11, 1965 (MLKJP, GAMK).

OTHER SOURCES:

Address to rally prior to Selma March, Selma, Alabama, February 1, 1965 (MLKJP, GAMK).

"A Letter from Selma: Martin Luther King from a Selma, Alabama Jail," *New York Times,* February 5, 1965. Copyright © 1965 by the New York Times Co. Reprinted by permission.

Instructions from Selma Jail to movement associates, February 1965 (MLKJP, GAMK).

"Let Justice Roll Down," *The Nation,* March 15, 1965

Statement on brutal beating of three white ministers, March 10, 1965 (MLKJP, GAMK).

Handwritten draft of statement regarding death of James Reeb, March 11, 1965 (MLKJP, GAMK).

Statement announcing judge's permission to stage march to Selma, Montgomery, March 16, 1965 (MLKJP, GAMK).

Statement regarding the address made by Lyndon Baines Johnson on the situation in Selma, March 16, 1965 (MLKJP, GAMK).

Interview in Selma, Alabama, March 24, 1965 (MMFR, INP).

Address at St. Jude's, Montgomery, March 24, 1965 (MLKJP, GAMK).

Address at Selma to Montgomery March, March 25, 1965 (MLKJP, GAMK).

Address and Press Conference at St. John Baptist Church, Gary, Indiana, July 1, 1966.

Where Do We Go From Here: Chaos or Community? (New York: Harper and Row, 1967), pp. 1–2.

Form letter to supporters, June, 1965 (WAR, INP).

27. WATTS

PRINCIPAL SOURCES:

"A Cry of Hate or a Cry for Help?" Special to the *New York Times Magazine* draft (MLKJP, GAMK).

Statement on arrival in Los Angeles, August 17, 1965 (MLKJP, GAMK).

"Feeling Alone in the Struggle," *New York Amsterdam News,* August 28, 1965.

OTHER SOURCES:

"A Christian Movement in a Revolutionary Age," Rochester, New York, September 28, 1965 (CSKC, INP).

"Beyond the Los Angeles Riots, Next Stop: The North," *Saturday Review* 48 (November 13, 1965): 33–35.

"The Crisis in Civil Rights," Chicago, July 1967 (MLKJP, GAMK).

28. CHICAGO CAMPAIGN

PRINCIPAL SOURCES:

"Why Chicago Is the Target," *New York Amsterdam News,* September 11, 1965.
Where Do We Go from Here.
"The Good Samaritan," sermon at Ebenezer Baptist Church, Atlanta, August 28, 1966 (MLKJP, GAMK).
"One Year Later in Chicago," handwritten draft, February 1967 (SCLCR, GAMK).
Quoted in *Federal Role in Urban Affairs Hearings,* testimony before Subcommittee on Executive Reorganization, Committe on Government Operations, U.S. Senate, December 15, 1966.

OTHER SOURCES:

Statement to the press, Chicago, July 7, 1965 (MLKJP, GAMK).
The Chicago Plan, press release, Atlanta, January 7, 1966 (MLKJP, GAMK).
Address to Freedom Rally at Soldiers Field, Chicago, July 10, 1966 (MLKJP, GAMK).
Statement on West Side Riots, Chicago, July 17, 1966 (MLKJP, GAMK).
"Why I Must March," address, Chicago, August 18, 1966 (MLKEC, INP).
Statement on nonviolence, Grenada, Mississippi, September 19, 1966 (MLKJP, GAMK).
"A Gift of Love," *McCalls* 94 (December 1966): 146–147.
Keynote address, National Conference for New Politics, Chicago, August 31, 1967 (MLKJP, GAMK).
Press conference, Liberty Baptist Church, Chicago, March 24, 1967 (MLKJP, GAMK).
"What Are Your New Year's Resolutions?" sermon at Ebenezer Baptist Church, Atlanta, January 7, 1968 (MLKJP, GAMK).
Interview with Merv Griffin, on *Merv Griffin Show,* July 6, 1967 (MLKEC, INP).
"Conversation with Martin Luther King," in James M. Washington, ed., *Testament of Hope* (San Francisco: Harper and Row, 1986; 1991 ed.), pp. 657–679.
Quoted in Flip Schulke, *King Remembered.*

29. BLACK POWER

PRINCIPAL SOURCE:

Where Do We Go from Here, chapter 2.

OTHER SOURCES:

Address during Meredith March, West Marks, Mississippi, June 12, 1966 (MLKJP, GAMK).

Address at mass meeting, Yazoo City, Mississippi, June 21, 1966 (MLKJP, GAMK).
"It Is Not Enough to Condemn Black Power," signed advertisement in *New York Times,* July 26, 1966.
Statement on Black Political Power, Grenada, Mississippi, June 16, 1966 (MLKJP, GAMK).
"Conversation with Martin Luther King."

30. BEYOND VIETNAM

PRINCIPAL SOURCES:

"Journey of Conscience," draft of address, 1967 (CSKC, INP).
"Beyond Vietnam," address at Riverside Church, New York City, April 4, 1967 (MLKJP, GAMK).
Press conference in Los Angeles, April 12, 1967 (DJG, INP).
"To Chart Our Course of the Future," Address at SCLC staff retreat at Penn Center, Frogmore, South Carolina, May 22, 1967 (MLKJP, GAMK).
Address at SCLC's Ministers Leadership Training Program.

OTHER SOURCES:

"My Dream—Peace: God's Man's Business," *New York Amsterdam News,* January 1, 1966.
Press conference, Los Angeles, California, April 12, 1967.
"Why I Am Opposed to the War in Vietnam," sermon at Ebenezer Baptist Church, Atlanta, April 30, 1967 (MLKJP, GAMK).
"To Serve the Present Age," sermon at Victory Baptist Church, Los Angeles, June 25, 1967 (MLKEC, INP).
Press conference on riots, Ebenezer Baptist Church, Atlanta, July 24, 1967 (MLKJP, GAMK).
Keynote address, National Conference for New Politics.
The Trumpet of Conscience (San Francisco: Harper and Row, 1967), p. 37.
Sermon at Ebenezer Baptist Church, Atlanta, November 5, 1967 (MLKEC, INP).
"What Are Your New Year's Resolutions?" sermon at Ebenezer Baptist Church, Atlanta, January 7, 1968 (MLKEC, INP).
"A Testament of Hope," *Playboy* 16 (January 1969): 175.

31. THE POOR PEOPLE'S CAMPAIGN

PRINCIPAL SOURCES:

Statement on Washington Campaign, Atlanta, December 4, 1967 (MLKJP, GAMK).

"Showdown for Non-Violence," *Look* 32 (April 16, 1968): 23–25.
"Movement to Washington."
Address in Memphis, Tennessee, March 18, 1968 (MVC, TMM and MLKJP, JMK).

OTHER SOURCES:

Address at SCLC staff retreat at Penn Center, May 22, 1967.
"What Are Your New Year's Resolutions?"
Address at mass meeting, Waycross, Georgia, March 22, 1968 (MLKJP, GAMK).
"A Testament of Hope," *Playboy.*

32. UNFULFILLED DREAMS

PRINCIPAL SOURCES:

"Unfulfilled Dreams," sermon at Ebenezer Baptist Church, Atlanta, March 3,
     1968, in *Knock at Midnight,* pp. 191–200.
"I've Been to the Mountaintop."
"The Drum Major Instinct," sermon at Ebenezer Baptist Church, Atlanta, Febru-
     ary 4, 1968, in *Knock at Midnight,* pp. 184–186.

INDEX

◆

Now you can order superb titles directly from Abacus

☐ A Knock at Midnight	Clayborne Carson & Peter Holloran (eds)	£7.99
☐ Freedom in Exile: The Autobiography of the Dalai Lama	Dalai Lama	£9.99
☐ Ancient Wisdom, Modern World	Dalai Lama	£8.99
☐ Long Walk to Freedom	Nelson Mandela	£12.99

The prices shown above are correct at time of going to press. However, the publishers reserve the right to increase prices on covers from those previously advertised, without further notice.

Please allow for postage and packing: **Free UK delivery.**
Europe; add 25% of retail price; Rest of World; 45% of retail price.

To order any of the above or any other Abacus titles, please call our credit card orderline or fill in this coupon and send/fax it to:

Abacus, P.O. Box 121, Kettering, Northants NN14 4ZQ
Fax: 01832 733076   Tel: 01832 737526
Email: aspenhouse@FSBDial.co.uk

☐ I enclose a UK bank cheque made payable to Abacus for £ . . . .
☐ Please charge £ . . . . . . to my Visa, Delta, Maestro.

Expiry Date [ ][ ][ ][ ]   Maestro Issue No. [ ][ ]

NAME (BLOCK LETTERS please) . . . .

ADDRESS . . . .

. . . .

. . . .

Postcode . . . . Telephone . . . .

Signature . . . .

Please allow 28 days for delivery within the UK. Offer subject to price and availability.

Chapter Two

It was as if the earth had turned to quicksand under Arabella's feet. She stared at the woman who'd stolen her rightful future—her husband, her unborn children and her home. Her eyes took in the sweetly wholesome face, the flaxen hair and the figure that tapered from voluptuous bosom to...

Oh, merciful heaven...

Sally's robe was tied several inches above her waist. Below the knot, the bulge of her pregnant belly was slight but unmistakable.

It was too much. Chilled, exhausted and shocked beyond her capacity to cope, Arabella felt her world crumbling like a plaster wall in an earthquake. She wanted to run back outside, track down McIntyre and demand that he take her... somewhere. Anywhere but here. And yet when she tried to turn away, her legs refused to cooperate. Sally's face blurred before her eyes. Charles's hands reached out to steady her as she reeled. Then her legs buckled beneath her, and everything went black.

McIntyre stabled the horses, fed them some hay and toweled their wet coats before leaving the barn and stumbling up

the steps of his rambling log and stone house. He felt like the raw edge of hell; but he'd be lucky to get much sleep before dawn, when he'd have to round up some help and go after the mired buckboard.

Blast the woman! Why couldn't she have gotten Charlie Middleton's damned letter and stayed in Boston where she belonged? He'd known how things stood when he'd picked her up in town. But it hadn't been his place to tell her. That, as he'd made clear, was Middleton's job.

He'd been hard on her, letting her wait in the rain, then telling her that story about the royal flush. When the stage pulled in, he'd been settling a quarrel between two friends. He could've dropped everything and rushed outside. But his friends had needed him. And given what he knew, he'd been none too eager to face Charlie Middleton's jilted fiancée.

By now Arabella would have learned the truth about the man she'd loved and trusted. McIntyre could imagine how she'd take the news after coming all this way. It might have been kinder to tell her in town. But then what? She'd have been stuck in the rain in Buffalo Bend with no place to stay and no easy way to leave. For all he knew, she might've tried to jump out of the wagon and drown herself.

Hellfire, she'd nearly done just that, going after her damnfool wedding dress in the flood. The woman was a willful brat. Middleton would have an easier life with sweet, patient Sally. But McIntyre couldn't help admiring the little redhead's spunk. Even half drowned and spitting fury, he had to concede she was uncommonly pretty.

That made him even more eager to see her leave. Charles had been reluctant enough to do his duty by Sally. Throwing the woman he'd *wanted* to marry into the mix wouldn't do the newlyweds any favors as they settled into married life. And the last thing McIntyre wanted was to see Sally hurt again.

Yes, it would be better for all of them if Arabella Spencer

left—and left soon. If he never saw the little snip again, it would suit him just fine.

A glance at the clock next to the massive stone fireplace told him it was nearly 3:00 a.m. Since he would need to rescue the buckboard at first light or risk losing the cargo to thieves, it was scarcely worth going to bed. But he was chilled to the bone, and the old hip wound, a souvenir of Gettysburg, was throbbing. Even a couple of hours of sleep would be better than nothing.

Dragging himself into the bedroom, he peeled off his wet clothes and left them in a heap on the rug. Naked and shivering, he crawled between the worn flannel sheets and closed his eyes. Morning would be here all too soon.

Arabella stirred and woke. A streak of sunlight, falling between the drawn drapes, stabbed her eyes. She turned over with a moan. Her sleep-blurred eyes glimpsed yellow flowered wallpaper, a quilted coverlet and a tall mahogany bedpost. Where was she, and how did she get here?

She stretched cautiously, wincing in pain. Her body felt as if every muscle had been pounded like a slab of beef. And last night she'd had the most horrible dream about Charles…

"Arabella?"

The voice jarred her to full awareness. She raised her head to see Charles standing in the doorway, dressed in a white shirt and a leather vest. His once-pale skin had acquired a healthy tan, but the gentle blue eyes and light brown curls were just as she'd remembered. Talons of pain clenched around her heart.

"Last night wasn't a dream, was it?" she whispered.

He shook his head. "Arabella, dearest—"

"How could you?" Jerking upright in the bed, she flung the words at him. "How could you do this to me? To *us*?"

"I wrote you a letter."

"You wrote me a letter! A letter I never received! Is that all you've got to say for yourself?"

He sighed. "I suppose I do owe you an explanation. May I sit down?"

She nodded toward a bedside chair, then took a moment to adjust the pillow behind her back. The faded flannel nightgown she was wearing felt several sizes too big. How she came to have it on was something Arabella didn't even want to know.

She glared at her ex-fiancé, now another woman's husband. "No more surprises, Charles. Tell me the truth—the whole sordid little story."

He fiddled with his thumbs, avoiding her gaze. After a long moment he cleared his throat. "Sally kept house for her brother on the next spread north of here. When I moved to the ranch last summer, she came over with an apple pie, expecting to find a family. Instead she found me. She was shy at first, but over time we became…friends."

"Friends." Arabella cast him a withering look. "Did you tell her you were engaged to be married?"

"Of course I did. I even showed her your picture. But she was lonely and so was I. Her brother was out on the range for days on end, so it wasn't hard to find time together. Mostly we just talked or went for rides. She even taught me how to fish. We behaved ourselves pretty well until the big January blizzard. She happened to be here the day the storm blew in. There was no way she could leave. One thing led to another…" He stared down at his thumbs.

"Oh, Charles!" Arabella felt as if she were scolding a wayward child. It was a feeling she'd had many times before with him, dating back to when he actually *was* a child, and could never seem to keep himself out of mischief. He was always genuinely sorry afterward, and faithfully promised to mend his ways…until the next time temptation got the better of him.

Everyone had said his character would become steadier as he grew to manhood, but if recent events were any indication, he still had quite a bit of maturing to do.

"Why didn't you tell me then?" she asked.

He shook his head. "Afterward, Sally was upset. She said she'd done a bad thing, sinning with a man who was already promised. When she left here, she told me she never wanted to see me again."

"And what about you? Were you even sorry?"

"Sorry?" He made a little choked sound. "I'd betrayed you and taken advantage of an innocent girl. I despised myself for what I'd done. But the one thing I knew for sure was that I didn't want to lose you. When I didn't hear from Sally, I sent you the tickets and put the finishing touches on the house. Everything was going as planned until three weeks ago."

"I can just imagine." Arabella masked her pain with icy calm. "Go on."

"I heard a knock at the door. When I opened it, there was Sally on the porch, crying her eyes out. Her brother was with her, looking as mean as a grizzly bear. He'd brought along a preacher and the biggest shotgun I'd ever seen." His voice choked with tears. "If I'd refused to marry her, I've no doubt the man would have killed me. Oh, Lord, don't hate me, Arabella! I didn't mean for this to happen!"

He looked like a little boy who'd been caught with his hand in the cookie jar. Arabella felt frozen inside. "You're not worth hating, Charles Middleton. All I can do is wish you and your bride the best and get out of your life."

Charles reached for her hand, catching it tight. "You've got to understand. Sally's a sweet girl, a fine girl. I care for her. But, so help me, it's you I love, Arabella. If there's a way, any way at all…"

Disgust thawed Arabella's composure. She jerked her hand away. "I can't believe you'd suggest such a thing! Shame on

you, Charles! You've made your bed, so lie in it with that poor girl and try to be a decent husband! As for me, I'm well out of this mess. As soon as my trunk arrives, one of your hired hands can drive me back to Buffalo Bend."

He rose, his mouth set. "Your trunk was on the front porch this morning. But you can't leave yet. The bridge is washed out. Even if you could get to town there's no place to stay, and the stage only comes through every ten days—less often if the weather's bad. For now, I'm afraid you're stuck here."

"Stuck here. In this house, with you and your bride." Arabella felt as if she'd just pronounced her own prison sentence. This was unthinkable—a nightmare with no escape. She thrust out her chin, fighting tears. "Very well, I'll stay if I must. But the less I see of your lying face, the better!"

He flinched as if she'd slapped him. Good. The cheating bastard deserved that and more. But her own self-control was cracking around the edges. "Get out," she muttered. "Just go."

"Your trunk will be in the hall. I'll have some breakfast sent up."

When she didn't reply he walked out, closing the door behind him. As his footsteps faded, Arabella gave in to fury. She had loved Charles, trusted him completely. But he was weak and deceitful. While she'd been dreaming about him and planning their future, he'd been sleeping with another woman—*sleeping* being the polite word for an act so intimate that Arabella could scarcely imagine it. Then, as if nothing had happened, *he'd sent her the blasted tickets!*

If he hadn't gotten the wretched creature with child, Arabella would have married him and never been the wiser—until the next time he strayed. Oh, there would always be a next time. A man didn't change that much.

How could she have been such a fool?

Turning over, she punched her pillow—once, then again and again. Was it Charles or herself she was pretending to

beat? It didn't make much difference. The release felt like something she needed.

A solid blow split the stitching of the pillowcase. Feathers exploded in a blizzard of white, falling around her like the fragments of a shattered dream.

All her hopes, all her plans—her wedding, her home, her future family—everything was gone because of a scheming little Montana prairie flower with an apple pie and a man too weak-willed to keep his word. What had she done to deserve this? And what was she going to do now?

Clutching her ribs with her arms, she doubled over in the bed. As the feathers settled around her, Arabella's body shook with hard, dry sobs.

A light rap at the door riveted her attention. Swiftly composing her features, she sat up. "Who is it?"

"Breakfast." The voice was a woman's, the word so faintly spoken that it barely penetrated the wood.

Arabella sat up, adjusting herself in the bed and smoothing back her unruly red curls. At least the hired help wouldn't be expecting her to answer any questions. "Bring it in," she said.

The door opened slowly. The young woman who stepped over the threshold with a tray was uncommonly tall and dressed in faded calico. Her hair fell over one shoulder in a thick flaxen braid. Arabella's spirits sank to a new low. The last person she wanted to see this morning was Charles's wife, Sally.

"I hope you like ham and eggs," she said. "I brought fresh biscuits, too, and—" Her dove-gray eyes shot open as she noticed the feathers. "My stars! What happened?"

Arabella bit back a stinging retort. She was starved, and that breakfast did smell good. Her stomach growled. "Excuse me." Her politeness was brittle. "I'm afraid I took out my frustrations on that pillow. I'll be happy to pay for a new one."

"No, no!" Sally set the tray across Arabella's knees and

began scooping up the feathers. "I can mend it. No trouble at all. Oh, and I washed your muddy clothes and hung them to dry. Your beautiful silk gown had some mud stains, but I managed to get the worst of them out. Maybe you can add a row of lace to cover what's left of them, along with the watermarks."

"Thank you. That gown was my grandmother's." Arabella nibbled a piece of flaky biscuit. Strange, how the dress she'd saved for her wedding had been salvaged by the very woman who'd laid ruin to her plans. It was as if she'd stepped into a world of smoke and mirrors, where nothing was as it seemed—including Sally's friendly manner. What schemes and plans lay behind that sweetly smiling face?

"My grandmother was married in that gown," Arabella added. "She and my grandfather were happy together for almost fifty years. I thought it might give me luck to wear it." She shrugged. "So much for luck."

"You're so pretty, Arabella. Even prettier than your picture. Surely you'll get other chances."

Other chances. Arabella's spirits sank a notch deeper. True, there were men standing in line back home. But none she wanted to spend her life with. Her heart had always been set on Charles.

Cheating, lying, two-faced Charles, who'd fathered another woman's child and married her only because he was forced to.

Assuming a mask of politeness, Arabella changed the subject. "This breakfast is delicious. My compliments to your cook."

Sally flushed. She had skin like a ripe peach, with the lightest dusting of freckles across her classic nose. There was a part of Arabella that wanted to fly at her and yank that long golden braid until she screamed. But what purpose would that serve now?

"I'm the cook," Sally said. "There's a Chinese man who does the heavy work and washes up in the kitchen, but I enjoy cooking and cleaning—and it does save Charlie a bit of money."

Arabella choked on a bite of airy scrambled egg. She'd assumed that Sally had set out to snare herself a rich husband. But Charles's wife seemed as guileless as she was pretty.

That, or she was putting on one humdinger of an act.

"Charles has plenty of money, Sally," Arabella said. "In fact he's quite wealthy. He can certainly afford to hire more help for you."

"Oh, but I don't mind." Sally was stuffing handfuls of feathers back into the pillowcase. "I've worked hard all my life. I'm used to it."

"But you're expecting a baby. You're certainly going to need a woman's help soon."

"My mother raised seven children in a log cabin without any help at all. I'm strong, just like she was. I'll manage fine."

Putting the pillowcase aside, she sat down on the foot of the bed. "I know you'll be needing some time to yourself. I'll have Chung bring in your trunk and fill the bath. But before I go, there's something I want to say."

Her work-worn hands clasped and unclasped in her lap. She wore no wedding ring—evidently that hadn't been included in the shotgun ceremony. Someone should tell Charles to buy her one.

"I know you have every reason to hate me, Arabella," she said. "You came here expecting to be married. Instead you found…me." Her hand brushed the curve of her growing belly. "I never meant for you to be hurt. When I found out about the baby, I planned to raise it on my own. I kept the secret from my brother for as long as I could, but he finally noticed. He was the one who forced Charlie to marry me."

She shook her head. "I can't blame Stewart. He was only try-ing to do the right thing."

"Do you love Charles?" Arabella was startled by her own question.

She nodded, blinking back tears. "If I didn't love him, this—" Her hand stroked her belly again. "This never would have happened. But he was yours. I never meant to take him away from you."

Arabella's emotions caromed between anger and pity. Sally had Charles. She had his house, his child and the status of being his wife. But how much was that worth if her husband claimed to love another woman?

What a mess! Arabella could hardly wait to be on that train back to Boston.

"I was thinking this morning," Sally continued. "You've traveled all this way. Maybe there's still some good that can come of it. My brother, Stewart, is a good man. He's kind and responsible, and he has his own ranch, bigger even than this one. Now that I've married Charlie, he's all alone. What if you and he—"

Arabella's fork clattered to the tray. "Your brother?" she gasped. "What makes you think I'd be interested in the man who forced you and Charles to marry?"

Sally's face fell. "You could give him a chance while you're here. Stewart's a quiet man, but he can be pleasant once you get to know him. He's even a war hero. He won a medal for bravery at Gettysburg."

A war hero? No wonder he was able to scare Charles into the wedding ceremony. Mean-as-a-grizzly, shotgun-toting Stewart, Charles had described him. He'd probably scared the Rebels to death.

"We invite him over for dinner every Sunday," Sally said. "He's coming this evening. You might enjoy spending some time with him. What have you got to lose?"

Arabella chose not to answer the question. But it did start her thinking. Paying a little harmless attention to another man might show Charles that she was capable of moving on. And Sally was right about one thing—even if Stewart proved to be a troll, what did she have to lose? She'd be leaving on the next stage out of Buffalo Bend.

Arabella drained her tea and set down her fork. "All right, Sally. No promises, mind you, but I'm willing to meet your brother."

"Oh, but you've already met him. Didn't he tell you who he was?"

Arabella's jaw went slack. She groaned as the truth sank home. How could she not have seen the resemblance—the height, the strong features, the deep-set gray eyes.

"Stewart McIntyre." Sally's smile confirmed her worst fears. "My brother's the man who brought you here."

Stewart surveyed the banquet laid out on the white linen tablecloth. Sally had outdone herself tonight, with roast chicken, braised potatoes and carrots, hot buttered rolls and a fresh apple cobbler with cream for dessert. Much as he relished a good meal, he worried that his sister was working too hard. Maybe it was time her husband took a firm hand and hired more help.

Not that Charlie Middleton took a firm hand in much of anything. Stewart didn't have a high opinion of any rancher who wouldn't get his fingernails dirty. And after what Charlie had done to his sister, he could scarcely abide the man's company. But he accepted these weekly invitations to keep in touch with Sally and make sure she was well taken care of.

He'd been of a mind to make his excuses tonight. With Arabella Spencer in the house, tensions were bound to be running as high as the Missouri in flood. But early that morning, when he'd delivered Arabella's trunk, Sally had met him on

the porch and begged him to come. Sensing that she needed his support, he'd said yes.

They sat around one end of the long table, Sally on her husband's right and Arabella on his left, directly across from Stewart. From where he sat, there was no way to keep his eyes off her.

She'd cleaned up right fine since he'd left her, shivering like a wet pup at Charlie's gate. Her pale yellow gown was simple but elegant, with a pert little ribbon at the throat. Her fiery locks were twisted up and pinned at the crown of her head, leaving a few loose curls to tumble around her heart-shaped face. He noticed for the first time that her eyes were the color of fresh spring grass.

She looked like a little porcelain doll. And the sidelong glances Charlie Middleton was giving her made Stewart want to stand up and punch the bastard.

It had been his worry all along—that the presence of Charlie's former fiancée would put a strain on his sister's marriage. Seeing Arabella for the first time had doubled his worries. Sally was a beautiful girl with a true and tender heart. Given time, Charlie might see her fine qualities and grow to love her. But Arabella Spencer was a dazzler—lively, spirited and confident of her charms. If she made up her mind to get Charlie back, poor Sally wouldn't stand a chance.

Maybe he should've left the damned woman back in town!

"Sally tells me you're a war hero, Mr. McIntyre." Arabella had turned her wiles on Stewart now. She was clearly trying to make Charlie jealous. Stewart fought the urge to get up from the table and walk out, away from all of this nonsense. Only Sally's pleading eyes kept him in his seat.

"Oh, call him Stewart, Arabella. We don't hold with formality in these parts." Sally's gaiety was as brittle as glass.

"Very well, Stewart." She smiled and batted her impossibly long eyelashes. "I was told you won a medal at Gettys-

burg. There must be a good story behind that, if you'd care to entertain us."

Stewart took the time to spear a drumstick from the white china platter. "It was a long time ago, and it's hardly fit for entertainment. If I told you what Gettysburg was really like, you wouldn't be able to finish your dinner."

Her delicate brows shot up. "I'm sorry, I was only—"

"I was nineteen years old and scared spitless. What I did involved killing boys as young and scared as myself. I threw away the medal, and I've since done my best to forget the whole miserable experience. Is that entertaining enough for you, Arabella?"

Charlie had gone pale around the mouth. "Really, Stewart, Arabella was only trying to make polite conversation."

"Fine. But let's make polite conversation about something else." He knew he'd been harsh, but of all subjects for Arabella to fix upon, that was the worst choice. Remembering the war was the last thing he wanted to do.

Stewart drizzled gravy onto his mashed potatoes. Without looking up, he could feel three pairs of eyes—Charlie's blazing with proper outrage, Sally's overflowing with dismay. And Arabella's, most likely shooting daggers from their emerald depths.

"Since you had to go back to get your wagon, maybe you can tell us about the road," she said. "As soon as it's fit to travel, I mean to be gone from here."

"Then you'll have to wait for a while," Stewart replied. "What I saw of that road's not much better than a hog wallow. So you might as well settle in and enjoy your stay. Montana can be a pretty place in the spring when the wildflowers are in bloom. Have you had a chance to look around?"

"I'm still recovering from last night. So far all I've managed to do is sleep, bathe and dress."

"I'm sure Stewart would be happy to show you around,

Arabella." Sally's voice quivered with hope. Good Lord, was this his sister's attempt at matchmaking?

Arabella's silence expressed how she felt about Sally's suggestion. Stewart breathed a sigh of relief. He'd already had enough of Miss Arabella Spencer.

"I'll be busy rounding up spring calves," he said. "If I took time off to play guide, I could lose a few of them."

"I'd be happy to take you out for a ride." It was Charlie who spoke up. "The sidesaddle I ordered is waiting in the barn. We could go first thing tomorrow morning."

Stewart saw the hurt that flashed across his sister's pretty face. At that moment he could have lunged across the table, grabbed his brother-in-law by the collar and shaken him until his teeth fell out.

Flashing Stewart a look of dismay, Arabella shook her head. "After last night, I'm so sore, I couldn't ride a hobby horse. Don't trouble yourself, Charles. I'll see the country in my own good time."

"You're sure?"

"Quite." As if to punctuate the word, she jabbed a carrot slice with her fork. "And now, if you don't mind, this delicious dinner is getting cold."

She lowered her gaze and attacked her plate with the ferocity of a small red fox. The meal was finished in snatches of awkward small talk. Stewart was relieved when the last bite was eaten and the chairs were pulled away from the table.

He was about to take his leave of his sister and go when Arabella stepped in front of him. "I'm in need of some fresh air, Stewart," she said. "Would you be so kind as to walk me around the yard? It's dark out, and I don't want to risk a misstep."

"Certainly." Stewart offered his arm and allowed himself to be led out onto the porch. He knew better than to expect a pleasant evening stroll. Arabella's request had been more

like a summons from the Spanish Inquisition. The little red-head wanted answers and would stop at nothing to get them. Any way it went down, this was not going to be pretty.

Chapter Three

The night sky was a sea of stars. Arabella's eyes traced the arc of the Milky Way, like a spill of crystal sand across the vast, dark bowl of the heavens. Boston's misty nights were lovely in their way. But Montana's dry, clear air sharpened the senses to razor keenness. In the chirr of tiny grass-dwellers she could make out individual voices. The wings of a night-hawk sliced the air above her head. Stewart's horse, tethered by the gate, snorted in the darkness. Arabella could hear the sound of its teeth cropping the fresh spring grass.

Beneath her light touch, Stewart's arm was as taut as steel cable. He was silent, waiting for her to speak.

She cleared her throat. "You might have told me," she said in her sternest voice.

"It wasn't my place to tell you. I agreed to meet the stage, in case you were on it, and give you a ride to the ranch, but after that, you were Charlie's problem. It was up to him to break the news."

"So you let me blather on about getting married, when all the time you knew!"

"What would you have done if I'd told you?"

"I don't know. But at least I'd have been prepared." She

gazed past the fence, toward the hulking silhouette of the barn. "At least I know why you've been so hateful toward me."

She caught the sharp intake of his breath. "Hate is too strong a word, Arabella. I don't hate you. But I'm protective of my sister. Sally's happiness means the world to me."

"And you see me as a threat to her."

"Aren't you?"

The question brushed the hair trigger of Arabella's temper. "What exactly are you implying?" she snapped.

"That you're a beautiful woman who knows how to use her charms, and that you have everything to gain by doing so. I saw the moon-calf way Charlie was looking at you tonight. All you'd have to do is crook your pretty little finger, and—"

Arabella's palm struck his face with a slap that sent a jolt of pain up her arm. It was like striking granite. "How dare you?" she gasped. "The very idea that I'd want Charles back, or that I'd plot to take him away from the mother of his child—"

His frigid expression silenced her. "That's enough, Arabella. I'll go now. You've made your point—but don't forget mine. Hurt my sister and you'll answer to me."

He strode to his horse, untied the reins and swung into the saddle without looking back.

"Go, then!" Arabella hurled the words after him. "See if I care! I never want to see you again, Stewart McIntyre!"

Her words were lost amid the clatter of departing hooves.

Stewart took the tall buckskin at a lope, thundering over the two-mile trail that linked his ranch to Charlie Middleton's. Arabella's palm print burned like a brand on his face. Damn fool, that's what he was. He should've been man enough to stay and smooth things over with her. At least her outrage showed she had no intention of getting in the way of Sally's marriage. Maybe he should have apologized for offending her. Instead he'd bolted. But wasn't that what he'd always

done at the first tingle of attraction to a woman—thrown up a barrier and run like a scared jackrabbit?

Pretty little dolls like Arabella Spencer had always made him feel awkward and ugly. But Arabella wasn't just pretty. She was smart, spirited and damned sexy in her ladylike way. Everything Charlie might see in her in her, Stewart saw, too. A man, even a married one, would have to be crazy not to want her in his bed.

Charlie hadn't been able to keep his eyes off her all evening—it was clear to Stewart that his brother-in-law had every intention of winning back Arabella's affection. And Arabella *had* loved Charlie—since they were children, if he remembered correctly. If Charlie used the days before the stage returned to woo her in earnest, would she be able to resist returning to his arms? *Sally* had certainly found those arms all too tempting.

The comparison brought him back to thoughts of his sister. Growing up, she'd been the baby of the family. As the first-born, Stewart had always looked after her. She'd been fifteen when their mother died. By then Stewart had acquired his ranch, and he'd taken her in. He'd hoped one day to see her married to a good man. But he'd been unable to protect her innocence from the likes of Charlie Middleton.

Had he been wrong to force the marriage? At the time he'd thought it the only thing to do. Middleton had been responsible for Sally's pregnancy. He had ample means to take care of her and the baby. And Sally had said she loved him.

Lord help him, had he ruined his sister's life?

He'd honestly believed they had a chance to be happy. Then Arabella had shown up, with her delicate beauty, fine clothes and lively manner, to set everything topsy-turvy.

Arabella had insisted she didn't want Charlie back. Stewart believed her. She'd been cruelly betrayed by the man and had every reason to hate him. But she could still be swayed

by sentiment, and long-held feelings. It didn't matter that she didn't *plan* to steal Charlie away. After all, Sally hadn't *planned* to fall into an engaged man's bed. Things didn't always go according to plan.

As he rode, the night breeze cooled his burning face. But lower down the heat smoldered, fueled by his imagination. Now he knew why Charlie had struggled so hard against the idea of wedding Sally. What man wouldn't fight against losing the chance to see those russet curls tumbling over his pillow, those mischievous absinthe eyes, challenging a man to take her and ravish her ripe little body until she yowled like a cat in heat…

Damn!

The truth of it was, he wanted her. How could any man with fire in his belly *not* want her? But he couldn't let desire cloud his judgment. He'd be better off without her around. They all would. When the next stage pulled out of Buffalo Bend, it would be his sworn duty to make sure Arabella Spencer was on it.

Any way you looked at her, the woman was trouble.

Arabella lay awake in the darkness, staring up at the ceiling. The memory of Stewart's words and the scorn in his voice stung like lye. It was bad enough that he viewed her as evil and conniving. But what galled the most was his notion that she'd be stupid enough to want Charles back.

She should have hit him even harder.

From the other side of the wall came the rhythmic creak and thump of shifting metal bedsprings. Merciful heaven, couldn't Charles and Sally have put her in a different room? Arabella knew little more about marriage than what she'd read in her aunt Pearl's doctor book. But she could guess what was going on.

Charles had said he still loved her. But that didn't stop

him from taking his pleasure with his wife. Surely he would
know that Arabella could hear them. But maybe he didn't
care. Maybe he was even trying to make her jealous.

She should get down on her knees and thank the good
Lord she hadn't married the jackass. Poor, sweet Sally had
done her a favor.

Hurt my sister and you'll answer to me.

Stewart's threat came back to her as she slipped out of
bed, pulled on her light woolen robe and pattered down the
stairs. For a moment, she envied Sally. As an orphan and
an only child, Arabella had always felt that she was largely
on her own. Yes, she'd had the doting aunts who'd raised
her, and plenty of friends, but she'd never had a protector,
a hero willing to go to battle to defend her from harm. Yet
her brother's protection wouldn't be enough to shield Sally
in this case. Unless something changed, Sally was liable to
get her heart broken.

She was a lovely young woman in her own way. But she'd
grown up on the frontier in a log cabin, and it showed. She
needed someone to take her in hand, someone to help her be
more of a lady.

Sally needed a friend.

Opening the front door, she tiptoed across the porch and
sank onto the top step. The air was cool and fresh. A sliver
of crescent moon hung above the distant hills.

Don't get involved, her sensible side argued. *Mind your
own business and leave as soon as you're able.*

Sound advice. Charles and Sally had created their unhappy situation. Her meddling could make it even worse,
especially if Stewart saw it as an attempt to break up his sister's marriage.

Blast Stewart!

He'd deserved that slap for judging her so harshly. Arabella
wasn't accustomed to being judged. After the death of her

parents in a tragic accident, when she was little more than a baby, two maiden aunts had taken her in and raised her with all the tender pampering a girl could want. She'd had friends, clothes, parties, dancing and riding lessons. Everyone had loved her—especially Charles Middleton. True, she might have been spoiled, but not in a bad way. What had happened to make her the villainess in this melodrama?

She felt so utterly alone. Coming to Montana was supposed to open a new chapter in her life—a chapter that would be filled with the family she'd always longed for. Instead she was left with nothing.

A touch against her arm triggered a start. Her muscles tensed for a sprint to the door. But it was only a dog, a shaggy mutt that looked to be part collie, working its damp nose beneath her hand. Arabella liked dogs. This one smelled of wet grass and probably had ticks, but at least it was friendly. She scratched its ears and was rewarded by the vigorous thump of its tail. Even a scruffy dog was better than no friend at all.

"Where did you come from, boy?" Her fingers found a worn leather collar, its strap molded to its rusty buckle. The dog appeared well fed. Most likely it belonged here.

Stretching out at her side, the dog laid its head on its muddy paws. Lost in thought, Arabella gazed up at the vast expanse of stars. Her aunt Phoebe had always said that everything happened for a reason. Could that be true? Arabella thought she'd come to Montana to marry Charles. But maybe she'd been brought here for an entirely different purpose.

It was a deep thought—too deep for tonight. She yawned, suddenly tired. Surely by now Charles and Sally would be asleep.

The dog had begun to snore. Easing to her feet, Arabella crept back into the silent house and closed the door behind her.

* * *

She woke at first light the next morning. A quick glance from between the drapes showed mauve ribbons of cloud above the distant hills. The crystalline warble of meadowlarks greeted the prairie dawn. It was going to be a beautiful day. But the prospect of dealing with Charles and his marriage was enough to curdle Arabella's mood like vinegar in milk. She felt like a prisoner. If only she could escape, even for a few hours…

The notion came in a flash. Charles had mentioned the sidesaddle in the barn. Where there was a saddle, there was bound to be a bridle and a spare horse. She would slip out of the house and go for a morning ride.

Her spirits rose as she turned up the bed, splashed her face and dressed in her smart new riding habit and boots. Secrecy was vital. If Charles knew where she was going, he'd insist on going with her. Since Sally's pregnancy made riding a risk, she would be alone with him. That was the last thing she wanted.

Twisting up her hair, she pinned it in place and topped it with a rakish straw hat. The hat was new, with a long, curling feather tucked into the brim. Arabella had bought it especially for riding on the ranch. With a final, satisfied glance in the mirror, she closed the door behind her, stole down the stairs and crossed the porch. The dog was still there. It raised its head, shook its tangled coat and followed her toward the barn.

The only other sign of life was a thin curl of smoke from the bunkhouse chimney. Charles had mentioned last night that most of his hands were out on the range rounding up calves for branding. Only two men remained here to take care of the chores. Neither of them was in sight to help her.

The saddle and bridle were easy to find, and the dappled gelding in the second stall seemed docile enough to ride. Straining with effort, Arabella hefted the new saddle onto its

back and tightened the cinch. Minutes later she was stealing out the back door of the barn.

The horse seemed nervous, snorting and dancing as if to rid itself of an unaccustomed weight. Maybe the animal wasn't used to a sidesaddle. But never mind, it would settle down before long. Arabella urged the gelding to a trot, putting distance between herself and the ranch. The dog loped along behind, ignoring her attempts to send it home.

At the top of a rise, she reined in to get her bearings. By now the sun was up. Rolling plains, carpeted with wildflowers and glistening with morning dew, spread around her in all directions. To the far west, snowy peaks jutted above the horizon. The vastness boggled Arabella's imagination. She had never seen so much land or so much sky. The beauty of it almost brought her to tears.

Looking back the way she'd come she could still see the ranch, but from this distance the buildings looked like toys. She willed herself to memorize the lay of the land and note the position of the sun. It wouldn't do to get lost in this wild country where so many places looked the same. Maybe it was a good thing the dog had come with her. At least the shaggy mutt seemed to know its way around.

Nudging the horse to a trot again, she headed west, with her face toward the mountains. Damp earth, fresh grass and wildflowers perfumed the air. The sun climbed the sky as she rode. A herd of pronghorn antelope raced over a hill and out of sight. High overhead, a golden eagle circled on outstretched wings. What glorious country this was. It was almost a shame she'd soon be going back to Boston.

Her aunts and her friends would wonder what had happened. Arabella detested lies and liars, but the truth was so humiliating. Maybe she could just say that Charles had changed and was no longer the man she'd fancied herself in love with. That was close enough to the truth, wasn't it?

Glancing back, she could no longer see the ranch. Never mind, she was sure she could find it again. All she had to do was turn around and ride with her back to the distant peaks.

But which way were the mountains? She turned the horse one way, then another. Rolling hills blocked her view in every direction. And the sun was at the peak of the sky.

Could she be lost? Certainly not, Arabella told herself. She was just…disoriented. She would find her way again in no time. All she needed to do was head for higher ground.

Mounting a ridge, she gasped in wonder at the sight below. Buffalo—hundreds, perhaps thousands of them—were pouring out of a hollow and spreading onto the plain. She'd glimpsed the huge animals from the train and from the stage, but never so close or so many. There were great lumbering bulls, and cows trailed by gangly brown calves. The earth rumbled beneath their pounding hooves.

Mesmerized, Arabella urged the horse closer. Almost under the gelding's belly, a flock of prairie chickens whirred out of the grass. The nervous horse screamed, reared and bucked. Arabella flew off the sidesaddle, her boot catching in the single stirrup. Hot pain shot up her leg as her foot pulled loose. She lay on the ground, writhing as the horse bolted over the hill and vanished from sight.

The dog circled her, uttering agitated little barks, almost as if it wanted to play. Arabella's hat lay nearby, where it had fallen. Seizing the hat in its jaws, the big mutt bounded off through the grass.

"Come back here!" Arabella shouted. But her cry was lost in the great silence of the prairie.

Stewart peered through his binoculars, scanning the hills for any sign of stray calves. The smaller ones, even with their mothers standing guard, were easy prey for wolves and coyotes. It was vital that he bring them in to the safety of the

pasture. This afternoon he saw none. But as he lowered the glass, he noticed a low, brown shape moving through the distant grass. A solitary wolf? He raised the binoculars and sharpened the focus.

Blasted dog. He'd always been a roamer, but what was he doing clear out here? Swinging out of the saddle he gave a sharp whistle. Tail flying, the dog bounded toward him. Stewart dropped to one knee as sixty pounds of burr-tangled canine hurled itself joyfully at his chest. Although Slocum was Stewart's dog, he was equally attached to Sally and made regular visits to her new home. But he didn't usually venture this far out alone.

"You old rascal, what're you— What the hell is this? Did you bring me a present?" Stewart worked the crumpled hat free of the dog's dripping jaws. It was like no hat or bonnet he'd ever seen, woven of fine dark straw that was almost as soft as linen. The ridiculous feather sewn into the grosgrain band had suffered from Slocum's drooling grip, but it was clearly meant to be something special.

Stewart swore out loud. Only one person he knew within fifty miles would wear a hat as silly as this one. Still muttering he swung back into the saddle.

"Come on, boy. Show me where you found this."

Arabella dragged herself forward through the long, prickly grass. She'd tried walking in the direction the horse had gone, but between her missing boot and her throbbing ankle, she could barely take a step. Given the choice between lying where she'd fallen and crawling as far as she could make it, she'd chosen the latter.

The gray gelding was bound to find its way home. When it arrived with her boot hanging from the stirrup, someone would know she was in trouble. Charles would have riders out combing the prairie for her.

Surely they'd find her and everything would turn out all right. But what if something went wrong? What if it was all up to her? She couldn't just wait to be saved. She had to keep moving.

The hot rays of the afternoon sun beat down on her. To protect her fragile skin, she'd slipped off her light jacket and draped it over her head and neck. It kept her from burning, but the underside was like an oven. Sweat had glued her thin cotton blouse to her skin. Her palms were scraped raw from the sharp grass and prickly weeds. The dry membranes of her throat felt as if they were cracking and curling like old paint.

She yelped as her hand came down on something sharp. Her stomach clenched in fear; but it was only a thorn. Dizzy with relief, she used her teeth to pull it out of her skin. She'd heard there were rattlesnakes on the prairie, as well as wolves and coyotes. And Stewart had mentioned something about Indians. Maybe he'd only said it to scare her. That would be like Stewart. But the dangers out here were real and deadly. Not least among them was the chance that she could die of thirst and exposure before anyone found her.

Arabella could feel her strength ebbing. Fighting the urge to rest, she inched forward, dragging her body along the ground. She'd lost track of time, but the angle of the sun told her it was getting late in the day. The thought of spending the night out here, alone in the dark, filled her with terror. And what if it stormed? She'd heard tales of terrible thunderstorms on the prairie. Nothing scared her more.

Now she could hear something coming toward her, approaching light and swift through the long grass. Was it a wolf? An Indian? Too weak to run or fight, she hunkered low and braced herself for the attack.

It came in the form of muddy feet and a slobbering tongue as the dog bowled her over. Struggling to right herself, Ara-

bella heard the snort of a horse and a grating voice she knew all too well.

"What the devil are you doing out here?"

She would never have believed she could be so glad to see Stewart McIntyre.

He was off his horse now, crouching beside her. One strong hand lifted her, propping her back against his knee. The other hand tipped an open canteen to her mouth. Arabella drank greedily, gulping water like a winded horse.

"Easy…easy there…" He tilted the canteen away. "You'll make yourself sick. What happened?"

Her voice emerged as a croak. "Horse spooked and threw me. My boot caught in the stirrup—twisted my ankle when it tore loose. Hurts too much to walk."

"You were out riding alone?"

"Should I have taken Charles up on his offer to come with me?"

His look darkened as her barb hit home. "Never mind. Sit back and give me your foot. I'll have a look at that ankle."

Kneeling, he peeled off the dirty, threadbare remnant of her stocking which had dragged along the ground as she crawled. Cradling her foot in one hand, he pulled loose the stickers embedded in her tender flesh. For such a rough-spoken brute of a man, he had an amazingly gentle touch. Arabella closed her eyes as his big, callused fingers worked their way up her foot toward her ankle. Her breath hissed inward as he pressed the swollen spot.

"There?" He probed cautiously. Arabella clenched her teeth to keep from crying out. Stewart probably thought of her as a spoiled baby. She wanted to prove him wrong.

"It doesn't feel broken," he said, "but I'd guess you've got a nasty sprain." His free hand stripped the bandanna from around his neck. "We'll wrap it as best we can. When we get back to my house, we can cold pack it."

"*Your* house?"

"We need to get you out of the sun, and it's the closest place. I'll send a man to Charlie's to tell them you're safe." Stewart's hands wrapped the folded bandanna under the arch of her foot and twice around the ankle. The dog sat close by, watching.

"Is that your dog?" Arabella winced as he tightened the wrapping.

"I feed him. But Slocum's pretty much his own animal. You're lucky he decided to be yours today." Stewart tied the ends in a snug knot, then stood and pulled her to her feet. "It's too far to go for the wagon. You'll have to ride behind me."

As she balanced on her solid right foot, he lifted off his weathered felt hat and dropped it onto her head. "That should do a better job of shading you than that silly gewgaw the dog brought me."

She glowered from under the outsized rim. "I'll have you know that hat's the latest fashion in Boston. I paid a pretty penny for it."

"Now, why doesn't that surprise me?" With a mutter, he climbed into the saddle. One hand seized her arm and swung her up behind him, as if she weighed no more than a rag doll.

"Hold on tight." Tucking her jacket into a saddlebag, he kneed the buckskin to a brisk trot. For the first instant, the momentum threw Arabella backward. Recovering, she flung her arms around his ribs and hung on tight. Her straddled legs nested behind his.

A breeze had sprung out of the west, rippling across the long grass. How like the sea the prairie was, Arabella thought. Beautiful, dangerous, always changing yet always the same, not unlike the man who'd just rescued her.

Stewart's body was as solid as the trunk of an oak. He rode with ease, his big hands skilled and sure. His body smelled of prairie grass and clean, masculine sweat. Only the wide

brim of the hat saved Arabella from the impulse to press her face against his back and inhale him into her senses. He was, in his own way, a compelling man, as powerfully male as the huge buffalo bulls she'd seen rumbling out of the hollow.

She'd always told herself she preferred gentle, refined men, like Charles, but Stewart's masculine closeness was having a strange effect on her. Where her pelvis rested against his taut rump, a delicious heat was spreading outward into her thighs. Enhanced by the motion of the horse, the tingling sensation spiraled upward into the core of her body. She stifled a moan. Common sense told her this was wicked, and that she should pull away. But without falling off the horse, she had no place to go. Besides, the sensation was… Heaven help her, she didn't want it to stop. Was this how girls like Sally got into trouble?

"How's your ankle?" Stewart slowed the horse to a walk, easing the sweet torment on her body. There was a roughness to his voice. Had he been aware of her response to him? Was that why he'd slowed down?

"It's no worse." Arabella had almost forgotten about her injury. As she remembered, her ankle began to throb once more. "How far do we have to go?"

"Not much farther. My ranch is over that next hill." He glanced at the sky, where clouds were scudding in from the west. "Good thing. Looks like it could rain in a bit. Have another drink." He passed her the canteen. Arabella took her time, savoring the sweet, clear water until it was gone.

"I never asked you. What were you doing out on the prairie before you found me?"

"Looking for strays."

"Did you find any?"

He chuckled, a surprising sound. "Just one."

"I saw buffalo. A big herd of them."

"Hope you didn't get too close. Those big bulls would kill

you given the chance. And where you find buffalo, there are liable to be Indians tracking them."

Arabella shuddered. "Have you had much trouble with the Indians?"

He shook his head. "I stay out of their way, and they don't bother me. But it wouldn't take much to stir them up. A pretty red-haired woman, out there by herself…" He let the implication hang. "You were lucky this time, Arabella. You're not to go riding alone again, understand?"

She tried to ignore the burst of pleasure she felt at his protective tone. "For a man who has no claim on me, you're being downright bossy, Stewart McIntyre. Are you offering to go with me next time?"

"If that's what it takes—and if I don't ship you out on the stage before then."

"Ship me out? You sound as if that's *your* decision."

"Believe me, nobody wants you gone more than I do."

Though pleasantly spoken, the words stung. It shouldn't matter that this gruff giant of a man didn't want her around. But somehow it did.

They had come over the crest of the hill. Stewart's ranch lay on the plain below. Arabella wasn't sure what she'd expected, maybe a log cabin with a broken-down wagon in the yard and a deer hide hanging over the door. But the corral, barn and sheds looked immaculately built and tended. A small creek, bordered by willow and cottonwoods, ran through the property, shading a house that appeared to rise out of the land itself.

To please her, perhaps, Charles had remodeled his house to look like an Eastern home—the pillared porch, the white exterior with dark green shutters, the picket fence and paved walkway. Stewart's rambling home, built low to the land was all logs and natural stone, with an overhanging shingled roof

shading the wide front porch. It looked as if it belonged here, like a natural part of the vast Montana prairie.

"Did you build the house?" she asked Stewart.

"Every stick and stone of it. I started when I came here, after the war. This was a wild place then, before the railroad. In some ways, it still is."

They started down the hill. The dog raced ahead of them, tail high through the grass. A hawk, circling overhead, flapped its wings and soared skyward. Beyond the outbuildings, cows and calves grazed in a fenced pasture. There was something welcoming about this spot, an air of peace that seemed to reach out to Arabella and embrace her. But how could that be, when its owner wanted nothing more than to see her gone?

She didn't understand it at all.

Stewart dismounted at the corral where Miguel, the shy teenage boy who helped out around the place, was waiting to take the reins. After instructing the lad to deliver the news of Arabella's rescue to Charlie's Ranch, he reached up to lift her down from the horse.

Even after her long crawl through the weedy grass, she looked beautiful. Her russet curls tumbled over her shoulders, awakening an urge to curl the silken strands around his fingers. The way her damp blouse clung to every curve of her perfect little body was enough to make his mouth go dry. From under the brim of his hat, her eyes blazed green fire.

He'd been acutely aware of her on the ride. The pressure of her bouncing crotch against his rump had triggered a heat surge so intense that he'd slowed the horse rather than lose his dignity altogether. And she'd felt something, too. He'd sensed it in the tightening of her arms around his ribs and the rapid jerk of her breath. She'd been all but panting. His imagination had gone crazy.

Lord help him, if he had a brain in his head, he'd hitch up the wagon and have Miguel drive the woman back to Charlie's place right now. But he could imagine the sympathy an injured Arabella might stir up there. Brotherly duty demanded that he keep the little bundle of temptation here with him.

Still sitting astride the horse, she lifted his hat off her curls and dropped it onto his head. Her hands braced against his shoulders as he swung her off the horse and caught her. She fit perfectly, her shoulders nested against his chest and her legs dangling over one arm. Since she couldn't walk, it seemed only sensible to carry her to the house.

When Stewart had built his house it had been with a future family in mind. He'd even imagined carrying a bride up this very path. But the years had passed, and it hadn't happened. Most of the women who came to this untamed country were either wives or whores, and the few eligible females were swiftly snatched up by more charming suitors. With time Stewart had come to accept his bachelorhood as a permanent state. After all, what could he offer a woman, with his scarred face and body and his solitary nature?

Sally's arrival had saved him from becoming a recluse. His vulnerable young sister had brought out his tender instincts and given him someone to nurture and protect. He'd always known she'd grow up and marry one day. But he hadn't anticipated the loneliness her absence would leave in his life.

Thunder, still faint, rumbled behind them as he carried Arabella toward the porch. Her head settled against his chest. His clasp tightened around her as he mounted the steps.

Arabella Spencer fit into his arms as if she belonged there. But she was an Eastern woman. She'd want an elegant Eastern husband—someone like Charlie who was soft, polished and courteous. She'd never choose a rough-spoken ex-soldier

like him. Even if she weren't a threat to Sally's marriage, he'd be a fool to think of asking her to stay.

No matter how much he might want her to.

Chapter Four

Stewart's ranch house was even more striking inside than outside. Arabella had grown up with flowered wallpaper, draped windows, crocheted doilies and ceramic whatnots on every shelf and table. It was the way people lived, especially if they had a little wealth to show off. By comparison, the interior of Stewart's home was as stark as the prairie and, in its way, almost as beautiful.

Massive logs, oiled to a golden gleam, supported the walls and the open-beamed ceiling. The front, broken by wide glass windows, was formed of river stones, as was the cavernous fireplace at the room's far end. Gingham pillows, braided rugs and a bright, crocheted afghan—touches most likely added by Sally—lent color and warmth.

"I've never seen anything like this!" Arabella gazed around the room as Stewart lowered her to the buffalo robe that covered the couch in front of the fireplace.

He tossed his hat onto a nearby chair. "I was studying architecture when the war broke out. I never went back to school, but I always wanted to build something using my own ideas. This is it."

"But it's so different—people would love it! You could make a lot of money building homes like this!"

He shook his head. "The business would take away the pleasure. As for the money, ranching gives me enough for my needs. Now, let's have a look at your ankle."

Stewart pulled up a low footstool and sat down. He was so tall that his knees jutted like a grasshopper's. Arabella bit back a smile as he cradled her foot between his hands and began loosening the knotted bandanna. Such gentle hands. How would it feel, she wondered, to be loved by this big, gruff, surprisingly tender man?

But what was she thinking? Stewart viewed her as the enemy. The only thing he had in mind was to send her packing back to Boston.

She winced as he pulled the bandanna away. "The swelling's worse," he said. "Hold on, I'll get some wrappings and some cold water."

He left the room. Arabella heard him rummaging in what she presumed to be the kitchen. A moment later she heard the opening and closing of the back door. She waited, her ankle throbbing as her eyes explored the room.

Ceiling-high shelves crowded with books framed both sides of the fireplace. From where she sat, she could make out a few of the titles. There were books on history, architecture, travel and astronomy, novels by Charles Dickens and Jane Austen, Shakespeare's plays, Greek myths and volumes of poetry. Arabella had always loved to read. If Stewart was a reader, his sister probably was, too. Maybe she'd underestimated Charles's sweet, pigtailed bride.

Lightning flashed through the front window. Thunder crashed across the sky as the first raindrops spattered against the roof. Arabella shivered. She had yet to master her fear of thunderstorms. Her parents had been killed when lightning struck a tree, spooking the horse that pulled their buggy. The

animal had plunged off a steep road, toppling the rig into the creek bed below. Only Arabella, a toddler then, had survived. She had no memory of the accident, but she'd been told about it. As long as someone was with her, she didn't mind a storm. But when she was alone, it was as if the terror had been etched into the marrow of her bones.

She was struggling with her nerves when Stewart returned with a bucket and a loose bundle of muslin wrappings. His wind-tousled hair was damp with rain. At the sight of him, her fear took wing.

"Blowing up a big one out there," he said.

Arabella remembered the youth he'd sent to Charles's place. "Will the boy be all right?"

"He should be. The ranch isn't far, and he can stay there till the storm's done. Sally will give him a good meal and a bed if need be." He glanced toward Arabella. "If the rain keeps up, there's a chance you could be stuck here overnight."

Her pulse slammed.

"There's a bed in Sally's old room," he added, as if reading her thoughts. "And if you don't mind cowboy grub, you'll find me a fair to middling cook. Now let's see about cleaning you up and packing that ankle."

With the sun gone, the room had grown chilly. Stewart took a moment to touch a match to the logs and tinder already laid in the fireplace. As the crackling warmth spread around her, Arabella settled back into the pillows. Beyond the front windows, rain streamed off the roof enfolding the porch in a shimmering gray curtain.

Along with the wrappings, Stewart had brought a washcloth. Dipping it in the bucket, he leaned toward her and began sponging her dust-caked face. His touch was light, the water deliciously cold. Arabella might have closed her eyes, but then she'd have missed the chance to study his arresting face. His eyes, set deep beneath the dark ridges of his brows, were

the color of the rain, their pupils deep and penetrating. His features, sharp but rugged with high cheekbones, reminded her of a painting she'd seen in a museum—George Catlin's majestic portrait of a Mandan chief. Although he didn't really look like an Indian, Stewart had the same presence, the same quiet dignity.

Her eyes were drawn to the scar that slashed a lightning streak from his temple to the corner of his mouth. She knew he'd been in the war. Had it been a saber that marked him? A bayonet? She quelled the urge to reach up and trace the pale line with a fingertip. Maybe one day he would open up and tell her about it. But what was she thinking? After she left Montana she would never see Stewart McIntyre again.

"Hands." He dipped the washcloth again and wiped her scratched, bloodied palms. "I've got some pine tar salve in the kitchen," he said. "It works fine for horses—no reason it shouldn't work for you. But first, the ankle."

Settling back on the footstool he steadied her foot between his long legs. One hand dipped a length of wrapping in the bucket and laid it, still dripping, on her skin.

"Creek water. The cold will ease the swelling," he muttered without looking up. "You're damned lucky you didn't break a bone or snap a tendon. Maybe next time you'll be more careful."

"Are you saying there might be a next time?"

His glance was a warning. She chose to ignore it.

"I know what you think of me, Stewart. In your eyes I'm a Jezebel, out to wreck your sister's marriage. But you don't know me at all."

He continued wrapping her ankle. The cold was beginning to feel good now; and the brush of his fingers against her skin sent tingles of pleasure up her leg.

"Until I came here, I'd never known anything but love and

kindness," she said. "If that makes me a spoiled brat, so be it. But it doesn't make me evil."

"Did I ever say you were evil?" He didn't look up but she could feel the tension in his hands.

"I grew up next door to Charles Middleton. He asked me to marry him when he was twelve and I was ten. There was never a thought that I might not be his wife one day. You can't imagine how I felt when I arrived here and learned how he'd betrayed me. I'll not easily forgive or forget what he's done."

Stewart tied the ends of the wrapping into a snug knot. "But he still loves you. I saw that last night. And for all I know, you still love him."

Arabella's temper surged. Wasn't the man listening to her? If words wouldn't get through to him, maybe she should try something else. Gripped by a sudden impulse, she seized the sides of his head, yanked him toward her and burned a hot, angry kiss onto his mouth.

For an instant he went rigid. Then his arms caught her close. His lips crushed hers, powerful and demanding. She'd been kissed by Charles, of course, and by a few silly boys at parties, but never like this. She'd always been so proper, so restrained—but something about Stewart made her lose control. She moaned as his mouth coaxed hers to open. The thrust of his tongue trailed flame along her sensitive nerves. Dizzy with a whirl of new sensations, she arched against him, offering her throat, her breasts, wanting to be kissed, to be stroked and touched by that compelling mouth and those big, gentle hands.

"Damn it, Arabella," he muttered. "I've wanted you from the first time I saw you!"

A response stirred in her throat. "I need…" The rest of her words dissolved in a moan as his hand cupped her breast through the damp linen blouse. Her nipple shrank to an aching nub under the pressure of his palm. Her free hand fum-

bled for the buttons. "Yes," she whispered as his thumb slid beneath her lace-edged camisole to brush and tease her bare nipple. "Oh, yes…"

Thunder rattled the windowpanes as the storm broke in full fury. Arabella's heart drummed in counterpoint with the pounding rain as he bent and kissed her mouth again. Her fevered body responded, hands pulling his head lower to her barely covered breasts. The heat shimmering through her veins was beyond anything she could have imagined. All she could think of was how badly she wanted more.

To aid the wrapping of her ankle, she'd bared her left leg to the knee. Now his palm found her naked calf, sliding upward to the lacy hem of her drawers. Arabella whimpered, feeling the yearning ache where she wanted him to touch her, and knowing that nothing less would be enough. When he seemed to hesitate, she found his hand and slid it beneath the loose fabric to rest on her thigh.

A groan escaped his throat. "Arabella, we mustn't…" he murmured.

Arabella's kiss stopped the words she was beyond hearing. Her hips arched against his hand. As her right leg moved aside, her foot struck something solid. With a clatter the bucket spilled onto the floor.

"Oh!" She felt the shock of the ice-cold splash. Pulling away, Stewart scrambled to right the bucket and sponge up the water with the leftover wrappings. When he stood, she saw that a wall had slid into place behind his eyes.

"Arabella, I…" She could see him trying to frame an apology, and knew she couldn't bear to hear it.

"Please don't," she interrupted. "We…we both got carried away, that's all," she added, desperate to save face.

He cleared his throat. "I need to see to the stock," he said. "It might take some time. Will you be all right to hobble around in here?"

"I suppose so." Shaken by his sudden shift, Arabella mouthed the words.

"The salve's on the kitchen counter, and there's stew warming on the stove. When you're ready to sleep, you'll find Sally's room down the hall. There's a necessity under the bed."

"Stewart, I—"

"Not now." Reaching out, he traced a fingertip along her cheek. "We can talk tomorrow, after we've both had time to come to our senses."

Without giving her a chance to respond, he turned and strode out through the kitchen. The back door slammed in the wind. Arabella reached for the afghan and pulled it around her shaking shoulders. Her cheek felt cold where his finger had brushed it. Thunder boomed across the sky like mocking laughter.

Merciful heaven, what had she done?

By the time Stewart reached the barn, where he kept a spare slicker, he was soaked to the skin. Not that it mattered. After what had happened in the house, he'd needed a good, cold dousing. Lord help him, he'd believed he was under control. Then Arabella had kissed him and blown that notion all to hell.

What had she wanted? If she'd wanted to prove she could make him respond, she'd succeeded. For a few minutes there, his need for her had overwhelmed everything else. And oh, how she had responded… In that moment, her desire for him had been as real and as powerful as his craving for her. But it had been just a moment of passion, and nothing more. He couldn't let himself believe she might truly care for a man like him. He was too awkward, too homely, too old at thirty and, although well-off, most of his money was in the land. He was nowhere near as eligible and appealing as Charlie Middleton.

He needed to get himself under control. If he went back

in the house right now, he'd be tempted to pick right back up where he left off—and he had a sinking suspicion that she'd let him. If he allowed their mutual passion to play out, if he fully explored the heat and desire between the two of them, then he didn't think he'd be able to let her go. Not back to Boston, not back to Charlie and Sally's house—not out of his arms or his heart ever again.

But that wasn't going to happen. With Miguel gone, he could find enough chores to occupy him for a couple of hours. He wouldn't go back into the house until she was in bed, safely tucked out of his sight.

Donning the slicker over his wet clothes, he saddled a horse and rode out to the pasture to check on the calves. Range cows were used to stormy weather, but the smaller, weaker calves could get chilled. Circling the pasture, he rounded up the cows with younger calves and herded them toward the open shed at the near end. Some hay tossed down from a storage rack would give the mothers an added incentive to stay put.

The horse he'd ridden would need a rubdown after the short gallop. The pigs and chickens would need attention as well, to make sure their pens weren't flooding in the storm. There was a weasel-size hole in the coop that couldn't wait till tomorrow. The milk cows were running low on hay; and that was only the beginning.

By the time Stewart finished the chores, night had fallen. Rain sheeted off the roof of the barn as he bolted the doors and turned back toward the house.

The windows were dark, but a lantern glowed on its hook next to the back door. Had Arabella lit the wick and hung it there? Since he hadn't done it himself, there could be no other explanation.

Shedding his slicker and muddy boots on the back porch, he stepped into the kitchen and closed the door behind him. He was chilled beneath his wet clothes. It was time he peeled

them off and hauled his tired body into bed. But there was one thing he needed to do first.

Stealing down the hall, he paused before the room that had been his sister's. The door stood ajar. He eased it open.

Arabella lay asleep in the narrow bed, her curls spilling over the pillow. In the darkness, Stewart could just make out her pale face. With her eyes closed and her sweet mouth at rest, she looked as innocent as a child.

Gazing down at her, Stewart felt something tighten around his heart. From the start, he'd done his best to convince himself he didn't like her. But in the measure of things, Arabella was bright and spunky, with a ready wit and a courageous heart. He remembered her reckless plunge into the river to save her wedding gown. He pictured those small hands, scratched and bloodied from crawling across the prairie. And the way she'd turned to living flame in his arms…

Tearing his gaze away, he backed out of the room and left the door as he'd found it. He could drive himself crazy thinking about Arabella. But that didn't mean any good would come of it. She'd be leaving soon, and that would be best for them all.

Weary as sin, he dragged himself back to his own room, stripped off his wet clothes and crawled into bed.

Only after he'd left did Arabella dare to open her eyes. She'd lain perfectly still, heart pounding, while Stewart stood in the doorway, gazing at her. What did it mean when he'd lingered a few moments in the darkness? Was he having second thoughts about what had happened between them and how he'd ended it?

She'd gone to bed hurt and angry. But as she felt his presence in the room, she'd found herself yearning to have him bend over and touch her. She'd imagined herself reaching up,

pulling him into her arms. At least she might have spoken to him. Now it was too late.

She was in dire need of sleep. The day's misadventure had worn her out; but thoughts of Stewart had kept her on edge. Now that he was safe indoors maybe she could finally relax.

Fluffing the pillow, she turned over and closed her eyes. Lulled by the steady tattoo of the rain she began to drift…

A deafening thunderclap shook the house. Arabella opened her eyes with a gasp. What time was it? Was she still dreaming?

The dream had haunted her since childhood, returning again and again—no images or words, just the sensation of crashing through space, tumbling over and over to the boom of thunder and the echo of screams. Aunt Phoebe, who'd done some reading on the subject, said the dream could be the buried memory of the accident that had killed her parents. Arabella would never know for sure. She only knew that, whenever it came, the dream left her terrified beyond words.

Lightning flashed hot blue through the bedroom window. Thunder roared across the sky, so loud it seemed to fill the universe. Suddenly Arabella was on her feet, bolting out of the room and stumbling down the hall in her shift—toward the one source of comfort and safety.

Stewart was a light sleeper by nature. He'd been snoring soundly, but the presence of someone in the room quickly roused him to full alertness. He raised his head and opened his eyes.

Arabella stood in the doorway, ghostly pale in her white shift. Her hair fell in tangles around her face. Her eyes were as wild as a spooked mare's.

"What is it?" he managed to ask.

Her lips parted, but no voice emerged. He could tell that

she was shaking. Outside, the storm had redoubled its fury. Wind and rain lashed the house.

"What is it, Arabella?" he asked again.

Lightning flashed through the window. The thunderclap was louder than the cannon fire he remembered from the war. Arabella cowered in terror, wrapping herself in her arms. Her strength had always ignited a passionate response in Stewart, but somehow her vulnerability moved him even more deeply.

Stewart knew what he needed to do. He also reminded himself that he was naked between the sheets, a sure recipe for disaster. But then a solution dawned. Turning back the quilt, he exposed the top side of the sheet that covered him.

"Come here before you catch your death, girl," he murmured, brushing the surface he'd smoothed for her. She came with a little whimper, huddling into the bed as he covered her with the quilt. Stewart wrapped her in his arms. She was soft and warm and smelled faintly of lavender soap.

They lay spooned, chastely separated by a thin layer of cotton flannel. Stewart's body had responded at first touch, springing to full, quivering arousal. He did his best to keep his hips pulled back from her rump, so she wouldn't feel it and be alarmed.

The effort was pure torture. Arabella was the most desirable woman he'd ever known. But, so help him, the last thing Stewart wanted was to ruin her the way Charlie Middleton had ruined his sister.

Stewart's bed felt warm and safe but Arabella was still trembling.

"What's the matter?" he asked her again.

"Just a bad dream. The thunder makes it worse. I know it's silly but I can't seem to help it."

"Nothing's silly if it makes you afraid. Tell me about it."

Arabella's story began haltingly, then spilled out of her

in a rush—how her parents had died in a storm, and how, despite no conscious memory of it, the tragedy still haunted her dreams.

"Sometimes I dream about the war." His lips skimmed her hair. "The thunder makes it worse—it reminds me of artillery fire. I tell myself that's silly, too. It was over a long time ago. But there's a part of my brain that doesn't quite believe that. Maybe it's the same with you."

She turned to face him in the bed. "Hold me tight, Stewart," she whispered. "Maybe the thunder will go away for both of us."

A groan quivered in his throat as his arms tightened around her. His skin was cool and smelled of rain. She realized for the first time that he was naked beneath the sheet. Somehow that seemed all right. More than all right. A freshet of excitement pulsed through her body.

He muttered something that sounded like "Maybe you should go back to bed." Arabella couldn't make out the words, but that didn't matter because in the next breath they were kissing, and she was lost in the taste of his lips, the roughness of his stubbled beard, the sheer masculine power of the man. Her arms slid around his neck, fingers raking his thick hair.

Now that they were face-to-face she could feel the rock-hard jut of his sex against her belly. The thought that *she* was causing that reaction sent a jolt of heat to the aching core of her body. Moisture slicked her thighs. The sensations that swirled through her were as old as nature, yet frighteningly new. A lady, she reminded herself, would leap out of bed or fight tooth and nail for her virtue. But she was lost in a storm of delicious yearnings. All she could think of was flinging aside every rule of propriety and common sense she'd ever known to give herself to this man.

"Stewart…" She tugged at the sheet. "Please, I need you…"

He exhaled raggedly. Shifting in the bed, he kissed her again, gently this time. "Lie still, Arabella," he whispered.

His hand found its way beneath her thin cotton shift to cradle her breast. She moaned as he caressed her, his skillful touch triggering ripples of pleasure. "More," she murmured as his hand paused to rest on the flat of her belly, then moved downward to cup the wet nest of curls that framed her secret place. Her hips strained upward. She whimpered with need.

His fingertips opened her gently, parting her labia like rose petals, taking time to stroke each one. She gasped as he found the sensitive bud in the center. Brushing a kiss across her mouth, he moved his hand and began a delicate, feather-like caressing.

"Oh…" Arabella murmured. "Oh…!" The feeling was so exquisite she almost wept. Her legs parted. Her hips thrust upward, seeking more pleasure. He could have taken her easily, but that, she realized, wasn't his intent. He was holding himself back, doing this for her.

The pulsing deepened. She could feel the hot, liquid contractions in her womb, swelling like drumbeats. Almost sobbing now, she gasped his name. Something clenched like a fist inside her. With a little cry she tumbled over the edge.

Gently his hand withdrew. He leaned over her where she sprawled on the sheet, utterly drained. A ghost of a smile flickered at the corner of his mouth.

Her hand brushed the scar on his cheek. "I didn't know anything could be like this…" she whispered.

He skimmed a kiss across her mouth. "Go to sleep, Arabella. I don't think the thunder will wake you now."

She sighed and closed her eyes, already drifting. Outside, the storm's fury was moving east, leaving a soft rain in its wake.

Dawn came early on the Montana prairie. But even before the first dim rays silvered the clouds, Stewart was awake. He'd

lain sleepless most of the night, feeling Arabella's warmth beside him and listening to the sweet murmur of her breath. He could be happy waking up like this every morning of his life. But he knew better than to think it was going to happen.

Rising on one elbow, he watched the soft light steal across her sleeping face. He loved Arabella. That was the plain, simple truth of it. He'd loved her since that wild night when he'd picked her up in the rain and delivered her soaked and shivering to Charlie Middleton's gate. He loved her beauty, her stubbornness, her courage. And he loved the vulnerability she'd shown in his arms last night. Her complete trust had touched him more than anything he'd ever known.

But even last night couldn't change the fact that she didn't belong here. Arabella Spencer was a city woman. She might think she could be happy on the prairie, but she'd soon come to miss Boston—the parties and dances, the fashionable shops, the company of friends, all the things Montana couldn't offer her.

Then there was the threat to his sister's marriage. For Sally, the presence of her husband's ex-fiancée would be an open invitation to heartbreak. He knew now that Arabella would never take Charlie back, but as long as Charlie continued to long for her, he could never make Sally truly happy. For that reason alone, Arabella couldn't be allowed to stay.

So he couldn't allow himself to want her—especially not as his wife.

Arabella stirred and stretched in the morning sunlight. Even with her eyes closed, she could tell it was going to be a beautiful day—especially if she could spend it with Stewart.

There was no reason she had to leave just yet. After she dressed and freshened up, she could offer to make him breakfast. Then, if he had time, she could ask him to show her

around his ranch. But right now, all she wanted to do was move close and snuggle against his side.

Shifting in the bed she reached out to embrace him. Her hand groped in confusion, finding nothing where he'd been but the cool, empty sheet. Stewart was gone.

Startled wide-awake, she sat up. Only then did she see the folded sheet of paper tucked under his pillow. Her hands shook as she unfolded it and read the note, written in an architect's precise script.

Dear Arabella,
By the time you read this I'll be on my way to help the men with the spring roundup and branding. There's coffee on the stove and a tray of fresh biscuits in the warmer. I've left instructions for Miguel to hitch up the buggy and drive you back to the Middleton Ranch. If I don't see you before you leave for Boston, have a safe and pleasant journey. I hope you'll think of me now and again, as I will surely think of you.
Stewart

Arabella's throat jerked. She reread the note, battling the urge to crumple it and stomp it into the floor. Temper tantrums were for spoiled babies, and she was a grown woman. It was time she started behaving like one.

Her hand wiped away a furious tear. After spending the night in his bed, this was the last thing she'd expected. She'd thought Stewart liked her, maybe even loved her. She'd drifted off to sleep with happy dreams dancing in her head—living here on the ranch with him, sharing his everyday life, waiting on the porch to welcome him at the end of each day…

What a silly, romantic little fool she was!

She'd given him a piece of her heart, and the wretched man had taken it and run off like a sneaking coyote.

Arabella wasn't accustomed to being cast aside by men. And now it had happened twice in the same week. Pride dictated that she toss her curls, pack her trunk and go back to Boston, where a bevy of rich, handsome, eligible men would be vying to court her. She could pick from the best.

But she would never find another man like Stewart McIntyre.

Chapter Five

"You have such beautiful hair, Sally." Arabella plied the brush, letting the silky gold strands slide through the bristles. "Just wait till I'm finished with you. You're going to look like a princess."

Sally's laugh was musical. "I'm hardly a princess, Arabella. Pigtails will do me fine for the ranch."

"But you're the wife of a gentleman rancher now. There'll be times when you want to look like a lady."

Again, Sally laughed. "All right, have your fun. But remember our bargain. Today you get to do my hair. Tomorrow I get to take you fishing."

"I'll probably drown." Arabella curled a sun-kissed lock around her finger. In the three days since her return to the Middleton Ranch, she'd discovered how easy it was to like Stewart's sister. She was a softer, gentler version of her brother. Sally was bright, warm, practical and very much her own person. Despite the strained circumstances, she was exactly the wife Charles needed—a steadfast rock to balance his somewhat flighty nature.

The real challenge was getting Charles to see that. So far Arabella had managed to avoid being alone with her ex-fiancé.

But his manner toward her hadn't changed. Sooner or later the confrontation would come. She would have to be ready.

"I'm still curious about what happened at Stewart's place," Sally said. "You've been mighty tight-lipped about it."

Arabella shrugged. "Well, there isn't that much to tell."

Except that I fell in love with him.

"Stewart's always been shy with the ladies," Sally continued, chatting on. "The more he likes a woman, the faster he runs away. I expect that's why he's never married. He'd make a wonderful husband and father. But that's not likely to happen—not unless some girl has the gumption to toss away her pride and go after him with all flags flying."

With all flags flying...

The hairbrush slipped out of Arabella's hands and clattered to the floor. The color rushed to her face as she bent to pick it up. It was clear that Sally had spoken for her benefit. But she'd never pursued a man in her life. In Boston society, that sort of thing just wasn't done.

Did she love Stewart enough to throw away her pride? But why ask that question? His note had made it clear that he didn't plan to see her again. How could she pursue a man when he was someplace else? It wasn't as if she could ride out and track him down on the prairie.

Twisting Sally's hair into a shining coil, Arabella began pinning it into place. The motions were so familiar and automatic that they proved no obstacle to her wandering thoughts. Her time here was running out. Before long the roads would be patched, the bridges would be rebuilt and the stage would resume its scheduled run.

Would she be on it?

She blinked away a furtive tear. Once she'd been anxious to leave this wide-open country. But that was before she'd lost her heart. What she needed now, more than anything, was a reason to stay.

* * *

Stewart pushed back his hat and used his bandanna to wipe his sweating face. He'd spent the past four days roping and branding—and the past four nights dreaming about Arabella.

Those dreams—hellfire, they were enough to drive a man crazy. Arabella in his bed, her voluptuous little body meeting his thrusts as he filled her with his seed. Arabella at his side, holding his babies, railing at him and teasing him and filling his life with love and passion as their family grew.

He'd hoped that being on the range would help him forget her. But it hadn't worked. She'd been on his mind the whole time. More than he'd ever wanted anything in his life, he wanted that little green-eyed spitfire for his own.

So what was he doing out here with the cattle when the woman he loved could already be on her way back to Buffalo Bend? He'd never considered himself a stupid man. But he'd be an idiot if he let her get away without even trying to convince her to stay.

Win or lose, it was time he laid his cards on the table. Proposing to Arabella could be the biggest mistake he'd ever made. She could spit in his eye and tell him to go to hell. After the note he'd left her to find following her night in his bed, he wouldn't blame her. Worse, she could say yes and then later discover she couldn't really be happy with him after all. But unless he asked her, he'd never know what he might have missed.

It was a chance he had to take.

After leaving a few instructions with his men, he turned his horse toward the Middleton Ranch and nudged the animal to a trot. Roused from a doze under the chuck wagon, the dog shook its muddy coat and raced after him.

The fishing lesson had been a grand success. Sally had driven the buckboard to a small creek overhung by willows.

There she'd shown Arabella how to string a line, attach the fly and cast it into a quiet hole. She had a collection of beautiful flies, hooked into the fleece of a sheepskin folder. Fashioned of tiny feathers, wound with silk thread on to a barbed hook, they were as exquisitely detailed as real insects. Some were nearly as small. Stewart had made them over the winter months, Sally explained. Each one was a painstaking work of art.

Casting the line had taken some practice. At first, Arabella's fly had snagged the willows more often than it landed in the water. But once she got the knack of it, she'd taken to the sport like a natural. Between the two of them, she and Sally had brought home a nice stringer of trout.

The morning's activities had worn Sally out. After lunch she'd gone upstairs to rest. Twenty minutes later, when Arabella had looked in on her, she'd found Charles's wife asleep on the bed with one arm curled protectively over her rounded belly. Arabella had covered her friend with a quilted throw, stolen back downstairs and walked outside, onto the front porch.

The builder of Charles's house had chosen the spot for its sweeping view of the countryside. From where she stood, Arabella could see all the way to the mountains, where black clouds were boiling over the horizon. Her ears caught the faraway whisper of thunder. Another storm, and it was moving fast. Soon it would be overhead.

Would Stewart be safe on the open range? She couldn't help worrying. But Stewart had spent years on the Montana prairie. To him, a spring thunderstorm would be nothing to fear. The only thing Stewart seemed to fear was *her*.

With all flags flying... Sally's words came back to her as she watched the clouds spread across the sky. Was that what it would take to win the man—an all-out, shameless pursuit? Was she up to the challenge?

A cool breeze struck her face, smelling of rain. As the distant thunder grew closer, Arabella turned and went back inside the house. Charles had stocked his study shelves with books. She could always pass the afternoon reading. Maybe that would take her mind off the storm.

The study was off the entry hall, across from the parlor. The door stood ajar. Arabella was about to cross the threshold when she glimpsed Charles at his desk, his head bent over his account books.

He hadn't seen her. It would be easy enough to sneak up to her room and avoid him, as she'd been doing all week. But sooner or later, the reckoning would have to come. With Sally asleep upstairs, now was as good a time as any for what she had to tell him.

Steeling her resolve, she opened the door. "May I come in, Charles?" she asked.

For an instant he looked startled. Then he rose. "Of course. Sit down, Arabella. Can I get you something to drink?"

"No, thank you. And I believe I'll stand. What I came to say won't take long."

"That's too bad. I was hoping you and I would get more time together." He walked around the desk and took her hand. "I have some news. Not welcome news for me, I'm afraid. One of my men rode a horse into town yesterday. He brought back word that the bridge is up again, and the road's been repaired. The next southbound stage will be coming through Buffalo Bend in three days."

Three days. Arabella felt her heart drop.

Charles's sky-blue eyes widened. "What's this? I thought you'd be happy. Does that downcast look mean you'll be sorry to leave me?"

She shook her head. "Charles, I—"

His hand tightened its grip on her fingers. "I knew it! You do still care for me, don't you?"

She tore her hand away. "Of course I still care for you! We've been best friends since we were children! That's why I can't let you go on making a fool of yourself!"

His expression froze. "A fool? Whatever do you mean?"

"Grow up, Charles!" She hurled the words at him. "You're married to a wonderful woman, and she's about to make you a father. Be a man, for heaven's sake! Give her the loyalty and consideration she deserves!"

He sighed, looking sheepish. "I do love Sally, you know. She's ten times better than I deserve. But, Arabella, I love you, too. I'll always love you."

"Well, I don't love you!" She watched his face go pale. "If you must know, I'm in love with somebody else."

He stared at her as if she'd told him night was day and the moon was made of butter—as if it had never occurred to him that her feelings could change.

"I'm in love with Stewart," she said.

"With *Stewart*? That big, overgrown—?" He shook his head in disbelief. "And does Stewart feel the same about you?"

"I don't know. I only know that if he asked me I'd marry him this minute."

As Arabella spoke the words she knew they were true. She loved Stewart to the depths of her soul, and she couldn't leave without giving herself another chance with him.

"That's why I'm telling you now, Charles. I don't know what's going to happen with Stewart, but if I stay, things will have to be different between us. We could end up being neighbors. Your wife could end up being my sister-in-law. But no matter what happens with Stewart, you have to understand that there will *never* be anything but friendship between you and me ever again. Do you understand?"

His eyes had taken on that lost puppy look. Once it would

have melted her heart. Now it made her want to grind her teeth. "But we still *can* be friends, can't we?" he asked.

"Of course we can. But nothing more. You'll be giving all your love to your beautiful wife and your child." She thrust a finger at his chest. "For heaven's sake, Charles, don't you know what a lucky man you are to have a woman like Sally? Breaking her heart would be the worst thing you could ever do."

He sighed again. "You were always the wise one, Arabella. You're right. I am lucky. And I'd be crazy to risk losing my wife and child through my own foolishness. All I can do is wish you well. You deserve the best life has to offer."

"Thank you. So do you."

"Friends?" He held out his arms for a hug.

"Friends." She stepped into his embrace. They'd been companions most of their lives; but looking back over the years, it seemed they'd been more like brother and sister than sweethearts. It was time for both of them to move on.

"Be happy, Charles." Arabella was stretching upward to plant a sisterly kiss on his cheek when she heard a footstep and the subtle squeak of a door hinge.

Startled, she turned to see Stewart standing in the open doorway, unshaven and dusty from the range. His face was rigid with shock.

He couldn't get out of there fast enough. Without a word, Stewart stepped back into the entry and strode outside, letting the front door slam behind him.

He'd always been a man of action, a man who'd charge fearlessly—even recklessly—into any situation, no matter the odds. But now, all he could do was run.

Lord, how could he act sensibly when he couldn't even think straight? He had to get away from here before he did

something crazy. Vaulting into the saddle, he kicked the horse to a gallop and headed for the gate.

"Stewart!" Arabella had rushed out onto the porch. "Stewart! Stop! This isn't what you think!"

As he thundered down the drive, he willed himself not to look back at her.

Arabella collapsed on the top step of the porch and buried her face in her hands. Her intentions had been entirely good. How could she have made such a mess of things?

Stewart had long suspected her of scheming to break up his sister's marriage. Now she was certain that he believed he'd seen proof of it, and he wasn't the sort of man to change his mind. She had lost him for sure; and after she heard his story, Sally would never want to be her friend again. The best she could do for all concerned was leave.

Hot tears scalded her cheeks. She smeared them away with her hand. At least Charles hadn't followed her outside. He was probably scared of what Stewart might do to him.

The storm clouds that roiled overhead matched her mood. Sheet lightning flickered against the blackness. Out of habit, she counted between the flash and the thunder. Four seconds. Four miles. Not so close yet but the wind had freshened. The storm was moving in fast.

She could no longer see Stewart. Horse and rider had vanished behind a low hill. From there they could be headed in any direction. Even if she tried, she'd have no hope of catching up with him.

Something cool and wet touched her arm. The dog, its fur coated with dust and mud, pressed against her side. It must have come here with Stewart and decided to stay.

She stroked its head, heedless of the smudges on her yellow dress. Whining, it pushed its nose into her hand. "What is it, boy?" she asked. "Are you trying to tell me something?"

The dog's tail thumped against the porch. Pawing at her skirt, it gazed at her with eager, golden eyes. Such an intelligent animal. Arabella remembered how it had run off with her hat and led Stewart to her rescue when she'd fallen off her horse.

Could the dog lead her to Stewart now?

Lightning cracked across the sky, chased almost immediately by an earsplitting boom of thunder. Terror gripped Arabella's throat. The storm was closing in. If she left now, she would be in the open—but so would Stewart.

Stewart knew the prairie well, but that didn't make him immune to danger—especially if he was feeling betrayed and prone to recklessness. What if something were to happen to him? What if he were to die—like her parents had died—without ever knowing that she loved him?

Arabella was on her feet now, running across the yard with the dog at her heels. Raindrops spattered the ground as she dashed into the barn. The gray gelding that had thrown her was in its stall. Despite her bad experience, she knew the animal was swift and sturdy. She would choose it any day over the carriage horses and the showy bay Charles favored. But no more sidesaddle for her. She found a well-used Western saddle, lifted it onto the gelding's back and buckled the cinch.

Outside the barn, she hiked up her skirts and mounted the nervous horse. The dog was dancing with anticipation. "Find your master, boy," she said. "Go!"

The dog was off like a shot, with Arabella flying along behind. The rain was coming down hard now. Within seconds it had plastered her clothes to her skin. The memory of her nightmares stirred and rose—the thunder, the screams... She willed them away. All that mattered now was finding Stewart and forcing him to hear the truth.

She could only hope he would listen.

* * *

Stewart had ridden straight out onto the prairie. He hadn't wanted to go home, where Arabella's sweet fragrance still lingered in his bed. And he was in no condition to go back and face his men. All he wanted to do was crawl into a hole and lick his wounds like a wild animal.

What was he going to tell Sally? Nothing, for now, he resolved. There was too much danger that her distress could harm the baby. But the next time he caught Charlie Middleton alone, he would threaten to shoot off the bastard's balls if he didn't behave himself. As for Miss Arabella Spencer... he didn't know what to think, or what to believe. It was as if the world had turned upside down. His eyes and his mind told him one thing, but with all his heart and soul, he didn't want to believe it.

Lightning cracked the roiling sky. The boom of thunder seemed to shake the earth. The strike had been close—too close. In a storm like this one, the open prairie was a dangerous place to be. It was time he headed for shelter.

Rain streamed down as the clouds opened. Stewart scanned the country around him. He'd been riding aimlessly, but he recognized the hollow between two low hills. In a shallow canyon was an abandoned homestead with an old sod shanty. Last time Stewart had seen it the shanty had barely been standing, but as least it might offer some protection.

Pushing the horse to a gallop, he made for it.

Numb with cold and terror, Arabella urged her horse through the streaming rain. The dog was a brown blur in the long grass. It was all she could do to keep the creature in sight. What if it wasn't leading her to Stewart at all? What if it was just out for a run?

A hundred yards to her right, lightning struck a burned-out tree stump. The crack of thunder was like a cannon going off

inside her head. The gelding screamed and reared. Arabella clung to its neck, sawing at the reins. Seconds crawled past as she struggled to quiet the frightened animal. Little by little, she managed to bring the horse under control.

Exhausted, she sagged in the saddle and glanced around for the dog. The shaggy mutt was nowhere to be seen. Fear crawled up her throat as she whistled and called. There was no bark, no rustle in the grass; no response at all. Arabella was lost in the storm.

She had little choice except to keep moving. But with the deadly lightning so close, she realized it would be safer to dismount and lead the horse. Now that she no longer knew where she was going, there was no reason to hurry.

Speaking calmly to the skittish gelding, she slid to the ground and took the reins. Her boots were spongy with water, the sharp-edged grass knee-high. She was soaked to the skin, shivering with cold and nauseous with terror. Her sprained ankle, which was still healing, had begun to throb. But she didn't dare allow herself to rest. If she sat down she might not have the strength to get up again.

Was Stewart somewhere out here, cold, miserable and alone just as she was? Arabella battled a growing hopelessness. Even with the dog, finding him would have been a matter of luck. Now not even luck would be enough.

She needed a miracle.

Stewart huddled in the driest corner of the old soddie. Most of the roof had caved in, but at least the walls lent some protection from the wind and the lightning. Too bad he had no walls against the bittersweet memory of Arabella in his arms.

Could he have been wrong about what he'd seen? Now that he'd had time to think, the question tormented him. She'd come running after him to explain, but he'd stormed off without giving her a chance. What if he'd stayed long enough to

listen? If he'd misjudged her, he could pay the price to the end of his days.

The horse snorted and stirred in the shadows. Stewart had led the animal inside the walls to protect it from the lightning, which had been known to kill men and animals on the open plain. He remembered Arabella's story of how her parents had died, and the fear that was buried inside her, deeper than memory. At least he'd left her in a safe place. No matter what she might have done, he could never wish her harm.

He loved her too much for that.

The horse nickered, pricking its ears. Stewart was instantly alert, moving toward the Winchester he kept slung from the saddle. Before he could reach it, a wet, muddy canine hurtled through the crumbling doorway, flinging itself on him in a paroxysm of joy.

Stewart managed to shove the squirming, licking animal to arm's length. "Fool dog," he muttered, "don't you even have the sense to stay out of the rain?"

The dog wheeled toward the doorway, whining and yipping. It was a behavior Stewart had come to recognize. "What is it, boy? Do you want me to follow you?"

The dog yipped and trotted outside. Knowing it would be safer to go on foot, Stewart slung the rifle over his shoulder and hurried into the storm. Whatever the mutt wanted him to see, he could only hope it wasn't far off.

Minutes later he spotted the bulky outline of a horse through the rain. His heart plummeted as he recognized the gray gelding from the Middleton Ranch. It was the horse Arabella would have taken if she'd come after him.

With a prayer on his lips, Stewart plunged ahead. Arabella was terrified of thunder and lightning. She would never have ventured out in a storm like this one—not unless she was crazy enough to love him.

He could have stayed and listened to her. Instead he'd

mounted up and galloped away. If the worst had happened, he'd have no one to blame but himself and his damned foolish pride.

He had nearly reached the horse when he saw her. She'd fallen to her knees in the grass, her head drooping forward. Was she praying or merely exhausted? It didn't matter. Nothing mattered except that she was alive, and he'd found her.

At the sound of her name she looked up. Stewart strode forward, caught her in his arms and lifted her like a child. Shivering, she curled against his chest. She was so precious, and he loved her so much. He would do everything in his power to make her happy.

"Stewart—" She looked up at him. Her lips were blue with cold.

"Hush, it's all right. Don't try to talk, Arabella." He strode toward the old sod house, the horse and dog trailing behind.

"No, I have to tell you." Her hands gripped the front of his rain-soaked shirt. "When you saw me with Charles, he was wishing me well, as an old friend. That was all. I'd just told him that I…" She hesitated. "That I was in love with you."

"Hush, I know, my love." All doubt vanished as he spoke. "I should have known all along. If you'll forgive me, I want to spend the rest of our lives making it up to you."

She pressed her head against his chest as he carried her into the crude shelter and settled against the wall. "Let me warm you," he whispered as he held her close.

The rain would soon be letting up. Already, through the clouds, Stewart could see a glimmer of sunlight. Before long the storm would pass. Then they would mount up and ride home side by side, under a blue Montana sky.

Maybe there would even be rainbows.

Epilogue

One week later

The setting sun had turned the clouds to flame. Ribbons of gold, pink and vermilion streamed above the western peaks, casting the prairie in a rosy glow. A flock of wild geese, flying north, winged across the sky.

Arabella rested her head on her husband's shoulder as the buggy pulled over the last hilltop. "Look," she whispered. "Even the sky is celebrating with us."

"I think the sky is telling us it's almost bedtime." Stewart chuckled as he lifted the reins to drive forward.

"No, wait." Arabella laid a hand on his arm. "Give me a moment to look down at the place from here. It's so beautiful. And I'm seeing it for the first time as my new home."

"Whatever pleases you, love." He slipped an arm around her shoulders, pulling her close. The ranch house nestled below the hill, a perfect symphony of logs, stone and glass that harmonized with the land where it lay. The windows glowed in the golden light.

"I think I realized I was in love with you when I first saw your house," Arabella teased.

"Well, now you have both—the house and me. I hope you're pleased with yourself, Mrs. McIntyre."

"More than pleased. Now let's go home."

Arabella's wedding had been far different than she'd imagined. There'd been only a few days to plan it before the circuit preacher came through. Grandma Peabody's silk wedding gown was splotched with water stains that not even Sally had been able to remove. Arabella had chosen to wear it anyway, for luck. The wreath of wildflowers in her hair had matched the bouquet she carried down the aisle of the little white church. She had never felt more beautiful. And when she looked up into Stewart's eyes to recite her vows, his love had flowed through her like warm sunlight.

In attendance at the simple ceremony were a few friends from town, as well as Charles and Sally who'd smiled and held hands the whole time. A special guest of honor, Stewart's dog, had been bathed, brushed and adorned with a garland of ribbons and daisies around its shaggy neck. During the ceremony, the wayward mutt had wandered off to romp in a puddle with a canine friend, then returned to the church, leaving muddy footprints down the aisle. A wedding picnic at Charles and Sally's had capped the festivities.

In other words, the day couldn't have been more perfect.

Stewart pulled the buggy up to the front walk and turned the horse over to Miguel, who waited with a shy grin on his face. Arabella was about to climb to the ground when Stewart swept her up in his arms.

"Remember the first time I carried you into this house? I was wondering then how it would be to carry you home as a bride," he said.

Arabella laughed. "As I recall, I was thinking along the same lines. Let's find out."

She nestled against Stewart's chest as he carried her across

the porch. Some things, she'd learned, didn't work out according to plan. And life's unexpected gifts could be the dearest blessings of all.

* * * * *

THE BRIDE WORE BRITCHES

Kate Welsh

Dear Reader,

You can't imagine how excited I was when I was asked to participate in this anthology. I've written a few very short stories for magazines, but I've never written in novella length. My excitement grew when I learned I would be able to link this story to the series I've been working on for Harlequin® Historical.

The question about my writing I'm asked most often is "Where do you get your ideas?" My answer is always "Everywhere." The inspiration for this novella came from my husband's sister. She married his best friend—his childhood friend. That happened after what we all laughingly call "the miracle." She was an unashamed tomboy, who had a date one Saturday night when my husband and his friend happened to be heading somewhere as well—being a man, my husband doesn't remember where. As they were readying themselves to leave, my sister-in-law came downstairs, all prettied up for her date. His friend looked up and lightning seemed to strike him. He asked a now infamous question. Watch for it, because Dylan asks it, too. My sister-in-law, who is now my best friend, answered in much the same way as Rhiannon Oliver.

I hope you enjoy this tale inspired by our family history. There's always something exciting happening in Tierra del Verde, so watch for other installments of the characters who settled the Wild West in Texas's beautiful Hill Country. You can find out what sent them west in the first books of the series. They're at www.Harlequin.com.

Kate Welsh

To Deb and John. Thanks for the inspiration.
I love telling your story! Hope you have
many more happy years together. All my love, Kate.

Chapter One

Tierra del Verde, Texas—March 1879

Rhiannon Oliver pulled the buckboard to a stop in front of Wheaton General Store. She glanced up and down the main street and smiled a little sadly. The town had grown because of the stagecoach line having put them on their route. Sadly a few families had moved on because of the growth.

Unfortunately with progress came problems. Strangers drifted in and out of town more often now. Which forced her to continue wearing a disguise of britches and loose shirts that had come about accidentally when her figure had begun to blossom six years ago. With her mother long dead, neither Rhia nor her father had known what to do other than pretend she was a son. But she wasn't.

Since her father's death two years earlier, she'd had no one to rely on but herself. Her friend's mother had filled in, so in some personal matters she hadn't been completely bereft of a woman's counsel. A woman alone was in danger, however, so what had been a convenience for her father now had to be continued for her safety.

Recent Comanche raids worried everyone, too, especially

since no one had been able to track the raiders or find evidence they even existed. Some called them Ghost Warriors. Some looked at the bigger operations with suspicion but the source of the murderous raids remained a mystery.

Rhia just kept putting one foot in front of the other trying not to let resentment take root in her soul because no one saw past the disguise. Two cowboys walked along then, passing her without notice. Rhia sighed. Yep. *Still invisible.*

She set the brake and jumped down. Her gaze fell immediately upon a poster tacked to the upright of the covered boardwalk. Spring Social. April 4. Rocking R. Five To Midnight. Apparently Alex Reynolds and his wife were hosting again.

She would stay home. Again.

Tying her old horse, Jessie, to the hitching rail, she watched with a smile as Scout, her border collie and constant companion for as long as she could remember, took a flying leap from the wagon's seat to the boardwalk. Rhia grabbed her basket of eggs and ran lightly up the steps. She and Scout entered the general store together—the way they did everything else.

"Good afternoon, Abby," she called out to the proprietor as the screen door smacked shut behind her. "I hope you need eggs."

Abby Wheaton peeked around the back room doorway, her green eyes sparkling. "I just sold the last to Reiman House. Your timing's perfect." She pushed the curtain aside, carrying several dresses. "Let me hang these before they wrinkle then I'll be right with you."

Rhia set her basket on the counter and went to the empty display table where Abby started to lay the dresses. The scent of freshly ironed cloth rose from the neat stack. "Here," Rhia said, "let me hold them while you hang them. It would be a shame to see them wrinkled."

Scout padded over to the stove and lay down as Rhia took the dresses by their hangers. She handed them to Abby one

by one, admiring each while Abby hung them. Rhia found herself wishing for at least one of the pretty garments Abby had made. Ready-made dresses was an idea Abby had brought with her from the East. "These are really lovely, Abby."

Abby looked over at her, eyes narrowing shrewdly. "You know, I let those britches fool me for a while. You'd love to be able to wear dresses."

Rhia laughed, her nerves showing in the shakiness of her voice. Abby had stated a fact not a question and now Rhia felt a bit like an unmasked bank robber. She shrugged, pretending indifference. "Daddy taught me never to buy on credit. If this year's wool prices stay where they are, maybe I'll be back for one of these," she said, but it probably wasn't wise to step out from behind the mask.

"Oh, I remember the penny-pinching days."

That was what was nice about Abby. Though married to the town's banker, a man of means, she came from working stock, the daughter of a Pennsylvania coal miner. She knew what living without meant.

Rhia came to a dress that looked like it might fit her. She hesitated and took a moment to gaze at it. "Raul and I plan to start shearing tomorrow," she said, hearing the wistful tone in her voice and praying Abby hadn't.

Abby took the dress and looked over the pretty blue frock, giving Rhia an extra moment to covet it. If she bought anything, it should be new shears, not an impractical dress she shouldn't wear in public.

"Are you coming to the spring social?"

The tinkling of the bell over the door made Rhia glance over her shoulder. She nearly sighed aloud. Dylan Varga. She couldn't remember a day since meeting him when she hadn't loved him. He was her best friend's older brother and, with womanhood, her puppy love had deepened and begun to fill

her entire being. Unfortunately, she might as well be part of the shelving for all the notice he gave her.

Maybe if I dropped the disguise that'd change. But that presented complications. She'd promised her father to make Adara a success, which meant living alone. She couldn't fail him. That was far more weighty a worry than risking a final rejection from Dylan.

She glanced Dylan's way again, holding the remaining dresses in front of her like armor, hoping to avoid that stomach-flipping effect his nearness always caused.

Dylan took his hat off, his black hair shining in the sunlight, and closed the door. Then he smiled. Oh, no. Now she even felt it when all he did was smile in her direction.

"Good day, Mrs. Wheaton," he said, then to Rhia he added with a grin, "You thinking of buying a dress, Rowdy? You don't want the sun to fall out of the sky, do you?"

She notched her chin. Rowdy. He'd named her that the first time he had to rescue her when she'd climbed too high in a tree. She'd liked it, that pet name he called no one else—but it had grown tiresome. His sister wore pants while working at Belleza, their family sheep ranch. Her pants were the more costly Levi Strauss jeans. At $1.25 a pair, Strauss's jeans cost what an acre of good Texas land did. Farrah's father could afford what Rhia couldn't.

That her clothes didn't reflect the real her rankled. She wasn't a tomboy like Farrah. She wanted to dress like a woman but her position as a woman alone wouldn't allow it.

"Actually," Rhia heard Abby say, "we're looking for the right one for Rhiannon to wear to the spring social. I hope you'll be escorting your sister since your mother and father won't be attending."

His golden eyes widened at Abby's whopper but he refrained from any smart-mouthed comments about Rhia wearing a dress and attending a dance. "The don won't step foot on the Rocking R because I work there," Dylan replied. "He

demanded Alex Reynolds fire me. Alex being Alex refused. Still, I don't think the don would forbid Farrah from going. I doubt she'd want to go, but I'll ask."

"Oh, she'll come," Abby assured Dylan. "Now if you'll excuse us, I need to get Rhiannon settled in the back. Come along, lovie." She ordered compliance with a look. "I'm sure Mr. Varga won't mind waiting a moment."

Stunned, Rhia stared at the back of Abby Wheaton's head then followed meekly. What would it hurt to try on one or two of Abby's pretty frocks? She didn't *have* to buy one. Thankful Dylan wasn't too close, she walked past him. Having him too near was another thing that caused her stomach to do that strange dance. Surely she could outlast Dylan's business there. It would give her a chance to wallow in all that pretty finery.

"Abby, I told you I can't buy a dress," she whispered. "You know how Daddy felt about credit. And are you sure Farrah is going? She hates socials."

"Oh, she'll be going or my name isn't Abaigeal Kane Wheaton," Abby said, stepping close and working at the buttons of Rhia's oversize shirt. "You're leavin' here with a dress. We'll take a little bit each time out of your egg money till it's all paid off. You won't even notice it missing. I know what it's like to be ashamed of my clothes. You deserve this. Don't be denyin' you want to go. Or that you want to be im-pressin' that big lug out there. Callin' you 'Rowdy.' I never heard such a thing. Now strip and try on one these dresses. I'll be right back with a crinoline after I've waited on him and sent him on his way. We're going to knock him senseless come the fourth," Abby whispered.

Rhia stared after Abby. The woman was a force to be reck-oned with. Especially since Rhia had never wanted anything as much as she wanted to knock Dylan senseless with that blue dress and what she looked like in it. Rhia hurried to get it on praying it fit—forgetting all the reasons it was a bad idea.

Chapter Two

At almost dusk on April 4, Dylan waited impatiently in the gig outside his parents' hacienda. His mother had stuck her head out the door for just a moment to ask him to wait there. Which really meant the don still wouldn't receive his own son.

She'd also told him Farrah had asked her friend Rhiannon Oliver to ride along. It was going to be a bit of a tight fit in the two-person gig.

God, at least Rhia always managed to scrub off the stink of working with sheep. He knew that smell having been forced to care for them while growing up. Instead he always caught the faint scent of wildflowers whenever he was in the same room with her.

Strange.

He looked up and saw his mother staring out at him from Farrah's upstairs bedroom window. He smiled and blew her a kiss. His thoughts swung back to her and her difficult position between the warring men in her life. And guilt followed. He couldn't imagine being separated from his own child and he was sorry for his part in her heartache. But he had to live life his way and that didn't include sheep ranching.

His mind slid to his sister. What had sparked her atten-

dance tonight? Farrah's pretty face and tall stature managed to make her in a pair of Levi Strauss's blue jeans a sight most of the men around Belleza and Tierra del Verde enjoyed seeing. Of course, knowing they'd be looking elsewhere for work kept the men on Belleza from acting on any attraction they felt toward her. Farrah's prickly demeanor took care of the rest.

Farrah's surprise companion tonight put them off with her appearance alone. Unlike Farrah, Rhia had always been too plump and too unkempt. From a couple years after her mother's death, every time he'd seen her, she'd had a beat-up old Stetson rammed down on her head. She made herself real inhospitable to a man, no matter that she was a good, hardworking person. To his knowledge no man had ever given Rhiannon Oliver a second look. Of course, he doubted Rhia minded. All she seemed to care about was following in her daddy's footsteps running Adara.

The door opened and his mother came out again. He jumped down and went to her. God, he'd missed her.

"The girls will be along," she said. "Your father said I could come get a hug."

Dylan wrapped his arms around his mother and held her for a long moment. "*Cabra vieja*," he growled.

His mother whacked him on the shoulder as she stepped back. "Who are you calling an old goat?"

"The don." He kissed his mother's smooth cheek. "Certainly not the prettiest woman in the state of Texas."

She clearly fought a smile. "Flattery won't get you out of hot water. You should be ashamed. He's your *father*."

"You're right, but I loved my grandmother too much to call him a son of a bitch."

"Language," she scolded. "One of you has to bend first. He's not going to live forever, then it'll be too late."

"Talk to *him*. He's the one who refuses to compromise. He won't even let me into the house so I *can* talk to him. I'd

have been happy to stay. He's the one who needed to bend. Instead he escalated this. He disowned me. All I asked for was a piece of land to raise horses."

His mother sighed and stroked his cheek. "I know. You have your life and dreams just as he did when he left Spain." She forced a smile. "He had to give up his dreams for you the way his father did when we came here. But enough talk of problems. Smile. You're the luckiest man in Tierra del Verde tonight." She stepped to the side. "You'll be escorting the two prettiest young ladies in Texas to the social."

Dylan looked first to Farrah walking toward him. She did indeed look like a lady for once with her chestnut hair waving around her shoulders and wearing a pretty dress instead of jeans.

Then his eyes slid to Rhiannon as she drew closer.

His heart turned over in his chest.

She was dazzling. Not a bit plump. And the dark-as-night hair she usually kept hidden under that beat-up hat was so silky it even managed to capture the last dying rays of the sun. It hung down her back in adorable waves and framed her face while flirting with the breeze. Her creamy complexion made his fingertips yearn to touch its softness. He was suddenly grateful to that hated old hat for the shade it had provided. Her ebony lashes, thick and full, framed her cornflower-blue eyes.

She wore a pretty blue dress with a full skirt he'd swear was the same color as her incredible eyes. The sash around her middle accentuated her slender waist and hips. He retraced the path of his perusal back up to her eyes where he found himself ensnared.

Why had he never noticed how pretty she was? Why had he never noticed her at all except as someone to tease? "Rhia? Where the hell have you been?"

Her chin notched up. "I've been ready to leave for an hour.

Farrah and your mother were arguing over her dress. Why blame me?"

"No. No. I'm not. I meant…uh…where did you come from?"

She looked at him as if he'd lost his mind. "From Farrah's room?" she said real slowly the way folks talked to someone not quite right in the head.

Maybe he *had* lost his senses. He'd certainly lost his touch. He was usually a lot more polished with a woman who'd caught his eye. But then again, the soiled doves at the Golden Garter weren't exactly a good test of his prowess.

"I meant you look…nice," he finished, knowing that wasn't a strong enough word but settling. As tongue-tied as he felt God alone knew what might have popped out.

Silently he took Rhia's hand to help her into the gig he'd borrowed from Alex. And nearly gasped. What the hell was that? If his eyes hadn't told him different, he'd have sworn her touch had set his hand afire. By handing her up first he'd insured that she'd be pressed close to him in the two-seat gig. He ought to be able to untie his tongue on the way so he could charm her into walking in on his arm.

A few hours later Dylan watched from the side of the room as yet another admirer claimed Rhiannon for a dance. They were like bees drawn to the last flower of summer. He'd only gotten to partner her in one dance and that had been a square dance.

Checking his watch, he realized the night was nearly over. He tried to take comfort from the knowledge that she'd walked in on his arm and would be leaving the same way. But it didn't help that George Bentley had her hand in his as the caller signaled them to allemande left then promenade.

Finally Bentley had to let go as they each moved on to other partners. Dylan felt better about it as it was Joshua

Wheaton, the town's banker and husband to the miracle worker who'd made Rhia's pretty blue dress.

Funny, Dylan wouldn't have thought Rhia could dance—if he'd thought about her at all. Or that she'd be so delicate and pretty under what she usually wore. He ached to hold her in his arms and wished he could claim her for a waltz.

He looked across the handsome gold room with its gas chandeliers and wall sconces. They made the place almost as bright as day. Alex Reynolds stood near one of the open windows.

Dylan walked over and breathed in the scent of the early blooming wildflowers. Alex was his boss but he'd become more friend than employer since Dylan had played a part in rescuing Alex's wife from a kidnapper. "Do you think those yahoos know how to play a waltz?" Dylan asked, nodding toward the piano player from the Golden Garter and the three others sawing on their fiddles.

Alex grinned. "They'd better. They promised to practice it all this week. I have the last dance reserved with Patience. It's supposed to be the waltz. You going to try for a chance to lead out the belle of the ball?"

Dylan followed Alex's gaze to Rhia. She *was* the belle and he wanted her in his arms. He found himself moving back toward the dance floor, making sure he stood right where Rhia and her partner stopped. Quickly stepping forward, Dylan cut off George Bentley's approach. "This is the dance you promised to me," Dylan lied.

Miraculously Rhia didn't call him on it. She did look confused, though, when she said, "Oh, yes. I suppose I must have forgotten." Her breathing was a bit labored, too. He should lead her to the lemonade table to cool off but he was feeling selfish. He wanted her all to himself.

The little quartet struck up an odd version of a waltz.

Though he'd heard it played more expertly, it was sweet music anyway. Because Rhia was in his arms, looking into his eyes.

"I can't believe I finally have the belle of the ball all to myself."

"Hardly a belle and I doubt this is as grand as a ball. You've visited both sets of your grandparents. Farrah told me how grand everything is in England and Spain."

He grinned. "Tonight, my belle, here with you like this, it all seems pretty grand to me." He couldn't seem to curb the things he said to her any more than he could take his eyes off her. "You look so beautiful tonight. I'd like the opportunity to get to know you better, Rhia."

Chapter Three

Rhia stared up at Dylan aware of everything in the room and nothing except the feeling of being held by him. The musk-and-lime scent of his nearness. The sparkle in his golden-honey-brown eyes. The security of his strength surrounding her.

She didn't know what to say in answer to the words she'd dreamed of hearing almost her whole life. "You've known me since I was six years old," she finally managed to say. "I hardly remember a time when we didn't know each other."

He shook his head. "I've known the girl running tame after Farrah. I've let her ride along when I took my sister into town. I've waved to her across the street. I've teased her and called her Rowdy. But I don't think that's who you are. There's more to a person than recognizing them or even knowing they like the ices at Reiman House or the licorice at the General Store. I don't know your hopes. Your dreams."

And I don't know yours, either, she thought as she stared into his rich, honeyed gaze. Really all she knew about him these days was that he and his father were on the outs, but not why. And she knew that being near him flustered her, made her nervous. But not in a way that made her feel…afraid.

It was an exciting kind of nervousness. Like riding full out while a thunderstorm was bearing down on you.

But she never courted danger.

She was careful. Farrah said too careful. She planned each move she made. Until she'd looked at a blue dress and thrown caution away with her disguise.

Rhia forced herself to examine why she'd done what she had but she came to no conclusions. Dylan's proximity seemed to scramble her thoughts and tie her tongue in knots. Yet his words hadn't thrilled her as she'd thought they should. Why?

The music came to a halt and she was saved from needing to make further comments when the voice of their host thanked the men on the instruments and all the guests for coming to celebrate spring.

The evening was over.

Farrah rushed up then. "The band played longer than planned. We should be going. Papa will be waiting up and you know how grouchy he is when he's kept up so late."

Rhia wanted to protest but Dylan, who'd continued to hold her in his arms, abruptly let her go and jerked back. The loss of his heat made her shiver in the warm room. She felt instantly bereft and resentful of her friend's intrusion.

"I'll bring the gig around," Dylan said. "The stable boys are probably harnessing up the mare right now." He nodded to them and walked away.

"You certainly made use of all those dance lessons Mama forced on us over the years," Farrah said, looking a bit cross.

Rhia considered her friend. "She forced them on *you*. I liked them."

Farrah frowned but joined arms with Rhia and they moved toward the doorway and down the stairs that led to the big rear yard where the many wagons and coaches were parked. There was already a bustle of activity as guests began to head home.

"Why should I let some man lead me around a dance floor

as if I'm too stupid to know where to put my feet?" Farrah complained, taking up the argument again. "It's a metaphor for the way they treat us. What's wrong with wanting to be the master of my own fate?"

"Nothing." Rhia patted Farrah's hand. Don Alejandro ruled his home with an iron fist. Nothing was beyond his control. She was as independent as Farrah wanted to be but Rhia knew it wasn't all her friend thought it was. "Life on your own isn't as easy as you seem to think it is. If I make a mistake, I could lose everything. Raul follows my orders but never does more than what I specifically tell him to do. Angus is just plain cantankerous. He refuses to take orders at all." She shook her head. "He's always liked sheep more than people."

"You seem to handle it so easily I forget Adara could fail. Are you worried about coming out from behind the disguise? The men flocked around you tonight like a swarm of bees to a newly opened bloom."

"I feel...exposed," Rhia admitted. "And confused. I kind of wish I'd resisted dressing up and coming tonight. The other half of me wouldn't have missed it for anything." They reached the busy yard. A breeze blew softly from the west carrying a sweet scent on the air. "When Abby made me try the dresses on, it was to needle Dylan. But I'd already been thinking how sick I was of hiding behind baggy men's clothes. I'd gotten to where I was more afraid of ending up some strange smelly hermit than of the consequences of being seen for who I am. I'm still not sure what I feared more but now there's only one possible consequence left to face."

Farrah squeezed her hand. "Are you afraid no one will come calling or that whoever does won't treat you as an equal once you marry him?"

"I didn't think ahead. I just reacted, you know? Abby all but shoehorned me into the first dress. But when I looked in the mirror, I wanted to be the person staring back at me. I

didn't think further than that." She gazed at Dylan where he waited. "There's only one man I'd want to come calling anyway," she muttered under her breath.

"Maybe I should give that man a little push in your direction," Farrah said.

She'd heard! Rhia stopped dead in her tracks, pulling Farrah to a stop, too. Farrah was unpredictable and likely to do anything once she got an idea in her head. "Don't you dare say one word to him. I'd be mortified. Promise me."

Farrah sighed. "Fine. Now let's go. Papa's going to be fit to be tied that I'm out this late. Which means he and Dylan will have another fight."

She followed Farrah hurrying toward the gig where Dylan awaited. But George Bentley came rushing up the path from the side garden. "Miss Oliver, I wondered if you would—"

"Sorry, Bentley," Dylan said as he stepped between them. "I have to get my sister and Rhi— Uh…Miss Oliver home then be back here to catch some shut-eye. Days around here start with the dawn. We don't keep bankers' hours."

Rhia nearly groaned in relief at Dylan's interruption. George seemed nice but he was a bank teller as Dylan had just pointed out. They had nothing at all in common.

She scrambled into the gig with Dylan's help and Farrah followed. He walked around the gig and looked up with a smile. "Now to take the two prettiest ladies in Texas home."

Farrah emitted an unladylike snort but all Rhia could think about was what he'd said. And this time she wouldn't let sour thoughts intrude.

That was pretty hard to do, though, because it was the last thing Dylan said on the whole ride. He just drove and seemed to brood. Silent. Stiff. Farrah peppered the air with meaningless small talk.

But she'd been a bit uncommunicative herself, caught up in her confused thoughts. When they arrived at Belleza, Rhia

was shocked, having ignored the passing scenery. Farrah's smug grin told the story of what she'd missed. Her former friend had apparently talked Dylan into dropping her home first. Now Rhia would be alone with Dylan.

I'll throttle her.

Rhia was as close to heartbroken as she'd been since her father took his final breath. Dylan would never be interested in her even all gussied up and looking her best. Couldn't Farrah see that? Rhia stiffened her back. Well, so what! She didn't need him. She didn't need anyone.

Still, she didn't know how she'd live in Tierra del Verde knowing that at any time she might see him courting some woman who'd moved there, then hearing of their marriage or later about the birth of their children.

She tightened her hands where she had them tangled in her lap. Becoming a smelly hermit didn't sound half bad right then. She should have stayed hidden. She'd come out into the open. Exposed herself. Probably weakened her standing as a landowner. She'd certainly made herself look vulnerable. And all for nothing. Now she'd have to face the consequences. Alone.

Then she got to wondering what she'd done earlier to put Dylan off. He'd insisted she dance with him and she hadn't stepped on his feet or lost her place even once while they'd danced. Had her anger over trivialities shown in her manner while they'd been dancing? It must have. He'd changed somehow after the band ceased playing. The moment Farrah had given him an excuse, he'd all but fled the ballroom. Which meant, unplanned and ill-timed as this night had been, she'd exposed everything for nothing.

The ride to Adara wasn't as silent as the ride to Belleza but it was full of the same kind of meaningless small talk. Just as they topped the rise overlooking Adara's homestead, Rhia took one last deep breath, sure it would be the last time

she got to enjoy Dylan's earthy lime and leather scent along with his warmth pressed against her shoulder.

Then she noticed the silence and all thought of her failure that night fled. The ominous feel of impending disaster crawled over her. She put a staying hand on Dylan's forearm. "Stop," she whispered. "Something's wrong. The sheep are too quiet. Especially for a night with a full moon."

Dylan canted his head listening, too. He hadn't acted on her hunch alone but at least he'd listened for the worrisome silence. Would he have questioned another man or taken him at his word?

Then, without another whispered word between them, he pulled the gig to the side of the road into the shadow of a big oak. "Wait here." His reply barely audible, he pulled his revolver from the holster on his hip, flipped it over and offered her the pistol grip. "Tie up the rig and hide. Use it if you have to but, Rhia, save a bullet." Then he yanked his Winchester from under the seat, jumped down and headed into the shadows.

The sharp sound of Dylan cocking the Winchester brought his last words to her thoughts. *Save a bullet.* What he'd left unsaid was—*for yourself.* A woman alone was in danger.

Chapter Four

Dylan ducked under a low-hanging branch of a big old oak. Moving through the dense woods, he kept his steps as silent as possible. When he emerged from the cover of the brush, it was with a sinking heart.

In all directions the full moon revealed Rhia's northern-slope flock—still, silent, slaughtered. He made his way to a shadowy form on the ground. Angus, her grizzled old shepherd. He'd been murdered and it looked like the work of the Comanche.

Most of the tribe had signed a treaty but apparently this band of renegades had something other than peace in mind. He'd just bent down to close Angus's sightless eyes when a thought occurred to him. Comanche raided for food, horses, useful goods and, yes, murder and mayhem. But it was unlike them to kill innocent animals in this wasteful way. They'd have stolen as many as they could for hides and food but they'd never kill this many animals so indiscriminately.

Puzzled, he looked below toward *the* homestead and sniffed. The breeze carried no smell of smoldering lumber. Adara's house, barn and cabin looked to be intact. Yet in every other raid so far, the band had torched the buildings.

He rose turning slowly, deep in thought. With almost all the residents of town and the surrounding area attending the dance on the Rocking R, Rhia's nearest neighbor, flames lighting up the sky and the smell of smoke on the breeze would have brought men running. But why would a renegade band of Indians know about the Spring Social?

Wanting to get back to Rhia, Dylan moved through the dead flock to the access road. He walked back up the hill. When he saw the faint silhouette of the gig, he called out, "Coming in," not wanting to get shot full of holes.

Rhia crept out and went to the mare's head, taking hold of the bridle, the revolver in her grip. "What happened?" she demanded, a small quaver in her voice.

"I'm sorry, Rowdy. There's been a raid. Angus is dead." He saw her flinch and her shoulders sagged when he added, "And your northern-slope flock is wiped out. I don't know about the others. The buildings look intact from up here but I didn't want to take the time to check and leave you alone and vulnerable."

That Rhia didn't argue a bit about her being vulnerable told him she was badly rattled. He took the revolver from her lax grip and put it back in his holster. "I'm nearly sure the at-tackers are gone," he went on but didn't add, *because Angus is already cold.* "Let's go see how bad it is."

Rhia nodded and silently walked to the seat of the gig. Shaking, she needed his help to climb up. Her expression looked as if she held on to her composure by a tenuous thread. He was tempted to leave straightaway but decided there was no use having her imagine it as worse than it was.

He climbed up next to Rhia and snapped the reins. They'd gotten as far as the yard when two figures stepped out from behind the big elm tree that dominated the site. Dylan nearly had his revolver out of its holster before he recognized Raul Hernandez and his wife, Consuela.

The two approached. Raul had his sombrero in his hand, looking apologetic. His woman had a belligerent tilt to her head. "We are sorry, Miss Rhia," Raul said. "We can stay no longer. Angus is dead, no?"

Dylan nodded when Rhia stayed silent, staring toward the destruction filling the clearing ahead.

"We leave now," Consuela Hernandez said. "They will get us *all* if we stay."

"How did they miss you two?" Dylan asked.

"We hide in the cave near the stream," Raul replied.

"Didn't you even try to help Angus?" Dylan demanded of Raul. The man's face crumpled and he looked away. Dylan liked to think he'd have tried but did any man know how he'd act until death came knocking?

"He would not have come to help Raul," Consuela snapped.

More composed now, Raul explained, "I have Consuela and the *bebé* she expects. I stand no chance against so many. Howling and shooting comes from the north and warns us. Before we get to the cave, Angus...he no longer screams. They come look for us as if they know we are here but the cave the *señorita* shows us is well hidden."

Consuela nodded, looking around at the mess Dylan's eyes had finally adjusted enough to see. "They go through *sus casas*, Señorita. They make much mess but take only money jar and *armas y balas*."

Dylan frowned, thinking. "Guns and bullets make sense, but money?" Then he glanced next to him to see if Rhia had picked up on the inconsistencies. But she just sat there. Silent as her dead shepherd and sheep. Completely unlike the Rhia he knew. He wanted to wrap her in his arms and keep her safe.

The thought shocked him. Was it the dress or had he seen a part of her she usually hid from the world? He'd never thought of her as needing protection. She'd always been so

strong and capable. This feeling was as out of place as the peculiarities of the raid were.

He stifled a sigh at the destruction littering the clearing ahead. Torn curtains hung out of broken windows. Pieces of crockery and cloth items had been trampled into the ground.

"I have to go for the sheriff then take Rhia to Belleza. You two can pack up and use her wagon to get to town." He wasn't happy about the couple's desertion of Rhia but he couldn't say he didn't understand. They'd had quite a scare. Lesser men had cleared out after the first raid last year.

"You can talk to Sheriff Quinn or Ranger Kane about what you heard and saw when you get there."

Dylan turned to Rhia. "*Querida,* can I get you anything from the house before we leave?"

She glanced toward the house again, then just shook her head. He'd expected an argument or maybe even tears. They'd have scared the bejezus out of him but her soundless answer, like the lost look in her eyes, was as haunting as the ranch's silent little yard.

Minutes later he'd turned the gig around and headed toward town. After reporting the raid to the law, he'd take her on to Belleza. She was nearly as close to his mother as she was to Farrah. He wasn't looking forward to dealing with his father but tonight it was Rhia who mattered.

He also had to talk to the old man about taking precautions. They could just as easily have attacked Belleza. At least Rhia had been thinking ahead. He was sure Raul and Consuela were only alive because Rhia had shown them the cave where they'd all played as children.

His thoughts went back to Farrah and his mother. The most ferocious guards on Belleza were the dogs whose job it was to protect the sheep from predators.

Dogs.

Dammit! He hadn't seen evidence of Rhia's dog, Scout,

on that hill or Angus's dogs, either. He hoped they'd successfully run from the sound of the guns. Maybe it was just as
well he hadn't thought to look. He didn't think Rhia could
take another loss tonight.

With Rhia sitting next to him frozen in shock, Dylan was
at a loss as to what to say to her. So, as he had on the way
to Belleza after the social, he drove in stony silence fighting
the instinct to hold her and promise to always keep her safe.

He'd been so consumed with desire for her earlier he hadn't
thought about the poor timing of her sudden emergence as a
desirable woman. Now because of the waltz and, influenced
by her nearness, what he'd said during it, he had to be very
careful how he offered comfort. He didn't want to hurt her
but he wasn't ready to take on a wife. Especially not one who
stubbornly clung to the idea of making her father's dream
come true by making a success of Adara. She couldn't be
the woman for him no matter how much he wished it were
otherwise.

The stop in town to alert Ryan Quinn about the raid took
only moments, then they headed for Belleza.

As he drew the gig even with the front door of his parents'
hacienda, it flew open and the don stormed out in full high
dudgeon. "I care not if the rest of the females of the area are
allowed to dance at that Englishman's to all hours. What were
you thinking to bring your sister home so late? And what have
you been doing with Rhiannon Oliver all this time? What if
someone discovers you've been—"

"Shut. Up." Dylan's voice cracked into the air and shocked
the old man into silence. "Get Mama," he told Farrah who'd
followed her father out of the house. Dylan jumped to the
ground and scooped Rhia unresisting into his arms. When he
turned, his father blocked his path to the house. Dylan wanted
to simply walk away as he usually did but tonight was different. Dylan ordered, "Stand aside. This is no time for you to

get on your high horse about bloodlines. Rhia's had a nasty shock. Adara was raided while she was gone."

Miraculously his father gave way but he followed them inside, demanding, "Why bring her here?"

Dylan refused to react to the don's coldheartedness. He set Rhia on the small divan and stepped back as his mother and sister rushed to her. He turned to face his father and through gritted teeth said, "I brought her here because she needs Mother."

By moving to the beehive fireplace in the far corner of the room, Dylan forced his father to follow. The sound of Rhia answering Farrah's question calmed him a bit. All he could think was, suppose she'd been there when they'd struck. There was no question in his mind that she'd have tried to help Angus. She'd be dead now, or worse. A captive.

"Are they all dead?" the don snapped.

"The couple who lives there are lucky they escaped with their lives but they've moved on. Old Angus is dead. The whole place has been ransacked. I couldn't leave her there," he whispered fiercely. "Surely you can see that." Dylan ran an angry hand through his hair and leaned even closer to the stubborn old coot. He felt like shouting but had to whisper so Rhia wouldn't hear. "At least half of her flock is dead. If you're turning her away, I'm sure Alex and Mrs. Reynolds would be happy to take her in."

That got the old man's back up. "I wouldn't consider turning away a neighbor in need."

"Funny. That's how you sounded." Knowing his father, what the don meant was he wouldn't consider allowing Alex Reynolds to outshine him.

"I've asked her to sell Adara to me several times since Henry Oliver died. I knew she'd never make it out there."

He'd probably offered half what the place was worth. Dylan glanced at Rhia. She already seemed better, looking angry

and determined. The knot in his stomach eased. Rhia would recover from this. If the don tried to push her toward selling out now, she'd probably hand him his head. But that thought brought the knot right back. The next thing she'd do was head on home. Alone. She had a stubborn streak that ran deeper than anyone he'd ever met.

Except maybe himself.

He had to take the don's mind off making another offer for Adara. And he knew exactly how to do it. "You have to take steps to increase Belleza's security. Your men aren't trained with guns. It's dangerous."

The don's face darkened in anger. "I refuse to arm men of a lower class. How I run Belleza is no longer your concern."

Farrah stood and the other two followed suit, beating a hasty retreat, exactly as he'd hoped they would if he stirred up trouble. His sister and mother had witnessed enough battles. Dylan usually walked away when the don started shouting. This time, he'd stick till his father heard him out.

"I may have given up my inheritance to Belleza, but the safety of my mother and sister is at stake. The way I see it that gives me the right to comment on how well you protect them. These raids aren't stopping. They're getting even uglier. What makes you think you're not going to face what others have? Arm the shepherds. Failing that, hire guards you feel you can trust! If you don't, *you* might not live to regret it. But *Mama and Farrah* may. Do you really want your last thoughts to be of them as Comanche captives?" He couldn't help but be pleased to see the old man pale.

"I'm borrowing a horse," Dylan said and stalked toward the door. Maybe he'd finally won one of their arguments.

An important one.

Chapter Five

Rhia settled with Farrah in Elizabeth Varga's sitting room as they'd been doing since she and Farrah were in their teens. She glanced around. The architecture of the room, like the rest of the home, was Spanish, but the decor was unashamedly British. Farrah's mother clung to her roots as did her husband. The mix might work for them but not for their children who were unashamedly Americans. Texans.

"I'm so sick of the arguments between Papa and Dylan," Farrah lamented. Rhia focused on her friend. She sounded disconsolate and looked near to tears.

Elizabeth Varga shook her head and reached over to squeeze her daughter's hand. "They love with great passion and disagree the same way. It is their nature. Dylan will never follow your father's path and your father sees Dylan's stand as a criticism of him. I only hope Alejandro comes to understand his son before it's too late. If a rift grows too wide, a bridge can never be built to traverse it."

Though Rhia agreed with Elizabeth's wisdom, she grew distinctly uncomfortable with all the personal talk. She didn't belong at Belleza. Don Alejandro didn't even want her there and never had. She'd heard him protest her arrival somewhere

in the distance. She'd always known he objected to her but she ignored his insults because Farrah needed their friendship as much as Rhia did.

She wasn't letting him chase her away now any more than she ever had, she assured herself. But she couldn't stay there. She had problems to solve. A lot of problems. It had nothing to do with bruised feelings.

It didn't.

Angus needed burying. Poor Angus. He'd died as he'd lived. Alone among his sheep. Her father hadn't been the first to have a man on his payroll who preferred to remain anonymous but it was so very sad that she didn't have more than his Christian name to put on his marker.

Hearing of his death had been a shock. She'd always hoped to reach him. To hear his reasons for being so secretive. Now that would never happen. She would mourn the emptiness that had existed between them. Lost opportunities to love were always the saddest.

"I have to get back to Adara. Raul and Consuela left, which means the place is deserted," she said when she realized the two women had fallen silent and were staring at her.

"You can't go back there alone," Farrah insisted.

"Of course I can. I can't let the place and the remainder of the flock go unwatched. And I have to find out about Scout. I can't believe I forgot to look for him. Dylan would have told me if he'd found him dead, wouldn't he?"

"Of course he would," Elizabeth said and squeezed her hand. "And you'll go *nowhere* tonight, young lady. Especially not to look for a dog."

Scout might only be a dog to most folks but he was her only family. If she'd been at Adara instead of that darn dance, he'd have been safe at her side in the cave. She should have looked for him earlier but the wanton destruction of her parents' dream had stunned her. She'd gone numb all the way

to her core, unable to break through what felt like a wall. It had been as if someone had locked her inside her head. It was still nearly as frightening as the all-encompassing effect the raid would have on her life.

Now all her anger, fear of the future and desperation about Scout—emotions she should have felt earlier—came rushing to the fore. This time Rhia sat straighter, determined to fight back. She rose. "The don doesn't want me here. I have to leave."

"Do you think I let that man rule me?" Farrah's mother said, conviction in her tone. "This is my home as well as his. I want you here. He'll welcome you to our breakfast table in the morning or he'll sleep in his study for a week. On his very short settee!"

Hardly noticing Farrah's chuckle, Rhia protested, "But Adara—"

Elizabeth Varga took her hand. "Let Dylan handle Adara tonight. I'll make sure he plans to go back and that at least one of our men goes along to see to your flock." She gave Rhia's hand a little squeeze. "Think. You cannot go there alone with my son for propriety's sake. It's bad enough he took you to town with him to inform the sheriff. And Farrah may not travel along as a chaperone. It's too dangerous and I won't have you all at risk. These Ghost Warriors could be watching."

They could be. All right, she would stay. Rhia sat down with a sigh and got a pat on the shoulder as a reward. It actually felt good to be pampered. It was the first time in years she had been. Rhia took an instant to savor the moment. Foggily she recalled Dylan caring for her earlier. Had he really called her *querida*? Or had it been hopeful, desperate thinking on her part?

"Farrah, find your brother," she heard Elizabeth say, "and remind him Scout is missing."

But at that moment a triumphant bark echoed through the house. Popping to her feet, Rhia smiled. "Scout." Toenails rapidly clicked up the stairs and along the hall toward her. In seconds she was on her knees, wrapping her arms around the exuberant dog. "You're all right! They didn't hurt you or take you." She took his head in her hands and looked into his golden eyes. "I was so worried."

She heard a masculine chuckle as Scout licked her face and neck. Dylan stood in the doorway, a slight smile curving his beautifully sculpted lips. "I see he found you. I'm sorry I didn't think to look for him earlier. He must have followed us all the way to town and then here. I'm heading back to Adara. The don is lending me two men to help out. But he won't have a dog in his hacienda. Suppose I take Scout along with me?"

"You can take us both."

"No, he won't," Elizabeth said. "I've told you why. Go on with you, Dylan. And, son, good for you for storming in when you arrived. Did you manage to fix anything between you and your father?"

Dylan's lips thinned as he shook his head. "Let's go, Scout."

Rhia signaled Scout to go with Dylan. Scout protested with a high-pitched whine and a sloppy tongue lick on her cheek. She shook her head. "Go on, buddy. Go with Dylan." With his head down and a last wistful look over his furry shoulder, Scout followed Dylan close on his heels.

The next morning finally dawned with light creeping across the ceiling. Rhia had been staring at it for hours. If she'd slept at all, it had been in tiny snatches. Dylan's mother had meant well but Rhia's thoughts had bounced from problems to losses to Dylan and back to problems, losses and Dylan throughout the night.

Exhausted, she admitted to herself she would probably

sell Adara if not for the deathbed promise she'd made to her father. Having sworn to make his dream of success come to fruition, she had no choice but to plod ahead. Which meant she would now have a lot of unexpected expenses to deal with just to make the house habitable again.

Joshua Wheaton was a fair banker and would no doubt let her take out a mortgage on the free and clear property but that didn't sit well. One more setback like this one and she could lose it all if a bank held title and she found herself unable to make the payments.

To avoid that, she'd have to use credit at businesses around town to replace some of what had been destroyed. If she owed a little here and there and couldn't pay it back right away, she wouldn't lose Adara.

Rhia pushed herself out of bed. Her body felt leaden as she put on the dress she'd worn to the social, having no idea where her usual clothes were at that moment. She went down to eat at the table in the courtyard where the family took many of their meals. The don made his usual bid to buy Adara for much less than it was worth. Even though exhausted with the day barely begun, Rhia needed to stand on her own feet. Having lost her appetite, she asked to borrow a wagon so she could go into town to try to hire a shepherd. The don lent her an old wagon and she left for town.

During the ride, she tried to steel herself for the inevitable. Unless she found and hired a man of Angus's advanced age, there was bound to be talk. With the help of the Ghost Warriors, she may have traded invisibility for notoriety in one short night. Never in her life had she so regretted a decision as she did buying the blue dress and going to the social.

Her emotions felt like a fish just pulled from a stream, flopping back and forth, leaving her unable to decide how or what she felt. She tied up the wagon at the town square, blink-

ing away useless tears. Used to invisibility, she couldn't help notice the attention she drew as she walked along the pathway.

Straightening her shoulders, Rhia moved across the square to the posting board. She tacked up her notice for a shepherd, distressed that no one had posted as a job seeker.

She decided to walk over to Abby's General Store and leave the ancient, badly sprung wagon at the square. Once again she noticed folks watching her. But then she heard two women talking and could have sworn they'd used her name before realizing she was behind them. One of them glanced back and, looking a little shamefaced, grabbed her friend and pulled her to the side. But then, as if some silent communication went between the two, they put their noses in the air and stepped back even farther, holding their dresses aside lest their hems brush Rhia's as she passed. Perplexed, she walked on.

Between the square and the bank, three different men who'd partnered her the night before stopped her, voicing varying degrees of concern for her welfare and reputation. Others stopped her, too. The topics ranged from invitations for meals at the hotel to outright insulting proposals of marriage without even the meal. All the men had two things in common—they all had plans for Adara that were contrary to hers and they mentioned they were all willing to overlook her having been seen alone with Dylan in town the night before. To a man, they assured they didn't think anything untoward had happened but it felt to Rhia as if they were trying to push her down the aisle by offering to rescue her from shame. She turned them all down, of course. And explained to each one in the most reasonable tone she could muster that Adara had been raided and that she'd needed Dylan's help to summon the sheriff and his gun in case the raiders were still around.

Not only was it all infuriating, but the haunting fact was
that the only man she was interested in walking down an aisle
toward was Dylan. And he persisted in seeing her as a sister,
no matter that he'd professed to want to get to know her better and had later called her *querida*.

"Miss Oliver," George Bentley called as he rushed toward
her from the side door of the bank. In seconds he'd blocked
her way on the boardwalk. "You simply must have tea with
Mother and me. She has a reputation for strict adherence to
propriety. It would make my day and go a long way to tam-
ing these preposterous rumors."

She frowned. They must all know about the raid and about
Angus's murder. None of them knew she and Angus hadn't
been close. That she wouldn't be deeply grief-stricken by
his death. How could they be so thoughtless? She stepped
to the side.

"I'm sorry, Mr. Bentley," she said. "This isn't a good time."
As she tried to pass him, he took hold of her arm.

"Because of your losses? I understand. Any rancher would
be upset at your business setbacks but your reputation is more
important."

"Business setbacks? More important?" She gave him a
long hard look. "A man *died*, Mr. Bentley. Raul and Consuela
could easily have been killed, as well. I lost nearly half my
stock, not to mention that most if not all of the mementoes
I had from my parents are damaged if not utterly destroyed.
I'd advise you to let go of my arm before I'm tempted to push
you into that horse trough behind you."

He let go with an affronted huff and Rhia walked on. She
was about to pass the bank's front doors when Lucien Avery
stepped onto the boardwalk. Avery was a wealthy rancher
with a large spread out near her place. If she wasn't mistaken
he'd danced with her the night before, too. "Good day, Miss

Oliver. I just heard about your terrible misfortune. I wanted to extend my deepest sympathy for your losses."

Finally a man who isn't shockingly callous. "Thank you, sir."

"Have you given much thought to your future in town with all this talk? I imagine you'll want to move on. After all, Don Alejandro will never allow his son to marry so far beneath his station even if the two of them aren't on the best of terms. I'll be happy to purchase your property to facilitate your departure."

Rhia fisted her hands. "I'm not interested in—"

"Now, now. Don't be too hasty," he cajoled. "You haven't heard my offer. I'll give you ten percent over the highest offer you get from anyone else."

"You'll have to look elsewhere for more water for your cattle, Mr. Avery. My parents are buried on that land. Adara isn't for sale. And I don't give a hoot in hell what the don thinks of me. Never have. Never will. Excuse me."

He stepped in front of her as Mr. Bentley had. "If your reputation doesn't concern you, you should at least think about how lucky you were not to be a casualty last night. You could be as dead as your shepherd is right now. This is a dangerous time for a young woman alone."

She stared at him. Concern? Or threat? She couldn't tell so she forced a smile. "I'm tougher than I look," she told him and this time he stepped aside.

By the time she'd reached the sanctuary of Abby's store, Rhia had sworn off men entirely and off the women of the town as potential friends, too. Tierra del Verde had changed more than she'd thought.

Chapter Six

Hell-bent-for-leather, Dylan rode into town with his sister. An hour earlier, Farrah had torn onto Adara shouting as if the hounds of hell were on her heels. Rhia had left for town unescorted. What she thought she'd accomplish there was anyone's guess.

Since he wasn't happy that Farrah was out riding around alone, either, he'd let her ride along rather than take the time to take her home as he had the night before.

They reined in their mounts and jumped to the ground next to Belleza's old supply wagon where it stood tied to the hitching post near the town square. But Rhia was nowhere to be seen.

Mr. Johnson hailed them. He was the town's undertaker and barber and the worst gossip around. He said he'd seen Rhia tack something up in the square. Dylan went to look and found her advertisement for a shepherd. When Dylan got back to Farrah, Johnson was telling her that quite a few men had stopped Rhia to talk and she'd seemed upset by whatever they'd said.

After that Dylan walked his gelding, Rory, along the street

on one side, checking in shops, looking down alleys. Farrah did the same thing on the other side.

Joshua Wheaton stepped out of the bank and said something to Farrah, then walked across the street toward Dylan. His sister followed in Josh's wake.

"Can I assume you thundered into town looking for Miss Oliver?" he asked.

"She rode in from Belleza alone," Dylan explained. "Did you see her?"

Josh nodded. "I saw Lucien Avery stop her just outside the bank. She seemed upset by something he said then she hurried over to my wife's store."

"When Papa offered to buy her out at breakfast she got really upset. Maybe Mr. Avery offered, too," Farrah ventured.

Dylan frowned. Dammit. What was wrong with their father? Had he no compassion at all?

Josh frowned, too. He also looked thoughtful. "I was going over to Abby's store, to make sure everything is all right," he said, "but Miss Oliver may need a friend."

"I'd better go check on her," his sister said. "Don't take too long to calm down, brother mine. She isn't likely to stay put for long and you wanted to keep her away from Adara." Farrah mounted and wheeled her mare off toward the general store.

Dylan narrowed his eyes in thought. "I'd love to know what Avery said to upset her," he muttered.

Wheaton raised an eyebrow. "I'd guess your sister is right. He probably offered to buy her out. Or he could have mentioned the gossip that's circulating. Maybe both."

Dylan tethered his mount to the hitching rail and looked at Josh. "What gossip?" he asked.

"Someone saw her in town last night with you. And the news spread like a wildfire. I had to go over to the saloon to

talk to Walther about his mortgage on the Garter. Even the men in there were talking about her. And not in a good way."

"Dammit. For crying out loud. Was I supposed to leave her alone out there to contend with the dead?" Dylan gritted his teeth. Why hadn't he taken the time to leave her with his family before he headed into town? He had to fix this. He turned toward Abby's General Store and Josh fell into step beside him.

"I'd never dishonor Rhia in any way. People should learn not to say anything if they can't say something good."

Josh gave a sharp nodded. "I know. But she left the social with you and hours later, she came riding into town still in your company."

"Came riding in after we discovered her place torn up and her shepherd dead. Pardon me all to hell if I wasn't thinking about anything but getting Quinn and Kane out there and not leaving her there alone."

"I know. You wanted to protect her but you did the opposite. Folks are adding two and two and coming up with five or six. Eastern mores are moving west. Wagging tongues aren't going to be stilled easily. Maybe you should think about marrying her. Just last month you were grousing that the women coming in on the stage were either bound for the Garter or looking for a big ranch owner."

"I meant I'd be looking in a year or two and I didn't like how things were going," Dylan protested. "I'm not ready for marriage. I haven't saved enough to buy a place."

"She wouldn't be opposed to working by your side, building Adara into a fine horse ranch."

"Yes, she would. Rhia's dead set on seeing her father's dreams of a successful sheep ranch realized. And you know how I feel about sheep. I don't want my kids teased and tortured the way I was."

"Well, my friend, I have to tell you, she won't live this down alone."

His mother was going to skin him alive for putting Rhia in this position. He was ready to skin himself. Where had his penchant for careful planning gone last night? "Am I supposed to give up my dreams because of a few thought-less decisions?"

"Maybe it would just be a dream postponed. There's some more land out by her place available. You could do there what you wanted to do at Belleza. And at least you care about her. From what I heard over at the Garter, there will be other of-fers coming but not good ones. If you don't help get her out of this, she's going to wind up ostracized or with someone who not only doesn't care about her but who doesn't respect her or her dreams."

Josh was right. This wasn't about him, was it? He'd always wanted only good things for Rhia, even when he'd thought she was peculiar, because she was one of the kindest people he'd ever met. And now, through his carelessness, her chance to be courted properly by one of the respectable men who'd partnered her last night was ruined. She deserved better than people treating her poorly.

Rhia's fixation on raising sheep aside, last night he'd been sorry her emergence as an attractive woman hadn't fit into his timing and plans. He'd even been annoyed with all the men partnering her. Because, dammit, even though he wasn't ready to take on a wife, he'd wanted her. That waltz he'd in-sisted on had proven that to him.

So timing aside, there was only one course of action. He'd have to offer to marry her. There didn't seem to be any way around it. Feeling a bit like a condemned man and conversely like the luckiest yahoo in town, Dylan looked at Josh.

And Josh grimaced. "Take a little advice. Give Miss Oli-ver a choice even though neither of you has one. But make

no mistake, you've got to talk her around to seeing this as the only way it can be."

Dylan sighed. He knew Rhia. She was going to dig in her heels and dare anyone to criticize her. But he knew how cruel people could be. They would indeed condemn her. His thoughts somersaulted more than his stomach as he strode toward Abby's store.

How in hell was he was supposed to talk Rhia into marrying him when he was so ambivalent about marrying her? He wanted her. Sure. But he wouldn't lie. It was attraction. Lust. He certainly didn't love her nor did he want to. He'd seen the heartache his mother's love for his father had caused her. All he could claim was that he cared about Rhia's welfare and that he wanted her physically. If she rejected him, he didn't know how he'd keep her safe from the circling vultures.

He winced. If she said yes to his proposal, he would become a sheepherder after all. *Madre de dios!* He glanced up and wondered if the One the priests called *Lamb* of God was up there laughing at him.

Probably.

Chapter Seven

"Farrah, try to understand. I have to go home." Rhia put down the now empty teacup. Abby had promised tea would make her feel better. It hadn't. Because there she sat in Abby's back room, wondering how many times she'd have to repeat the same thing. This time she added what they both knew to be true but had never acknowledged. "Your father doesn't want me at Belleza. You know he doesn't. And he never has. He thinks I'm beneath him and therefore beneath you. Now he'll hear all this talk and be sure of it. He'll say my being there will sully your reputation by association."

"Since when do you care what my father thinks?"

"Normally I might go back to Belleza just to watch him stiffen up when I get too close. But I'm not that strong right now."

"Why don't you stay with us?" Abby offered as she walked in from the front of the store where she'd been taking care of a customer.

Embarrassed that she appeared to be so needy, Rhia shook her head. "Thanks, Abby, but I promised my father I'd take care of the ranch. Town is too far from Adara. Besides, I've had all I can take of town people for a while."

"Then you have to stay with us at Belleza, at least until you can hire replacements. You can't be out there alone," Farrah said again.

"That could take weeks," Rhia argued. "After word of Angus's death gets around, I doubt anyone from these parts will hire on with me. That means sending a letter or a wire to San Antonio to advertise in the *Express*. In the meantime, I can't leave my mother's home all torn up and open to varmints—the four- *or* two-legged kind."

The bell over the front door jingled another arrival. Abby sighed. "Why did everyone in town have to pick today to need something?"

"They're probably coming in the hope of getting a glimpse of the fallen woman," Rhia sneered.

"Where is everyone?" Dylan called out.

Abby stood and pointed at Rhia. "You stay put," she ordered and rushed out to the shop. "We're back here having a bit of tea."

"We? Please tell me that includes Farrah and Rhia," he said, worry rife in his tone.

Farrah frowned and said, "He sounds upset, doesn't he? I'd better go see what's wrong."

"Maybe he heard his name linked with mine," Rhia grumbled. Before they'd found Adara raided, he'd seemed to regret everything he'd said to her all evening. After, he'd started talking to her like a big brother.

Farrah rolled her eyes and went into the store.

Which left Rhia to ponder her options. Was her name really so ruined that life would become more difficult for her or was it just a few—well, all right, several—small-minded citizens without enough to occupy themselves? And as far as going home, at least there she wouldn't have to deal with unearned scorn. Besides, would she really be in that much danger at Adara? Was there any reason to think they'd be back?

She should just go ask Dylan what he thought. She needn't mention the talk in town today. She doubted anyone would really repeat any of those things to him. They'd all be too cowardly. So he'd never know.

Unfortunately she didn't have the energy to even stand much less walk out to the other room. Instead she propped her chin on the heel of her hand and closed her eyes. What was wrong with her? She couldn't let any of this defeat her. Her problem was that both of these trials had come upon her within hours of each other.

No, she wouldn't let it get to her this way. Rhia started to push herself to her feet to go ask Dylan's opinion but he stepped into the room. Rhia settled back into the chair.

He seemed to fill the room with his essence. Shrink it. "Rough morning?" he asked, tilting his head just a little. His every gesture was so familiar. So dear.

"There weren't any postings up in the square for shepherd work or really anyone looking for a job. Farrah tells me you buried Angus. Thank you. I'll visit his grave as soon as I get home."

His eyes locked with hers. "Thanks aren't necessary. I'll show you the grave. You'll miss him even though he was..."

She managed to chuckle. "Grumpy. Cantankerous. Difficult."

"Well, yeah. But he was a constant in your life and the last one left who started the place with your father."

She swallowed. "I know, which is why I—"

"I need you to listen to me," he interrupted, settling in the chair across from her at the small table. Then oddly he fell silent which seemed strange, as he'd wanted her to listen. Had he heard what they were all saying? God, she prayed not. Dylan leaned his elbows on the table and clasped his hands lightly. "You're in a bad position right now. I wanted to help. I never meant to make it worse but apparently I have."

"Then you've heard."

"What? You thought I wouldn't? It's about me, too, you know."

"But it isn't really your problem."

"You think I can let my thoughtlessness ruin your life and do nothing?"

"Dylan, I come into town once a month. Stop at Abby's for supplies and leave. I'll just come to the back door for a while—"

"No back doors. You did nothing to be ashamed of. I'm the one who has to fix this and there's only one way I can." He took a deep breath, reached a hand toward her, only to let it fall back to the table. "I want you to marry me."

She could hardly catch her breath for the pain. How could the six words she'd longed to hear falling from his lips hurt so badly? All because he didn't love her. He couldn't even look at her.

He was being forced by circumstance.

By gossip.

By his own chivalrous nature.

Rhia started to shake her head but he stopped her by raising a staying hand. "Wait," he ordered, "hear me out. Adara would remain yours to run as you see fit. I'd never take that from you. I just want to protect you and your reputation. You can't hide what everyone saw last night. That horse has left the barn."

Her response, full of resentment, burst from her lips unbidden. "You never even *saw* me before last night." And, as it was too late to take back the accusation, she went further. What the heck! *In for a penny, in for a pound,* Daddy always said. "Don't pretend you'd be sitting there if I hadn't looked so different last night."

He blinked. "You're mad that I didn't see through your disguise? Not my fault you did such a good job all these years.

But you showed up looking like you do with your hair done up all pretty. It changed everything. They all see you as a woman. A lady."

"A lady who spent the last two years running her own place. Alone."

"Dressed as a no-account squatter. Then everyone saw you all prettied up and we all realized how many years had gone by. And then came the raid and you were so fragile all of a sudden. It scared me witless. I was so worried about you I didn't think to take you to Belleza before going to town."

She was so busy trying to work out exactly what he'd said and if there was a compliment buried in there somewhere, she nearly missed what he meant. "So you want to marry me to do penance for not thinking like a few mean-spirited people around these parts?"

"You are the stubbornest! There's *plenty* of talk. Not just a few gum-flapping idiots. Josh was in the Garter and heard your name bandied about. *In a saloon, Rhia.* You won't stay a lady in anyone else's eyes with you living out there alone with no husband. Especially not after all that happened last night."

She clenched her hands into fists. "This isn't fair."

"No. It's not. But like Josh says, the town's changing. Growing up. Getting civilized. With that comes rules. *And* gossip. A woman can't break rules, Rhia."

"And because of some Eastern idea of propriety with nothing to do with living in Texas, you think you should marry me?" Stunned, bleeding inside, she managed to add, "You're from nobility. In your father's eyes, I'm the child of a gutter-snipe from London's Seven Dials section and an Irish house-maid from Five Points in New York City. The don would pitch a fit."

Dylan grinned, his golden eyes sparkling. "Now you're just trying to seduce me with a chance to get the don's goat even more than I already do. See, you're the perfect wife for

me." Then he grew serious again. "Women coming west by train don't understand this place. You know what hard work it takes to make a dream rise out of a scrap of land. You're what I want in a wife and in the mother of my children."

"I know I'm not the perfect wife for anyone. You just feel obligated."

That turned him serious again. "Look, I'm not going to pretend what I don't feel. I respect you too much for that. But I'd like to think I measure up in the husband department a little better than the early-morning bunch over at the Garter. And a hell of a lot better than that drifter in there who hasn't taken a bath in a month of Sundays."

He did. And he knew he did. "This isn't fair to *you*." It was she who didn't measure up to what he really wanted. Was there ever anything worse than being only an obligation to the man you love? Of course it wasn't unfair to her. He'd always been her dream lover. She'd lain in bed and hugged her pillow, pretending it was him for so many years, she no longer found it odd to wake still holding on for dear life to a sack of goose feathers.

"*Querida*, life doesn't have to be fair," he whispered, his brown eyes clearly assessing her. "Just *good*. We can be good together. We respect each other. I'd like to think we like each other. Lots of folks don't have that starting out."

"By not fair I meant what if you meet someone you love someday but you're already stuck with me?"

"Not going to happen. I don't want love. It just makes for hurt feelings and broken dreams. I won't pretend I don't want a real marriage but that can wait till you're more used to me as more... As more than a brother."

Brother. There, he'd said it and her heart sank a bit more. She'd never seen him as a brother. That was his feeling he was talking about. A blush heated her face and she looked away but nodded so he wouldn't try to explain further. God,

could this get worse? She *was* ready. She'd been *ready* for years. And he thought she was a *lady*? He clearly wanted one because this was all happening because he thought he needed to save her reputation. If he'd thought she wasn't a lady, he'd never have offered marriage. He'd have laughed at the gossip.

"I'll send one of the don's men for that piece of garbage he lent you. I'll see the livery readies your buckboard. Farrah can ride with you and I'll follow," he said. "Maybe on the way, you could talk to her. Or maybe wait and talk to Mama."

Would this never stop getting worse?

She found herself asking the very same thing of Farrah on the ride back to Belleza.

"But it's wonderful. We'd be sisters!" Farrah exclaimed.

"How can you not understand? He. Doesn't. Love. Me," Rhia said between her teeth. Then she slapped the reins so hard against the horse's hide they took off in a jerking dash. She had to saw back on the reins and use the brake to slow them down again.

Farrah laughed. "He will soon then. How could he not?"

"Before last night I hid who I was. Now he sees me as more than I am—as a lady—and he still doesn't love me."

"More than you are? You are a lady. Being a lady is about more than pretty manners, lovely dresses and fancy hairdos. Or the right ancestors before you add that. It's about purity and goodness and kindness—all qualities you have in abundance."

Rhia huffed out a breath. "But he doesn't even *want* to love me. He said he doesn't want love. Oh, and he can wait for a *real* marriage till I get used to him as more than a brother so forget him being attracted to me."

Farrah sighed. Took a breath then said, "That was nice of him, wasn't it?"

"I never thought of him as a brother. That's his feelings for me so forget any passion on his part. I'd settle for a little

passion, hoping love would follow no matter what he says he wants or doesn't. But I may as well *be* his sister for all the desire he feels."

Farrah squeezed Rhia's hand over the ribbon of leather threaded through her fingers. "He'd probably shoot me for saying this but he didn't take his eyes off you all last night."

"Probably the same protective way he watched you."

"He didn't even glance my way. He didn't forget I was there, he practically forgot anyone else was. I may not want to attract a man but I know what it looks like."

"Oh…" Now that changed things a little. Maybe he truly had been talking about her feelings.

"But what about your father? I can't let Dylan make things worse on my account. He'll never get back in your father's good graces if we marry. I said as much to him but Dylan made a joke of it. Like he's happy not in the don's good graces."

"Don't confuse my father with yours. They're as far apart as the East is from the West. Dylan's only concern at Belleza is Mama and me. You can't live your life to suit anyone but you, Rhia. That isn't what this is really about. I know you love my brother and have for years. Ask yourself this—how will you feel when he marries someone else and you're all alone on Adara?"

Rhia closed her eyes. "I already have thought of that. Angus would seem cheerful compared with the shrew I'd become. But it still hurts not to have love returned. And to hear it said so plainly as he did."

"I've seen every day of my life how much that hurts. Dylan feels as he does because of Mama. Our father swept Mama off her feet but what he loved was her dowry. What Dylan doesn't understand is that he's half in love with you already. He just doesn't recognize it because he has no idea what love looks like. You know more about love than anyone I know.

Opposites are supposed to be perfect for each other. You two are. You can teach him about love. So are you going to accept or not?"

Rhia mentally asked herself again. Could she watch Dylan marry someone else, knowing he could have been hers? The answer was still the same. Defeated, she sighed. "I guess I only have one other question. Considering that your father already doesn't talk to Dylan unless he's forced, what do we do about arranging a wedding?"

Farrah grinned. "We leave that up to my mother and Dylan. Our job will be to make sure you outdo the dress you're wearing. I'm going to enjoy seeing my brother finally happy."

From your lips to God's ears, Rhia thought.

Chapter Eight

Rhia brought the wagon to a stop in front of Belleza's hacienda and Dylan rode around them to the hitching post. Quickly tying Rory off, he hurried over to help the women down. And nearly stopped dead in his tracks.

Women. They really are *women.*

In the last day his world had shifted. The *girls* he'd waited for last night had suddenly grown up in his mind. How had he failed to notice the years passing in their lives yet remain aware of his own age?

Reaching up, he grasped Rhia around her slim waist and lifted her to the ground. It was a near thing but he resisted the urge to pull her against him and let her slide along his body. If he'd lost that battle, she'd know what a struggle it would be to give her the time he'd promised.

If indeed she consented to marriage at all. What woman wanted a shotgun wedding when they'd done nothing to deserve it?

Farrah cleared her throat, having jumped down on her own while he'd stared down at Rhia. "I'll go get Mama," she said. When he glanced at her, she wore a knowing grin and winked before spinning away.

They must have talked about his proposal. He covered his latent desire with a teasing grin. "Got an answer for me, Rowdy?"

She nodded. Opened her mouth to speak but not much by way of sound came out. She cleared her throat. "On one condition." She seemed to force the words out. "Promise you won't let Belleza swallow up Adara. I promised my father I'd make it a success for him. I promised, Dylan."

"I'd sooner cut off my right arm than be in league with my father." He didn't add that he'd rather try to herd chickens than go back to tending sheep but he couldn't provide for her safety at Adara if he spent his days working miles away at the Rocking R. She needed his gun as well as his name. "Adara is yours," he said and added, "you have my solemn promise." Somehow he'd save enough money to add land and horses and see that his part of the operation grew so their children wouldn't suffer the way he had.

"I'm willing to accept your proposal but with one more condition. I run Adara. I might want to bounce ideas off you but the decisions will be mine."

"I already told you the operation is yours. I'm man enough to take orders from a woman." He hoped he hadn't sounded as gloomy as he felt. He'd be working sheep again. *Damn.*

His tone must have sounded okay to her because she looked up at him with such gratitude and caring in her eyes it took his breath away. He leaned forward, drawn to her by that expression, intent on the sweet experience of their first kiss. Her pretty cornflower eyes drifted closed, her thick sooty lashes the perfect foil to her porcelain-doll complexion. He'd brought his lips within an inch of hers when his father's strident voice jerked them out of the moment.

"Dylan! I demand to know what you told that upstart sheriff!"

Dylan stepped back and turned toward the hacienda as

the don stalked around the corner with Farrah tripping behind him.

"Why?" he asked. Sheriff Quinn and Kane, the Texas Ranger now assigned the area, had both spent a couple of hours at Adara looking at tracks, the wounds on the dead animals and helping him bury Angus. Just as Dylan had thought, there were things about each of the recent raids that didn't add up to Comanche being involved. The Hernandezes' survival made no sense. Day or night, no one hid from the Comanche.

Instead of pushing Dylan further and probably knowing it was a waste of breath, the don glared at Rhia. "What about you?" he demanded.

Before Dylan could object to the don's disrespectful tone, Rhia said, "I barely spoke to him."

She seemed unsurprised by his father's treatment—used to it in fact. Which could only mean the don always treated her this way.

Dylan's anger grew. "Don't take that tone with Rhia. It isn't a way to talk to any woman, especially not your future daughter-in-law," he added, waiting for the explosion Rhia had predicted. Now he understood why she knew he'd object.

The don's face darkened even more. "You cannot—"

"Watch it!" Dylan snapped. "I *can* and *will* be more than proud to take her as my wife and it'll be as soon as I can arrange it. As I said last night, this is America. We're all equal no matter where our parents came from." He flicked a look from his father's eyes to his feet and back up again. "And thank God we aren't judged by *who* they are, either. That isn't a position I'd ever want to be in considering how rude you are."

Farrah jumped in then clearly trying to once again be the peacemaker. "Papa, Sheriff Quinn probably heard you'd offered to buy Rhia out from Joshua Wheaton. I mentioned you'd made Rhia another offer this morning. I saw the sheriff

ride into town but he stopped to talk to Mr. Wheaton. Then the sheriff turned around and rode out again. I guess to come here. Dylan, I'll go tell Mama your happy news."

"So this is why the Anglo sheriff questions *me*? *Me*, Don Alejandro Alvaro Varga. Do I look like a Comanche? A thief? A murderer?"

Dylan coolly pretended to study his father then shrugged nonchalantly. "Better be more careful what land you try to buy, *Don Alejandro*, especially from raid victims. It could be misconstrued." Since he'd promised not to tip Quinn and Kane's hand, Dylan turned away to watch his mother rush from the hacienda. For her sake, Farrah's and his own he prayed his father wasn't involved in the deepening mystery about who was behind these raids. They would all be so ashamed if the don was responsible.

His mother wore a wide smile, obviously thrilled with their marriage plans, clearly unaware of the don's mood. Remembering the shadows of destruction at Rhia's place, he extracted a promise from Rhia that she would remain with his family and not attempt to return to Adara. In turn, he promised to keep watch over the place, couching his request in a need to maintain the greatest measure of propriety before the wedding.

Ignoring the don, his mother scolded Dylan again for his carelessness last night and instructed him to make arrangements for a wedding in a week or two. Then she bundled Rhia and Farrah inside as the don was getting all set for another tirade. Dylan ignored him and mounted up but he glanced back as Rhia entered the hacienda. A worried feeling stole over his soul. He felt as if he'd left a prize foal with one hoof poised over a snake den.

That feeling, while unsettling, gave him hope for the future. As he'd told her, many happy marriages had begun with

less than they had between them. He had always cared about her so protecting her with his name already began to feel less like a life sentence. He went whole minutes without a spirit of doom settling over him. It was a doom that always stemmed from business concerns. He truly was attracted to this new Rhia who'd emerged at the social. He'd only tried to step back because of bad timing financially and Rhia's plan to keep Adara a sheep ranch.

Worries and recriminations were a waste of time and energy. He had no real choice. He'd made a huge blunder by taking her into town with him and now he had to fix it. Still, life might turn out pretty good eventually. Just not like he'd planned. He sighed and prepared to get on with arranging a wedding for as soon as possible not in a week or two as his mother suggested. He wanted Rhia away from his father.

Dylan encountered Father Santiago on the road as the priest was leaving town. He'd been called to another of the missions he served to perform the last rites and probably a funeral mass for the same person. From there he'd go on to make his regular rounds. Though he sympathized with Dylan's reason for speed, commended him for facing his responsibility and even agreed to skip reading the banns, he could do no more to speed things along. He'd be back in time to marry them the following week on Friday or Saturday.

Dylan rode to the Rocking R to draw his last pay from Alex then rode back to Adara, to assess the damage and make a list of supplies. Once there he stood in the midst of the wanton destruction, grateful he had a week to make repairs before Rhia saw the destruction in the light of day. As the list grew, Dylan's hope of buying the land to the east dimmed. Every pane of glass was broken, the furniture, the doors, the dishes. The list went on. And on.

As he picked up the broken pieces of Rhia's world, he re-

membered something. Rhia always referred to the sweet little house as her mother's. She always referred to the surrounding land that made up the enterprise portion of Adara as her father's. But they'd both been gone for some time.

So why was no piece of this place Rhia's?

Not the broken dishes, the dented pots, or even the faded curtains that had been torn asunder had changed from the days his mother used to take him and Farrah for visits. There was no trace of Rhia anywhere.

He picked up the broken pieces of a teapot to toss them into the waste bin but he stopped, remembering the first time he'd met Rhiannon Oliver. It had been his eleventh birthday and her sixth.

His mother had urged them into the carriage for a ride to welcome Henry Oliver's wife and daughter to the area. Henry Oliver had come ahead to build a house for his family then he'd sent for them.

His mother had brought a pie along that day. Dylan had felt so grown up having been given the job of keeping the treat safely balanced in his lap all the way there. That sunny day Mrs. Oliver had greeted them with a broad welcoming smile, inviting them into the little house to share the pie and a cup of tea.

From that very pot—the pieces of which lay in his hands.

He, Farrah and Rhia had become fast friends after that day as had Theresa Oliver and his mother. For six years they'd repeated the ritual, especially on that day of the year, until Mrs. Oliver died in childbirth along with her baby when Rhia was twelve.

Dylan sighed and wrote "glue" on his list for town so he could mix up a batch and fix the teapot. He only hoped he could put the shards of Rhia's life back together as easily. And that his own life didn't wind up as full of unwanted feelings as he felt at that moment.

* * *

Dylan paced to the window of San Rafael's tiny sacristy then turned back toward where his groomsmen sat slouched nonchalantly in their chairs. He, Josh Wheaton and Alex Reynolds all wore nearly identical black suits but his friends wore nearly identical grins. Amused by his nervousness.

In truth, he hadn't had time to even think about the wedding his mother had insisted upon because he'd been working so hard trying to put Adara's homestead back together. Or as back together as his savings had allowed.

They only had a plate apiece and a few dented tin cups and bowls. But the walls were painted on the inside as were the clapboards outside, along with the doors and window trim. Abby had made curtains and cushion covers for the chairs as a wedding gift.

Dylan raked a hand through his hair then tried to loosen his collar a bit. He'd thought he'd settled himself about the marriage so his nervousness was a surprise. He'd barely had time to sleep. He probably wouldn't sleep tonight, either.

Tonight, Dylan repeated to himself. That's what had him nearly jumping out of his skin. If she even smiled at him, he wasn't sure he'd be able to keep his hands off her. And a broken promise was no way to begin their marriage.

Chapter Nine

Rhia stood in Abby's bedroom looking into the mirror at the stranger staring back at her. The white silk gown was so beautiful it made her eyes flood with tears. She fingered the delicate lace that formed the high neck of the gown.

And it truly sank in. She covered her mouth, blinking away tears. Rhiannon Oliver, the girl who eight days earlier had arrived at the Varga hacienda in britches to dress for the spring social, was about to marry the man of her dreams.

Farrah's mother had insisted on buying the dress—a betrothal gift, in memory of Rhia's mother, who couldn't be there.

So how could I refuse?

She turned to the side, admiring the way the straight princess front belled out a tad in back then fell into a train trimmed in flounces of Brussels lace. Cuffs of matching lace fell to her wrists from the middle of her forearm. Her veil was made of light net and lace and was attached to silk flowers.

"Beautiful," Farrah whispered behind her, her tone almost reverent. "Dylan isn't going to see another person in that church once he catches sight of you."

Rhia whirled, her heart leaping with joy. "Oh, you came. I was so afraid your father wouldn't let you."

"I told you we'd be here. Mama went to see Dylan at the mission."

Rhia could see Farrah looked worried behind her smile. "Your father didn't come."

"Don't let that bother you," Farrah said. "It won't upset Dylan."

Rhia sighed. "I didn't want to be responsible for widening the rift between them."

"Mama's wrong, *hermana*. That rift is a canyon. And you aren't responsible. Papa is."

Through gathering tears, Rhia smiled at being called sister by her best friend. "I'm so sad for Dylan. I always knew Daddy loved me."

"Dylan will have *your* love, now. It'll be enough."

"He told me outright he doesn't want love in this marriage. I don't think he believes in it."

"He believes it exists. But you're going to have to love Dylan until he knows he can trust in it. He already trusts in you."

She'd loved Dylan for years already. That wasn't about to change. She would give him all the love and time he needed. She'd need patience. "I can do that," she promised, praying she wouldn't have to wait too long.

"Don't you look just like the picture?" Abby said from the doorway, her green eyes sparkling, her smile wide and pleased.

"The dress is gorgeous," Farrah said. "My brother will be awestruck."

Abby laughed. "And isn't that what a special gown for a woman's wedding is supposed to be all about? I've been waiting for a special bride to wear this one from the day I saw it in the catalog."

Rhia turned and rushed to give Abby a hug. "I don't know how to thank you. Or how to repay you for all your kindness."

Abby blinked away the mist of tears. "I'm grateful for this week at your side as I doubt I'll ever have a daughter to fuss over." She swirled into the room, letting out a watery laugh. She and Farrah both wore the kind of full-skirted dress Western women favored. Abby's was emerald and Farrah's was sapphire.

"And don't we look wonderful in *our* new dresses, Miss Farrah?"

Farrah gazed at herself in the mirror and crossed her arms. "Just so we're clear. I wore this for your sake, Rhiannon Oliver."

Abby rolled her eyes at Rhia and laughed. "So, we're all set?" she asked. "My brother has the carriage all hitched and ready to take us to the church."

Rhia took a deep breath. "I'm as ready as I'm gonna get."

"Stop," Farrah shouted. "I nearly forgot. Mama says you have to have…ahem…something old, something new, something borrowed, something blue and sixpence in your shoe," she recited in one breath. "It's for luck." She dug into her reticule and pulled out a tarnished coin. "Mama kept this sixpence from her wedding. And since it's old and borrowed and your dress is new all you need now is something blue."

Abby chuckled. "And I have that for you in the hall. From Dylan. It came with a note." She rushed out then back in with a bouquet of flowers tied with a blue satin bow. "I added the blue and a bit of arrangin'. He is a man and therefore ham-handed," she teased.

The flowers were wonderful and bright. Wildflowers every one. Rhia's hands shook as she opened the note.

Rowdy,
I felt pretty terrible this morning because all I have to

give is a ring to show my esteem. Then, as I headed for
town, I noticed Adara is in full bloom.

The daisies made me think of how small and delicate
you look but how strong I know you are. The bluebonnets remind me of your eyes when they darken up because you're riled. Then I noticed a few Indian blankets
scattered around. I didn't think they matched the others
but I remembered an old-timer called them fire wheels.
Fiery. That's you past riled all the way to furious. I'll
try to avoid that. I promise. Last time you tried to bean
me with my own baseball. Remember?

I hope having these will be a little like having a small
part of your parents with you. I also hope this wedding
with all the trimmings makes up for how mean some
people were to you.

Deepest regards,
DV

Rhia blinked away tears that had gathered as she'd read.
Esteem. Regards. She prayed that would be enough if his love
never came her way. She clutched her beautiful bouquet and
prayed for patience all the way to San Rafael's.

When she got there and peeked into the sanctuary there
were more of the same flowers on the altar and she found she
could smile again. How many flowers had Dylan picked? He
must have denuded every meadow on Adara! And he *must*
care. He must care *a lot*.

How far behind could love be?

A few minutes later Rhia stood alone in the nave still
clutching her precious bouquet, watching Abby and Farrah
walk down the aisle of the sanctuary ahead of her. The pews
were full of people who'd watched her grow and had lent their
support through the last week. And there were the newcomers
from the East who hadn't known her. They'd turned a trag-

edy into a scandal and because of them Dylan was about to sign away his life and she her heart.

Just as despair nearly swamped her again, the strains of the same music she and Dylan had waltzed to floated from the balcony overhead. It was the same group of men from last week's Spring Social. Dylan's doing, she was sure.

She saw him then, stepping in front of Father Santiago up by the altar. He held his hand out. But, standing there with no support, she couldn't seem to take that first step. Clutching her flowers, her connection to her parents, she took one step toward Dylan and their uncertain future.

Maybe he realized how hard it was for her to be alone right then because he walked up the aisle toward her.

They met halfway.

It was late afternoon when she and Dylan rolled to a stop at the top of the hill overlooking the heart of Adara. The Wheatons had hosted a late-morning breakfast at their house for everyone who'd attended the ceremony. Mr. Reiman over at the hotel had even sent over a fancy cake as a gift. They'd put what was left of it and their other gifts in the back of the fancy rig Josh and Abby insisted they use. Because Scout and cake were a bad combination, she'd left him behind for a day or two with the Wheatons. Dylan would get Scout when he returned the rig.

"Close your eyes, Mrs. Varga," Dylan purred into her ear, making her shiver. Making her want.

Then apprehension spread through her. It was time to return to reality. Rhia closed her eyes with a silent sigh. This was near where she'd waited while Dylan investigated the silence that had shrouded Adara. She didn't really want to look at the house anyway. She knew destruction lay below.

As he started the rig downhill, Rhia found herself dreading the first sight of her mother's house. Though her memory

of that night was foggy, she'd seen the debris in the shadows. Her father had been so proud of the sweet little house he'd built for his beloved wife.

Trying to brace for destruction, she imagined the windows boarded-up, maybe the door fixed but scarred. Dylan was only one man after all. That he'd tried was all that mattered.

"Hoah!" Dylan called and the horse stopped. The seat shifted, telling her he'd scrambled down. Then he took her hand from below. "Keep 'em closed and stand up so I can get you down."

She stood, wobbling a bit. "Dylan Varga, I feel like I'm six years old again and you're torturing me with blindman's bluff."

He took her by her waist and, laughing, lifted her down as if she were still that tiny girl. "Oh, *querida*, you are no longer a mere girl." His voice, so close and deep, made her open her eyelids in the next instant. Then as his lips moved toward hers, she let her suddenly heavy eyelids drift closed. This kiss, unlike that first chaste one he'd given her in church, had her stomach flipping and her toes curling. Like the other kiss, this one ended too quickly. Dylan jumped back so suddenly it left her teetering. "Open your eyes!" he said abruptly.

Startled, reeling with confusion, bereft of him, she opened them and stared at him. She didn't understand him at all. Especially not his strained grin when he gestured toward the house.

She looked then, and blinked in shock. It didn't look like her mother's house. Not anymore. But it gleamed.

"I hope you like it. All the paint is Patience and Alex's wedding gift."

The previously dull, whitewashed clapboards were painted the color of buttermilk. All the trim, the shutters, and front door—the *new* front door—were bright white.

"I know it looks different," he said, "but—"

"It's beautiful," she interrupted sure by his tone he was worried. "How on earth did you do all this?"

"I had some help. Josh and Alex pitched in a couple of days. Then Abby's brother Brendan Kane came out and it turns out a Texas Ranger can be an able carpenter. A few cowboys from the Rocking R spent some hours here, too. Everyone felt awful about the raid and the gossips in town."

He paused then, as if nervous. It was the first time she'd considered him unsure of anything. Then he said, "Oh, and I hired Juan away from my father. Juan was sick of being screamed at and belittled, so we have a shepherd who's also good with horses. He cleaned up the Hernandezes' cabin and moved in. He took care of the livestock and the dogs leaving me free to work on your house. Our house now."

"Still, this was a lot of work. I could have helped. It wasn't necessary for you to work so hard on your own."

He grimaced. "Yeah. It was. There was a lot of damage, Rhia, and I didn't want those memories to linger. We have to look forward. It doesn't matter what put us here. We need to do our best with the lot we've been dealt."

She hated that she was the lot he'd been dealt while she'd gotten her fondest wish. Some men would have been in a vindictive frame of mind, put her to work on the mess and brooded. But, though Dylan hadn't wanted this marriage, he wanted to make the best of it. She still felt guilty that Dylan had given up his job, his freedom and further infuriated his father. All for a life he'd never have chosen freely.

Dylan led her to the front porch where he'd even added some of the pretty fretwork Abby had on her house. "Ready?" he asked, turning back to her after opening the door.

She nodded bracing herself for all the damage he hadn't had time to fix inside. She took a deep fortifying breath then it came out in a long squeal when he swept her off her feet. "What are you doing?"

He laughed and she felt the sound rumble through his chest. His golden-honey eyes danced with mischievous delight when he smiled down at her. "Have to do this. Mama made me promise not to let evil spirits pester you."

"I never knew your mother was so superstitious. First that 'old, new, borrowed and blue' rhyme. Now this. That coin they made me put in my shoe has given me a blister. You'd better not drop me, Dylan Varga."

He laughed as they cleared the doorway, then he bent to set her on her feet in the front room. She looked around. The board and batten interior walls were freshly painted in the same buttery color as the outside. The seat cushions of the sofa had new cotton duck covers. The curtains had been replaced with the same color gingham and there were matching seat cushions on two new rockers positioned across from the sofa.

"Where did the chairs come from?"

"Brendan Kane made them. They're a wedding gift."

She blinked against tears stinging the back of her eyes. "I hardly know him. Everyone's been so kind. Well, not everyone, but this goes a long way toward making up for what those townsfolk said, doesn't it?"

"To my way of thinking, it does," Dylan said. "Brendan promised to help me build new tables for the parlor when this raiding calms down."

The little front room looked wonderful but over the smell of fresh paint she noticed the faint odor of kerosene. "I guess the lamps broke," she said and looked down. The rag rug her mother had made just before she'd died was missing.

"I soaped up and rinsed the rug but it's still airing out on the corral fence."

She bit her lip, nodded and looked toward the kitchen. It, too, was clean as a whistle but there used to be six chairs and now there were only two. She walked to the kitchen and

braced her hands on the backrest of one of the ladder-back chairs. The shelves were mostly empty of dishes and bowls. But in the center of the table sat her mother's sunny-yellow teapot with a little bouquet of daisies and bluebonnets in it. The teapot had been lovingly glued back together. She sighed and ran her fingertip across a flower petal.

Dylan had tried so hard. She forced a smile. "Thank you," she whispered but her voice broke.

He was there in a heartbeat, his arm around her shoulder. "I glued it and put a tin can inside so at least it could be a vase. The flowers…it was the strangest thing. Yesterday there wasn't a bloom to be picked and this morning the whole meadow was wild with color."

"I guess Adara wanted me to have a pretty wedding bouquet and flowers at the church. Thank you for listening to her."

"Her?"

"Mum teased Daddy that Adara was her rival for his affection. But it was just a tease. After she was gone, I used to hear him cry in his room at night. At least now they're together."

"I put a bunch of their things that were torn up and broken in the barn. I thought you should get to decide what to keep and what to say goodbye to. There are enough unbroken pieces for me to put two more chairs together."

Rhia nodded, looked up at him and smiled. "I'll look over all of it soon but it's okay. You're right, it's time to build new memories—a new life."

He blinked and let go of her, stepping back in the same moment. "Uh…right." His eyes widened. "Oh, the bedrooms. I forgot them." He raked a hand though his thick black hair. "I took the smaller one. I'll put your things in the bigger room. That reminds me, I should unhitch the wagon and check with Juan. And bring everything in, too." Then in a blink he was gone.

He'd all but *run* from her at the mere mention of the bed-rooms. She'd told herself she could handle his subtle rejection. They were still only friends. Not even partners. Maybe she shouldn't have told him she would make all the business decisions. Maybe she should have shared some of the burden of the place.

Maybe when she trusted his methods with the sheep more and when he trusted her heart more, they'd be more to each other. Then they'd share burdens and their love. She had to be patient.

But with his indifference standing right there where he had a moment before, the loneliness she'd been battling for such a long time seemed to swallow her whole.

She'd been stuck miles away from town, working day and night, hardly seeing anyone except the silent Hernandezes and occasionally Farrah. Now, when she finally had some-one to share her life with, he'd jumped away like she was a rattler about to strike.

Drained after so many ups and then one last, huge, down-hill slide into despair, she stumbled into the place that had always brought her solace. Her parents' room. She'd hoped that through some miracle it had gone untouched. But the bed was all that remained. Not even her mother's quilt had survived. She'd watched her mother piece it together back in Philadelphia while they'd waited to travel to Texas.

Tears came in a torrent then and she threw herself across the bed. She wept for all that was gone. For the years alone. For all the lonely, loveless years that seemed to lie ahead.

Oh, God, what have I done?

A hand pressed on her back and rubbed. "Shh," she heard over the sound of her own anguish. "Rowdy, stop. They were just things. We'll get new ones as soon as we can afford to."

She rolled over, going from anguish to anger in half a heartbeat. "Things? You think I'd cry over *things*?" She

screamed out her pain. "It's not their things but what they represented. My parents. People who loved me. Now even those are gone."

"I'm sorry."

She couldn't stop. She had to tell someone, tell *him* what was buried in her heart. What she'd never let herself admit even to herself. "Do you have any idea how alone I've been? Angus growled at me or ignored me. Raul just took orders. Consuela said it would be too hard to move on if we became friends. I'd come in from the field and she would tell me what she'd made for dinner and had done in the house, then she'd rush off to their cottage. This last week was the first meal I ate with anyone except Scout in two years. We're going to have to teach him to eat off the floor again because I took to putting his bowl on the table. At least that way there was a pair of eyes looking at me."

Rhia sat up. Dylan's eyes, his lips were mere inches away. "It's like the center of me is empty. I feel so…so hollow."

"Oh, Rowdy," he whispered and cupped her cheek, then spanned those terribly lonely inches in a blink and covered her lips with his. His firm, roving mouth on hers started to fill some of those empty places inside her.

But not all. "Fill me," she whispered against his lips when she felt him start to pull away. "Fill me up so I know I'm not alone anymore."

Chapter Ten

Dylan did the only thing he could think of in response to her pain. He kissed her. Gently. As innocently as his raging need for her would allow.

But those tortured words in her hoarse, anguished voice echoed in his head, threatening his tentative control. He lifted his head and stared into her tear-filled eyes. Those tears shimmered, reflecting luminescent blue in the sunlight that flooded the room.

Then she said, "Fill me. Fill me up so I know I'm not alone anymore."

And all his good intentions about taking it slow and waiting for the physical part of their marriage flew right out that brand-new window next to the bed. He reached for her. Tunneling his fingers into her fancy wedding hairdo, he dropped his head again, unable to resist taking her sweet lips now that those words had fallen from them. He should say something but didn't trust himself to utter even a word. He hoped she understood what it was she'd asked for. A man couldn't resist starting the rest of his life in the face of this much temptation.

And so he took her mouth with his, more forcefully this time, parting her lips, swirling his tongue past them, revel-

ing in her sweet taste. He dragged one hand out of her hair, fingers of the other still tangled in her curls. He caressed her cheek and neck with his knuckles using a featherlight touch. His hand shook as he fought for control. Or was that her quaking?

Dylan hadn't any idea. Lost in the feel and taste of her, he no longer knew where she ended and he began. He slid his fingers gently, lightly, over her neck and lower, over the soft slippery silk of her dress. It was wondrous yet torturous because he knew her skin would feel so much better. Then he cupped her breast and knew it was his hand shaking.

Her gasp when he fondled the lush globe nearly drove him mad with desire. He rolled her nipple between his index finger and his thumb, earning a sensual moan and himself a gnawing ache he had to wait to assuage.

She moaned again, fisting her hands in his hair, and threw her head back. "Fill me," she begged again, breaking his heart with her need for a connection to another person. He'd never realized before today how alone she'd been. He was grateful she'd turned to him for the warmth and affection she needed.

Grateful he would be the one to teach her about passion.

His control on the thinnest of tethers now, he pulled back and looked into her eyes. The blue had darkened to the color of the paintbrush that bloomed all over Adara's meadows.

"No," she sobbed, "you can't stop. I need more. I need *you*. I need to belong to you. I need you to belong to me."

He groaned against her neck. And just like that, everything he'd sworn to keep in check bubbled up, spilled out.

Set him on fire.

For his little wildflower.

"I need you, too, Rowdy girl," he gasped. "But we have to get you out of that pretty contraption you're wearing." Before he turned savage and tore her beautiful gown, he urged her off the bed to stand between his thighs. He started working at

the satin buttons running down her back but his hands shook enough to make him fumble. He cursed roundly, earning him a muffled giggle.

He took a deep breath, trying to settle down before he sent tiny buttons flying everywhere. What kind of cruel person had designed this means of torturing bridegrooms? Ought to be staked to an anthill, that was for sure.

Finally, after a few tries, the first button gave up the battle and fell open. Then another. He got the knack after that. But he was on fire, his erection was so hard it was practically screaming for freedom. By the time he'd bared her to her waist, undid the hook of her crinoline and untied the damn tiny drawstring of her pantaloons, his whole body thrummed. His need was so strong it scared him. Thank God his tiny new wife didn't have one of those corset contraptions on.

Maybe he should run for the hills but now that he'd gone this far there'd be no stopping. Running for the hills sure didn't make any sense to the rest of him. He couldn't remember why he'd said they should wait. Stupid idea. He needed her more than he needed to listen to reasons that no longer mattered.

Not with her shivering. Quaking. Calling his name.

And not with her whole beautiful back from neck to her cute round bottom bared. Not with her right there for his taking. Unable to resist the call of all that creamy skin, he nibbled his way from her nape all the way across the sharp planes of her shoulders and listened with pure satisfaction to the sweet music of her gasps and moans.

Nope. He wasn't going anywhere but right there with her.

Needing to see her, all of her, he stood and ran his hands down her arm taking all that silk and lace along for the ride. In seconds the dress, crinolines and drawers were in a pool at her feet and all she wore was her shoes and stockings. She turned in the circle of his arms, and he looked his fill of her

curvaceous, compact body. The best things—the very best things—really did come in small packages.

A blush stole everywhere his eyes roved. She tried to look him in the eyes but looked down then sucked a shocked little breath. He guessed she'd caught sight of his erection, straining for freedom. Then the little torturer of his youth—not about to play a passive part—reached out and ran her knuckles over him.

He cursed.

She giggled.

Then biting her lip, her expression a little uncertain, her breath coming out in little pants, she went to work on the buttons of his trousers. He stood there rooted to the floor, panting like a stallion scenting a mare. But when he sprang free into her hand, he spit out another curse, scooped her up and lowered her to the mattress in the space it took for his next breath.

He'd planned to take off her shoes and undress himself but then he caught sight of her hot gaze on him and followed her down instead. Kissing those swollen lips couldn't wait. Neither could trailing his mouth down to her pert nipples.

He braced himself on one forearm and cradled her breast in his palm then drew her taut nipple into his mouth. Soon he moved on to the other as she raked her fingers through his hair, then kneaded the taut muscles of his arms. He'd never felt anything like having her hands on him as she panted with growing excitement.

Nearly at the end of his tether, he ran his hand downward, exploring the firm skin of her hips and belly until he came to her nest of black curls and found her center—wet and ready.

She shouted his name, trembling under his fingers and pulling at his shirt, running her small hands up his ribs and over his back. She seemed to be urging him on. He stood that. He did. He even helped her get his shirt off. But the sensu-

ous feel of her silky skin against his and her cry of "Closer. Please, closer" in a low raspy voice completely undid him.

After that every thought but the most primitive fled. He shoved his pants farther down on his hips and pushed her knees apart with his. He entered her as carefully as he could but her gasp this time was of shock and pain, not glory.

As if doused by cold water, he froze, managing to ignore his own need in favor of hers. He kissed the tears that flooded her eyes, letting their personal history take over. "That full up enough for you?" he teased.

She gifted him with a watery chuckle. "A…a little too, I think."

"No," he soothed. "It'll get better, wildflower," he whispered against her lips, "give it some time. You tell me when you're ready for more." He closed his eyes reaching for a memory to help him keep that promise.

Just like that, he was back there on the spring day he'd taught her to swim in Adara's clear cool lake. Looked like he was teaching her something new this spring, too. "You'll see, wildflower. I'll see it gets real good real, real soon. That's no brag, I promise."

"And you never break a promise. Right?" She moved under him a bit as if testing the waters.

It was a point of honor for him. He never did.

He kept this promise, too. It got a lot better for her and him. Right after he kissed her again and carefully moved in her. She let out a beautiful little gasp. It was full of delicious joy followed by a tiny shriek, hot with need. His own need flooded back with a vengeance. He wanted to race for the end but forced himself into a slow rhythm. He felt the surprising strength in her when she wrapped her arms around him and in the undulating motion of her body as she caught his rhythm. It took him by surprise when she started to shudder and quake under him, around him. He'd never felt such unbridled hap-

piness knowing he'd brought her such pleasure. Needing to watch her face as she came apart for him, he braced himself and arched his back to look down into her beautiful face. And then he had to follow her or die.

And if he had, it would have been with his boots on.

Chapter Eleven

Rhia threw her arm over her eyes, trying to block out the sunlight and cling to her dream—she and Dylan making sweet love. Though she was desperate not to lose the dream, it started to fade as her sleepy senses pushed past the fog that dulled her mind.

There was sunlight on her face. She usually woke to the subdued light of dawn. She frowned. The sun rose on the other side of the house. Curiosity drove her ahead, willing her to face the day.

She opened her eyes and stared up at the ceiling. This was her parents' room. An ache registered in her muscles. Muscles she'd swear she'd never used before. It hadn't been a dream. She slid a hand across to where Dylan had slept. He wasn't there but still, it all flooded back.

Dylan. The wedding. His kindness. Everything that had led to him trying to comfort her.

Her love for him and her own need to belong to someone had welled up from some deep place inside her, overwhelming her pride. He'd made love to her but didn't love her. She blinked back welling tears. Her pain was no excuse. She'd agreed to the terms of his proposal. As he had to hers.

So, instead of finding a way to thank him for his rescue from her uncertain circumstances and scorn, for relinquishing his chance to ever find a woman he could love the way she loved him, she'd thrown herself at him—begged him. Which made her no better than a soiled dove at the Garter, trying to earn a dollar.

Remembering the way he'd made love to her and the number of times he'd turned to her in the night, she thought sadly that Dylan was a passionate man. Which only meant she'd tempted him beyond endurance. She wasn't foolish enough to think his passion had anything to do with feelings for her.

Her face heated. How was she going to face him? Abby had tried to fill in her spotty knowledge of the human mating ritual but she hadn't told her a thing about the awkwardness she'd feel the next day.

She imagined Dylan had let her sleep as yet another kindness. Rhia shook her head. Though the idea of hiding in there with the door bolted held real appeal, it was time to do what she'd always done—put one foot in front of the other. She rose to face the day.

There were eggs to collect, sheep to be sheared and probably fences to check. She washed, dressed in her same old baggy work clothes, and felt the sharp pang of hunger before she remembered she no longer had a cook.

That stopped her in her tracks. Had Dylan thought she'd be the kind of wife who could cook? Sew? Knit? If so, he was in for a rude awakening. After her mother died, Rhia had lost count of the meals she'd burned. She'd get it all going just fine, then her mind would skip to the ranch work that needed doing. She'd follow that thread of a thought on into deeds and forget about the kitchen until smoke leaked from the house. Which was why her father had always hired a shepherd with a wife to cook for them.

Spying the leftover cake from their wedding, Rhia cut a big

hunk, and ate it on the way to the shearing shed. She noticed Dylan's mare, Annie, in the corral and stopped to give her a quick pet. Then she chatted with Juan about where they stood in the shearing and some of the load lifted from her shoulders. Dylan had thought to shear, and skin the sheep she'd lost to the raiders, which would recoup some of her losses.

Grabbing her shears, she got right to work on a ewe she pulled from the holding pen. Shearing time was measured by the number of sheep handled, not by the clock. She and Juan worked in silence but for the din of the bleating sheep.

Fifty ewes later, Rhia's arms and back ached as she caught a particularly stubborn sheep and finally rolled it over to rest against her knee. "Why are you fighting me?" she crooned as she started clipping its belly. "Don't you know how hot you'd be in a few weeks if we don't get this done?"

"She's probably just hoping to make your life even more miserable than it already is with this job to do," Dylan said from behind her.

Startled, feeling at a distinct disadvantage bent over a recalcitrant sheep the way she was and still dreading facing him, she lashed out, "I wasn't aware my life was all that miserable. I'm sorry if you feel I've dragged you into a pit of misery."

"I didn't say that exactly but I had hoped after yesterday I'd seen the last of the no-account drifter." He nodded toward her clothes. It sounded as if he was teasing but she couldn't help thinking there was more than a grain of truth to what he said.

Which meant she was doomed. How was she supposed to keep her promise to her father and look like the person she'd been last week? She couldn't.

Rhia stared at Dylan over the struggling sheep. She'd been raised to respect hard work as the path to success and security. She hadn't been raised to care how she looked or to sit

around being waited on. In other words, she wasn't a lady like Dylan's mother.

Too bad! He'd said he didn't want that. Apparently he'd been wrong. She guessed she wasn't the only one having emotional revelations suddenly crop up the way her loneliness had.

He'd been determined to rescue her. He'd said the perfect wife for him had to know what it meant to put in a hard day's work. That's what he'd gotten.

All he'd gotten.

Distracted, the shears slipped in her palm. She dropped the sheep before she hurt it and rounded on Dylan in a pure fury. "Now that tears it!" she shouted and heard a door at the other end open then shut. Juan had fled. Smart man.

"I look like a no-account drifter? Suppose you go over to the Rocking R and herd cattle wearing a dress. Or pick up a pair of sheers here with your skirts tangling in a ewe's hooves, then tell me how your day went."

Dylan took a breath. "Look. I'm sorry for the remark about your clothes. It just drives me crazy to know you wore that getup to hide and that you're still hiding. I want more for you than that. But the truth is, we need you to help with the shearing to get to market before my father drives prices down because of the volume he'll have for sale. I rode over there. He hasn't started shearing. I'm sorry I hurt your feelings."

She nodded. "What exactly did you mean by calling my life miserable? Do you see this marriage as having dragged you into misery?"

Dylan's eyes widened and he raked his fingers through his hair. "You don't know what the don and I fought about, do you?"

"You call him *the don*," she said, her tone sarcastic as she planted her hands on her hips. "That pretty well says it.

I figured you two had another battle and he ordered you off Belleza. So you went to work for the Rocking R."

She could see anger build in his eyes as he shook his head. "You have it backward. He disowned me because I went to work on the Rocking R. And I did that because I hate sheep and anything to do with them. They're smelly and stupid and cause trouble wherever they're raised."

Rhia could feel the blood draining from her face. Who was this man she'd married? Did she know him at all?

Apparently not.

She put a hand in the middle of his chest and pushed him back out the shed door. "Get off my place, now. You set me up when you took me to town the night of the raid. It got you ahead of all those others in town who lined up to court me all of a sudden. Which means you didn't marry me to save me from disgrace. You planned to take over here so you could bring cattle here. You want to destroy my parents' dream."

Eyes narrowed, lips thin, Dylan took a vibrating breath. Then another. "You're wrong, Rhia. You don't know what it's like to grow up being tormented for being the son of a sheepherder. They just left you alone 'cause you were a girl and you were rarely in town.

"You talk about your parents' dream. Well, I had one, too. I gave it up to try to help you make their dream and yours come true. But I wanted more for me and eventually my wife and children than the stigma cattle ranchers tack on to those who run woolies. The town's growing. Changing. Look at the gossip over you and me going in to report the raid. There's a school now. I wanted my kids to be able to go there and not get tripped in the street or not get pushed in the mud because of how their father earns a living. I'd think any woman would want the same for her children.

"As for me leaving Adara, we consummated this marriage,

Mrs. Varga. And you asked for it. So I guess you're stuck with me." He turned and stormed away.

Oh, God. What have I done?

"Dylan," she called but it came out as barely a squeak. Her breath, her anger, and all the starch drained right out of her along with her ability to stand. Numb, she slid downward, the outside wall of the shed at her back. She hugged her knees. "Dylan," she whispered.

Too drained to even cry, she just sat. And tried to think. Was she sorry for Dylan or herself? Had she betrayed her parents by loving Dylan? Or had Dylan betrayed her?

She didn't know.

She didn't know anything anymore. So she sat there and watched the breeze stir the leaves on the big elm overhead. And thought of nothing—nothing at all.

Not much time could have passed when she felt Dylan crouched down in front of her. "Rowdy, honey, I'm sorry." He touched her arm.

She lifted her head and stared into his earnest golden eyes.

"Despite my feelings about raising sheep, you're the boss of this outfit and it's your dream we'll work toward. And what I said about last night was plain unforgivable. But I hope you'll forgive me anyway. Last night was special." He smiled. "I hope for both of us."

She nodded and tried to smile back. How could she hold back forgiveness when everything she'd done since she'd seen that darn blue dress had trapped him in a life he clearly hated?

"Thanks," he said quietly.

"Your dream, Dylan. What was your dream?" Her voice sounded so thin and reedy it shocked her.

"I wanted to breed horses. That's what Annie was all about. She'd throw gorgeous foals. Alex has a stallion he was going to let me breed to her. I'm good with horses. I could train them and if I cut some of the ones with good lines out of

wild herds, I might be able to breed in mustang endurance. With horse racing getting more and more popular, I think I could do really well."

"Maybe someday we could buy more land. I've been trying to save for some. I'm sorry, Adara isn't big enough for both right now, but maybe someday," she said.

He nodded but there was a deep sadness in his eyes he tried and failed to hide. "Enough of that. Let me see that hand."

She blinked. "Hand?"

"There's blood on my shirt from when you pushed me out of the shed. You must have cut your hand or you have some mean blisters. Now let me see your hand."

Her hand did sting some.

She put her palm up and he spit out a curse. "It's both. Let's get you up to the house and get this looked after."

He was so sweet and gentle. He took care of her hand but then he got all polite and stiff, his eyes still sad. He excused himself. He had things to think about, he said. Then he made her promise not to go back to shearing. Next thing she knew he was out the door. And she was alone.

Not knowing what to do, she figured she'd try to cook dinner. Since she was supposed to stay in the house, maybe she could keep from burning it to a cinder.

It wasn't easy with her hand all bandaged but she had the stove going and a stew on to simmer within an hour. At loose ends in the sparkling-clean house, she went to make up the bed and blushed at the evidence of last night's activity. She stripped the sheets, grateful for the new ones the Presbyterian minister and his wife gave them as a wedding gift.

As she tucked in the blankets, she wondered about the damage to her mama's pretty quilt. Yesterday Dylan said he'd put the damaged things in the tack room of the barn. That was something she could do with herself.

In the barn she stopped to pet Jessie's velvety old nose.

Dylan's mare, Annie, trumpeted for attention and Rhia went to the stall and stroked her neck and cheek. "You really are a beauty."

With a deep, defeated sigh, Rhia left the stalls and headed for the tack room. She found the quilt right off and was relieved she had enough skill with a needle to fix it. Mum had kept swatches of their old clothes Rhia could use to make repairs. They were in a yellow wooden box Daddy built. Mum had been going to make a quilt for the baby. Then they'd both been gone. Now Daddy was gone, too.

It wasn't hard to find the bright yellow box. The lid was crushed and broken. She lifted the pieces with care and laid them aside in the hope that Dylan could glue it the way he had the teapot.

She smiled at the memory of the wildflowers he'd had waiting for her on the table. In her bouquet. On the altar at the church. Dylan had made their wedding day special even when she was the last woman he'd have chosen to marry.

Feeling sad already, she got even more so as she looked through the swatches, remembering the clothes they'd come from. Her dresses. Her mother's. Her father's shirts. At the bottom of the pile lay a letter addressed to her grandparents in New York. They were both gone, too.

She frowned down at the envelope and ran her fingertips over her mother's handwriting. Curious, Rhia opened it. The date explained why it had never been posted. Mum had written it the day before her death.

In it she talked about Adara and the reasons they'd decided on raising sheep. It wasn't for any great love of them. Her mother confessed to not liking them a bit. She called them smelly and stupid.

Rhia fought a smile. Dylan's exact words.

Her parents had picked sheep because it was easier to build a herd. Required fewer men. And there were the drives north

with cattle on long dangerous trails they'd considered and rejected. It hadn't mattered to them what made Adara a success, as long as they gave their children a good future.

Rhia closed her eyes, she'd been so wrong.

Then a thought occurred to her and she knew exactly what she intended to do about it. Their birthdays were tomorrow.

The only question left was could she do it on time?

Chapter Twelve

Dylan sat staring at the lake. It spread out before him, so still it perfectly reflected the trees surrounding it. They remained the bright green only seen in spring.

Spring.

Supposedly the season of promise. Of renewal. Of life. Not destruction, heartache and pain.

If only he'd kept his mouth shut. Rhia hadn't needed to learn about his hatred of raising sheep or his reasons for it. She had so many worries with the uncertainty of starting a life together. Clearly a lot of men had made their true interest in her clear in town last week. They'd all wanted her land. It made sense that she'd read the motives of those men into his actions toward her.

So she'd lashed out in anger.

He frowned and looked down at the stone in his hand, then hurled it into the lake. No, she'd been feeling more than just anger. Hurt had added teeth to it. He'd never seen her strike out in anger at anyone, even as a child. He rubbed his hand over his chest where she'd shoved him backward out of the shed.

It surprised him that he could read her so well sometimes

and not at all the rest. Like he'd understood she was hurt as well as angry but not why. He got to his feet, unable to sit while his thoughts had him so churned up. He stared at the lake and shoved his hands in his pockets. Could you wound someone who was indifferent to you? He didn't think so.

He paced to the water's edge. It made no sense. She hadn't responded to his proposal as if she had any feelings for him. It had taken his sister to talk her into the marriage. Even the censure the people in town hadn't been incentive enough. Had his unemotional approach put her off? Could it be she cared about him as more than a friend?

A thrill shot through him at the idea that she might love him. Why that would be, he didn't understand. It wasn't as if he wanted to love her in return. What kind of person did that make him?

Not one he was proud to be. He wasn't a taker. That *wasn't* who he was. Agitated, Dylan started walking along the shore-line needing the motion. The action.

He kicked a stone. He *hated* that he'd hurt her.

Even the act of taking her virginity had made him cringe for her pain. He thought back to the second time he'd made love to her. He'd looked in her eyes and his heart had turned over with wanting for what he'd seen there.

He stopped and blinked. Love was something he'd sworn he'd never want. Yet he did. He wanted hers. He hadn't wanted to love anyone, either. But he must love her. What else could cause this aching need to be with her? To protect her? To make sure she was happy?

He loved her. With all his heart.

What a prize idiot! He'd left his family over sheep but had married her in spite of them. He'd do anything to keep her safe and make her happy. Anything!

He stopped walking, suddenly sick to his stomach. She must feel awful. There were only two things she could give

him as his wife. One—her love—was something he'd said he'd never want. The other—her body—he'd said he could wait for as if he'd been indifferent.

She must think she'd gotten everything with this marriage and he'd gotten nothing. He spun around and started back the way he'd come. He had to tell her. But how? How to let her know and ease the guilt he now understood?

He swallowed. There was only one way to fix this. And that was to show her he loved her above everything. He had to do it. She had to know nothing was more important to him than she was.

That only left one question. Could he do it by tomorrow and give her the best birthday gift possible? The gift of knowing how much he loved the woman she was.

He arrived back at the house and found only the scent of burning food. A pot sat on the hot stove untended. Burning. He grabbed a hot pad and ran it outside then went back in to open all the windows.

Where the hell was she? "Rowdy?" he called.

No answer.

He checked the bedroom thinking maybe she was tuckered out from the hard morning she'd put in. Nothing made your back hurt more than a day shearing woolies. But Rhia was nowhere to be found. Which meant she was working. With those hands!

He stomped out to the shed but she wasn't there. While he was there he took a look at her shears. They were in bad shape. It was a wonder she had any unblistered skin left on her poor hand.

He checked the barn next. And heard a scuffing sound in the tack room. Was she never still? He grinned. She had been last night after each time they'd made love. She'd been played-out and satiated, her body pliant. He liked that he could affect her the way nothing else did.

Dylan looked into the tack room and drank in the sight of her sitting on the floor, surrounded by a large pile of ruined goods. She was busy sorting. "Hey there, wildflower. You forget something?"

"I'm not shearing. I came out to see how bad the quilt Mum made was damaged. I think I can fix it. That got me started on going through all this."

"I meant did you forget something at the house?"

She frowned, her forehead wrinkling adorably. "The house? No, I—" Her eyes widened and she dropped whatever it was she'd been looking at. "Oh, my God, dinner." She scurried up and moved toward him and the doorway. "Get out of the way."

He grabbed her around her waist. "It's too late. I'm not sure even the buzzards want whatever was in the pot."

She let her head drop on his shoulder. "Stew. It was stew. I'm the worst wife ever. I didn't make us dinner last night or breakfast this morning and now I burned tonight's dinner."

He kissed her exposed neck. "I liked what I had for dinner last night," he murmured, thinking he could as least hint at how much she'd pleased him in bed. "Let me be the judge of your success as a wife. I think there's some ham in the springhouse. Let's slice it up and make sandwiches then top it off with wedding cake."

"I had cake for breakfast," she confessed.

He chuckled. "So did I. I didn't want to wake you. And cake has milk, eggs, flour. It's really puffy griddle cakes. Right?"

She groaned against his chest. "Stop, Dylan. I still ruined good meat and vegetables. I never told you why we always had a cook after Mum died. I can't cook. If I could remember I was in the middle of cooking, I could probably make a passable meal, but something always steals my attention."

He gave her a little squeeze to reassure her. "How many

women can shear sheep, repair a fence *and* keep a kitchen? It's okay. We'll cook together. I'll make sure you don't get distracted and help with the chopping. I'm good at that. I used to hide from the don in the kitchen. Cook put me to work. We'll be partners inside and you're boss out here. How's that for a deal?"

She nodded. "I'm sorry."

He let go, stepped back and tilted her chin up with a crooked finger. "Stop apologizing. If I'd been the one cooking you'd wish it had burned."

They supped by the lake on thick slabs of bread, ham and more of their wedding cake. When she got cold, he warmed her up until she burned. He muffled her cries with his mouth and gloried in her response. But he didn't tell her how he felt. Not then. Not on the walk back to the house. Or before, during or after they made love again.

He wasn't sure she'd believe words. He wanted to show her. Prove how much she mattered. And by tomorrow afternoon, she'd believe him.

Dylan rose early the next morning and crept from bed as he had the day before. He'd told Rhia he was going to take Annie to the blacksmith in town to cover his real plans. He saddled Rory, put a leader on Annie then headed for the Rocking R. His heart was a mite heavy but he knew he was doing what was right.

He concluded his business with Alex quickly and left for town with a wad of cash on a mission that needed Abby Wheaton's touch. After he'd finished there, he'd hurry back to give his bride her birthday gifts.

Chapter Thirteen

Rhia lay in bed fighting a smile and pretending to sleep as Dylan snuck out of the room on cat feet. As soon as she heard the front door shut, she jumped up, washed and dressed in her pretty blue dress. She grabbed the last of the cake and ran to the barn, to hitch up old Jessie.

She felt lighter than air as she all but danced through the chore. The decision she'd made, the dinner by the lake, the closeness they'd shared afterward, had changed something between them. Or maybe it had just changed something in her.

What did it matter if Dylan never *said* "I love you"? He showed her with more than just passion, though there was plenty of that. He treated her as if she were precious to him. He cared. Deeply. It was in his every action. Words came cheap. It was actions that mattered.

Actions had always been enough between her and her father. He'd shown his love but rarely talked about it, yet she'd been secure in that love. She was going to choose to believe Dylan loved her.

Shortly she'd be dealing with the reason why Dylan didn't understand love. His father.

The cut on her hand burned, protesting her grip on the seat

as she climbed onto the wheel of wagon, then swung into the seat. Once seated, she took up the reins, thankful Jessie was such an easy animal to control. Dylan had been so worried about her hand, he'd made her promise to stay away from the shearing in the shed, another example of the way he cared for her. She smiled. She'd had other plans for her day anyway.

She was off to change Adara's direction. Change the dream to suit a future with Dylan.

A weight lifted from her shoulders even as she stopped in front of Belleza's hacienda, ready to face the don.

Farrah rushed outside. "Happy birthday," her new sister called. "I planned to ride over with gifts later. What on earth are you doing riding around by yourself? Dylan's going to be fit to be tied."

Rhia laughed. "If your father agrees to my proposal, I don't think Dylan'll even think about how it came about." She climbed down with Farrah's help, not yet used to wearing skirts. Rhia eyed her friend's Levi Strauss jeans with envy. Remembering Dylan cupping her bottom last night, Rhia had a feeling he wouldn't cringe if she wore those.

They walked into the inner courtyard. "Papa," Farrah said, "Rhia's here to see you."

The don looked up from his meal, his eyes narrowed. "Have you learned you married a man with no means? If you come to plead his case, you waste your time, *señora*."

"Dylan doesn't need anyone to plead for him." She stood straighter. Prouder. She was through deferring to this old toad. "I've come with a business proposition." She saw Farrah melt into the interior. "I have two hundred and fifty ewes. Twenty yearling rams. And fifteen mature rams. They're good stock. And for sale." She named her price and saw his interest before he schooled his features and tried to bargain her down. When she threatened to sell elsewhere, he capitulated.

She left with thirteen hundred dollars and an escort to the

Rocking R. There, Alex Reynolds listened to her offer to buy the half-Arabian stallion Dylan was so interested in. Clearly confused at first, Alex finally shot her one of his irreverent grins and agreed to her price. She paid him three hundred dollars and he promised to get the balance of her money safely to the bank for her. Then he sent her home with an escort to control the big high-spirited stallion.

Dylan had never even dreamed of owning the stallion and soon he'd be culling the wild mustang herds for mares to breed with him. Dylan would be in business. They might have a few lean years but they'd be together and their children wouldn't be taunted as he had been.

She was thrilled to get home before him. Determined, she stoked the fire in the stove and got out the ingredients for a cake. It came out of the oven without a single singed spot. While it cooled, she made boiled ham, carrots and potatoes. Then she iced the cake and had just set it on the table when she saw Dylan, trotting down the lane. He must've needed to leave the mare with the blacksmith but Scout was with him.

She clasped her hands together and started out the door but stopped and ran back to take the dinner off the stove and set it on the warming shelf. When she stepped outside Scout raced up onto the porch barking his enthusiastic greeting. She ruffled his fur and hugged him while watching Dylan enter the barn. She rushed to the barn and she found Dylan scratching his head and staring into the stall holding Midnight.

"Happy birthday," she said, sneaking up behind him and grabbing his muscular arm.

He whirled around, more than a little confused. "What's he doing…?"

"I changed the dream. To *your* dream. I sold my sheep. To your father. We get to finish this last shearing. We can use the money from that and what's left from the sale of the

flock to build your corrals and fence your paddocks. And I guess build a stable and anything else you need."

He stared at her for a long moment, then he erupted in laughter. She'd expected him to be happy but not to laugh like a crazy man. Next thing she knew, he grabbed her and took them flying into a hefty pile of fresh hay. She screamed as she landed on top of him, then he rolled onto his side, laying her in the fragrant hay. They stared at each other.

"You've been busy, Rowdy. But so have I." He jumped up and rushed to his horse, pulled a roll off the saddle they dug into his saddlebag. He rushed back and sat next to her, handing her a box. "Happy birthday to you."

She opened the box and found a set of new shears. She sputtered a laugh. "Abby'll take them back. I'm sorry if I spoiled your surprise."

He handed her another, much bigger bundle. She untied the cord and delved inside. There were two pairs of the Levi Strauss jeans she'd coveted just that morning and two blouses. There was also a pretty yellow dress. All of which said he understood her. Except… "I thought you'd spent all your savings fixing the house. This isn't on credit, is it?"

He snorted out a laugh. "Nope. I sold Annie to Alex."

Her eyes widened. "That's why he looked so confused. And amused. He could have warned me!"

Dylan chuckled. "Too much fun for him to spoil, I'd guess."

"He'll sell her back, right?"

Dylan nodded then he took her gifts and set them aside, pulled her into his arms and over him as he fell back into the hay. His expression turned serious as he cupped her face with both hands. "I love you, Rhiannon Varga."

She stared. "Did you—? You love me?"

He grinned. "More than life. Hell, more than I hate sheep and that's powerful. I married you in spite of them, didn't I?"

His eyebrows pulled into a V. "You forget something, wild-flower? You love me, don't you?"

It was her turn to grin. "Dylan Varga, I've loved you for what seems like my whole life."

"And I'm going to love you for the rest of mine," he promised and sealed the deal with a long, lingering kiss.

* * * * *

SOMETHING BORROWED, SOMETHING TRUE

Lisa Plumley

Dear Reader,

Thank you for reading "Something Borrowed, Something True"! I'm thrilled to be a part of the *Weddings Under a Western Sky* anthology, and I'm happy to introduce you (or welcome you back) to my favorite Old West town, Morrow Creek! I've written several books set in this cozy Arizona Territory town, and it's always a pleasure to return for a visit.

If you like Nellie and Everett's story and would like to know more about my books, please visit my website at www.lisaplumley.com, where you can read free first-chapter excerpts from all my historical, contemporary and paranormal romances, sign up for my reader newsletter or new book reminder service, catch sneak previews of my upcoming books, request special reader freebies and more.

I'm also on Harlequin.com, Facebook and Twitter, so please "friend" me on the service of your choice. The links are available on www.lisaplumley.com. I hope you'll drop by today!

Lisa Plumley

Chapter One

∽∽∽∽∽

"The first thing necessary to win the heart
of a woman is opportunity."

—Honoré de Balzac

April 1884
Morrow Creek, northern Arizona Territory

When a man couldn't pick out his own blasted fiancée from the crowd of people on a train platform, it was probably time to rethink a few things. Like the way he was living his life. The honorable intentions he clung to. And the damnable, meddlesome *vaqueros* he employed, depended on, and trusted... far too much.

Standing hip deep in confusion at the Morrow Creek train depot, Everett Bannon reckoned this was what he deserved for letting down his guard. He deserved cinders and sparks. He deserved hordes of travelers, cheery train whistles, and puffs of sooty coal smoke. He deserved a mail-order bride—arriving on today's 10:17 train from San Francisco—that he *hadn't* ordered.

The *vaqueros* at his ranch had ordered her. *For him.* Secretly. Giddily. Most of all, inconveniently. Now it was up to Everett to deal with the imminent arrival of one Miss Nellie Trent—and to squash her expectations that they were to be wed.

He hoped she didn't bawl. He couldn't cope with bawling.

Feeling altogether provoked by this unexpected turn of events, Everett paced the length of the depot platform. The springtime sun shone down on him. The morning breeze threatened to steal his hat. Travelers streamed past—but none of them wore the red hat "with a jaunty blue ribbon" that his hypothetical bride-to-be was supposed to be sporting. None of them gazed at him with knitted brows, trying to match his rugged face to his farcical written description. None of them brightened at his approach. None of them seemed hopeful... and therefore vulnerable.

Everett knew all about romantic hopefulness. He wanted no damn part of it. Not anymore. His calamitous experiences with his former ladylove, Miss Abbey O'Neill, had taught him that. He was better off without sentimental mush like loving. And needing. And hoping. So, he reckoned grumpily, was Miss Nellie Trent—wherever she was.

"Patrón!" Casper—one of his interfering ranch hands—clomped his boots in Everett's wake. "Wait! You forgot your armband!"

Turning, Everett was nearly blinded by the hank of blue fabric that Casper foolhardily waved at his face. It was frayed. It was spotted. It stank of saddle leather and stale tobacco.

It could have been worse. It could have been a sock.

Squinting at it, Everett wasn't entirely certain it *wasn't* a sock. It did have a particularly hard-used aspect to it—the same quality that every ranch hand's worldly goods acquired after some time in the bunkhouse. What's worse, Casper

seemed—even more foolhardily—hell-bent on tying it on Everett's arm.

He jerked away. "I'm not wearing that."

Casper blinked in surprise—something Everett should have expected. After all, the lanky boy was the newest, greenest, and—therefore—most reckless of all his ranch hands.

"You *have* to wear a blue armband, *patrón!*" Casper said in a tone of earnest concern. "How else will Miss Trent find you?"

"I'll find her myself." *Then I'll send her away.*

Stubbornly Everett set his jaw in silent confirmation of that plan. That was the reason he'd come to the depot at all. He intended to meet Miss Nellie Trent, explain the mistake his *vaqueros* had made, buy his "fiancée" a return train ticket… and hope she was a reasonable woman who wouldn't kick up too much of a fuss about canceling their impending "wedding."

"Heck, this will help with finding her!" Not the least bit daunted by Everett's refusal to be earmarked for love, Casper fixed the length of blue fabric around his arm. He wrenched a firm knot with a yank of his cowpuncher's fist, all but brimming over with misguided optimism and youthful naïveté. "There. Now you look the way you're s'pposed to look to meet your bride!"

With a saint's forbearance—because Casper was too gullible to know any better, and because the older men had doubtless been the ringleaders in this whole imbroglio, even if they were letting Casper stick out his neck—Everett shook his head. He sighed. "For the twelfth time…I'm *not* getting married."

"I know you're fixin' to send her away, *patrón*. You told us so already this morning." Casper broke off to rub his nose with the heel of his hand, the gesture unaffectedly boyish. He grinned. "If I recall correctly, you told us Miss Trent would be 'back on the train before her feet touched the ground.'"

Everett *had* said that. He'd also said a lot more during this morning's kerfuffle, when the men had revealed their unasked-for matchmaking. In rejecting their scheme, Everett hadn't bothered with mollycoddling. The words *damn fools*, *pack your duffels* and several colorful profanities had been spoken.

"I meant what I said." It was his way. Always had been. "I don't want a wife. I don't need a wife. I won't have a wife."

"You'll change your mind when you see her," Casper alleged with an imprudent grin. "I bet five dollars you would!"

Everett frowned. "You have a bet running? On me *getting married*?"

Casper and his compatriots nodded. Casper did so gleefully. The others… *Hellfire.* They nodded gleefully, too. Everett didn't know what the world was coming to when a man couldn't even trust his own *vaqueros* not to stab him in the back with Cupid's arrow.

Audaciously a few of them had even followed him on horseback along the mountainous road between his sprawling ranch and the town of Morrow Creek. Presently more than half his troublemaking ranch hands loitered between the train tracks and the bustling ticket office—hoping, he knew, to see the spectacle of their hard-nosed *hacendado* being overcome by love.

The odds of that happening were very long indeed. Once, Everett had thought he was a typical Western male: gruff but affable. Now he knew he was not. Despite the longtime admiration of his men, he was…lacking. At least to the *feminine* mind, he was. The day he'd learned that had been one of his worst.

No right-thinking woman wants to live on a hardscrabble ranch with a burly, unrefined oaf for a husband, Everett.

Honestly. Did you think I would settle for this? For you?

Those had been Miss Abbey O'Neill's parting words to

him. The memory of them still stung. Not long after that, she'd absconded from town to elope with Astair Prestell, the famously cultured author, during his whistle-stop speaking tour of the territory.

Although Everett did not miss Miss O'Neill in the way he'd thought he would—unaccountably, he did not miss her at all—he didn't like knowing that he'd turned up wanting. In any arena.

Far better, he'd decided, to give up on "love" for now.

But his men had no compunction about meddling in their *hacendado's* affairs. They'd banded together, contacted a mail-order marriage bureau and written several letters to his "fiancée" on Everett's behalf. He still didn't know exactly what those letters had said—what they'd promised. The possibilities of that concerned him. Who knew what a miscreant bunch of whiskey-swilling, knuckle-dragging *vaqueros* from a half dozen different countries and cultures considered to be "romantic"?

The possibilities made Everett shudder. When Miss Nellie Trent arrived—*if* she arrived—she might be expecting a very peculiar courtship. What sort of woman agreed to that? To *him*?

"Don't look so worried, *patrón*. This is one bet *I* aim to win. *Fácil.*" Smiling at Everett, Pedro patted the pocket where he kept his bankroll, apparently ready to risk everything on the outside chance his boss would find love. Before coming to Morrow Creek, Pedro had been a faro dealer in the southern presidio of Tucson. Swarthy and debonair at almost fifty years old, the man still sported the heavy silver rings that proved his expertise at the gaming table. "Not even you can resist a pretty woman. You won't be able to help yourself. Just like me."

To prove it, Pedro winked at a passing woman wearing a

full-skirted pink dress and carrying a parasol. She blushed. She giggled. Finally she relented and coyly waved at him.

"*Da.* Sooner or later, wedding fever strikes everyone," Ivan opined in his lingering Russian accent, oblivious to the flirtation that Pedro had embarked upon. The hulking blond kept his attention fixed on the gingham-lined basket of baked goods he'd brought along for the trip. Ivan selected a snickerdoodle, then pointed it at Everett for emphasis. "Marybelle and Edina told us so, and they would know." At his mention of the ranch house cook, Ivan appeared momentarily distracted. Then downright dreamy. Then he recalled himself. "This time of year, no man for miles can resist getting hitched. It's springtime wedding fever. That's what Edina said. All you need is a willing bride."

"Which *we* have found for you!" Oscar boasted in his jovial and precise German-accented speech. Keeping a finger hooked in his latest philosophy text—just one in a never-ending series of books that accompanied the dark-haired recent immigrant to roundups, roll calls and every meal the aforementioned Edina served up—Oscar nodded sagely. "A new woman can change things for you, *patrón*. A new woman can cure your broken heart."

Everett didn't want to talk about his "broken heart." Especially not with a ranch hand who'd once quoted poetry to him as an excuse not to tame the latest prize mustang he'd wrangled. Pointedly Everett cast a warning glower in his men's direction.

"The next man who says 'broken heart' will find himself mucking out horse stalls—alone—for a solid month. Understand?"

His *vaqueros* saluted. "Yes, *patrón*. We understand."

They *sounded* suitably contrite. But given the lasting (and incongruous) expressions of schoolgirlish eagerness on their (mostly) grizzled and beard-stippled faces, Everett didn't feel

he'd sufficiently impressed on them the importance of never pulling such a ludicrous stunt again. He crossed his arms for good measure. Then he deepened his frown to a fearsome degree.

"I don't want any more of this matchmaking nonsense. What if I'd already promised myself to some other woman?"

They all sobered. "What other woman?" Ivan demanded, warily clutching his basket of goodies to his midsection. "Not Edina!"

"No, not Edina, *mi amigo*." Pedro shook his head at Ivan's protective feelings toward the cook. "We were very careful about picking out Señorita Trent," he told Everett in a self-assured tone. "No one else will be such a perfect lady for you."

"Auch wenn." Carelessly Oscar shrugged. "That may be true. But our *patrón* does not agree. Perhaps he is too inconsolable to agree." The German gave Everett a long-suffering look. He closed his book—something Oscar rarely did—demonstrating the gravity of their situation. "The agency guaranteed satisfaction. Once you have rejected Fräulein Trent, *patrón*, we can request another—"

"No one is going to *reject* Miss Trent!" Everett blurted.

He couldn't help it. Put that way, it sounded horrible. While he did not consider himself to be especially softhearted *or* softheaded—and he would have had to have been both to agree to this "wedding"—there were lines that even the strongest, toughest, most uncompromising *hacendado* refused to cross.

What he proposed doing with Miss Trent was not a rejection of *her*. It was merely…changing their supposed deal. Unless she refused to accept a return ticket, of course. That was still possible. Then what in tarnation would he do with her?

Why in blazes had his men stuck him in this position?

Aggrieved all over again by their preposterous plan, Everett paced some more. His battered boots clunked along the

platform; his plain work shirt and britches kept him respectably—if not stylishly—clad. He wished he'd uncovered his men's cockamamie scheme earlier. By the time he'd learned of it, it had been too late. His "fiancée" had already been on her way.

"I'm simply going to...return Miss Trent to the city. That's where she belongs. She'll be happier there." *With a citified man like Astair Prestell.* Defensively Everett lifted his chin. "I'm going to thank her for coming, then pay her to leave."

They all gawked at him. "*Pay her? She's not a prostitute!*" Casper sounded indignant. Two bright red spots bloomed on his cheeks, betraying the fact that he'd visited Miss Adelaide's place only once—and then merely to "chat" with one of the girls. "You can't give her money outright like that. It ain't proper."

"A ticket, I mean. I'll pay for a return train ticket." Everett had explained this to them already. "It's the least I can do," he said. "How else am I supposed to get rid of her?"

"Get *rid* of her?" At that, Ivan and Pedro gasped. They traded fretful glances. "*Patrón*, you don't *deserve* her!"

Damnation. Now he'd been judged and found wanting by his men, too! "How do you know that? None of you have met her."

Oscar raised his eyebrows. "We've corresponded," he reminded Everett archly. "Miss Trent has lovely penmanship and exemplary grammar, two fine qualities for a potential wife."

"Lovely penmanship *and* good grammar?" Everett gave them a sardonic, helpless grin. "Well then. I just changed my mind!"

His *vaqueros* weren't amused by his joke.

But that probably didn't matter anyway. At this rate, Everett reckoned the argument was moot—especially after he

swept the assembled travelers with another decisive glance. "She's not here," he announced. "I don't think she's coming."

"She's coming. She paid a fee," Oscar said dourly, "just like we did. I only hope she was not as idealistic as we were."

Everett swiveled. "There was a *fee* involved?"

His *vaqueros* shrugged. A chorus of yeses in a variety of languages rang out. Oscar's was last. "*Ja*. We all contributed." He raised his mournful gaze to Everett's face. "If it brings back your soul to you, *patrón*...then it will be money well spent."

Doubly troubled now, Everett shook his head at them. This was typical of his longtime *vaqueros*. His ranch hands were commendably dedicated and hardworking. They were also much too willing to come together for a "cause" they believed in.

Last year, they'd pooled their salaries to buy new featherbeds for the girls at Miss Adelaide's place. A few months ago, they'd joined forces to run a roughhousing regular from that same cathouse out of town. Weeks ago, they'd decided their lonesome *hacendado* needed a wife...so they'd ordered up one.

Against all reason, Everett didn't want to disappoint them. These men would likely never have wives or weddings themselves; they had already given their hearts to the solitary *vaquero's* life. He understood the loneliness of that life. He understood its compromises. He'd accepted them for himself. But that didn't mean Everett intended to go along with this nonsense.

He didn't have to. He had blue skies, spirited horses, plenty of mescal and all the faro-playing, joke-telling, smoke-a-cigar-in-peace breathing room a man could ever want. He didn't need anything else. No matter what his ranch hands said.

"Well, Miss Trent doesn't rate highly in punctuality," Everett groused, on the verge of abandoning this fool's quest

in favor of enjoying a lager at Jack Murphy's saloon. "You say she's 'pretty' and 'perfect,' but all I see is 'unreliable.'"

Overhearing his words, a female passerby stopped.

Smartly she glanced at Everett.

"That's too bad," she said cheerfully. "Because there are also 'intelligent,' 'intrepid' and 'irresistible' to consider. I have it on very good authority that those attributes apply to Miss Trent as well." Warmheartedly she smiled at him. "Fortunately she's also 'easygoing.' She might be willing to prove it by giving you another try at your description."

Her impish grin called to mind secrets and surprises and unknown wishes granted. It called to mind a woman who was reputedly pretty, perfect and proficient at penmanship and syntax. It called to mind other hasty character assessments that Everett had made...and had lately been proven wrong about.

After all, at one time, he'd believed Miss Abbey O'Neill truly cared about him—and was capable of fidelity, besides. He couldn't have been more wrong.

If he were wise, he'd be more careful this time.

Looking at the woman who'd so boldly approached him, Everett had a jumbled impression of blue eyes, freckled skin and tawny hair. He registered her soot-smudged dress, dark gloves and crumpled red hat. Beneath its blue-ribbon-bedecked crown and woefully bent brim, her face appeared singularly pert and vivacious. Her lips pursed. Her cheeks bloomed. Everett had the unmistakable sense that she had not been exaggerating when she'd called herself intelligent, intrepid...and irresistible.

Was *this* Miss Nellie Trent at last?

His mind whirled. Studying her more closely, Everett no longer heard the metallic squeal of train wheels or the hubbub of conversation. He no longer felt the platform beneath his boots. He no longer sensed his *vaqueros* nearby. He *did*

hear his own heart pounding double-time in his chest. And he *did* feel his body tingle with a curious sense of…anticipation? Eagerness?

Oddly enough, it felt like…recognition. It felt the same as when Everett rode across the foothills after a long time away and spied his hard-won *hacienda* in the distance. It felt *good*.

That made no sense whatsoever. This woman *could* be Miss Nellie Trent. She could also be an impossibly nosy bystander.

Either way, she gazed at him interestedly, oblivious to his bafflement, as though genuinely expecting him to reconsider the various qualities he'd attributed to his unknown "fiancée."

"No? All right, then. Maybe later." Her lively smile dazzled him. "When it comes to hearing my finer qualities enumerated, I am willing to wait just as long as it takes."

Belatedly Everett regained the use of his addled brain. "I see. I don't guess those qualities will include modesty?"

She laughed. "Touché, Mr. Bannon!" Her gaze dropped to the grubby blue band on his arm. "It *is* Mr. Bannon, isn't it?"

"It was when I woke up this morning."

Another peal of laughter. "You *are* delightful!" Shaking her head in apparent wonderment at that, the woman lightly touched his arm. "And here *I* was worried you'd be some fusty old coot."

As she lifted her hand, Everett experienced an inexplicable fondness for the tied-on blue armband that had identified him to her. He never wanted to remove it. "If I was, I reckon you'd be the type of woman to tell me so. Immediately upon meeting me."

"Ah. You mean I'm too forward, don't you?" She tilted her head as though the idea had newly occurred to her. "I see. I'll list that attribute right next to 'unpunctual' in my personal ledger." A brief smile. "Although I'm not usually late.

Today I was unavoidably delayed in meeting you. It won't happen again."

She did not elaborate, and he couldn't ask her to. Despite her blithe tone and merry eyes, Everett couldn't help feeling his comment had bothered her. He wanted urgently to recall it. "It's no trouble. You're probably just tired and hungry," he assured her gruffly. "Train travel can take its toll on anyone."

"All the same…I'll try to do better. I'm *very* interested in this marriage we've arranged, you see." With a winsome smile that would have tempted any man into unwanted matrimony, she extended her gloved hand. "I'm very pleased to meet you, Mr. Bannon. I, of course, am Miss Nellie Trent. Your bride-to-be."

Hopelessly charmed by the bustle-wearing, blue-ribbon-sporting, outspoken force of nature that was his potential "fiancée," Everett took her hand in his. Warmth passed between them, leaving him surprised and shaken. And just like that, Everett realized that his *vaqueros* were right.

He *did* need something more. He needed Nellie Trent.

Chapter Two

"Are my lodgings very far from here?" Nellie asked.

Interestedly she examined the town of Morrow Creek, nestled in the valley beyond the train depot. It was full of lumber-framed buildings and false-fronted shops and at least one two-story hotel. It bustled with people and wagons and the usual horse traffic. To her ever-curious mind, the admittedly minor and fairly typical town of Morrow Creek looked… *thrilling*.

But then, most unexplored situations seemed thrilling to Nellie. That was part of her nature. She loved new places, new things, and new opportunities. She loved challenges and risks. She loved throwing herself into life with zeal and open-mindedness. That was part of what made her *her*.

It was also part of what made her good at her job with the San Francisco *Weekly Leader* newspaper…part of what had brought her here to the Arizona Territory—and to Everett Bannon—in the first place.

"Are your lodgings far from here?" Everett Bannon repeated her question in his rumbling, shiver-inducing deep voice. "Well, about that—" He broke off. He took off his flat-brimmed hat. He squinted into the distance. He raked

his hand through his hair, then sighed. "I'm afraid there's something I need to tell you."

"Yes?" Pertly Nellie waited. "What is it?"

He hesitated anew, still frowning at the hat he held in his capable-looking hands. "You see, the trouble is, I didn't—"

"Don't say it, *patrón*!" blurted one of the men who stood behind her groom-to-be. The patrician *Mexicano* gave Nellie an apologetic look. *"Por favor,"* he begged Everett, "don't do it!"

There was a fraught moment, during which everyone stilled. Passersby glanced at the man who'd spoken; the other men all watched Everett Bannon. Clearly he was in charge here.

Just as clearly, Nellie reasoned privately, he'd meant what he'd said about sending her away the moment she arrived.

She'd overheard that much of their conversation, of course, shortly after she'd stepped off the train. Her first order of business had been to locate her blue-armband-wearing "fiancé." Her second had been—sensibly enough—to begin surreptitiously eavesdropping on his conversation with his cadre of ragamuffinish men before making her presence known to them.

A woman who'd offered herself up for a mail-order marriage couldn't just waltz into such an arrangement willy-nilly. She had to prepare. She had to gather as many details as she could.

So far, she'd sussed out that Everett Bannon did *not* want her here—but his men did. From the charming man with the silver rings to the curly-haired, book-toting poet and the shy, fair-haired young man standing next to him, to the giant with the enormous appetite and the gingham-lined basket of goodies, they all appeared deeply interested in making sure their "*patrón*'s" engagement went off without a hitch.

Nellie didn't want to let on her awareness of those facts,

however. She still hoped she could salvage this opportunity. She couldn't do *that* if Everett Bannon put her back on the return train, lickety-split. So, with no other option immediately presenting itself, she waited to see what would happen next.

"Pedro, you and the others head back to the ranch," Mr. Bannon finally said, delivering a quelling look to the dark-haired man with the Spanish accent. "You have work to do."

"But *patrón*! You can't possibly still mean to—"

"*Work like mucking out stalls.* Don't make me ask again."

For a heartbeat, they all quieted. Then the bashful-looking young blond man gestured toward Nellie, his expression adorably hopeful and inquisitive. "But…wait. What about…?"

"I said I'd handle this." Mr. Bannon put on his hat with a decisive yank, casting his square-jawed face in shadows. "All of you say goodbye to Miss Trent now, and get on down the road. I don't want to find any work left undone when I get back."

Incredibly they still wavered. Even beneath the stern, hazel-eyed gaze that Everett Bannon gave each of them in turn, they held fast to their positions. Did his marriage mean so much to them that they would risk his ill temper for it? Evidently, it did. Despite everything, Nellie felt impressed by their loyalty. To have earned that, Mr. Bannon must be quite a man.

"Will you be *alone* when you get back?" asked the largest man, his tone mistrustful as he cradled his basket of baked goods. "Or will you be accompanied by…*someone*?"

His not-at-all-subtle head tilt indicated Nellie—who was dying, by then, to intervene on her own behalf. The passivity of just standing there was making her feel downright itchy.

It would have been more in her nature to argue her case—to offer a rebuttal or try a negotiation or propose some sort of blandishment. All those tactics had gotten her quite far in her journalism work. Two of them had gotten her *here*, in fact.

But Nellie doubted such aggressive strategies would endear her to an old-fashioned rancher who lived in a tiny territorial settlement like Morrow Creek. So instead, as an alternative to asserting herself, she settled on shifting in place in the travel-dusted, boy-size work boots she wore under her skirts, hoping she could outlast Mr. Bannon's current bout of reticence.

Unfortunately it appeared to be of the abiding variety, and Nellie's store of patience was definitely *not* infinite.

Perhaps, neither was Mr. Bannon's. Because next he crossed his arms over his broad chest, making his muscles flex with impressive amplitude beneath his plain white shirt. "Ivan, do you want me to quit buying cone sugar for Edina's baked goods?"

The big man, Ivan, went pale. "*Nyet.* I do not want that."

"Then quit pestering me. All of you, get going."

Nellie felt almost positive this standoff was concluded.

"Your soul, *patrón*!" the poetic one cried in a German accent. He waved his book. "*Bitte!* Think of your soul!"

Then again, perhaps she was wrong. Mustering up a soup-çon more patience, Nellie rocked up on her boot heels. She vastly preferred wearing useful footwear rather than sporting typical high-buttoned, fashionable but *impractical* ladies' shoes. She preferred, overall, being nimble to being prim or well-behaved. If that made her a bit unconventional, well… Nellie didn't mind.

"My 'soul,' Oscar?" Mr. Bannon asked in an amused voice. For an instant, his gaze touched Nellie's directly, then roved over her face and personage in turn. "Have you seen Miss Trent? Next to her, a soul feels about as meaningless as a handful of penny candy. A man would give up heaven itself to have her."

Shocked by his lyrical turn of phrase, Nellie gawked at him. Maybe there *was* hope she could stay on in Morrow Creek.

Maybe there was hope Everett Bannon would truly like her.

Nellie certainly liked *him.* Now more than ever—now that he'd come up with such a quixotic notion about his soul…and her own supposedly irresistible claim upon it. This was by far the most unusual group of rough-riding Western males she'd ever encountered, and she'd only been here a short while so far!

The men of Bannon's ranch seemed similarly taken aback by his statement. One of them jostled another. They all grinned.

"But I doubt a mail-order contract is the way to accomplish such a miracle," Mr. Bannon went on. "And the longer you no-goods hang around, the unlikelier my chances get. So skedaddle."

"Wirklich?" Oscar exclaimed. "Then you're *not* going to—"

"I'm going to speak with Miss Trent *alone,*" Mr. Bannon interrupted firmly. "I believe I owe her that much, at least."

At that, all his men blanched. But Nellie was too busy daydreaming about her handsome "fiancé's" unexpectedly starry-eyed nature to let their obvious consternation discourage her. Because, in a single statement, Everett Bannon had just made her mission in Morrow Creek a personal one—a very personal one.

In that moment, Nellie didn't want Everett Bannon to simply accept her as his mail-order bride; she wanted him to accept *her.* She wanted him to say more sweet words. She wanted him to liken her blue eyes to the springtime bluebonnets sprouting between the railroad ties. She wanted him to hold her hand.

She wanted…*him.* She wanted to know everything about him.

Because even while aggrieved, as he was now, Everett Bannon was…*wonderful.* His features were even, his eyes

kind, his dark hair as long as his collar and as shiny as silk. She wanted to touch it—to sift her fingers through it—and felt shocked by that untoward impulse. She didn't know where it had come from. She'd never been intimate with a man; she'd never even come close. For all her bravado and all the inroads she'd made into what was largely a man's world back in San Francisco, she was still a good woman with all her morals and personal strictures intact.

But oh…how Everett Bannon tempted her to abandon them!

Especially *this* Everett Bannon—the one who spouted romanticisms and watched her blush…however inexpertly she did so. Her own feminine wiles were certainly rusty, but his masculine appeal seemed more than intact. Most likely, he could have had his choice of marriageable women in town. For the umpteenth time since she'd stepped off the train, Nellie wondered why a man like him required a mail-order bride.

He was neither asocial nor ugly. He was not infirm or indigent. He appeared respectable. He owned property. He gave every impression of intelligence and good humor. So why—

"It's been a pleasure meeting you, ma'am." The reticent young man stopped in front of her, apparently having been ordered to do so—again—while Nellie had been woolgathering. He gulped, nodded, then shook her hand. "Goodbye, ma'am."

"Wait!" Nellie lay her hand on his forearm. With concern, she gazed into his face. "I don't even know your name."

He shrugged. "I reckon that ain't gonna be necessary."

Then he screwed up his face in almost comical determination and strode away toward town, his posture ramrod straight.

Pedro smiled at her. "Do not worry," the *Mexicano* said with a gallant sweep of his arm. "He is always as skittery as a preacher in a whorehouse. He will be fine. I'll make sure of

it myself." With elaborate gentility, he held her gloved hand in his, then bowed over it. "*Encantado*, Señorita Trent. *Adiós*."

The somber-eyed poet, Oscar, followed him. "I will treasure your letters always," he confessed, tenderly squeezing her hand.

Nellie blinked. *Oscar* had her letters? But why? How?

She could not pursue the question. The bearish Russian, Ivan, approached her next. "Give him this," he advised with another significant nod toward Mr. Bannon. With elaborate care, Ivan pressed something in her hand. "It will work magic for you. It always has for me." With his covert mission accomplished, Ivan tipped his hat to her. "*Ycnex*. That means good luck."

Unaccountably touched by their kindness, Nellie held on to whatever he'd given her. "Thank you. Thank you all so much!"

Curtly Ivan nodded. Oscar bowed. Pedro blew her a kiss.

Mr. Bannon looked on in disgruntlement. "Quit it. Next you'll all be caterwauling, and I didn't bring my handkerchief."

Glancing at him, Nellie grinned. His gruff demeanor didn't fool her. He clearly felt a great deal of affection toward his men. "Hmm. You must have left it in your other suit."

At that, Mr. Bannon glanced down at himself. He regarded his plain, button-placket shirt, brown canvas trousers, braces and scratched-up boots, then frowned. "I only own one suit."

"Well, then. If that's true, you'd better quit looking at that ensemble as though you'd like to start a bonfire with it."

He started. "Are you...*teasing* me?"

"It certainly sounds as though I am."

"But no one teases me." His frown seemed proof of it.

"Then I think *I* will be the necessary exception. While I am here, I've decided to tease you as often and as mercilessly as possible, Mr. Bannon," Nellie declared, alluding for the first

time to the possibility that he might make her leave, "until you either give me a genuine smile or— Nope. No, that's all I want. A genuine smile from you. *Then* I will be satisfied."

He seemed on the verge of giving her a genuine smile just then, merely at her mention of her just-discovered plan. But with what must have been a mighty effort, he resisted. Mostly. A corner of his mouth still quirked. Satisfyingly so. She loved having an effect on him, however meager it was. For now.

"I'll wager you do not always get your way, Miss Trent."

"Ah. Now that's where you'd be wrong. Because I *do* traditionally persist *until* I get my way. Indefatigability is the secret, you see." She picked up her two slim satchels—all her baggage—from the spot where she'd set them at her feet, ready to have this settled once and for all. "Also, you simply *must* call me Nellie. And I will call you Everett! If we're to be married, we may as well begin as we intend to go on— informally."

It was a bluff, plain and simple. Nellie reasoned that he would not turn her away—not now. Not after he'd said all those lovely things. She rarely misjudged a bluff, but this time…

Worryingly Everett gazed at her satchels. He glanced over his shoulder at his men, most of whom were already at the hitching posts where they'd left their horses. He took off his hat again, turned it in his hands, then put it back on.

It was, she'd learned, a signifying gesture. He'd decided something. Now he was going to tell her what it was.

"We're not going to be married," Everett said flatly. "I didn't order you from the mail-order marriage bureau. My men did it for me. They wrote all those letters to you, too."

"Mmm." Nellie thought about that. Yes, that answered several niggling questions she'd had about this whole process. "That explains their peculiar emphasis on the rangeland, the bunkhouse furnishings and the variety of livestock present."

He winced. "I believe they took turns writing to you."

"Then Oscar must have sent me the poetry. And Pedro the pressed flowers. And Ivan the stale cake crumbs, and—"

"I didn't even know you were arriving until an hour ago," Everett confessed, seeming unwilling to indulge her attempts at humor. "I didn't want to turn you away outright—"

"Because I'm better than penny candy."

At that, he briefly closed his eyes. Almost imperceptibly, he nodded. So did Nellie. When Everett opened his eyes again and looked at her, something indefinable passed between them. Something laden with possibilities, risks...and potential success, too. Nellie had never experienced anything like it.

It moved her in a way nothing ever had. It made her want to linger near Everett by whatever means possible—a bold idea, perhaps, but Nellie had never been a woman who'd shied away from *those*. Given the stirring and unexpected way he made her feel, staying near Everett Bannon might be the boldest idea of all.

"But I didn't want to lie to you, either," Everett went on doggedly. "So here it is—I will gladly buy you a return train ticket. And I will happily invite you to stay at my ranch house—with my cook and housekeeper in attendance as chaperones, of course—until you feel strong enough to travel." His gaze swerved to hers, full of indomitable honesty and integrity. "But I'm very sorry to say that I cannot promise to marry you."

Evidently on tenterhooks, he waited for her response.

Doubtless, he expected her to be crushed—to have no other options for marriage. But there were things that Nellie knew about herself that he did not—beginning with the fact that she'd always expected to end up a spinster...and ending with the fact that, with one reckless touch of his hand, Everett Bannon had made her hope for something more. Now, she hoped for *him*.

"I see." Attentively Nellie nodded at him, fighting a powerful urge to dismiss his wrongheaded notion that she might be too fragile to travel again immediately. No one had *ever* suggested that Nellie Trent was anything but sturdy, tomboyish and inconveniently ambitious—especially for a woman. No one had ever tried to cherish or protect her. She was "unusual" and occasionally "unruly"—especially to the men in her life—and that was that. It could not be helped. "Why did your men believe you might not only promise to marry me but actually do it?"

"I don't know."

"You *must* know."

"I can't begin to guess." Everett blew out a breath, seeming overwhelmed. "You've met them. You must understand."

"I thought they were very kind," Nellie insisted. "You're fortunate to work with men who are so devoted to you."

"Yes. I am." Mulishly Everett said nothing more.

"They seem to believe marriage would be good for you," she prompted leadingly. "There must be a reason for that."

He refused to speculate—at least for now. But the jut of his jaw suggested there *was* a reason. Innate curiosity demanded that Nellie uncover what that reason was. She simply had to.

"All right, then. That's fine. You can tell me later."

Brightly Nellie unwrapped the item Ivan had given her. She saw that it was an unfamiliar cookie-shaped thing and wrinkled her nose in confusion. *This* could be magical?

"Why does Ivan believe this cookie is magical?"

"Because he believes everything Edina touches turns to gold," Everett grumbled. Then added, "Is that all you have to say?"

"Er…" Nellie thought about it. She raised her cookie. "Would you like half? I'll share with you. Frankly I'm famished. The stops along the way left much to be desired."

When he did not answer, she transferred her gaze from the cookie to his face—and received an unwelcome surprise.

Why was Everett gawking at her? Confusedly Nellie waggled the cookie at him in an enticing manner. "Please. Take some."

He did not. Perhaps he thought she was being too forward again. He'd accused her of that once already. She didn't want to irk him needlessly now. Stymied, Nellie considered what her most ladylike female friends might do in this situation. Aha!

"It's *far* too much for me to eat all by myself," she fibbed demurely, knowing full well she could have gobbled that cookie and another one besides. But she wanted to impress Everett Bannon somehow. She wanted to make him *see* her. She wanted to learn more about him, too. Attempting to fulfill his stated vision of her as a dainty flower of womanhood seemed a good way to do those things. Regrettably Nellie preferred being brash and—occasionally—groundbreaking. Being decorous was hardly her forte.

She did, however, try her best. "You must have some of it," she urged with her most winning smile. "Please do."

Her offer did not have the desired result. Everett only put his hands on his hips. "Do I not suit you?" he demanded roughly.

"What?"

"I've just said I won't marry you. You traveled hundreds of miles to hear me say it." Appearing markedly confounded, he shook his head. "And now all you want to talk about is cookies?"

Oh. Nellie blinked. "I'm sorry, Everett," she told him cheerfully. "I thought you'd already guessed. *I* don't want a wedding, either! And I certainly can't promise to marry you." She chuckled. "That was never my intention at all."

He seemed put out. "It wasn't?"

"Well, I *did* intend to proceed a bit further with the engagement shenanigans and all the wedding to-dos before saying this," Nellie declared, "but frankly, your not wanting to be married comes as something of a relief to me! I was concerned about hurting your feelings with *my* not wanting to be married. But since you're being so straightforward, I think I can be, too." She examined the rapidly emptying depot platform around them, then looked up at him. "I'll tell you all about it on the way to your ranch, Everett. I accept your offer to stay."

Chapter Three

⟨⟨⟨⟨⟩⟩⟩⟩

Never in a thousand springtimes had Everett expected to find himself driving along the rutted road between the town of Morrow Creek and his *hacienda* with a fetching woman by his side. Not today. Not ever. He'd thought that Miss Abbey O'Neill's desertion had stolen that possibility from him forever. He'd thought she'd made him give up. Forever. But now, today...

Now, Everett had a new beginning to look forward to.

At least it felt that way. Despite Miss Trent's much-too-nonchalant acceptance of his refusal to marry her, Everett felt things were different somehow. Things were different inside him.

I don't want a wedding, either! he recalled her saying an instant later. *And I certainly can't promise to marry you.*

Well, there was *that* to contend with. Nellie didn't want him—at least not for a husband. But Everett reckoned he might be able to change her mind. He could be damn persuasive when he wanted to be. However contrarily, right now he wanted to be.

He wanted to persuade Nellie to smile at him. He wanted to hear her say his name, to feel her touch his arm again,

to watch her crinkle her nose in amusement when she teased him.

Everett didn't know how it had happened, but he was smitten. If he'd guessed right, Nellie was smitten, too.

Why else would she have accepted his offer of lodgings?

Gratified, Everett returned his attention to the road, his team's tracings held lightly in his hands. Beside him, Nellie jounced on the hard plank seat with her skirts spread around her, gazing with interest at the landscape they passed. Her curiosity entranced him; her evident appreciation of the sometimes hardscrabble territory he lived in made him feel that perhaps—if he was lucky—they had something in common.

"I thought springtime would never come," Everett surprised himself by admitting. "Around here, it's been…bleak lately."

"Really?" With her usual high-spiritedness, Nellie looked around. "I can't believe it's ever less than beautiful here. The hills, the grass, all the trees with their tiny, green, newly unfurling leaves, all those wildflowers…they're stunning!"

"They're temporary," he felt compelled to say. He set his jaw in a harsh line. "Eventually the grass will wither. Those leaves will turn brown. The wildflowers will die away."

"All the more reason to enjoy them now! Oh! Listen."

At her urging, he did, prompted by the cute way Nellie cupped her ear. Birdsong floated to him, barely audible above the wagon's creaking and the clomping of his horses' hooves, carried on the same breeze that had threatened his hat earlier.

Nellie sighed. "I certainly don't hear *that* at home."

"At home? In San Francisco?" Reminded of the life she'd left behind to come here, Everett glanced at her perky profile. She nodded, making him worry anew. "Do you like it there?"

"Of course! It's a very exciting place to live."

Exciting. Everett acknowledged that with a grumble. Undoubtedly, he reasoned unhappily, Nellie already missed

the highfalutin life she'd carried on in the city. She probably viewed her time in the territory as a lark. She probably considered him a yokel who wasn't worth marrying. After all, she'd already looked askance at his homespun clothing.

Frowning at his britches, Everett shifted in his seat. If he wanted to impress Nellie Trent, it occurred to him, he would have to be more like the men who appealed to her— the men who appealed to *all* women: citified men. Men who wore suits.

Men like Astair Prestell, who were cultured and erudite.

Everett was neither of those things. He was…ordinary. He read newspapers, not literature. He didn't know any sonnets. He could not have identified a fine wine or doled out a gossipy tidbit to save his skin. Although he was clean and neat and possessed a strong, healthy body, he did not normally adorn that body with any of the concoctions urbane people favored.

He didn't own a drop of cologne. He didn't gussy up his hair with shiny pomade. In fact, for the first time in his recollection, Everett had cause to regret the slapdash way he'd combed his hair that very morning. And his shaving job… Stealthily he raised his hand to his jaw to gauge the effects of his typically casual appointment with his straight razor.

Hellfire. The stubble there could have kindled a fire.

He had to do something to remedy that. Straightaway.

"So you're probably wondering why I registered with a mail-order marriage bureau and came all this way," Nellie said, "only to reveal that I don't intend to get married at all."

Everett had been wondering about little else since she'd announced her nonintention to marry him. Miraculously, given this chance now to find out more, he managed not to leap on it with both big, booted feet. He held his response to a brief nod.

It damn well nearly killed him.

"The truth is, Everett, that I'm not an ordinary woman."

He couldn't help nodding. "I could have told you that."

He sweetened his statement with a mischievous sidelong glance, caught Nellie blushing, and found himself surprised by that. She didn't seem the timid, tittering, rosy-cheeked kind of woman he was used to. She seemed different. He liked that.

"Well. Thank you." Nellie clasped her hands in her lap, her posture graceful and her demeanor refreshingly direct. He liked that, too. She inhaled deeply—and affectingly. "I will assume, of course, that you meant that in a complimentary manner."

How else could he have meant it? "Of course I did."

"Good. Anyway, as I was saying, I'm not an ordinary woman. I'm..." Here, Nellie faltered. She cast him a helpless glance.

Hmm. The more she hesitated, the more Everett rethought his original assessment of her candor. It seemed such a natural part of her, as inherent as her freckles or the curve of her waist. Yet there were those odd moments—like when she'd tried to forcibly feed him her cookie, claiming she couldn't possibly finish one of Edina's wee *bizcochitos*—that made Everett wonder if Nellie Trent was truly the woman she appeared to be.

Then, finally, Nellie rallied. "I'm a journalist!"

"A journalist?" Everett experienced a sinking sensation. He gripped the weathered leather tracings harder, his mind filled with the disheartening realization that—most likely— a female journalist would doubly insist on having a sophisticated man.

But he was Everett Bannon, damn it! He would not go down without a fight. He liked Nellie. She liked him. They could—

"Yes. But only for the ladies' society pages!" she assured him hastily, her cheeks growing pink again. "Only to write

about parties and art and recipes! And only until I'm married!"

Her rusty-sounding giggle didn't suit her. Plagued by a feeling he was missing something crucial here, Everett pointed out the obvious. "I thought you didn't want to get married."

"I didn't." She flashed him an alluring smile. "I'm becoming more amenable to the idea by the moment, though. In fact, if you could provide me with more of those delicious cookies, I might even be persuaded to consider—"

"You're teasing me again. I warned you about that."

"I am. But only a little." Nellie grinned. "It made you quit frowning about my work at the *Weekly Leader*, didn't it?"

He'd been frowning? If he had been, Everett knew, it had only been because he was planning how to become appropriately sophisticated. But he would have sooner died than admit it.

"Yes, you were frowning. You looked fit to spit nails. But I'll have you know I'm not so very unusual. These days, many women perform clerical work or take factory jobs in the city—"

Everett had had enough of "the city." "What's your newspaper got to do with me? With mail-order marriages?"

With your irksome lack of interest in marrying me?

"I'm writing a story for the newspaper about them."

He was glad to see her directness had returned. He enjoyed that side of her. "A story about mail-order marriages?"

"Yes." Warming to her revelation, Nellie nodded. "The mail-order marriage bureaus claim that anyone can fetch themselves a 'perfect match' for the cost of a few fancifully written letters and a postage stamp. I believe that's misleading—and maybe even fraudulent! So I set out to discover the truth about things."

"By positing yourself as a potential bride," he guessed.

"Yes!" She brightened. "That's how all the best investigative journalism is done these days. Not that I get much chance at that. I'm mostly relegated to—" Abruptly she stopped. Then added, "Let's just say I had to lobby very stringently with my editor to be allowed to go forward with this story."

"But you believe in it."

"Absolutely!" Her expression shone with true zeal. "Who knows how many people are pinning their hopes—and their hard-earned money—on these marriage bureaus? If they're as damaging as I think they are, the bureaus' dealings ought to be exposed before more vulnerable women and men become tangled up in them."

Her dauntless expression endeared her to him all the more. It required a courageous woman, Everett thought, to take on a challenge the way she had. He admired that about her.

As for the rest, though... "Then you don't believe in love?"

"Of *course*, I believe in love! Especially—" Nellie broke off, seeming on the verge of saying more. She gave him a brave, warmhearted look. Quietly she added, "Especially today, I do."

Her gaze met his, full of hopefulness and inquisitiveness—and budding fondness, too. Everett was sure that's what it was.

"Today has been...a good day," he agreed roughly.

She nodded...and in that moment, their newfound camaraderie grew a little bit more. Like the wildflowers that bloomed along the roadside, their mutual interest seemed to be both hardy and fast growing. It sounded fanciful—but Everett knew that those pricklepoppies, brown-eyed Susans and pink primroses were weedy fighters at heart. They might look delicate, but they were inherently unstoppable. They *belonged* in that grass. If they were squashed or uprooted, they rallied like tumbleweeds.

"Also," Nellie said enthusiastically, "if my articles about this issue are successful, it could mean a promotion at the

Weekly Leader! I've worked very hard at my job, Everett. It would mean a lot to me if I could be assigned more of the—"

"Most interesting ladies' luncheons and parties?" he asked, sensing again that there was something she was withholding.

"Well, of course." Nellie gave a vigorous nod. "Parties! That's what I meant to say." She gave another unpracticed titter. "Only the most radical career-minded woman would want to write about anything other than crudités and ball gowns!"

"Humph. Writing about parties sounds like a punishment, not a job."

Nellie bit her lip. "To *you*, it might. But you're a man!"

Illustratively she gestured at him. To Everett, her motion seemed to paint him as some sort of hairy, hulking, ham-handed brute with all the common sense and usefulness of a horsefly.

"I *do* know how to use a pen and paper," he informed her.

"And I *adore* writing about bustles and fruit punch!" With a sort of wounded dignity, Nellie shot him an inquisitive look. "Don't I appear to be the sort of woman who likes those things?"

"Since the moment I met you at the depot this morning," Everett told her truthfully, "you've seemed to be the sort of woman who isn't sure what sort of woman she is."

Nellie crossed her arms. "You could not be more wrong."

"No, I'm right," he insisted. As proof, he added, "One minute you're traveling hundreds of miles on your own, the next you're insisting you can't eat an entire cookie by yourself. You say you don't want to be married, then you say you might." Everett fixed her with an assessing look, allowing the horses to move at their own pace. "You tell me you like writing about female fripperies for your newspaper…but it's the possibility of writing a real exposé that makes you sit up straighter and wave your arms and look lively. It's the chance of stopping people being taken advantage of by mail-order

marriage bureaus that sets your hair afire. A man would have to be blind not to see it."

"Then perhaps you are not as ably sighted as you think." Decorously Nellie folded her hands in her lap. "Because I am *very* dainty and ladylike, and I cherish writing about hats."

Somehow, Everett strongly doubted it. Also, she wasn't the only one who knew how to tease someone. Piqued by her seeming assertion that he was wrong about the observations he'd made about her—observations he *knew* damn well were correct, because his attentiveness had never failed him before, and neither had his intuition—he delivered a ludicrous statement of his own.

"Yes. And I, like every man, want a compliant, trusting, wishy-washy, swooning female straight from *Godey*'s magazine to call my own," Everett deadpanned. "It's all I dream about while baling hay and building fences and rounding up wild mustangs."

Her blue eyes brightened—and not at his wit, either.

"You round up wild mustangs?" Fervently Nellie clutched his arm. "Can I go with you next time? That sounds *fascinating*!"

If she would continue touching him, Everett knew, he would allow her to go anywhere with him. He was definitely in over his head. "It's not very dainty," he warned. "It will be noisy and dusty and dangerous." Then, belatedly reminded of his quest to impress Nellie with his supposed sophistication, he added, "Besides, we could have ourselves a poetry reading instead."

Nellie made a face. Then she caught him watching her.

"Oh! Outstanding! Poetry!" she enthused. "Only…perhaps we could have a tiny excursion to see your horses first? I promise I'll try to bear up under the noise and dust and danger."

At the valiant tilt she gave her chin, Everett guffawed.

"You know, I believe you will." Full of wonder at this contradictorily fascinating woman he'd found, he urged his team of horses onward at full chisel. He wanted to get on with discovering Nellie's secrets—and that was something best done at home. "I'll promise to try not to scare you too much with my swaggering virile ways and coarse language and clumsy shave."

Her eyes sparkled at him. "We have ourselves a challenge."

"Pshaw," Everett scoffed, rubbing his chin. "I'm not that bearded yet. It isn't even noontime. The truly notable stubble won't emerge until supper. And as far as my swagger goes—"

"No, I mean with our 'marriage,'" Nellie said, smiling. "I still want to write my story for the *Leader*, Everett, and since I'm already here anyway..." She bit her lip again, inciting in him an unholy urge to do the same to her mouth himself... very, very gently. "Would you mind very much *pretending* to be engaged to me for a while longer yet?" Nellie asked. "I know your men believe you were going to hurl me back onto the train a while ago—"

"I was never going to *hurl* you anyplace. I'm not a beast." Why did she persist in believing he was ungentlemanly? Gaily she overlooked his disgruntled tone and continued.

"—so they might require convincing of our newfound and immediate rapport." With a decisive air, Nellie slid across the wagon's bench seat. She looped her arm in his, then snuggled up to him until their bodies touched full-length along one side. Engagingly she gazed upward. "Do you think this will do?"

It was doing plenty for Everett already. At her nearness, his whole body tightened. Her warmth touched him. Her bosom pressed against his arm. Her softness felt evident, even through all the layers of her dress and petticoats and corset and whatever else she had on. Imagining it, his wits went walking.

With effort, Everett managed not to drop the tracings and

pull her into his arms right then. "Do I think this will convince my *vaqueros* we're going through with our 'engagement'?"

"Yes." She seemed concerned. "Are you all right? You seem…distracted. If this is too much for you to take on, I—"

"No." He cleared his throat. "Let's do it. I feel confident I can take on everything at hand and make you feel glad I did."

His head swam with visions of doing exactly that. Lustily Everett pictured himself holding Nellie closer, bringing his mouth to hers, making her open herself to him, so sweet and hot and ready to share herself with him as he kissed her and kissed her, both of them shedding their clothes and losing their minds. Their coming together would be sensual, of course, but also—

"Excellent!" Nellie blinked at him, innocent and pure.

Innocent. And pure. Recognizing those qualities in her, Everett tardily remembered where he was and what he was doing—which was *not*, he reminded himself strictly, taking advantage of a woman who might or might not aspire to great heights of journalistic excellence…but who definitely trusted him to help her carry off the mission that had brought her to Morrow Creek.

He would *earn* her trust, Everett promised himself then. He would help Nellie research that investigative story of hers, he would pretend to be her fiancé, and he would convince anyone who looked at them that he was boots over hat in love with her.

Not that doing so would be much of a stretch. He felt half spoony already, and that was only the effect of meeting her. Who knew how much more besotted he'd become if given a few days?

No, the difficult part would be doing all of those things *sophisticatedly*, Everett knew. The difficult part would be impressing Nellie with his intellect, style and essential re-

finement without accidentally letting slip his too-manly ways—the aspects of him that had already cost him love once before.

With Nellie, things would be different, Everett swore. With Nellie, *he* would be different. For her. And if he was lucky, he thought as they rounded the next turn and his *hacienda* and its pastures and outbuildings came into view, maybe she would even agree to stay after her story for the *Weekly Leader* was written.

Chapter Four

"...The tricky thing about it," Edina said as she puttered around the kitchen of Everett's ranch house on the morning after Nellie's arrival, "is that the bride doesn't know beforehand that it's her *groom* who's kidnapping her. All she knows is that she has to make a choice—and if she chooses wrong, the glorious wedding she's been dreaming about will go up in smoke. Poof!"

The jolly, apron-wearing cook threw up her floury hands in demonstration, making sure that Nellie understood the significance of the prewedding tradition she'd been describing. It was only one of many head-spinning old-world customs that Edina had insisted everyone in the territory—especially the *vaqueros*—held very close at heart. According to Edina, the ranch hands were hoping Nellie and Everett would include several of their most beloved traditions in their upcoming nuptials.

"It's a test, really," Edina went on, going back to her stoneware bowl of biscuit dough. "You probably ken that much. But it's certainly not fair to the poor bride! She hasn't even had a chance to sew that last lucky stitch on her wedding dress."

"Zut alors!" Marybelle, the housekeeper, shook her head. "The bride must not sew her own wedding dress! It is bad luck."

"No, it is bad luck to wear a green wedding dress."

"Or a red dress." Marybelle shuddered. "That is almost as bad as seeing a nun on the way to the church and being struck barren. *Non,* Nellie must let *us* sew her wedding dress for her."

"Oh! That would be lovely!" Feeling almost as though the dress in question would truly be hers—and not just a footnote in her story for the *Weekly Leader*—Nellie took an enlivening sip of coffee. "Honestly I hadn't given much thought to what I might wear. I'm not good with fashion. I'm a truly awful seamstress."

Edina and Marybelle stared at her in patent disbelief.

Oh. Fashion and sewing skills were essential for ladies, Nellie recalled too late. "I mean, I don't enjoy sewing."

The two women blinked, still seeming not to comprehend her.

Perhaps some diversion would be best. "What about the wedding itself?" Nellie asked brightly. "You've told me about several prewedding traditions, but what about the wedding?"

"At the last wedding I went to, I got a daisy pin for a favor," Edina shared. "The unmarried ladies wear theirs upside down, you know. *I* lost mine before the end of the night!"

Mystified by the significance of that, Nellie raised her brows in confusion. Seeing her, Marybelle rushed to explain.

"She thinks that means *she's* next to be married," Marybelle said in her enchanting French-accented speech. "But I put more stock in catching the bouquet, myself. At the last wedding I attended, *I* did that. So I believe *I'm* the next to be married."

Edina disagreed. Their conversation had the tenor of a longstanding rivalry—leavened with affection, to be sure, but

a rivalry, all the same. Propping her booted feet on the rungs of the nearest ladder-back chair, Nellie listened with interest.

Idly she reached down to pet the tabby cat that had padded into the kitchen and taken up residence underneath her seat. Nellie didn't know its name, but like everything and everyone else in Everett's home, the cat had welcomed her unstintingly.

"I will have a traditional ceremony, the way we do in Brittany," Marybelle was saying. "Children will block the road with wedding ribbons, and I will cut them with fancy shears. To reach me, my groom will have to remove briars from the road—"

Edina snorted. "Likely they'll be tumbleweeds, you mean."

"—and I will toss my garter and have a *chiverie*!"

"Oh, I do love me a good shivaree!" Edina agreed with Marybelle readily for once. "Staying up till all hours, having a wee nip of whiskey, crowding around the hapless married couple while they try to have it off in their wedding-night bed—"

Appalled at the very notion, Nellie gawked at her. She couldn't help picturing herself and Everett, clad in nightwear with blankets pulled up to their chins, surrounded by boisterous Westerners wielding cowbells and hard liquor at midnight.

While the idea of Everett in bed with her held a certain undeniable…*intrigue*—making her wonder exactly what he *did* wear to sleep—the rest of that scenario left Nellie feeling aghast.

Catching her horrified expression, Edina placidly went back to patting out her biscuit dough. "Not that we'll do anything like that to you and Everett, dearie," she promised.

"Oh, *non*," Marybelle agreed coolly—and not entirely convincingly. "We and the *vaqueros* will leave you alone for your wedding night's *l'amour*. All we ask is that you indulge us with a few harmless *les traditions* in the days before the wedding."

"And during the wedding ceremony itself," Edina put in.

"Bien sûr." Marybelle nodded. "During the wedding, too. You will have your maids of honor, to confuse the evil spirits. You'll need to distract them from making mischief for the true bride."

"I could think of no one nicer than the two of you," Nellie opined, beginning to feel guilty that she couldn't *promise* the positions of honor to Marybelle and Edina, "to stand with me."

At that, both women gave girlish smiles. Their pleasure only added to Nellie's burgeoning sense that she was unavoidably hoodwinking these kind people. Everyone at Everett's ranch had greeted her with open arms. And she was repaying them by being only half truthful about the real reason she'd come there.

But she couldn't write an accurate story for the *Leader* if she didn't experience an authentic mail-order marriage—at least in part—could she? That meant Nellie had to carry on as she was.

"You'll need hearty groomsmen, too," Edina added, filling her pan with several more biscuits. She'd already made at least three dozen of them. "To be sure you're not stolen away by rival cowboys."

"Rival cowboys?" Nellie laughed. "I don't think that will be a problem. For one thing, they won't want me. For another—"

"Won't want you?" Her two new friends regarded her owlishly. "Why not?"

"Well, because I'm not strictly marriageable," Nellie said. "I never have been." That's what had made her ideally suited for her story on the mail-order marriage bureaus. That's what had finally convinced her editor, in fact, to let her write it.

When Nellie had come to him with her "groom's" writ-

ten request for her, via the mail-order marriage bureau, he'd taken one look at "Everett's" letter and offered a blunt reply.

Well, if those people at the marriage bureau have found someone who wants to marry you, Miss Trent, then I guess they are a bunch of shysters, just like you said they might be, he'd told her, applauding her instincts. *Go ahead and prove it!*

Thus emboldened, Nellie had set out to do exactly that.

Marybelle gave a musical laugh. "Monsieur Bannon would disagree with you about that. He seems to find you eminently marriageable. We all noticed it yesterday, when you arrived."

"Well, he's...*contracted* to marry me. That's different."

"*Non.* You don't understand," Marybelle insisted. "You have made Monsieur Bannon a changed man! He was so gloomy in the days following Miss O'Neill's traitorous departure, but now—"

At her mention of the mysterious Miss O'Neill, Edina slapped down a biscuit with extra vigor. She muttered a curse.

"—now he is like himself again," Marybelle said happily, "only better! And that is only because *you* are here at last."

Nellie sincerely doubted that. Although..."He *did* have the vitality to argue with me on the drive here yesterday."

"You see?" Edina gave a nod. "He is restored! By you!"

"And he *did* have the vitality to tell me," Nellie went on, troubled anew by the recollection, "that he wanted a 'compliant, trusting, wishy-washy, swooning female straight from *Godey's* magazine' to call his own." Worriedly she clenched her coffee cup. Miserably she stared into it. "I'll never measure up."

Marybelle and Edina laughed. "He said *what*?"

Too mortified to repeat it, Nellie adjusted her boys' boots instead. She should have cleaned them last night; they still bore a layer of caked-on mud, earned when she'd sojourned along the railway track during the train's stops, exploring things.

"Never mind." Nellie sipped more coffee, feeling herself growing a tiny bit...jealous? Casually she poked at her boot heels, striving to seem nonchalant. "Who is Miss O'Neill?"

At that, both women began talking to beat the band. It was as though they'd been *dying* to tell the story of their beloved *hacendado* and the duplicitous woman who'd cruelly wronged him.

In short order, Nellie learned all she cared to know about Abbey O'Neill. She learned how Miss O'Neill had "pretended" to care about Everett, how she had strung him along ("And several other men, too!" a scandalized Edina confided) all through their courtship, and how she had heartlessly abandoned Everett to elope with a man who she'd decided offered better prospects.

Hearing the name of Miss O'Neill's paramour, Nellie gasped. She knew of Astair Prestell; everyone did! His writings were legendary and varied. His speaking engagements were said to be even more memorable. Astair Prestell was witty, sophisticated...

Well, he was altogether dissimilar to Everett Bannon, that was for certain. Astair Prestell was a person of importance in society. Everett was...a man of good character in Morrow Creek.

"Our *patrón* was devastated by Miss O'Neill's betrayal," Edina said in an outraged tone. "She made a laughingstock of him, running off like that!"

Marybelle shook her head. "He is better off without her. In time, his heart will heal. I believe that." She gave Nellie a warm look. "Especially now that *you* are here to love him."

"Yes." Swamped with empathy for what Everett must have gone through, Nellie nodded unthinkingly. "Poor Everett."

Edina and Marybelle traded meaningful glances, as though Nellie's gesture signified her intentions to save their *patrón*

from heartbreak. But as much as she wanted to, Nellie wasn't sure she could carry it through.

After all, her own editor at the *Weekly Leader*—a man who knew her thoroughly, had hired her himself, and often professed his esteem of her writing talent—had believed she would not find herself a single potential groom from among the entire catalog offered by the mail-order marriage bureau. He'd believed she was simply *that* lacking in feminine appeal and suitability to become a bride. Worse, this man—whom she trusted—had believed that her apparently glaring deficiency would even come through *on paper*!

Nellie knew she was a good person. She didn't believe she needed to be silly, superficial, or overly concerned with petticoats to be a "real woman." When it came down to it, she didn't believe *any* woman needed to behave in a particular way.

She'd always been happy breaking down barriers, proving herself the equal of men in her workday life, and forging her own way with things. She'd always been happy…period.

But she'd never before been smitten with a man the way she was with Everett Bannon: instantly, giddily and overwhelmingly. And she'd never before been filled with such longing to impress anyone—not the way she yearned to impress Everett right now.

Without a doubt, Nellie was out of her depth. What if Everett truly *did* want a swooning, simpering, idiotic girl, like the "ideal woman" personified by *Godey's Lady's Book*?

Nellie couldn't possibly manage *that*.

Unfortunately the only alternative was revealing her true self to Everett *now*, then trying to bear his inevitable disdain.

Everett would try to hide it, of course. He was honorable that way. He was chivalrous and kind and engagingly down-to-earth. He wasn't like the popinjays and braggarts who filled San Francisco society; he was real and true. Nellie had

seen that in dozens of ways already, beginning with the way Everett had sat down to his usual shared evening meal with all his ranch hands, Marybelle, Edina and her last night, and continuing with the way he'd treated Nellie so far—respectfully and generously.

She couldn't afford to lose his positive regard already… not when things between them felt so very new and captivating. Not when she'd only begun to daydream of kissing him—just a peck!—and finding out if his beard stubble felt soft or scratchy.

When she was around Everett, Nellie reflected dreamily, she felt…*overwarm*, all the time. With a single glance, he could pull August heat out of a springtime day and leave her sweltering.

"*Regarde.* Look!" Marybelle nudged Edina, pointing her chin at Nellie. "She is daydreaming about her wedding. Sweet, *non*?"

"Very sweet!" Both older women fairly cooed with delight.

Nellie only frowned, struck by a new thought. "Are you *sure* it was Astair Prestell whom Miss O'Neill ran away with?"

Marybelle gave a languorous Gallic shrug. "*Oui. Bien sûr.*"

Edina narrowed her eyes menacingly. "I will never forget his name. I will never buy one of his blasted books, either!"

"Of course not. Me, either." Nellie soothed, stifling a smile. She liked these two women already. Under different circumstances, they might have become close friends. "It's just that he is so *very* sophisticated and witty and well-mannered—"

"I suppose," Marybelle allowed grudgingly. Edina only gave a dismissive wave of her floury hand, urging Nellie to go on.

"Well, that's not quite the sort of person I'd expect to find here in the territory, that's all," Nellie said. "I'd—"

She broke off, startled by a noise around the corner.

She didn't want to be caught gossiping by one of the *vaqueros*. She didn't want anyone to tell Everett that she knew about his ordeal with Miss O'Neill. It was bad enough it had happened; for Everett, having the whole imbroglio spoken about would undoubtedly only be worse. It would only be painful.

Contrary to her fears, a noticeably buoyant Everett sauntered in an instant later, all broad shoulders, neatly combed dark hair and clean-shaven jaw. The noise she'd heard, she realized, had been his boot heels ringing against the floorboards. Now, he offered up a bright morning smile.

It was, it occurred to her, exactly the "genuine smile" she'd sought from him—under threat of further teasing—at the train depot. She hadn't expected it to be quite so...*heartwarming*, though. Everett was *charming*.

"Don't listen to their bad-mouthing me, Nellie," he said breezily, obviously having overheard part of what she'd said. He cast his housekeeper and cook a chiding glance. "Folks around here wouldn't know sophistication if it plumb fell on them."

"Youch! Maybe it already has!" Squinting at her precious *patrón*, Edina shielded her eyes with her hand. She guffawed. "Leastwise, *something's* assaulting my poor eyeballs right now. My money's on that hideous necktie of yours. But if you say it's 'sophistication,' I reckon I'll have to take your word for it."

"Yes. You will," Everett said with a satisfied grin. "Nellie already has. Maybe you should follow her lead, Edina."

Still smiling, he gave Nellie a meaningful, solidarity-filled look. Belatedly she realized that he'd overheard her describing the "sophisticated, witty and well-mannered" Astair Prestell—and had mistakenly decided she'd been describing *him*.

Well, there was no sense disillusioning him now. Especially not since he appeared—endearingly—to have gussied

himself up specifically for the occasion of spending the day with her.

"Mon Dieu!" Looking at Everett, Marybelle shied away, too. "You will spook the horses with that ensemble."

Everett chuckled. "Very funny." He strode confidently across the room, poured himself a cup of coffee from the speckled enamelware pot on the cooktop, then sipped. "I have it on good authority that a four-in-hand necktie is very stylish."

"Since when do *you* care about what's stylish? You must've had to drag that suit outta mothballs." Edina squinted again. *"Patrón*, are those *spectacles* on your face, too? Humph. Maybe if you took them off, you'd be able to see how funny you look."

At that, Everett's expression changed. A tiny hint of vulnerability softened his mouth, making him appear…*kissable.*

No! Nellie scolded herself. *No.* Not kissable!

Everett clearly had gone out of his way to look nice for their first full day of being "engaged," and his housekeeper and cook simply weren't used to his newly dapper appearance. Or to his until-now undetected need to wear eyeglasses.

Everett required a show of camaraderie right now, not more teasing, Nellie decided. She had to think of *his* needs—not her own selfish, sinful urgings to cup his face in her palms, touch her lips to his lips, inhale that leather-and-tobacco scent that clung to his skin and clothes, rub her body all over his—similar to the way she had in his wagon yesterday, when she'd brazenly cuddled up to him to "pretend" to be attracted to him—and make herself all breathless and needful and… and… Well, she didn't know what else. But she felt quite certain, just then, that Everett did. She wanted very much for him to share that knowledge with her. She truly, breathlessly did. But first…

"*I* think you look *very* handsome today," Nellie told him loudly. To prove it, she reached for his hand. He took it.

He tossed her another gratified smile, wholly ignorant of the thrills that chased through her body at his touch. His hand felt warm and strong and faintly callused, Nellie observed, and when Everett looked at her again, his eyes were... They were...

They were partly *hidden* by those silly spectacles he had on! An offense like that should have been a crime of some sort.

Displeased with that realization, Nellie did her best to rally. She could hardly begrudge Everett the ability to see clearly. Especially if—as likely was the case—he needed those eye-glasses to read the thick book he held in his opposite hand.

Although on further reflection...Nellie could have sworn she'd glimpsed that very same book in Oscar's hand yesterday. Truly. And she *still* felt resentful that those eyeglasses had stolen her view of Everett's stirringly warm and intense hazel eyes. And to be one hundred percent honest, she didn't en-tirely approve of the necktie that had so nettled Edina, either.

But she *did* wholeheartedly approve of the man who wore it, Nellie reflected anew, and that was all that really mattered.

Gently Everett rubbed his thumb over the back of her hand, making another series of thrills rush through her. Bereft of the ability to speak under such heady circumstances, Nellie only gazed, undoubtedly wide-eyed, at her supposed "fiancé."

"Yep. They're adorable together," Edina judged brusquely.

"*Ah oui.* They are *enchanteur.*" Marybelle pressed together her hands in a prayerful position. "Everything will be fine now." She signaled Edina. "Come! Hurry up with those bis-cuits. We must begin sewing, or Nellie's dress won't be ready."

At that, Nellie started. She couldn't allow Marybelle and Edina to slave away on a dress she would never wear. She

had to stop them somehow, without rousing suspicion. She had to—

Abruptly Nellie followed Everett's glance toward her feet. She realized, to her dismay, what he must be looking at.

Her boots. Her muddy, disreputable, *boys'* boots.

Reflexively she yanked them under her skirts again. She'd thought she'd been doing so well in her quest to appear ladylike and demure. Evidently making herself over into Everett's dream woman would be more challenging than she'd expected—and more necessary than ever, as well. She'd noticed, at dinner last night, that Everett had flawless table manners and rarely made a misstep himself. She would simply have to do better than this!

Distraught, Nellie opened her mouth to formulate an excuse for her hoydenish ways. But before she could even begin, Everett squeezed her hand. All her self-chastising thoughts fled.

"Come with me." Cheerfully he pulled Nellie to her feet. "We have a month's worth of wedding fripperies to get to and only a week to do it in. So we'd better get started."

Chapter Five

Striding toward the paddock at his easternmost pasture with Nellie by his side, Everett felt as giddy as a schoolboy. Until that moment, he hadn't realized exactly how fraught with tension his arrival in the kitchen had felt to him. But now...

Now he knew Nellie liked him. She truly did.

His plan was working! He had successfully impersonated a sophisticated man. For her sake. And maybe, possibly, his own.

When he'd arrived in the kitchen, Everett had half expected Nellie to laugh at him. He'd expected her to tease him the way Edina and Marybelle had. Or to reject him outright the way Miss O'Neill had. Instead Nellie had gazed at him with respect and admiration. She'd complimented him on the outfit it had taken him thirty-six vexatious, swearword-filled minutes to assemble. She'd taken his hand in hers and she'd smiled, and in that moment, Everett had known everything would be all right.

He should have known it would be, he chided himself now as they continued alongside the grassy area where his tamest horses grazed. He'd heard Nellie's opinion of him with his own ears.

It's just that he is so very sophisticated and witty and well-mannered, she'd been telling Marybelle and Edina in an awestruck tone when he'd come downstairs, and Everett saw no reliable reason not to believe her. Everyone knew that overheard statements were the most honest. Nellie's remark had certainly seemed to be authentic. Especially since she'd followed up by admitting with typical forthrightness that Everett was *not quite the sort of person* she'd expected to find in the territory.

He could tell, by now, that she was changing her mind.

Silently congratulating himself on having carried off his plan so far—despite a few subtle missteps while navigating the multiple forks he'd uncharacteristically insisted Marybelle set for dinner last night—Everett smiled at Nellie. Her strides were steady and sure, purposeful enough to make her skirts swish, and he couldn't help remembering the appealingly self-assured way she'd been perched at his kitchen table when he'd arrived, with her feet propped on the chair rungs and her posture alert.

Nellie Trent was no coy, helpless damsel, he reckoned approvingly as he watched her tramp across the windswept landscape. She was energetic and interesting. She was fascinating and smart and alluring. She was…capable, it seemed, of enchanting all the creatures, big and small, on his ranch.

Even now, he saw, his old dog trotted at her heels, tongue lolling in canine adoration. And when he'd come downstairs, his tabby mouser had been curled up beneath her chair. And every one of his *vaqueros* had quit work to tip his hat at her, grinning from ear to ear. Pedro, of course, had offered a courtly bow.

Glancing again at her doggy companion, Everett grinned. He knew exactly how that helpless mutt felt—entranced and ensnared.

"All right. That's it!" Stopping abruptly, Nellie yanked

her hand from his. "You're staring at my feet again, aren't you?" Accusingly she frowned at him. "You can just quit wondering, because I'll admit it—I'm wearing boots." She lifted her skirts a few inches to confirm it, offering a tantalizing glimpse of her stocking-clad legs in the process. Knitted cotton hosiery had never looked better. "Boys' boots. I like them. They're comfortable. They fit me. This pair is a little muddy at the moment, but that's remedied easily enough. It doesn't make me any less ladylike!" She jutted out her chin. A pause. "Well?"

Confused by her beleaguered tone, Everett looked down. "Well…" He searched for a proper reply. "You have nice knees."

She yelped in surprise. Her skirts dropped. *"Knees?"*

"Before, in the kitchen, I could only *wish* I could catch a glimpse of your knees. But now…it's kind of you to oblige."

"I wasn't showing you my knees!" Nellie informed him with another lift of her chin. "I was showing you my boots. Since you were so all-encompassingly curious about them, and all."

"Nope. You were showing me your knees." Everett grinned, recalling the moment with fond remembrance. He'd distinctly glimpsed her shapely calves, exposed knees…and the most elusive, most *haunting* hint of a curvy inner thigh adorned in dark stockings. But perhaps that last had been his overactive imagination. "Whatever your intentions were, I've seen boots before. I don't need a refresher on what they look like."

"I see. So your eyes just naturally wandered upward?"

"Naturally." He took her hand again. "You have a surpassingly fine figure. I couldn't help myself." He remembered his newfound gentlemanly persona and added, "Of course, I'm very sorry if that offends your ladylike sensibilities."

Nellie didn't even appear to be listening. Instead she was gazing at his shoulders in a preoccupied fashion. "My what?"

"Your ladylike sensibilities."

She blinked. "Oh! Yes. *Those.*" Her mouth formed a delectable moue of distress. "You're correct. Formally I am offended by that comment, of course. It was impertinent and overfamiliar."

"And yet," Everett pointed out, "you're smiling."

"Posh." Nellie tried to suppress her grin. "I am not. It would not be at all ladylike if I were, say, *thrilled* to hear you remark favorably on my figure. That would be unthinkable."

"Your eyes are lovely, too. And I like your lips."

Appearing mesmerized, she touched them. "My lips?"

Damnation. He was probably not supposed to mention them in polite company. It was just like him, a rough-and-tumble Western man, to forget that. "I'm sure," Everett hedged, searching for a courteous alternative, "they have interesting things to say."

"Not without my running them, they don't." Now Nellie's grin turned mischievous. "Exactly whom do you think is in charge of me? Hmm?" Playfully she nudged him. "Does your mouth do things all on its own, without any instructions from you?"

Everett nodded. "It's been trying to subvert my good intentions all day." He lowered his gaze to her lips. "It wants me to kiss you. I keep having to remind it we've only just met."

"Strictly speaking, that's true," she agreed, shifting her gaze to his mouth…and holding it there with another preoccupied look on her face. "It doesn't feel that way, though."

"No, it doesn't." He took a step nearer, still holding her hand. He lifted it to his chest, letting Nellie feel his heart thumping along underneath his shirt and necktie and suit coat. He raised her hand higher. Keeping his gaze pinned on hers, Everett brought her hand to his mouth. Very softly, he

kissed it. "There. Maybe that will keep my subversive impulses at bay."

Shakily Nellie exhaled. She nodded, her eyes enormous and blue and affectionate. "It ought to," she pronounced. "After all, I am a demure lady. And you are a bespectacled gentleman. Between the two of us, we ought not want anything more."

"No," Everett agreed. Even *he* wasn't convinced. All of him yearned to pull Nellie still closer…to kiss her properly. "We are both far too sophisticated to give in to our urges."

"Yes," Nellie breathed, moving a hairsbreadth closer. "We are. Far, *far* too sophisticated." She paused. Then, "Only…"

Instantly Everett felt doubly alert. "Only…?"

"Only we *might*, purely for the sake of our 'engagement,' try out a very minor kiss," Nellie proposed. Devilishly, she raised her eyebrows. "It wouldn't have to mean anything."

"It would mean *everything*."

"Or it could mean everything." A nod. "Yes, please."

Everett nearly groaned aloud. "You really *are* a lady. Only a lady would request a kiss in such a well-mannered fashion."

At that, Nellie perked up. "Well, then! Let's do it!"

"Not here." Lacing his fingers in hers, Everett hauled her sideways. Within moments, the shadow of the barn enveloped them, providing a slice of blissful privacy. The springtime coolness mingled with the earthy scent of freshly plowed soil and the perfume of budding flowers. With his back to the sunshine and his front to everything that mattered to him just then, Everett leaned Nellie against the barn wall. Reverently he brought his hand to her face. He stroked her cheek. *"Here,"* he told her.

Another preoccupied look. "Here what?"

"Here is where I'm going to kiss you."

She nodded. "If you don't hurry up, I won't be at all convinced of your impassioned response to your fiancée."

"Are you always this bossy?" Grinning with delight at her puckish expression, Everett brought his other hand to her face. Gently he cradled her jaw in his hands. "This can't be rushed."

"Can it be helped along?" Cooperatively Nellie looped her arms around his middle. She levered herself nearer, making her skirts collide riotously with his trouser legs. "How's this?"

Perfect. It was perfect. That was all Everett could think about. Nellie, in all her directness and enthusiasm, could not have been more wonderful, or more ideal for him. He trembled at feeling her body crowded against his, all soft and warm and giving. He wanted to give *her* everything...to let her know how much it meant to him that she was there, with him, just then.

Instead his borrowed spectacles—a remnant of a former *vaquero* who'd forgotten them when he'd moved on—fogged up.

He'd hoped they would make him appear scholarly. They only succeeded in making him appear...damp. Everett whipped them off.

"It's good," he managed to say with a nod. "Very good."

"I like you without your eyeglasses on," Nellie nattered on as he, having stowed his spectacles, returned his hands to her face. She seemed cheered by the notion that she was being useful. "You have magnificent eyes. And it's only fair that I help with our kiss, since this was my idea in the first place."

"*Your* idea?" If she only knew the largely sleepless night he'd just spent thinking of her. "I won't give you credit for this. Not in the slightest. Not after how much I've wanted—"

"You must!" she insisted with a sincere expression—and a twinkle in her eyes. "It's the only gentlemanly thing to do."

"Right now," Everett said honestly, "I'm no gentleman."

Then he tilted Nellie's head upward, lowered his mouth to hers...and gave in to every ungentlemanly impulse he'd ever had.

Her mouth tasted like honey, her lips felt like heaven, and before Everett had so much as begun coaxing her to open herself to him, he knew he could never get enough of this—enough of *her*. Kissing Nellie was like leaping into the sunshine after a long, cold winter. It was like searching for something long lost, then finding it unexpectedly in a half forgotten pocket. It was like being split in half and then becoming whole again. It was...

"Amazing," Nellie said when he'd lifted his head again. She blinked at him, then traced her fingers over his cheek. "I guess the marriage bureau was right—you *are* ideally suited for me."

"I thought you said they are scurrilous fraudsters."

"Potentially," she reminded him, still looking dreamy. *"Potentially,* they are scurrilous fraudsters preying on the hopes of naive men and women. That was my original hypothesis, at least. But the proof of that remains to be found—and the plain fact is, the evidence at hand just can't be ignored."

Everett wanted to kiss her again. Again and again and again. Instead he made himself converse. "It can't?"

"No." With her gaze lingering on his face, Nellie shook her head. She frowned in thought. "It seems to me that we really *are* wonderful together. Surely *all* kisses aren't like that."

Everett squared his shoulders. "Like what?"

"Magical. You must have felt it."

He wanted to jump for joy. Somberly he said, "Yes, I did."

"Well, then! What if we're *meant* to be together?"

He was having trouble thinking clearly. "If you're expecting philosophy from me, *especially* after that kiss—"

"You *did* have the book for it close at hand. Remember?"

Hellfire. The book he'd borrowed from Oscar. Evidently it had been too effective in convincing Nellie of his erudition. Now she expected deep thoughts and contemplation from him.

On the verge of confessing that the book—in German, no less!—had only been for appearance's sake, Everett stopped. His plan was working. He was impressing Nellie. He had to continue.

"The only way to find out about our future is to live it," he said firmly. "Starting with our 'wedding.' Come on."

Chapter Six

When Everett clasped her hand and urged her toward the barn door, Nellie did not think she could move. She felt too languid, too preoccupied with Everett's mighty shoulders and hard-muscled chest and big, nimble hands…too itchy for more things like kissing to concentrate on mundane matters like a mail-order marriage—particularly a *sham* mail-order marriage for a newspaper story for the nearly forgotten *Weekly Leader*. Her original reason for coming to town felt further away with every passing minute.

But then Everett parted the barn doors. He let them roll aside with all the fanfare of a big-city play on opening night, and Nellie glimpsed what was inside, and she livened up quickly.

"Oh, my word!" Awestruck, Nellie stepped inside. She wheeled around, taking in her surroundings. "Everett! This is— This is—"

"It's all my *vaqueros*' doing," he said, pausing to put on his dratted eye-obscuring spectacles again. Although they made him appear duly bookish and wise, Nellie preferred him without them. He gestured at the barn's interior. "Do you approve?"

"Approve? I'm flabbergasted!" Eagerly she hurried past rows of empty stalls, taking it all in. "It's beautiful!"

Contrary to every expectation she would have had, it *was* beautiful. The ranch hands had cleaned, scrubbed and polished. They'd stacked hay bales, tied ribbons to the beams and draped cottony bunting from the rafters. They'd hung safety lanterns. They'd created a cozy seating area. They'd *decorated*. Somehow, incredibly, they'd managed to turn a barn into…a cathedral.

Or something that felt very much like it.

"Is *this* where we're getting married?" she asked.

Everett seemed too enchanted by her reaction to respond at first. Then, he nodded. "Unless you'd prefer somewhere else."

"Somewhere else? I wouldn't think of it!" Hugging herself, Nellie turned in a circle. She grinned. "It's so…unconventional!"

That meant it was *perfect*. At least it was for her.

"Oh." Everett frowned. "No one wants 'unconventional.' You're being polite and ladylike again."

His words dashed her hopes in a heartbeat. Brought back to earth by his commonsense statement, Nellie remembered how silly she was being. Of *course* no one wanted "unconventional." She'd been hearing that all her adult life—sometimes about herself.

With effort, she rallied. "What I meant was, this appeals to me because I don't have a family to invite to a conventional wedding," Nellie said as matter-of-factly as she could. Through long practice, she was able to shrug. "My friends and coworkers would hardly fill up two pews, much less half a church!"

"I'm sorry. I didn't know that." Everett's sympathetic gaze followed her. "I read all your letters—Oscar gave them to me last night," he went on, "but they didn't mention—"

"No, they wouldn't have." Giving him a smile, Nellie went

to him. She took his hands in hers. "It's all right, Everett. I was an only child, and my parents died a long time ago." She offered him a squeeze. "Do you think I'd have turned out this way if I'd had someone watching over me for all these years?"

Contrary to her expectations, he took her joke seriously.

"I like the way you turned out," Everett said.

Nellie wished she could believe that. But Everett didn't know the real her...and if she succeeded, he never would.

"Someone else likes the way you turned out, too," Everett teased. He nodded toward her feet. For an instant, Nellie thought she was going to have to display her "unconventional" boots again. Everett must have been disappointed to have glimpsed them. He'd been polite about them, of course, by pretending to be more interested in her knees than her wardrobe.

"Have you noticed your entourage?" he asked now, gesturing toward the shaggy dog who'd been following her around. By now, the cat from the kitchen had joined the lovable mutt, too. "Counting my dog, my cat and the mare who was nosing around after you outside, you have a veritable menagerie started."

Nellie laughed. "Now you're just being silly. Horses don't follow around people! They're not like dogs and cats."

Everett shrugged. "The evidence at hand, as you say, can't be ignored." His eyes glimmered at her. "Around these parts, Nellie, you are *beloved*. By my livestock, my *vaqueros*—"

"Ha! If only that were true," Nellie joked, unable to hear more talk like that. But, tellingly, her voice cracked on the words. She *did* want to be beloved, if the truth were known. She wanted to lavish affection on Everett—and on his various animals and his ranch hands and Edina and Marybelle, too. She wanted to give away her pent-up love. She wanted to quit holding it close for fear that no one would want it if she offered it.

She hadn't known she'd been doing that until right now.

"You *could be* beloved," Everett assured her, pulling her closer, "if you wanted to be. If you would accept an ordinary man and a barn-bound wedding and a passel of funny traditions."

Nellie was afraid to hope for so much. "Well, I *am* powerfully curious about all those traditions," she allowed.

"We'll be getting to them shortly," Everett promised. "All fifty-nine of them that my ranch hands made me promise to try."

At his wry but accepting grin, she practically fell in love on the spot. Why did Everett have to be so remarkable…and so increasingly out of her reach? The more he revealed his almost flawless, gentlemanly self, the less she measured up to him.

"And I *do* fancy the idea of getting married in a barn," she added insouciantly, trying her very hardest not to envision that selfsame ceremony. But it was no use. In a heartbeat, Nellie pictured Everett standing handsomely and earnestly by her side while she said her vows in a dress handmade by Marybelle and Edina. If only that reverie could be more than just a dream!

"Well, my barn has never looked better," Everett confirmed.

"But I'm afraid I just don't see an *ordinary* man around here," Nellie told him, playfully pretending to look for one. Smiling, she brought her hands to his suit coat lapels and patted them in demonstration. "All I see is a fine gentleman!"

"A fine gentleman? *That's* what you see?" Everett stalked nearer, seeming displeased by her compliment. He glowered down at her. "Look closer," he said, then he kissed her again.

Swept away beneath his kiss, Nellie clutched his lapels and just held on. Her heartbeat galloped; her breath left her in a single surprised utterance. All she could feel was wanting. All she could do was kiss him back. Because there had

never been anything she'd wanted more than to kiss Everett. There had never been anything she'd *needed* more than to feel his mouth on hers, his hands on her waist, his body pressing insistently closer.

Kissing Everett was like finding a lucky penny that never could be lost again. It was like understanding the meaning of poetry and music and art in a single instant. It was like wanting a drop of water and being presented with an ocean.

Nellie had never dreamed of having as much as she felt in Everett's arms. She had never known she could be so passionate, so needful…so wrong. It was wrong to do this to Everett and his ranch hands. It was wrong to pretend, even for a good cause.

But oh, how she wanted to go on doing it!

Surely the Almighty would understand why she needed to do this. Surely He would forgive her this one lapse in a lifetime filled chockablock with efforts to see more, do more, *be* more.

Surely He would give her a few minutes more of this.

Instead the tall, blond *vaquero* rushed inside the barn like an unwanted heavenly timekeeper, putting an awkward end to Nellie's prayers for more time alone with Everett. Guiltily, she and her "fiancé" leaped apart while the ranch hand came nearer.

It took Nellie a solid ten seconds to recollect that, as an officially engaged woman, she was *allowed* to socialize with her fiancé. She was allowed to gaze wistfully at Everett, to indulge her impulse to hold his hand…to satisfy her curiosity about him.

It was the most liberating realization she'd had all week.

"Aha! *There* you are, *patrón*!" The lanky *vaquero* pointed outside, oblivious to the barn's fancifully decorated interior. "Come quick! You're already late for the bunkhouse jamboree."

Everett quirked his dark eyebrow. "You must be mistaken."

"No, I ain't! Last night, at dinner, you said you'd come."

"To a jamboree?" Everett sounded skeptical. "Impossible. I make it a practice never to attend jamborees—*especially* if they're happening in the bunkhouse. A shindig, maybe. A party—"

Nellie didn't believe him. "Why not? It sounds like fun!"

"Fun? This won't be a fancy, *big-city* soirée, like you're used to," Everett warned. "This won't be a ball or a gala—"

"It'll be a jamboree!" the *vaquero* supplied obligingly.

"—or anything like what you're missing from San Francisco."

Nellie frowned. She wasn't missing anything. But this wasn't the time to say so—especially since she, as a *Godey's*-style "wishy-washy, swooning female," ought to have been wanting a fashionable diversion to occupy herself with. So, dutifully, she smiled at the *vaquero*. "We'd be delighted to attend."

"Thank you, ma'am." The youth shot Everett a victorious look, then swept off his hat. Holding it in his hand, he gave Nellie a bow. "I'm Casper Dietson, ma'am, at your service."

"I'm pleased to meet you, Mr. Dietson." Nellie shook his hand. "I was very sorry not to get your name yesterday before you went to town, nor last night in all the hubbub at dinner."

"Shucks, that's all right, ma'am." Casper plunked on his hat. "I didn't reckon it was safe to tell you my name until now. But now that you're here *for good*, I guess it's all right."

At that, Casper delivered a delighted grin to his *patrón*.

Under his glowing approval, Everett bore up stoically.

Then Casper took a second hasty glance. "What's that you've got on yourself, *patrón*? A suit? And specs? Ain't that somethin'? I never known you to tolerate fancyin' up like that."

Stone-faced, Everett blinked. He tugged at his hat, indi-

cating a decision was at hand. "I guess I was wrong about that jamboree, Casper. Miss Trent likes parties. So I do, too."

His acquiescence had a revitalizing effect on the *vaquero*.

"Well, I suppose you oughtta like the jamboree! It's on account of the two of you that we're having it!" Casper chuckled. He beamed at them both. "It's for your engagement!"

"Well, isn't that nice?" Nellie nudged Everett. "Dearest?"

He recognized her cue and smiled. "Perfect, sweetheart."

Casper squinted at them both. Then he shook his head. "If you two don't beat all," he said happily. "You're as cute as a pair of june bugs! I aim to tell all the fellas that right now!"

The *vaquero* hurried off, clearly pleased as punch with his *hacendado's* new love match…and dying to share his excitement.

Everett stiffened. "I've got to stop him."

"What for?" Nellie put her hand on his arm. "We *want* all your men to believe we're crazy about one another, don't we?"

"Of course we do. For your newspaper story." Unmoving, Everett compressed his mouth. He cast her a plaintive look, full of nicked male pride and patent disbelief. "It's just… He said we were *cute* together, Nellie. He called me a june bug!"

She suppressed a grin. "I heard him."

"So—" as though it were obvious "—I have to stop him."

At that, Nellie gave him a long look. "You know what? Even when you're disgruntled and childish, I think you're adorable."

"*Childish?*" His jaw tightened. "*Adorable? Impossible.*"

"You keep saying that," Nellie told him, unable to hold back a grin. "To you, 'impossible' seems to signify agreement."

Before Everett could respond to her banter, Casper halted at the barn door. "Come on, you june bugs!" he shouted with a hurry-up gesture. "Git your feet moving. Time's wastin'!"

Nellie laughed. "Come on, june bug!" She gave Everett a poke. "We don't want to miss the party in our honor, do we?"

"Heaven forbid." With a chivalrous gesture of his powerful arm, he escorted her ahead of him. "After you, Miss Trent."

A few steps onward, Nellie realized he wasn't alongside her. She stopped. She looked back. "Aren't you coming?"

"Yes. First I'm consoling myself by watching you walk ahead of me. It's the least I deserve." Everett lifted his devilish, dancing-eyed gaze from the vicinity of her bustle to her face. "From where I'm standing, the jamboree's already happening."

She laughed. "You're incorrigible."

"Absolutely." He grinned. "I think you like it."

"Why, Mr. Bannon!" Nellie gave her bustle a coquettish wiggle. "Would you look at that? I think I just might."

Everett's husky laugh was enough to make her day.

For a heartbeat, as they smiled at one another, Nellie felt certain they were in perfect harmony. She took unabashed delight in Everett's scandalous appreciation of her physical charms—even swaddled, as they were, in boys' boots and last year's dress and a halfhearted attempt to style her hair in a fetching fashion—and she imagined that he, for his part, found an equal enjoyment in her teasing and unladylike repartee.

But then Casper hollered for them both again, wanting them to hurry, and Nellie snapped out of her impracticable reverie.

She could not make decisions based on what she *felt* about Everett, she reminded herself. She had to act based on what she knew to be true about him—what she *knew* to be true about herself. Everett had told her he wanted a swooning, compliant lady. However much Nellie tried, she could not be that for him. Not forever, at least. So unless Everett informed her otherwise between the bunkhouse jamboree in their honor

and the "wedding day" they'd ostensibly reach in a week or so, Nellie would have to make do with what was real.

If she could *remember* what was real, that was...

She was meant to be using this time to recover from her arduous train journey—not to fall in love with her host. She was supposed to be writing a newspaper story about disingenuous mail-order marriages—not enacting a similar fraud on herself.

If she fell entirely in love with Everett, would that make it all right? Nellie wondered. Or would that only make it hurt more on the inevitable day when Everett delivered the return train ticket he'd promised her...and made it plain he could not love her back?

"Cheer up, my beautiful bride-to-be." Catching up to her, Everett gave her a consoling squeeze of his hand. "If you're dreading having to endure a rustic territorial party, we'll only stay long enough to make the *vaqueros* happy. I promise."

Nellie gazed up at him. "How long will that be?"

Hours, she hoped to hear. *Days. Years and years and years.*

But Everett didn't seem to understand. "Not long," he said brusquely, then he offered her a smile and took her away.

Chapter Seven

When Everett saw Nellie glance up at him and, in her sweet and undeniably sensuous voice, ask him how long they'd have to tolerate the *vaqueros'* engagement party in their honor, he couldn't help being gutted. He'd wanted her to *want* to accompany him there. He'd wanted her to *yearn* to be by his side—the way he increasingly longed to be by hers—no matter where they went.

Instead her dolefully voiced question had let Everett know unequivocally that no matter how sophisticated he tried to be, he could never be the man Nellie wanted. He could never be the man she needed. He could never, ever, be the man she loved.

But that didn't mean Everett intended to quit trying.

Because Everett Bannon, in his heart of hearts, was not a man who quit. When Nellie had arrived, he'd felt reborn. His reaction to her, contradictorily, had proved he could not stop.

There was too much at stake to stop. Everett had thought he could stop caring, stop wanting, stop needing; now, with Nellie nearby, he could do nothing else. He'd thought he was done with living cheerfully and well; with Nellie at his side, every new moment was a celebration. He'd thought there

was nothing more for him to discover; with Nellie there to provoke laughter and surprise and contradictory reactions to everything, Everett knew, beyond a doubt, there was *everything* left to discover.

All the world's secrets could be found in Nellie's heart.

Everett knew he could unlock them. All he had to do was try. He knew he could win. All he had to do was throw himself into every manner of mad shenanigans and prewedding hoopla.

So, over the course of his *vaqueros'* rowdy jamboree—and at all of the many events that followed it over the next several days—Everett did exactly that.

He indulged every tradition. He tried every good-luck charm. He got fitted for a wedding suit, wore a "fruitfulness-enhancing" leafy Slavic headpiece, and slumbered with apples, asparagus and gold coins under his pillow to ensure (variably) a happy marriage, a sweet-tongued wife and future prosperity.

He tripped his way through folkloric dances—laughing as Nellie blushed and skipped and showed admirable prowess with the complicated steps—and selected himself some trusted groomsmen. He let a roving medicine showman predict his prospects…and smiled along with Nellie when those prospects were good.

But Everett didn't restrict his efforts to bunkum like springtime flower selecting and itinerant fortune-telling. He also spent every moment he could with Nellie, talking and sharing and laughing and stealing kisses. In hardly any time at all, he could scarcely envision his household without her in it.

Simply put, Nellie *fit* there. She fit with him.

She understood the wildness and vitality and freedom of the West. She seemed to like it, too. In her hands—and with his *vaqueros'* instructions—a lasso became a thing of grace and beauty. Blessed by her smile, Everett's ranch hands and

horses and hodgepodge of pets became something more than they'd been.

Thanks to Nellie, his band of miscreants became a family.

Everett didn't want to lose that. But as he sat at a late-night campfire with his entire world surrounding him—however meager it was—watching Nellie be adorned with garlands of woven flowers in some almost-forgotten marital tradition that Ivan had insisted they observe, Everett had no idea how to hold on to it.

It was possible, he knew as he smiled anew at Nellie, that *he* was the only one who felt the pull between them. It was possible that *she*, as a citified sophisticate with more suitors than shoes, was still merely *pretending* to care about him.

If she was, Everett decided as he got to his feet to go to her, then she was doing a mighty convincing job of it. Because as he took Nellie's hand and led her away from the firelight, he could feel the heat and need between them. He could feel the unusual strength of their bond, as tenacious and surprising as the fast-growing wildflowers along the road to town. He could *know*, in his heart, that providence had brought her to him.

All he had to do now was make her his forever.

And because he was man enough to do so, Everett drew Nellie into the same space near the barn door where he'd first kissed her. He caught hold of her dewy flower garlands, then smiled.

"Pretty," he said. "But not half as beautiful as you."

He kissed her, hungrily, the way he'd dreamed of doing while watching her "prepare" for their wedding. Then Everett delved his hands in her hair and kissed her again. He needed to feel her mouth against his—needed to sweep his tongue against hers and steal the same breath and give her... *everything* he had.

"I guess they work, then," Nellie said when he raised his head at last. Playfully she dragged her strands of flowers over

his chest, his neck, his face. "They're supposed to make me irresistible to you, so that you want to have the wedding."

"Oh, I want to have the wedding." He kissed her again, letting her know with every thrust of his tongue that he spoke the truth. He pinned her against the barn's rough exterior wall, heedless of the raucous celebrating still going on near the campfire. He roved his hands over her sides, her waist, her derriere. "I want to have *you*, Nellie. I want you so much."

"Yes." Breathlessly she caressed him, too. Her hands touched his back, his nape and then his hair with what felt like wickedly seductive intent. "Oh, Everett. If only you knew!" Eagerly she kissed him. "Marybelle told me it would be *'la torture'* to wait for our wedding night. Edina warned me as well. But I never dreamed it would be like this! I wish—"

Gasping, Nellie stopped. She tossed her head while Everett pressed his lips to her neck, her earlobe, her waiting mouth.

"I wish we were getting married tomorrow!" he said roughly.

At the same time, Nellie blurted the very same thing.

In unison, they laughed, the spell of their kisses momentarily broken. This had been happening between them, too—this eerie synchronicity that suggested something more.

"See what just happened there?" Nellie pointed out with an elfin look. "*Now* do you want to discuss whether we're truly meant to be together, the way the marriage bureau claimed?"

"Shysters," Everett judged. "Fraudsters." He kissed her again, lightheartedly this time, but he couldn't help being reminded of her question to him days ago, after they'd shared their first kiss on this very same spot. Knowing she would persist—another quality he loved about Nellie—he shook his head. "I can't rightly say. I don't have my philosophy book."

And she, most likely, would expect erudition from him—scholarship and wisdom he would have stolen from one of

Oscar's many books—as patently false as his need for eyeglasses.

Why in tarnation had he hatched this plan at all? Everett wondered. Right now, it was only separating him from Nellie. He couldn't truly be her man, and he wasn't sure he was helping her with her blasted newspaper story, either—despite all the note-taking and writing she'd done so far. That had impressed him, too—her dexterity with words. But for some reason, her fluent ability to describe her thoughts wasn't evident just then.

"Oh. You can't say? All right then," Nellie told him with her usual sprightliness. "Maybe you'll tell me later."

It was her customary rejoinder—one that, Everett had learned, signified disappointment as much as resignation. He wished the two didn't come so automatically to Nellie.

He wished harder that she wouldn't feel them at all.

He wasn't sure what he'd done to upset her—and the tempting curve of her mouth prevented him, quite reasonably, from delving into the matter any further. Driven by craving and passion and a need to assure Nellie that he *did* care for her, even if he didn't have the fancy authorial words to say so, Everett kissed her again. He held her close. He let his actions speak as best as they could, in the darkness surrounding his barn and his land and his poor woebegone heart, and if gestures had meanings, then his kisses meant everything. They were promises. And entreaties.

"Come away with me, Nellie," he urged in a husky voice. "Just for the night. Come away, right now. No one will know—"

"*Everyone* will know. Your household is overflowing!"

Everett shook his head. "If we slip away now, no one will see. They're busy weaving Russian flower garlands."

"I saw Ivan give one to Edina," she said chattily. "Do you think they'll be next to be engaged?" Then, looking up at

him, Nellie seemed to realize how inadequate her attempts to distract him were. "Not that *we're* truly engaged, but you know—"

"Please." He sweetened his request with another kiss. In his arms, Nellie was pliant and warm and breathless, and he knew she was close to agreeing. "We'll be alone all night."

"Alone? Together?" Her gaze looked tremulous. "But I—"

"Say yes, Nellie. I can tell that you want to. I—"

I want to, too! Everett meant to say, but before he could, Nellie sharpened her gaze. She pulled back abruptly.

"You *can't* tell that about me. You can't! Even if I *am* outside a barn kissing you, I'm a good woman, Everett," Nellie insisted. Sudden tears swam in her eyes. Her chin wobbled. "I am! Maybe not *exactly* the kind of woman you said you wanted—"

"Precisely the kind I wanted," he swore, feeling his meager powers of volubility deserting him like dandelion fluff on a seedtime breeze. *"You're* the woman I want, Nellie! Why else—"

Why else would I be wearing spectacles and a suit? Everett wanted to shout. *Why else would I carry around books and sleep with apples under my head?* But again Nellie cut him short.

"If this is a test, I hope I've passed," she said.

He boggled at her. "A test? Of what?"

Nellie crossed her arms over her chest, making him miss the feel of her arms around *him*. A long moment passed. The balmy April breezes lifted her skirt hem and ruffled Everett's shirt. A coyote howled. In the gloom, Nellie's face turned downcast.

"I have a great deal of work to do," she declared. "Our 'wedding' is just days away, and I've scarcely written enough material to fill a single column inch at the *Weekly Leader*."

"You're thinking of work? *Now?*"

"Well." With a single backward step, Nellie seemed to put a mile's worth of distance between them. "That's what I'm here to do, isn't it? Although we ought to discuss how to break off our 'engagement,'" she went on in a reasonable-sounding tone. "I think *you* should be the one to do it, on account of your—"

"I *won't* do it!" This time, it was Everett's turn to fold his arms over his chest. He glowered at Nellie, hoping she could sense the depth of his dislike of that notion. He wasn't ready for this. "Are you saying you don't want to get married?"

"Are you saying you *do*?"

Caught, Everett frowned. He wanted to cast aside his pretenses, show himself for the man he was...be *loved* for the man he was. If he was honest with himself, that was *all* he wanted.

Despite that, fear held him silent.

Fear held him silent, stubborn...and woefully alone.

No right-thinking woman wants to live on a hardscrabble ranch with a burly, unrefined oaf for a husband, Everett, he remembered Abbey O'Neill telling him all those months ago. *Honestly. Did you think I would settle for this? For you?*

He couldn't ask Nellie to make the sacrifice that Abbey had refused. Nellie was better than Abbey—better than anyone he knew. Everett couldn't ask her to throw away her work, her talent, her dazzling life in the city, all for his sake.

What he *could* do was sacrifice, this night, for her.

"Let's see this through a few more days," he said. "That will be enough time—" *to get a return train ticket, savor our last few hours together, stamp your memory on my heart, where it can never be erased* "—to put things as they should be."

At that, Nellie's wounded gaze swerved to his. She gave him an unsteady smile. She reached for his hand. Her touch felt more necessary than the air Everett breathed...more heart-

breaking than all the moments leading up to this had been or ever would be.

"Gentlemanly to the end?" Nellie said with a faint nod of approbation. She inhaled deeply, then nodded. "I understand."

Everett didn't want her to understand. He wanted her to come away with him, to be with him…to love him. But if this was what he got instead, he vowed to make the most of it.

"You won't want this later," Nellie said in a confusingly wry and self-deprecating tone, "so I'll give it to you now."

Still holding his hand, she levered upward. She looked into his eyes, brought her mouth to his, then kissed him. Softly. Slowly. Sweetly. He'd have sworn her heart and soul was in that one point of contact between them…but as soon as Everett had that fanciful thought and opened his eyes to verify it, she was gone. All he could glimpse in the darkness around him were shadows and faraway flickers, too hazy to make out or hold on to.

Then the darkness filled with sound of a strumming guitar. A dozen hoarse male voices raised in song. Everett knew then that fate had recognized Nellie's departure, too. The song on the air was one his *vaqueros* had written specifically for her on the day of her arrival in Morrow Creek. They played it now like a love song. Like an epic ballad. Like one of the sonnets that Everett had tried—and bungled—reading to Nellie himself.

Inhaling a fortifying breath, Everett joined in, too. After all that Nellie had given him, it was the least he could do.

At least it was…for now.

Chapter Eight

From the night of the campfire onward, Nellie's course of action was plain. She couldn't spend any more time laughing with Everett, exploring his ranch hand in hand, or learning about esoteric wedding customs and the quirky traditions of his *vaqueros'* diverse homelands. As much as she'd loved getting to know Everett and his life in the West, she had to move on.

The strain she'd been under—and the way she'd cracked under that strain when Everett had asked her to slip away with him that fateful night—had made that truth more than evident. She wasn't cut out to be a rancher's compliant wife. The effort of pretending she was was devastating, both to her and to Everett.

Nellie knew, in retrospect, that he hadn't been disrespectful of her. Likely *he'd* felt the connection between them, too… and had wanted to deepen it by being alone together.

In her heart of hearts, Nellie had wanted that, too.

But then, as now, she hadn't been able to face that. She hadn't been able to let Everett throw away his future on an impulse fueled by a single tender moment and a moonlit spring night. Everett deserved more than that. He deserved

more than a tomboyish wife who loved his ribald jokes more than his sonnet readings, his rolled-sleeve Henley shirts more than his neckties and suits, and his wide-open lands more than his tidy library. He deserved…*everything*. Everything Nellie couldn't give him.

Everett would never be happy with a hoydenish wife like her, Nellie knew. And she couldn't change her ways—not lastingly, at least. It gave her too much pleasure to tramp through the fields, twirl her heavy borrowed lasso and watch the mustangs run. She didn't want to make either of them miserable; that's what staying together would accomplish. Yet, contradictorily, Everett refused to end their engagement.

He *had* to be the one to do so! In the same way that he'd categorically refused to discuss canceling their wedding, Nellie refused to humiliate him the same way Miss O'Neill had. She refused to run. She refused to toss him away heartlessly.

The only thing to do was to make Everett reject *her*. And the only way to do *that* was simple to discern.

Nellie had to let him see *her*. The real her.

The unconventional, boots-wearing, unacceptable *her*.

So, when Everett happened upon her practicing her new lasso-twirling skills with his ranch hands' help, Nellie spun that hank of braided leather with twice her usual vigor. When she accompanied Everett to their next round of engagement parties and traditional soirees and prewedding activities, she strode ahead of him with stamina and enthusiasm. When dining, Nellie shunned delicate pastries and pies in favor of spicy dishes full of chilis; when dancing, she moved with abandon; when relaxing in the evenings, she forewent her earlier attempts at ladylike needlework and substituted pen and paper instead.

"Read to me what you've written," Everett said on one of those nights. And because Nellie was trying to make him

see how unsuitable she truly was for him, she went ahead and did so.

When she'd finished, she lowered her paper. "Well?"

"You have a knack for detail and an evocative turn of phrase. You're even more talented than I thought, Nellie."

Flabbergasted, she stared at him. "You're supposed to say, 'Those are silly scribblings,' or 'Describe the dresses more.'"

"Your article is an exposé of mail-order marriage bureaus," Everett said mildly. "It's not about dresses."

"But a tidbit about fashionable reticules could probably be worked in someplace," she retorted. "Isn't that correct?"

With big hazel eyes, Everett gazed at her as though she were mad. "Are those the kinds of things you usually hear?"

Defensively she jutted her chin. "Sometimes. Of course."

"The only 'of course' thing about that is that you've been listening to the wrong people," Everett told her. Then he adjusted his spectacles and went back to reading his book.

"German philosophy isn't usually read upside down," Nellie pointed out huffily. "And your eyeglasses are on crooked."

But Everett only smiled at her and went on reading.

Her other efforts to make him end their engagement were similarly futile. Nellie kissed him in the upstairs hallway, late at night after everyone else had gone to sleep, hoping to prove how horribly unladylike she was…and had nearly succeeded in starting a house fire with her own body heat for her trouble. She took to showing off her muddy boots, loudly proclaiming her ineptness at cookery and boldly feeding the mustangs carrots.

Everett only watched her with an implacable expression and said, variously, "My boots are muddy, too." Then, "Edina would bawl if you tried to take away her biscuit-making bowl." And finally, blithely, "Watch your fingers. That one bites."

In despair, and with only days left until their "wedding,"

Nellie finally snatched up a bottle of Old Orchard from the hidden stash in the kitchen, marched out to the eastern barn and proceeded to make herself unavoidably, unfemininely drunk.

Unfortunately Everett found her before she got very far.

"You might have invited me here for a drink yourself," he said as he sauntered inside, limned by the afternoon light from the window in the hayloft, looking handsome and broad-shouldered and breathtakingly necessary for her overall happiness, "rather than leading me on this wild-goose chase." He put his hands on his hips. "Marybelle told me you were down by the creek."

"Aha!" Wild-eyed, Nellie pointed the whiskey bottle at him. "That's what I *told* her to tell you! It was a clever diversion."

"Well, I can't say you weren't thorough." With something akin to admiration, Everett came nearer. He sat on a hay bale beside her, close enough that she could smell his intoxicating shaving soap. "Edina claimed you were at the telegraph office in town. Ivan insisted you were hiding *bizcochitos* in the attic. Oscar said you'd gone to become a dance-hall girl at Jack Murphy's saloon." He grinned. "His was the most entertaining."

"I see." After taking another bitter swig from her bottle, Nellie hugged it to her chest. Inside she felt hollow and desperate—but also a tiny bit hopeful, too. Did Everett's continued pursuit of her mean he cared...a little? "Is that all?"

A chuckle. "Not by a long shot." Squinting roguishly at the bunting and ribbons overhead, Everett recalled more details for her. "Several men pointed me toward the mountains, claiming you'd found a gold strike. Pedro challenged me to a duel, simply for asking about you. He said he would fight for your honor."

"That's sweet. And Casper?"

"Casper confessed everything in five seconds flat. Then he spent the next fifteen minutes begging forgiveness for deceiving me in the first place." A sardonic grin. "That boy hasn't got a sneaky bone in his body."

"Humph. I guess that's how you found me in here, then?"

"No." Shaking his head, Everett gazed fondly at her. His face was clean-shaven, his hair unmussed, his suit rigorously tidy. She longed for the Everett Bannon she'd *first* met—rugged, straight-talking and a little bit wild. "I saw you go in here."

"Then why did you question everyone else?"

"I wanted to see how far their loyalties went."

"Oh." Nellie considered that. "How far did they go?"

"All the way to *defying me* and back." Everett seemed put out by that—and a little bit amused, too. "I never thought I'd see the day. I told you—they all love you." Illustratively he angled his head toward the barn door. "I'll have you know, there are six horses, one cat, one dog and a hungry stray bunny outside right now, all waiting for you to come out."

But *Everett* wasn't waiting for her, Nellie couldn't help thinking. And that was all that mattered to her, now and later and all the painful times in between. *Everett* didn't want her.

At least he didn't want the real her. The *wild* her.

Maybe the original Everett she'd met would have…

Banishing the thought, Nellie gave her Old Orchard bottle a rebellious swish, readying herself for more. She didn't really want to drink any more. To her, whiskey tasted like vinegar… only slightly *less* toothsome. But this was her last-ditch effort to do the right thing by Everett, and she didn't want to fail.

"I don't even like bunnies," Nellie lied. Then, screwing up her face, she valiantly took another hefty swallow of whiskey.

Reflexively she shuddered. Everett gave a knowing laugh.

"It's a good thing the bunnies have the sense to like you anyway, despite all your protests," he said. "Just like the rest

of us do." Quietly he covered her hand with his. He squeezed. "Before you get too out of hand, give over that bottle."

Defiantly she clasped it harder. "If you're wanting to be paid for it, I can do that. I have my own money, you know."

"I don't want to be paid for it." Everett peered at its sloshy, foul-tasting contents. "Besides, I wouldn't have the first idea how much to charge for two and a half swallows."

"Humph. I have an excellent job at the newspaper," Nellie informed him proudly, beginning to feel the disorienting effects of the whiskey despite Everett's low estimation of her consumption so far. "Did I ever tell you how I got my job?"

"You did not. I'd like to know."

She examined him, decided he meant it sincerely and loved him a little bit more because of it. "I read a horribly offensive and sexist article in the *Leader* and wrote to the editor in protest. He liked my writing well enough to offer me a job."

"I'm impressed."

Not enough to marry me! her poor sorrowful heart cried, but Nellie forged on in spite of it. "When I arrived and he realized I was a woman, he rescinded his offer." She heard Everett's swearword in response to that and smiled in acknowledgment. "It took me all afternoon to persuade him to hire me. But I did it."

"I don't doubt you did." For a moment, all Everett did was gaze at her, proudly, affectionately and—if she wasn't mistaken—sadly, too. "You're an extraordinary woman, Nellie. Truly."

At that, she scoffed. Everett's sad, stoic tone scared her. She didn't understand it. She didn't want to. And yet...

"If *I'm* so extraordinary, why do *you* sound so miserable?"

"Because—" Everett began, then he broke off. He squeezed her hand in his again. "Because I don't want any of this."

That was blunt. The depth of her despair upon hearing his words shocked her. Morosely Nellie stared at the dust motes

floating in a beam of sunshine. The barn would never host a wedding now. It looked so lovely, yet it would remain empty.

She'd *so* wanted it to be filled to the rafters with the wedding vows that she and Everett would exchange. Her heart hurt with the effort it required to suppress her longing for that.

"I don't want to hold you back," Everett was saying, "and I don't want the world to be without your newspaper stories."

She had the impression he'd been talking and she'd missed something. Perhaps, Nellie realized belatedly, she was more susceptible to the effects of demon drink than she'd thought.

"Don't worry," she told him, doing her best not to weep. "Everything in my story will be positive. None of it will reflect poorly on you or your *vaqueros* or your *hacienda*." Drawing in an empowering breath, Nellie squared her shoulders. She even, miraculously, managed to sound composed. "It turns out that I was wrong about mail-order marriage bureaus. They're not frauds. They really can find ideal matches for people. I know that because they found me *you*, and I feel that *we, together*—"

To her dismay, her throat closed up on the words. Nellie could not speak. She couldn't see through the haze of tears filling her eyes, either. Drat! Why was this so difficult?

Doing the right thing was supposed to be, if not easier, then at least heartening. But Nellie didn't feel heartened. Sitting there, close enough to feel Everett's warmth and hear his breath and know his kindness, she only felt…alone.

So alone. And sad. And hopeless and tipsy and bereft.

"You asked me before if I thought we were meant to be together," Everett was saying now, forcing her to recall those times she'd foolishly shared her feelings—her fantasies that somehow, some way, they were *destined* for one another. "I didn't have an answer for you then. But now I do." He drew in a ragged breath. Then, "The answer is no, Nellie. It has to be no."

Stunned, she let his words wash over her. As gently said as they were, they threw into harsh relief her earlier hopes that Everett's pursuit of her, here to the barn, meant he cared.

That her inability to drive him away…meant he cared.

Wordlessly Nellie nodded. The motion made her tears fall on their joined hands. Embarrassed, she pulled away.

But Everett reclaimed her hand. Urgently he pressed something in her grasp. "That's why I got you this," he said, sounding hoarse and angry and bewilderingly formal. "So you can be happy. So you can go back to the city and be happy."

Dazed, Nellie opened her hand. A train ticket lay there.

Everett was sending her away. Here, in the place they were supposed to have been married—if her daydreams had come true—he was giving her the ticket he'd promised. He did not love her.

She'd succeeded.

Victory had never felt more bittersweet.

"I see." With tremendous determination, Nellie stood. She wobbled a bit, but she did it. She nodded. "Thank you, Everett."

Through her teary vision, she glimpsed his expression. He appeared aghast—probably at having provoked her tears at all. Men, her editor had informed her, did not like emotional women.

Unfortunately he'd also said there was no other kind.

For no good reason other than the fact that she was at a loss for what to do next, Nellie handed Everett the bottle.

"If you'll excuse me," she said, "I think I might be ill."

"Oh! I'll help you." Sounding aggrieved, Everett stood. Gentlemanly to the end, just as she'd suspected, he reached for her. "Let me help you. I'm sorry, Nellie! Let me help. Please."

But Nellie Trent hadn't been an unconventional, inconvenient, tomboyish woman all her life for no reason. The reason was, it turned out, that her sporting ways allowed her

to run. So before Everett could touch her—before he could break her heart all over again by pitying her—Nellie turned and ran away.

Forever.

Chapter Nine

With his head in his hands and his unwanted whiskey bottle on the kitchen table in front of him, Everett moaned in agony.

"Why?" he groaned. "Why did it take me so long to see what was happening?" An idea occurred to him. With extreme bias, he wrenched off his stupid borrowed eyeglasses. He hurled the spectacles away from him, letting them *clink* to a stop on the oak tabletop near Marybelle's basket of clean laundry. "It's probably these damn spectacles," Everett groused. "I could hear that Nellie was upset, but I couldn't see what was wrong. I was confused. It was dark. She'd been drinking. Drinking!"

He had actually driven a good woman to drink, Everett realized. He was a monster. However, drinking sounded like a fine idea for the likes of him, Everett realized tardily. He grabbed the Old Orchard. He took a searing, useless glug.

It didn't help. He was still faced with the reality that he'd sent away Nellie—likely crushing her heart in the process—and he didn't have the first idea how to remedy the problem.

Why hadn't she been *thrilled* to return to San Francisco, the way he'd thought she would be? Why had she *cried* instead?

Could it be that she *hadn't* been pretending to care about him? If it was, he'd been a fool to push her away.

Melancholically Everett looked up. At least a dozen of his *vaqueros* stared back at him—most of them with distinct belligerence, resentment, or some combination of the two.

"If you want sympathy, *patrón*," Pedro announced, crossing his arms sulkily, "you won't get it from us. We miss Nellie."

"Da," Ivan said, apparently too riled up to eat for once. "This is not the way springtime wedding fever is supposed to go. This is not the way Edina said it would be. Right, Edina?"

"Absolutely!" The cook stepped up to the big Russian's side, stalwartly laying her hand on his shoulder. "The boys went to all that trouble to make everything perfect for you and Nellie, and you ruined it."

At her words, Everett flinched. He drank more whiskey.

"I was lying for part of it," he told her brokenly. "She wanted an answer from me. When it comes to Nellie, the answer is always 'yes!' *Always* 'yes!'" Everett babbled, awash in raw-feeling memories. "But if I'd said that, she'd have stayed."

"Then that's what you should have done," Marybelle said staunchly. "You should have said 'yes' a thousand times."

His housekeeper was right. She was right a thousand times. And yet… "I couldn't let her stay," Everett insisted in his own defense, unable to reconcile his good intentions with the calamity that had just occurred. "I *tried* to help Nellie once I realized she was crying, but she was fast. Too fast for me."

"She was too *perfect* for you, you mean," Oscar accused with his expression unforgivingly flinty. "Nellie was poetry and light and hope and joy! And *you*, *patrón*, are—"

"Gonna git her back," Casper interrupted gaily. "Right?"

They all stared expectantly at Everett. He frowned.

"Springtime wedding fever is not about misguided sacrifice and broken hearts and cast-off eyeglasses," Marybelle

urged him. "It is a time for *l'amour* and kisses and wedding dresses!"

She traded a look with Edina, reminding Everett that his housekeeper and cook had been diligently at work on a gown for Nellie. She'd even tried it on, he knew. The women had all shooed him from the house before he caught an "unlucky" glimpse of her wearing it. Now, Everett wished he'd looked anyway.

It would have been a memory worth keeping close forever.

"I don't have 'springtime wedding fever,'" he grumbled, irked to have his feelings for Nellie reduced to the equivalent of a bout of sniffles. "That's nothing more than a myth."

"*Sí*. What you've got is *nada*," Pedro said fiercely. "No Nellie, no wedding, and no good reason for any of it."

But Everett did have a reason. "She would not have been happy here," he told them stonily. "She is a citified woman. She needs a citified man. A man like Astair Prestell. Someone who—"

"Someone who will bore her to tears with useless jabbering and endless pomposity?" Edina inquired. "That kind of someone?"

Everett slumped. "A gentleman," he stated carefully. "Who—"

"A gentleman who wears suits?" Casper inquired, an oddly comprehending look on his face. "A gentleman who wears specs and neckties? A gentleman who shaves twice a day and totes around a boring ol' inch-thick book everyplace? That kinda 'gentleman'?" Wrinkling his brows, Casper gestured at Everett. "'Cause you already are one of them, *patrón*. You made yourself into one."

Everett shook his head. "It's fakery. It's all fakery. I'm no more a gentleman than my mustangs out there are," he said. "Nellie deserves better. She deserves...*everything*."

His *vaqueros* glared judgmentally at him. So did Edina and Marybelle. Everett fancied that even his cat and dog scowled.

"You are wrong about Nellie," Oscar said, cutting straight to the heart of the matter. "She is not like Miss O'Neill. She does not want a *Schwätzer* like Astair Prestell for a husband."

"*Non.* Indeed, she does not!" Marybelle nodded vehemently.

Everyone else only gawked at her. There was silence.

Then, "You know what *Schwätzer* means?" Edina asked, turning wide-eyed to her friend. "How on earth do you know that? I mean, Oscar said it like it was something awful, so I guess we all agreed with that part, but you seemed to know it for certain."

Coyly Marybelle said, "I may have been studying *Deutsch.*"

Oscar brightened. "*Wirklich?* Marybelle, that is *wunderbar!*" He smiled at her. "I am very impressed by you."

The housekeeper smiled serenely. "*Vielen Dank.*"

At that, Oscar seemed almost beside himself with joy. He grinned at Marybelle. She cast him a flirtatious glance back.

"Well, I reckon Edina and Ivan ain't gonna be the only ones gettin' themselves hitched soon," Casper said gleefully. "Do you s'ppose you can line up weddings like whiskeys and do 'em one right after another? 'Cause the barn's already decorated—"

"There aren't going to be any weddings," Everett interrupted harshly. "Not this week. Not in my barn." He didn't think he could stand it. Not after all that had happened. "I made a hash of things with Nellie. She's gone. It's too late."

"*Patrón.*" Pedro tsk-tsked. "It is *never* too late for *amor.*"

"That might be true for Edina and Ivan," Everett agreed. "And for Marybelle and Oscar." Although he was still dumbfounded by their budding romances, he was pleased for all four of them. "But it's not true for me. I know what I'm not,

and I'm *not* what Nellie needs. No matter how much I want her, I can't—"

"How do you know?" Ivan asked bluntly.

"How do I know what?" Everett gulped more whiskey. It still didn't help. His *vaqueros'* sour moods didn't help, either.

"How do you know you're not what she needs?" Edina clarified, easily seeming to understand what Ivan had meant.

Wistfully Everett remembered when he and Nellie had shared a similar synchronicity. The recollection made him feel worse.

With the last of his patience, Everett tried explaining *again* about Miss O'Neill—about her judgments about his ranch and his character and what right-thinking women wanted and needed.

He didn't get far.

"That is *absurdité*! You must fight for the woman you love!"

Oscar's outburst earned him a startled gasp from Mary-belle. In an aside to her, the gallant *vaquero* confided, "I may have been learning some of *le française*, as well. For you."

In response, the housekeeper swooned. Oscar winked.

That was it, Everett decided. The world had gone crazy.

Oscar did not wink; he was far too solemn for that. His ranch hands did *not* berate him; they were much too deferential to do so. And he did not, it occurred to him, have to stay here and listen to this. Resolutely Everett pushed back his chair.

Unsteadily he rose, bottle in hand. "I'm leaving."

"Yahoo!" Casper leaped to accompany him. "I'm going, too!"

Everett blinked. "Going where?"

"To fetch Nellie, of course."

"I'm not going to fetch Nellie."

But his *vaqueros* and Edina and Marybelle had already assembled themselves to accompany him. Eagerly they waited.

"You must!" Marybelle urged. "Go get her."

Everett scowled. "I wouldn't begin to know how."

"Apologize," Edina said readily. "Sweep her off her feet. Ask her to go away with you! It will be romantic."

"I already tried to get Nellie to go away with me," Everett said, remembering that balmy moonlit night. "She told me no."

Nellie's rejection of him then had solidified all his fears—that she didn't want him, couldn't love him, didn't need him. Everett didn't want a second dose of that hurtful tonic.

"The old ways have a solution for this, *patrón*," Pedro said. "If you are not sure of your lady's affections, you must—"

"No more traditions." Stanchly Everett held up his hand, cutting off Pedro before his *vaquero* could finish. "No more customs. No more wedding fripperies." He scoured them all with a pain-filled look. "Haven't you all done enough?"

For a moment, they lapsed into regretful stillness.

Then, from Ivan: "*We* have done enough, *patrón*. Have you?"

Everett frowned. About to insist that he *had* done enough—because he *had* loved Nellie, and he *had* tried to do what was right by her, and he *had* believed the right thing was sending her away—Everett was forced to reconsider.

He'd accepted this whole imbroglio the way he'd done everything else so far in his life—with curmudgeonly equanimity. He hadn't tried to fight. He hadn't done anything except enjoy Nellie's company…and then send her away. Maybe it was time, Everett decided, to fight for what he wanted—to fight for *Nellie*, no matter what the risk was to him.

She was worth it. Together, *they* were worth it.

With a decisive gesture, Everett set down his whiskey bottle. He reached for his hat, then tugged down the brim.

"This 'old ways' solution," he asked Pedro. "What is it?"

He could scarcely hear the specifics over the din of cele-bratory whoops and shouts from his improvised family. But before very long, Everett figured he had enough...if he com-bined it all with love and courage and a little bit of luck, be-sides.

It should have been her wedding day, Nellie realized as she paused over her satchel with an armful of petticoats. It should have been her time to declare her love for Everett, dance amid the hay bales beneath his barn's ribbon-bedecked timbers, and find out if Edina and Marybelle were right about the fun to be had during a raucous midnight chiverie.

She should have been finding out what Everett really *did* wear to sleep in...how he felt in her arms and how she felt in his. She should have been loving him. Instead, Nellie reck-oned morosely, she was packing for a return trip to San Fran-cisco that she did not want. She was preparing to go back to a life that had never felt emptier or—paradoxically—more constricting.

She was giving up before she'd truly gotten started.

If she could have packed away her feelings as readily as she'd packed away her belongings, things might have been different, Nellie knew as she stuffed in her petticoats and snapped shut her satchel's latch. But she couldn't stop think-ing about Everett. She couldn't stop wishing things could have been different between them. She couldn't stop won-dering *why* he'd finally decided to give her that train ticket and send her away.

In her most fearful moments, Nellie believed it was because Everett had glimpsed the real her...and then disapproved. But—

A banging sound outside her window cut short her thoughts.

Nellie jumped, staring in that direction. She had arranged this hotel room—admittedly hastily—after leaving Everett's ranch yesterday. Everyone had assured her that the Lorndorff Hotel was reputable. She'd been promised she would be safe there until it was time for her train's departure.

The thumping sound came again, louder this time.

Evidently, Nellie realized, she'd been misinformed. Someone—or something—was outside her hotel room window.

But she had not traipsed across several states and territories on her own during her time as a reporter for the *Weekly Leader* to surrender meekly to any threat. With a second glance at her packed satchels, she judged her escape route to the door and then lifted her chin with inherent pugnaciousness.

She'd been through too much to back down now, Nellie decided. Whoever was outside the window of her hotel room had chosen the wrong woman to pester this morning.

It might feel…*invigorating* to confront whatever was happening outside, Nellie thought as she eyed the drawn draperies with her fists tight, and assert herself against it.

Likely it was a squirrel. Or a cat. Or yet another bunny. Everett hadn't been utterly wrong about her erstwhile menagerie.

Just in case, Nellie armed herself. She stood tall.

A shadow crossed her window. More thumping could be heard.

The window sash lifted. Before she could yell for help or even reconsider her position, a dark-haired man stepped inside.

Nellie gawked at him. *"Everett? Is that you?"*

At her outburst, he turned around fully. He *looked* like Everett. Except he was dressed in rugged canvas pants and a white Henley shirt, not a suit and tie. And he wasn't wearing spectacles. And his hair was all mussed from climbing inside. And she'd have sworn he was sporting three days'

growth of beard, even though it had only been yesterday since she'd seen him.

"You look so...wild," Nellie blurted. "And so *manly*!"

The devilish grin he threw her only reinforced that rogue impression. "This is who I am, Nellie," Everett said. "I'm wild and I'm rough and I don't wear eyeglasses. I don't like suits and I've never written poetry and I can't abide wine."

Frozen in place and entirely unsure what to do next, Nellie clutched the makeshift weapon she'd grabbed: a broom left over from a maid's recent hotel room visit. It wobbled in her grasp.

Audaciously Everett eyed it. "What are you going to do with that?" He grinned again. "Clean up my muddy footprints?"

"Better yours than mine." With nothing left to lose, Nellie stuck out her boys' boots proudly. "This is who *I* am, Everett. I'm ambitious and smart and I don't like sewing. I loathe *Godey's Lady's Book* and I've never had a fainting spell. Ever."

He nodded. "Did you finish writing your article?"

"I forwarded it to my editor already, along with a proposal that I be allowed to work on a freelance basis. I know more than ever now that writing about parties and hors d'oeuvres will never make me happy." Still confused by seeing him there, Nellie set aside her broom. "I'm not planning to stay in town, if that's what you're wondering," she assured him. "I'm leaving shortly—"

"I have a better idea." Everett held out his hand. It trembled slightly. "Come with me, Nellie. *Be* with me. Please."

Even more perplexed by that, she wrinkled her brow. "Didn't you hear me? I just told you I *don't* like sewing. I *don't* like ladylike pursuits like reading about fashion and giggling inanely. So I can't imagine why in the world you would—"

Love me in spite of it all, Nellie finished silently.

"I know. And I love that about you," Everett said.

She blinked. "I must have gotten tipsier than I thought. I thought you just said—" She stopped. "No. I'm imagining you."

At that, he gave a husky chuckle. "Tipsy? Over two and a half swallows of whiskey? Yesterday? I doubt it."

"But I must be!" *Because you're here.* "I must—"

"Come with me, Nellie." Again Everett offered his hand. He wiggled his fingers enticingly. "Springtime is a time for second chances, and I'm asking you for mine, right now. I'm sorry for what happened yesterday. I'll try never to hurt you again. I didn't understand—I should have asked you what you wanted, instead of trying to decide for myself what you wanted."

Nellie frowned anew. "I *like* being outdoors, Everett," she specified with her heart pounding, just so he'd be sure to know the truth. She couldn't move on until she knew he understood. "I like hearing your bawdy jokes, and I like kissing you and I like *you*, so much, in every way, boldly and unstoppably and in no way politely, and I know that makes me less than perfect—"

"You're wrong," Everett told her with evident certainty. This time, he didn't wait for her to take his hand. *He* caught hold of *hers*, then he squeezed her tightly. "You *are* perfect, Nellie. I can't believe you'd think anything else."

"But I don't know how to embroider," Nellie pointed out, quite notably, she thought. "Surely you'll want a wife who—"

"I want *you*," Everett said. "And if you want me, too, then nothing else matters. Not eyeglasses or boots or bustles."

Entirely overwhelmed by that, Nellie gazed at him. "I didn't like your spectacles," she confessed. "Or your suits. Or your poetry readings. I like you best as you are right now."

"Fine. I'll give away my eyeglasses, hide away my suits

and never read a sonnet again. Now can we run away to-gether?"

At that, she laughed. "You can't mean it."

"I just climbed to the second floor of this hotel, opened your window and came inside," Everett pointed out, looking more rascally—and more irresistible—than ever. "I mean it." His grin broadened handsomely. "In case you hadn't noticed, Miss Trent, I'm officially kidnapping you. This is a roman-tic, unplanned elopement we're having. The least you could do is cooperate."

"If you want cooperation," Nellie said sassily, a little of her verve returning with him, "then you've got the wrong girl."

Then she realized the astonishing thing he'd just told her, and the truth hit her at once. *This* was the kidnapping tradition Edina and Marybelle had told her about! This was… It was…

It was *Everett*, showing her he loved her with a wedding to prove it or without one. And right now, given the way she'd been dithering, he probably believed it would be without one.

Without *her*.

All she knows is that she has to make a choice, Edina had said about the traditional bride in the scenario she'd been describing days ago. *And if she chooses wrong, the glorious wedding she's been dreaming about will go up in smoke.* Poof!

At the remembrance, Nellie shook her head. She glanced at Everett next, saw the heartrending vulnerability in his face, and knew that this choice was no real choice at all.

"I would rather have *you* than all the fancy weddings in the world," she told Everett truthfully. "I would rather be by your side in a horrible rainstorm than inside, alone by a cozy fire, without you. I would rather take my chances loving you—"

"*Loving me?* Did you just say—"

"—than know I would be blessed by leaving you. If it comes down to you or a beautiful barn wedding…I choose

you, Everett. I choose *you* every time, again and again. I choose you. Forever."

Again, he asked, "Did you just say 'loving me'?"

His astounded expression almost broke her heart. "Not yet. Not exactly. But I do." Impulsively Nellie took his face in her hands. She gazed into his eyes and spoke every truth she'd ever tried to hide. "I love you, Everett. I love your strength and your generosity and your way of tugging down your hat when you decide something important. I love your smile. I love your hands. I love your bristly beard stubble—" here, she rubbed her palm delightedly over it and discovered that it felt both soft *and* scratchy "—and I love your gruff ways and your tender heart. I love *you*, Everett! If I ever gave you cause to doubt that, I'm truly sorry. It was only because I was afraid. I was afraid you wouldn't love me back. But now you're here—"

"I'm here because I love you back," he said simply.

"—and everything is all right because of it." Decisively Nellie turned. She snatched up her satchels. With one in each hand, she bit her lip, then gazed inquisitively at Everett. "Do I jump in your arms now? Do you carry me over the threshold? Do we walk away arm in arm? What happens next?"

His intent, loving gaze swept over her. "Next I tell you I love you, Nellie. Because I do." Bravely Everett inhaled. "I love your smile and your vitality and your touch. I love that you can keep up with me. I love that you keep me on my toes!" He delivered a chuckle that warmed her clean through. "I love your kindness and your graciousness. I love your knack for writing and your talent with a lasso. I love…everything about you."

He brought her close, then confirmed his words with a kiss. With her hands still full of her baggage and her heart still full of her newfound second chance at love, Nellie could only hold on…and kiss Everett back with all her soul.

"As far as what comes next goes," Everett continued, wrapping his arms around her middle and smiling, "I guess we'll have to decide that together, just like everything else."

"Well, then," Nellie said. "I have an idea."

"I'm not at all surprised," Everett told her gladly.

And not long after that, she shared it with him.

Chapter Ten

Ten minutes later, Everett emerged from the front entrance of the Lorndorff Hotel with Nellie held close in his arms.

Squinting against the bright springtime sunshine, he stepped over the hotel's threshold with exquisite care, making sure there was no chance of tripping or falling. This wasn't the main door of their eventual home together, so the usual superstitions about a hapless bride bringing about bad luck on her wedding day—and hence needing to be carried over the threshold by her groom as a safeguard—didn't strictly apply. But after having been baptized in the mores of at least six different cultures' wedding traditions, Everett was taking no chances. He wanted his future with Nellie to be long and happy.

Right now, he could envision it no other way.

Secure in his arms, Nellie peered toward the street. She clutched her hastily grabbed satchels and squinted, like Everett had, against the glare. "Are they there?" she asked in a low voice, heedless of the curious townspeople who were beginning to stop and gather on the raised sidewalk nearby. "You said they'd all come with you to town. You said they'd all be there."

They're there, Everett was about to say…but then his *vaqueros* did it for him. As they had on that fateful night near the campfire, his ranch hands lifted their voices together to sing their song about Nellie. It was unaccompanied by guitar music. It was off-key and unquestionably rowdy. But it was, this time, a celebration…and to Everett, that's all that mattered.

Because Nellie loved him, and he loved her. In a world full of uncertainty and long odds and hard choices, they'd somehow had the good fortune to find one another, the audacity to fall in love…and the courage to claim that love, no matter what.

If that wasn't a miracle on the order of steam engines and ready-made shirts and good tinned beans, then Everett didn't know what was. He smiled, then set Nellie on her feet.

She set down her satchels. He straightened his shoulders. Then, hands clasped, they raised their arms in the air.

The din that greeted them was overpowering. It was loud and joyous and contained not a whit of ladylike or gentlemanly behavior—but it did contain plenty of hollering and a good deal of whooping. It came from all his ranch hands and Edina and Marybelle and all their friends and neighbors, too. And that was exactly the way Everett and Nellie liked it. Together.

"Aha. They're there," Nellie said, grinning beside him.

"You have no idea," Everett told her. "I heard that later they're planning to 'surprise' us with fireworks and mescal."

His wife-to-be—his *real* wife-to-be this time, and not his sham mail-order bride—squeezed his hand tightly.

"Not much surprises you, dearest," she teased. "Does it?"

"Only how lucky I am to have found you, sweetheart," Everett returned ably, again recognizing what she wanted. "That will surprise me for the rest of my life."

And as Everett delivered Nellie his most genuine smile yet, he knew that it was true. He *was* lucky. Beyond lucky.

"You know," Nellie mused aloud, "I think we *are* adorable."

"Yes," Everett agreed, feeling sappy and overcome, "but I'll still wallop any man who calls me cute as a june bug."

"Hmm. Then I guess, since I'm a woman, that'll just have to be *my* province." After a hug that felt as big and as strong as her generous heart, Nellie nudged Everett to head toward home. "Git your feet movin', june bug!" she said with a nudge and a saucy laugh. "We don't want to miss a minute."

"I'm piling up memories already," Everett told Nellie, picking up her satchels to carry. Then he followed her full-chisel toward their future. Because from where he stood, that future looked to be full of laughter and singing and a whole heap of loving…and, if he didn't miss his guess, a wedding night to remember, too. Reminded of that, he gave her another grin. "I aim to give you a few more memories to cherish later, too."

On the verge of being surrounded by all their *vaqueros* and friends, showered in well wishes, and feted as the savior of the most *formerly* woebegone man in Morrow Creek, Nellie stopped.

"Too late." She kissed Everett full on the mouth. "I've already started in on those happy memories. There's one now!"

Then she wrapped her arms around Everett, lifted her head at a jaunty angle and prepared to give him what he felt certain would be an interesting, invigorating and love-filled life.

Now and forever after…just the way Everett wanted.

* * * * *

HISTORICAL

Where Love is Timeless™

HARLEQUIN® HISTORICAL

COMING NEXT MONTH
AVAILABLE JUNE 19, 2012

RENEGADE MOST WANTED
Carol Arens
(Western)

AN ESCAPADE AND AN ENGAGEMENT
Annie Burrows
(Regency)

THE LAIRD'S FORBIDDEN LADY
Ann Lethbridge
(Regency)

TEMPTED BY THE HIGHLAND WARRIOR
The MacKinloch Clan
Michelle Willingham
(Medieval)

REQUEST YOUR FREE BOOKS!

 HARLEQUIN® HISTORICAL:
Where love is timeless

2 FREE NOVELS PLUS 2 **FREE GIFTS!**

YES! Please send me 2 FREE Harlequin® Historical novels and my 2 FREE gifts (gifts are worth about $10). After receiving them, if I don't wish to receive any more books, I can return the shipping statement marked "cancel." If I don't cancel, I will receive 6 brand-new novels every month and be billed just $5.19 per book in the U.S. or $5.74 per book in Canada. That's a savings of at least 17% off the cover price! It's quite a bargain! Shipping and handling is just 50¢ per book in the U.S. and 75¢ per book in Canada.* I understand that accepting the 2 free books and gifts places me under no obligation to buy anything. I can always return a shipment and cancel at any time. Even if I never buy another book, the two free books and gifts are mine to keep forever.

246/349 HDN FEQQ

Name _____ (PLEASE PRINT)

Address _____ Apt. #

City _____ State/Prov. _____ Zip/Postal Code

Signature (if under 18, a parent or guardian must sign)

Mail to the **Reader Service:**
IN U.S.A.: P.O. Box 1867, Buffalo, NY 14240-1867
IN CANADA: P.O. Box 609, Fort Erie, Ontario L2A 5X3

Not valid for current subscribers to Harlequin Historical books.

Want to try two free books from another line?
Call 1-800-873-8635 or visit www.ReaderService.com.

* Terms and prices subject to change without notice. Prices do not include applicable taxes. Sales tax applicable in N.Y. Canadian residents will be charged applicable taxes. Offer not valid in Quebec. This offer is limited to one order per household. All orders subject to credit approval. Credit or debit balances in a customer's account(s) may be offset by any other outstanding balance owed by or to the customer. Please allow 4 to 6 weeks for delivery. Offer available while quantities last.

Your Privacy—The Reader Service is committed to protecting your privacy. Our Privacy Policy is available online at www.ReaderService.com or upon request from the Reader Service.

We make a portion of our mailing list available to reputable third parties that offer products we believe may interest you. If you prefer that we not exchange your name with third parties, or if you wish to clarify or modify your communication preferences, please visit us at www.ReaderService.com/consumerschoice or write to us at Reader Service Preference Service, P.O. Box 9062, Buffalo, NY 14269. Include your complete name and address.

HHI1B

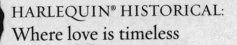

HARLEQUIN® HISTORICAL:
Where love is timeless

Fan-favorite author
MICHELLE WILLINGHAM

brings readers another captivating tale from

The MacKinloch Clan

*Highland warriors prepared to fight fiercely
for their country…and for love*

After years of brutal torture, Callum MacKinloch is finally free of his captors—but his voice is still held prisoner. He never let anyone hear him scream. When Marguerite discovers Callum waiting to die, her heart aches for the warrior beneath the suffering—but they can have no future. Yet she is the one woman with the power to tame the rage locked inside him. Maybe he *can* find another reason to live…for her!

Tempted by the Highland Warrior

The adventure continues this July.

HH29698

*Carol Arens, Harlequin® Historical's newest
Western author, brings you an exciting tale of a most
improper convenient marriage! Set against the backdrop
of the Wild West, with an utterly unforgettable rebel
cowboy, it's certainly not to be missed!*

*Here's a sneak peek of
RENEGADE MOST WANTED*

Emma flashed Matt Suede what she hoped was a seductive smile. She leaned into his hug and became distracted by the playful dusting of freckles frolicking over his nose and across his cheeks.

Matt bent his head, whispering in for a kiss.

Emma pressed two fingers to his lips, preventing what promised to be a fascinating experience.

"Matt, honey, you did promise me a proper wedding. I don't think we should keep the preacher waiting."

Matt's arm stiffened, his fingers cramped about her middle. There was a very good chance that he had quit breathing.

The marshal let out a deep-bellied laugh that startled poor Pearl and made her whiney. "Looks like you been caught after all, Suede."

"If you ain't The Ghost, you can't deny being the groom," someone snickered.

"Since you don't see a spook standing here, I believe you're looking at the groom." Matt Suede's voice croaked on the word *groom*.

"The problem is, I don't recall you having a steady girl, Suede," the marshal said. "Just to be sure you and the lady here aren't in cahoots, I think the boys and I will just go along to witness those holy vows."

A man slapped his thigh and let out a roaring hoot. "Singing Trigger Suede goes through with this marriage and we'll know he's telling the truth."

"You've got the wrong bank robber, boys. The next hour will see me hitched and tied."

Matt bent his mouth close to her ear. His breath warmed her cheek.

"You sure you want to do this, ma'am?" he whispered. The men standing nearby wouldn't hear him, since they stood close to the barn door, and the traffic traveling down Front Street drowned his words to anyone but her. "I'm better than that old drunk, but only a little."

Find out what happens next
in RENEGADE MOST WANTED in July
from Harlequin® Historical and look out for future books
by the evocative Carol Arens!

Love Inspired HISTORICAL

celebrating
15
YEARS

DOROTHY CLARK

brings you another story from

PINEWOOD
WEDDINGS

When Willa Wright's fiancé abandoned her three days
before the wedding, he ended all her hopes for romance.
Now she dedicates herself to teaching Pinewood's children,
including the new pastor's young wards. If she didn't know
better, Reverend Calvert's kindness could almost fool Willa
into caring again. Almost.

Wooing the Schoolmarm

Available July wherever books are sold.

For my fierce and feisty sister-in-law, Jenny.
One of the best perks of marrying your
brother was getting you as friend.

Michelle Major grew up in Ohio but dreamed of living in the mountains. Soon after graduating with a degree in journalism, she pointed her car west and settled in Colorado. Her life and house are filled with one great husband, two beautiful kids, a few furry pets and several well-behaved reptiles. She's grateful to have found her passion writing stories with happy endings. Michelle loves to hear from her readers at www.michellemajor.com.

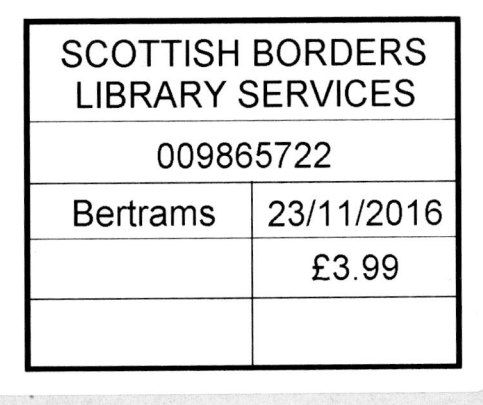

Chapter One

"It's so white."

April Sanders flicked a glance in the rearview mirror as she drove along the winding road up Crimson Mountain.

Her gaze landed on the sullen twelve-year-old girl biting down on her bottom lip as she stared out the SUV's side window.

"It's pretty, right?" April asked hopefully. "Peaceful?" She'd come to love the mountains in winter, especially on days without the sunny skies that made Colorado famous. The muted colors brought a stillness to the forest that seemed to calm something inside of her.

"It's white," Ranie Evans repeated. "White is boring."

"I like snow," Ranie's sister, Shay, offered from her high perch in the booster seat. Shay was almost five, her personality as sunny as Ranie's was sullen.

April didn't blame Ranie for her anger. In the past month, the girls had been at their mother's side as she'd lost her fight with cancer, then spent a week on their aunt's pullout couch before they'd landed in Colorado with April.

Even this wasn't permanent. At least that's what April told herself. The idea of raising these two girls, as their mother's will had stipulated, scared her more than anything she'd faced in life. More than her own battle with breast cancer. More than a humiliating divorce from her famous Hollywood director husband. More than rebuilding a shell of a life in the small mountain town of Crimson, Colorado. More than—

"Can we make a snowman at the cabin?" Shay asked, cutting through April's brooding thoughts.

"You don't want to go outside," Ranie cautioned her sister. "Your fingers will freeze off."

"No one's fingers are freezing off," April said quickly, hearing Shay's tiny gasp of alarm. "You've both got winter gear now, with parkas and mittens." The first stop after picking up the girls at Denver International Airport had been to a nearby sporting-goods store. April had purchased everything they'd need for the next two weeks in the mountains. "Of course we can build a snowman. We can build a whole snow family if you want."

"What we *want* is to go back to California."

April didn't need another check in the rearview mirror. She could feel Ranie glaring at her from the backseat, every ounce of the girl's ill temper focused on April.

"Mom took us to the beach every Christmas. Why wouldn't Aunt Tracy take us to Hawaii with her? Why

couldn't you come to Santa Barbara? You used to live in LA. I remember you from when I was little and Mom first got sick."

April tightened her grip on the steering wheel as memories of her friend Jill rushed over her. Taking the turn around one of the two-lane road's steep switchbacks, she punched the accelerator too hard and felt the tires begin to spin as they lost traction.

Ignoring the panicked shrieks from the backseat, she eased off the gas pedal and corrected the steering, relieved to feel the SUV under her control again.

"It's okay," she assured the girls with a forced smile. April was still adjusting to driving during Colorado winters. "The road is icy up here, but we're close to the turnoff for the cabin." She risked another brief look and saw that Ranie had reached across the empty middle seat to take Shay's hand, both girls holding on like the lifeline they were to each other.

It broke April's heart.

She pulled off onto the shoulder after turning up the recently plowed gravel drive that led to Cloud Cabin. The quasi "remote wilderness experience" was an offshoot of Crimson Ranch, the popular guest ranch in the valley, and had opened earlier in the fall. The owners happened to be April's best friend, movie actress Sara Travers, and her husband, Josh. April had first come to Crimson with Sara three years ago, both women burned out and broken down by their lives in Hollywood.

April knew this town could heal someone when they let it. Crimson—and Josh's love—had done that for Sara. April also recognized that she'd held herself

back from the community and hadn't truly become a part of it.

Throwing the SUV into Park, she turned to the backseat and met the wary gazes of each of her late friend's precious girls. "I'm sorry your aunt couldn't change her plans for the holidays." She took a deep breath as frustration over Tracy's callous attitude toward her nieces threatened to overtake her. "I'm sorry I couldn't come to California for these weeks. I have a work commitment here that can't be changed."

"I thought you were a yoga teacher." Ranie snatched her fingers away from Shay's grasp. "Who does yoga in the snow?"

"No one I know." April wanted to unstrap her seat belt, crawl into the backseat and gather the surly girl into her arms and try to hug away some of the pain pouring off her. "There's a guest coming to stay at the cabin for Christmas. I need to get there and make sure everything is in order before he arrives. He's a writer and needs to finish a book. He wants the privacy of the mountains to concentrate."

She was already behind, the detour to the airport in Denver pushing back her arrival at Cloud Cabin a few hours. "My job is to cook for him, manage the housekeeping and—"

Ranie offered her best preteen sneer. "Like you're a maid?"

"Like I take care of people," April corrected.

"Like you're taking care of us because Mommy died." Shay's voice was sad but still sweet.

"I am, honey," April whispered around the ball of emotion clogging her throat. She smiled at Ranie, but

the girl's eyes narrowed, as if she knew being with April was anything but a sure bet for their future.

April turned up the brightness of her smile as she looked at Shay. "Only about a quarter mile more." She turned to the front and flipped on the radio, tuning it to a satellite station that got reception even in this remote area. "How about some holiday music? Do either of you have a favorite Christmas song?"

"'Rudolph,'" Shay shouted, clapping her hands.

April pulled the SUV back onto the snow-packed road. "How about you, Ranie?"

"I hate Christmas music," the girl muttered, then added, "but not as much as I hate you."

Despite the jab to her heart, April ignored the rude words. She turned up the volume and sang along until the cabin came into view. A driver was bringing Connor Pierce, who was flying into the Aspen airport, to the cabin. The fact that the windows were dark gave her hope that she'd caught at least one break today, and he hadn't arrived before her.

April needed every advantage she could get if she was going to successfully manage these next two weeks.

"No kids."

Connor Pierce growled those two words as soon as the willowy redhead walked into the kitchen.

Maybe he should have waited to speak until she'd spotted him standing in front of the window. Unprepared, she'd jumped into the air, dropping the bag of groceries as she clutched one hand to her chest.

Her wide brown eyes met his across the room, a mix of shock and fear in her gaze. Scaring a woman half

to death was a new low for Connor, but he couldn't stop. "They need to go," he snapped, fists clenched at his side. "Now."

To the woman's credit, she recovered faster than he would have expected, placing a hand on the back of a chair as she straightened her shoulders. "Who are you?"

The fact that she didn't scurry away in the face of his anger was also new. Most people he knew would have turned tail already. "What kind of question is that?"

Her eyes narrowed. "The kind I expect you to answer."

"I'm the paying guest," he said slowly, enunciating each word.

"Mr. Pierce?" She swallowed and inclined her head to study him more closely. He didn't care for the examination.

"Connor."

"You don't look like the photo on your website."

"That picture was taken a long time ago." Back when he was overweight and happy and his heart hadn't been ripped out of his chest. When he could close his eyes and not see a car engulfed in flames, not feel his own helplessness like a vise around his lungs.

She didn't question him, although curiosity was a bright light in her eyes. Instead, she smiled. "Welcome to Colorado. I'm sorry you got to the cabin before me." She bent to retrieve the groceries, quickly refilling the cloth bag she'd dropped. "I was told your flight arrived later this afternoon."

The smile threw him, as did her easy manner. "I took an earlier one."

After placing the bag on the counter, she walked forward, her hand held out to him. "I'm April Sanders. I'll be making sure your stay at Cloud Cabin is everything you want it to be."

"I want the kids gone." He didn't take her hand, even though it was rude. She was tall for a woman but still several inches shorter than him. Her long hair was pulled back in a low knot, revealing the smooth, pale skin of her neck above the down coat she wore. The light in her eyes dimmed as her hand dropped.

"I don't know what you mean."

"I saw you come in," he said, hitching a finger toward the window overlooking the front drive. "Are those your daughters?"

She shook her head.

"They can't be here."

"They aren't *here*. They're with me in the smaller cabin next door."

"It doesn't matter." Their voices had drifted up to him when the girls spilled out of the car. The older one, her dark blond hair in a tight braid down her back, had kept her shoulders hunched, arms crossed over her chest as she took in the forest around the house. Connor had felt an unwanted affinity to her. Clearly, she was as reluctant to be trapped in this idyllic winter setting as he was.

It was the younger girl, bright curls bouncing as she pointed at the two log cabins situated next to each other on the property, who had brought unwanted memories to the surface. She'd given a squeal of delight when a rogue chipmunk ran past the front of the SUV. Her high-pitched laugh had raked across Connor's nerves,

making him want to claw at his own skin to stop the sensation.

She was dangerous, that innocent girl, threatening his stability on a bone-deep level. "I'm at this cabin to work." He kept his gaze on the window. "I need privacy."

"I'll make sure you have it."

"Not with kids around."

She'd moved so quietly Connor didn't realize April Sanders was standing toe-to-toe with him until he turned back. Up close, with the afternoon light pouring over her, she looked young and too innocent. He'd never seen anything as creamy as her skin, and he had a sudden urge to trace his finger along her cheek and see for himself if it was as soft as it looked.

It was a ridiculous thought. Connor didn't touch people if he could help it. Not for three years, since that drive along the California coast when he'd held his wife's hand for the last time.

Although he knew it to be untrue, he'd come to believe he could hold on to the memory of his wife and son more tightly if he kept himself cut off from physical contact with anyone else. He'd never felt the need before now.

The fact that this woman—a stranger—made him want to change was almost as terrifying as the deadline looming over his head. He took a step back.

"They have no place else to go," she said, the gentle cadence of her voice at odds with the desperate plea he didn't want to see in her eyes. "I promise I'll keep them out of your way."

Connor stepped around her, reaching for the sheet

of paper on the table at the same time he dug in his pocket for his cell phone. "I'm calling Sara Travers."

"No." April snatched the paper with the contact information for Crimson Ranch out of his hand. "You can't." The sheer audacity of the action gave him pause.

"Are you going to hold me here against my will?" He almost laughed at the thought of it, but Connor also hadn't laughed in a longer time than he cared to remember. "I'll call my editor. He'll contact Sara. I assume she's your boss?"

"Please don't." Her voice hitched on the plea, making alarm bells clang in Connor's brain.

"You're not going to cry," he told her. "Tell me you're not going to cry."

She took a breath, blinked several times. "Sara is my boss at the ranch, but she's also my friend. She and Josh just left for a holiday vacation, and I don't want her to worry." April's voice had gone even gentler, almost defeated. Another long-buried emotion grated at his nerves. "She doesn't know about Ranie and Shay yet. If you tell her…"

"She'll make you get rid of them?" he asked, allowing only a hint of triumph to slip into his tone.

"She'll want me to keep them."

He was intrigued despite himself. "Who are those girls to you?" When she only stared at him, Connor placed his cell phone on the table. He couldn't believe he was considering the possibility but he said, "Tell me why I should let them stay."

Chapter Two

April's mind raced as Connor crossed his arms over his chest, biceps bunching under his gray Berkeley T-shirt. He was nowhere near the man she'd expected to be working for the next two weeks at Cloud Cabin.

Connor Pierce was a famous author—not quite on a par with John Grisham, but a worthy successor if you believed the reviews and hype from his first two books. She'd checked his website after Sara had asked her to take on this job as a personal favor.

April had worked full-time at Crimson Ranch when she and Sara had first arrived in Colorado. Although in the past year the yoga classes she taught at the local community center and at a studio between Crimson and nearby Aspen had taken up most of her time, she'd booked off these two weeks. April had been a yoga instructor, as well as a certified nutritionist, to Hol-

lywood starlets and movie actors before her life in California imploded. Apparently Connor Pierce had an extremely stringent and healthy diet, and April felt more comfortable than the ranch's new chef in tailoring her cooking to specific requests.

Based on his publicity photo, Connor was a pudgy, bearded man with a wide grin, so the strict dietary requirements his editor had forwarded hadn't quite made sense. They did for the man in front of her. He was over six feet tall, with dark hair and piercing green eyes in a face that was at once handsome and almost lethal in its sharp angles. As far as she could tell, he was solid muscle from head to toe and about as friendly as a grizzly bear woken from hibernation.

"Ranie and Shay lost their mother last month and their dad has never been in the picture. Jill was an old friend of mine and gave me custody of the girls when she died." She took a deep breath, uncomfortable with sharing something so personal with this seemingly emotionless man. "I can't possibly keep them, but—"

"Why?"

"You ask a lot of questions," she muttered.

He raised one eyebrow in response.

She grabbed the bag of groceries and walked toward the cabinets and refrigerator to put them away as she spoke. "The girls have family in California they should be with on a permanent basis. I'm not a good bet for them." She ignored the trembling in her fingers, forcing herself to keep moving. "They're with me temporarily over the holidays, but I can't send them away. If it's such a problem, we'll go. I'll get you settled, then Sara will find—"

"They can stay."

April paused in the act of putting a bag of carrots into the refrigerator. Connor still stood across the kitchen, arms folded. His green eyes revealed nothing.

"Why?" she couldn't help but ask, closing the refrigerator door and taking two steps toward him. "What made you change your mind?"

"Now who asks too many questions?" He ran a hand through his short hair. "Just keep them quiet and out of my way. I'm over seven months behind on the deadline for my next book. I have until the first of the year to turn in this book before they terminate my contract and…"

"And?"

"I'm here to work," he answered, which wasn't an answer at all. "I need to concentrate."

She nodded, not wanting to push her luck with this enigmatic man. "The food you requested is stocked in the pantry and refrigerator. Cell service is spotty up here, but there are landlines in both cabins. I'll have dinner ready for you at six unless you call. You won't even know we're here with you." Grabbing the empty cloth sack from the counter, she started past him.

He reached for her, the movement so quick it startled her. She stared at the place where his fingers encircled her wrist, warmth seeping through the layers she wore. It was odd because for such a cold man, his touch almost burned.

"I'll know you're here," he said, his voice a rough scrape across her senses. "But keep the girls away from me."

"I will," she promised. Something in his tone told her his demand was more than a need for quiet so he could work.

He released his hold on her a second later and she left, stopping outside as the cold air hit her. She took a couple of breaths to calm her nerves. Yes, she'd have to tell Sara about Ranie and Shay, but not yet. Not until April could find a way to do it without revealing how weak and broken she still was.

And that could take a while.

She hurried across the snow-packed drive, worried that she'd left the girls alone for too long. The cabin was quiet when she entered through the side door.

The caretaker's cabin was much smaller than Cloud Cabin, which had been built to house family reunions and groups of guests who wanted a wilderness experience away from town. In addition to the oversized kitchen, Connor had his choice of five bedrooms, including two master suites, a huge family room and a game room, plus a workout area in the basement. There was a big patio out back with a fire pit and hot tub, but April had a hard time picturing Connor relaxing in the steam and bubbles. It was also better if she didn't try to picture him bare chested because, despite his surly attitude, she'd felt a definite ripple of attraction to Connor Pierce. That was a recipe for disaster.

The girls weren't in the kitchen so she headed upstairs. In this cabin there were only two bedrooms, on either side of the narrow hallway. Sara and Josh had built it to accommodate the small staff needed when there were guests on-site. While construction had been completed in late summer, they'd only taken a few bookings for the fall and hadn't expected anyone to be staying here over the winter months. It wasn't exactly easy to access, although maybe that's what appealed to Connor—or at least to his editor. April knew his debut

book had been made into a movie and the sequel was set to release in the spring. She imagined there was a lot of pressure for another blockbuster in the series.

The door to the second bedroom was closed and she had to press her ear to it before she heard voices inside. Both girls looked up when she walked in. "It was so quiet I thought you two might be napping."

Ranie rolled her eyes. "I'm twelve. I don't take naps."

Shay smiled. "I do sometimes, but not today. Mommy used to nap a lot."

April remembered how tired the cancer treatments had made her. All that medicine to make things better, but there were difficult side effects at every stage. "What are you doing?"

Shay held up a tangle of yarn. "I'm finger knitting. I can make you a scarf if you want."

"I'd like that," April said, coming forward to sit on the edge of the other twin bed. "Who taught you to knit?"

"Mommy taught Ranie, and Ranie taught me." Shay pointed to her sister's lap. "She's really good. She can use needles and everything."

April placed her hand lightly on Ranie's knee. "May I see?"

The girl stood up abruptly, shoving what was in her hands into a bag. "I'm not that great. Mostly my rows are crooked. It was just something to do when we sat with Mom."

April tried not to let the girl's constant rejection hurt her, but it was difficult. Ranie looked so much like Jill. "Your mom sent me a sweater one year for Christmas," she told Shay, aware Ranie was listening

even as she pretended to ignore them. "I have it with me if you'd like to see."

"Mommy made the best sweaters." Shay tugged her fingers out of the yarn, which to April's eyes looked more like a knot than a scarf. "I mess up a lot."

April reached for the deep red yarn, but Ranie stepped forward and snatched it away. "You're getting better, Shay." She stretched out the jumble until April could see where it almost resembled a scarf. "I'll unknot this and you can keep going."

Shay beamed. "Ranie is the best. She can teach you, too."

"I'd like that."

"Don't you have work to do?" Ranie asked, flipping her long braid over her shoulder. "Taking care of the big-shot author?"

"I'll have time," April told her. "Would either of you like a snack before I start prepping dinner?"

"Can we make the snowman now?" Shay asked, going on her knees to look out the window above the bed.

April thought about the promise she'd made to Connor Pierce. "Because Mr. Pierce is writing a book, he's going to need quiet. I know it's fun to play in the snow, but—"

"I can be real quiet," Shay assured her, not turning from the window. "Ranie and me had to stay quiet when Mommy was sick."

"Ranie and I," April and Ranie corrected at the same time.

When April offered a half smile, Ranie turned away. April sighed. Between the cabin's grumpy houseguest and her own ill-tempered charge, this was going to be

the longest two weeks of her life. "Maybe it would be better if we found things to do inside the house."

"He doesn't want us here," Ranie said, her tone filled with righteous accusation. "That's why we have to be quiet. He doesn't want us."

April would have liked to kick Connor Pierce in the shin or another part of his anatomy right now. "He needs to concentrate," she said instead, wanting to make it better for these girls who'd lost so much and were now in a strange state and a strange cabin with a woman who had been their mother's friend but little to them. "It isn't about you two."

"So we can't go out in the snow?" Shay shifted so she was facing April. "We have to stay inside the whole time? That's kind of boring."

Feeling the weight of two different stares, April pressed her fingers to her temples. She should call Sara right now and find someone else for this job, except then she'd have to make holiday plans for these girls. Her work here was a distraction, different enough from real life that she could keep the two separate. It was too much to think of making Ranie and Shay a part of her world. What if they fit? What if she wanted to try for something she knew she couldn't manage?

A remote cabin and its temperamental guest might be a pain, but at least it was safe. Still, she couldn't expect the girls to entertain themselves for two weeks in this small cabin, and neither could Connor.

"Get your snow gear from the shopping bags I left in the front hall," she said after a moment. "As long as we're not making a ton of noise, we can play in the snow as much as you want."

"Mommy liked to rest," Shay said, too much knowl-

edge in her innocent gaze. "Sometimes the medicine gave her headaches, so we know how to be quiet." She wrapped her arms around April for a quick, surprising hug and then scrambled off the bed.

"I'll get your stuff, too," she told Ranie before running from the room. "We're going to build a snowman." April could hear the girl singing as she went down the steps.

Ranie was still glaring at her, so April kept her tone light. "I'd better put on another layer. My sweater and coat are warm but not if we're going to be outside for a while."

"It's me, right?" Ranie's shoulders were a narrow block of tension.

"What's you?"

"The author doesn't want me around," Ranie said, almost as if she was speaking to herself. "It can't be Shay. Everyone loves Shay."

"It isn't about either of you." April risked placing a hand on Ranie's back, surprised when the girl didn't shrug it off. "He's here to work."

"Aunt Tracy bought Shay a new swimsuit," Ranie mumbled, sinking down to the bed.

"For a trip to Colorado in December?"

The girl gripped the hem of her shirt like she might rip it apart. "She wanted to take her to Hawaii with their family."

April shook her head. "No, your aunt told me the trip was only her, your uncle Joe and the boys."

"Tyler and Tommy are annoying," Ranie said.

April smiled a little. "I imagine nine-year-old twin boys can be a handful."

"I guess Aunt Tracy always wanted a little girl,"

Ranie told her, "because I overheard Mom talking to her toward the end. She'd wanted us to live with Tracy, but Tracy would only agree to having Shay." Her voice grew hollow. "She didn't want me."

"Oh, Ranie, no," April whispered, even as the words rang true. Jill's sister had been just the type of woman to be willing to keep one girl and not the other. How could April truly judge when she couldn't commit to either of them?

But she knew the girls had to stay together. "I talked to your aunt before they left on their trip. It's only for the holidays. We have a meeting scheduled with an attorney the first week of January to start the process of transferring custody. She's going to take you both in the New Year. You'll be back in California and—"

"She doesn't want me." Ranie looked miserable. "No one does now that Mom is gone. That author guy is just one more."

"It's not you." The words were out of April's mouth before she could stop them. She hated seeing the girl so sad.

"You're lying." Ranie didn't even pause as she made the accusation and paced to the corner of the room. "Everyone loves Shay."

"Something happened to Connor Pierce that makes it difficult for him to be around young kids."

"What happened?" Ranie stepped forward, hands clenched tightly in front of her. This sweet, hurting girl had been through so much. Once again, April wanted to reach for her but held back. She shouldn't have shared as much as she had about Connor, but she couldn't allow Ranie to believe she was expendable to

everyone she met. At least this way, Ranie could help
shield Shay, keep her out of Connor's line of sight.

April met Ranie's clear blue gaze. "His wife and son
died in a car accident a few years ago. The little boy
was five at the time."

"Shay's age," Ranie whispered. The girl's eyes
widened a fraction.

Good. The news was enough of a shock on its own.
April didn't have to share anything more. Not the images she'd seen online of the charred shell of a car after
the accident and fire that had killed Connor's family.
Not the news report that said he'd also been in the vehicle at the time of the crash but had been thrown clear.

She hoped he'd been knocked unconscious. The
alternative was that Connor Pierce had watched his
family die.

Connor glanced at the clock on his phone again,
staring at the bright numbers on the screen, willing
them to change. When they did and the numbers read
6:00 on the dot, he jumped out of the chair in front of
the desk, stalked toward the door, then back again.

He knew April was in the kitchen, had heard her
come in thirty minutes ago. He'd been staring at the
clock ever since. Minutes when he should have been
working, but the screen on his laptop remained empty.

Every part of his life remained empty.

When his editor had suggested taking two weeks
at a remote cabin to "finish" his manuscript, Connor
hadn't argued. He hadn't wanted to explain that he
still had over half the story to write. It had even made
sense that a change of scenery might help him focus.

That's how it worked with writers, right? A quiet

cabin in the woods, an idyllic setting to get the creativity flowing. What Connor understood, but wouldn't admit, was that his inability to write came from the place inside him that was broken. There was simply nothing left, only a yawning cavern of guilt, regret and sorrow. Emotions he couldn't force himself to mine for words to fill a manuscript, even one that was seven months past due.

He shut the laptop and headed downstairs, the scent coming from the kitchen drawing him forward. That was as unexpected as everything else about April Sanders, since food was no longer something from which Connor derived pleasure. He ate for energy, health and to keep his body moving. He didn't register flavor or cravings and lived on a steady diet of nutrition bars and high-protein meals that were bland and boring.

Nothing about April was bland or boring, a realization that fisted in his gut as she turned from the stove when he walked into the room.

"How's the writing going?" she asked with a smile, as if they were friends. She wore a long-sleeved shirt that revealed the curve of her breasts and waist, with a pair of black yoga pants that hugged her hips. April was slim, with the natural grace of a dancer—someone aware of her body and what it could do. Her hair was still pulled back, but the pieces that had escaped to frame her face were curlier than before.

"I could hear the kids playing outside," Connor said, and watched her smile fade. This was who he was now, a man who could suck the warmth out of a room faster than an arctic wind.

"We stayed on the far side of the caretaker's cabin

and the girls weren't loud," she answered, pulling a plate from a cabinet.

"I still heard them."

She glanced over her shoulder. "Were you pressing your ear to the window?"

He opened his mouth, then shut it again. Not his ear, but he'd held his fingertips to the glass until they burned from the cold. The noise had been faint, drifting up to him only as he'd strained to listen. "Why were they outside? It's freezing up here."

"Shay wanted to play in the snow." April pulled a baking tray out of the oven and set it on the stove top. "They're from California so all this snow is new for them."

"Join the club," he muttered, snapping to attention when she grabbed a foil-wrapped packet on the tray and bit out a curse.

She shook out her fingers, then reached for a pair of tongs with her uninjured hand.

He moved closer. "You need to run your fingers under cold water."

"I'm fine," she said, but bit down on her lower lip. "Have a seat and dinner will be—"

He flipped on the faucet as he came to stand next to her. Before he could think about what he was doing, Connor grabbed her wrist and tugged her the few feet to stand in front of the sink. He couldn't seem to stop touching this woman. He pushed up her sleeve and positioned her hand under the cold water from the faucet. "If the burn is bad enough, it will blister your fingertip."

"I wasn't thinking, but I'm not hurt," she said softly, not pulling away.

She was soft against him, the warmth of her both captivating and an irritation against the shell he'd wrapped around himself. She smelled subtly of lavender, and Connor could imagine April standing in a field of it in the south of France, her red hair a beautiful contrast to the muted purple of the plants. Fanciful thoughts for a man who'd become rigid in his hold on reality.

"It's better to be safe."

He didn't want to examine why he kept his grasp on her wrist and why she didn't pull away. She wasn't going to blister—the burn from the foil was a surface injury at most. That meant… He met her gaze, gentle and understanding, then jerked away as if he'd been the one scalded by the heat.

"What do you know about me?" he asked through gritted teeth.

She took a moment to answer, turned off the tap and dried her hand before looking up to him. "Only what I've read in old news reports."

Gripping his fingers on the edge of the granite counter, he forced himself to ask, "And what did they tell you?" He'd purposely not read any of the press after the crash.

"Your wife and son were with you during the promotional tour for your last book release three years ago. There was a car accident on the way to an event—another driver crossed the median and hit you head on—they were both killed."

"We all should have died in that wreck," he whispered.

"You were thrown from the car. It saved your life."

She didn't dispute his observation, which he appreciated. Part of why he'd initially cut so many people

out of his life after the accident was that he couldn't stand hearing any more theories about why he'd lived while Margo and Emmett had died. That it was fate, a greater plan, some universal knowing to which he wasn't yet privy.

Connor knew it was all nonsense. If there had been any sense in the tragedy, it would have been for him to perish while his beautiful wife and innocent son survived. Anything else was blasphemy as far as he was concerned.

"Unfortunately, it did," he agreed, wanting to shock her. He'd spent hours wishing and praying for his own death in the months after the accident. His whole reason for living had been stolen from him, and he hadn't been strong enough to save either his wife or son. He'd wallowed in grief until it had consumed him. The pain had become a part of his makeup—like another limb or vital organ—and it pushed away everyone and everything that didn't make it stronger.

Eventually, the grief had threatened to destroy him, and Connor had shut it down, his will to live stronger than his wish to die. But in excising the pain, he'd had to cut out other parts of himself—his heart, the connections he had to anyone else in the world who he might fail with his weakness. Perhaps even his creativity. The ability to weave stories was so much a part of him that he'd taken the gift for granted. Except, now it was gone, and he had no idea how to get it back.

The feel of April brushing past pulled him from his thoughts. She placed a plate of food on the table at the one place setting and bent to light the candle that sat in the center of the table.

"That's not necessary," he told her, his voice gruff.

"I light candles for all the guests." She straightened. "Would you like wine with your meal?"

"Water, but you don't have to serve me."

"Actually, I do," she said with a wry half smile. "It's my job, and I'm good at it."

"Why aren't you asking me questions about the accident?"

She studied him for a moment, a hint of pink coloring her cheeks. "Do you want to talk about it?"

He shook his head.

"That's why," she said simply, and walked back to the kitchen to fill a glass from the water dispenser in the refrigerator.

The fact that she wasn't pushing him made Connor want to tell her more. As soon as people started asking questions, whether it was his editor, the therapist his publisher had hired, or one of his sisters or his mother, Connor shut down.

Yet the need to share details of the nightmare that had defined his recent life with April was almost overwhelming in its intensity. His chest constricted, an aching reminder of why he kept silent. To talk about Margo and Emmett was to invite pain and sorrow back into his life. Connor couldn't do that and continue to function.

"I'm going to check on the girls," she told him after placing the water on the table. "I'll be back in a few minutes—"

"What if I want you to stay while I eat?"

She paused, meeting his gaze with those big melty chocolate eyes. There was something in them he didn't understand, not pity or wariness as he would have expected. It looked almost like desire, which he couldn't fathom. He had nothing to offer a woman like April,

someone so full of light and peace. The darkness inside him would blot her out, muting her radiance until she was nothing. That's how the darkness worked, he'd realized, and there was little he could do to stop it.

"Then I'll stay," she said.

He let a sneer curl his upper lip. "Because it's your job?"

She didn't blink or look away. "Because you asked me."

A lightning-quick bolt of emotion passed through him, forcing him to take a step back when all he wanted to do was move closer to her. The unfamiliarity of that urge was enough to have him piling the silverware and napkin on the plate, then picking it up along with the glass. "I'm going to eat in my room. I have work to do on an important scene for the book."

"You can leave your plate outside the bedroom door," she said in that same gentle voice. What would it take to rattle a woman like April? "I'll clean it when I get back."

"Fine," he said, purposely not thanking her or acknowledging the effort she'd put into the meal that smelled better than anything he'd eaten in ages. His rudeness was another shield, and he'd need as many as he could create to resist the things April made him feel.

Chapter Three

April let herself into the main cabin before sunrise the next morning. The girls were still sleeping and, before leaving the caretaker's cabin, she'd prepared a pan of cinnamon rolls to bake when she returned. She needed to make breakfast for her cantankerous guest but didn't want to take the chance of seeing Connor again so soon. The previous night had jumbled her nerves in a way she barely recognized.

Connor Pierce was arrogant, ill-mannered and a borderline bully. But the pain she'd seen in his eyes when he spoke of the accident that had claimed his wife and son touched her at a soul-deep level. Just as his actual touch made her skin heat with need. Her reaction was inappropriate at best and, more likely, damaging to a heart she'd learned the hard way to protect and guard.

Thankfully, he hadn't reappeared last night when

she'd returned to clean the kitchen. His empty plate had been left on the counter, the cabin quiet as she'd put everything away. A light had still burned in the upstairs window when she'd walked across the dark night to her cabin but that had been the only indication Connor was still awake.

April was grateful since she wasn't sure she would have been able to resist questioning him more on the heartbreak of losing his family. There was no doubt the grief had been substantial, and she could use advice on how to guide Ranie and Shay through the sorrow of losing someone they loved, even if the circumstances were totally different. April had thought she understood heartbreak after her divorce but later realized that the scars from Daniel leaving had more to do with rejection and humiliation than love.

She started coffee, preheated the oven and then unpacked the lidded container she'd prepped at the other cabin. There was a nonstick muffin tin in the drawer next to the oven, and she began to dump egg-white-and-vegetable mix into the openings. Each move she made was quiet and purposeful so as not to make noise. Her goal was to get everything ready, then leave before Connor woke.

"You're up early."

April jumped at the sound of that gravelly voice behind her, the mixture sloshing over the side of the glass bowl. "Is your goal to give me a heart attack?" She set the bowl on the counter and grabbed a wad of paper towels to clean up the mess.

"You spook easily," he told her. "It's the only time you raise your voice."

"You shouldn't sneak up on people. It's rude." Toss-

ing the paper towels into the trash can under the sink, April turned, planning to enlighten Connor Pierce on what she sounded like when shock turned to anger. The words caught in her throat at the sight of him standing on the far side of the island wearing only a pair of loose gym shorts, his chest broad and hard and glistening with sweat.

Glistening. Oh, my.

"There's a workout room downstairs," he said, wiping a small white towel across his face and down his front. April followed the movement, the muscles and smattering of hair across his chest making her mouth go dry. She'd thought herself immune to men and the heavy pull of attraction since her divorce. Many of her girlfriends in Crimson were involved with handsome men, but April had never noticed any of them other than with the affection reserved for brothers.

What she felt for Connor was different and dangerous.

Instead of berating him more for startling her, she asked, "Do you need anything?" and hated that she sounded breathless.

"A shower."

Spoken in his deep voice, those two words sounded like an invitation. April felt her cheeks color. She grabbed the muffin tin and shoved it into the oven, hoping the heat that wafted out would provide a decent excuse for her blush. "I can have breakfast ready in about twenty minutes. Are you always up at this time?"

"I don't sleep much."

"Too inspired?"

She'd been referring to his writing, but one side of his mouth kicked up like he'd taken the question an-

other way. "Not yet," he answered. "But there's time for that."

She didn't understand his mood this morning. He was relaxed and almost flirty, different from the tense, bitter man she'd encountered yesterday.

"Working out helps me," he offered, as if reading her mind. "Gives me an outlet that I find calming."

"I teach yoga," she said with a nod. She opened the dishwasher and started putting away the clean dishes. "It does the same thing."

"Do you teach at Crimson Ranch?" He moved closer, took a seat at the island. Connor seemed unaware of the effect his upper body was having on her, and she tried to ignore her reaction. Even if he hadn't been a guest, this man was not for her.

She filled a glass with water and placed it on the counter in front of him. "During the summer months, I teach at the ranch. There's also a community center in town that offers classes, and another studio between Crimson and Aspen."

"You've done yoga for a while?" he asked, taking a long drink. A droplet of water traced a path along his strong jaw, then over his throat and down the hard planes of his chest. He wiped it away, then met her gaze. It took April several seconds to realize he was waiting for an answer to his question.

"Almost fifteen years." She concentrated on unloading the dishwasher as she spoke. "I had some injuries from dancing when I was younger, and yoga helped my body heal. I owned a studio in California for a while." She'd loved the studio she'd built from the ground up, but it had become one more casualty of her illness and then the divorce.

"But you teach for other people here?"

April felt her eyes narrow. Connor was a little too insightful. The woman who owned the private studio outside of town had offered to sell the business to April on several occasions. Marty was in her seventies, ready to retire and move closer to her adult children and their families, but she felt a loyalty to the local clients she had in the area. April knew the older woman had received offers from at least two national chains, but Marty hoped her studio would remain locally owned.

"It gives me more flexibility," she answered.

"Do you travel?"

She focused her attention on the basket of knives and forks. "No."

"Have a big family?"

She shook her head, not liking where this line of questioning was leading.

"Why is flexibility important?"

How was she supposed to explain? It was the answer she always gave, and no one had ever questioned her answer. Not until Connor.

April loved Colorado and the town of Crimson, but as much as she was grateful for a new start and the friends that were part of it, there was something missing. A broken piece inside that prevented her from truly committing to this town the way Sara and so many of their friends had in the past couple of years.

There was too much at stake for April, because if she devoted herself to making a life here the way she had in California and then lost it again, she wasn't sure she'd survive. It was easier to play the part of caretaker and helpful friend. Those roles allowed her to be a part

of the community without investing the deepest pieces of her heart and soul in anyone.

Giving too much—feeling too much—left her vulnerable to pain, and she'd had enough pain to last a lifetime.

"Why do you care?" she asked, slamming the empty silverware basket back into the dishwasher and closing the machine's door. She hated how this man riled her but couldn't stop her reaction to him any more than she could deny the attraction she felt. All she could do was ignore them both.

He pushed the empty glass across the counter. "Just making conversation," he said as he stood, his gaze steady on hers. There was a teasing light in his eye, and awareness danced across her skin in response. He didn't seem upset by her rudeness or realize how out of character it was. But *she* knew and it scared her. "We're the only two people here so—"

"Actually, we're not." She placed her palms down on the cool granite and leaned toward him. "There are two sweet, sad girls in the other cabin who are afraid to make a sound in case they get me in trouble."

"They don't belong here," he said, the warmth in his voice disappearing instantly.

"They don't belong anywhere," she countered. "That fact doesn't make it easier to manage. I'd think you would understand—"

"I'm here to work." He pushed away from the island. "Not to play grief counselor."

"How's the writing going? Is being alone in this cabin inspiring you?"

She thought he'd walk away so was surprised at his quiet answer. "I'm always alone."

Just when she'd worked up a good temper, one that could hold her attraction at bay, he'd done it again. Let a bit of vulnerability slip through the impenetrable shields he had to curl around her senses.

April understood *alone.* She knew the emptiness of loneliness but also the safety it provided. She didn't want to have that in common with Connor, because it was a truth she hadn't shared with anyone else in her life. If he recognized it in her...

"You don't have to be," she said quietly, and the words were as much for her as him. She wanted to believe them even as the fear that lived inside her fought against it.

"Yes, I do." He ran a hand through his hair, the damp ends tousling. "I'm going to take that shower."

"Breakfast will be ready when you're finished. I'll—"

"Leave it," he snapped. "I don't need you to wait on me."

She opened her mouth to protest, but he held up a hand. "Don't worry. I won't complain to anyone. It's distracting to have you in and out. Leave the food and I'll take care of myself. I'm used to it."

He didn't wait for an answer before stalking from the kitchen.

April blew out an unsteady breath. She was making a mess of this. Sara still had ties to Hollywood and continued to act when the right roles came along. Not as much since expanding the ranch, but the studio that held the movie rights to Connor's books was important to Sara. It's why her friend had agreed to arrange two weeks at the cabin for him. It was also why Sara had asked April to step in and help. April's talent was

caring for people. It was something she enjoyed and a gift she used both at the ranch and while teaching her yoga classes. She normally had an easy way with even the most demanding guests.

But she was at her worst with Connor, and she hated it. As abrasive as he could be, he was also her client, and he'd survived a life-altering tragedy that should make her more sympathetic to him.

She imagined that Connor hated sympathy—she had during her battle with breast cancer. The pitying looks and fake support from the women she'd thought were her friends had added an extra layer of pain to her life. Those so-called friends had said the right things but quickly distanced themselves when the treatments robbed her of strength, her looks and most of her dignity. Only Sara had remained at her side, driving her to and from appointments and helping her to move when Daniel had filed for divorce in the middle of her second round of chemo.

The oven beeped, drawing her from her thoughts. She removed the egg muffins and placed them on a rack to cool. Pulling a plate from the cabinet, she set the table, poured a small glass of juice, then set a bowl of cut melon next to the plate. Connor may not need someone to look after him, but that was April's job here. She was going to take care of that man whether he liked it or not.

Hand lifted in front of the heavy oak door, Connor drew in a breath, the cold air making his lungs burn. He welcomed the sharp stab of pain because physical pain helped him remember he was still alive. It was part of the reason he worked out so compulsively—

pushing his body to the point of exhaustion gave him a sense of connection to something. Also, Connor had vowed never to be weak again. His weakness was the reason Margo and Emmett had died.

What he was about to do was madness, but he knocked on the door anyway.

It took only a moment for it to open, and he was looking down at a young girl with angelic blond curls, huge blue eyes and a smudge of something across her cheek. The impulse to wipe his thumb across her face was a punch to the heart. He almost turned and ran, even though that would mark him as the coward he was. Emmett had always had a smear or stain on some part of him. His son's favorite food had been peanut-butter-and-jelly sandwiches, and there was normally a telltale spot of grape jelly on the corner of his mouth and sticky fingers, leaving marks on everything the boy touched.

Connor had often balanced writing with parenting duties if Margo had an appointment or meeting. His preoccupation with his work had sometimes left Emmett, even at five, to slap together sloppy sandwiches for both of them. Emmett loved being in charge, and Connor had been happy to have something to eat that he didn't have to make. After the accident, he'd spent hours wishing he could have a daddy do-over. He would have put aside his precious words to take care of his more precious son.

"Are you a delivery man?" the girl asked when he stared at her.

He shook his head, not yet trusting his voice when memories threatened to pull him under like a riptide.

"Mommy said Santa Claus uses real delivery people to help bring toys at Christmas so they don't feel left out because he's got a sleigh and they don't. Last year Santa had the delivery man bring me three sparkly ponies and a new set of markers." She wiped the back of her hand across her nose. "Do you like to draw?"

"I like to write," he answered automatically. "At least I used to."

She nodded. "I'm good at writing. My teacher said my big *G* is perfect."

"Shay, shut the door." Another voice drifted forward. "It's freezing."

A moment later, a different girl appeared behind the little one. They were clearly sisters, although the older girl's hair was a darker blond and her eyes a deeper blue. "Who are you?" She placed a hand on her sister's shoulder.

"He likes to write, Ranie," Shay announced. "But he's not helping Santa."

"I need to talk to April," he told Ranie.

"She's getting ready to take us to town," Shay answered before her sister could speak, "to buy games to help us be quiet. The man who lives next door hates kids." She bounced on her small feet. "We're going to see the lights and get hot chocolate."

"I don't hate kids," Connor muttered, shifting under Ranie's gaze. He was certain the girl knew exactly who he was.

"That's good," Shay told him. "You should stay away from the other man. He might not like grown-ups either."

"No doubt," he heard Ranie mumble.

Instead of making him angry, Connor had the strange

urge to smile. He liked this girl standing sentry, still holding on to her sister as she tried to fill the doorway with her small frame. "Where's April?"

"I'll get her." Ranie went to close the door in his face, but Shay stepped forward.

"We have to invite him in," Shay said, grabbing his hand and tugging him forward before he could react. "He's nice."

He fought the need to jerk away from her small hand and allowed himself to be led into the smaller cabin.

"Shay, you don't know that he's nice. This man—"

"What's going on?"

As the door clicked shut behind him, he looked up to see April silhouetted by the late-morning light. She wore a pair of dark jeans and knee-high boots with a thick gray sweater. It was the first time he'd seen her hair down, the gentle red curls falling over her shoulders.

Shay didn't let go of his hand, and Connor could feel the imprint of her soft skin like a brand. The pain was fierce, radiating up his arm and through his chest to the empty place where his heart used to be.

"You left your phone at the other cabin." He pulled the device from his coat pocket with his free hand and held it out.

"I could have taken it at the door." Ranie reached forward and pulled Shay away from him. "You don't hold hands with a stranger," she scolded.

"He's not a stranger." Shay pushed a curl off her forehead. "He's April's friend. He had her phone." She glanced up at him. "Right?"

April took the phone from his hand, her cool fingers

brushing his palm. "Mr. Pierce is staying next door at the cabin," she told Shay, ruffling the girl's hair. "He's busy working, so it was nice of him to bring the phone to me."

Shay glanced between April and Connor, her mouth dropping open. "But the man living next door hates kids. You don't hate me, do you?" she asked him, her blue eyes wide with disbelief.

"Shay, shut up," Ranie said on a hiss of breath.

April threw Connor an apologetic look. "I never said—"

"I don't hate you," he told the little girl.

She pointed to her sister. "See, he's nice and my friend and April's friend and you shouldn't say 'shut up.' Mommy didn't like it."

"Mom isn't here." Ranie glared at Shay. "She's—"

"Enough." April's tone was firm. "You girls go get your coats, hats and mittens and we'll head to town."

Ranie stalked off down the hall, but Shay continued to stand next to him, her chin quivering the tiniest bit. "Do you want to go to town with us and get hot chocolate?"

He started to shake his head when she added, "Because I know you're nice even if Ranie doesn't think so. She gets extra grumpy because our mommy died, and that makes her act mean. But she's really just sad inside."

The wisdom in those words leveled him. Connor had been used to being angry since the accident. He had cut people out of his life and pushed them away with his moods until the rage inside him felt like all that was left. What if he had held on to the anger so he didn't have to feel the lingering sorrow of loss?

"Will you go?" Shay asked again when he didn't re-

spond. "It's a long way down the mountain, so April said this trip is special."

"Shay," April said quietly, "that's nice of you to offer, but Mr. Pierce has—"

"I'll go."

The girl smiled and clapped her hands. "I knew we were friends. I'm going to go get my winter coat. April bought it for me new because in California we don't have snow. You should wear gloves and a hat because there's an ice-skating rink in the park downtown and if it's not too crowded we can try it."

Connor watched her run down the hall and disappear around a corner before he met April's dubious gaze. "Does she always talk that much?"

She gave a small nod. "Shay talks and Ranie sulks. Why did you tell her you'd come to town with us?"

"Because she asked me," he responded, echoing her words from last night.

Her eyes widened a fraction, but she didn't acknowledge the repetition. "What about writing?"

He shrugged. "I need a break."

"What about needing the girls to be quiet?" she asked, her mouth thinning. "I'm not going to demand they don't talk."

He wanted to press the pad of his thumb to her full lower lip. This need to touch her, to be near her, was a slippery slope that could only lead to complications for both of them. It had driven him across the property when he should be working. Now the thought of April and the girls leaving him totally alone up here on the mountain had him agreeing to a jaunt into town when he hadn't allowed himself to be social or out in public for years. He was used to being alone, had meticu-

lously carved out the solitary existence he lived. But he couldn't force himself to turn around.

"I realize that was an unfair request." He tried to offer a reassuring smile, but his facial muscles felt stiff from underuse. "I'd like a do-over. Please."

Part of him hoped she'd refuse and he could crawl back into the reclusive hole that had become his life. At least there he was safe. A deeper piece of him needed the companionship and acceptance April could provide. As much time as he spent alone in his apartment in San Francisco, he thought he might go crazy if left by himself on Crimson Mountain. He couldn't let—

"We'll leave in five minutes." April said the words so softly he barely heard her. "And it's going to be fun, so prepare yourself."

Something in his chest loosened and it was easier to flash her a genuine smile. "Are you insinuating I'm not fun?"

She let out a little huff of laughter. "Of course not. Connor Pierce, life of the party."

"That's me."

"Grab your stuff, Mr. Party Pants." She held his gaze for several long moments, then shook her head. "This should be interesting."

"Thank you, April." He wanted to say more, to assure her he'd thought this through and it was a good idea. But he hadn't and, as insignificant as a visit to town seemed, the weight of it suddenly crashed over him, making it difficult to catch his breath. He opened the door, the biting-cold air a welcome distraction.

Fun was no longer part of his repertoire, so he had five minutes to retrieve parts of himself that he'd shut

away after the accident. He'd asked for this, and he had to figure out a way to manage it. It was one afternoon in a small mountain town. How difficult could it be?

Chapter Four

As it turned out, April could have promised silence to Connor on the way into town. Neither of the girls spoke as they made the slow drive down the curving mountain road. Glancing in the rearview mirror, April saw that Ranie kept her gaze firmly out the window, although the girl seemed lost in her thoughts rather than intent on the view. Shay couldn't seem to take her eyes off Connor, who was sitting still as a statue next to April. The little girl was studying him as if he was a puzzle with a missing piece.

Two missing pieces, she thought. She'd endured losses in life but couldn't imagine the pain he must have felt losing his wife and son. The need to comfort and care for him crawled up her spine, coming to rest at the base of her neck, uncomfortable and prickly like an itch she couldn't quite reach. That inclination

in her was her greatest strength and biggest weakness, but mixed with her body's reaction to Connor, it was downright insanity.

Sara was forever trying to find a man for April. It had become her friend's singular mission to see April happy and in love. April had gone on dates with a few nice men, but ended things before they got remotely serious.

She'd been in love once, thought she and her ex-husband had been happy, but understood now that was only an illusion. When her marriage had ended, she'd vowed never to make herself vulnerable to anyone again. She'd convinced herself she was content on her own. It had been easy enough to believe, especially since she hadn't felt the heavy pull of physical desire for a man since her divorce.

Until a rushing awareness of the man next to her had buried all of her hard-won peace in an avalanche of need and longing she could barely process.

As if sensing the thread of her tangled thoughts, Connor shot her a glance out of the corner of his eyes. Barely a flicker of movement, but she felt it like an invisible rope tugging her closer. His gaze went back to the road after a second, and she noticed his knuckles were white where his fingers gripped his dark cargo pants. He was nervous, she realized, and somehow that chink in his thick, angry armor helped her regain her composure.

There was so much sorrow and loss swirling through this car, and it was up to her to ease the pain. Christmas was a time for joy and hope, and she was going to give a little bit of it to these three people under her care.

"I forgot to turn on the radio," she said, making her voice light.

Ranie groaned from the backseat. "Not more corny holiday music."

April flipped on the radio and the SUV's interior was filled with a voice singing about grandma and a reindeer. "That's called karma," April told the girl with a laugh. "You said 'corny' and that's what we've got." She sang along with the silly song for a couple of bars and felt her mood lighten. Maybe it was so many winter breaks spent working retail during high school and college, but holiday music always made her feel festive.

"Santa and his reindeer fly," Shay said brightly as the song ended. "Why would the grandma get run over if she was walking?"

"Kid has a point," Connor muttered.

April smiled at his grouchiness because at least he was talking and he'd loosened his death grip on his pant legs. "Maybe it was when Santa's sleigh was taking off after delivering presents," she told Shay, "so he was still on the ground."

"But shouldn't he take off from the roof?" Shay asked.

She glanced at Connor for help. He arched his brow and didn't say anything.

April turned off the mountain road onto the two-lane highway that led toward downtown Crimson. She met Ranie's gaze in the rearview mirror as she pulled up to a stop sign at the bottom of the hill.

The girl rolled her eyes, then looked at her sister. "Maybe they didn't have a chimney at their house," she said, her tone gentler than April would have expected from the sullen tween. "And Santa was parked in the

backyard. Remember how Mom told you he's magic? That's how he can deliver all the toys and find kids even if they're visiting family for Christmas."

"So even though we're not with Aunt Tracy in Hawaii, he'll know to find us in Colorado?"

Ranie nodded. "Yep. Besides, it's just a song, Shay. Santa wouldn't really run over someone's grandma."

"Thanks, Ranie." The young girl reached over and took her sister's hand. April saw Ranie's eyes close as her chest rose and fell with a breath so weighty it was a wonder the girl's shoulders didn't cave under it. April wanted to cry for the unfairness of a twelve-year-old who was her sister's emotional anchor.

Tears wouldn't help these girls. But holiday spirit might. She turned up the volume for a classic remake of "Baby, It's Cold Outside" and sang the part that Margaret Whiting had made famous. "Want to be the man?" she asked, glancing at Connor as she eased onto the exit for downtown.

"I *am* a man," he answered, his tone grumbly.

"She meant in the song, silly," Shay called from the backseat.

"I don't know the words."

"April knows the words to all the Christmas songs," Shay said.

"It's like a curse," Ranie added.

One side of his mouth curved.

"What's your favorite holiday song, Connor?" April asked, slowing the car as they hit the steady stream of traffic that bottlenecked Crimson's main street throughout the winter ski season.

He gave her a look like she'd just asked whether he wanted his hands or feet cut off first.

"Everyone has a favorite song," she insisted. "Shay's is 'Rudolph the Red-Nosed Reindeer' and Ranie's is…" She paused, holding her breath.

"'Silent Night,'" the girl said on an annoyed huff of breath.

April didn't bother to hide her smile. "Give it up, Connor. I'm guessing you're not the 'Rocking Around the Christmas Tree' type. If I had to pick—"

"'O Holy Night,'" he told her.

"Nice choice," she said with a smile then turned her attention back to the road. She found a parking space a couple of blocks off Main Street. The snow was packed down on the roads, but the sidewalks had been cleared. "The lighting of the big tree in the town square was last week, so we missed that," she said as Connor and the girls got out of the car. "But the stores are all decorated so it's fun to shop and—"

"It's never fun to shop," Connor said, glancing around at the historic buildings and painted Victorian storefronts that made up downtown Crimson. "This place looks like a movie set."

April smiled. "It's beautiful, right?"

"It looks fake," he corrected.

She started to narrow her eyes, then forced an even brighter smile on her face. "The best part about Crimson is that it's not fake. This is a real town filled with people who love the holidays. It's a wonderful place to live."

Shay returned her smile. "I like it."

April felt a pang of guilt at the hope in the girl's eyes. "Of course, California is a wonderful place to live, too. Your aunt Tracy—"

"Can we just go?" Ranie asked, stomping her boots

against the sidewalk. "I'm going to freeze to death if we stand around any longer."

"Right." April took a breath. "Let's check out a few of the shops." She tugged gently on one of Shay's braids. "There's a great little toy store around the corner."

Shay slipped her hand into Connor's as they started down the sidewalk. "We'll need lots of games and toys so we don't bug you when you're writing the book."

Connor's jaw tightened and April watched him try to pull his hand out of Shay's, but she held tight. "Um... okay."

"You should probably buy us extra. That way we'll be really quiet."

"If that's what it will take," Connor said around a choked laugh.

A laugh. It was like music to April's ears.

"And Ranie wants a new iPad." Shay was skipping now. "If they have those."

"Connor is not buying your sister an iPad," April said quickly.

Ranie glanced back at Shay. "Nice try, though."

They got to the front of the toy shop, and Shay let go of Connor's hand to press her fingers to the glass. "It's a winter wonderland," she said, her tone rapturous.

It was true. The toy store had one of the best window displays in town. It was a mini version of Santa's workshop, with elves positioned around a large table filled with wooden trains and boats and stuffed bears and smiling dolls. Above that scene a sleigh pulled by tiny reindeer was suspended from the ceiling and, from one side, Santa Claus watched the whole scene.

"They have holiday decorations in California," Ranie muttered.

"But it seems more Christmasy when it's cold and snowy," Shay said, and sighed happily. "Like this is a place Santa Claus would live."

Connor cleared his throat. "You know Santa really—"

Ranie stomped on his foot at the same time April elbowed him.

"Hey," he yelled, wincing.

"What were you going to say about Santa?" Shay asked, turning from the window.

"I was going to say that Santa lives at the North Pole." He threw a look to April and then Ranie.

"Sorry," April whispered.

"But," he continued, focusing on Shay. "I'm sure Crimson is one of his favorite stops on Christmas Eve."

She nodded, serious. "So he'll find us even though we're not with Mommy or Aunt Tracy?"

"He'll find you," he assured the girl with a small half smile.

April's heart pounded in her chest. Connor Pierce wasn't as dead on the inside as he pretended to be. The way he looked at Shay convinced her his heart wasn't totally broken. It could be fixed and, because it was her way, she wanted to fix it. To fix him.

The door to the shop opened, several mothers with a gaggle of small children between them spilling out. There was giggling and happy shouts as the group headed down the sidewalk.

"Let's go in," she said, and held the door. Shay ran through and Ranie followed. April glanced back at Connor. He looked as if he'd seen a ghost. His face had gone pale and the lines bracketing his mouth and eyes were, once again, etched deep.

"Are you okay?" She turned to call for Ranie and

Shay, but they'd disappeared into the crowded store. "Let me find the girls and—"

"No." He ran a hand through his dark hair. "I can't go in there. I saw a sporting-goods store on the next block. I'll meet you there." He pulled out his wallet, grabbed a hundred-dollar bill and pressed it into her palm. "Buy them whatever the hell they want to shut them up."

She opened her mouth to argue, but he was already striding away.

"What's wrong with Connor?"

Ranie and Shay had returned to the open doorway, staring at April.

"He needed to...uh..."

"Get away from us," Ranie supplied.

April shook her head and moved into the store. "No, that wasn't it. We'll meet up with him in a bit."

"But I want him to help me pick out a game," Shay said. It was the first time April had heard the young girl whine. "I like him."

Ranie sniffed. "He doesn't like—"

"Then let's pick out some fun stuff," April interrupted. "I'm sure he'll want to see it all."

Ranie rolled her eyes again but led Shay toward the wall of board and card games at the side of the store.

April sighed as she followed them, glancing over her shoulder, hoping to see Connor making his way through the other customers toward her. He wasn't there. Suddenly, all of her hope and holiday spirit seemed insignificant in the face of his overwhelming grief.

Connor ducked into a narrow walkway between two buildings a few storefronts away from the toy shop. He

pressed himself against the cold brick and tried to calm the nausea roiling through him. His legs trembled and his heart raced. He could barely catch his breath from the panic choking him.

Why the hell had he agreed to leave the cabin? He'd been a hermit for three years and somehow chosen a popular mountain town two weeks before Christmas as his first outing. A trip to a toy store? What a disaster. There was a reason he lived in seclusion. He wasn't capable of handling anything more. The pounding of his heart was proof of that.

In just one day, April had made him feel more alive than he had since the accident. Like a deluded moth fixated on a bright flame, he'd been stupid enough to believe that meant he had hope. He'd even relaxed around those two girls, almost as broken as him. But an isolated cabin wasn't real life. The prickling under his skin had started the moment he got out of the car and only intensified as Shay took his hand and led him along the crowded street.

The toy store was too much. As soon as he'd heard the children's laughter, which had sounded so much like Emmett's, he'd lost it. Emmett would be almost eight years old now. How would he have changed? Would his sweet laugh have deepened or gotten louder? What would be on his Christmas list? Would his son still believe in Santa Claus?

If Ranie and April hadn't stopped him, Connor would have told Shay there was no Santa. He really was a demented embodiment of Ebenezer Scrooge if he was cracked enough to ruin an innocent girl's belief in Christmas magic.

This was why he was better off alone.

A cold wind rushed between the buildings and he realized he was nearly shivering, more because of the adrenaline draining out of him than the temperature. But he took a deep breath and made his way to the sporting-goods store, feigning interest in a display of backpacks as he worked to regulate his nerves. A well-meaning salesclerk approached him and then quickly backed away at the look Connor shot him. He was holding it together by too thin a thread to make small talk.

A touch on his arm a few minutes later had him spinning around. "I don't need help," he growled, then stopped as April arched a brow.

"That's right," she said softly. "You've got it all under control."

"I shouldn't have come with you today." He glanced over her shoulder to where Ranie and Shay were standing a few feet away, eyeing him warily. Several stuffed shopping bags sat at their feet.

"Maybe not," she agreed, and the fact that she'd already given up on him was an unexpected disappointment.

"Take me back to the cabin," he demanded.

She shook her head. "We're going to the bakery for hot chocolate and muffins and then ice skating."

"I want to go back…" He cleared his throat when several customers glanced their way, and then said in a quieter tone, "I'm the guest."

She took a step closer. "You chose to come with us today, and it's too far to drive you up the mountain and then come back down." Her smile was so sweet it almost made his teeth ache. "Suck it up, Connor," she whispered. "These girls deserve some fun and we're going to give it to them."

He glared but her smile only deepened, daring him to defy her. Somehow that challenge calmed his demons. Everyone else he knew coddled him and, while his grief was real, being handled with kid gloves as if he was liable to crumple at any moment only gave more power to the sorrow slowly eating away at him. For whatever reason, April expected more.

Panic attack be damned, he wanted to give it to her.

He reached out and lifted a lock of her copper hair, rolling the soft strands between his fingers. A blush colored her cheeks and his body went from ice to fire in the span of an instant.

Connor didn't understand what it was about this woman that gentled the pain inside him, but even he wasn't fool enough to walk away. "Okay."

Her lips parted in surprise, and if it wasn't for Ranie and Shay still watching, he would have claimed them as his. He didn't like to be touched but craved contact with April like she was a toddler's well-loved security blanket.

"Let's have some damn fun," he whispered. He grabbed the shopping bags and stalked past the girls back onto the crowded sidewalk.

April pressed her fingers to her forehead as she led her motley crew into the Life is Sweet bakery a few minutes later. Connor was so tense she could almost see it radiating off him like a current. Ranie was back to her normal sulking and even Shay seemed subdued, as if afraid she might set off Connor again and send him running from their little group.

For whatever reason, the young girl felt a connection with the surly, standoffish man. April couldn't explain

it any more than she could understand her own attraction to him. Shay had taken great care in picking out toys and games, even adding a few she thought Connor might like to play.

"For when he needs a break," she'd told April shyly.

"That's nice," April had answered, her throat clogging at the girl's inherent generosity.

"When he takes a break, he isn't going to want to hang out with us," Ranie had said. "We're the problem."

"We're not a problem," Shay had argued. "It's just like when Mommy needed rest. After she napped, she was always happy to see us."

"We're everyone's problem," Ranie had said under her breath, but she hadn't corrected Shay.

These three damaged souls were April's responsibility for the next two weeks, and she didn't have a clue how to help them. A trip to town had seemed so simple back at the cabin. But Connor was clearly having difficulty with the crush of holiday shoppers, and his black mood was quickly seeping into the rest of them, like sludge coating everything in its path.

The smell of fresh-baked pastries gave her a bit of hope as the bells over the bakery's door jingled merrily. As usual, Life is Sweet was filled with customers, drawn by the scent and the promise of the town's best cup of coffee. The walls were painted a cheery yellow and cheery spruce garland had been strung from the wooden beams across the ceiling. A tree sat in one corner, decorated with strings of popcorn and cookie cutters tied to bright red ribbon. Who could stay bad-tempered in the face of so much cheer?

Connor Pierce, by the looks of him. He was star-

ing at the other patrons like they were part of the holiday apocalypse and might transform into zombies at any moment.

"I thought you were working at Cloud Cabin this week."

April turned to see Katie Crawford, the bakery's owner, making her way from the display counter toward them. Katie was a Crimson native and, although she knew almost everyone in town, always had room in her life for another friend. One of the best things about coming to Crimson had been having true friends in addition to Sara.

"We came down for a little holiday shopping," April said, stepping forward to hug Katie. "You look amazing."

"I feel like a beached whale." Katie rubbed her round belly and flashed a wry smile. "I'm getting bigger every day. This little guy or girl is kicking all the time."

Katie was almost seven months pregnant with her first baby. "I bet Noah loves that," April answered.

"He sure does," Katie agreed. Her husband, Noah, worked for the Forest Service in town. It was a shared joke among their friends that the man who hadn't taken anything seriously in life for so many years was now an overprotective, earnest father-to-be. "Let me clear off a table for you." She tilted her head toward Connor and the girls. "I didn't realize there was a family staying at the cabin."

Connor's expression tightened further at Katie's suggestion.

April quickly motioned the girls forward. "These are the daughters of a friend of mine. They're staying

with me over the holidays." She searched Katie's face, but her friend seemed to accept the simple explanation. April breathed a little sigh of relief. "Ranie and Shay, this is my friend Katie Crawford. She makes everything you see and smell in the bakery."

"Welcome to Crimson," Katie said with a warm smile that even Ranie returned.

As April hoped, it was difficult not to be comforted by the atmosphere of Life is Sweet. Connor still stood stone-faced a couple of feet behind them.

She gave him a pointed look and he moved forward. "This is Connor Pierce, Cloud Cabin's guest."

"Welcome to Crimson," Katie said, shaking his hand. "I hope your Christmas with us is a merry one."

"I'm here to work," he muttered in response.

"That's why Ranie and I have to be quiet," Shay announced. "We got games to keep us busy so we don't bug him."

April saw color rise to Connor's cheeks. At least he had the good sense to be embarrassed.

Katie seemed to take it all in stride. She led them to a table near the window. "Do you want the usual?" she asked April. When April nodded, she turned to the girls. "How about a hot chocolate for each of you?"

Shay smiled. "With whipped cream and marshmallows?"

"Of course." Katie placed her hand on Ranie's shoulder. "What about something to eat?"

"I guess a cookie would be good," Ranie said softly.

"Perfect." Katie clapped her hands together. "I have a batch of chocolate-chip cookies about to come out of the oven. Would you two like to see the kitchen?"

Both girls looked at April.

"Wash your hands when you're back there," she told them.

Katie's gaze shifted to Connor. "For you?"

He looked at his feet. "Nothing."

Katie shot April a questioning look but said only, "Let me know if you change your mind."

The girls took off their bulky coats, then followed Katie through the heavy swinging door that led to the kitchen.

As soon as they were out of sight, April rounded on Connor. "This is *not* sucking it up," she said on a hiss of breath.

"I'm here when I don't want to be," he answered, sinking into one of the café table's metal chairs. "Doesn't that count?"

April sat next to him. "No."

He glanced up at her.

"I mean it, Connor." She peeled off her gloves and set them on the tabletop.

He blew out a breath. "I'm sorry. I really am. I thought I could have a normal afternoon, but there's nothing normal about me, April. It's not an accident that I keep to myself. You can see I'm not fit to be around people." A muscle ticked in his jaw, and he looked so miserable that she felt a stab of sympathy for him.

"When was the last time you did something social?"

He gave a harsh laugh. "Does a funeral count?"

"Oh, Connor."

"Don't feel sorry for me," he whispered. "Those girls need and want your sympathy. I'm fine the way I am."

But he was the opposite of fine, and April hated it.

Hated that he had no one in his life to pull him away from his grief, even if he went kicking and screaming.

What she'd been through was nothing compared to his experience, but she wondered if she would have fallen into a deeper sorrow for what she'd lost if she hadn't had Sara to look after her. What about Ranie and Shay? Was having each other enough to see them through the pain of their mother's death?

All of her frustrations bubbled to the surface before she could rein them in. "I guess I don't need to feel sorry for you when you do such a bang-up job of it yourself."

His gaze crashed into hers. "I don't feel sorry for myself."

She knew she should stop talking but couldn't seem to keep her mouth shut. "I can't imagine what you've been through, but you hold on to your isolation like it's a precious gift. Is that what your wife would have wanted for you?"

He went absolutely still, and she realized she'd crossed some invisible line. "You know nothing about her," he whispered, his voice raw.

"You're right," she continued, despite the warning bells going off in her head. "But if she loved you half as much as you loved her, she would have wanted you to be happy. To cherish her memory and your son's by living, Connor. Not by—"

"Stop." He slammed his palm onto the table. "I can't be happy. I won't let myself."

People from the tables around them stared, but April ignored everything except the man sitting across from her. Pain was etched into every inch of his face. "Why?" she whispered.

"Because," he answered, drawing in a ragged breath, "it would mean I've let go of Margo and Emmett. I won't lose them any more than I already have."

The honesty in that statement sliced through her. This was Connor, tied to tragedy and holding on to the past even though it kept him from living now. By the time she'd gathered her composure to argue, he'd stood.

"I don't want to ruin the girls' fun this afternoon. They should have a chance to be happy again, and you can help them. But not me, April. There's no help for me."

"That's not true."

He reached down and pressed a finger to her lips. The gentle touch sent a shock wave of longing through her. His skin was warm, so at odds with the ice in his voice. "Enjoy your time here. Take them skating. I'll meet you back at the car when you're finished."

And he walked away.

Tears clogged April's throat and she focused on her breathing as a server brought two hot chocolates and her tea to the table. What if she couldn't help him? What if he was meant to be locked in that self-imposed prison for the rest of his life? The thought rocked her to her core. She didn't want the connection she felt to Connor, but she didn't want to let it go.

A few minutes later Katie and the girls returned to the table. Ranie and Shay each held a plate with two cookies.

"Look at all that whipped cream," Shay cried as she slipped into a seat and then stuck out her tongue to lick off one of the chocolate shavings. "Marshmallows, too. This is the best."

Ranie's gaze darted around the bakery as she sat. "Where is he?"

"He had some things to do in town."

"Things like avoiding us," Ranie mumbled.

April threw a helpless smile at Katie. "Merry Christmas," she whispered.

"That's the famous author, right?"

April nodded.

"He's different than I imagined, based on his books," Katie said gently. Thanks to its proximity to Aspen, Crimson saw plenty of famous visitors each year. Most people in town took it in stride.

"I think he's different than he used to be," April answered.

Shay dipped a spoon into the hot chocolate and scooped up a mini marshmallow. "He's grumpy because he has so much work to do."

April placed a hand on the girl's thin shoulder. "Sweetie, it's more than the work. Connor had a wife and son who died in a car accident a few years ago. He misses them."

Shay nodded. "I miss Mommy. It's sad when people die."

April saw Katie's eyes widen. Maybe it had been a mistake to come to town, after all. Sara might be on vacation, but there were plenty of other friends she'd need to avoid if she didn't want to talk about the situation with Ranie and Shay. Her reputation in town was that of a mother hen, the one who took care of everyone around her. While that might be true for her friends, she couldn't imagine allowing the girls to stay with her permanently.

April had arranged her life so that *permanent* wasn't

part of it. She had no real commitments to anyone or anything, and if that was a bit lonely, it was also safer. She couldn't be hurt if she wasn't truly involved.

"It is sad," she told Shay. "So we'll have to be extra patient with Connor."

"Even though," Ranie piped in, "he's a big jerk."

April didn't bother to correct her. "Even though," she agreed, and earned the ghost of a smile from Ranie. That was something.

She glanced up at Katie, who was eyeing the three of them curiously. "You should call me later," her friend said, clearly interested in the story April wasn't sharing.

"Service is spotty at the cabin." April sipped her tea.

Katie frowned. "There's a landline, right?"

"Thank you for cookies and drinks," April answered, ignoring the question. She pulled her wallet from her purse, but Katie shook her head.

"A Christmas present for your guests."

Both girls thanked Katie, who was still studying them as if trying to puzzle out the deeper meaning. April felt herself tense, but at that moment one of the women behind the counter called to Katie.

"You go on," April told her. "The bakery is slammed, and they need you."

Katie hesitated.

April finally relented. "I'll call you soon."

With a satisfied nod, Katie hugged both girls and then April. "You've supported every single friend you've made in town these past few years," she said, her dark brown eyes sincere. "Maybe it's time you let us return the favor."

"Thank you," April whispered, hating that her voice shook a little.

When Katie walked away, she plastered the smile back on her face. "Who's up for ice skating?"

Chapter Five

Connor had walked the streets surrounding downtown Crimson since leaving the bakery and was now cold to the bone. He hadn't worn gloves or a hat, and both his fingers and head felt practically frozen. He'd lived his whole life in northern California, so while he was used to damp cold, the bone-chilling air of the Colorado mountains was an entirely new sensation.

One plus to turning into a human Popsicle was that it had helped him get his burning emotions back under control. He'd had to get away from the crowds and April's too-knowing gaze. Not because she was out of line in speaking about Margo and Emmett but because the truth in her words shamed him.

Margo would have wanted him to go on with his life and find happiness again. Her parents had visited him several times after the funeral to try to convince

him of just that. April and those girls made him smile, lifted his heart out of the blackness that had surrounded it for so long. But it felt like a betrayal to his wife and son's memory to feel anything but emptiness.

He dug his knuckles into his chest, trying to keep everything buried. Alone in his small apartment north of San Francisco, it had been easy to pretend that sorrow and guilt were all there was to him. It was the only way to make sure he would never again feel the pain of so much loss.

He made his way from the picturesque residential neighborhood with cozy houses decorated with lights and garlands back toward the equally charming business district and came to stand at the edge of the outdoor ice rink. The rink was large, occupying most of a public park that stretched the length of a city block. Many groups of skaters twirled around the wide oval shape. He spotted April and Shay on the far side of the rink, holding hands and moving slowly. April looked steady on her skates, but Shay was hanging off her arm as if April was the only thing balancing the girl.

He scanned the other skaters but couldn't find Ranie. Finally he noticed her bright blue parka at the edge of the rink. He could see her gripping the edge of the wall, but she wasn't moving and her face was buried in her arms. Without thinking, he started toward her.

"You'd better get going," he said when he was in front of her across the wall. "This is a skating rink, not a parking lot." She didn't move and he immediately regretted the stupid joke. His brilliant social skills were making a mess of things once again.

When she raised her head to glare at him, her cheeks

were stained with tears. His heart lurched. Still not as dead on the inside as he wanted to be.

"Hey," he said, placing his hand awkwardly on her arm. She jerked away, then started to lose her balance and reached for him. He grabbed both her arms and held on tight. "I'm sorry. Bad joke."

"I don't care about anything you say," she snapped. "I can't skate."

"Well, you're holding on to the wall like a champ, so you must have gotten this far somehow."

She shook her head. "I'm stuck here. I can't move."

"Sure you can." He loosened his grip on her. "I'm going to let go and—"

"No!" Her voice was pure panic.

"It's okay," he said. "I've got you." He looked for April's copper hair amid the skaters gliding toward them but couldn't see her. At the speed she and Shay were moving, it would take another several minutes for them to make it to this end of the rink.

"I'll fall if you let go."

"You were doing fine before I got here."

"I wasn't."

"Everyone falls when learning to skate, Ranie. A few bruises and you'll be fine."

"I'm afraid. Please help me, Connor." She sounded miserable, whether from her fear or having to ask him for help, he couldn't tell.

He should have kept walking. He didn't want to be involved, but he couldn't make himself desert this girl now. Not when he could actually help her. The fact that she would rely on him, even if only because she was desperate, poked at something deep inside him. It was

nothing, an inconsequential turn around a skating rink. But it was something he could do.

"I'm going to let you go and—"

"Fine. Who needs you anyway?" She bit down on her lip.

"For a second while I hop over the wall."

"Oh." She nodded and took a breath.

He hitched her up so she could hang on to the wall while he boosted himself up and over. His boots slid as they hit the ice, and he very nearly landed flat on his back. After righting himself, Connor took hold of Ranie's arm. "Let go now."

"I can't," she whispered. "I'll fall."

He bent and wrapped his arm around her waist, pulling her closer to him. He hadn't been this near another person, let alone a child, since the accident.

"I've got you, Ranie. Trust me."

Those were the wrong words, because Connor wasn't someone this girl should trust. But she lifted her hands from the wall, grabbing tightly to his coat sleeve. Her whole body was stiff as he walked across the ice, dragging her along with him as he went. The rink seemed even more crowded now, and he focused on moving through the center to make a small circle that would put them back at the break in the wall that served as the skaters' entrance and exit. He glanced at the frightened girl still holding on to him and saw that her eyes were squeezed shut.

"Not much of a skater?" he asked, keeping his tone conversational.

She gave a sharp shake of her head.

"Why did you agree to this little outing anyway?"

"Shay was excited. She's never ice-skated. And

April really wanted to make her happy after you were such a jerk."

He smiled at her blunt words. "This wasn't your first time?"

"No."

"Bad experience?" He steered her toward the edge of the rink. "Open your eyes. We're almost to the exit."

She did and let out a shuddery breath. He stepped onto the rubber mat in front of the exit and helped Ranie off the ice. The girl took two steps forward and sank onto one of the metal benches surrounding the rink. Connor glanced over his shoulder and caught April's gaze. She held Shay's hand, the young girl smiling from ear to ear as they sailed over the ice. He could read the question in her eyes but motioned for her to take another turn around the rink. He expected her to ignore him, but instead she and Shay glided past the break in the wall.

Connor looked down at Ranie, who had her elbows on her knees and her face in her hands. Panic licked down his spine. Why the hell hadn't he let April take over? Clearly, the girl was upset about something and he was wholly ill equipped to deal with whatever it was.

With a sigh, he sat down next to her. "Tell me about you and skating."

She shook her head.

"That's okay. I'm happy to think you're a wimpy girl."

She sucked in a breath and dropped her hands. "You really are a jerk," she said, glaring at him.

He nodded. "Are you going to tell me?"

"It's stupid."

"I guess you want me to think you're wimpy *and* stupid?"

She mumbled something under her breath that he pretended not to hear. "My mom took me skating when I was little. Shay was a tiny baby and Mom got a baby-sitter for her so we could have a fun afternoon together. It was an indoor rink because we were in California, but she fell and sprained her wrist."

"And that scared you?"

The girl shrugged. "Maybe. I don't remember. She went to the doctor for a splint and asked them about a lump she had under her arm. That's when we found out she had cancer."

Again Connor wished he hadn't waved April away. And why had she listened to him? He was the last thing this girl needed right now. He scrubbed a hand through his hair and whispered, "That sucks." It was all he could think of at the moment.

Ranie gave a small laugh. "You're bad at giving comfort."

"No doubt," he agreed.

"But thank you for rescuing me."

"What happened out there?"

"I don't know." Her thin shoulders slumped like they carried the weight of the world. "I didn't think it was a big deal, but I started skating and suddenly I was afraid. Like something bad might happen if I fell. I'm all Shay has left and…" She broke off, wiped a mit-tened hand across her cheeks, then said, "You're right. I'm stupid and wimpy."

Connor cringed. "I didn't say that exactly."

She rolled her eyes. "You sort of did."

"I was trying to get you to talk to me."

"I know." She sighed. "I bet you regret it now."

He stood and turned to her. "Hold that thought." He jogged over to the ticket booth, grabbed his wallet from his back pocket and then pushed a few bills toward the teenager working behind the counter. He told her his shoe size and, skates in hand, returned to the bench next to Ranie.

"What are you doing?"

"I'm putting on ice skates."

"You're going to leave me and go skating after what I just told you?"

He cut her a look. "No, we're both going back out there."

"No way." Ranie crossed her arms over her chest, the puffy down jacket making her look more substantial than she was.

Both Ranie and Shay were delicate and fine-boned, much like April, although they weren't related. Emmett had been solidly built, "husky" as the clothes Margo bought for him were called. Connor had mistakenly thought that the boy's sturdy body would keep him safe, but there wasn't much anyone could do when jackknifed on the highway on a rainy night.

The familiar wave of grief pounded him, making it difficult to suck air into his lungs, and he closed his eyes and prepared for it to take him under.

"Hey."

He felt a gentle nudge on his arm. Blinking several times, he opened his eyes to find Ranie staring up at him. His sorrow started the slow slide back into the dark crevice that was its home.

"I'll go with you," she said, "Just don't look like you're going to freak out on me."

"I'm not going to freak out," he muttered.

"Right. Because this moment is about *me*. This is my freak-out. You got yours earlier."

He couldn't help but smile at her attitude. "Are you distracting me?"

"I think we're distracting each other," she told him, and looped her hand around his elbow. "You better not let me fall."

He led her toward the ice. "The whole purpose is to get okay with falling."

April and Shay met them at the edge of the rink. They moved so that they weren't blocking the steady stream of skaters getting on and off the rink. Ranie didn't let go of his arm.

"What's going on?" April asked, eyeing the two of them like she wasn't sure what to make of them together. Connor understood the sentiment.

"Connor is teaching me to ice-skate."

"You told April you didn't need help," Shay said. "She can teach you. She's good." She tugged at Ranie's free arm. "Better than him."

"No doubt," Connor agreed, earning a frown from both April and Ranie. How was it that those two weren't related when they could give such well-matched death glares? He sighed, maneuvered Ranie so she could hold on to the wall and crouched down in front of Shay. "You look like a pro out there, Shay," he said. "I bet this isn't your first time on skates."

"Is so," she said, chewing on her bottom lip and looking over his shoulder. Her nose and cheeks were bright pink and her blond hair had escaped its braid to curl around the edges of the knit cap she wore. After a moment she met his gaze. "April taught me. She's nice."

Connor understood that part of what she was thinking went unsaid. "I'm sorry I wasn't nice earlier." Despite the cold, he felt a bead of sweat roll between his shoulder blades. Her innocence reminded him so much of his son. But both April and Ranie were right. He'd had a time for his own freak-out, and there would be plenty more once he was alone again.

As difficult as it was, for two weeks he could help these girls maneuver through this new life without their mother. It's what Margo would have expected from him and what he'd wish for his own son if the situation was reversed. The familiar rhythm of wanting to change the past pounded in his chest, but he forced it away. "Sometimes when I'm sad it makes me grumpy."

"You're sad because your family died."

He swallowed. "Yes."

"I bet you were nice to them."

"I tried to be," he whispered. "I loved them very much, just like your mommy loved you." He slipped off his glove and reached out to touch the tip of her nose. "I'm going to try to be nicer to everyone because my wife and son would have wanted that."

"Mommy made videos and wrote letters for Ranie and me to look at on our birthdays every year. She said she'll tell us things we need to know like how to make friends and be smart and stuff." She smiled. "You can teach Ranie to skate, but I still bet you're not as good as April."

"I'm not that great," April said as Connor straightened.

He met her dark gaze. "You looked pretty darn good to me."

"Oh," she whispered, color rising to her cheeks.

Ranie gave a patented teenage groan. "Let's go before I freeze even more."

Connor winked at April, surprised he could still make the gesture, and led Ranie back onto the ice.

"You're giving me whiplash," April said as she and Connor stood behind the skating rink's wall and watched Shay and Ranie circle the rink.

Connor shot her a look out of the corner of his eye. "I'm not even moving."

"It's your attitude. You need to pick whether you're going to be a jerk or a decent human being. This back-and-forth is making me crazy."

Crazy might be an understatement for how she felt with Connor. Earlier today she'd written him off after he'd stalked away at the bakery. She'd figured her attempt at drawing him out of his isolation had failed and she'd maneuver through the Christmas holiday as best she could. Until he'd shown up at the ice rink, patiently taught Ranie how to skate, and then spun and raced with Shay while the young girl giggled. Ranie had actually laughed and, once she felt comfortable, the girl was a natural on skates. There was a connection between these girls and Connor that April didn't understand but could still appreciate.

He'd been so gentle with the girl the first time she'd fallen. After a few moments Ranie had gotten up with a huge smile on her face, dusted the ice off her legs and kept going. It was the tenderness that affected April the most. She could deal with moody Connor and even handle her attraction to him. But the gentleness was so at odds with who he pretended to be that it slid into her

soul and made her want more than either one of them was willing to give.

"I'm out of practice with the human part," he said quietly.

"Yet suddenly you're willing to work on it?"

He turned to her more fully. "Isn't that what you wanted?"

She sucked in a deep breath of the cold mountain air, hoping the pain in her lungs would help clear her mind and make sense of the emotions tumbling through her.

"Yes," she said after a moment.

"But…"

But she was afraid. Afraid to trust her feelings after so long, especially when they could only lead to disappointment. Afraid to admit how much she cared for those girls after only a short time with them. Giving them back was going to be the hardest thing she'd ever done, but she still didn't have a choice.

If her cancer had taught her one thing it was that life was uncertain, and April's life most of all. She'd tried making plans, had had her future mapped out and it had all turned to hell, leaving her alone and heartbroken. She couldn't risk that again. In some ways it was easier with Connor as the bad guy. She could concentrate on his issues instead of her own failings. But a Connor willing to try was another thing entirely.

"I'm glad," she answered finally.

"You're a bad liar," he said with a small laugh, and tucked a loose strand of hair behind her ear. He wasn't wearing gloves and she loved the warmth of his finger where it touched her cold skin.

She'd stuffed her hat in her pocket after coming off the ice and now brushed her hair over one shoulder,

then waved to the girls as they skated by. "I'm sure I have terrible hat hair."

"You look beautiful." His hand slid around the back of her neck and pulled her closer. Nerves zipped around her stomach and she gazed into his dark eyes. "I don't want to fight with you." His lips brushed against hers, soft for a man with so many hard angles.

"I work for you, Connor."

He nipped at the edge of her mouth. "You work for Crimson Ranch."

"You're the guest," she whispered, but when he would have pulled back she fused her mouth to his. It was reckless, but the past few years of being alone had suddenly become too much. She needed to kiss Connor Pierce like she needed her next breath.

It was everything she'd imagined and nothing she expected. His lips were gentle, searching. He made her feel that they had all day to savor each other, instead of a few stolen moments while the girls were busy on the ice. He slanted his mouth over hers, but all too soon they broke apart.

"I like being the guest," he whispered as his hands dropped away.

Her head felt fuzzy and she touched her fingertips to her lips, surprised they seemed to be the same as they were minutes earlier. Foolish as it was, that kiss had released something inside her that she hadn't realized she'd shut away. It was more than awareness or attraction. She wanted Connor even though, in Crimson, she'd built her life around supporting others, never taking anything for herself.

He waved to the girls and she fought to regain her composure as they came off the ice.

"I'm getting cold," Shay said, her teeth chattering. The sun had just started to dip behind the mountain and the temperature was already dropping. April was used to the double-digit fluctuations in temperature from day to night in the mountains, but it was often a surprise to people new to Colorado. "Can we go home now?"

Home.

The truth came rushing back to April as guilt hit her like a punch to the gut. These girls had no home and neither did she. Yes, she had a cozy apartment in town but it wasn't the same as a home. Not for her. It was a place to keep her belongings and a base of operations. Nothing more. She hadn't had a real home since she'd packed her bags and walked out of the sprawling Mediterranean house she'd shared with her husband.

The fact that Shay could lose her mother and be taken from the only home she'd ever known and, in the space of a day, think of a temporary cabin as home humbled April. She was used to friends coming to her for advice but realized she had so much to learn about hope and resilience from these girls.

"Yes," she said, swallowing around the lump in her throat. "Let's go home."

They walked to the car in the waning afternoon light, Shay chattering the whole way as she held on to Connor's hand. A few kind words and all was forgiven. April wished it was so easy as an adult.

Ranie, who was leading the way down the sidewalk, suddenly stopped. "Be quiet," she said on a hiss of breath. "Listen."

All four of them stood in silence next to the Jeep.

"I don't hear anything," April whispered, but then she did. A tiny sound. Definitely a meow.

Oh, no.

Ranie held out her hand, eyes trained on the snow-covered garbage can near the corner. Dark was coming now and shadows filled the space under and around the metal can. "Give me your phone. Please."

April dug in her purse and then handed it over.

The girl flipped on the flashlight app and shone the light toward the trash can. Two yellow eyes stared out at them.

Connor moved closer and crouched down.

"Be careful," April whispered.

Connor threw her a look. "It's a kitten."

"It *sounds* like a kitten," April argued. "Who knows if—"

Shay clapped her hands. "It's a kitten," she shouted as Connor pulled the small animal out from under the trash can.

"Shh." Ranie handed the phone back to April before taking the bundle of fluff from Connor. "You'll scare him."

"He's tiny," Shay whispered, her eyes double their normal size.

"He's freezing." Ranie tucked the small animal into her parka.

"Me, too," her sister said.

April hit the remote-start button on her key fob. "Everyone in the car. We'll think better when we're warm."

The girls climbed into the backseat while she and Connor got in the front. She flipped on the overhead

light and turned toward the girls. "There's an animal shelter just outside of town. If I call now—"

Ranie shook her head and kept her gaze on the kitten. All April could see was a tuft of black hair peeking out of her coat.

"We have to keep him," Shay whispered, reaching out a finger to stroke the kitten's fur.

"He needs to see a vet."

"We'll take him on the way home."

April threw Connor a "help me" look.

"What will you name him?" he asked.

"Not funny." April swatted his arm. "Girls, you can't keep him."

"Sure we can," Ranie said, finally glancing up. "If you say yes. He's purring."

"I can hear him," Shay said. "Can I hold him?"

Ranie shook her head. "Not until we get back to the cabin. He's warm in my coat."

"He can be warm in my coat."

"We're not taking him to the cabin," April told them, struggling to keep her voice even. "We're taking him to the animal shelter." She pulled out her phone. "I know the woman who runs it. She does a great job matching animals with homes."

"He has a home," Shay announced. "With us." April started to argue just as the girl added, "Mommy sent him."

"Well played," Connor whispered under his breath.

April narrowed her eyes at him, then adjusted in her seat so she could talk directly to the girls. The car had warmed enough that she could no longer see her breath, and both Ranie and Shay had pink-tinged cheeks and shiny eyes.

"What do you mean?"

"I told Mommy I wanted a puppy for Christmas, but she said they were too much work but maybe we could get a kitten."

April bit the inside of her cheek to keep from cursing. "When did she tell you that?"

"Halloween." Shay smiled. "I dressed up like a doggy." She petted the kitten's head again. "But I love cats, too."

At the end of October Jill would have known only a miracle could ensure another Christmas with her girls. The fact that she'd made the promise at that point in her illness was so like her. And now April was here to deal with the aftermath and this sweet girl's expectations.

She glanced at Connor. "You can't think it's a good idea that we bring a kitten to the cabin."

"It's not coming to my cabin." He shrugged. "Besides, I like cats."

"If Connor Grumpy Pants likes cats, we have to keep him," Ranie said with a giggle.

Connor pointed at her. "Respect your elders."

She only laughed more.

April shook her head. How had she become the outsider in this group? She straightened in her seat and wrapped her fingers around the steering wheel. She'd gone from being responsible for herself to worrying about these girls, this man and now a kitten.

"We still have to get to a vet," she muttered. "I don't know a lot about cats, but that kitten is just a baby. He should be with his mama."

"Ranie's his mama now," Shay said, wonder in her voice. "I'm his auntie. What if he's a girl?"

"The vet will be able to tell us," Connor offered. "Maybe you should wait to name him until we find out."

"This doesn't mean I'm keeping him forever," April said as she threw the car into gear and eased onto the road. The traffic in the downtown had lightened as darkness unfolded. She flicked a glance at the clock on the dash. "One of the local vets is a yoga client of mine. We'll head to her office."

"Sucker," Connor whispered.

April rolled her eyes. "You know the constant commentary doesn't help."

"It makes me happy, and it's good when the guest is happy."

An hour later and a hundred dollars lighter, April pointed her car toward Crimson Mountain. Darkness had fallen completely and only the muted silhouette of the peak was visible under the soft moonlight. The wide-open spaces they drove past on either side of the highway were dotted with the soft glow of the various properties situated outside of town. Sometimes when she'd driven back to town from Crimson Ranch, she'd thought about the houses filled with happy families gathered around their kitchen tables and imagined what it would be like to have a family of her own.

Now she had a full car and more people depending on her than she would have ever guessed, not to mention a new pet. She almost giggled from the absurdity of the way her life had changed so quickly. Oblivious to her musings, the girls sat in the backseat, both of their heads bent over the kitten, which now slept in a tiny ball curled inside Shay's jacket.

It had taken quite a bit of coaxing for Ranie to share

him. The girl had kept the kitten, whom they'd named Jingle after he was confirmed a boy, close during the visit to the vet and a trip to the local pet store for supplies.

The vet had guessed him to be about seven weeks old, too young to be away from his mama and littermates. But he was on his own, so they'd received instructions on how to care for a baby kitten, and even purchased a bottle from the pet shop so the girls could feed him with it.

April felt a bit of panic at the thought of all it would take to keep the small ball of fluff alive and healthy in the next few weeks. She liked animals and dog-sat for a few of her friends, but she'd never been solely responsible for an animal. Growing up, her mother had been fastidious about the house and had never entertained the idea of a pet. Even a goldfish had been deemed too much mess. Her ex-husband had felt the same way, and April had never questioned either rule or the fact that she had no input making it.

Now she knew why. The kitten terrified her.

"He's going to be fine," Connor said softly, as if he could read her thoughts. "If he survived living under that trash can, your cabin is going to seem like the Taj Mahal."

She adjusted the radio so that the sound was playing from the speakers in the back of the SUV and turned up the volume. "I can't keep him," she whispered, sliding a glance at Connor, "and I doubt the girls' aunt will let them bring him to her house."

"Then think of it as being a foster mom for a couple of weeks. He's with you until he's old enough to be adopted by a family who wants him."

"Do you have any pets at home?"

His mouth thinned. "Not anymore."

April sucked in a breath. "You don't mean—"

"My wife, Margo, had a dog. He'd been hers before we were married and was almost twelve. She loved that mutt like a second child. After the accident, I couldn't—" He broke off, cleared his throat. "Her parents took him. It gave them some comfort to take care of something she'd loved so much."

"But not you?"

He cleared his throat. "I didn't deserve any comfort."

The words broke another piece of her heart for this man. She reached for his hand just as headlights from the other side of the two-lane highway cut through the night. At the same time, the Jeep's headlights caught on a huge shape in the middle of the highway. A few stray elk crossing. April slammed on the brakes and dimly registered Shay's high-pitched scream as the back end of the SUV fishtailed across a patch of ice.

Luckily, most of the road was dry and the car lurched to a stop as one of the massive animals turned to look at her. Illuminated in the beam of headlights, the elk's dark eyes shone. It paused for only a moment, then trotted across the double yellow line and off the shoulder to follow the others. The truck on the other side of the road had skidded across the median, and then jackknifed directly in her path. The driver rolled down his window and waved before taking off again.

Forcing her fingers to relax their death grip on the steering wheel, she pulled off the highway onto the gravel shoulder. She flipped on the car's interior light and turned to the backseat. "We're fine," she said,

meeting both Ranie and Shay's frightened gazes. "Clearly, I still have a ways to go at mastering the art of winter driving in Colorado. Is the kitten safe?"

Shay nodded, opening her arms to show the small animal sleeping peacefully. April smiled despite the adrenaline pounding through her. Her smile disappeared when she flicked a glance at Connor. He sat completely still, staring unfocused out the windshield into the darkness. His fingers were pressed to either side of his temple like his head was pounding.

"It's okay," she whispered, placing her hand on his arm.

He flinched away from her touch. "Get me to the cabin," he said through clenched teeth.

She realized in an instant that whatever he was seeing out the front of the SUV had nothing to do with tonight and everything that involved the accident that had claimed his family. Once again, she wanted to wrap him in her arms and offer whatever comfort she could. Whatever he would take.

"Connor, this wasn't the same—"

"Now," he demanded. "Drive me back now."

The range of emotions in his voice overwhelmed her. Desperation. Panic. Anger. Worse was the fear pouring off him in waves, as if it were a physical force she could reach out and touch. It felt like he was holding on to his composure—and maybe his sanity—by the thinnest thread.

Pulling back onto the darkened highway, she pasted a smile on her face. "Well, this day has turned out to be quite an adventure," she said brightly to the girls.

Shay smiled back at her in the rearview mirror, but Ranie was watching Connor.

"That's one resilient little cat," April continued, hitting the button to turn off the interior light. She had a feeling Connor needed the darkness outside to mask whatever demons were pummeling him from the inside.

He'd made progress today. All of them had. Despite her doubts, she'd wanted to believe there had been some real healing. Now she worried that for the man sitting next to her, any effort she made might never be enough.

Chapter Six

"How's the kitten?"

At the sound of Connor's voice, April whirled around in the cabin's quiet kitchen. The plate she was unloading from the dishwasher crashed to the floor and splintered into a dozen pieces, much like her nerves.

She hadn't seen Connor since they'd returned from town to Cloud Cabin two days ago. He'd darted from the Jeep even before she'd come to a complete stop and disappeared without another word. The girls and the cat had needed her attention, so she'd settled them in the caretaker's cabin before returning to the main cabin to look for him. But there had been no answer when she'd called his name. Obviously, he was there. Where else would he have gone? But as much as she wanted to force him to talk to her, it wasn't her place.

What did she have to offer him anyway?

She'd made a simple dinner of soup and salad and

left it on a tray outside the bedroom door, then returned to her cabin to make dinner for the girls. She'd come back after they'd gone to bed to find the dishwasher loaded and running but no other outward signs of him.

She'd been tempted to call Sara on her vacation and walk away from this job. They'd been here less than a week. Surely Sara could find someone to take April's place. She could move the girls to her small apartment in town or get in the car and drive to the coast. They could rent a house on the beach for the holiday, something that felt like a vacation. Something that wouldn't feel like real life or a glimpse at a future she was too scared to grasp.

But she hadn't made the call.

Instead, she'd left a written schedule of when she would come to the cabin to make meals and check in each day. She figured if he needed her beyond that— and her foolish heart had hoped he might—he could walk across the driveway to her cabin.

Of course he hadn't. Other than the clean dishes in the dishwasher and a light under his bedroom door, there was no indication anyone was in the house. Last night she'd awakened at three o'clock and gone to her window to check the main cabin. The soft yellow glow had illuminated the pure blackness of the forest at night. It seemed appropriate that the cabin remain dark other than that one shining beacon, so she'd taken to working with only the small pendant above the sink to light her way when she came over before sunrise.

Now he stood in the doorway of the kitchen and flipped on the recessed lights. He wore a loose pair of fleece pants and a white T-shirt that was—damn him—fitted across his broad chest and shoulders in a

way that made her mouth go dry. His hair was rumpled like he'd been regularly running a hand through it, and the dark stubble that covered his jaw was quickly turning into a beard.

He looked wild and more than a little dangerous, a strange glint in his green eyes as his gaze raked over her. She'd tossed her down parka over the back of one of the kitchen chairs and wanted to hop over the pieces of scattered plate to wrap it around her.

He arched a brow. "Do you always wear pajamas on the job?" His voice was back to a gravelly rumble. It made parts of her body come to attention, parts that she wished would ignore Connor Pierce.

"Are you done hiding?" she shot back. Tearing her gaze from him, she stepped to the pantry and pulled out the broom and dustpan. When she turned around, he was gone, and she hated the instant disappointment that fluttered through her.

But then he returned, walking toward her with so much purpose she actually took a step back. "Let me clean up," he said, pointing to her bare feet. "You're not wearing shoes."

All business. Right. She handed him the broom and dustpan, careful to make sure their fingers didn't brush. "I took off my boots at the door," she said, proud that her tone was even and emotionless. "Jingle is fine, and I'm in my pajamas because I wasn't expecting to see you. You've been like a ghost with an appetite."

His head was bent as he swept, but she saw one corner of his mouth twitch. "Nice unicorns," he said softly.

She ran a hand over the well-worn cotton of her favorite pajamas. They had pictures of unicorns jumping

over rainbows covering them, a gift from Sara after April's surgery.

"Did you really leave your inner sanctum to poke fun at my pajamas?"

"No, but it's a bonus." He swept the broken dish pieces into the dustpan, and she pulled out the drawer that held the trash can so he could dump everything in it. He leaned the broom against the counter. "I need to get the vacuum and go over the floor. There may be pieces I missed."

"I can—" April lost her train of thought, yelping as Connor took a step toward her and lifted her into his arms. She was pressed against him from chest to toe, and the scent of mint and spice swirled around her.

After moving her to the far side of the kitchen, away from any remaining shards, he released her. She forced her knees not to buckle. "Don't walk in here without shoes until it's been vacuumed."

"You can't pick me up like that." She patted her fingers to her chest, hoping that would calm her pounding heart. Her reaction to this man was intolerable when he obviously didn't have the same response to her. "I'm not a child."

"You're light as one," he said, scrubbing a hand over his jaw.

The scratching sound was like some sort of unwelcome mating call and April fidgeted as heat pooled low in her belly. First thing to add to her list of New Year's resolutions was finally allowing Sara to set her up on a date with one of Josh's bull-riding friends. Clearly, self-enforced celibacy had negative ramifications.

"What are you thinking?" Connor asked, his voice tinged with amusement.

No way was she sharing her thoughts with him at this moment. Instead, she said, "I'll get the vacuum."

He grabbed her wrist as she moved past. "I wanted to thank you."

She stilled, staring at where his big hand gripped her wrist, olive toned against her pale skin. How could someone who admittedly spent most of his time indoors have such beautifully colored skin?

"April," he whispered, "look at me."

Glancing up through her lashes, she sucked in a breath when her gaze met his. For once, his eyes weren't guarded, and the look he gave her was so tender and intense it made her dizzy with longing.

Stupid longing.

"Thank you for taking care of me these past couple of days."

She sniffed. "It's my job."

He acknowledged her words with a small nod, or maybe it was the bitterness creeping into her tone that he recognized. "How are Ranie and Shay?"

"Do you really care?"

"Yes." He sighed. "Even though I don't want to care. The other night...on the highway...it affected me. Hearing that scream when the car slid on the road and the headlights moving closer." He paused and a shudder ran through him. "I'm sorry I disappeared, but I wasn't fit company for anyone after that."

"It's fine." She tried to hold on to her anger even as it slipped through her body like grains of sand through her fingers. She needed that anger. It was safer with this man. Safer for her heart. "You don't owe me an explanation."

"I want to give you one anyway." His hold on her

gentled and he rubbed his thumb over the sensitive flesh on the inside of her wrist. "I've missed you, April. I've spent the past three years alone, and suddenly I'm lonely without you. I stopped caring. I didn't think I had it in me to care, and I'm still so turned around. Every little thing sets me off and I can't stop it. But I also can't stop wanting to be near you. It doesn't make sense."

She closed her eyes against the onslaught of emotions that poured through her at his words and the gentle pressure to her skin.

"Do you know," he asked, shifting so close now that she could feel his breath against her hair, "that I listen for the door to close after you leave and rush down to the kitchen because your scent lingers after you're gone?"

She huffed out a laugh that sounded breathless to her own ears. "Are you saying I smell?"

"Like lavender and vanilla. I've made an idiot of myself the past two days following traces of you around the house."

"Why are you telling me this?"

"Because I want you to know what you do to me, even if I should stay away. It's better for both of us if I turn around and walk back to my bedroom until you're gone."

She waited a moment, but he didn't move. "You're not walking."

"Hell if I can make myself go."

"Don't go," she whispered. Slowly, as if she were gentling a stray animal, she lifted her hand. Her finger brushed the prickly strands of his dark beard, and his lips parted.

"I forgot to shave," he muttered.

"Too busy?"

He took a breath, released it and then nodded. "Writing."

"Connor," April whispered. "That's wonderful."

He shrugged and looked away. "Who knows how long it will last. But the words are coming. So damn many, drowning me with their force. It's like…"

She pressed her palm to his cheek, gratified when he leaned into it. "Like what?"

"Like it used to be." He said the words softly, as if they were an apology. April could feel the tension in his body and wished, just for a moment, she could transfer his pain to herself. Give him a few seconds of remembering what it was like to live without the weight of guilt and sorrow bearing down on him.

"Look at me," she said, moving closer to him, pressing into his warmth. His arms came around her waist, his hands splayed open against her back. She could feel their heat and strength through the thin cotton of her pajama shirt. So much talent flowed out of those hands. The worlds he created within his imagination and put on paper for readers to discover. "You have a gift, Connor Pierce."

"It's not—"

"Don't say it. Whatever you're thinking." She brushed her lips over his. "Those words are in you. The stories you write are part of you."

"How can they still be there when I'm dead inside, April? They were part of my life before, but now I'm—"

"You're here," she told him, and held her hand to his chest. His heartbeat was strong and sure under her palm. "With me. Now."

"You make me feel things I'd thought I lost the capacity to feel. You make me want things—" His voice

broke off as he drew in another deep breath. He leaned down until their foreheads touched. They stood that way for several long moments, her lips just grazing his. She breathed him in and it felt like she was pulling his essence into her lungs. Like he was part of her. A part she thought she'd lost after the illness and heartbreak that had changed who she was inside.

"I'm sorry I can't be the man you deserve," he whispered. "I'll hurt you and girls. I hurt everyone—"

"Not now." She pressed her mouth to the base of his neck, tasted the salt on his skin and wanted more. "This moment is ours."

He claimed her mouth then, kissed her until the feel and taste of him was all she knew. Everything else burned away in the flame that was her need for him. He pulled her closer, if that was possible. Their tongues tangled and his hands skimmed under the shirt and up her spine, sending tingles as they moved. His kiss was demanding and consuming, and every inch of her body burned for him. For more.

His lips trailed over her jaw and he nipped at the sensitive flesh of her earlobe. "Will you stay?"

The simple question rocked her. How was it that such a longing could have been buried inside her and she'd never guessed? Even at her most in-love-and-alive, she'd never felt anything quite like the force of her desire for Connor. Still, she shook her head. "I have to go back in case the girls need me. If Shay wakes up…"

"I understand," he said, pulling his hands from underneath her shirt.

No, her body screamed. *Don't let him go.*

"Come with me," she told him, lacing her fingers with his.

He stared at her, his eyes unreadable once more. She hated that he could slip behind his mask so easily. She wanted to break through until she saw every bit of him, good and bad. She wanted to *know* him and, in return, allow him access to all the secret places she kept hidden from the rest of the world.

"This isn't real life. We aren't—"

"I don't care." She bit down on her bottom lip. She knew what they were and what they weren't, but now that she'd awakened to her longing, she wasn't willing to abandon her desire so easily. "We're here now. It doesn't need to be more than that. We can agree—"

He squeezed shut his eyes, then looked at her again, his gaze empty. "It's a mistake, April."

"Make it with me, Connor."

She prepared herself for his rejection. Instead, he lifted her hand to his lips, turned it over and placed a tender kiss at the center of her palm. "Are you sure?"

"Right now," she answered honestly, "yes."

For some reason, that made him smile. "You're all sweetness on the outside but you have a core of pure steel."

"Is that a compliment?"

"Right now, yes," he said with a wry grin. "I'm coming with you."

"I'm glad."

As she led him through the smaller cabin, April pointed to the second floor and placed a finger over her lips. Connor was grateful for the sleeping girls because he wasn't sure he could actually form words at this moment.

He'd never expected to be in this place again. Want-

ing. Needing. The ache he felt for April went beyond the physical. It was elemental, as if in the span of a few short days she'd become a necessary part of him, vital to his very existence.

He'd never believed in a muse, but something about April had given new life to his creativity. He'd written close to a hundred pages in the past two days, and it wasn't the garbage he'd forced onto the page over the previous six months. The drivel that had prompted a call from his editor and a suggestion that he start over on the story. He knew as the words were pouring out of him that they were the best he'd even written.

Every time he thought about the beautiful redhead now leading him up the stairs, his fingers itched for the keyboard again. Not as much as they itched to touch every inch of her delicate skin. To know if it was as creamy everywhere as the places he'd seen and touched. He wanted it all, and he was worried that he might never get enough.

It was stupid since, after the holidays ended, he'd be back to his solitary life. The isolation that had once felt like a refuge now loomed like a dark, desolate wasteland.

But he wouldn't think of that now.

She turned to him in the doorway of the bedroom at the end of the hall. "Well, this is it," she said, tucking a lock of hair behind her ear, then untucking and then retucking. Nervous. She was nervous.

Connor smiled despite himself.

"We're good?"

"Sure." She smiled, crossed her arms over her chest. "Yep. We should…um…I mean I know what to do. It's just…"

He stepped closer, cupped her cheek and kissed her gently. "What's going on, sweetheart? It wasn't that long of a walk across the driveway."

"You're the one who said it was a mistake."

He licked the seam of her lips. "I'm an idiot. Ask Ranie."

She laughed. "That girl likes you. A lot."

"And you, April?" He tugged at the hem of her shirt. "Do you like me?"

"Against my better judgment," she admitted.

He pulled back, searched her deep brown gaze. "Tell me now, April. Is this a mistake?"

"No, but…" She pressed her lush, kiss-swollen lips together. "I haven't been with a man since my husband."

"I haven't been with a woman since my wife."

"You don't understand. I haven't been with a man since my *cancer*." Her arms wrapped tighter around herself. "My *breast* cancer."

She said the words like they were a challenge—as if she expected him to run from the room at the mention of her cancer. The knowledge of what she'd been through shocked him, but he wasn't scared by it. It only made him admire her more. "I'm sorry, April."

She shook her head. "Don't you dare feel sorry for me," she whispered. "I'm a survivor. But it's changed me. It's changed my body."

"I don't feel sorry for you," he clarified. "I'm sorry for anything that caused you pain, but never doubt that you are beautiful." He stepped closer. "*I* think you're beautiful."

"You haven't seen me."

"I've seen the most important parts," he said, lean-

ing in to kiss her forehead. "Your intelligence." He slowly drew one finger down the side of her face, over her neck and collarbone to the center of her chest. "Your beautiful heart." He lowered his mouth to brush against hers. "Although I'm partial to this part of you, as well."

She kissed him back, but her body remained stiff. He took her hands in his and slowly drew her into the room, shutting the door behind them. "Tell me what you want me to know," he said when she sat on the edge of the bed.

She blew out a breath. "The cancer was caught early, so I opted for a lumpectomy and then a course of radiation and chemo as my treatment plan. There's a scar and… I'm not a young girl anymore. My body—"

"Is perfect," he interrupted. "Because it's yours." He pulled his shirt over his head and turned so that his back was to her. He heard her gasp and let his eyes drift closed. "During the accident, my seat belt malfunctioned and I was thrown from the car as it rolled. I landed against the edge of the guardrail."

Her fingers traced the length of his scar. Other than the hospital staff, no one had touched that part of his body. He was surprised to find that the skin there was still sensitive after all this time, or maybe it was simply a reaction to April's touch.

He shifted to look at her and found her eyes bright with unshed tears. "No, April. No crying."

She swiped at her cheeks and nodded. "I haven't dated or been with a man since my divorce because I'm afraid to show anyone that part of me. The physical reminder that I'm not who I was."

"We don't have to—"

She reached for the hem of her pajama top. "I want to, Connor. With you." Her smile was wry. "Even if it's only temporary. I have to start somewhere, right?"

Those words sent a stab of jealousy piercing through him. He had a feeling that once he started with April he would never want to finish. To think of another man with her after he was gone was a sharp pain in his chest. But then she lifted her shirt over her head and let it drop to the floor and all he could say was "Thank you for starting with me."

She wore a pale pink satin bra, the soft color a perfect complement to her creamy skin. His gaze snagged on the jagged edge of an incision he could see above the fabric. At this moment, he wanted to throttle her ex-husband for letting her go and also express his gratitude for the man's stupidity since it allowed Connor the gift of having April here with him.

He wanted so badly to touch her, but forced his hands to remain in his lap. "There's one thing," he said. "I wasn't expecting this and I don't have protection."

A wisp of sadness flitted across her gaze before she smiled. "One benefit to the cancer, I suppose. My treatment sent me into early…" She paused, as if the word was too difficult to say out loud. "I can't get pregnant."

"I'm sorry."

She shrugged. "Some things weren't meant to be."

"This *is* meant to be," he whispered, leaning forward again. He took her mouth, planning to go slowly. But as soon as her tongue touched his, all the desire he'd banked came howling back to life inside him. He needed her now. All of her.

As if she was responsible for the very beat of his heart. As if touching her could somehow sew together

all the shattered bits of his soul and make him a whole person again. It was foolish, he knew, and too much to expect of anyone. She had scars of her own, and not just the one on her body.

He'd spent so much time wallowing in his own grief that he'd forgotten how it felt to offer comfort and pleasure to another person. Now he wanted to rediscover that piece of himself. The one that wasn't buried in sorrow. The one that could feel something besides pain and regret.

He forced himself to slow down and savor the moment. Every sigh and moan that escaped April's beautiful mouth. Damn, but he loved her mouth. He kissed her with every part of himself, pulling her closer and then lowering her onto the bed. His fingers found the clasp of her bra and flicked it open. She stiffened as he drew the straps down her arms.

"Beautiful," he murmured as her breasts were revealed to him. He kissed the scar that traveled the edge of one breast as he cupped the other one in his hand. She let out a sound that was half sob and half moan as he gently sucked her nipple into his mouth.

Her hands reached around his back, her fingernails lightly scratching a path over his spine.

"Let me see you," he whispered as he raised his head to look into her eyes. "I want all of you."

She nodded and he stood, flipping down the covers as he did. She backed up onto the sheets and he reached for her pajama bottoms, curling his fingers into the waistband of her panties at the same time. He tugged the material down over her hips, revealing every inch of her to him. She looked at him shyly from beneath her lashes. With her copper hair tumbling over her

shoulders and her skin milky white in the early morning light that filtered through the curtains, he was almost brought to his knees. She was the most beautiful thing he'd ever seen. She was long and curvy in all the right places, her body clearly sculpted by the yoga classes she taught.

"You're staring," she said, her mouth curving slightly.

"I could look at you all night."

She laughed, a husky sound that made him want her all the more. "I'd rather you join me." She crooked a finger at him. "Are you waiting for an official invitation?"

He shucked off his pants and boxers, realizing his fingers were trembling as he did, and then climbed onto the bed. He felt like an untried schoolboy with April, excited and nervous and so damn grateful to be exactly where he was. That gratitude was new for him, and he concentrated on that. Focused on making April believe she was as beautiful as the way he saw her.

Her skin was smooth and he skimmed his hands up her legs. "I want to touch you everywhere," he whispered, and pressed a kiss to her belly.

"I don't think I have enough patience for that right now," she said, pulling on his shoulders until he brought his mouth to hers.

"We have time," he said, and deepened the kiss. She wrapped her legs around his hips in a silent invitation that he was happy to accept. Sliding into her was like nothing he'd ever felt. It was as if she'd been made for him, the way she tasted and smelled the perfect combination to stoke his passion even higher. He licked a trail down her neck, sucking lightly when she

squirmed. Her fingers kneaded the muscles of his back and she arched into him, moaning when he changed their movements.

"You feel so good," he said.

She whispered his name on a sigh and then opened her eyes to gaze into his. The pressure inside him built and they continued to move together.

"So good," she repeated, and he felt her body stiffen and then tremble around him. Her tiny moans and the flush that colored her cheeks spurred him on and he came inside her, shuddering at the power of his release. She held him and he continued to drop gentle kisses at the base of her throat before scooping her into his arms and turning so that she was sprawled across him.

They lay like that for several minutes and Connor finally felt his heartbeat return to normal. She lifted her head, resting her chin on his chest. He could feel her gaze but wasn't ready to open his eyes. Couldn't risk her seeing what this moment meant to him. He had no intention of changing his plans. This was temporary. A holiday fling.

His stomach tightened, rejecting his brain's intention, but he ignored it. He'd become a master at ignoring his feelings. There was no reason to change now.

"What are you thinking?" she asked softly, and he was struck by the wariness in her tone. How was it possible that this woman could read him so easily?

"No words," he said, schooling his expression as he met her gaze. "There are no words for how amazing that was."

She studied him for a moment before flashing a quick smile. "Even from the writer?"

No words, he wanted to tell her, would keep his

heart safe from being destroyed when this ended. All the ways he didn't want it to end scared the hell out of him so, instead of answering, he kissed her again. As if he could wrench out every bit of pleasure from her and somehow make it enough to allow him to walk away.

Chapter Seven

Connor pressed his fingers to the cold glass the next afternoon as he watched the girls and April play in the small clearing behind the cabin. They were bundled up in parkas, hats and mittens. It had snowed again over-night, and April's bright hair seemed to sparkle against the reflection of the pristine layer of snow enveloping the ground and surrounding trees.

Ranie was on her knees, rolling a ball of snow across the clearing. Shay applauded as the ball, clearly intended to be the base of a snowman, got bigger. She started to shout something to her sister, then clapped a mittened hand over her mouth. April said something he couldn't make out before glancing up at his bedroom window.

Instinctively, he backed out of sight. He hadn't seen her since he'd left her bed late last night. She'd been

asleep next to him, her hair fanned out in glorious waves across the pillow. She'd looked so peaceful and content, and he'd wanted to stay wrapped around her all night long. But he was afraid that would send the wrong message about what was between them so had sneaked out, back to the stillness of his own cabin.

Instead of sleeping, he'd sat down in front of his laptop. He'd expected to stare at the blank screen, his frustration mounting until his head was a jumble of anger and disillusionment. But, as had happened over and over in the past few days, his fingers had flown across the keyboard, pumping out words and scenes that had been locked inside him since Margo's and Emmett's deaths. He was so close to the end of the book, and his momentum continued to grow.

It triggered both relief and guilt, because somehow losing his gift had seemed a form of penance for living when his family had perished. It had been inadequate punishment, but it was something.

Now he had his story *and* April. It was almost too much. The unfamiliar happiness that washed through him was both a balm to his sorrow and a jab at the misery that had been his constant companion.

With one last glance out the window, he forced himself to sit back down at the bedroom's rolltop writing desk. He'd sent off an email to his editor early this morning, telling her he'd be delivering the story she was waiting for by the end of his two weeks at the cabin. Now he opened her response, an enthusiastic paragraph about pushing up release dates and a potential media tour. Panic gripped Connor's chest and he slammed shut the laptop screen.

Another happy shout drew him to the window. Al-

though she faced Shay, April pointed at the cabin, her back to him. Connor had a perfect view of Shay's face as her sweet smile faded and she dropped her head to stare at the ground. He could almost hear April's sigh as she bent to wrap her arms around the girl.

In that moment he'd never felt like a bigger ass. Those girls, who had lost so much, couldn't even enjoy a day out in the snow because he'd demanded peace and quiet. The truth was that at the start of his career, before he'd had a home office, he'd often written in bustling coffee shops, proud of his ability to block out background noise as he concentrated. Even after Emmett was born, he'd heard the sounds of baby cries from his desk when Margo came home from work and took over the parenting. There was no reason for him to insist on perfect quiet other than his wolfish agitation at hearing young voices.

But the sounds didn't poke at his sanity the way they had after the accident. At that time, any high-pitched sound reminded him of Emmett and the boy's scream in that last moment before the truck had slammed into their vehicle. It was one of the main reasons Connor had become such a hermit. He was afraid of being swallowed by panic and not having the ability to snap himself out of it. But he'd grown weary of giving his demons so much power.

He hurried down the stairs, shrugging into his coat as he grabbed a pair of gloves and knit cap from the storage bench by the back door. The sunshine bouncing off the snow had him squinting, and he took a pair of sunglasses from his coat pocket and slid them on. April and both girls looked up as he rounded the corner to the back of the house.

April moved toward him quickly, her thick boots crunching in the snow. She held out her hands as if to physically stop him. "It was just a little shout," she said, her voice pitched low. "It's hard to stay quiet when you're five, but she's trying."

He looked over her shoulder to the girls. Ranie had come to stand next to Shay, her arm wrapped protectively around her sister's shoulders. The older girl glared at Connor as Shay chewed on her bottom lip. He realized he hadn't seen the girls since he'd fled after their trip to town and now they expected he was here to complain and yell.

Great. *Now* he felt like a bigger ass.

"I've come to help," he said quickly.

April blinked like he was speaking a foreign language.

"With the snowman," he clarified.

"Did you fall and hit your head sneaking away last night?"

"I didn't sneak away," he said through clenched teeth. "You were asleep."

She poked him in the chest. "Because you *snuck* out of bed without waking me."

He took off one glove and tapped his finger to the tip of her cold nose. She drew away, making him smile. "You're beautiful when you're angry, but not as beautiful as you are with your hair spread out over the white sheets and not nearly as lovely as when I was deep in—"

"Okay, girls," April called, whirling away from him but not before he saw the blush coloring her cheeks. "Connor's going to help us with the snowman."

"Do we still have to be quiet?" Shay asked, continuing to nibble on her lip.

April glanced over her shoulder, one brow arched. If eyebrows could speak, hers would be saying, *See what a jackass you are.* But he didn't need her to enlighten him.

He shook his head, moving toward the girls. "You can be as loud as you want," he said, crouching in front of Shay. "I've gotten a lot of writing done this week and I appreciate how you've helped me. Things are going well enough that I can take a break, and even when I go back to work, you can make noise."

"I don't want to bother you," she said quietly.

"You don't, sweet girl. How's that baby kitten?"

Shay's face immediately lit with pleasure. "He drinks from a bottle and sleeps with me and Ranie. We're going to bake cookies after the snowman. You can help and then you'll see him."

"He doesn't want to bake cookies," Ranie muttered.

"Do I get to lick the batter bowl if I help?"

Shay nodded. "Yep. We each get a spoon. At least that's how Mommy did it."

"Sounds like a plan to me," April said from where she stood a few feet away.

Connor straightened. "Are you better at making snowmen than ice skating?" he asked, sliding a glance at Ranie.

Her mouth dropped open. "I was great at ice skating."

He shrugged. "With some coaching. You need help with Frosty?"

"I can roll a way bigger snowman than you."

"We'll see about that," he said with a grin. "How

about a wager? Whoever builds the biggest snowman gets first dibs at the batter bowl?"

Shay giggled. "Ranie loves cookie dough."

He pointed at the older girl. "Then you'd better get rolling."

"You're on," she said, returning his smile before she took off for the corner of the clearing where the snow was deepest.

Connor turned to April.

"How do you do that?" she asked. "Make things good with her so easily? Other than when she's holding that cat, I can barely get her to crack a smile."

He leaned in close. "Maybe I have a gift with words *and* prickly women."

"I am *not* prickly," she protested.

"I know. You're perfect." He glanced over to make sure Ranie and Shay were busy, then brushed his mouth across April's. She tasted like cold and mint, and he wanted nothing more than to wrap his arms around her until she was warm and pliant under him. "I didn't sneak away," he said as he reluctantly pulled back.

She gave a delicate snort.

"I walked away quietly," he added, earning a small smile.

"You're good when you make an effort."

"I'm going to make more of an effort." He leaned in again. "Later tonight."

This time she laughed for real, and it was more rewarding than any glowing review of his books.

"April, will you help me find a nose for Ranie's snowman?" Shay called. "We're helping her beat Connor."

April reached down, grabbed a handful of snow and

threw it directly at his face. "You'd better get rolling," she said, and ran off to join the girls.

His demons were silent as he watched her go. She was the only thing he'd found that could effortlessly keep them at bay. They were no match for the joy she brought to his slowly brightening life.

With a tremor of unfamiliar hope unfurling inside him, he bent to the ground and started rolling.

"You know there are carbs in that pizza crust." April nudged Connor as he helped himself to another slice later that night.

"What's a carb?" Shay asked, wiping her hand across her mouth.

"Napkin," April said at the same time as Connor, and then slanted him a small smile.

Shay bounced up and down in her seat. "Jinx," she called out. "You owe each other a soda."

April had no idea what she was talking about, but Connor answered, "The jinx machine is out of order. Please insert another quarter."

Ranie rolled her eyes, but Shay's gaze widened. "How do you know about jinx?"

Connor took a breath. "My son loved getting jinxed," he said after a moment.

Shay nodded. "I wish I could have met him. I don't have many friends my age."

"He would have been eight next month." Connor placed the piece of pizza back on his plate. "But he loved playing with kids of all different ages. I'm sure you would have been good friends."

Silence descended for a moment and then Ranie pushed away her chair from the table. "Shay, let's clear

our plates and I'll show you that new app I downloaded on my iPad."

The younger girl lifted her hand to her mouth. She reached for her napkin and wiped it across her lips. "I'm sorry you're really bad at making snowmen," she said to Connor, and then followed Ranie to the kitchen.

April tried to hide her smile as Connor turned to her.

"Really bad?" he asked.

"Pretty awful," she told him.

"He was just a little off-center. It gave him character."

"His head fell off before you'd taken two steps away."

"Maybe," he admitted, "making snowmen isn't one of my gifts."

She rested her head on his shoulder. "You have others."

He pointed to the two empty seats across from them. "I can sure clear a room."

"Is it difficult to talk about your son?"

He took so long to answer she wasn't sure he was going to. Then he said, "To some people, but not Shay. She's so matter-of-fact about it. Most of my friends and family either tiptoe around the subject or immediately start to cry when they see me. After the accident, Margo's mom would call me every day to tell me details of Margo's life when she was a girl." He closed his eyes for a moment, the soft Southern drawl of his mother-in-law's voice echoing in his mind. "Some of the stories I'd heard before, but the constant barrage of details when I was already so broken…" He opened his eyes again, met her gaze as she tipped her head to look at him. "I stopped taking her calls. I turned off my machine. I couldn't…"

MICHELLE MAJOR   *113*

"It's okay."

He shook his head. "Her parents were as heart-broken as me. They lost their only daughter. I didn't protect my family. I was too weak—"

"I read more reports about the accident on the internet," April told him. She felt him stiffen. "You couldn't have done anything."

"I could have gotten them out of the car before it caught on fire. I was too fat and out of shape to move when it mattered." He pushed the abandoned plate toward the center of the table. "It's why I got healthy. No carbs. Lots of protein and exercise. I won't ever fail someone I love again." He gave a gruff laugh that broke her heart a little. "Of course, there's no one left alive who I love."

Another jab to her heart. Of course she didn't expect him to love her. Of course she wasn't falling in love with him. She'd barely known him for a week. They'd spent one night together. Maybe it was the best night of her life, but that didn't matter.

Her heartache was insignificant compared to how his had been broken, but she was too raw to offer him any comfort right now. Instead, she pasted a bright smile on her face. "So the pizza was a pretty big deal?"

"Don't forget the cookies."

"You inhaled a half dozen."

There was a rustling under the table and then a black ball of fluff clawed at her pant leg. Jingle jumped into her lap.

"He looks good. I think he's grown in the past few days."

"He makes them really happy," she said, "and it's going to be terrible when they have to give him back."

"Maybe they won't."

"There's no way Jill's sister will let them keep a kitten."

"April," he said softly. "Those girls belong with you."

"No." She jumped up from her chair, dropping the kitten onto the table as she did. Ignoring the sudden trembling in her fingers, she collected the pizza stone and both their plates. "That's not an option, Connor."

"Why?"

"Does it matter?" She stalked over to the kitchen sink and dumped the plates and pizza stone into it. She went to open the dishwasher, but Connor was next to her, blocking the door. "You don't get to do this," she said.

"Why?" he asked again, and she couldn't tell whether he was repeating his question or wondering about her anger. She opened herself, gave her temper free rein in a way she normally wouldn't. She'd learned early on to control what she felt until her optimism had become an inherent part of her. Yoga helped with that. Whenever she felt pressure building, she'd go through her favorite restorative sequences until her equilibrium returned.

But she had no center of balance with Connor. She was like his snowman, continuously off-center and on the verge of toppling over.

She gave him a small push and he backed up a step, far enough that she could open the dishwasher. Flipping on the faucet, she rinsed the plates and began to load them. "You wrap yourself in your tragedy like it's a warm blanket. It's defined you, and anytime you're uncomfortable you pull it up to your chin like a protective layer. You don't get to hide behind your demons

and still demand that I put aside mine. I honor what you've been through and how it's shaped you, Connor."

"You've pushed me every day since you showed up at that cabin," he answered, but there was no anger in his tone.

She lifted her gaze to his, and his green eyes were lit with understanding. She didn't want understanding. She was baiting him because his anger would mute the other emotions tumbling through her.

"It's not the same."

"Those girls need a family, April. They need you."

She almost laughed at that. Because if anyone was needy in this scenario, it was her. All the need and desire she'd locked away was now pushing on the door of her heart. She could feel the barricades starting to crumble and was working overtime to shore up the cracks in her armor. That involved not allowing herself to even entertain the idea of keeping Ranie and Shay.

"I'm not a good bet for them," she said, drying her hands on a dish towel and then slamming shut the dishwasher. "Their mother died and if my cancer returns…"

"You can't live your life letting the fear of a future that may never happen run it."

"Watch me."

"You'd be good for them," he said softly.

She shook her head. "I'm not good for anyone." No matter how much she tried, how much she gave to her friends and the Crimson community, her deepest secret was that it was all a mask. Everything she did was to prove that she added value and was worthy of the love and friendship people offered her. Because she didn't believe she was worthy of it just for being who she was.

He reached for her, pulled her close and wrapped

his arms around her. She tried to stay stiff, to ignore how right it felt to be surrounded by the strength and heat of him.

"We're quite a pair," he whispered, and all the effort she'd made to fortify her defenses didn't matter. They fell away in an instant, as if he'd snapped his fingers and worked some kind of strange, desperate magic. She sagged into him and let him support her. All her tarnished edges and dusty corners. She didn't hide anything, only pulled air in and out, matching her breathing to the steady rhythm of his heartbeat.

"You're making an effort," she whispered after a long minute. "That counts."

"You're giving those girls a Christmas they won't forget," he answered. "And dragging me along for the fun. That counts, too."

She sniffed. "I'm not dragging you—"

He cut off her words with a gentle kiss. "Thank you," he said. "For being you."

"April?"

Shay's voice was uncertain. April pulled away from Connor and turned to where the girl stood in the kitchen doorway, a book held to her stomach.

"Are you ready for the story?" she asked.

Shay nodded, then her blue gaze flicked to Connor. "I was wondering if Connor would read it to us tonight?"

Oh, dear. April supposed she didn't need to push Connor when Shay was around. That sweet girl was determined to bring him back to life. She smiled at him over her shoulder. "Each night leading up to Christmas we read a different story out of the Christmas book bought the other day. They're short but if…"

"Dragging me," he whispered, "in the best way possible."

He stepped around her toward Shay. "It just so happens that in addition to my mad skills making snowmen, I'm a master story reader."

Ranie had come to stand next to her sister. "This should be a treat," she muttered, but a smile lit her eyes.

"Can we have cookies while we listen?" Shay asked April.

April nodded. "One more each. You get settled on the couch with Connor and I'll put them on a plate."

Her cell phone rang as she turned for the counter, and she recognized Sara's number. "Are you checking up on me from paradise?" she asked as she accepted the call.

Sara's throaty chuckle sounded through the phone. "I'm having a margarita in your honor."

"I don't drink margaritas," April answered with a smile.

Sara laughed again. "You should, my friend. You should."

"How's vacation and why are you calling? Is everything okay at Crimson Ranch?"

"It's fine and vacation is perfect. I should try it more often."

"You'd get bored and bug that handsome husband of yours," April told her.

"Oh, I'm *bugging* the heck out of him on this trip. He's not complaining." Sara sounded happy and relaxed, and April was glad for her. "I wanted to check in on our cabin guest. Connor's editor called to thank me. She said he's going to finish his book during this trip. Apparently, the studio that made the first movie

is interested in film rights. I don't know what you've been doing, April, but as usual you've got the magic touch with difficult guests."

"He's not too bad," she said quietly, glancing at the doorway that led to the cabin's small hearth room.

"Really? I heard he went off the deep end after he lost his wife and son, and now he's a total antisocial hermit."

"April, come on." Shay ran into the room and skidded to a stop in front of her.

April fumbled for the mute button on her phone but ended up holding her fingers over the microphone.

"Connor and Ranie are having a pillow fight and you need to referee." The girl was bursting with excitement and shouting at the top of her lungs. "Bring the cookies to distract them."

She held a finger over her lips and whispered, "I'll be there in a minute. Don't run in the house."

Shay heaved the impatient sigh of a five-year-old, and then turned and sprinted back out of the room. "April's got the cookies," she yelled, her voice carrying even after she'd disappeared.

"Sara, I need to go. Have a—"

"You're kidding, right?" Her friend sounded stunned. "You can't hang up without an explanation. Pillow fights and cookies? Who is Ranie? And is there a child at the cabin?"

April made a pathetic attempt at white noise. "Sorry, Sara, you're breaking up."

"You can't pawn me off with fake static. What's going on, April?"

April sighed, pressed a hand to her forehead. She hadn't drunk more than an occasional glass of wine

since her cancer diagnosis, but this was a moment she could have used a shot of hard liquor. For medicinal purposes, of course. "It's under control. You have to trust me."

"Of course I trust you." Sara's voice gentled. "But I need to know you're okay. I know how you take on more than you should because you can't say no. The point of being up on the mountain with a hermit was that you'd have time to relax, too. Whatever is going on there—"

"I'm fine," April lied. "Everything is fine."

Shay yelled for her again.

"I need to go. Enjoy your vacation and I'll talk to you when you're back in town."

"If you need anything," Sara said quickly, "call me. Anytime. Take care of yourself, April."

"I will." The lie stuck in her throat. She swallowed, then made her voice bright. "Merry Christmas, Sara. Give Josh a hug for me and I'll see you in the New Year."

"Merry Christmas" was the last thing she heard her friend say before ending the call.

Everything might not be fine, but that was her own fault. She'd let her heart get involved with the three people waiting for her in the next room. They meant something to her, different from what she'd expected and more than she could handle without being hurt. But she'd committed to doing her best to heal those girls and Connor. No matter what life had thrown at her, April had always believed Christmas was a time of magic. She wasn't going to give up on that now.

The sound of raucous laughter spilled from the hearth room into the kitchen. Laughter was a good

reminder of how far they'd come in just a few days. She plated the warm cookies and, humming a holiday tune under her breath, moved toward the happy sounds.

Chapter Eight

A loud crash from downstairs made Connor jerk away from his keyboard. He glanced over his shoulder at the closed bedroom door. Was April trying to get his attention?

It seemed unlikely since she'd been avoiding him all day. Maybe she was angry again that he hadn't spent the whole night with her, but he'd made a point of waking her before he'd crawled out of her bed around midnight. She'd given him a sleepy kiss and a smile before falling back to sleep. He'd assumed that meant she was okay with him leaving. The truth was, even if he'd wanted to stay, the words were pounding through his brain at such a fever pitch he couldn't sleep. He'd returned to his cabin and stayed at the computer until the sky had turned pink and orange with the dawning of a new day.

Only then had he forced himself to rest for a few hours before heading down to the treadmill in the basement. He'd timed his workout so he might see April making breakfast, but she hadn't made an appearance all morning. It was easy enough for him to fry a couple eggs, and he'd had a small stab of guilt at the fact that he was sleeping with a woman who, in a roundabout way, worked for him. Maybe he should make her breakfast? Or dinner. He'd checked the refrigerator and pantry and figured he could whip together some sort of decent meal for her and the girls.

He'd been the one to cook most of the meals when Margo was at work, and he expected the thought of cooking for someone else to feel uncomfortable. Instead, he liked the idea of doing his part for the woman who had already done so much for him.

But April hadn't come to the house at lunch and the small cabin next door had remained quiet all day. He could have texted her, but something had stopped him. Maybe there was another reason she was staying away. Maybe he'd shown her too much of himself, and it was more than she was willing to take on. He wouldn't blame her, even as disappointment coiled around his gut.

Anger rose to the surface, sharp and familiar. She *did* work for him. Even if she'd decided she wanted nothing more to do with him, she still had a job. He stalked toward the stairs, letting the demons he'd kept under lock and key have free rein inside him. They stretched and yawned, then gnashed their teeth, prepping for a fight he didn't exactly want but couldn't seem to stop himself from seeking.

He came up short as he turned the corner for the

kitchen. Ranie was on her knees with a towel, wiping up what looked to be enough water to fill a bathtub. Shay stood on a chair pulled to the counter chopping carrots with…damn, was that a butcher knife in her hand? April was nowhere in sight.

"Hey, girls," he said softly, not wanting to startle a five-year-old wielding an eight-inch knife. "What's going on?"

Ranie froze on the floor, glancing up at him.

Shay turned and the look in her eyes wrecked him. "We're making you dinner," she said with a hitch in her voice. "But you don't have any food in the cabinets. Ranie's real good at noodles or mac n' cheese. You only…"

"Sweetheart," he said, stepping closer. "Put the knife on the counter."

Ranie straightened and, after moving behind Shay, grabbed the knife out of her sister's hand.

"We'll figure out something," the older girl told him, her chin tipped up. "You have eggs. I can make eggs. Go back to whatever you were doing and—"

"Why are you two making dinner?"

"We want to," Ranie said. At the same time Shay whispered, "April's sick."

Ranie nudged the girl's shoulder. "Be quiet, Shay."

Connor's mind raced and spun as he tried to assimilate the scene before him and the little girl's words. "What do you mean she's sick? Is she at the other cabin still? What's wrong?"

The two sisters looked at each other, an entire silent conversation occurring before his eyes.

"I'll see for myself," he said, already turning and heading for the door. He shoved his feet into boots and

was shrugging into his coat when the girls came rushing after him.

"No." Ranie shouted that one word into the silence.

Connor stopped, his hand on the doorknob. "Tell me what's going on."

"She says it's just a stomach bug." Ranie dropped her gaze, wrapping her thin arms around herself. "She doesn't want you to see her right now."

"She's *really* sick," Shay whispered, and looked so miserable that Connor instinctively opened his arms. With a muffled sob she ran into them and he lifted her against his chest, her weight insubstantial and yet unsettling as her shoulders shook and she cried into his shirt.

He murmured soothing words into her hair. She smelled like sugar and sweat and child. A universal scent that wrapped around his soul, tugging tendrils of memory from their hiding place. His demons quieted, as if lulled by her nearness, watching and waiting to see what would happen next.

Ranie took a step closer and put a soft hand on her sister's back. "Our mom threw up a lot during that last round of treatment. It upsets Shay and…" She clamped her mouth shut, her blue eyes frightened and so big against her pale skin.

"It's going to be okay," he said, and opened his embrace to include her. She allowed herself to be held for only a few moments before pulling away. Shay still clung to him, though, and Connor found that he didn't want to let go of her. He shifted her in his arms so he could hold her as he walked and then led the two girls across the driveway to the smaller cabin.

He held open the front door for Ranie. "When did it start?"

"I guess in the middle of the night," Ranie admitted reluctantly. "She was sick when we woke up this morning."

He started to ask why she wouldn't want the girls to tell him but wasn't sure he wanted to know the answer to that question. April was comfortable being the one to take care of those around her, but what if it was more than that? What if she didn't trust him?

After all he'd shared with her about his weakness and failing his family, she didn't have much reason to have faith in him. But, damn, if he didn't want her to.

He lowered Shay from his arms at the bottom of the staircase. "You two pack your bags while I check on April."

Both girls gave him a look of such horror the ice spikes of guilt hammered into his gut. Apparently, one day of fun in the snow wasn't enough to balance how he'd treated them when they'd first arrived. These girls did not trust him.

"Everyone is moving into the main cabin so I can take care of April," he said gently. "So I can take care of all of you."

Shay nodded and Ranie let out a shaky breath. He could almost see the weight lift from her shoulders. Connor cursed the heavy burden of responsibility this girl had been forced to carry when she should have been focused on being a kid.

"Jingle can come, too, right?" Shay asked. The tiny animal peeked his head around the corner from the hallway.

"Put him in the carrier and bring him along. Once we get April settled, I'll come back for his supplies."

"I can hold him," Shay protested. "He doesn't like the carrier."

Connor shook his head. "I don't have time to chase a kitten through the snow. He can have free rein in the cabin, but he has to make the trip in his carrier."

"Fine," she muttered.

Ranie patted her shoulder. "You get Jingle, and I'll start packing."

As Shay took off down the hall toward the kitchen, Ranie met Connor's gaze. "Thank you," she whispered, her eyes darting toward the cabin's second floor.

"Everything is going to be okay," he told her, and once she'd disappeared after her sister, he headed up the stairs.

He heard the telltale sound of violent retching before he even opened the bedroom door. The bed was empty so he moved toward the bathroom. She was kneeling on the tile floor, hanging on to the side of the toilet as if she was having trouble staying upright.

She stiffened as he crouched behind her and gathered her thick hair into his hands and away from her face. A moan escaped her lips in between heaves, whether from what was going on inside her body or his presence, he couldn't tell. He guessed the latter.

His suspicion was confirmed when she stilled a few minutes later, shallow trembles the only thing racking her body.

"Go," she whispered, her voice hoarse and shaking. "Don't need you."

To prove her point, she shifted away from him like

she was going to stand but crumpled into a heap after just one step.

"Ah, sweetheart," he murmured. "You might not need me, but I'm going to lose my mind if you won't let me help you right now."

Her only response was a soft groan.

He knelt beside her, rubbing his palm over her back. "Let me help you."

She shook her head, her mass of copper hair dull and tangled as it draped over her face, hiding her from his view. Counting on her body's current frailty to prevent a fight, he took her shoulders and eased her around so he could see her face.

Damn. He stifled a gasp at the sight of her sallow skin and chapped lips, the shadows bruising the sunken hollows of her eyes. She didn't look at him and her body was so limp in his arms he couldn't tell if she was still awake. He traced the blue veins of her eyelids with his thumbs.

She stirred as he drew the washcloth over her forehead and cheeks.

"Stomach bug," she croaked out. "Leave me—"

"I'm taking you to my cabin," he told her, surprised when she gathered the strength to fight him. Her skin was burning, and he figured she was half-delusional, thanks to the fever. Although she flailed, there was no strength in the movements and he easily subdued her, gathering her closer. He hoped to heaven this was only a stomach bug. The thought that it might be something more serious made it hard to draw air into his lungs.

"We're going to give it one night," he said as he stood, cradling her in his arms. "Then I'm bringing in a doctor."

"No doctor," she whispered, her body going rigid again. Then she sighed and sagged against him, her breath raspy on his neck.

He headed for the door and found Ranie waiting in the hallway. "She's in bad shape," the girl said, and it wasn't difficult to read the panic in her gaze.

"We'll take care of her," he said with a confidence he didn't feel. Maybe he should call a doctor right away or at least contact someone from Crimson Ranch to let them know what was going on.

As if reading his thoughts, April struggled in his arms. "No," she groaned in a croaky voice that was and wasn't hers.

He didn't answer her as he maneuvered down the hallway. Because even if it was only a virus, no one should trust him with the responsibility of nursing another person back to health. He'd already proved that he couldn't take care of someone who was important to him.

The revelation of his feelings for her had his knees starting to buckle before he clamped down the lid on his emotions. The constant refrain he'd told himself in the past few days…this is a fling, she doesn't matter…held no weight in his heart as the girls led their silent parade through the frozen afternoon air to the other cabin.

Even if what between them ended, April was his. She was in his heart, part of his very makeup. She'd breathed life back into him when he'd thought it was impossible. Stomach flu or something else, he was going to take care of her. He was going to prove that she could depend on him.

The next few days passed in a fevered haze for April. She slipped in and out of sleep as her body seemed to

turn in on itself. Even during the cancer treatments, the surgery and the searing pain of recovery, she'd remained conscious of each moment.

Whatever was ravaging her body now had taken it over completely. There were short bursts of lucidity and she clung to those and the details of life swirling around her.

Connor holding her hand. The feel of a cool cloth against her forehead. Struggling to the bathroom or heaving over the bucket at the side of the bed. A girl's voice softly singing Christmas carols. The downy feel of a kitten's fur against her neck. An unfamiliar presence in the room. A doctor?

She'd protested the clinical hands on her, the cold metal of a stethoscope and a pinpoint of light shone in her eyes. Then Connor's strong hands soothing her. A glass of water tipped to her dry lips.

Now she blinked open her eyes, the raw ache in her throat propelling her awake. She felt as if she'd crawled her way through a hot, dark desert, pulling sand into her lungs until they were filled with an abrasive scrape.

A rustling across the room and Connor was beside her.

"Hello, sweetheart," he murmured, and she had the random thought that no one had ever called her that before. Desperately she wanted to be someone's sweetheart. This man's sweetheart.

But not as desperately as she needed a drink.

"Water," she whispered.

He held a glass to her lips and, while swallowing made her wince, it was a cool balm over the fire that burned her throat.

She glanced up at him from under her lashes and

other memories poured into her mind, like a thick soup that meant to choke her. Memories of waking from terrible dreams, the kind that had plagued her during her radiation and chemo, and being comforted in Connor's embrace. Embarrassment followed quickly. She knew from when Sara had cared for her during her treatment, April had a tendency to talk in her sleep. What had she said in the thrall of the fever? What had she revealed when she'd worked so hard to keep her secret fears hidden?

She coughed a little and Connor moved the glass away, dabbed at her chin with a soft cloth. She'd sworn after the cancer that no one would see her so weak again, and a part of her hated that he'd been forced into the role of playing nursemaid.

Perhaps he didn't mind, but she'd watched the way her husband had changed. The difference between how he had looked at her when she'd been whole and healthy and the disgust and pity in his gaze after her diagnosis.

The thought of Connor seeing her that way was more than she could bear.

Tears clouded her vision before she could stop them and immediately he scooped her into his arms, rocking her back and forth like a father would a child who'd scraped a knee. She knew she should fight, show him she was still strong, but the truth was twofold. She wasn't strong and the comfort of being held was too appealing. She wasn't ready to let him go.

"I'm fine," she said, her voice raspy, and she forced herself to pull away.

He gave a tired laugh. "You scared me."

She scooted back against the headboard, shocked

when her arm muscles protested the work of supporting her as she moved. "I'm sorry."

How many times had she said those words to her husband? *I'm sorry I'm sick. I'm sorry I'm not the woman you married. I'm sorry you don't love me anymore.*

Bitterness filled the emptiness in her belly, making her hunger for more than just food.

"Sweetheart, you have nothing to be sorry about."

That word again. *Sweetheart.* Connor's voice was so gentle. She forced herself to meet his gaze, steeling herself for whatever she'd find there.

The tenderness radiating from him was the last thing she'd expected. Again tears pricked her eyes, but this time she blinked them away.

"How long have I been out?"

"Three days." He ran a hand through his hair, and she realized he looked almost as exhausted as she felt. "The fever broke yesterday, shortly after the doctor was here."

"I said no doctors."

"You said a lot of things," he told her. "That one I ignored. Sara insisted—"

"You called Sara?"

"Right away," he answered matter-of-factly.

"It was a stomach bug."

"April," he said on a sigh. "I haven't ever seen a person that sick from a virus. I wasn't taking any chances." He looked away, out the window with the curtains that were drawn so only a bit of light filtered through.

She bit her lip. He'd watched his wife and son die in that car accident. Of course he'd wanted a doctor to

take responsibility for her. She was surprised he hadn't shipped her off to the ER so she'd be out of his hair.

No. That was unfair. Connor wasn't her ex-husband. She couldn't lay the shortcomings of another man at his feet.

"Will you open the curtains?" she asked softly, and he stood to do her bidding. "I'm sorry you were worried. And Sara... I'm surprised she didn't fly back from her trip."

He smiled at her over his shoulder. "You know her well. The doctor who made the house call was her brother-in-law."

April cringed. "Jake Travers drove up the mountain to check on me?"

"Only then did Sara agree to stay on her vacation." The mattress sagged as he sat on the edge of it again. "He gave you three liters of IV fluids but said you should still take it easy."

"I feel awful that everyone was so put out by me. He has a family of his own and—"

He placed a finger over her mouth. "He didn't mind, and his wife—"

"Millie?"

"Yes, Millie. She's called twice to check on you." He pulled his phone out of the pocket of his flannel shirt and smiled at the screen. "It seems like half the town has called or texted for updates on your progress. You have a lot of people who care about you."

"I wish no one knew," she said on a sigh. "I don't want people to think that I'm..."

"Human?" Connor asked, one side of his mouth curved.

"Sick," she whispered.

He frowned. "You were sick, April."

"I mean really sick," she clarified. "Most people know my history and—"

"A stomach virus is different than cancer."

"I know," she mumbled, although feeling weak and dependent on other people was universally awful no matter the reason. "It's difficult for me to not be the one taking care of others." She glanced around at the room she was in, suddenly realizing it wasn't her bedroom. "I'm at the main cabin?"

"It was easier to take care of you here."

"What about the girls?"

"They're here, too. In fact, if you're up for it, I know they'd love to see you awake. Both of them have been worried."

"I didn't want them to tell you I was sick."

He flashed a wry smile. "They told me anyway."

She shook her head. "That was stupid and selfish of me. Those girls shouldn't have to feel responsible for anyone but themselves. After everything they've been through…"

"Don't beat yourself up, April," he said, reaching out to take her hand. "Ranie and Shay care about you. They just wanted you to feel better."

"I don't deserve them," she whispered, her chest squeezing. That was why she couldn't keep them. She didn't deserve that kind of devotion, and her instincts around taking care of herself were twisted. She should never have asked the girls to hide her illness from Connor.

Being sick had affected more than April's body. It messed with her mind, bringing back too many memories of not being able to care for herself or having to

rely on her husband during her cancer treatments. That experience had changed her, and while she hated the way it had distorted her view of herself and the world around her, she didn't know how to fix it.

"Hey," he told her, tracing his thumb in circles on her palm. "How about you give yourself a break for a minute?" He leaned forward and pressed a kiss on her forehead so gentle it almost broke her heart. "Let's concentrate on the fact that you're on the mend."

"Three days," she muttered. "That means…it's two days until Christmas Eve."

"Yep."

She gave a little groan. "I don't have anything ready. No tree, no presents. I wanted to go to town once more to buy gifts." Disappointment and guilt warred inside her, both vying for equal measure. "I'd hoped to give the girls a special Christmas with their mom gone. Now, it's ruined."

"Nothing is ruined," he assured her. "The best gift those girls can get is you feeling better."

She nodded, even though she didn't agree. She was no one's best thing. "I'm going to brush my teeth and splash water on my face before I see them."

He stood as she moved her legs from under the covers, then caught her as she stumbled when her feet hit the floor. Her head spun as she realized how truly weak her body was.

"Slow down," he murmured against her hair. "I've got you."

Her nerves bristled at his words, but he only wrapped his arms more tightly around her. After a moment, she let herself sag against him. "Thank you," she whispered. "For taking care of me and the girls. I

should have said it earlier, but the stupid virus seems to have taken my manners along with my dignity."

"I'm glad to be the one who was here to look out for you."

She tipped her face to meet his gaze. "Do I even want to know what I said in my sleep?"

He couldn't quite hide his grin. "Probably not, but I got lots of creative story ideas."

She groaned again. "Your book. Oh, Connor. I'm sorry. You're supposed to be working on the book, not holding my hair back while I puke."

"I like your hair," he said as he led her slowly toward the bathroom, "and I brought my laptop into your room to work while you slept. Turns out you're inspiring even when feverish and nauseous."

"I'll remember that." She paused, placed her hand on the door frame. "I'm okay from here."

"Are you sure?" He loosened his hold but didn't quite let her go. "The last thing we need is for you to fall and crack your head open."

"I'm fine. I should make myself something to eat after I see the girls."

"I'll heat up some soup."

"We don't have soup."

"The girls and I made it."

She felt her eyes widen. "You made soup?"

"I found a recipe on Pinterest."

"Oh, no." She swallowed another groan. "You were reduced to searching Pinterest?"

"Ranie set me up with an account."

"Well, thank you. But I can take care of—"

He bent his knees so his gaze was level with hers. "I'm not done taking care of you, April. You might be

uncomfortable and you can fight me all you want. I'm not walking away."

She sniffed, swiped her fingers across her cheeks. "I like you better when you're a jerk."

He laughed. "That can't be true."

"It's a lie, but things were simpler when you were a jerk."

"Things were simpler when I was alone, but it didn't make me happy." He tucked her hair behind her ears. "You make me happy." He lifted a strand of her hair and cringed. "Even with dried…something stuck in your hair."

"I'm a mess."

"You'll feel stronger after you eat. I'll get the girls."

By the time she'd washed her face and brushed her teeth, April felt almost human again. She looked like hell, pasty and drawn, and her hair was a dirty, stringy mess around her face. She ran a brush through it and then gathered it into a ponytail.

The girls were waiting quietly next to the bed when she walked out into the bedroom. Ranie held on to Jingle like he was keeping her grounded. Connor stood next to the older girl, Shay clinging to his hand. He must have been an amazing father. The thought made her heart ache for him all over again. For what he'd lost and the capacity for caring he was slowly regaining.

"I'm so glad to see you both," she said, lowering herself onto the bed, then opening her arms. Shay launched herself into them immediately, but Ranie held back.

"Are you sure you're okay?" Ranie asked as the kitten squirmed and jumped onto the bed, sniffing at April before curling into a ball at her side.

April nodded. "I need food and a shower, but I'm fine."

"I'll work on the food," Connor said, and left the room.

April stroked the kitten's silky fur. "I remember this guy keeping me company."

"He's a good boy," Ranie whispered. "He was worried about you."

"You threw up a lot," Shay said quietly, tucked against April's chest.

"I'm sorry if I scared you." April rubbed the little girl's back. "Thank you for taking care of me and for letting Connor know I was sick."

Ranie shifted a bit closer. "You aren't mad about that?"

"No, sweetie. You did exactly the right thing. It was wrong that I didn't tell another adult right away. You shouldn't have had to take care of me."

"It's not a big deal," Ranie whispered, sitting next to April.

April adjusted her hold on Shay so she could wrap an arm around Ranie's shoulders.

"Ranie took care of Mommy," Shay added. "But she never puked as much as you."

April drew in a breath. "I was sick after my treatments, too, but this was different. You both understand that, right? I was sick with a stomach virus, but I'll be healthy again. It isn't like—"

"Mommy felt better for a long time." Shay's voice was painfully matter-of-fact. "Then she got sick again."

"I'm not going to…" She paused and then said, "This had nothing to do with cancer." She wanted to tell the girls she wouldn't get sick again, but how could she make that promise? Yes, it had been more than five

years since her diagnosis and the odds were good that she'd be fine. But she lived with the knowledge that her cancer could return at any time. She couldn't commit to Ranie and Shay for the long term. How could she take the chance on these two beautiful girls being forced to watch her battle the same disease that had claimed their mother?

She cleared her throat and pasted a smile on her face. "Tell me about what you've done in the past couple of days."

Shay bounced up and down on her knees. "We baked cinnamon bread and played card games. Connor knows one called poker and I'm really good at it."

"Great," April muttered with a laugh. "He's turning you into a card shark."

"She's got skills," Connor said from the doorway. Shay dropped off her lap and Ranie stood as he carried in a tray. "Although it's a little early to decide on a career as a professional poker player."

"I can't be a poker player." Shay pushed her hair away from her face. "I'm going to be a cancer doctor when I grow up," she told them. "So no one else will get sick."

April swallowed back her emotion and smiled. "Your mom would be proud of you," she whispered. Was there no end to this girl's ability to slay her?

Connor waited for her to get comfortable on the bed and then placed the tray across her lap. It held a steaming bowl of chicken soup, a glass of juice and a piece of toast on a small plate. Her stomach grumbled as the comforting scent of soup hit her.

"Ranie did most of the work," Connor told her.

The older girl shrugged. "I like to cook, and Connor helped."

"I cut vegetables," he said with a laugh. "That's prep work."

"Ranie's going to be on the Cooking Channel," Shay said, bouncing up and down.

April spooned up a bite of soup. She closed her eyes to savor the flavors of garlic and roasted vegetables. The warm broth soothed her chafed throat as she swallowed. "It's delicious," she told the girl, and was rewarded with a wide smile.

"You have your mother's smile," she whispered, and Ranie gave a small nod. "Thank you again," April said, taking all three of them in with her gaze, "for all you've done the past few days. I feel so…" She wouldn't say *loved* even though that was the truth of it. "I feel so lucky."

"Now that you're better," Shay announced, trailing one finger over the edge of the quilt. "You should maybe take a bath. You kind of—"

Ranie clapped a hand over her sister's mouth, but April laughed. "Trust me," she told the girl. "I can smell myself, and that's bad."

Shay grimaced. "Real bad."

"After the soup, it's off to the shower for me."

"Shay, let's go finish our puzzle," Ranie suggested. "And you still need to make your bed and get out of your pajamas."

Shay nodded and then leaned closer to April. "I love you even though you smell."

Without waiting for an answer, she turned and walked out of the room. Ranie rolled her eyes and followed.

April froze with the spoon halfway to her mouth.

"Do you remember what it was like when emotions were that simple?" Connor asked.

April took another bite and a sip of juice before answering. "No," she said softly. "My parents got divorced before I was a year old. I don't think things were ever that simple."

"Emmett loved me like that." He sank down into the chair in the corner of the room, elbows on his knees and head in hands. "It was pure and constant and I didn't appreciate it the way I should have. I took both of them for granted, as if their love was my due because Margo had married me and I was Emmett's father. Like that word meant he was mine forever."

"He should have been," she said, and moved the tray off her lap. She got out of the bed slowly, a hand on the nightstand for balance, but found she was steadier after the soup and juice. "I'm sure they both knew how much you loved them." She came to stand in front of him, reaching out to push the hair off his forehead.

"I wish I'd told them more." He lifted his gaze to look at her. "The fact that Shay can still say the words so easily is a miracle. Especially when…"

April pressed her lips together. "When I'm going to let them go?"

"You don't have to—"

"Please, Connor, don't do this. Not now." She stepped out of reach when he would have pulled her closer. "I'm going to shower."

"Are you strong enough?"

There had been many days during her cancer treatment when she hadn't been strong enough to do more

than stare at the ceiling. She wasn't that woman any longer. "I'm fine."

In reality, the shower exhausted her. She hated feeling so weak even though she knew it would pass quickly. By the time she turned off the water, she felt dizzy again. She was mustering the strength to climb out when the shower door opened.

A moment later she was wrapped in a fluffy white towel as strong arms lifted her onto the bathroom tile.

Connor turned her to face him. "Can you stand on your own?"

She gritted her teeth and nodded.

Expression serious, he efficiently dried her body and hair and then helped her into a plush terry-cloth robe. She started to protest as he scooped her into his arms, but he whispered, "Let me take care of you, April. Even if you don't need it, I do."

She did need it and, more importantly, she wanted it more than she'd wanted anything in a long time. He carried her across the bedroom and gently placed her on the bed.

"You changed the sheets?"

A half smile pulled up the corner of his mouth. "I'm full service."

She laughed but it quickly turned into a yawn.

"Rest now," he murmured, tucking the blanket and quilt around her. "The girls and I will be here when you wake up."

Even if she'd wanted to argue, her eyelids were too heavy. She drifted off to sleep feeling more cherished than she had a right to.

Chapter Nine

The sound of muffled voices greeted April when she woke again. The muted light coming through the window told her it was late afternoon. She must have slept for hours. She swallowed and stretched, finally feeling on her way to normal.

She realized the voices weren't speaking. They were singing Christmas carols. Climbing out of bed, she re-tied the sash of the robe and stepped toward the window. This bedroom faced the front of the cabin, and she could see Connor, Ranie and Shay dragging a sled with a pine tree tied to it up the driveway.

Connor was doing most of the hauling, an ax slung over one shoulder. Every few feet Ranie adjusted the tree when it started to drag while Shay skipped next to him, singing at the top of her lungs. All three of them were singing, Ranie's soft voice complementing Shay's

enthusiastic soprano while Connor sang harmony. It was the most mangled and adorable version of "Joy to the World" April had ever heard.

They'd cut down a Christmas tree from the forest. The three of them were engaging in a Christmas ritual without her involvement. And…she watched a few more seconds…they all appeared to be having a great time.

Her suitcase was sitting next to the dresser, and she quickly put on sweatpants and a roll-necked sweater before making her way downstairs.

Connor was heaving the tree through the door. "Can I help?" she called from the bottom of the stairs.

He turned, his cheeks flushed with cold, and gave her a wide grin. "You look beautiful," he said, and she felt a blush color her own cheeks.

Shay ran toward her, wrapping cold arms around her waist for a tight hug. "She doesn't smell bad anymore."

Ranie was the only one who looked doubtful. "Are you sure you should be out of bed? What if you have a relapse?"

"It was a virus," April told her gently. "I'll be good as new by tomorrow morning. In fact, I feel fantastic now."

"Okay, then. Good." Ranie's shoulders dropped an inch, as if releasing the tension that had held them so tall.

"You can help us decorate," Shay cried happily. "Will you make hot chocolate? Connor burns it."

"One time," he protested, moving closer until he stood in front of April. "I burned it one time."

Shay shared a look with her sister.

Connor threw up his hands. "What?"

"You make really bad hot chocolate," Ranie said with a grin.

April raised her brows. "How can you mess up cocoa?"

"Let's talk about my chicken soup again."

"You said Ranie did the work on that."

He made a face. "After plenty of debate, we found the perfect Christmas tree."

Shay jumped up and down. "I picked it."

Connor grabbed her and lifted her up high. "I cut it."

April glanced at Ranie, who sighed. "I supervised."

"Come on, Ranie," Shay said when Connor deposited her on the ground again. "Let's open the box of ornaments." The girls laced fingers and headed into the family room.

"Ornaments?" April asked.

"The girls found Christmas decorations in the basement storage room," Connor explained. "We thought it would be a nice surprise for you."

Heat spread through her, and she crossed her arms over her chest to curb the urge to launch herself at him. She'd always loved Christmas, but having these three to share it with made the holiday even more special. It was funny, but a few days in this cabin and it felt more like a home to her than anyplace else on earth.

"You really are beautiful," he whispered, leaning in to brush a soft kiss across her lips. He smelled like cold and pine, but his mouth was warm and soft on hers.

"I look like I've spent three days puking my brains out," she said with a laugh.

He smiled against her mouth. "Your hair is clean."

"Quite an accomplishment."

He pulled back and glanced over his shoulder. "I

need to carry the tree into the family room. There was a tree stand in one of the boxes, so they must have expected someone would celebrate the holidays here."

"More like leftovers from Crimson Ranch. They weren't planning on guests at Cloud Cabin. You were important enough for an exception."

He turned and hefted the tree onto his shoulder. "More like my editor was desperate for me to finish the book."

"And?" she asked, leading the way into the family room.

"I'm close," he told her, and she could hear the pride in his voice. It was so different from how he'd sounded that first day in the kitchen, and she was grateful to be a part of the change in him over the past week. She only hoped it would last even after he returned to his life away from Colorado.

Ask him to stay.

She stopped as the thought popped into her mind, leveling her with its intensity, and was immediately prodded in the back with the tip of a pine tree.

"Sorry," Connor said, his voice muffled under the weight of the tree.

"My fault." She quickly moved into the family room and fisted her trembling hands together. Connor Pierce was a client, nothing more. Maybe more, but not a man she could plan a future around. He'd made it clear he had no room in his heart for anyone other than his wife and son.

April didn't believe that for a second, but he did and she had to honor it.

She raised her eyes and felt a gasp escape her lips. The cabin's cozy family room had been transformed

into a holiday wonderland. Stockings dangled from the rough-hewn wood mantel while snowmen figurines and nutcrackers were displayed on the bookcase. There were bright and festive throw pillows decorating the sofa and leather club chairs and, in the corner, a space had been made for the tree. A clear tub of ornaments sat next to the metal tree stand, strands of lights piled on the lid.

"I love it," she said, tears filling her eyes.

"Then why are you crying?" Shay asked, coming over to wrap her arms around April's waist.

"They're happy tears," April told her, running a hand over the girl's soft hair. Connor propped the tree against the wall and grinned at her.

"I only have happy smiles," Shay announced.

"Your smile makes me happy, too." April met Ranie's bright blue gaze and then Connor's piercing green eyes. "Thank you for doing this. It means a lot to me."

Pink tinged Ranie's cheeks. "It wasn't a big deal. We were kind of bored anyway."

Connor nudged her. "You just didn't want to lose to your sister and me at poker again."

The girl visibly relaxed at his gentle teasing. "You should stop corrupting me," she muttered. "I'm an innocent kid."

"Come on, kid," he said, "and help me get this tree in the stand."

When April stepped forward, he shook his head and pointed to the couch. "Sit down until we're ready for ornaments. You still need to take it easy."

"Have you always been so bossy?"

"Not at all," he told her with a wink. "You bring it out in me."

Shay took April's hand and led her to the leather sofa. The family room was a bigger version of the one in the caretaker's cabin. The walls were painted a warm gray and the river-rock fireplace surround went all the way to the vaulted ceiling, giving the room the feeling of a true mountain lodge. The furniture, while new, was overstuffed and comfortable, as if it had been part of the cabin for years. Thick rugs covered the hardwood floors, and both the coffee table and the end table had been built from reclaimed wood.

"I don't know how to put up a Christmas tree," Ranie said, her arms still folded over her chest.

Connor bent to adjust the tree stand. "I'm going to lift the tree. Your job is to guide it into the stand." At Ranie's dubious look, he grinned. "Trust me, you've got this. You're my Christmas wingman."

No, April wouldn't ask him to stay. But her heart would go with him when he left. She couldn't resist this man who thought he had nothing left to give but continued to break through the walls of a fragile girl as if it were the most natural thing in the world. April had started these two weeks thinking she'd be the one to save these three, but it was Connor who had made the biggest difference. She loved him for it, for the effort he was making and how he made her feel. For the man he used to be and the one he was rediscovering inside himself.

No, she wouldn't tell him any of that. Instead, she held the knowledge close to her heart, letting the golden light of it warm her and give her strength.

Within a few minutes they had the tree up and the fasteners tightened around its base.

"Just in the nick of time," she said as Jingle darted into the room and headed for the tree. The branches

rustled as the kitten climbed and then poked out his head from midtree height.

"He's our first ornament," Shay said, clapping her hands.

"That cat is a menace," Connor muttered, but was smiling as he reached in and plucked the small animal out of the branches.

Ranie took the kitten and cradled him in her arms. April said a silent prayer that the girls' aunt would allow them to keep their new pet when they went to live with her in California. Connor's gaze was a thick weight on her, but she avoided it, shifting to pull the tub of ornaments closer. It would hurt too much to see the censure she knew she'd find in his eyes. The silent suggestion that she keep these girls in Colorado with her. She couldn't. Or she wouldn't. Either way, the outcome was the same.

"Lights first," she said, keeping her tone light. Connor placed his hand over hers and squeezed.

He bent closer and dropped a tender kiss on the top of her head. "Let's just enjoy our Christmas together," he whispered. "It's all that matters right now."

The words were somehow both a pardon and an apology. Because she wasn't the only one who was too afraid to change her life. As ashamed as she was at her own weakness, the fact that he could understand and absolve her was a balm to the gaping sore that was her heart. She would hold on to their connection and try to ignore the tendrils of pain waiting to take over when the holidays were through.

Connor sat on the couch in the darkened family room, staring at the lights on the Christmas tree. Ice

clinked as he raised the glass of bourbon and sipped, the liquor burning a path down his throat. The last time he'd had a drop of hard alcohol had been a month after the funeral. He'd woken up, head pounding, in a pile of his own vomit, surrounded by empty liquor bottles.

At some point during his drunken blackout, he'd apparently gathered the framed photos his wife had lovingly arranged around their house and smashed the frames and then ripped apart the pictures inside. The images had been saved digitally and could be replaced, but the destruction had pierced something deep in his soul. It was his job, as the one left behind, to cherish Margo and Emmett's memory, not ruin the reminders of the life they'd had.

After that, he'd cleaned up his act and gotten healthy. He'd also sold their home and moved to an apartment in the heart of downtown San Francisco. He'd hoped a new location would help him mend all the broken pieces inside him, but he'd only retreated further into himself, willing to make his body healthy but unable to loosen grief's stranglehold on his heart and mind.

Only April and her girls had been able to manage that.

He heard a rustling in the doorway and looked up to see April walking toward him. The Christmas lights reflected off her long hair, making the copper highlights dance in their glow.

"How are you feeling?" he asked. She'd laughed and smiled as the girls had decorated the tree earlier, snapping pictures with her phone when Connor lifted Shay to place the star on top. But soon after, she'd grown tired. He could tell it frustrated her, but she'd allowed him to tuck her back in bed.

"Embarrassed that you're still having to do the work around here." A line of tension appeared between her eyes. "I'm fine now and hope by tomorrow morning I'll be back to normal. If not, I can call Sara and have her find someone to take over for me."

He sat forward, placed his drink on the coffee table, and then grabbed her hand and pulled her into his lap. "You're not getting rid of me yet," he whispered into the curve of her neck. "We're having Christmas here at the cabin. The four of us."

She sighed, her breath a soft wisp at the base of his throat. "It's not fair—"

At those words, he barked out a laugh. "We both know life isn't fair. We also agree this is our time. Right?"

He felt her nod against him. "I don't like feeling that I'm not contributing."

"You're the glue holding us together," he told her, kissing the edge of her jaw. "You make all of this work."

She pulled back to look him in the eye. Her brown eyes were wide and uncertain. "But I have no idea what I'm doing."

"Most people don't," he said, tracing the delicate skin under her eyes with his thumbs. "They do it anyway."

She smiled at that. "It's close to midnight. What are you doing down here?"

"I finished the book. I sent it to my editor an hour ago."

"Connor, that's excellent." She wrapped her arms around his neck and hugged him. It had been a long time since he'd had good news rewarded with a hug. He was surprised at how much the gesture meant to him. "I'm so proud of you."

He dropped a kiss on her shoulder, inching the soft cotton of her pajama top out of the way. "I wasn't sure I could do it," he admitted. "I never believed in the concept of a muse, but you're the reason for this."

She let out a breathy sigh that made heat pool low in his belly. "No. You're the reason. You wrote the words. This is your accomplishment."

"I'm glad I get to share it with you."

She shifted closer, nipped at the edge of his mouth. "Any ideas on how you want to celebrate?"

"Mmm." He lifted the hem of her shirt and splayed his fingers across her back. "Lots of ideas. Creative ones." He drew back. "But I don't want to go too fast for you."

"I like fast." Her gaze was cloudy with passion, her skin flushed.

Damn, she was so beautiful.

"You're still recovering."

She wiggled her brows. "I like slow, too." She bit down on her lip. "I feel fine, Connor. My body needs to move. I'm stiff and sore from lying in that bed for so long. So I can either bring out my yoga mat for a stretching series or—"

"I can help you move those muscles."

She nodded. "That's my preference." She leaned in close, kissing him in a way that was both an invitation and a demand.

He couldn't think of a better way to celebrate than with April in his bed. He stood, holding her in his arms as he made his way through the house and up the stairs. When her tongue touched his, he almost tripped into the hallway wall.

"Hold that thought," he whispered, pulling away and

concentrating on breathing. The last thing he needed was to bang her into something or make so much noise they woke the girls.

He hurried down the hall into his bedroom, gently nudging shut the door with his heel. "Where were we?" he asked against her mouth.

The kiss resumed and he quickly tugged his shirt over his head and then grabbed the hem of hers. He would never tire of looking at her body. It was like a breathing work of art, and he had every intention of giving it the adoration it deserved.

Unlike the first time they'd been together, he took his time with her, kissing and teasing and enjoying the noises she made, every shiver that he felt across her skin. He held the weight of one breast in his hand, bending to lick the rosy tip. When she moaned, he went to his knees in front of her, trailing kisses down her belly to the waistband of her flannel pants. He pulled them over her hips, his breath catching as each perfect inch of her was revealed.

He touched her, tasted her, and when her legs started to tremble, he scooped her up. Kicking back the covers, he laid her flushed and languid across his bed and was transfixed by her beauty. If the night ended now, he would be content.

Then she opened her eyes and crooked a finger at him. "This party is just getting started," she said, and for the rest of the night they celebrated in the best way possible.

April left Connor sleeping in his bed early the next morning. Although she'd only gotten a few hours of rest, she finally felt back to normal. Better than normal.

She was content in a way that was new and refreshing, and even if the sensation was fleeting she planned to savor it while it lasted.

She was also anxious to get back to a routine. Although Connor might like taking care of her, she wouldn't let herself grow accustomed to it.

After prepping for a breakfast of pancakes and fruit salad and brewing a pot of coffee, she made her way to the small exercise studio in the basement of the cabin. Cloud Cabin might look rustic, but it was set up with all the modern amenities a guest could want. The room was cool, so she adjusted the thermostat before pulling a yoga mat from the shelf and unrolling it.

She moved into her first pose, hands clasped in front of her in prayer position and took several deep, cleansing breaths. With each inhalation she could feel herself growing stronger.

A noise had her whirling toward the door. Ranie stood there watching her, still dressed in her pajama pants and a T-shirt.

"Are you better?" the girl asked. Her tone was casual, but she worried her hands together nervously as she waited for an answer.

"I am, sweetie. I've got breakfast ready to make, but I thought I'd do a little yoga while everyone else was still sleeping. You're welcome to join me."

April had made the offer to Ranie each time she'd started a session of yoga, but the girl had always turned away. This morning she took a hesitant step forward. "I'm not very athletic," she muttered. "I'm always on the C team for sports at school."

"Yoga is a balance between the spiritual and the physical. It can calm your mind at the same time it

works your body." She moved to the bookshelf and took out another yoga mat. "The beautiful thing is that anyone can benefit from it."

"In that case, you'd better grab two mats."

At the sight of Connor standing in the doorway, a jolt of awareness went through April. All the things they'd done last night, the ways he'd touched her, came rushing into her mind and she had to look away. When she glanced back, he was grinning as if he knew exactly where her mind had gone. He was wearing a faded T-shirt that fit tightly over the broad planes of his chest and a pair of baggy basketball shorts.

"You do yoga?" Ranie asked doubtfully.

"No. Do you?"

"Yes." Ranie bit on the edge of her fingernail. "I'm starting this morning."

"Me, too."

"Guys don't do yoga," she told him with a sniff.

"Of course they do," April said before Connor could answer. "Both men and women have practiced it for centuries." She rolled out the two mats next to each other a few feet behind hers and then pushed a piece of weight equipment off to the side. "Lots of famous men do yoga. Like Sting."

Connor came to help her move the heavy bar. "We know what he's famous for," he whispered, low enough that Ranie wouldn't hear.

April rolled her eyes, remembering the famous musician's quote from the early nineties when he'd extolled the virtue of tantric sex. She'd just gotten her teaching license then and there'd been a short-term upswing in couples joining the studio where she worked.

"Who's Sting?" Ranie asked, coming to stand on her mat.

Connor turned to her. "You're kidding, right? Tell me you know who the Beatles are."

"Of course." Ranie shrugged. "Mom had one of those cars for a while but decided it wasn't big enough."

He thumped the heel of his hand to his forehead. "For Christmas, little girl, I'm getting you an old-school turntable and a stack of albums."

Ranie flashed a calculating smile. "How about a subscription to Spotify?"

"How about we get started so we're not eating breakfast for lunch?" April stepped onto her mat, then glanced at Ranie. "Sting is a singer. He was in a band called The Police before launching an übersuccessful solo career."

Ranie's expression remained blank. "Never heard of him. Mom only liked country music."

"Never heard of Sting?" Connor asked, clasping a hand to his chest, his tone pleading. "Start the yoga before this girl reduces me to tears."

"There are different schools of yoga. I primarily teach in the Vinyasa tradition, which links your breath to movements. We'll start with sun salutations." The studio was warmer now, or maybe it was Connor's intense gaze on her. She shrugged out of her sweatshirt, leaving her in only a pale yellow athletic tank top over a sports bra.

She moved into the first pose, explaining the purpose and how they should be breathing as they moved. From there they continued with the series, focusing on synchronizing their breath through each one. Despite

claiming not to be an athlete, Ranie had a natural grace as she moved her body into each new position.

Connor was another story. He was in shape but, in the way of many men, clearly he hadn't paid any attention to his flexibility. He wobbled as he held downward-facing dog and landed facedown on his mat when he tried to straighten from another position.

Ranie giggled as she watched him, which he didn't seem to mind. April shifted into her role as teacher like slipping into a favorite pair of jeans. One of the best things about teaching was working with new students, helping them find the ease within the effort of the poses and connect the body with each breath.

Almost an hour later she took one last breath, completing the final sequence. "How do you feel?" she asked both Connor and Ranie.

"That was…" As Ranie searched for the right word, April held her breath. Somehow, what this girl thought about the practice April loved mattered on a deep, soul level. After a moment, Ranie smiled. "It was awesome. I could do that every day."

A bubble of pure joy burst in April's chest, sending happiness radiating through her. "You *can* do it every day. Yoga will go with you wherever you are." She gentled her tone, hoping Ranie would accept her next words. "I remember coming to visit your mom when you were just a toddler. We did yoga each morning, and you'd be right there with us. Crescent lunge was your favorite. Every time we turned around, you'd be in that pose."

"Mom had a framed photo of me like that in her bedroom," Ranie said with a nod. "I'm going to go upstairs and get dressed. Shay will be waking soon."

"What about you?" April turned to Connor.

"Well," he began, tapping a finger on his chin as if debating. Suddenly he reached out and yanked her into his arms. He kissed her deeply, his hands moving up and down her back, sending shivers of sensation wherever he touched. "I don't know that I'm cut out for yoga, but watching you do it is one of the hottest things I've ever seen."

She laughed against his mouth. "You just liked seeing me bend over."

He pulled away, his green eyes so bright they looked like spring grass after a heavy rain. "That's an added benefit. But you're a natural teacher. The way you worked with both of us and kept things moving and clearly have so much passion for what you do. Why don't you teach classes full-time?"

"Mostly I do," she said, stepping out of his embrace and rolling up the mats. He grabbed the one he'd been using but continued to watch her. "Remember, I'm here as a favor to Sara. But I had to sell my studio in California after my divorce to pay for the medical bills insurance didn't cover. It was another painful reminder of how cancer had changed my life. There was a full year I couldn't do yoga. The very thought of moving into a pose made me sick to my stomach."

His gaze turned solemn. "I get that. You know I get that."

"It was different. Losing your family and losing my business don't even show up on the same radar. I'm embarrassed at how I let the circumstances of my life define who I was." The understanding that she still did that, although it wasn't as obvious from the out-

side, shamed her. But she didn't think she was strong enough to overcome any more than she already had.

"But now you're teaching again?"

"I started doing classes for the guests at Crimson Ranch. A studio near Aspen asked me to be one of their instructors and, eventually, that became where I work most often. A lot of people who visit this area want to keep up with their practice while they're here and fitness is important to many locals, too. It's good for their bodies to balance out all that skiing and rock climbing."

"And running on the treadmill," he added, pointing a finger at his own chest.

"That, too," she agreed. "And I like to stay busy."

"You like to take care of people."

"Yes." She paused in the act of returning the mats to their place on the shelf. "The woman who currently owns the studio has offered to sell it to me."

"Perfect," he told her, taking the yoga mats from her hands. "When will that be finalized?"

She laughed. "Don't get ahead of yourself. I haven't agreed to anything."

"Why?"

"Owning a studio is a big responsibility."

"You've done it before, and you loved it."

"Things were different then."

"Things are different now."

She shook her head. "Not in the same way. I should get moving on breakfast." She started for the door. "Thanks for being game to do a session with me. I think—"

"Hold on." He placed his hands on her shoulders and spun her to face him. "Don't blow me off, April."

"I'm not."

"Why wouldn't you want to own a studio again?"

"Maybe I want to keep my options open. I have nothing tying me down right now. I can take off on a moment's notice if I want to. I'm a total free spirit."

At those words he flashed her a doubtful smile. "You're the least likely person to 'take off' that I know."

She bristled at the words, even though they were true.

"That's not a criticism. I like how grounded you are, but it's clear this community and the people in it mean something to you. This is your home. You love teaching yoga. Why wouldn't you want to have your own studio again? Is it the money? Because I—"

"It's not the money, and I'm not taking any of yours." She tried to pull away, but he held her steady. "What if I bought the studio and then I got sick again?" Unable to continue meeting his gaze, she focused on a small patch of sweat on the front of his T-shirt.

"What if you crossed the street and got hit by a car?" he asked in response.

"It's not the same thing."

"It is," he argued. "You've told me you've made it to the five-year-survival milestone. Even I know that's a big deal. Yes, there's a risk that you'll get sick again. There's a better chance that you'll stay healthy. There are no guarantees in life, and you can't just dump something that means so much to you because you're afraid it might not work."

"Does that apply only to me or are you going to take your own advice?"

"I finished the book."

"I'm not talking about the book," she snapped. "I'm

talking about the self-imposed isolation you plan to return to after Christmas. I'm talking about opening yourself to the possibility of being happy again. Of loving—"

"No." He released her so abruptly she stumbled back a step. "That part of me is gone. It died with Margo and Emmett."

"I've seen how you are with the girls," she argued. She wouldn't mention the way he made her feel. This wasn't about the two of them. This was him needing to admit he could love again. Even if it wasn't with her, he deserved a second chance at love. "You're not dead, Connor. You're here. Now."

"Don't try to fix me, April." The words weren't angry, only empty, which was worse. "I told you I don't have anything to give. I don't deserve…" He broke off, stalked to the edge of the room and back to her. "I'm not going there with you. If you want to live your simple little life, it's none of my business. In a few days, I'll be on a plane back to California. We have no hold on each other. Right now, what matters to both of us is Ranie and Shay. It's Christmas Eve, and I don't want to fight."

"Me neither," she whispered, although it was a lie. She wanted to push and prod this man until he admitted his heart was capable of mending. But he was right—she had no hold on him. And how could she pressure him for something she wasn't willing to give? Because in a few days, she'd be on a plane returning those girls to California. No matter what. "My friend Katie texted last night. She's closed the bakery to customers today and is hosting an open house for family and friends."

"I'm neither," he muttered.

"She invited all of us. I think it would be nice for the girls to get out of the cabin for a bit, and I'd like to pick up a few more Christmas gifts for them. I got some things when they first arrived, but tomorrow needs to be special."

"Everything you do is special," he whispered, and the honesty in his tone made her heart melt a little more.

No matter how frustrated he made her, she was a useless puddle of goo around this man. "Will you come with us?"

He shook his head. "I didn't handle a trip to town so well the last time."

"You're different now."

"It's been a week," he said with a wry smile.

She put aside her own worries and took his hand. "A lot can happen in a week."

He brushed a delicate kiss over her knuckles. "Why can't I say no to you?"

Chapter Ten

Why hadn't he said no?

Connor pressed two fingers to his forehead, which was throbbing so hard he thought a vein might actually pop. He stood off to the edge of the bakery, pretending to look at the display of mugs and small gifts housed on a farmhouse-style set of shelves. He could feel April's worried gaze and looked up long enough to give her a thumbs-up. She did the same and added a shoulder shrug and an apologetic smile.

But she had nothing to feel sorry about, and it was clear she belonged to this community and her friends. They'd been polite, if wary, when she'd made introductions earlier. He doubted there was a person in this room who didn't know his story, which made his skin prickle as if it were shrinking with every overly kind smile he received.

There seemed to be a line of people waiting to speak to her, and even now she was surrounded by a group of women who were taking turns giving her supportive hugs and gentle back pats. He wondered if they were sympathizing that she'd had to care for the broken-down author while the rest of them were enjoying Christmas vacation.

"That was the fakiest thumbs-up I've ever seen."

He turned to find Ranie at his side, arms crossed over her chest in her signature posture.

"*Fakiest* isn't a word."

"Neither is fun if this party is any indication."

He nodded at where Shay was busy at a café table, decorating cookies with a group of children her age. "Your sister might disagree."

"Because she's a little kid."

He arched a brow. "And you're so wise and mature?"

A dismissive sniff was his answer.

"I can ask around to see if there are any Christmas pageants being performed tonight. We might find you a gig as one of the three wise guys who visited the baby Jesus."

"You're not like other adults," she answered after a moment.

He nodded. "I'm real messed up."

"I'd say you're just real. Everyone else looks at me like they know exactly what happened with my mom. April's friends are nice, but they give me extralong hugs and I don't even know them."

"Hugs aren't too bad."

"You don't give out a lot of hugs," she countered.

He made his voice even. "Do you want one?"

"No. I just don't want people to pretend like noth-

ing's wrong when they look at me as if I'm some baby bird with a broken wing. Like they have to be extra careful."

"I like that imagery," he told her. "Have you ever thought about writing down your thoughts?"

"Like in a diary?" she asked.

"Sure. A journal works. Or poems. Or whatever interests you."

"Did you keep a journal after your wife and son died?"

"I kept a tight grip on the liquor bottle."

She barked out a laugh. "I don't think you're supposed to admit that to a kid."

"You like real, remember." He put a hand on her back, not quite a hug, but letting her know she wasn't alone. "Losing a family member changes you. It's a hole that can't be filled." He believed the words, but lately the hole inside him hadn't felt so cavernous.

"I think it takes time," Ranie told him. "At least that's what the adults say."

"They say that because they're afraid of your sadness, and hope is an easy thing to offer."

Her blue eyes flicked to him, and he cursed himself. What the hell was wrong with his mood? He wasn't supposed to be bringing down a twelve-year-old girl with his own baggage. That was a total jerk move.

"I'm sorry," he said quickly. "Don't pay any attention to me."

"April's pretty good at filling holes," she said softly.

"Yep." He looked to where April stood, the circle of friends surrounding her bigger than it was a few minutes earlier. She touched the woman in front of her

on the cheek and then wrapped her in a tight hug. His heart sped up. "She gives good hugs, too."

Ranie groaned. "Eww. Don't corrupt me."

At that moment, a tall, strapping man with blond hair, blue eyes and shoulders wide enough to look at home on a football field approached them. A boy who looked to be a year or two older than Ranie was with him.

"I'm Logan Travers," he said, holding out a hand. "Josh's brother."

Connor shook his hand. "Connor Pierce."

"You're the one staying at Cloud Cabin?"

"I am."

"I built that cabin."

"You do good work."

Logan nudged forward the boy next to him. "This is Jordan Dempsey. He lives here in town." The boy said a quiet "hello, sir" and grasped Connor's hand.

"Nice to meet you, Jordan." Connor turned to his side before realizing Ranie had stepped all the way behind him. He moved so she could be seen, earning him a dark look. "This is Ranie. She's staying with April over the holidays."

"Hey," she whispered, offering a small wave to Logan and Jordan.

Logan nudged Jordan again. The boy cleared his throat. "It sucks about your mom. My dad left town a while back so I don't see him, but at least I know he's still alive."

Ranie stared at the kid for a minute then said, "Um…thanks…I think."

Logan placed a large hand on Jordan's back. "Too

much information, buddy. Didn't you want to ask her something?"

"Oh, right. Katie has a basketball net out back. Do you want to go shoot some hoops? Otherwise, they're going to rope us into helping the little kids with their cookies."

As if on cue, Katie glanced from the crowded cookie table in their direction.

Connor cleared his throat. "Ranie likes—"

"Sure," she said, stepping fully away from Connor. He had the ridiculous urge to pull her back. She glanced up at him. "Will you let April know where I went?"

He nodded. "Don't go anywhere else, and come right back in if you need me."

She gave him a funny look. "Need you for what?"

From somewhere long forgotten, he summoned his best fatherly stare. "Anything."

"Relax," she whispered. "It's just basketball." She turned to Jordan. "You lead the way, but I have to warn you I'm not very good."

"Doesn't matter," he said. "Anything is better than putting sprinkles on cookies."

Connor watched as they disappeared through the swinging metal door behind the display counter.

"He's a good boy," Logan said.

Connor felt his eyes narrow. "He better be." Unfamiliar protective instincts raged through him. "She's young."

"They're both kids. Are you close to April and the two girls?"

Connor blinked as his mind registered how his at-

titude must look. "Not exactly. But I'm looking out for them while I'm here."

"Josh told me you're a writer."

"Uh-huh."

"Pretty famous, right?"

"In some circles."

Logan let out a deep laugh. "For someone who makes a living with words, you sure don't use many of them when you speak."

"What do you want to talk about?" Connor asked with a sidelong glance. "My dead wife and kid?"

To his credit, Logan didn't react to the rude and inappropriate question. "About as much as I want to unload about the drunk-driving accident that killed my sister."

Connor closed his eyes and let out a breath. The thing about being so wrapped up in his own grief was that he forgot that his story, while tragic, wasn't new or even all that rare. Most people carried pain or tragedy within them. It was only a matter of who could cope the best. He hated to admit that he'd felt a lot like Ranie at this gathering, mistrustful of the kindness in the eyes of the people he met and sure that all they felt for him was pity.

He'd been too long out of the real world. He'd had friends in California once, but he'd cut them out of his life after the accident. In doing so, he'd forgotten how to act like a normal person. April was helping him, giving him strength with her unconditional caring. He owed it to her to make an effort.

He laughed since that was exactly what he'd prom-ised her.

"Something funny about my sister's death?" Logan asked, his tone icy as the top of a fourteener in a blizzard.

"No, of course not." Connor turned fully to face the other man. "I'm sorry. I was laughing at my own ignorance and insensitivity, although come to think of it, neither of those is funny." He shrugged. "Basically, I'm a jackass."

Logan stared at him for a moment, then threw back his head and laughed. "When you decide to use the words, you sure do make them count."

Make an effort. Make his words count.

If Connor took only those two maxims from his time in Colorado, it would be a gift he could never hope to repay. He might not be able to make the changes April wanted him to, but he could begin the promise of rebuilding a life outside the walls of his apartment.

"Tell me more about building Cloud Cabin," he said to Logan, and started down the path of once again becoming part of the world around him.

"Wake up, April. It's Christmas. Santa found us."

April blinked several times as her eyes adjusted to the faint light of her bedroom. Only a dim cast of blue light filtered in through the curtains, which meant the sun hadn't yet risen. There was a weight on top of her that she quickly realized was Shay. The girl's face was only inches from hers.

A sticky finger tapped on her cheeks. "Are you awake yet?"

"I'm awake," she said around a yawn. "What time is it?"

"Time for Christmas presents," Shay shouted, hopping off the bed to flip on the light switch.

April shaded her eyes with one hand as she struggled to wake up. Normally, she was an early bird, but she wasn't sure this hour even counted as morning. Add in the fact that Connor had kept her awake until the wee hours of the night, and she was definitely not at her perkiest.

"It's too early for this," Ranie muttered from the doorway. Apparently, April wasn't the only one who could have used more sleep.

She swung her legs over the side of the bed and pointed at Shay. "Are you eating a candy cane?"

The girl flashed a wide smile. "Santa filled our stockings, too. Connor said I could pick one thing."

"Breakfast of champions," Connor said, appearing in the doorway behind Ranie.

"You're awake already?"

"And I made coffee." He stepped into the room and handed her a steaming mug.

"Oh, thank you," she said with a grateful breath. "I lo—" She ducked her head. "You're the best."

"Can we open presents now?" Shay was practically buzzing with energy. It had been a long time since April had witnessed a child's excitement on Christmas morning. As tired as she was, she couldn't help but smile.

"Give me a minute to wash my face and I'll be down," April told her.

"Your face isn't even dirty," Shay complained.

"Let's go, squirt." Connor took Shay's shoulders and turned her toward the door. "You can count your presents while you wait."

Her eyes wide, Shay darted from the room and Ranie followed.

Connor turned and cupped April's face in his hands. "Merry Christmas," he whispered with a gentle kiss. He tasted of toothpaste and spice, and April realized that the taste of him was just one more thing she'd miss when he was gone.

She forced a smile, determined not to let thoughts of losing him crowd her mind today. "You know, I didn't fill stockings last night," she told him. After the girls had gone to bed, she and Connor had wrapped the gifts she'd bought and placed them under the tree.

"Maybe Santa Claus really paid a visit to the cabin," he said with a wink.

She kissed him again and he took the mug from her hands, placing it on top of the dresser so he could pull her in tight. After a few minutes, she moved away, her breath ragged. "I need to get moving. Counting presents will only keep her busy for so long."

"I can buy you some time." He pressed one more kiss to the tip of her nose. "I'll have her put on boots so we can go outside and look for reindeer prints."

She stopped at the door to the bathroom, glanced over her shoulder. "Hoofprints?"

He ran a hand through his hair, looking almost embarrassed. "You know they leave a trail of sparkles on the ground under where they take off."

"I actually did *not* know that. Connor Pierce, you've been hiding your holiday spirit."

"Merry Christmas," he said with a smile, and then he was gone.

Just as April walked down the stairs fifteen minutes later, Connor and the girls were stomping back into the house, their boots coated with fresh snow.

"I saw the reindeer tracks," Shay called, slipping off

her coat and boots and rushing toward April. "They left red and silver sparkles in the snow."

Even Ranie looked impressed. "It was cool," she said, and glanced at Connor before picking up the coat Shay had dropped on the floor and hanging it on a peg.

April took Connor's cold hand as he came toward her, and laced her fingers with his. "How did you know to make reindeer prints?" she whispered.

"It was one of Emmett's favorite things about Christmas morning."

April smiled around the lump in her throat. "Thank you for sharing that tradition with us."

"Come on, people," Shay called impatiently from the family room. "We're ready to open presents now."

April settled on the couch with Connor across from her in one of the leather club chairs. "Let the Christmas madness begin," he announced.

Shay let out a squeal of delight, but instead of digging into her own gifts, she took two small bags from deep under the tree and handed one to April and the other to Connor. "Open them," she said, her cheeks flushed and her eyes bright. "They're from Ranie and me."

April swiped her fingers under her eyes and sniffed. "Are you sure you don't want to start with your gifts?"

Shay shook her head.

"They're not a big deal," Ranie said, her eyes watchful.

April started to assure her they were, but Connor said, "Let's open them and find out."

The girl grinned at him, and April was once again amazed at the bond that had formed so quickly between the three of them. All of their rough edges seemed to fit

together perfectly, and another wave of sadness washed over her knowing Ranie might not get that type of understanding from her uncle in California. The kind of soul-deep knowing she'd be lucky to have from any other man in her life.

"Are you gonna cry the happy tears again?" Shay asked.

"Probably," April admitted, and tore off the wrapping paper on the small package. Inside was a pinecone figure. The arms and legs were pipe cleaners, and plastic googly eyes had been glued to what would be the head. Wrapped in one pipe-cleaner arm was a small roll of blue felt.

"We made them while you were sick with the craft kits you bought us." Shay placed a finger on the felt. "This is your yoga mat. Connor has a book."

"I love it," April whispered, and glanced at Connor. He was staring at the pinecone figure, a slight smile tugging one corner of his mouth. "Let me see yours, Connor."

He held it up, and she noticed his hand was shaking just a little. "The book says '#1 bestseller' on the cover."

"That's what you want, right?" Ranie asked.

"Yes," he said softly. "Thank you both. This is a *very* big deal."

April pulled Shay in for a tight hug. "Thank you so much. I'll keep it forever."

"Put them on the coffee table," Shay said, her eyes dancing. "We made ones for Ranie and me, too. They can all be together."

The waiting Christmas gifts momentarily forgotten, Shay ran to a corner of the room, bent at one of

the low cabinets under the bookshelf and pulled out
two smaller decorated pinecones. She ran back over
and arranged the Connor-and-April pinecones on either side of the smaller two.

"It's a pinecone family," she said, and April's heart
cracked in two. They weren't a family. These two
weeks were like make-believe, a time Shay would remember years from now as a fuzzy series of events, if
she thought of this holiday at all. Or maybe the memory these girls would hold hadn't even been made yet.
What if what they carried with them was the impending end? The point where the woman their mother had
entrusted with their future walked away because she
was too scared to commit to them.

"They look great," April managed, her throat raw
from the effort of holding back tears.

"They were Shay's idea," Ranie said, looking between April and Connor as if she couldn't figure out
what about a few decorated pinecones was making the
adults react so strangely.

Connor cleared his throat. "How about I put them on
the mantel to be safe and you girls start on your gifts?"

"Presents!" Shay shouted, oblivious to the effect
her sweet gifts had.

She dropped to her knees next to the tree, and April
pulled out her phone. "Let me get a few pictures of
you."

Shay posed for a couple of seconds, then reached for
a brightly wrapped package. "I can't wait any longer."

Connor came to sit next to April as Shay held up
a bright pink princess costume. "Oh, it's just what I
wanted," she said, and twirled in a happy circle. "You
next, Ranie."

The girl held a wrapped box on her lap. "Is everyone going to watch?"

"Yes," Shay said with an exasperated sigh. "You know we each take turns opening presents."

Ranie sniffed. "Maybe April does it different."

"That sounds perfect to me," April told her, and got an eye roll in return.

"We don't have all morning here, kid." Connor rubbed his stomach. "Breakfast casserole is waiting."

Again, April was about to scold him for his attitude, but Ranie smiled. "Give me a break. It's not even seven a.m."

"You get the point," Connor shot back. "No more delays. I command you to open that gift."

"As if you're the boss of me," Ranie said, and stuck out her tongue. But she was already carefully unfolding the corners of the wrapping paper.

"Why does she like you so much," April whispered while Ranie was distracted with her gift, "when you're so mean?"

Connor scoffed. "I'm not mean. I'm direct. There's a difference." He linked their hands together. "Sometimes she takes things too seriously, especially herself. It breaks her out of it when I give her a little grief."

"Unorthodox therapy," April said, "but no denying it works."

Ranie gasped as she pulled a pair of designer sheepskin boots out of the box. Her eyes flicked to April. "These are the boots I saw when we got to Colorado that first day," she said, her voice soft. "You said they were too much money with everything else."

April smiled. "Christmas is about going a little overboard. Do you like them?"

"I love them." Ranie stood and came to April, giving her a small hug. "Thank you so much. They're perfect."

"Wow. You're welcome. I'm glad you like them."

Shay grabbed another gift. "Me next."

The girls continued to open presents until there was nothing left under the tree. Ranie was more animated than April had ever seen, and it tugged on her heart in a way she didn't want to examine. She knew Jill had been sick for a while and wondered exactly how much responsibility Ranie had taken on in the house and if she'd ever been able to be a carefree kid.

"How about stockings?" Connor asked.

Shay jumped up and ran toward the fireplace. "I love stockings!"

Connor handed the girls theirs and then placed one decorated with a needlepoint angel stitched on the front in April's lap.

"You didn't have to get me anything," she told him.

"I know. That's what makes it Christmas."

Ranie's harsh gasp drew April's attention. "Are these real?" the girl asked, her eyes wide on Connor.

He nodded. "You have pierced ears, right?"

"Yes, but…" She held up a pair of tiny diamond earrings. "I've never had anything like this."

"Merry Christmas," he said, almost sheepishly.

"Oh, it's so pretty." A delicate gold bracelet dangled from Shay's fingers.

"What's the charm on it?" April asked, leaning closer.

"It's the sun."

"Perfect for you, Shay, because you are a ray of sunshine."

The young girl beamed. "Now you, April."

April pulled out a small box from her stocking. "Do I sense a theme?"

Connor shrugged. "I snuck out of the party to shop but didn't want to be gone too long. There's a jewelry store next to the bakery."

"You really didn't have to—"

"Open the gift, April."

Unwrapping the shiny paper, April felt like a kid. Other than an annual Secret Santa exchange at the yoga studio and the occasional White Elephant party, she hadn't received a Christmas gift in years. As she opened the velvet box inside, her breath caught in her throat.

She glanced up at Connor, whose expression was an adorable mix of hope and nerves. "I'm out of practice with gift giving," he said softly, "but diamonds are always good, right?"

"These are better than good." She fingered the delicate diamond hoops. "They're perfect." The earrings were understated and gorgeous, and she could wear them every day, even to a yoga class. The last man who had bought her jewelry had been her ex-husband.

He'd insisted on her wearing large and sometimes gaudy stones, as if having a wife decked out in jewels helped prove his status within the Hollywood community. The jewelry had been the first thing she'd sold to pay off her medical bills.

"Try them on," Shay said, and with trembling hands, April fastened an earring in each ear.

"They look nice," Ranie told her.

At that moment Jingle came bounding into the room and pounced on a stray bow. The girls laughed, both jumping up to play with the kitten.

"Thank you," April told Connor as he tucked her hair behind one ear. She leaned forward and brushed a soft kiss across his lips.

"There's something else in the stocking," he said.

"Connor, no," She shook her head. "I thought we were just doing gifts for the girls. I don't have anything—"

"You've given me so much already." He cupped her face with a tenderness that brought another round of tears to her eyes. "Let me do this."

She dug in the bottom of the stocking and pulled out... "A flash drive?" She gave him a crooked smile. "Thanks. I can always use—"

"My new book is on it. I know it's already with the editor, but I was hoping you'd read it, too. I mean if you have time and—"

She threw her arms around him, burying her face in his neck so he wouldn't see how much she was affected by his gesture. For Connor to share something so personal with her, it must mean...no. She wouldn't let herself go there. She couldn't allow the hope for more to creep into her mind and her heart. It would only make the end harder to bear. "This is turning out to be an amazing Christmas" she whispered instead.

"Yes, it is," he agreed, and held her close.

Chapter Eleven

Connor ended the call with his editor and walked back into the cabin's bright kitchen. "Who wants to play a game of cards?"

"I do," Shay answered, bouncing on her knees on the chair. "So does Jingle."

Connor scooped up the kitten, which was pawing at the downturned cards Connor had left on the table. "Are you feeding this thing rocks?" He set the kitten onto the floor and watched him dart to the other side of the room. "He's probably doubled his weight since we found him."

April lightly pounded her palm on the table. "Hey, let's focus here. What did your editor think of the book? She loved it, right? Of course she loved it, because it's a fantastic story. It's flawless. Un-put-downable."

"That's not a word," Ranie said, but she was smiling.

"It should be," April countered. "I have bags under my eyes from staying up half the night to finish it."

Connor didn't bother to point out that reading wasn't the only reason she'd been up late, and he tried to ignore the fact that April's praise for his story meant more than anything his editor had said to him.

"What did she say?" April asked again.

"She liked it."

She raised her brows. "Liked?"

"Maybe she used the words 'guaranteed bestseller.'" Connor ducked his head, feeling color rise to his cheeks. That wasn't possible. He was a guy. Guys didn't blush. But he'd never felt comfortable with hearing praise for his work. Writing was personal for him, the characters milling about his head as the story formed and took a life of its own. He molded and shaped them, but they still came from a very private part of who he was. It was the piece he'd thought he'd lost when Margo and Emmett died. The part that April had helped him rediscover.

She and the girls gave a great cheer. He saw April start to rise from her chair, then lower back down again, folding her hands together on the table so tightly her knuckles turned white.

"Congratulations," she said, and the tone of her voice had changed to a hollow, thready rasp. "It looks like our work here is done."

He sucked in a breath as both girls turned to stare at her. He knew what she meant. His flight back to California was scheduled in two days. In the excitement of Christmas and keeping the girls busy, they'd been avoiding the inevitable conversation about him leaving. He still wasn't ready to tackle it.

But now that April had broached the subject, Ranie took up the mantle.

"Did you talk to Aunt Tracy?" she asked, glancing at Jingle, who was chasing the shadow cast on the floor in front of the window by the branches bobbing in the winter wind.

April bit down on her lip. "I did, and apparently your cousin Tommy is allergic to cats."

Ranie shook her head. "That's not true. They used to have a cat. I remember it."

"Obviously, something has changed," April snapped, and then ducked her head as if she regretted it. "I'm sorry, but you knew there was a good chance you wouldn't be able to bring Jingle to California. It's why I didn't want—"

"I don't want to go to California." Shay threw her cards on the table and jumped from her chair. "The twins are gross. They burp and fart and Tommy eats his boogers." She bent and lifted Jingle into her arms.

April's heart stuttered as the kitten nuzzled into the little girl's neck. "They're boys, sweetie, but they'll get better." She glanced at Connor for support.

"Just watch out if they try to 'Dutch oven' you," he said, pointing at each girl.

Ranie grimaced. "I don't even want to know what that is."

"It's when—"

April slashed the air with her hand. "Not helping, Connor."

"Why can't we stay here with you?" Shay asked.

The question, which had been running on a constant loop inside April's head for the past few days,

still shocked her. Hearing the words spoken in Shay's sweet voice was like a punch to her heart.

"I would love to keep you," April told her, making her voice soft, "but Aunt Tracy is your family. She understands—"

"We don't even know her," Shay argued. "She won't let us keep Jingle and there are so many dumb rules in her house."

"She's a good mom to her boys." April could feel desperation rising like a tidal wave up her spine. She needed to convince these girls she was doing the right thing. But how was she supposed to when she couldn't quite believe it herself? "She'll take care of you."

"We want you to take care of us." The kitten mewed as Shay squeezed him tighter.

April's gaze flicked to Ranie, but the girl was staring at the floor, her arms held tight to her side. "I can't," she whispered.

"We'll be good," Shay said, and the fact that she thought April's refusal had anything to do with who she and her sister were or how they acted was another painful stab inside April. "We won't eat much, and we can help—"

"I might die," April yelled suddenly, and the silence that followed was so charged she expected to see electricity sparking the air around them.

Shay let out a small whimper.

"I'm sorry." April took a step closer to the girl, but Shay backed up until her legs hit the couch. "After everything you went through with your mommy, I can't bear the thought of putting you girls at risk of watching me get sick again."

Ranie moved until she was standing next to her sis-

ter. "You're not sick," she muttered between clenched teeth. "You just don't want us."

"That's not—"

The cat meowed and squirmed in Shay's arms, jumping to the floor and darting from the room. Shay started to follow, tears streaming down her face, then stopped and turned to April. "We don't want you right back," she screamed. "I hate you."

April sucked in a shattered breath and watched the young girl disappear up the stairs. She turned to Ranie. "I'm sorry. I don't want her to be upset. I'll make her understand."

The girl only glared at her. "She already does," she said, and followed her sister.

April watched her go, wanting to reach out but knowing she had nothing to offer either of the girls. She rounded on Connor. "You could have helped me," she snapped. "You could have helped me make it better for them. I can't keep them. They need to understand I'm too big a risk."

His green eyes, which this morning had been so full of light and affection, were blank as he stared at her. "Life is a risk," he said. "What you're giving those girls is a lame excuse."

"Lame?" she sputtered. "I had breast cancer, Connor. The same disease that killed their mother. I could get sick again. That's real. I could die."

He gave a laugh so odd and disturbing it made the hair on the back of her neck stand on end. "You could die tomorrow," he whispered. "You could step off a curb and get hit by a car. That's real, April. Life is a risk, and sending those girls away isn't doing them any favors. It isn't helping them. It's being a coward."

The truth of his words sliced through her, and all her pent-up fear and pain poured forth, flooding her with everything she'd tried to repress for so long. All the ways she was lacking stood out in stark relief, and she hated it. Hated herself at this moment. Hated Connor Pierce.

"Don't talk to me about being a coward," she said, her breath coming out in shallow pants. "Not when you're packing to return to your cutoff life, alone and hiding out and using your grief as a weapon against anyone who tries to get close to you."

"That's not what I do," he ground out.

"Then don't leave," she told him, and gasped at her own boldness. She hadn't meant to say the words, but she was too raw and open now to hold them back any longer. "Stay here with me, Connor. Help me be brave. Give me your strength and I'll give you mine and together we can—"

"There is no 'we.'" His voice was so cold it sent a chill through her.

"I love you," she said without thinking.

He shook his head. "Don't say that."

"You know it's true whether I speak the words or not." She took a step toward him, another piece of her heart shattering when he flinched away from her touch. "I know you feel—"

"You know nothing about me." His jaw was clenched so tightly his mouth barely moved as he spit the words at her.

"I know you want to pretend you don't care, but it's a lie." She pointed to the stairs. "You care about those girls. You care about me. You are still alive, Connor." She jabbed a finger at his chest. "In here."

He grabbed her hand and yanked it away from his body. "I see what you're doing, April. Everyone sees it. You make your whole life about other people, what they care about and what they need. You think if you work hard enough for your friends, they'll mistake that for you truly being involved. But you're just as cutoff as I am. We're the same, and we both know how this is going to end. How it was always meant to end. It ends with both of us alone. What if I said yes to you? What if I told you right now that I want to make a life with you and the girls? We could be a family if you just said the word. How would you answer?"

She swallowed, her gut suddenly twisted. *This is what you wanted,* she told herself. But she couldn't force her mouth to form the word *yes*. She wanted to. Wanted to mend the hearts of those girls upstairs. And she certainly didn't want to admit that she'd let fear rule her life. Yet, how could she deny it?

She bit down on her lip for several moments before finally asking, "What does it matter how I'd answer? You're not asking the question, are you?"

"Not when you're too afraid to answer it," he whispered, and walked past her.

April glanced around the kitchen and sucked in a harsh breath. There was a stack of Shay's drawings on the counter and the cards from the abandoned game were still strewn across the table. It was so different from her neat and tidy apartment.

Two weeks on the mountain and this cabin felt like home. The girls and Connor were the family she secretly craved. But he was right. She was scared to claim that future. If she got sick again, what would happen if they left her? What if she wasn't perfect, couldn't

take care of them and everyone walked away? What if watching them leave broke her heart in a way she couldn't mend?

Connor heard footsteps pounding down the stairs as he stared at his computer several hours later. The bluish glow of the screen was bright in the fading light of afternoon, casting shadows across the wool rug and hardwood floor. His editor had emailed again, this time to say they were fast-tracking the publication of his book and asking about dates for a possible six-city book tour.

The thought of traveling the country and standing in front of groups of readers made his stomach jump and turn. He'd managed the holiday party in Crimson because of April and the girls. To face people, to pretend to be human on his own, was a daunting prospect. But April had been right in what she'd accused him of in the kitchen. He was a coward, afraid to put himself out there again, and risk hurt and heartbreak.

Margo would expect more. His beautiful wife would have wanted him to be happy. She would have expected him to start to live again.

April shouted his name, her tone so chilling it made goose bumps rise on his skin. He raced to the edge of the hallway.

"It's Shay," she called from the bottom of the stairs, already shoving her feet into snow boots. "She's gone."

"And so is Jingle," Ranie said on a sob. "She took him and—"

"No." Connor hadn't realized he'd shouted the word until both of them glanced up. "I mean, that's impossible. It's freezing out, and it only stopped snow-

ing a few hours ago. She must be hiding, playing a trick because she's angry."

Ranie shook her head. The girl was panting for breath, her blue eyes wide and terrified against skin pale as a December moon. "I've looked everywhere, and she wouldn't do that anyway. Shay is afraid to be alone."

He thundered down the steps and grabbed his coat. "Then why would she run away?"

"I don't know," Ranie said on a sob. "She was so upset about Jingle. They're gone."

"We'll find both of them," April told her.

"This is your fault," Ranie screamed. "She ran away because you won't let us stay."

Connor saw April's head jerk back as if the girl had struck her.

"There's no time for that now," he said, laying a hand on Ranie's shoulder. "We all need to look for your sister."

He opened the back door and held up a hand. "I can see her boot prints," he said, pointing to the tracks in the snow leading toward the woods. "And it looks like…damn it."

"What?" April tried to peer around his shoulder. He took a step out into the fading sunlight and crouched low. "Look at the tiny paw prints mixed up with hers. It looks like Jingle got out and she went after him."

"Oh, no." April's gaze followed his. "They disappear into the forest."

"We need to find her soon," Connor said, looking at the girl's small tracks. The sun hung low over the craggy peak that rose to the west of the cabin. "Before we lose the light. We only have about an hour."

He shouted for Shay at the top of his lungs. The only answer was a hollow echo and the sound of a squirrel scurrying along a branch.

"She hasn't been out here long," April said, and her voice sounded like a plea. She called for Shay as well, but received no response. "Should I call the sheriff?"

Connor shook his head. "They'll take too long to get up here. Damn it," he repeated. "There are two sets of tracks. It's like the kitten was running back and forth at the edge of the forest and Shay was following. I can't tell which way she went."

Ranie let out a pained whimper. "We need to find her." She rubbed her gloved hands together. "It's freezing out here and her coat was still hanging by the door."

"We will," Connor said, letting no trace of doubt slip into his tone. "We're going to split up. You two take the south and west side of the house. I'll cover the north and east and check around the caretaker's cabin. Call for her and keep looking for tracks. She's out here."

April nodded but her eyes were as panicked as the girl's. Connor grabbed her arms and gave her a little shake. "We're going to find her. I need you to believe me."

"I do," she said without hesitation. She swallowed and then gave a more forceful nod. "I believe you." She gently nudged Ranie and they both headed to the far side of the cabin, taking turns yelling for Shay.

As their voices became fainter, Connor started calling again. He stood in place for a moment, studying the puzzle of footprints, trying to determine which way the girl had gone.

Icy tendrils of panic buzzed up his spine and before he'd taken one step, he was transported back to the

accident. It was like reliving a nightmare, images flashing in his mind as his body heaved under the weight of his failure.

Suddenly he was no longer on a snow-covered mountain. It was a rainy night on a curvy California highway and he could feel the heat of the flames licking at him as he tried to run, tried to find the strength to move toward the burning car. The mental picture changed again and he was on his knees, the car exploding in front of him. The heat from the fire burned his eyes and he blinked, suddenly finding himself on all fours in the snow, white and icy under his hands, the chilled wetness seeping in through his pant legs.

Not again.

The two words were like a mantra as he forced himself to stand. This was not that horrible night. He would not fail Shay the way he had his wife and son. He was strong now, capable. He wouldn't allow his fear and his weakness to paralyze him the way they had after the accident.

He examined the footprints again and then headed into the woods, his boots crunching in the snow. After taking a few more steps, he glanced over his shoulder and realized that due to the hill behind the cabin, he could no longer see either of the structures. Everything around him was a mix of white, brown and green, and it was clear how a young girl could have gotten quickly turned around.

Daylight was quickly fading, sending shadows across the ground and making it more difficult to see her trail. He continued to call and if he had to admit it, began to pray. Not to God or some higher spirit—his

faith was too shattered for that. Instead, he allowed his heart to reach out to Margo, wherever she might be.

"Help me," he whispered into the silence of the forest. "Help me rescue that little girl the way I should have saved you and Emmett."

His chest squeezed as he reached out to the woman he'd lost, or maybe to nothing. He was desperate enough at this moment not to care. An icy wind blew through the trees, battering his exposed skin, and he shouted Shay's name again.

This time when he listened for a response, there was…something. A soft whine from somewhere in the trees. His gaze darted around until it fell on a flash of color and he moved toward it as fast as he could in the snow, pushing branches out of the way as he went. He rounded a rock formation and saw a pair of pink snow boots sticking out from under the branches of an enormous pine tree.

"Shay," he shouted again, dropping to his knees and scooping her into his arms.

She blinked several times, relief clear in her sweet blue eyes, and then bent her head. "Jingle ran away," she whispered, her voice hoarse. "But I found him. I'm keeping him safe."

"I know, sweetheart," he whispered, seeing the kitten's black head poke out from her fuzzy sweatshirt. Her skin was pale, her tiny rosebud lips tinged with blue. He unzipped his coat and shrugged out of it as best he could without letting go of Shay. Wrapping her and the kitten in the thick down, he held her close and walked as quickly as he could back to the cabin.

"Stay awake, Shay," he told her. "April and your sister want to see your beautiful smile when we get back."

She gave a tiny nod, but her eyes drifted closed.

Connor yelled for April as he made his way through the trees and snow-covered debris of the forest floor. Every time he shouted, Shay opened her eyes, which he hoped was a good sign. She was shivering like an aspen leaf in a strong wind. He tripped over a fallen log and she jerked, the kitten mewling pathetically as he righted himself.

He heard April's answering call, and Ranie ran to the edge of the property to meet him as he came into the clearing. "Is she okay?"

"She'll be fine," he answered, hoping with everything he was that he told the girl the truth. April was at his side a moment later.

"Oh, Shay," she murmured, her worried gaze clashing with his.

"We need to get her inside," he said, forcing himself to remain calm and focus on the action it would take to warm the half-frozen child.

April nodded and when she turned her head, he realized she was on her cell phone. "I've got Jake Travers on the line. He wants to know if she's responsive?"

"Yes, she spoke to me. She seemed tired but lucid."

She repeated his words into the phone. "She's pale but her breathing seems regular. It'll be hard to tell until we get her into the house."

Ranie was crying quietly on his other side. "We're going to take care of her," he assured her, again with a confidence he wasn't sure he felt.

April disconnected and ran ahead, holding the cabin's door open for them. "Jake says to change her out of anything wet and use dry heat to warm her, start-

ing at the center of her body. He's on his way up to check on her."

He stomped the snow off his boots as he entered the cabin, then headed up the stairs to her room. "Shay, honey, are you awake?"

"I'll get a heating pad," April said from behind him.

The girl shifted in his arms, one side of her mouth curving into a faint smile. "Jingle's tickling me," she murmured, and then breathed out a sigh. He lifted the kitten away from her and handed him to Ranie, who wrapped her hands around the animal and held it close.

From what Connor could see, Jingle hadn't suffered any ill effects of his time exposed to the cold, likely because Shay had kept him warm with the heat from her body. He wondered if the cat had any idea how lucky he was to be loved by that little girl.

"Shay, you're going to be okay," Ranie said as Connor removed Shay's boots and his coat, then pulled back the covers and lowered her to the sheets. "Do you hear me?"

Shay's eyes fluttered open and she looked directly at her sister. "I saw Mommy," she whispered. "She was so pretty, Ranie, like she was before." Another wispy smile flitted across her face as her eyes closed again.

A flash of envy stabbed through Connor at the idea of seeing his wife and son again in the way he imagined Shay was describing. Almost immediately, he put the thought aside, because he didn't want to think what it might mean if Shay was having visions of her dead mother.

Ranie started to cry harder and, moving on instincts rusty from years of not being used, Connor wrapped his arms around the girl and murmured words of en-

couragement against her hair. No jokes, no teasing. Just the support of an adult for a child in need.

After a few moments, he turned her to face him and bent to look in her eyes. "She's going to be okay. I promise." He wasn't sure what prompted him to say those words, since he no basis on which to make that pledge. He offered up a silent plea to Margo for help, then took a deep breath.

"We're not helping her this way," he told Ranie firmly. "We need to believe she's going to be okay."

April hurried into the room. "Jake texted. He just turned onto the mountain road." She held a heating pad in her hand. "Let's do our best to warm her until he gets here."

Connor dropped a soft kiss on the top of Ranie's head. "I promise," he repeated, and started the process of warming the younger girl.

Chapter Twelve

April stood in the doorway to the girls' bedroom late that night, the hallway light illuminating the darkness enough that she could see the two of them curled up together under the covers of Shay's twin bed. Jingle was wedged between them, purring contentedly.

Jake had given the girl a thorough examination, and Shay had woken long enough to eat a bit of soup. April was so thankful that Shay seemed to be on her way to a full recovery.

According to what the girl told them, she'd opened the cabin's door to check the temperature before going out to play and Jingle had darted onto the porch and across the driveway. Without watching where she was going, she'd chased him into the woods, but by the time he'd finally slowed enough that she could catch him, she hadn't been able to find her way back to the cabin.

The thought of Shay lost in the frozen woods with darkness approaching still sent panic spiraling through April's gut. She couldn't imagine what would have happened if Connor hadn't found the girl when he did.

There was no talk about how angry Shay and Ranie had been with her earlier. April's belief that Shay had run away to punish her now seemed petty. The one good thing about her terror was that it put everything else into perspective. As Connor had said, life could change in an instant and she wasn't going to waste another minute living in fear.

She felt Connor's presence behind her and shifted so that he could stand next to her.

"It's a miracle that Shay's okay," she whispered.

His breath hitched but he nodded.

She leaned into his arm. "You saved her."

"You and Ranie would have found her if you'd been in the right area of the forest."

Shay hummed softly in her sleep and scooted toward Ranie, who automatically pulled her closer.

April quietly closed the door and laced her fingers with Connor's, leading him down the hall to her bedroom.

"I shouldn't…" he said, but didn't pull away. "My flight goes out early tomorrow and—"

"I need to talk to you," she interrupted. "Please."

His jaw tightened, but he nodded.

Nerves and fear and hope wove together in April's chest, making her heart beat like she'd just summited one of the high peaks that surrounded Crimson. "You were right." She bit down on her lip to keep from shouting the words at the top of her lungs. "You were right," she repeated in a quieter tone.

His brows furrowed. "About what?"

"About me living in fear. I've been letting the past dominate my life, which has kept me from the future I want. But I'm through with that. I'm going to keep the girls, Connor."

He sucked in a breath.

"At least," she clarified, "I'm going to ask them if they still want to stay with me. I hurt them by not committing sooner, and I have a lot of mistakes to rectify. But Jill entrusted them to me, and I want to honor her wishes."

"Because you feel obligated?" he asked carefully.

"Because I love them," she answered with a smile. "Having them with me is a gift, and I'm not going to throw it away. The future isn't a guarantee, but I'm meant to be their family, and they're supposed to be mine." She squeezed his hands. "Just like I hope you'll be mine."

His fingers slipped from hers. "I don't understand. This morning you were so sure."

"This morning I was stupid and afraid." She laughed. "I'm still afraid, but who isn't? I won't let it rule my life. Ask me again, Connor. The question from this morning about making a family with you and the girls."

She could see his chest rise and fall and she wanted to reach for him, to see if his heart was beating a crazy rhythm that matched her own.

"I didn't actually ask anything." He ran a hand through his hair. "I only proposed the possibility of a question."

The word *proposed* had a lovely ring to it coming from this man. "Such a stickler for language," she

chided gently. "You know what I mean. Ask me now." She let everything she felt show in her eyes and held her bruised heart out to him.

His face went completely blank.

Not a good sign.

"I…" He turned, placed his palms against the top of the dresser as if he needed the support. "I told you my heart died with Margo and Emmett."

She shook her head. "I don't believe you."

"It doesn't matter."

"That's not true." She laid her hand on his arm, the lightest touch, in an attempt to gentle him. April understood what it was like to do battle with internal demons, and she wanted…needed to bring Connor into the light. "I'll be brave for both of us, Connor. Your new book is a beautiful tribute to Margo and Emmett. But they'd want your life to honor them as well."

"Shut up," he roared, whirling on her so violently that she stumbled back against the bed. "You don't know anything about Margo and Emmett. You and I have nothing." He swept out his arm, gesturing wildly. "This is nothing but make-believe."

"No." She whispered the word, not even certain if he could hear her with whatever noise was clattering through his head right now. "What we have is real. Those girls sleeping in the next room are real. You were here when they needed you. You found Shay."

He gave a sharp shake of his head. "Anyone could have—"

"But, more importantly, you saved Ranie."

"She wasn't lost."

"Yes, she was. In the same prison of sorrow that has you trapped. But you helped her. She trusts you. She

needs you. You still have more to give, and I'm asking you to take a chance. Just try." She took a breath and then whispered, "Make the effort."

He grimaced and her instinct was to comfort him, to try to take away his pain despite the fact that her heart was shredded at his feet.

"I can't," he said, and walked out of the room.

It was as if he'd thrown her off a great cliff. At first there was only the sensation of falling, weightless and terrible. Then came the crash that shattered her until nothing was left but broken pieces.

April bent in front of the fireplace the next afternoon, carefully picking the pinecone figures out of the ash.

"I did that," Ranie said from behind her. "I'm sorry. I was mad about going to Aunt Tracy's and I threw them away."

Tapping the gray dust from the figure holding a yoga mat, April glanced over her shoulder and smiled. "It's a good thing we didn't light a fire last night."

The girl hesitated and then offered a tentative smile.

April turned and sat on the fireplace surround, patting the cool stone next to her. "What is it, sweetie?"

Slowly, Ranie lowered herself to sit, her hands clenched in fists on her thin legs. "What if you change your mind? I know I'm not all sunny and sweet like Shay, and I haven't been very nice to you. Are you sure you want me to stay, too?"

"Of course I am." April wrapped an arm around the girl's shoulders. "I'm not changing my mind, Ranie. Not now and not ever. No matter what happens."

"Are we the reason Connor left like he did?"

"What do you mean?"

"He didn't even say goodbye," she whispered.

"I'm sorry," April said, and pulled the girl closer. "He had an early flight and…" How could she make an excuse for something inexcusable? "I wish he would have handled it differently. He cared about you girls, but it's hard for him to admit that."

Ranie glanced up at April, her blue eyes unsure. "Sometimes Mom had boyfriends who wouldn't stick around once they found out about Shay and me. Back when Shay was a baby and Mom was healthy. She never said anything, but I could tell it made her sad. One of our neighbors would babysit and Mom would be so happy for a few weeks. Then she'd bring the guy around to meet us, and he'd be gone."

"I'm sorry. I'm sure your mom never blamed you. Those just weren't the right kind of men."

"But you really liked Connor and it makes you sad that he left."

April didn't bother to deny it. Even at twelve, Ranie could spot a lie without much effort. "I did like him, and I am sad."

"Me, too."

"But he didn't leave because of you and your sister." April took a deep breath and then added, "Or because of me. Some people are just too scared to let themselves be happy."

The girl nodded. "I was really angry when Mom died. I still am sometimes. I think about her and I hate that she's gone. I hate cancer. I hate being the girl with no mom. I wish I was like Shay, but I'm not."

"I understand," April admitted softly. "Sometimes I hate being defined by my breast cancer. I'm proud to

be a survivor, but there is 'before cancer' and there is 'after cancer' and that will never change for either of us. All I ever want you to be is who you are. Even when you're mad or grumpy, I want you here. Even when I'm scared or unsure, I'm not giving you up. We're in this for the long haul. Do you understand?"

Tears shimmered in Ranie's eyes. "I want to be happy again," she whispered.

"Oh, sweetie." April hugged her tight. "You will. We will together." And because it was the right thing to do for this girl, April forced away her own heartache and let the love she felt for Ranie and Shay fill her heart. She wished it could have been different with Connor, and there was no denying that every part of her ached for him. But sadness and regret wouldn't rule her life. Her future was here in Crimson with these girls.

She shifted and turned toward the fireplace once more. "Let's rescue the rest of our pinecone family. I'm ready to head to our new home for the three of us."

"Where's Connor?"

April frowned. "Back in California by now, I imagine."

"No, I mean his pinecone." Ranie picked the two smaller figures out of the fireplace. "It's not here. Did you already throw it out?"

"I didn't touch it."

Ranie made a face and gave a creepy groan April would have expected to hear in a Halloween haunted house. "It's like he disappeared and was never really here in the first place."

April might believe that except for the deep ache in her heart. "We know he was here, and I believe that being with us this Christmas helped him. I hope he remembers us and it makes him feel a little better

each time he does. He cared about you, Ranie. Don't ever doubt that."

"I know," the girl whispered. "It's hard to be happy after someone dies. I feel guilty sometimes when I smile or laugh, like I should always be missing Mom."

Thinking of how much emotional weight this girl carried on her shoulders made tears clog April's throat. "She'd want you to smile and laugh. You understand that, right?"

Ranie nodded, then stared at the two pinecone figures in her hand. "At first I felt bad that I liked you. I didn't want you to be nice because it felt like I was turning my back on my mom."

"I could never replace your mother, and I'd never try."

"I get that now," the girl answered, meeting April's gaze. "I'm happy we're going to be a family."

"Oh, sweetie, thank you." April hugged the girl tightly, so aware of the precious gift Jill had given to her. For someone who had thought she'd never have a family, the fact that for the rest of her life April would have the honor of caring for Ranie and Shay was tremendous. She sent up a silent prayer of thanks to her friend for entrusting her with these precious girls.

She gave the two pinecone figures Ranie held a pretend kiss with the one in her hand. "Let's find your sister and Jingle and head home."

Chapter Thirteen

"How is it possible that one person has so many mugs?" Sara Travers folded the lid on another cardboard box and taped the edges together.

It was New Year's Eve, and Sara, who had just returned from her vacation the previous day, had spent the whole morning helping April pack up her small apartment. Although the space had two bedrooms, April wanted a real house for the girls.

One great thing about the close-knit Crimson community was that people were willing to help out friends and neighbors. Her landlord had been the one to suggest the three-bedroom cottage only a few blocks from the elementary school. She'd quickly found someone to sublet her current rental so they'd be settled in their new home by the time school started next week.

"I like options for my tea," April said with a wink.

She stepped toward the window and looked down to where Ranie and Shay were making a snowman in the open space behind the building.

Sara came to stand beside her, wrapping an arm around April's waist. "I can't believe you didn't tell me about them when all of this started."

"It was temporary and I knew you'd—"

"Tell you to pull your head out of your butt and make a home for those girls?"

April laughed. "Pretty much. I thought I'd left my fear behind in California when we moved to Crimson."

"Yeah, right." Sara snorted. "Fear is like a barnacle. You have to scrape that sucker off with sandpaper."

"I don't think I've gotten rid of mine," April admitted. "I'm just learning to breathe through it."

"I like that plan." Sara stepped back and did an exaggerated mountain pose. "It's what makes you such a damn fine yoga teacher. You've got the Zen stuff down."

April turned to her. "You know, for the first time in as long as I can remember, I feel at peace. I still don't quite trust that I'm the best person for those girls, but I know I'm going to do my best to take care of them."

"Honey, you're the best person I know. You took care of me when I was a train wreck. If you can handle a washed-up Hollywood tabloid mess, you can handle Ranie and Shay." Sara put her hands on her hips and cocked a brow. "Speaking of hot messes, I heard you got quite chummy with Connor Pierce while he was here."

Absently, April pressed a hand to her chest. She'd gotten used to the ache that accompanied thoughts of

Connor, and now it felt almost like a companion. "It was kind of close quarters up at Cloud Cabin."

Sara leaned in. "Close as in 'between the sheets' close?"

April could feel heat rising to her cheeks and turned to the boxes stacked next to the bookshelf. "He let me read his manuscript. It was amazing."

"You slept with him," Sara whispered, her tone full of wonder. "You haven't gotten busy with a man since your divorce. That's a big deal, April."

"It wasn't." April was surprised how easily the lie rolled off her tongue. "We had a holiday fling. Nothing more."

"You don't do flings."

"I do," April said with a laugh that sounded hollow to her own ears. "When the guy runs away at the end."

"Oh, honey." Sara pulled her in for a tight hug. "Connor Pierce might be a brilliant author, but he's also a total idiot."

April sniffed and rested her head on her friend's shoulder. "I'm so glad you're back," she whispered with a sound that was somewhere between a laugh and a sob. "I'll be okay. The girls and I will make everything okay."

Sara stayed for lunch and then headed back to Crimson Ranch. She and Josh were hosting a big New Year's party later that night. April took the girls to buy school supplies and a few more clothes, since she wasn't sure when the boxes with the rest of their things that Jill's sister was shipping would arrive.

They played cards and then got ready for the party.

"Are all your friends nice?" Shay asked from the

backseat as April turned onto the dirt road that led to the ranch.

April glanced in the rearview mirror, thinking about how different this car ride was than that first day up the mountain. "They're all nice. You met most of them at the party at the bakery before Christmas."

Shay nodded, as if satisfied by the answer. "Will Brooke be there? She's going to be my friend at school. I like her."

Jake and Millie Travers's daughter, Brooke, was only a year older than Shay and April thought it was a good sign that Shay was excited to see her friend again.

"Yes, Brooke and her parents will be at the ranch tonight."

"I wish Connor was here," Ranie muttered, and then sucked in a breath, as if shocked she'd said the words out loud.

April wasn't surprised. She and Ranie had come a long way since their conversation at the cabin, but Connor was the one who'd been able to so easily smooth the girl's rough edges.

"What do you think he's doing for New Year's Eve?" Shay asked. This was a game the girl liked to play— what is Connor doing now? At different moments during the day, Shay would raise the question and then they'd all have to guess at the answer.

"I don't know, sweetie. Maybe he's going to a party with his friends."

"He can't be," Shay argued. "*We're* his friends."

"Who cares what he's doing?" Ranie snapped. "He left us, Shay."

"I know that," Shay answered softly. "Mommy left, too, but it doesn't stop me from loving either of them."

"Mom died." Ranie's tone was exasperated. "It's different."

"Have you girls ever seen fireworks above a mountain?" April made her tone bright, trying to push away the darkness of the heavy silence. "The town sets them off on the top of Crimson Mountain at midnight. The colors reflect off the snow and it's beautiful." She gave a small laugh as she parked the Jeep in the row of SUVs and trucks in front of the ranch's main house. "At least that's what I've heard. To tell you the truth, I've never been able to stay awake late enough to see them."

"Me and Brooke are going to be awake until the new year," Shay shouted. She bounced in her seat, the verbal sparring with her sister already forgotten. "I can stay up all night long."

April turned to see Ranie roll her eyes, but she was smiling at her sister. "We'll see about that, squirt."

Since she was an only child, Sara was the closest thing April had to a sister. She was getting used to the constant banter between the girls and the fact that she didn't have to mediate every exchange. Despite their differences in temperament, Ranie and Shay had a special bond and, once again, April felt a wash of gratitude that she'd been given the gift of caring for them.

They got out of the SUV, boots crunching in the snow as they approached the house. April could see people talking and laughing through the picture window, the bright warmth of the house's interior at odds with the bitterly cold night. A wistful sigh escaped her lips before she could stop it. Most of her friends in Crimson were half of a couple, and she suddenly realized that part of the reason she turned in early every

New Year's Eve was because she didn't have someone worth staying awake for to kiss at midnight.

It was time she opened herself to the possibility of finding love again. As much as she'd wanted it to be with Connor, there was no use pining for someone who couldn't love her back. A new year was a time for new beginnings, and she put dating on the list as her first resolution. The thought of being with anyone except Connor made the gaping void in her heart feel even more hollow.

Josh Travers greeted them at the door, and she was proud to introduce Shay and Ranie to him. They'd only taken a few steps into the house when Sara rushed forward and threw her arms around April.

"Nice to see you," April said, laughing at her friend's exuberance. "But you know it's only been a few hours since you were at the apartment."

"Don't be mad," Sara whispered in her ear. "Promise you won't be mad."

Before April could ask for an explanation, Shay's voice rang out in the now-silent room. "Connor's here!"

Everything disappeared except the man standing across the room, watching her from those piercing green eyes. His hair was shorter than it had been at Christmas, and the shadow of a beard covered his strong jaw. He wore a thick gray sweater and tan cargo pants with boots, and he looked rough and rugged, like he belonged in Colorado. In her world.

But she knew that was only an illusion, so her first instinct was to turn and flee. Then Ranie's hand slipped into hers. April forced herself to remain where she was as Shay ran forward, dodging other party guests to launch herself into Connor's arms.

April could feel the curious glances of her friends as he made his way toward her.

"Happy New Year," he said when he was standing only a few feet away.

"Connor," Shay said, practically bubbling over with excitement, "there's fireworks on the mountain at midnight. We're going to stay up and watch them."

"That's pretty late for a little girl," he answered, his voice gentle.

"April said I could." Shay wriggled in his arms and he lowered her to the ground. "And we're moving to a new house. Are you going to come see it? How long are you staying in Colorado?"

He smiled and tapped her on the nose. "That depends on my three favorite girls."

"You left," Ranie said softly, the two words at once a painful reminder and a condemnation, and exactly the sentiment April wanted to express.

"I'm sorry," he whispered, his gaze focusing on the girl. April tightened her grip on Ranie's hand, as if emotionally shoring up them both. "I was stupid."

"Truth," the girl muttered, and one side of Connor's mouth curved.

"I missed you, Ranie," he said. "There's no one to give me grief without you."

"Is that why you're here? Because email and text work a lot easier."

"I don't want email or texts. I want to be here. Now." He took a step toward the entry table and as he moved, his scent floated around April. Pine and spice—the combination almost brought her to her knees with the longing that poured through her. She tried to push her

need back under the surface. "I also have something that belongs with you."

He picked up a gift box from the table and held it out to the girl. April curled her hand into a fist as Ranie released it to take the box. She opened it and let out a small gasp. "I knew you took it," she whispered. Lifting the pinecone figure holding a book out of the box, she turned toward April. "It didn't just disappear."

"No," April agreed, then fixed her gaze on the man now standing so close she could see the gold flecks around the edges of his eyes. "But you did. Why did you come back, Connor?"

"For you," he said without hesitation. "I came back for you."

Hope sliced through her fragmented defenses as she scrambled to shore up all the cracks in the walls that guarded her heart. She wasn't sure she could handle this moment without falling apart again.

She watched Shay tug on the hem of his sweater, her reaction to his return so simple. "I'm going to play with Brooke. Don't leave without saying goodbye, okay?"

"I'm not leaving," he told her, and with a nod, she skipped away. He met April's gaze again. "I'm not leaving," he repeated.

"My life isn't simple," she answered. "And I'm done making things easy for you." Behind Connor's shoulder, she saw Sara give her the thumbs-up and then Josh pulled his wife away. Suddenly it was all too much. Connor's return. Her friends watching. The way her heart stammered inside her chest.

She whirled around and made it several steps toward the front door before a hand grabbed her arm.

"April, don't run away."

"Don't you dare say that to me." She shrugged off his touch, grateful that at least since she'd moved into the foyer, all of her friends wouldn't bear witness to this. Whatever *this* turned out be. Her heart and her mind warred inside her head. "I'm not the one who ran. I pushed through my fears and doubts and I'm making life happen." She pointed at him, then lowered her hand when she realized her fingers were shaking. "You ran, Connor. When things got complicated, you took off."

"I'm sorry," he said again, and drew in a deep breath. "And you're right." He bent so that they were at eye level. "I'm scared to death, April. Every day. Every hour. Every minute and second. I can barely think for the fear pounding through me."

"I know." She bit down on her lip, hoping the small flicker of pain would stem the tide of her tears. She turned away again, her hand on the door.

"But it's nothing compared to the way I miss you." His voice hitched on the last word. She squeezed shut her eyes and didn't turn around.

Wouldn't turn. Because if she looked at him now, she was a goner. And as bad as the past few days had hurt, there wasn't enough left of her heart to keep going if he broke it again.

"Every moment I miss you," he said quietly. "Every time I take a breath, so I've actually done some experiments with holding my breath that would make David Blaine proud. It doesn't help. You are my breath. You are my heartbeat. You're my whole world, April."

She heard a broken sound and realized it had come from her.

"Turn around, sweetheart." His voice was gentle, coaxing. "Please turn around."

She did and the look in his eyes leveled her. It was open and real, and everything she'd wanted was right there in his gaze.

"I don't want to trust you," she whispered, because it was the truth and it was difficult, but she was finished being scared of either.

"Then just give me a chance to prove you can." His hand lifted before he pulled it back, running his fingers through his cropped hair. "The way you showed me that I deserve more than the half-life I was living. The way you proved to me that I can love again. I love you so damned much, April. Give me a chance. Give me forever."

She swallowed, but there was no stopping the tears now. They flowed hot and fast. She swiped at her cheeks. "I love you, too," she whispered.

His smile was tentative, hopeful. "I'm going to hold you now," he said, moving closer, crowding her against the door. "I'm going to hold you and never let you go."

Then he was wrapping her in his arms and she buried her face against his shoulder and cried. For what they'd both been through, what they'd lost and found and almost lost again. Everything in her heart poured out. The dam that had kept her emotions in check for so long simply burst under the force of her love. It was messy and real, and true to his word, Connor only held her tighter.

"Those are happy tears, right?"

April lifted her head as Connor shifted. Shay and Ranie stood in the doorway from the foyer to the family room, all the people she loved in the world watching behind them.

"The happiest," she whispered, and opened her

arms. Both girls ran forward and the four of them hugged. The joy April felt in this moment was so complete, nothing could compare. Nothing except the peace that descended a few moments later. Because she'd finally found her family, and she was never letting them go.

Epilogue

Six Months Later

Connor looked up from the podium as he finished his reading and the crowd gathered in the San Francisco bookstore started to clap. He took a deep breath, only exhaling when his gaze found April and the girls standing at the back of the room.

She smiled, and both Ranie and Shay waved. Because it was summer break, they'd been able to join him in several of the six cities on his current book tour. Of course, after the first two readings Shay had decided that his book was too "growned up" for her taste, and the three of them usually arrived at the end of each appearance. Every single time, seeing them made his heart expand with love and gratitude.

He owed April more than he could ever repay. She'd

brought him back to life and given him the second chance he hadn't realized he'd so desperately needed.

The bookstore manager allowed a few minutes of questions from the audience before leading Connor to the table stacked with his books. He signed copies and spoke with fans for almost an hour before the event was over.

April and the girls were waiting for him in the tiny coffee bar next to the store's main entrance.

"We got ice cream," Shay announced, holding up a half-eaten cone. "But April said we still have to eat dinner at the party."

"Since you're growing like a weed," he said, nipping at the ice cream, "I'm sure it won't be a problem."

"Unless they serve brussels sprouts," she told him. "Those are yucky."

"Hey," April protested with a smile. "I roasted brussels sprouts last week. They were delicious."

"Whatever you say." Shay licked at her ice cream.

"Margo's mother is a wonderful cook," he told the girl, slipping into the chair between her and April. "She'll have something there you'll like."

"And you're sure they're okay with all of us coming to the party?" Ranie's blue eyes were filled with worry. "It's not going to be weird?"

"It might be weird at first," Connor admitted. They had a hotel room downtown but were driving out to the suburbs to have dinner with Margo's family and a few of Connor and Margo's mutual friends. He'd slowly gotten back in touch with the people who had loved his wife, bolstered by April's support and encouragement. He'd found that, instead of sorrow and guilt, sharing memories of Margo and Emmett now triggered a quiet

peace. That peace strengthened the love he felt for the family he'd lost, but also allowed him to move forward with the family he was creating with April and the girls. "The Malones are really nice and they love kids." He leaned over the table. "Just don't pick your nose at the table."

She snorted. "I don't pick my nose."

He flashed her a grin. "Then you should be fine."

"You had a lot of super fans in the audience tonight," April said, reaching for his hand. "Everyone was excited to meet the famous author."

"Not as excited as the author was to get back to his wife," he whispered, and lifted her fingers to his mouth, gently kissing the diamond band on her left hand. They'd married in a small service a week into the new year. It had been a whirlwind, but Connor had no doubt he wanted to spend the rest of his life with April at his side. They'd agreed that it was important for the girls that they get married before he relocated to Colorado to move in with them.

With Ranie and Shay as witnesses, they'd had a ceremony at Cloud Cabin. He'd joined them in their rental house, but they'd recently purchased an acre of land outside of town to build their dream home. April's friends had quickly become his friends, and living in the shadow of the rugged beauty of Crimson Mountain was just one more thing that added to his healing.

"Can I go look at books?" Ranie asked.

"Me, too," Shay shouted around her last bite of ice-cream cone, jumping up from her chair.

"Yes, but stay together," April told them with a gentle smile. "And don't plan on buying anything more.

We're going to need a whole room in the new house for the books you've collected on every stop of this trip."

Both girls looked at Connor.

He glanced at April out of the corner of his eye. "How can you say no to books?"

"You're totally throwing me under the bus," she said with a laugh.

"I'm not," he protested, drawing her closer and kissing the top of her head. "But we're talking about books," he whispered into her hair.

"One book each," she told the girls with a sigh.

They fist bumped and then headed for the children's section.

She pulled back, her dark eyes gentle. "How are you feeling about tonight?"

"Nervous but positive," he admitted. "When I spoke with Margo's mother earlier, she was excited about meeting you and the girls. I think the guilt and blame I carried was a burden for more than just me. They really were my family, and somehow it helps their healing to know that I'm moving forward." He leaned in for a kiss. "But I'm happy that this is the last stop on the book tour."

She smiled against his mouth. "We're going home."

Home.

The word that had left him hollow for so long now filled him with a happiness he hadn't believed possible.

"You are my home," he whispered, cupping her face between his palms. "I love you, April. I'll love you forever."

"I love you, too, Connor. Forever."

Connor understood that life held no guarantees, but through the darkness and light, with April at his side

he would appreciate each step on the journey. He'd never again take for granted the peace that filled his soul, and he intended to spend every day proving his love to April and the girls.

* * * * *

Be sure to catch Michelle Major's next book,
A FORTUNE IN WAITING,
the first book in
THE FORTUNES OF TEXAS:
THE SECRET FORTUNES *continuity,*
coming in January 2017!

And don't miss the previous installments in the
CRIMSON, COLORADO *series:*

ALWAYS THE BEST MAN
A BABY AND A BETROTHAL
A VERY CRIMSON CHRISTMAS
SUDDENLY A FATHER
A SECOND CHANCE AT CRIMSON RANCH
A KISS ON CRIMSON RANCH

available now wherever Mills & Boon Cherish
books and ebooks are sold.

MILLS & BOON®

Cherish™

EXPERIENCE THE ULTIMATE RUSH OF FALLING IN LOVE

A sneak peek at next month's titles...

In stores from 15th December 2016:

- **Slow Dance with the Best Man** – Sophie Pembroke
  and **A Fortune in Waiting** – Michelle Major
- **Her New Year Baby Secret** – Jessica Gilmore
  and **Twice a Hero, Always Her Man** – Marie Ferrarella

In stores from 29th December 2016:

- **The Prince's Convenient Proposal** – Barbara Hannay
  and **His Ballerina Bride** – Teri Wilson
- **The Tycoon's Reluctant Cinderella** – Therese
  Beharrie *and* **The Cowboy's Runaway Bride** –
  Nancy Robards Thompson

Just can't wait?
Buy our books online a month before they hit the shops!
www.millsandboon.co.uk

Also available as eBooks.

MILLS & BOON®

EXCLUSIVE EXTRACT

When Eloise Miller finds herself thrown into the role of maid of honour at the wedding of the year, her plans to stay away from the gorgeous best man are scuppered!

Read on for a sneak preview of
SLOW DANCE WITH THE BEST MAN
by Sophie Pembroke

Maid of honour for Melissa Sommers. How on earth had this happened? And the worst part was—

'Sounds like we'll be spending even more time together.' Noah's voice was warm, deep and far too close to her ear.

Eloise sighed. That. That was the worst thing. Because the maid of honour was *expected* to pair up with the best man, and that would not make her resolution to stay away from Noah Cross any easier at all.

She turned and found him standing directly behind her, close enough that if she'd stepped back a centimetre or two she'd have been in his arms. Suddenly she was glad he'd alerted her to his presence with his words.

She shifted further away and tried to look like a professional, instead of a teenager with a crush. Looking up at him, she felt the strange heat flush over her skin again at his gorgeousness. Then she focused, and realised he was frowning.

'Apparently so,' she agreed. 'But I'm sure I'll be far too busy with all the wedding arrangements—'

CHRISTMAS ON CRIMSON MOUNTAIN

BY
MICHELLE MAJOR

First Published in Great Britain 2016
By Mills & Boon, an imprint of HarperCollins*Publishers*
1 London Bridge Street, London, SE1 9GF

© 2016 Michelle Major

ISBN: 978-0-263-92044-4

23-1216

Our policy is to use papers that are natural, renewable and recyclable products and made from wood grown in sustainable forests. The logging and manufacturing processes conform to the legal environmental regulations of the country of origin.

Printed and bound in Spain
by CPI, Barcelona

'Oh, I doubt it,' Noah interrupted, but he still didn't sound entirely happy about the idea, which surprised her. Perhaps she'd misread his flirting earlier. Maybe he really was like that with everyone and, now the reality of having to spend time with her had set in, he was less keen on the idea. 'Melissa has quite the packed schedule for the wedding party, you know. She's right—you're going to have to find someone to take over most of your job here.'

Eloise sighed. She *did* know. She'd helped Laurel plan it, after all.

And, now she thought about it, every last bit of the schedule involved the maid of honour and the best man being together.

Noah smiled, a hint of the charm he'd exhibited earlier showing through despite the frown, and Eloise's heart beat twice in one moment as she accepted the inevitable.

She was doomed.

She had the most ridiculous crush on a man who clearly found her a minor inconvenience.

And—even worse—the whole world was going to be watching, laughing at her pretending that she could live in this world of celebrities, mocking her for thinking she could ever be pretty enough, funny enough…just *enough* for Noah Cross.

Don't miss
SLOW DANCE WITH THE BEST MAN
by Sophie Pembroke

Available January 2017
www.millsandboon.co.uk

MILLS & BOON®

Why shop at millsandboon.co.uk?

Each year, thousands of romance readers find their perfect read at millsandboon.co.uk. That's because we're passionate about bringing you the very best romantic fiction. Here are some of the advantages of shopping at www.millsandboon.co.uk:

* **Get new books first**—you'll be able to buy your favourite books one month before they hit the shops

* **Get exclusive discounts**—you'll also be able to buy our specially created monthly collections, with up to 50% off the RRP

* **Find your favourite authors**—latest news, interviews and new releases for all your favourite authors and series on our website, plus ideas for what to try next

* **Join in**—once you've bought your favourite books, don't forget to register with us to rate, review and join in the discussions

Visit **www.millsandboon.co.uk**
for all this and more today!